If you are looking for a comprehensive, accessible and thought-provoking overview of current research trends in political violence, this is the book to turn to.

Nils Weidmann, Professor of Political Science, University of Konstanz (Germany)

Peace and Conflict, as with its predecessors, proves to be an invaluable source of up-to-date information on conflicts around the world. Various facets of political violence and their respective recent trends are documented in detail. New trends and challenges in conflict research are admirably discussed, as are traditional and more recent attempts in mitigating conflicts, from peacekeeping missions to criminal justice. Combining chapters on these themes written by the leading scholars in the field makes this volume a must-have for scholars and practitioners alike.

Simon Hug, Professor of Political Science, University of Geneva (Switzerland)

Peace and Conflict 2017

Edited by David A. Backer, Ravi Bhavnani, and Paul K. Huth

First published 2018
by Routledge
711 Third Avenue, New York, NY 10017

and by Routledge
2 Park Square, Milton Park, Abingdon, Oxon OX14 4RN

Routledge is an imprint of the Taylor & Francis Group, an informa business

© 2018 University of Maryland and the Graduate Institute of International and Development Studies

The right of the University of Maryland and the Graduate Institute Geneva to be identified as the authors of this Work has been asserted by them in accordance with sections 77 and 78 of the Copyright, Designs and Patents Act 1988 and in accordance with United States copyright law.

All rights reserved. No part of this book may be reprinted or reproduced or utilised in any form or by any electronic, mechanical, or other means, now known or hereafter invented, including photocopying and recording, or in any information storage or retrieval system, without permission in writing from the publishers.

Trademark notice: Product or corporate names may be trademarks or registered trademarks, and are used only for identification and explanation without intent to infringe.

Library of Congress Cataloging in Publication Data
A catalog record for this book has been requested

ISBN: 978-1-857-43912-0 (hbk)
ISBN: 978-1-857-43932-8 (pbk)
ISBN: 978-1-351-21166-6 (ebk)

Typeset in Bembo
by Taylor & Francis Books

Contents

List of Illustrations		*vii*
List of Contributors		*xi*

1 Introduction to *Peace and Conflict 2017*   1
David A. Backer, Ravi Bhavnani, and Paul K. Huth

2 Generalizing Findings from Micro-Level Research on Peace and Conflict: Challenges and Solutions   4
Karsten Donnay, Andrew M. Linke, and Ravi Bhavnani

3 Tracing Armed Conflict over Time: A Reversal of the Recent Decline?   16
Håvard Strand and Halvard Buhaug

4 The Geography of Organized Armed Violence around the World   23
Erik Melander, David A. Backer, and Eric Dunford

5 Spatial Patterns of Violence against Civilians   34
Hanne Fjelde, Lisa Hultman, Margareta Sollenberg, and Ralph Sundberg

6 The Size of Rebel and State Armed Forces in Internal Conflicts: Measurement and Implications   46
Jacob Aronson and Paul K. Huth

7 The Prevalence of Conflict-Related Sexual Violence: When, Where and By Whom?   58
Ragnhild Nordås

8 Democracy, Democratization, and Civil War   68
Suthan Krishnarajan, Jørgen Møller, Lasse Lykke Rørbæk, and Svend-Erik Skaaning

9 Evolution of Global Terrorism: The Growing Lethality of Attacks   77
Gary LaFree and Laura Dugan

10 Are Global Human Rights Conditions Static or Improving?   88
Peter Haschke and Mark Gibney

11 The Peace and Conflict Instability Ledger 2017: A New Methodology and Ranking of Countries on Forecasted Risks   101
David A. Backer, Jacob Aronson, and Paul K. Huth

Contents

12 Refugees and Conflict Diffusion   142
Seraina Rüegger

13 Armed Conflicts Active in 2015   154
Margareta Sollenberg

14 Multilateral Peacekeeping Operations Active in 2015   179
Deniz Cil

15 Criminal Justice for Conflict-Related Violations: Developments during 2015   208
Anupma L. Kulkarni

Index   *234*

List of Illustrations

Figures

2.1	Integrating Conflict Event Data on Afghanistan, 2008	10
2.2	Data at Different Spatial Units of Analysis	13
3.1	Annual Frequency of Organized Armed Conflict, by Type, 1946–2015	17
3.2	Global Trends in the Severity of Organized Armed Conflict, 1989–2015	18
3.3	Internationalization of Armed Conflict, 1946–2015	19
3.4	The Role of Islamism in Internationalized Internal Conflict, 1991–2015	20
3.5	Spatial Trends in Armed Conflict, 1989–2015	21
3.6	Civil Wars in Muslim Countries or with Islamist Insurgents, 1946–2014	22
4.1	Conflict Zones in State-Based Armed Conflict, 2006–2008	27
4.2	Fatalities due to Organized Armed Violence, by PRIO-GRID, 1989–2015	29
4.3	Severity of Categories of Organized Armed Violence, by Administrative Division, 1989–2015	30
5.1	Spatial Distribution of One-Sided Violence in South and Southeast Asia, 2005–2013	35
5.2	Spatial Distribution of One-Sided Violence in Africa and the Middle East, 2005–2013	36
5.3	Spatial Overlap of One-Sided Violence Committed by State and Non-State Armed Actors, 2005–2013	37
5.4	One-Sided Violence Committed by the Lord's Resistance Army in Central and East Africa, 2001–2014	38
5.5	Spatial Overlap between One-Sided Violence and Different Types of Armed Conflict, 2005–2013	39
5.6	Spatial Overlap of State-Based Armed Conflict with One-Sided Violence Committed by State and Non-State Actors, 2005–2013	40
5.7	One-Sided Violence in Rural vs. Urban Locations, 2005–2013	41
5.8	Spatial Relationship between One-Sided Violence and Level of Economic Development, 2005–2013	42
5.9	One-Sided Violence and Lootable Resources, 2005–2013	43
6.1	Trends in the Median Size of Rebel Forces, by Region, 1975–2014	49
6.2	Trends in the Median Size of Rebel Forces, by Type of Warfare, 1975–2014	51
6.3	Comparing the Median Sizes of Rebel and State Forces, by Conflict Duration	52
6.4	Regional Trends in the Median Share of State Forces Committed to Counterinsurgency, 1985–2014	53
6.5	Rebel Force Size and the Distribution of Conflict Outcomes, 1975–2005	55
6.6	Rebel Force Size and Fatalities Inflicted, 1975–2014	56
7.1	Trends in Conflict Actors Perpetrating Sexual Violence, 1989–2009	60
7.2	Proportions of Conflict Actors Perpetrating Sexual Violence, 1989–2009	61
7.3	Correspondence between Sexual Violence by State and Non-State Forces, 1989–2009	62
7.4	Correspondence between Sexual Violence by States and Militias, 1989–2009	63
7.5	Mapping the Prevalence of Conflict-Related Sexual Violence, 1989–2009	64
7.6	Prevalence of Conflict-Related Sexual Violence, by Region, 1989–2009	65
7.7	Prevalence of Sexual Violence by Conflict Actors in Africa, 2000–2009	66
8.1	Disaggregation of the Electoral Democracy Index	70
8.2	Probability of Civil War Onset at Different Levels of Electoral Democracy, 1946–2010	71
8.3	Probability of Civil War Onset at Different Levels of Attributes of Electoral Democracy, 1946–2010	72
8.4	Probability of Civil War Onset at Different Levels of Indicators of Clean Elections, 1946–2010	73
9.1	Annual Number of Terrorist Attacks, 1970–2014	78
9.2	Annual Casualties from Terrorist Attacks, 1970–2014	79
9.3	Fatalities from Terrorist Attacks, by Region, 1970–2014	81
10.1	Global Annual Average PTS (State Department) Scores, 1976–2014	89

List of Illustrations

10.2	Word Counts in State Department Human Rights Reports, by Year, 1999–2015	91
10.3	Word Counts in Section 1s of State Department Human Rights Reports, by Year, 1999–2015	92
10.4	Annual Growth Rates of State Department Human Rights Reports, 1999–2015	93
10.5	Annual Growth Rates of Section 1s of State Department Human Rights Reports, 1999–2015	94
10.6	Within-Country Time Effects on Full Report Word Counts, 1999–2015	95
10.7	Within-Country Time Effects on Section 1 Word Counts, 1999–2015	95
10.8	Full Report Word Counts by PTS Scores, 1999–2014	96
10.9	Section 1 Word Counts by PTS Scores, 1999–2014	97
10.10	Within-Country Variability of Report Word Counts, 1999–2015	98
10.11	Within-Country Effects of Word Counts on PTS Scores, 1999–2014	99
11.1	Framework of Analysis for New Peace and Conflict Instability Ledger	103
11.2	Global Map of Classifications for Risk of Adverse Regime Change, 2015–2017	115
11.3	Global Map of Classifications for Risk of Internal War, 2015–2017	115
11.4	Global Map of Classifications for Risk of State-Based Mass Killing, 2015–2017	116
11.5	Global Map of Classifications for Risk of Non-State Mass Killing, 2015–2017	116
11.6	Global Map of Classifications for Overall Risk of Instability, 2015–2017	116
12.1	Annual Refugee Count and Prevalence of Armed Conflicts, 1960–2015	143
12.2	Refugees with Co-Ethnics in Countries of Asylum relative to Total Number of Refugees, 1975–2009	145
12.3	Refugees and Transborder Ethnic Kin Ties to the Country of Asylum	146
12.4	Estimated Risk of Conflict Onset for Countries with Refugees, 1975–2009	150
14.1	Regional Trends in Deployment of UN Mission Personnel, 1990–2015	180
14.2	Contributors of Personnel to UNTSO in 2015	182
14.3	Contributors of Personnel to UNMOGIP in 2015	183
14.4	Contributors of Personnel to UNFICYP in 2015	184
14.5	Contributors of Personnel to UNDOF in 2015	185
14.6	Contributors of Personnel to UNIFIL in 2015	186
14.7	Contributors of Personnel to MFO in 2015	187
14.8	Contributors of Personnel to MINURSO in 2015	188
14.9	Contributors of Personnel to JCC in 2015	188
14.10	Contributors of Personnel to UNMIK in 2015	189
14.11	Contributors of Personnel to UNMIL in 2015	190
14.12	Contributors of Personnel to UNOCI in 2015	191
14.13	Contributors of Personnel to MINUSTAH in 2015	192
14.14	Contributors of Personnel to IMT in 2015	193
14.15	Contributors of Personnel to EUFOR-Althea in 2015	194
14.16	Contributors of Personnel to AMISOM in 2015	195
14.17	Contributors of Personnel to UNAMID in 2015	196
14.18	Contributors of Personnel to MONUSCO in 2015	197
14.19	Contributors of Personnel to UNISFA in 2015	198
14.20	Contributors of Personnel to UNMISS in 2015	199
14.21	Contributors of Personnel to ECOMIB in 2015	200
14.22	Contributors of Personnel to MINUSMA in 2015	201
14.23	Contributors of Personnel to EUFOR-RCA in 2015	202
14.24	Contributors of Personnel to MINUSCA in 2015	203

Tables

9.1	Twenty Most Lethal Terrorist Attacks, 1970–2014	80
9.2	Fatalities from Terrorist Attacks, by Target, 1970–2014	82
9.3	Fatalities from Terrorist Attacks, by Tactic, 1970–2014	83
9.4	Fatalities from Terrorist Attacks, by Weapon, 1970–2014	84
9.A1	Countries Listed under Each Region	85
10.1	Summary Statistics for Word Counts in State Department Human Rights Reports, 1999–2015	90
10.2	Time Effects for Word Counts, 1999–2015	92
10.3	Relationship between Word Count Estimates and PTS Scores, 1999–2014	98

11.1	Types of Instability: Definitions and Data Sources	103
11.2	Factors in Models of Instability Risk	106
11.3	Estimations of Models of Instability Risk	110
11.4	Diagnostics for Models of Instability Risk	112
11.5	Countries Ranked in Top 25 for Any Type of Instability Risk, 2015–2017	118
11.6	Country Rankings of Risk of Adverse Regime Change, 2015–2017	120
11.7	Country Rankings of Risk of Internal War, 2015–2017	124
11.8	Country Rankings of Risk of State-Based Mass Killing, 2015–2017	128
11.9	Country Rankings of Risk of Non-State Mass Killing, 2015–2017	132
11.10	Country Rankings of Overall Forecast Risk of Instability, 2015–2017	136
12.1	Estimations of Models of Impact of Refugees on Conflict Onset	148
14.1	Overview of Multilateral Peacekeeping Missions Active in 2015	181

Boxes

13.1	Afghanistan, et al. vs. Taliban	155
13.2	Algeria vs. AQIM	156
13.3	Azerbaijan vs. Nagorno-Karabakh and Armenia	157
13.4	Colombia vs. FARC and ELN	158
13.5	Ethiopia vs. OLF	159
13.6	India vs. Kashmir Insurgents	160
13.7	India vs. Pakistan	160
13.8	Iraq, et al. vs. IS	161
13.9	Myanmar vs. KIO	162
13.10	Nigeria, et al. vs. Boko Haram	163
13.11	Nigeria, et al. vs. IS	164
13.12	Pakistan and Afghanistan vs. TTP	164
13.13	Pakistan vs. BLA, et al.	165
13.14	The Philippines vs. ASG, et al.	166
13.15	The Philippines vs. CPP	167
13.16	Somalia, et al. vs. Al-Shabaab	168
13.17	South Sudan and Uganda vs. SPLM/A–In Opposition	169
13.18	Sudan vs. SRF and Darfur Joint Resistance Forces	170
13.19	Syria, et al. vs. IS	171
13.20	Syria, et al. vs. Syrian Insurgents	172
13.21	Turkey vs. PKK	173
13.22	Uganda and DRC vs. ADF	174
13.23	Ukraine vs. United Armed Forces of Novorossiya and Russia	175
13.24	United States of America, et al. vs. Al-Qaida	176
13.25	Yemen vs. AQAP, et al.	177
15.1	Argentina	209
15.2	Bangladesh	210
15.3	Cambodia	211
15.4	Central African Republic	212
15.5	Chad	213
15.6	Chile	214
15.7	Côte d'Ivoire	214
15.8	Democratic Republic of the Congo	215
15.9	Former Yugoslavia	216
15.10	Guatemala	217
15.11	Kenya	219
15.12	Libya	220
15.13	Mali	221
15.14	Nepal	221
15.15	Romania	222

List of Illustrations

15.16	Rwanda	222
15.17	Sudan	224
15.18	Uganda	225

List of Contributors

David A. Backer is Assistant Director of the Center for International Development and Conflict Management and an Associate Research Professor in the Department of Government and Politics at the University of Maryland. His research focuses on conflict dynamics and post-conflict processes. He is Co-Director of the West Africa Transitional Justice Project and the Constituency-Level Elections Archive.

Ravi Bhavnani is Professor of International Relations and Political Science at the Graduate Institute of International and Development Studies (Switzerland). His research explores the micro-foundations of violence, examining the endogenous relationships among the characteristics, beliefs, and interests of relevant actors, as well as social mechanisms and emergent structures that shape attitudes, decision making, and behavior. He uses agent-based modeling and disaggregated empirical data to link theoretical conjectures to concrete evidence, thereby identifying processes that tend to generate specific outcomes.

Paul K. Huth is a Professor of Government and Politics and Director of the Center for International Development and Conflict Management at the University of Maryland. He is also editor of the *Journal of Conflict Resolution*. He has published books and numerous articles on subjects related to the study of international conflict and war, including deterrence behavior, crisis decision making, territorial disputes, the democratic peace, international law and dispute resolution, and the civilian consequences of war.

Jacob Aronson is a Post-Doctoral Scholar with the Center for International Development and Conflict Management at the University of Maryland, working on a project, funded by the Minerva Initiative of the US Department of Defense, to study the effect of foreign aid on different phases of civil conflict. His main research focuses on how organized combatants generate and wield coercive power. In addition, he is working on a project, in collaboration with the Smithsonian Institution, that examines the strategic logic of combatant targeting of cultural heritage sites and the impact of this targeting on key conflict dynamics. He received his PhD in Government and Politics from the University of Maryland in 2015.

Halvard Buhaug is Research Professor at the Peace Research Institute Oslo (PRIO); Director of PRIO's Conditions of Violence and Peace department; Professor of Political Science at the Norwegian University of Science and Technology (NTNU); and Associate Editor of the *Journal of Peace Research*. He leads and has directed research projects on security dimensions of climate change and geographic aspects of armed conflict. Recent publications include the co-authored *Inequality, Grievances, and Civil War* (2013) and articles in *Global Environmental Change, International Security, Journal of Conflict Resolution, Political Geography*, and *PNAS*. He is the recipient of the 2015 Karl Deutsch Award and an ERC Consolidator Grant.

Deniz Cil is a Post-Doctoral Scholar with the Center for International Development and Conflict Management at the University of Maryland, working on a project, funded by the Minerva Initiative of the US Department of Defense, to study the effect of foreign aid on different phases of civil conflict. Her main research focuses on the implementation of peace agreements following civil wars, and explores variation in the degree of implementation and the factors that incentivize parties to continue implementation. She also works on peace process outcomes, peace duration, and civilian organization in wartime. She received her PhD in Government and Politics from the University of Maryland in 2016.

Karsten Donnay is a Junior Professor of Computational Social Science in the Department of Politics and Public Administration at the University of Konstanz (Germany). His research brings together rigorous statistical and computational analyses of large-scale, geocoded data on human interactions with theoretical and empirical research questions in political science. Specific studies have explored the micro-foundations of violence, including the Israeli-Palestinian conflict and the conflict in Iraq.

List of Contributors

Laura Dugan is a Professor in the Department of Criminology and Criminal Justice at the University of Maryland. She is a Co-Principal Investigator for the Global Terrorism Database (GTD) and the Government Actions in Terrorist Environments (GATE) dataset. Her research examines the consequences of violence and the efficacy of violence prevention/intervention policy and practice. She received an MS/PhD in Public Policy and Management and an MS in Statistics from Carnegie Mellon University.

Eric Dunford is a PhD student in the Department of Government and Politics at the University of Maryland, College Park. His research focuses on rebel mechanisms for dealing with adverse selection and the consequences of different selection institutions on organizational duration and cohesion during civil war. In addition, his work addresses computational solutions to data issues inherent to conflict event data, specifically dealing with issues of data integration and transparency.

Hanne Fjelde is an Associate Professor at the Department of Peace and Conflict Research at Uppsala University (Sweden). Her research focuses on the relationship between political institutions and organized violence, civil war dynamics, and violence against civilians. Her recent publications include articles in *Journal of Conflict Resolution*, *Journal of Peace Research*, *British Journal of Political Science*, and *Political Geography*.

Mark Gibney is the Carol Belk Distinguished Professor at the University of North Carolina-Asheville and the inaugural Raoul Wallenberg Visiting Chair at the Faculty of Law at Lund University (Sweden) and the Raoul Wallenberg Institute. Recent book projects include *International Human Rights Law: Returning to Universal Principles* (2015); *The SAGE Handbook of Human Rights* (2014); *Litigating Transnational Human Rights Obligations* (2014); and *Watching Human Rights: The 101 Best Films* (2013).

Peter Haschke is an Assistant Professor of Political Science at the University of North Carolina Asheville and a principal investigator with the Political Terror Scale project. His current research explores mechanisms of state perpetrated violence in democracies. He teaches courses in comparative politics, electoral systems, conflict, violence, and human rights, as well as political methodology. He received his PhD from the University of Rochester.

Lisa Hultman is an Associate Professor at the Department of Peace and Conflict Research at Uppsala University (Sweden). Her research focuses in particular on the protection of civilians by international actors and her broader interests include topics related to peacekeeping and violence against civilians. Her recent publications include articles in *American Political Science Review*, *American Journal of Political Science*, *Journal of Conflict Resolution*, and *Journal of Peace Research*.

Suthan Krishnarajan is currently a PhD Fellow with the Department of Political Science at Aarhus University (Denmark). His research interests include the effects of economic crises on political instability events such as democratic breakdowns, coups, and civil wars.

Anupma L. Kulkarni is a Fellow with the Stanford Center for International Conflict and Negotiation. Her research focuses on the impact of truth commissions, international and national war crimes prosecutions, and reconciliation policies in Africa. She co-directs the West African Transitional Justice Project and the Liberia Reconciliation Barometer Initiative. She is currently working on two book projects: *The Arc of Transitional Justice: Violent Conflict, Its Victims and Redress in Ghana, Liberia, Nigeria and Sierra Leone* (with David Backer) and *Demons and Demos: Truth, Accountability and Democracy in Post-Apartheid South Africa*. She received her PhD in Political Science from Stanford University.

Gary LaFree is Director of the National Consortium for the Study of Terrorism and Responses to Terrorism (START) and a Distinguished Scholar and Professor of Criminology and Criminal Justice at the University of Maryland. He is currently a Fellow of the American Society of Criminology (ASC) and a member of the National Academy of Science's Crime, Law and Justice Committee. He has served as President of the ASC and of the ASC's Division on International Criminology. Much of his ongoing research is on the causes and consequences of violent crime and terrorism.

Andrew M. Linke is an Assistant Professor in the Department of Geography at the University of Utah. His research investigates violent conflict, political geography, and the effects of environmental change in Kenya using GIS and spatial analysis, large population surveys, and qualitative fieldwork. His recent articles have been published in *Global Environmental Change*, *Political Geography*, *International Interactions*, *International Studies Review*, and other peer-reviewed academic journals. He completed his PhD in Geography at the University of Colorado Boulder in 2013.

Erik Melander is a Professor in the Department of Peace and Conflict Research and Director of the Uppsala Conflict Data Program at Uppsala University (Sweden). He is the Deputy Program Leader of the East Asian Peace Program. His research interests concern gender, masculinities, conflict, and peace. He is co-author (with Christian Davenport and Patrick Regan) of *The Peace Continuum* (Oxford University Press, forthcoming) and co-editor (Grace Mania) of *Peace Agreements and Durable Peace in Africa* (University of KwaZulu-Natal Press, 2016). His other publications include articles in the *European Journal of International Relations*, *International Studies Quarterly*, the *Journal of Conflict Resolution*, the *Journal of Gender Studies*, and the *Journal of Peace Research*.

Jørgen Møller is a Professor in the Department of Political Science at Aarhus University (Denmark). His research interests include conceptualization of democracy and the rule of law, patterns of democratization, conflict and democratic stability, patterns of state formation and the international order, and comparative methodology. His work includes articles in journals such as *International Studies Quarterly*, *Journal of Democracy*, and *Sociological Methods and Research* and in books published by Routledge and Palgrave Macmillan.

Ragnhild Nordås is an Assistant Professor of Political Science at the University of Michigan, Ann Arbor, and a Senior Researcher at the Peace Research Institute Oslo (PRIO). Her research spans the areas of political violence, civil war, and state repression. In recent years, she has focused extensively on the causes and consequences of conflict-related sexual violence, with a major product being the Sexual Violence and Armed Conflict (SVAC) dataset compiled with Dara Kay Cohen (Harvard University). Nordås' work has been published in the *American Journal of Political Science*, *Journal of Conflict Resolution*, *Journal of Peace Research*, and *International Studies Quarterly*.

Lasse Lykke Rørbæk is an Assistant Professor in the Department of Political Science at Aarhus University (Denmark). He studies political violence, including ethnic conflict and civil war. His work is published or forthcoming in journals such as *Democratization*, *Conflict Management and Peace Science*, and *Terrorism and Political Violence*. He completed his PhD at Aarhus University in 2016.

Seraina Rüegger is a Postdoctoral Researcher at ETH Zurich (Switzerland). Her research interests include forced migration, trans-border ethnic ties, civil war, and politics in post-socialist countries. Her work has been published in *Conflict Management and Peace Science* and the *Journal of Conflict Resolution*. She received her PhD from ETH Zurich in 2013.

Svend-Erik Skaaning is a Professor of Comparative Politics in the Department of Political Science at Aarhus University (Denmark). His research interests include the conceptualization and measurement of democracy and human rights, political regime developments, and comparative methodology. He has published three books on democratization and the rule law with Routledge and Palgrave, as well as articles in journals such as *Comparative Political Studies*, *Journal of Democracy*, *Political Research Quarterly*, and *Sociological Methods and Research*.

Margareta Sollenberg is an Assistant Professor in the Department of Peace and Conflict Research at Uppsala University. Her research has focused on the relationship between foreign aid and armed conflict and various topics relating to conflict data collection. She has been involved in the Uppsala Conflict Data Program (UCDP) for the past two decades and has published on UCDP data in *Journal of Peace Research* and *SIPRI Yearbook* among a range of venues.

Håvard Strand is an Associate Professor of Political Science at the University of Oslo and a Senior Researcher at the Peace Research Institute Oslo (PRIO). His research topics include the relationship between political institutions and armed conflict, conceptual problems in the study of armed conflict, and consequences of civil wars. His research is published in outlets such as the *American Journal of Political Science*, *Journal of Conflict Resolution*, *Journal of Peace Research*, *Journal of Development Studies*, *Security Dialogue*, and *World Development*.

Ralph Sundberg is a Post-Doctoral Researcher in the Department of Peace and Conflict Research at Uppsala University (Sweden). His current research (with Lisa Hultman) is mainly focused on improving our understanding of how peacekeeping and peacemaking efforts can help protect civilians from violence and abuse in civil wars. He has worked extensively on data collection, emphasizing the spatial and temporal disaggregation of conflict data, reflected in articles in the *Journal of Peace Research*.

1

Introduction to
Peace and Conflict 2017

David A. Backer, Ravi Bhavnani, and Paul K. Huth

The Center for International Development and Conflict Management (CIDCM) at the University of Maryland has produced the *Peace and Conflict* book series since 2001. *Peace and Conflict 2016* began a new partnership between the University of Maryland and the Graduate Institute of International and Development Studies in Geneva, Switzerland, with Ravi Bhavnani joining David Backer and Paul Huth as a co-editor. *Peace and Conflict 2017*, the ninth edition in this series, marks a shift to an annual release cycle. The primary purpose of this change is to keep abreast with ongoing developments in the world so as to enhance the value of the publication, especially for those readers who seek more current material for use in regular cycles of planning, teaching, research, and reporting.

This edition contains a total of 14 substantive chapters that are organized into four sections. The first section, "Advancing Research" (Chapter 2), examines selected topics dealing with important developments in academic scholarship on peace and conflict and offers constructive suggestions for moving forward. In the second section, "Global Patterns and Trends" (Chapters 3–11), regular core topics are examined along with several chapters that feature timely cross-national analysis. The third section, "Special Feature" (Chapter 12), spotlights novel research related to a select topic, which varies from edition to edition. This year, the focus is the link between refugees and conflict in asylum countries. The fourth section, "Profiles" (Chapters 13–15), describes developments in civil wars, peacekeeping missions, and international criminal justice proceedings that were active around the world during 2015. The remainder of this introduction offers an overview of the individual chapters, highlighting new contributions.

In Chapter 2, Karsten Donnay, Andrew Linke, and Ravi Bhavnani provide a thorough review and assessment of the challenges facing scholars who seek to draw generalizable insights from micro-level research on peace and conflict. They discuss common problems of divergent theoretical concepts, differences in research designs, and methodological approaches, referencing specific examples. In response, they propose several practical steps that researchers can take to integrate varied types of data so that more comparable and potentially generalizable findings can be drawn from micro-level studies.

In Chapter 3, Håvard Strand and Halvard Buhaug analyze patterns in interstate and intrastate armed conflict from 1946–2015, relying on information compiled by the Uppsala Conflict Data Program (UCDP). One of the central themes is an apparent trend toward increasing levels of conflict across the international system that has emerged since 2011. For example, the authors report that the number of active armed conflicts in 2015 was at its highest level in 25 years, while annual conflict fatalities over the past several years have been much higher than during the period from 2001–2012.

Chapter 4 is a new contribution by Erik Melander, David Backer, and Eric Dunford, which features a discussion of the recently released UCDP-Georeferenced Event Dataset (GED) that now provides global coverage of armed conflicts from 1989–2015. They summarize key findings from work by researchers who have utilized this dataset to study sub-national conflict patterns. The benefits of the expanded data are also illustrated via maps that highlight how regional tendencies differ by type of violence and over time. They conclude by pointing to new opportunities for innovative research that takes full advantage of the spatial and temporal specificity of UCDP-GED to better understand dynamics such as conflict escalation and diffusion.

In Chapter 5, Hanne Fjelde, Lisa Hultman, Margareta Sollenberg, and Ralph Sundberg explore the spatial patterns of violence against civilian populations during armed conflicts. They draw upon georeferenced data from UCDP on one-sided violence (OSV) from 2005–2013. A notable finding is that OSV committed by state and rebel forces does not tend

1

to overlap spatially. The authors reason that this result is observed because opposing combatants often target different civilian populations, reflecting the strong influence of local conflict dynamics.

Another new contribution, by Jacob Aronson and Paul Huth in Chapter 6, examines the nature and impact of patterns in the sizes of forces during armed conflicts from 1975–2014. Drawing on their own novel dataset, they identify considerable variation in the strength of state and rebel forces committed to armed conflicts, albeit the asymmetry is less than commonly thought. Their results indicate that larger rebel forces are more threatening, since they are able to inflict greater losses on state forces and civilian populations, stand a much better chance of achieving favorable conflict outcomes, and significantly reduce the likelihood of suffering defeats.

Continuing with new contributions in Chapter 7, Ragnhild Nordås presents a careful review of global patterns of conflict-related sexual violence from 1989–2009. Her analysis reveals a steady increase in the number of armed groups committing conflict-related sexual violence until the early 2000s, after which the prevalence tailed off somewhat. She also discovers considerable variation in sexual violence, with about 14% of armed conflicts experiencing high levels of such violence, whereas 41% of armed conflicts lack reports of sexual violence by any combatants.

The next new contribution, by Suthan Krishnarajan, Jørgen Møller, Lasse Lykke Rørbæk, and Svend-Erik Skaaning in Chapter 8, investigates the relationship between civil war and both democratization and levels of democracy. Drawing upon new disaggregated data on political institutions and regime characteristics from the Varieties of Democracy (V-Dem) project, they show that intermediate levels of freedom of expression and association are associated with higher probabilities of civil war, whereas low and high values of those freedoms are not. In contrast, the degree of free and fair elections is negatively related to the risk of civil war in a linear fashion: as elections become cleaner, the likelihood of civil war decreases. Among other things, these findings illustrate the utility of more disaggregated data on political institutions and practices for addressing key debates about peaceful, sustainable transitions from autocratic governance.

In Chapter 9, Gary LaFree and Laura Dugan employ the Global Terrorism Database (GTD) to analyze more than 141,000 terrorist attacks around the world from 1970–2014. They focus on trends in fatalities caused by terrorist attacks and examine how they are distributed across a range of dimensions such as regions, countries, targets, and weapons. A key finding is that the level of fatalities has increased substantially over the past four years, with 2014 registering the highest to date. Two regions, the Middle East and North Africa, suffered the most fatalities in the recent uptick.

In Chapter 10, Peter Haschke and Mark Gibney tackle the question of whether global human rights conditions are improving, as some analysts have suggested. The authors answer this question through an examination of trends in the Political Terror Scale (PTS) dataset, responding in particular to charges by critics of a bias toward underreporting state repression in earlier years. According to the authors, the data exhibit little systematic evidence of such a bias. They contend, therefore, that the relatively flat trend line of human rights abuses presented in PTS is accurate, which unfortunately implies the absence of a global trajectory towards improving human rights.

In Chapter 11, David Backer, Jacob Aronson, and Paul Huth discuss the latest findings from the Peace and Conflict Instability Ledger – a worldwide ranking of the risk of countries experiencing large-scale political instability during the years 2015–2017. Of particular importance, the authors present a new array of models for forecasting that incorporate significant theoretical, data, and methodological improvements. The collective result of these improvements is that the new models generate much more accurate and disaggregate forecasts of instability, distinguishing risks of adverse regime change, armed conflict onset and offset, and large-scale violence against civilians. As expected, Africa and Asia are the regions with the greatest concentration of countries forecast to have extreme risks of instability.

Chapter 12, authored by Seraina Rüegger, is the "Special Feature" contribution for *Peace and Conflict 2017*. She tackles the question of whether refugee populations forcibly displaced by armed conflicts in their home countries pose security threats to the countries in which they receive asylum. For this purpose, she utilizes an innovative data set on refugee populations from 1975–2009, which records information on the ethnicity of refugees. Her analysis reveals that the risk of armed conflict within asylum countries only increases when refugee populations share kinship with pre-existing marginalized ethnic groups in those countries.

In Chapter 13, the first in the "Profiles" section, Margareta Sollenberg provides a summary of the origins and evolution of all armed conflicts active in 2015 that reached the level of war in 2015, or had escalated to war in prior years. Her analysis covers 25 major active armed conflicts across 21 countries.

In Chapter 14, Deniz Cil focuses on the 23 international peacekeeping missions that were active as of the end of 2015, including both UN and non-UN operations. Her profiles of each mission provide brief chronologies, as well as details about mandates, personnel, and budgetary support.

Finally, in Chapter 15 Anupma Kulkarni reviews legal activities taking place around the world during 2015 (and 2016 in some cases) that deal with possible violations by individuals under various international conventions pertaining to war crimes, crimes against humanity, genocide, and torture. Her profiles encompass 60 countries where violations occurred and/or those held responsible for violations were being prosecuted. Her discussion addresses legal proceedings undertaken by domestic courts, the International Criminal Court, and foreign courts based on principles of universal jurisdiction.

As with previous volumes, *Peace and Conflict 2017* features rich and varied content by researchers who are leading specialists in the field. As is the traditional hallmark of *Peace and Conflict*, this latest publication focuses on comparative analyses, typically global in scope, of patterns, trends, and relationships that are central to academic scholarship, as well as crucial to understand for those who seek to address pressing security problems in the realms of policy and practice. With this in mind, a common thread to all the chapters in *Peace and Conflict 2017* is to advance the boundaries of knowledge with analysis and reference material that has both theoretical and applied relevance, highlighting new datasets and methods contributing to findings that are well-substantiated, intuitive, and resonate with real-world circumstances.

The goal remains to target and welcome a diverse readership, including academia, policymakers, practitioners, activists, and the media. With these audiences in mind, we strive to ensure that the presentation is broadly intelligible, remaining rigorous without being overly technical. Frequent graphical visualizations help to bring the data analysis to life and amplify crucial findings from basic research. These hallmarks will be preserved as enduring foundations of future editions of *Peace and Conflict*. We appreciate your continuing interest in appreciating the complex subject matter of peace and conflict and believe that this latest volume has much to offer.

2

Generalizing Findings from Micro-Level Research on Peace and Conflict

Challenges and Solutions

Karsten Donnay, Andrew M. Linke, and Ravi Bhavnani

Introduction

Recent editions of the *Peace and Conflict* book series have closely followed and documented the evident turn towards emphasizing disaggregate empirical research on peace and conflict, often focusing attention all the way down to the micro level. Many of these more in-depth studies have contributed to advancing knowledge of major patterns, trends, and causal relationships that are highly relevant not only for scholarly understanding, but also for the needs of real-world application among policymakers and practitioners. Of particular note is work on participation in violence and victimization, the influence of combatant characteristics and group leadership, the consequences of migration and segregation, the impact of governance and reconstruction, and the effectiveness of peacekeeping (Donnay, Gadjanova and Bhavnani 2014; Donnay and Bhavnani 2016).

A frequent limitation of these studies is analysis confined to one or a small set of contexts. The narrow scope is often a function of demands that arise when conducting intensive forms of research, which factors into the nature of data requirements and considerations of study design. Investment in a greater level of detail tends to mean fewer contexts are explored. A downside is that generalizing beyond the specific contexts of disaggregate studies is not always straightforward. Whether findings have wider application, or are context-dependent, may remain uncertain without some further demonstration. The situation embodies the classic trade-offs between achieving greater internal validity, through more precise analysis that appropriately reflects local dynamics, and aspiring to sufficient external validity, through a rigorous, robust accumulation of evidence across contexts. Navigating those trade-offs, to extract the most insight possible from ongoing research, is critical.

The prospect that detailed micro-level studies can inform theory, policy, and practice rests on the premise that this research, after accounting for the specific empirical context, helps to shed light on fundamental causal relationships. In practice, however, studies that tackle the same set of questions may exhibit a lack of comparability and coordination, which can result in disparate findings that lead to diametrically opposed conclusions and policy implications. While divergent findings are to be expected in an emerging, vigorous research field (Kalyvas 2008), these issues have persisted in disaggregate studies of peace and conflict for more than a decade, which is deeply problematic.

Our basic concern, therefore, is that the micro-level research on peace and conflict continues to encounter the same problems that motivated the turn in this direction: an inconsistency in the findings across studies that address the same question, due to divergent theorizations, marked differences in conceptualization and measurement, and variation in empirical strategies and methodological approaches, including choices about levels and units of analysis (and associated samples of observations), model specifications, and specific estimation techniques.[1] Left unaddressed, those inconsistencies hamper the ability of scholars to reach common ground and derive robust applications to policy and practice.

In this chapter, we seek to chart a way forward, in the form of best practices for increasing the generalizability of micro-level studies. To start, we take a closer look at some of the fundamental challenges that confront micro-level research on peace and conflict. We pay particular attention to theoretical bases, empirical strategies, and methodological approaches, highlighting our concerns with illustrative examples. Next, we review and illustrate specific approaches that move us closer towards rectifying these issues, emphasizing methodologies for systematic data integration and disambiguation. We conclude with a discussion of these and other potential ways to increase the coherence of relevant research.

Fundamental Challenges

Micro-level studies on peace and conflict analyze a rich universe of individual or select country contexts in great depth. These disaggregate perspectives provide unique empirical leverage (Donnay, Gadjanova, and Bhavnani 2014). Yet studies addressing the same set of questions in the same context may yield diametrically opposite results without comparable, stringent standards for research designs and methods.

In this section, we discuss a number of fundamental challenges to achieving the generalizability of micro-level research. The challenges are illustrated via two sets of examples drawn from recent literature investigating the role of information-sharing mechanisms in conflict.

The first set of studies examines whether or not broadcasts from hate radio stations contributed to the actions of *génocidaires* during Rwanda's Hutu-led campaign of violence against Tutsi and moderate Hutu in 1994. Straus (2007: 609) finds evidence against "the conventional wisdom that broadcasts from the notorious radio station RTLM were a primary determinant of genocide." In contrast, Yanagizawa-Drott (2014: 1947) finds that such messages "had a significant effect on participation in killings by both militia groups and ordinary civilians." Both studies model the effects of a single radio station: *Radio Télévision Libre des Mille Collines* (RTLM).

The second set of studies investigates the impact of mobile phone communication on conflict. Pierskalla and Hollenbach (2013) find that mobile phone network coverage is associated with *higher* levels of conflict across regions of sub-Saharan Africa, as this coverage facilitates communication and therefore coordination among combatants. In contrast, Shapiro and Weidmann (2015) show that insurgent violence in Iraq is *lower* where network coverage exists, an effect the authors attribute to the local populations' ability to inform on militants.

In addressing the role of information – and associated technologies and media – in conflict, both sets of studies contribute to a vital academic debate with immediate policy relevance. Yet the contrasting findings from each set of studies fail to provide conclusive evidence that could inform both policy and practice. What are the theoretical and methodological issues that might explain these sets of contrasting findings?

Divergent Theoretical Bases

One fundamental challenge to the generalizability of findings from micro-level studies concerns variation in measurement, especially as a by-product of divergent theoretical foundations. The illustrative studies provide clear instances where one can identify marked differences in conceptualization and measurement, which are arguably sufficient to account for disparities in conclusions.

For example, the two studies on the impact of hate radio broadcasts in Rwanda nominally examine the same dependent variable: genocidal violence. Yet they differ substantially in terms of how they capture this variable. Straus (2007) employs a coding of the date when genocidal activities commenced in each administrative unit, whereas Yanagizawa-Drott (2014) relies upon counts of the numbers of perpetrators of genocidal violence. The former indicator focuses on whether any genocidal violence occurred, as a means of establishing the timing of *onset*. The latter indicator is concerned entirely with the *intensity* of violence, regardless of its timing. Consequently, these studies are susceptible to reaching dissimilar conclusions about whether and how hate radio affects genocidal violence because they conceptualize this outcome in contrasting ways, examining aspects of the violence that are different in nature (though not necessarily unrelated). Acknowledging the distinction is important when contemplating the inferences that can be drawn from this set of research. As it happens, the findings are not mutually exclusive. The results of Straus (2007) indicate that hate radio did not systematically affect the onset of genocidal violence, while the results of Yanagizawa-Drott (2014) indicate that radio broadcasts influenced the intensity of the observed violence. Such nuances in findings are observed regularly in the literature on peace and conflict.

The other pair of studies exhibits analogous discrepancies. Both studies examine conflict outcomes in relation to the geographical coverage of the cellphone network as the key explanatory variable. Pierskalla and Hollenbach (2013) analyze the onset of violence, whereas Shapiro and Weidmann (2015) analyze changes in the number of violent incidents. Thus, the studies differ in the conceptualization of the dependent variable, although each does rely on conflict event data for purposes of measurement. Here too, the results can be viewed as compatible: cell phone coverage increases the likelihood of conflict, but decreases the severity of this conflict, in a given location.

Different Empirical Strategies

Another fundamental challenge to the generalizability of findings from micro-level studies concerns variation in empirical strategies, specifically with regard to data collection and coding. The illustrative sets of studies exhibit conspicuous differences in terms of which sources are used and/or how they are employed in the analysis. Once more, these differences are plausibly sufficient to explain disparities in conclusions.

Both Straus (2007) and Yanagizawa-Drott (2014) document violence based on eyewitness accounts collected after the conflict, but their sources of those accounts are not the same. Straus (2007) derives dates for the onset of genocidal violence from in-depth field research and interviews, whereas Yanagizawa-Drott (2014) draws on records from the *gacaca* traditional justice process. In addition, both rely on information about hate radio coverage in the environs of Kigali and Mount Muhe, obtained from the International Criminal Tribunal for Rwanda (ICTR). Straus (2007) maintains, however, that the exact broadcast range of hate radio messages is unknown. Therefore, he compares the information from the ICTR with three further broadcast scenarios encompassing national coverage, urban coverage and limited coverage around Kigali.

Meanwhile, both Pierskalla and Hollenbach (2013) and Shapiro and Weidmann (2015) rely on institutionalized sources of conflict data. Yet their specific sources differ and exhibit notable contrasting features. Pierskalla and Hollenbach (2013) use the Uppsala Conflict Data Program's Georeferenced Event Dataset (UCDP-GED) (Sundberg and Melander 2013). This source is an example of passive, retrospective, remote recording of conflict events. The data are compiled by non-participants, after incidents of violence, using media reporting and other available written material. UCDP-GED is part of a broader universe of institutional initiatives, which also includes the Armed Conflict Location and Event Data project (ACLED, Raleigh et al. 2010), the Social Conflict Analysis Dataset (SCAD, Salehyan et al. 2012) and the Global Terrorism Database (GTD, START 2013). Meanwhile, Shapiro and Weidmann (2015) derive data from records compiled by the US military about significant activities (SIGACTS) in Afghanistan and Iraq. This source embodies active monitoring of incidents of violence in which US military units were engaged, as well as incidents that occurred in other locations where US troops were present.

Passive recording has advantages: data can be collected after the fact, without exposure to security risks, and efficiently leveraging information in existing digital sources that are open access – or at least not classified. Yet this approach has been frequently criticized for depending heavily on media reporting, which may significantly affect both the coverage and coding of violent events (Chojnacki et al. 2012; Weidmann 2013; Weidmann 2015a). A particular concern is the relative lack of coverage of smaller-scale violence, as compared to large-scale incidents (Donnay and Filimonov 2014).

Active monitoring can have strengths that usefully address certain shortcomings inherent in passive recording. In principle, first-hand, contemporaneous data collection can improve reliability. Also, the data collection can be designed prospectively, rather than being limited to whatever source material is available. The SIGACTS data, for example, offer coverage of a much richer array of activity observed throughout extended episodes of violence, whereas UCDP-GED is confined to violence involving organized armed actors. The active monitoring approach does hinge on the geographic and temporal coverage of participants and observers who are responsible for recording information. In that sense, the data derived from SIGACTS is not intrinsically different from UCDP-GED, which hinges on the extent to which journalists and media outlets provide coverage of events. When considering conflict dynamics, however, the coverage of a source like SIGACTS should not systematically depend on the severity of events (Weidmann 2015b), whereas one can expect media sources to vary along those lines.

These sorts of differences have implications for research. To the extent that Pierskalla and Hollenbach (2013) and Shapiro and Weidmann (2015) rely on data with dissimilar empirical coverage of violence, the findings of those studies are not comparable. In fact, a comprehensive study of reporting bias found in conflict event data conducted by Weidmann (2015b), which encompasses the work of Pierskalla and Hollenbach (2013), finds that the coverage of insurgent violence by SIGACTS does indeed seem to be more complete and independent of event severity. Weidmann (2015b) also demonstrates that using data derived from media reports introduces systematic differences in findings of analysis about the effect of mobile phone coverage on violence – suggesting a bias in coverage. According to Croicu and Kreutz (2017), however, studies based on passive monitoring that includes sources beyond news media articles should not be affected as substantially by reporting bias, unless conflict intensity is very high.

Stepping back, the differences between individual and institutional data collection warrant further reflections. Individual data collection, reflected in the pair of studies on Rwanda, tends to be far more detailed in terms of coverage, offers greater depth of inquiry, and provides unique empirical insights. Yet these data can be uneven, especially when the data collection and coding protocols are not the same across cases. Without consistent protocols, generalizing findings beyond a specific micro-level setting is difficult. Meanwhile, institutional data collection efforts, such as those reflected in the studies on Africa and Iraq, typically afford a greater degree of cross-case validity. In particular, the coding standards and procedures tend to be stable and comparable – at least within a given dataset (and any progeny). Nothing guarantees, however, that institutional data are complete and unbiased.

Ultimately, in the absence of protocols for systematic integration and disambiguation among datasets, whether they happen to involve individual and/or institutional forms of collection, judging their relative coverage and quality is nearly impossible. We return to these issues in the next section and discuss best practices that serve to mitigate such concerns.

Variation in Methodological Approaches

A further fundamental challenge to the generalizability of findings from micro-level studies concerns variation in methodological approaches, including choices about levels and units of analysis (and associated samples of observations), model specifications, and specific estimation techniques. In all of these respects, the illustrative sets of studies exhibit hardly any similarities. Not surprisingly, those inconsistencies make comparing results and deriving broader inferences about patterns, trends and relationships essentially impossible.

In the studies on Rwanda, Straus (2007) examines variation in the onset of violence across 145 communes, whereas Yanagizawa-Drott (2014) uses aggregate counts of perpetrators in 1,065 villages. Meanwhile, Shapiro and Weidmann (2015) consider the dynamics of violence in the 63 administrative districts in Iraq in which the mobile phone provider Zain operated,[2] whereas the spatial unit of analysis in Pierskalla and Hollenbach (2013) is a 55 km x 55 km grid cell. In both pairs, therefore, one study focuses at a higher level of geographic aggregation than the other study. Furthermore, the illustrative studies on Iraq differ with regard to their temporal units of analysis: Pierskalla and Hollenbach (2013) rely on an aggregate onset measure for a year (2008), whereas Shapiro and Weidmann (2015) consider district-month event counts.

Theory might indicate that findings at one level of analysis ought to be consistent with the findings at another level of analysis. This expectation could appear reasonable, but is not necessarily true. Units of analysis effectively define the boundaries or context for social interactions. Thus, differences in units are more than incidental technicalities – they can easily be central to the theoretical and conceptual pillars of any study, which are then consequential to the findings. Contradictory results associated with varying units of observation in quantitative analysis are by no means a new phenomenon. This circumstance is related to the well-known *modifiable areal unit problem* (MAUP, see Openshaw and Taylor 1979; Openshaw 1983), according to which the correlation between any two variables will likely differ with changes in the size and shape of spatial units of observation (e.g., communes vs. villages). In any event, comparison across studies becomes difficult if the overlap between units of observation is partially or entirely incomplete, and more so if the dependent variables fail to coincide precisely.

These issues are compounded when model specifications differ. Some of these differences we discussed already: studies may be interested in the same general outcome, but their operative conceptualizations are divergent and/or they opt to employ distinctive indicators of the same concept. This is clearly evident in our sets of illustrative studies. Even if the operationalization and coding of the dependent variable match exactly, model specifications are not always identical. Studies may consider the same factors and use the same indicators, but do so in distinctive ways (e.g., lags, interactions). More often, studies of a common topic exhibit at least certain differences in the factors they consider. Unless everything else about those studies is the same, comparison is hardly straightforward.

Estimation techniques add yet another layer where analyses tend to deviate methodologically. In this regard, Pierskalla and Hollenbach (2013) and Shapiro and Weidmann (2015) are the most directly comparable in terms of the nature of their approaches. Both studies use well-established statistical procedures and explore a range of alternative specifications to ensure the robustness of results. Yet the procedures ultimately differ. If one wants to compare the two studies and establish the generalizability of their findings, using as similar estimation techniques as possible is of paramount importance.

Establishing Consistent Empirical Bases

In this section, we focus on a specific challenge: the need for consistent empirical bases. As discussed earlier, when the units of analysis and/or the observations themselves deviate across studies, efforts to generalize their results lack necessary foundations of comparability. At the same time, empirical bases ought to be appropriate for the requirements of conducting research that is theoretically and practically meaningful, as well as methodologically rigorous. Thus, navigating this challenge has implications for essential choices with respect to study designs and analytical approaches.

Here, we present solutions that contribute to the generation of consistent, appropriate empirical bases, describing two novel tools. The first tool facilitates the integration and disambiguation of georeferenced, date-specific event data. The second tool enables the integration of data with various different spatial formats. Both tools help researchers to overcome methodological and practical hurdles to working with multiple sources of data, whether they have similar or disparate features. In so doing, we believe that the tools also provide a valuable means to improve the consistency and quality of research. Achieving such improvements entails that the data used in empirical analysis are more expansive, complete, and standardized. Employing the tools, following associated best practices, takes steps in this direction.

To emphasize, the tools are not meant to generate singular, definitive datasets. Instead, the tools yield versions of data that offer a better accounting of empirical reality, bolstered by formal, transparent, flexible, reproducible procedures that acknowledge uncertainty in measurement and can be leveraged to explore the sensitivity of results to specific aspects of the data assembly process. We believe, therefore, that the application of these tools in empirical research – especially micro-level studies of peace and conflict – enhances prospects of ensuring that findings are valid beyond select settings.

Throughout this section, we illustrate applications and tools drawing on the case of Afghanistan studied by Weidmann (2015b). His study is well-suited for comparison because of the emphasis on the implications of using different types of data sources, which rely on distinct forms of recording and reporting information, as well as the questions raised about the completeness and accuracy of coverage across event datasets in particular.

Data Integration to Improve Data Coverage and Quality

Many micro-level studies rely on a single existing or compiled dataset for the measurement of any given indicator used in analysis. This approach tends to introduce several limitations. With very rare exceptions, no single dataset will comprehensively measure a phenomenon of interest. Such incompleteness can arise even with datasets that purport to be exhaustive. For example, event datasets typically exhibit selective coverage, due to shortcomings inherent in the sources of raw information (e.g., media reports) that are used to compile these datasets, as we discussed above, and the nature of the process of coding this raw information. In addition, datasets that seek to capture the same type of events, occurring in the same location and during the same time period, are not necessarily consistent. Two event datasets may rely on differing sources or coding protocols and techniques (e.g., human vs. machine vs. hybrid), all of which introduce variation in measurement. Consequently, an event that appears in one dataset may be absent or recorded without identical details in another dataset. Other inconsistencies are encountered with event datasets. Their geographic and temporal coverage and precision often vary. The types of events that datasets capture can also vary. In particular, some event datasets are narrow in scope.

The immediate upshot of all these limitations is that no single dataset is likely to be decisive, as a fully complete, accurate, and sufficient representation of a relevant indicator of empirical dynamics. A further implication is that every decision by a researcher to choose one particular dataset will be expected to influence the results of analyses. In fact, the choice of a dataset can bias findings toward conclusions that might not be reached if a different dataset is used instead.

This apparent dependence of inferences on choices of datasets presents a serious problem for micro-level studies, including on topics about peace and conflict. The field needs to adopt a better means of proceeding that will ensure more consistent and appropriate measurement of phenomena, drawing upon available data in the smartest way possible.

One solution involves the systematic integration and disambiguation of datasets. In other words, the observations in multiple datasets are merged, while ensuring that the end product does not contain duplicate observations. *Integration* is designed to mitigate against under-representation of whatever is being measured. A merger of multiple datasets will augment coverage, assuming that each dataset is incomplete, but includes at least some observations that are not included in another dataset. The degree of overlap allows one to infer the robustness of the empirical basis: the more events that both datasets cover and also code consistently, the stronger the evidence. *Disambiguation* is designed to mitigate against the distortion of whatever is being measured, by limiting double-counting of observations that qualify as duplicates.

These strategies have been deployed constructively in several studies that contribute to the field of peace and conflict. Leading the way, researchers at the Human Rights Data Analysis Group (HRDAG, http://www.hrdag.org) have relied on the records from multiple diverse sources – often unstructured material – when assessing the extent and nature of casualties during conflicts in numerous countries around the world, including Guatemala (Ball, Kobrak and Spirer 1999), Timor-Leste (Silva and Ball 2006), and Syria (Price, Gohdes and Ball 2014). Building on the work of the HRDAG and others, Donnay et al. (2016) have recently introduced MELTT (Matching Event Data by Location, Time and Type), a protocol and automated tool that integrates and disambiguates any number of event datasets. The success of these approaches revolves around several crucial elements.

A basic element is addressing the core challenge of de-duplication among entries merged across multiple datasets. For example, MELTT identifies duplicate entries according to an assessment of the spatio-temporal correspondence of events reflected in entries, followed by a detailed comparison of other characteristics of events in closely corresponding entries. The recorded characteristics and their precise coding often differ substantially across datasets; only the measurement of location and timing tend to approach uniform standardization. Therefore, MELTT formalizes the task of comparing entries by using flexible taxonomies, which map event characteristics across datasets. This element of the procedure implies a degree of commonality across datasets being integrated. Fortunately, conflict event datasets usually record a number of characteristics such as type and severity, in addition to geo-coordinates and timestamps. Researchers have to identify which characteristics are to be treated as the same or analogous across datasets, as well as establish how the codes for a characteristic in one dataset relate to the codes for a characteristic in another dataset. Two codes may be identical, indicating equivalent measurement. Alternatively, codes may be similar to varying degrees, or merely fall within some broader category of the taxonomy, reflecting more substantial deviation in measurement.

All of this means that researchers must make inputs into the tool, by defining the relevant taxonomies, which requires judgments about the mapping of characteristics and codes. MELTT then structures and implements a versatile framework to use the taxonomies for purposes of undertaking disambiguation, incorporated into an automated procedure.

In the context of data integration and disambiguation, automated program-based procedures are usually superior to manual procedures for multiple reasons. Running the procedure necessitates that all specifications are declared and documented, including required inputs from researchers. None of the output is based on judgments beyond those that are made explicit. Consequently, the derivation of the output is fully transparent. The output should also be exactly reproducible by running the procedure with the same inputs. Given a list of datasets and the inputs from a researcher, which have the effect of fixing all the specifications, MELTT will always generate the same output.

In contrast, manual disambiguation is susceptible to variability and outright errors. People making comparisons by hand can arrive at different judgments and overlook information that indicates similarity or dissimilarity. Such issues materialize even in data-collection efforts that use multiple coders, with reconciliation of discrepancies in results, or conduct other sorts of quality checks. These issues reduce data quality. Also, the process of manual disambiguation may not be fully or at all transparent and is often difficult to reproduce, from both a practical and resource perspective.

On this count, automated computational procedures for integrating and disambiguating data are almost inevitably more powerful and efficient than manual procedures. Comparing information by hand can be laborious. As the number of dataset entries and/or items of information grow, the task multiplies exponentially. Each comparison may not be quick – certainly nowhere near instantaneous. Automated comparisons conducted computationally offer a massive advantage in speed relative to a manual procedure. The resource requirements and associated costs are thereby reduced tremendously, aside from programming and computational inputs. This approach also scales to handle larger volumes of data in a manner that is more readily feasible than employing a manual procedure. A further benefit of automated integration and disambiguation of data is that the process can be repeated with a rapid turnaround and at a very low cost in terms of time and resources. The ability to repeat the procedure has considerable value given datasets and other data sources are revised and extended on an ongoing basis. In addition, researchers may wish to refine the inputs and regenerate outputs. For example, a researcher using MELTT can opt to change their choices of datasets and the specifications of the disambiguation process, including the taxonomies, producing new results from the integration procedure in reasonably short order.

The important applications of such a tool are evident when one considers the findings of Weidmann (2015b). He manually compares the correspondence between the SIGACTS and UCDP-GED data on Afghanistan for 2008. The analysis identifies differences in the coverage of certain types of events: SIGACTS data provides a more complete picture of insurgent-initiated violence, but lacks coverage of both US- and ISAF-initiated actions, relative to the UCDP data. These circumstances are suited to integration and disambiguation of data, to harness the strength of each dataset and provide a fuller accounting of violence, while mitigating against duplicates.

As a demonstration, we illustrate the benefits of integrating multiple datasets on the conflict in Afghanistan using MELTT. Going beyond the manual integration of just insurgent-initiated violence that is reported in Weidmann (2015b), we consider all types of violence. Specifically, the automated procedure allows us to efficiently integrate the full SIGACTS and UCDP-GED data on violence in Afghanistan for 2008. One output is a measure of the relative coverage of each of the datasets. Because MELTT is designed to accommodate uncertainty in the coding of events, we can also deal with the various coding discrepancies noted by Weidmann – again, in an automated manner. To extend the scope of the demonstration, we include the Global Terrorism Database (GTD) as part of the integration. This source primarily covers insurgent-initiated attacks. The events included in GTD are identified via a comprehensive search of media reports, followed by automated pre-processing, then manual coding of event characteristics.

Figure 2.1 shows a summary of the main results of the integration process: the relative fractions of unique and duplicate events in the three datasets, a time-series graph of violence dynamics across Afghanistan, and a map displaying the geographical coverage of the respective datasets.[3] In each graphic, duplicate events are indicated in lighter shades of the colors corresponding to the three datasets. Given that SIGACTS features the most complete coverage overall, we treat this as the base dataset and display duplicate coding of events in UCDP-GED and GTD.

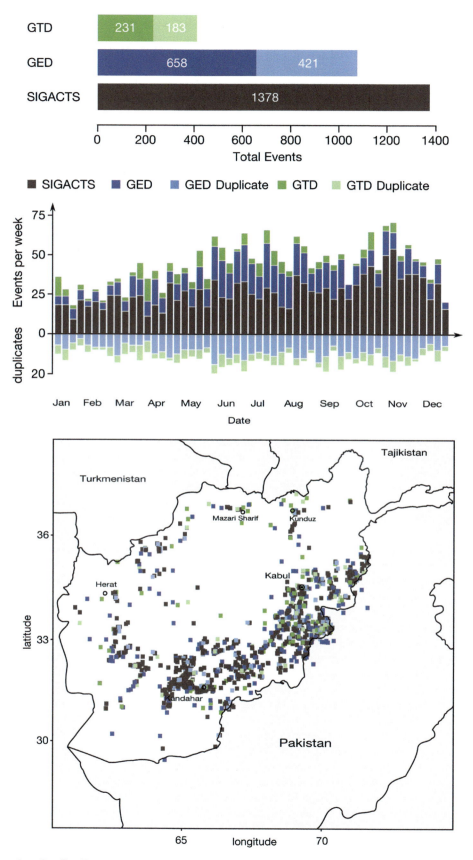

Figure 2.1 Integrating Conflict Event Data on Afghanistan, 2008

The results confirm the significant overlap between SIGACTS and UCDP-GED, especially for insurgent-initiated events, consistent with the findings of Weidmann (2015b).[4] At the same time, the results clearly show the complementary coverage of UCDP-GED. Of the 1,079 events reported in UCPD-GED, over 60% are not represented in SIGACTS; many of these are US- and ISAF-initiated actions.[5] In addition, both datasets appear not to capture a significant number of insurgent-initiated incidents recorded in GTD: of the 414 events coded in GTD, 56% are not represented in either SIGACTS or UCDP-GED. The coverage by the three datasets is relatively stable throughout 2008. The overall geographical coverage of the three datasets appears to be consistent, though local coverage differs markedly. Thus, consistent with what Weidmann (2015b) and others conclude, our demonstration confirms that the coverage of a single conflict event dataset is typically contingent on the nature of data collection and coding and may be subject to the biased inclusion or exclusion of certain types of events.

As such, we advocate systematic data integration and disambiguation as a best practice whenever multiple datasets cover a given setting. The results may reveal a high degree of overlap between the datasets. This finding need not imply wasted effort. Instead, the extent of overlap underscores the robustness of the empirical basis of an analysis. In most instances, however, integrating data from multiple sources will be a means to substantially improve empirical coverage, as demonstrated above. With the recent advent of methodological solutions such as MELTT and associated software tools, routinely applying this best practice becomes feasible for a wide range of researchers.

We caution that the solution is not a panacea. Even the product of integrating a variety of independently collected datasets is unlikely to provide complete, fully unbiased measurement of all of the "true" empirical dynamics. In many instances, therefore, integration may be only the first step in estimating how (in)complete these datasets really are. A next step can be to use techniques such as multiple systems estimation (MSE). Certain disciplines, including biology and epidemiology, have a long tradition of applying MSE. This technique is not usually applied in political science research, however, aside from some recent applications for deriving casualty estimates (c.f., Ball et al. 2003; Manrique-Vallier, Price and Gohdes 2013).

MSE is suited to contribute to the purposes we describe because of a focus on finding the extent of overlap among datasets and providing robust estimates of missingness. The technique uses statistics on which events were included in one dataset, but not others, to infer how many events neither dataset captured (Manrique-Vallier, Price and Gohdes 2013). In much the same manner, MSE could provide crucial information on the completeness of datasets once integrated, from which valuable estimates of how many events should be recorded altogether can be derived. These results can also be extended to extrapolate better estimates of other characteristics of events – for example, measures of overall casualties. More broadly, insight about the degree of missingness in datasets illuminates the empirical context for making inferences, which has direct implications for the generalizability of findings.

We acknowledge that the MSE technique has important limitations, which constrain application. For robust analyses without strong technical assumptions, MSE requires more than two datasets, which are independent of one another. This means datasets compiled using the same or similar sources and protocols are less than ideal candidates. Likewise, if datasets cover similar aspects of empirical dynamics in a particular setting, but fail to cover other aspects, then the application of MSE will not augment the scope of coverage to encompass all aspects – the technique is data-dependent. Also, MSE does not add any event-specific information. Instead, the technique can merely afford a better sense of how many events are missing across a number of datasets. Details such as where and when the missing events occurred will remain unknown.

Integrating Different Types of Data

As we discussed in the previous section, performing analysis at theoretically appropriate and comparable units of observation is critically important for the generalizability of findings from micro-level studies. Such analysis can be technically difficult to accomplish due to the nature of available data. Among the main hurdles are indicators for relevant variables that are measured at inconsistent spatial units. Unless theory clearly says otherwise, these indicators ought to correspond to the same spatial units.

When faced with inconsistencies in units of measurement, a solution is to achieve consistency through the imputation of indicators, as necessary, to a fitting common unit. Spatial imputation techniques, well established in the field of geography, are not necessarily part of the repertoire of many researchers in other social science disciplines, nor have they been included in widely used statistical software.

Implementation of imputations requires addressing the distinctive spatial characteristics of data, making important decisions in the process. Increasingly, many types of data are coded using geographic information systems (GIS), which facilitates imputation. Even GIS data, however, may have different formats. For example, population density is typically coded as raster data, whereas administrative districts and population settlement areas are demarcated as polygons. Meanwhile, event data may be coded as points, where possible. In merging diverse GIS layers that contain indicators of interest, decisions concerning the appropriate unit of analysis, as well as the assignment rules that determine each variable's numerical value in the common units, are central. These decisions ought to be transparent, standardized by protocol, and reproducible by other researchers. In practice, some researchers repeat analyses for alternative specifications that take account of considerations regarding spatial units of measurement, to demonstrate the robustness of results.

A key need is for tools that overcome technical constraints of working with complex spatial data and allow researchers to readily perform analyses at appropriate units of their choosing. At least three significant initiatives have taken major steps along these lines, with applications that contribute to standardization of data in the field of peace and conflict studies.

The first initiative is the PRIO-GRID dataset produced by the Peace Research Institute Oslo (Tollefson, Strand, and Buhaug 2012). This dataset reports dozens of relevant variables, such as violent event counts and socioeconomic, political, environmental, and geographic indicators, along a regular, highly granular spatial grid of 55 km x 55 km cells that covers the entire world. A constraint is that this dataset comes in only one form. Any researchers who wish to conduct analysis with spatial units of other sizes and shapes must take care of adjustments by themselves.

The second initiative is SpatialGridBuilder (Pickering 2016), a tool that transforms spatial data to any grid size. A constraint is that this stand-alone software package and interface is not set up to function directly with statistical and computational analysis platforms.

The third initiative is the data integration package *geomerge* for the R statistical programming language (Donnay and Linke 2016). This package, which builds on methodological innovations reflected in the first two initiatives, is designed to provide researchers with an easy-to-use tool that transparently and robustly integrates spatial data. The package aims for the middle ground between the overly-simplistic approach of relying entirely on existing off-the-shelf datasets and complex approaches to processing spatial data that require substantial GIS programming skills. The tool enables researchers to apply standard functionalities for their specific goals, as warranted. Any number and format of GIS layers can be aggregated in a series of spatio-temporal joins that assign each variable's numerical values to a target spatial resolution, which can assume any geographical shape. For these purposes, the package reflects existing best practices, including different types of spatial join assignment rules, zonal statistics, etc. (c.f., Bivand, Pebesma, and Gómez-Rubio 2013; Brunsdon and Comber 2015). In addition to merging different kinds of data, the tool automatically aggregates event counts to the designated spatio-temporal unit of analysis, whether this takes the form of district-months, grid cell-months or -days, or something else. Also, the tool returns the spatial lag values – encompassing first- to third-order adjacent units – of all variables, which facilitates spatial econometric and predictive modeling.

The *geomerge* package was developed for generic application, but is certainly relevant to the research on peace and conflict. Here, we demonstrate the versatility of the approach with reference to the data used in Weidmann (2015b).

Our initial illustration employs the tool to integrate static covariate data at different spatial units of analysis. Figure 2.2 (top panel) shows a population raster dataset (CIESIN, FAO, and CIAT 2005) joined with the administrative districts of Afghanistan, drawing the necessary spatial polygons from data compiled by the ESOC project at Princeton (https://esoc.princeton.edu/), as well as with 55 km x 55 km cells as found in PRIO-GRID.

The next illustration highlights why the choice of the spatio-temporal unit of analysis matters. Figure 2.2 (bottom panel) shows the comparison of grid cell-year and district-year counts of events of insurgent-initiated violence, integrated from SIGACTS, UCDP-GED and GTD, as discussed above. The maps convey different pictures about patterns of violence, depending on the choice of units, even though the maps are derived from the same raw data. This variation reinforces the need for researchers to repeat analyses for different choices of units, in order to evaluate the sensitivity of their findings. The *geomerge* package simplifies these robustness checks, allowing researchers to easily generate spatial panels for any spatio-temporal units. Because the package adopts consistent, reliable methodology, data joined to a given unit are fully comparable within and across settings because the same assumptions and assignment rules were used uniformly.

Conclusion

What insights can be drawn from the recent evolution toward micro-level research on peace and conflict? Because of the level of analytical detail, such research offers unique empirical leverage, illuminating key dynamics that are otherwise impossible to study. Yet micro-level studies often pose challenges for the generalizability of findings, which are essential to acknowledge and address. Generalizing insights obtained from micro-level analyses is vital for theory development and knowledge accumulation. Fundamental causal relationships will be illuminated only if studies of the same phenomenon in the same setting yield similar findings, and insights also "travel" beyond the specific settings examined in any single study or set of studies. Furthermore, generalizability hinges on the basic assumption that the empirical characteristics of the settings we study account for any differences in the relationships we observe from analysis.

This assumption entails that other sources of variation across studies ought to be minimized to the extent possible. As we have discussed in this chapter, these strict requirements are such that the theoretical and conceptual bases, the empirical

Micro-Level Research on Peace and Conflict

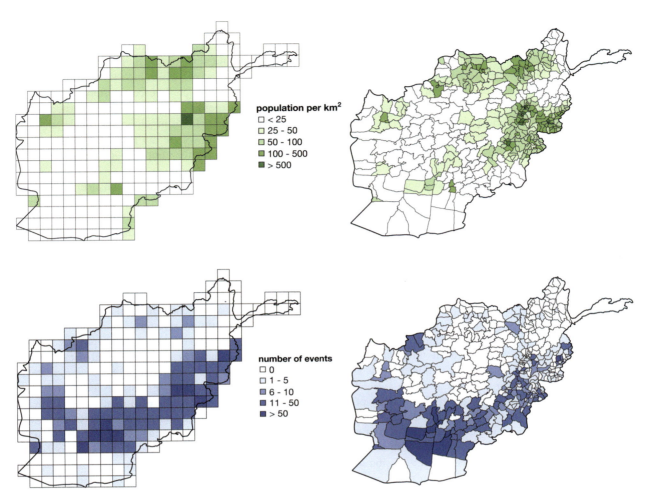

Figure 2.2 Data at Different Spatial Units of Analysis
Note: Data on population density (top maps) are drawn from CIESIN. Counts of conflict events (bottom maps) are derived from the integrated and disambiguated data using SIGACTS, UCDP-GED and GTD, as illustrated in Figure 2.1.

strategy, and the methodological approach should not be distinct to individual studies. Instead, studies must match sufficiently on those characteristics in order for substantive findings to be generalized, thereby supplying a firm basis for deriving implications for policy and practice. In other words, the comparisons of multiple studies must be apples to apples, or else the desire for broader inferences is undermined.

In practice, however, studies often diverge along key dimensions. Differences in theoretical bases, empirical strategies, and methodological approaches provide ample room to yield inconsistent findings, even if patterns, trends, and relationships are similar in reality. Without adequate attention to such issues, a real danger exists that important insights are lost amid diverse and even contradictory findings. Unless the dimensions of studies are comparable, it is impossible to tell whether disparities in findings are mere artifacts of specific choices made by researchers. The studies we review in this chapter – spanning Africa, Afghanistan and Iraq – highlight these concerns, providing tangible evidence that differences along dimensions of research compromise the comparability of findings across micro-level studies and ultimately their generalizability.

What then can researchers do to alleviate the concerns? The short answer is to aim for greater comparability. This recommendation may sound obvious, not to mention already demanded by the entrenched first principles of research. Yet all too often, studies are not entirely comparable, which tends to arise for several reasons. Researchers study different angles of a broad topic, in distinctive ways. Researchers also have disparate ideas about how to study the same topic. In addition, studying a topic in the same way may be complicated by variation, especially across settings, in the data that are already available or can feasibly be compiled. Compounding the problem, it remains the exception, rather than the rule, that published studies are released with the data necessary to replicate results, let alone the fuller extent of data that would allow other researchers to conduct (re)analysis and judge the rigor and robustness of findings.

Against this backdrop, we advocate a continued push for a greater degree of standardization across studies. Our call is hardly intended to insist upon complete uniformity, which would be nonsensical and squelch the gains that ought to be realized through novelty and innovation. Balance between standardization and distinctiveness is always needed. The former helps to ensure that comparability across studies is relatively straightforward, while the latter pushes research frontiers in suggestive new directions that demand careful replication in further studies. The conventional practice that each study offers multiple variants of an analysis, using different theoretical bases, empirical strategies, and methodological approaches, is fruitful. These variants can serve as robustness checks, yield more angles of insight, and provide additional results that contribute to worthwhile comparisons of findings across studies. In sum, we are not proposing for researchers to be forced into narrow lanes, but rather that they should be more attentive to the need for comparability and generalization of results.

In the context of studies on peace and conflict, we focus on the prospect of solutions that could enhance the extent of standardization in empirical strategies, which can be expected to carry over to methodological approaches too. Of central interest is the nature of measurement, especially the format, units of observation, coding, and coverage of data employed in different studies. Here, we think that major opportunities exist for achieving greater standardization. In this field (as with many), data are hard to develop. Researchers often rely on available datasets provided as public goods by various institutional initiatives. This circumstance has a number of implications. One implication is advantageous: a large share of researchers draws on the same array of data, which is already a major step toward standardization. Another implication is disadvantageous: researchers have off-the-shelf datasets to use, which provide a quick route to analysis that attenuates the incentive to devote attention to introspection about data and to further data development. The field can be advanced by researchers using consistent, suitable, combining existing resources with original primary research.

On these counts, we introduce and guide researchers to follow our recommended best practices by employing MELTT to integrate event data obtained from multiple sources and *geomerge* to join different kinds of spatial data. MELTT improves data coverage and quality, while *geomerge* enables data to be rendered at comparable units as appropriate for analysis – ideally, reflecting the level at which a causal mechanism of interest operates. These tools are fully standardized and transparent, contributing to the reproducibility of any study in which they are used. In particular, other researchers can easily test the sensitivity of findings to the decisions made in applying the tools. These practices are also consistent with the recent push in social science that advocates strict reproducibility of empirical research (King, 1995; O'Loughlin et al. 2015). In all those ways, tools such as these improve efforts to standardize peace and conflict research, aspiring toward the goals of validating analytical results within a specific setting and generalizing findings across settings.

Stepping back, micro-level research on peace and conflict is at a crossroads, where convergence on a set of minimal standards that ensure comparability across studies and clear commitments to transparency and reproducibility are warranted. The disparate findings discussed in this chapter, which can lead to diametrically opposite conclusions and policy implications, can be avoided in many instances if the best practices we (and others) advocate are consistently followed. At the very least, researchers will have a much more accurate measure of the robustness of their findings within and across studies. This outcome serves not only to provide a more nuanced and reliable basis for academic research on peace and conflict, but also helps to better inform debates that are central to policymakers and practitioners who are actively engaged in real-world settings.

Notes

1 For example, research on greed and grievances at the macro level features the very same problem of divergent findings driven by theoretical and methodological inconsistencies (Ross 2006).
2 Shapiro and Weidmann (2015) also analyze the impact of mobile phone technologies on violent events at the much more fine-grained spatial resolution of individual cell phone towers.
3 When identifying potential duplicate events, we allowed for a maximal coding uncertainty of 2 days and 10 km. Disambiguating events, we used rich taxonomies for type of event and geo-spatial coding precision.
4 The overlap of 421 events between UCPD-GED and SIGACTS identified in the automatized comparison using MELTT is consistent with the 434 events identified in the manual comparison performed in Weidmann (2015b).
5 The UCDP-GED data used here are drawn from the most current version 5.0 of the dataset, which features a broader coverage of events compared to the preliminary data used in Weidmann (2015b).

References

Ball, Patrick, Jana Asher, David Sulmont, and Daniel Manrique (2003) *How Many Peruvians Have Died? An Estimate of the Total Number of Victims Killed or Disappeared in the Armed Internal Conflict between 1980 and 2000. Report to the Peruvian Truth and Reconciliation Commission (CVR)*. Washington, DC: AAAS.
Ball, Patrick, Paul Kobrak, and Herbert F. Spirer (1999) *State Violence in Guatemala, 1960–1996: A Quantitative Reflection*. Washington, DC: AAAS.

Bivand, Roger S., Edzer Pebesma, and Virgilio Gómez-Rubio (2013) *Applied Spatial Data Analysis with R* (2nd ed.). New York: Springer.

Brunsdon, Chris, and Lex Comber (2015) *An Introduction to R for Spatial Analysis and Mapping*. London: Sage Publishing.

Center for International Earth Science Information Network, Columbia University (CIESIN), United Nations Food and Agriculture Programme (FAO), and Centro Internacional de Agricultura Tropical (CIAT). (2005) *Gridded Population of the World Version 3 (GPWv3): Population Count Grid*. Palisades, NY: Socioeconomic Data and Applications Center (SEDAC). Available at http://sedac.ciesin.columbia.edu/gpw.

Chojnacki, Sven, Christian Ickler, Michael Spies, and John Wiesel (2012) "Event Data on Armed Conflict and Security: New Perspectives, Old Challenges, and Some Solutions." *International Interactions* 38(4): 382–401.

Croicu, Mihai, and Joakim Kreutz (2017) "Communication Technology and Reports on Political Violence: Cross-National Evidence Using African Events Data." *Political Research Quarterly* 70(1): 19–31.

Donnay, Karsten, and Vladimir Filimonov (2014) "Views to a War: Systematic Differences in Media and Military Reporting of the War in Iraq." *EPJ Data Science* 3(1): 1–29.

Donnay, Karsten, Elena Gadjanova, and Ravi Bhavnani (2014) "Disaggregating Conflict by Actors, Time, and Location." In David A. Backer, Paul K. Huth, and Jonathan Wilkenfeld (eds) *Peace and Conflict 2014*. Boulder, CO: Paradigm Publishers.

Donnay, Karsten, and Ravi Bhavnani (2016) "The Cutting Edge of Research on Peace and Conflict." In David A. Backer, Ravi Bhavnani, and Paul K. Huth (eds) *Peace and Conflict 2016*. New York: Routledge.

Donnay, Karsten and Andrew Linke (2016) "Geomerge: Spatial Data Integration." Working paper.

Donnay, Karsten, Eric Dunford, Erin C. McGrath, David Backer, and David E. Cunningham (2016) "MELTT: Matching Event Data by Location, Time and Type." Paper presented at the Midwest Political Science Association's Annual Meeting, Chicago, April.

Kalyvas, Stathis N. (2008) "Promises and Pitfalls of an Emerging Research Program: The Microdynamics of Civil War." In Stathis N. Kalyvas, Ian Shapiro and Tarek Masoud (eds) *Order, Conflict and Violence*. Cambridge: Cambridge University Press.

King, Gary (1995) "Replication, Replication." *PS: Political Science and Politics* 28: 444–452.

Manrique-Vallier, Daniel, Megan E. Price, and Anita Gohdes (2013) "Multiple Systems Estimation Techniques for Estimating Casualties in Armed Conflicts." In Taylor B. Seybolt, Jay D. Aronson, and Baruch Fischhoff (eds) *Counting Civilian Casualties: An Introduction to Recording and Estimating Nonmilitary Deaths in Conflict*. Oxford: Oxford University Press.

O'Loughlin, John, Pauliina Raento, Joanne P. Sharp, James D. Sidaway, and Philip E. Steinberg (2015) "Data Ethics: Pluralism, Replication, Conflicts of Interest, and Standards in Political Geography." *Political Geography* 44: A1–A4.

Openshaw, Stan (1983) *The Modifiable Areal Unit Problem*. Norfolk: Geo Books.

Openshaw, Stan, and Peter J. Taylor (1979) "A Million or So Correlation Coefficients: Three Experiments on the Modifiable Areal Unit Problem." In Neil Wrigley (ed.) *Statistical Applications in the Spatial Sciences*. London: Pion.

Pickering, Steve (2016) "Introducing SpatialGridBuilder: A New System for Creating Geo-Coded Datasets." *Conflict Management and Peace Science* 33(4): 423–447.

Pierskalla, Jan H., and Florian M. Hollenbach (2013) "Technology and Collective Action: The Effect of Cell Phone Coverage on Political Violence in Africa." *American Political Science Review* 107(2): 207–224.

Price, Megan, Anita Gohdes, and Patrick Ball (2014) "Updated Statistical Analysis of Documentation of Killings in the Syrian Arab Republic." *Human Rights Data Analysis Group, commissioned by the United Nations Office of the High Commissioner for Human Rights (OHCHR)*.

Raleigh, Clionadh, Andrew Linke, Håvard Hegre, and Joakim Karleson (2010) "Introducing ACLED: An Armed Conflict Location and Event Dataset." *Journal of Peace Research* 47(5): 651–660.

Ross, Michael (2006) "A Closer Look at Oil, Diamonds, and Civil War." *Annual Review of Political Science* 9(1): 265–300.

Salehyan, Idean, Cullen S. Hendrix, Jesse Hamner, Christina Case, Christopher Linebarger, Emily Stull, and Jennifer Williams (2012) "Social Conflict in Africa: A New Database." *International Interactions* 38(4): 503–511.

Shapiro, Jacob N., and Nils B. Weidmann (2015) "Is the Phone Mightier Than the Sword? Cellphones and Insurgent Violence in Iraq?" *International Organization* 69(2): 247–274.

Silva, Romesh, and Patrick Ball (2006) "The Profile of Human Rights Violations in Timor-Leste, 1974–1999." *A Report by the Benetech Human Rights Data Analysis Group to the Commission on Reception, Truth and Reconciliation of Timor-Leste*.

(START) National Consortium for the Study of Terrorism and Responses to Terrorism (2013) *Global Terrorism Database*. Available from http://www.start.umd.edu/gtd.

Straus, Scott (2007) "What is the Relationship Between Hate Radio and Violence? Rethinking Rwanda's 'Radio Machete'." *Politics and Society* 35: 609–637.

Sundberg, Ralph, and Erik Melander (2013) "Introducing the UCDP Georeferenced Event Dataset." *Journal of Peace Research* 50(4): 523–532.

Tollefson, Andreas F., Håvard Strand, and Halvard Buhaug (2012) "PRIO-GRID: A Unified Spatial Data Structure." *Journal of Peace Research* 49(2): 363–374.

Weidmann, Nils B. (2013) "The Higher the Better? The Limits of Analytical Resolution in Conflict Event Datasets." *Cooperation and Conflict* 48(4): 567–576.

Weidmann, Nils B. (2015a) "On the Accuracy of Media-based Conflict Event Data." *Journal of Conflict Resolution* 59(6): 1129–1149.

Weidmann, Nils B. (2015b) "A Closer Look at Reporting Bias in Conflict Event Data." *American Journal of Political Science* 60(1): 206–218.

Yanagizawa-Drott, David (2014) "Propaganda and Conflict: Evidence from the Rwandan Genocide." *The Quarterly Journal of Economics* 129(4): 1947–1994.

3

Tracing Armed Conflict over Time

A Reversal of the Recent Decline?

Håvard Strand and Halvard Buhaug

Introduction: From Worse to Bad?

The number of active armed conflicts reached a 25-year peak in 2015, making this another bleak year for international peace and security. These circumstances reinforce the impression that the decline of war, heralded less than a decade ago, is not only halted but reversed. The number of new or recurring (vs. ongoing) conflicts was also at a record high. A positive development is that fatalities fell by 10% relative to 2014. Yet this improvement is set against a backdrop where annual conflict fatalities have been far higher in each of the last few years than was the case from 2001–2012.

The extent and lethality of armed conflict in recent years resembles the previous surge following the collapse of the Cold War, though there are important differences as well. The peak in conflict during the early 1990s was driven to a large extent by nationalist movements related to the breakup of the Soviet Union and Yugoslavia, resulting in a sharp rise in distinct separatist conflicts. The recent increase in conflict frequency is mainly the product of militant Islamism, spearheaded by *al-Qaeda* and the *Islamic State* (IS), whose modus operandi is unaffected by the demarcation of international borders. Put another way, today's conflicts involve a relatively small set of non-state actors, many of which are related in a more complex web of ideology and identity, fighting a large number of governments that draw on military and moral support from an ever larger number of countries.

In this chapter, we present and discuss three notable and related patterns of contemporary armed conflict: (1) the increase in conflict prevalence and severity; (2) the increasing internationalization of armed conflict; and (3) the increasing role of militant Islamism. While recent developments may give little room for optimism, at least in the short run, the situation today does not look equally bad on all dimensions.

The Entrenchment of a Worrying Trend

The Uppsala Conflict Data Program (UCDP), the leading provider of statistics on armed conflicts (Gleditsch et al. 2002), recorded 50 active cases – those with 25 or more annual battle-related deaths – during 2015 (Melander, Pettersson, and Themnér 2016). This figure is the highest since 1991 (51 conflicts) and the second highest ever recorded in the dataset, which covers from 1946 onwards. Moreover, the figure constitutes a dramatic continuation of the recent increase in conflict, amounting to over 50% growth since 2012 (33 conflicts). In this sense, the much-lauded "decline of war" (Pinker 2011), clearly visible in the statistics for the 1990s and early 2000s, appears to be not only halted but reversed (Figure 3.1).

Among the 50 active conflicts, there was just one interstate conflict (India–Pakistan over Kashmir) and 49 internal conflicts, 20 of which involved international participants.[1] Eleven new conflicts broke out in 2015 – the highest number of new onsets in a single year since 1948 (12 new conflicts). Eight of these 11 conflicts concerned the violent struggle to establish a so-called *Islamic State* in countries across Sub-Saharan Africa, Asia, and North Africa and the Middle East. Two more conflicts involved other Islamist organizations (*al-Shabaab* in Kenya and the *Macina Liberation Front* in Mali). The last new internal conflict came as a result of a merger between four separatist groups in the Indian northeast, claiming self-determination for the "Western South East Asia". In addition to the new conflict onsets, seven older conflicts restarted during 2015 after one or more year(s) of inactivity, bringing the total number of new plus restarted conflicts to 18 – second only to 1991 (19) in the entire post-World War II period.

If we focus on the number of countries experiencing active armed conflict, captured in the top panel of Figure 3.1, the situation appears to be slightly less dramatic. The number of these locations was 32 in 2015, well below the 37–38 locations observed during the peak in the early 1990s. In other words, many of the new and recurring conflicts are located in countries already engaged in armed conflict. Indeed, 13 of the conflict-affected countries in 2015 hosted two or more conflicts, with India, Mali, and Syria the sites of three distinct conflicts apiece, and Myanmar as many as four. We discuss the spatial distribution of conflicts in further detail below.

Tracing the numbers of armed conflicts and of locations of conflict is one way to assess trends in global security. Another, arguably more direct, indicator is the lethality of conflict. Figure 3.2 shows the global annual battle-related deaths in armed conflict over the post-Cold War period, highlighting the contribution of the three most severe conflicts to the total in each year.

Although this period has been remarkably peaceful by long-term historical standards, the results show that the level of violence varies considerably across years, with notable peaks separated by periods of relative tranquility. The peak years also are the years in which the most brutal conflicts account for the largest share of the global casualty number. This relationship is reminiscent of a power law distribution, first demonstrated by Richardson (1948), which basically means that large wars are much less frequent than small wars. Three unusually deadly periods stand out.

First, the start of the post-Cold War era was dominated by the final stages of prolonged civil war in Ethiopia, which had been ongoing since 1976 and involved a plethora of rebel organizations. In the late 1980s, an alliance (the Ethiopian

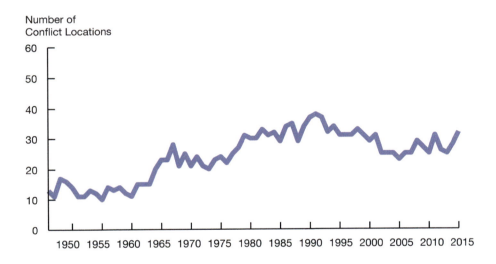

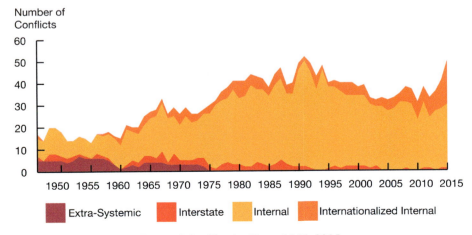

Figure 3.1 Annual Frequency of Organized Armed Conflict, by Type, 1946–2015
Note: Data based on UCDP/PRIO Armed Conflict Dataset (Melander, Pettersson, and Themnér 2016; Gleditsch et al. 2002).

People's Revolutionary Democratic Front) was formed among the largest of these rebel organizations, around the same time that the Ethiopian government lost military support from the by-then defunct Soviet Union. In just three years (1989–91), 86,000 people were killed on various battlefields in Ethiopia. In 1991, Ethiopia was overshadowed by the swift US-led liberation of Kuwait against the Iraqi invaders. About 22,000 people were killed in this war, almost all Iraqis.

The next peak is also connected to Ethiopia. Eritrea had achieved independence from Ethiopia after a lengthy separatist struggle that culminated with the events of 1991. In 1998, a minor border dispute between the countries escalated, pitting the presidents of the two countries – former allies in the fight against the Mengistu regime of Ethiopia – in a bloody trench war. Within two years, almost 100,000 people were killed, accounting for two-thirds of all conflict-related deaths worldwide in 1999–2000.

The third and most violent post-Cold War peak began in earnest in 2013 and is still ongoing. This new wave of violence is dominated by the wars in the Middle East and adjoining areas. The most severe wars are found in Syria, Afghanistan and Iraq, which together jointly accounted for around three-quarters of all battle-related deaths in this period.

The country that features most frequently on the unflattering top-three list of battle-related casualties is Afghanistan, with 22 appearances since 1989. The exceptions are 1990–1 and 2002–4. These relatively more peaceful years followed the Soviet withdrawal and the US invasion. respectively With the exception of 2002–5, more than 1,000 people have been killed in battle in Afghanistan every year since 1979. Iraq and Sri Lanka both ranked among the top three most violent countries in nine years, including four and three years, respectively, as the most violent country. In every year since 2012, Syria has generated the highest number of battle-related casualties.

A notable trend is the recent increase in battle-related deaths for the less severe conflicts, represented by the lighter shade in Figure 3.2. This increase is due partly to a rise in the number of active armed conflicts discussed earlier. Another reason is that the average conflict intensity has gone up in recent years. Compared to the 1990s, however, these less severe conflicts are not especially violent, implying that the recent uptick is largely the product of a handful of cases.

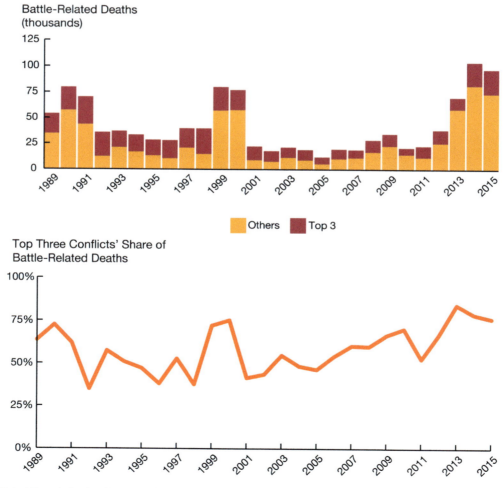

Figure 3.2 Global Trends in the Severity of Organized Armed Conflict, 1989–2015
Note: Data based on UCDP Battle-Related Deaths Dataset v.5–2015.

A further key difference between 1991 and 2016 is the addition of 2 billion people to the global population (World Bank 2015). This circumstance raises the overall demand for a large number of commodities, though the worldwide rate of poverty has fortunately been reduced (United Nations 2015). Such resource competition can spur conflict.

At the same time, the crude rate of deaths directly attributable to armed conflict has fallen considerably and remains at a very low level (Pinker 2011). These facts should be acknowledged as counterpoints to the recent negative trend toward a greater number of conflicts, including some with high intensity. The reduction is largely due to the near absence of interstate wars, which analysts have attributed to a more organized and interdependent world (Mueller 2009). The previous internationalist threat to world peace, communism, was backed by large and relatively resource-rich countries capable of waging war across the globe. These countries, either directly or through proxies, fueled the largest conflicts in the later parts of the twentieth century, along with their counterparts on the democratic side.

Internationalization of Armed Conflict

While internationalization of armed conflict in the form of interstate wars has waned since World War II, the number of internal conflicts with international participation has increased steadily over the last 25 years. Continuing this trend, 2015 saw a strong increase in internationalization of armed conflicts: more than 40% of the active internal conflicts involved at least one international actor – the highest share ever recorded.

The conflicts with the largest number of external actors were the government of Mali's fights against *La Coordination des Mouvements de l'Azawad* (CMA) and *al-Qaeda in the Islamic Maghreb* (AQIM), in which the Malian government received support (i.e., troops on the ground) from no less than 54 foreign countries. The two conflicts are listed separately in the UCDP/PRIO data since these two rebel organizations are pursuing different goals. All 54 countries are present in both conflicts, as a result of which Mali accounts for 108 instances of international involvement in internal armed conflicts. Other conflicts with high international participation include the Iraqi government's struggle against IS (12 countries) and the government of Somalia versus *al-Shabaab* (eight countries). In addition, nine states supported forces loyal to the Yemeni ex-president Hadi in their conflict against the Sana'a-based Houthi forces that overthrew the Hadi government in early 2015.

One reason for the increase in internationalized conflict (as well as the rise in conflict more generally) is the growth of militant Islamist ideology. During the Arab Spring, many countries saw civil society oppose the established political elites. Religious organizations were often best poised to dominate these movements, which in many cases, most notably in Egypt and Bahrain, were struck down by the military.

Figure 3.3 underscores this recent shift. This figure displays the number of foreign countries participating with troops in internal conflicts elsewhere, per year. Up until 2000, international involvement was uncommon and almost always involved non-Islamist conflicts. Military assistance was most often in the form of weapon supplies. A number of high-profile interventions were dismal failures, such as the Vietnam War and the Suez Crisis. The Gulf War in 1991 saw

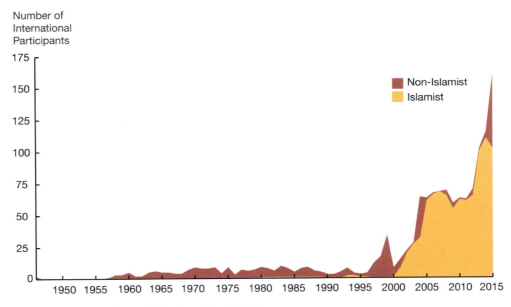

Figure 3.3 Internationalization of Armed Conflict, 1946–2015
Note: Data based on UCDP/PRIO Armed Conflict Dataset (Melander, Pettersson, and Themnér 2016; Gleditsch et al. 2002) and Gleditsch and Rudolfsen (2016).

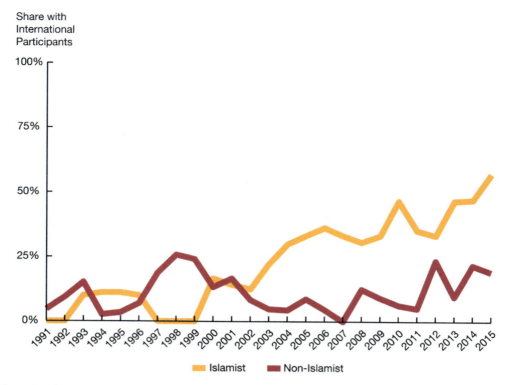

Figure 3.4 The Role of Islamism in Internationalized Internal Conflict, 1991–2015
Note: Data based on UCDP/PRIO Armed Conflict Dataset (Melander, Pettersson, and Themnér 2016; Gleditsch et al. 2002) and Gleditsch and Rudolfsen (2016).

a spike of international activity, as a broad coalition of states was formed to counter the government of Saddam Hussein.[2]

In the latter part of the 1990s, the extent of international involvement in armed conflicts started to grow. Notable examples included several conflicts in Africa, such as the civil wars in Zaire/Democratic Republic of the Congo, Liberia and Sierra Leone. In 1999, a large international coalition took to the skies over Serbia to end what was perceived as a genocide about to happen in Kosovo.

From 2001 onwards, the situation changed even more dramatically. No less than 902 dyads of armed conflict have been observed between governments and Islamist opposition organizations with the involvement of foreign governments. This figure accounts for 68% of all foreign interventions in internal conflict for the whole post-WWII period.

Not all conflicts involving Islamists rebels exhibit international participation, but the trend is toward increasing involvement. Figure 3.4 shows the share of internal armed conflicts since 1991 that are internationalized, differentiating between conflicts involving an Islamist rebel group and all others. The tendency towards greater international involvement became more pronounced during the late 1990s. Between 1997 and 1999, however, no Islamist conflict was internationalized. By 2015, well over 50% of the Islamist conflicts were internationalized, compared to 20% of other conflicts in 2015. In total, over 75% of conflicts were internationalized, a huge jump from the shares of less than 10% in the early 1990s, 20–30% in the mid- and late-1990s and 30–40% in the early 2000s.

Increasing Dominance of Militant Islamism

As mentioned above, every new conflict that broke out in 2015 involved, except one, militant Islamist actors. In addition, many of the ongoing internationalized conflicts involve multiple state governments who joined forces to fight IS-affiliated non-state actors across borders.

In effect, we are witnessing a concentration of conflict in the Muslim world. Figure 3.5 presents a simple visualization of the geographic distribution of armed conflict over time, comparing the initial post-Cold War years (1989–94) with the most recent period (2010–15). Much as one would expect, countries that have hosted conflict in both periods (shaded in orange) are largely located in the developing world, with distinct hotspots along the Sahelian belt and in the chain of countries from the Caucasus to South Asia. Elsewhere, notably in Latin America, Europe, and Southeast Asia, we find a

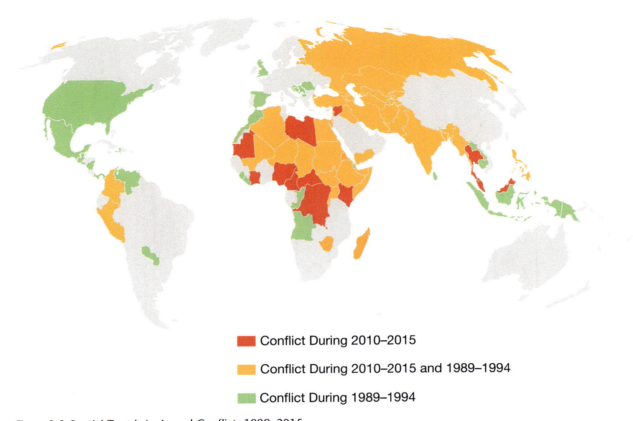

Figure 3.5 Spatial Trends in Armed Conflict, 1989–2015
Note: Data based on UCDP/PRIO Armed Conflict Dataset (Melander, Pettersson, and Themnér 2016; Gleditsch et al. 2002) and Gleditsch and Rudolfsen (2016).

number of countries that have successfully managed to end the conflicts of the first period (shaded in green). With the pending resolution of the long-standing Colombian civil war, the Americas may be devoid of active armed conflict – and the world may experience an entire continent at peace – for the first time in 45 years.[3] The other category is comprised of locations experiencing recent outbreaks of new conflict, which were at peace as of the early 1990s (shaded in red). All these countries – concentrated in Africa – are adjacent to countries with protracted conflict. This finding epitomizes the fact that contemporary political violence and instability are increasingly located in the Muslim world.

Gleditsch and Rudolfsen (2016) document this trend, as visualized in Figure 3.6. This figure focuses only on those conflicts that are labelled wars, which requires at least 1,000 battle-related deaths. Muslim countries have historically accounted for a fair share of the world's wars, ranging up to 60% between 1946 and 2000. From 2005 onwards, however, a pronounced shift is observed, whereby Muslim countries predominate on the list of conflicts. This shift transpired against a global backdrop in which 2005–11 was an exceptionally peaceful period – probably among the least violent in human history. Wars ended all around the world, except in the Muslim world. It remains to be seen whether the drop in the share over the past couple of years is symptomatic of a broader negative trend documented elsewhere in this chapter, or signals something more specific about the reduced vulnerability of Muslim countries to conflict.

A parallel trend is observed for Islamist insurgents. Between 1962 and 1978, no Islamist insurgency took part in any conflict that resulted in 1,000 battle-related fatalities. During the 1980s, Afghanistan was the main location for militant Islamism. Throughout the 1980s and especially the 1990s, ardent nationalism and ethnic rivalries were perceived to be more potent problems than militant Islamism. The landscape has clearly changed since the early 2000s. Today, 75% of all wars have an Islamist group directly involved. This involvement has been destabilizing and destructive, but has not generally resulted in taking control of state authority through force. The rise of the Taliban in Afghanistan represented the first case of military victory by a militant Islamic armed group. Very few similar victories have been observed. In Somalia, the Supreme Islamic Council of Somalia and its militant wing, *al-Shabaab*, won control over Mogadishu in June 2006, lasting to mid-December the same year. Apart from those cases, militant Islamism has not done very well in regards to winning power. In 2014, IS declared the territory it controls to be an Islamic state – a caliphate. At the time of writing, the future of this proto-state remains very unclear.

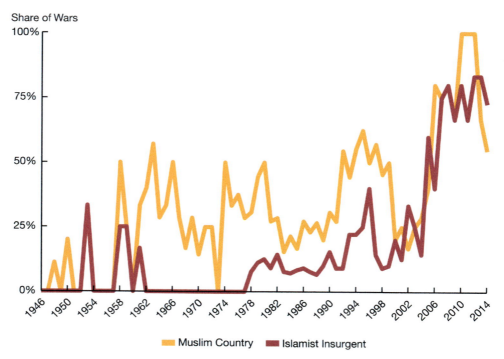

Figure 3.6 Civil Wars in Muslim Countries or with Islamist Insurgents, 1946–2014
Note: Figure 3 from Gleditsch and Rudolfsen (2016).

Conclusion

After a nationalist-infused explosion of armed conflicts in the wake of the collapse of communism, the world moved into an exceptionally peaceful period. The trend towards a more peaceful world was broken in 2011. For a few years, peace researchers have been uncertain as to whether we have observed a speed-bump or a more permanent change in the conflict picture.

Based on the data from 2015, we must acknowledge that the number of conflicts and the number of casualties are indeed at a higher level than they were five years ago. This increase must be seen in light of the war on terror as well as the changes that have occurred in the Middle East and North Africa region since the onset of the Arab Spring. It is very hard to predict whether this situation will persist. To avoid such an outcome, crafting some form of peace in Syria and other hot spots across the region, if only partial, should be a top priority of all international policymakers.

Notes

1 See http://www.pcr.uu.se/research/ucdp/definitions/definition_of_armed_conflict/ for the UCDP definition of armed conflict.
2 The 1991 spike is not present in Figure 3.3 as it was seen as a conflict between two countries, despite Saddam Hussein's claims.
3 Oceania is excluded.

References

Gleditsch, Nils Petter, and Ida Rudolfsen (2016) "Are Muslim Countries More Prone to Violence?" *Research & Politics* 3(2): 1-9.
Gleditsch, Nils Petter, Peter Wallensteen, Mikael Eriksson, Margareta Sollenberg, and Håvard Strand (2002) "Armed Conflict 1946–2001: A New Dataset." *Journal of Peace Research* 39(5): 615–637.
Melander, Erik, Thérése Pettersson, and Lotta Themnér (2016) "Organized Violence, 1989–2015." *Journal of Peace Research* 53(5): 727–742.
Mueller, John (2009) "War Has Almost Ceased to Exist: An Assessment." *Political Science Quarterly* 124(2): 297–321.
Pinker, Steven (2011) *The Better Angels of Our Nature. Why Violence Has Declined*. New York: Viking.
United Nations (2015) "The Millennium Development Goals Report 2015." United Nations.
World Bank (2015) *World Development Indicators*. http://data.worldbank.org/products/wdi.

4

The Geography of Organized Armed Violence around the World

Erik Melander, David A. Backer, and Eric Dunford

Introduction

In the previous edition of the *Peace and Conflict* book series, Donnay and Bhavnani (2016) highlighted the increasing availability and utilization of detailed event data as one of the noteworthy recent developments contributing to the cutting edge of research on peace and conflict. As an emergent common practice, these event data are both geocoded – identifying the coordinates of where each event occurred, most often pinpointing to a sub-national level and even a precise location – and date specific. This geographic and temporal granularity contrasts with conflict data that are reported with the country-, dyad-, or group-year as the unit of observation, on which many scholars in the field have traditionally relied. Thus, empirical studies using the existing event datasets have progressed to the stage of being well positioned to undertake more disaggregate analysis, employing study designs that reach closer to capturing where and when dynamics of conflict are actually theorized and observed to happen.

Donnay and Bhavnani (2016) also noted significant shortcomings of the available event datasets. In particular, many lacked global coverage. At the time, the Uppsala Conflict Data Program's Georeferenced Event Dataset (UCDP-GED) covered Sub-Saharan Africa and most of Asia from 1989–2014 (Sundberg and Melander 2013). The Armed Conflict Location and Event Data (ACLED) Project covered Africa from 1997 to the present (weekly releases since 2016), plus select countries – with less temporal coverage – in Asia and the Balkans (Raleigh et al. 2010). The Social Conflict Analysis Database (SCAD) covered Africa, Central America and the Caribbean from 1989–2013 (Salehyan 2012). Other available datasets affording comprehensive geographic coverage exhibited their own notable shortcomings. The Global Terrorism Database (START 2016), by construction, has been confined to a narrow subset of events unsuitable for a broad range of studies of conflict. In this regard, alternatives such as the Global Database of Events, Language and Tone (GDELT), the Integrated Conflict Early Warning System (ICEWS), and the Social, Political, and Economic Event Database (SPEED) are quite a bit more expansive. As Donnay and Bhavnani (2016) discussed, however, concerns exist about the reliability of these datasets, which are entirely machine coded. In addition, SPEED had not been kept at all current, leaving off at 2004. The shortage of suitable, reliable conflict event data offering global coverage and remaining current presented a conspicuous constraint on the feasible scope of analysis.

Subsequently, in October 2016, UCDP released a significantly updated version of UCDP-GED, which now affords the desired global coverage, from 1989–2015 (Croicu and Sundberg 2015). For the first time, geocoded data on events for the three categories of organized armed violence reported by UCDP – state-based conflict, non-state conflict, and one-sided violence – are compiled for the entire world.[1] No other dataset offers comparable coverage of all these categories of organized armed violence, detailed at the event level.

This chapter is designed to offer insight into the utility of this latest release of UCDP-GED. We start by offering relevant background on the dataset. Next, we review existing literature that employs UCDP-GED in analysis, to highlight the contributions to the field to date. We then present two perspectives on what the latest data reveals, mapping the fatalities from events for the entire world in order to examine trends over time and patterns with respect to the three categories of organized armed violence. Finally, we conclude with thoughts about the necessity of sufficient geographic and temporal coverage in conflict event datasets for the ability of researchers to make accurate, meaningful inferences about patterns and trends.

Background

The UCDP has an established record of compiling and disseminating an array of widely used data resources. All of the datasets are unified by shared, theoretically informed objectives of studying the dynamics of political violence. A specific focus is serious cases of violence, committed by organized armed actors, with lethal outcomes. Armed violence is qualitatively different from other types of contentious activity that are not characteristically violent, but may result in violence (e.g., protests, demonstrations, riots), let alone other political behavior. Events resulting in killings imply a greater severity of conflict than non-lethal events. Also, compiling useful data on lethal events is ordinarily more feasible, given the recording of information in various sources, than tracking non-lethal events.

In this section, we explain the rationale for compiling categorized, geocoded, date-specific conflict event data, detail the definitions of types of organized armed violence that are captured by UCDP-GED, and discuss the data collection process.

Motivations

The field of conflict studies, and the data that contributing scholars collect, have progressively moved toward greater specificity along several dimensions. This specificity is reflected in the categorization, location and timing of violence captured in datasets, coded at the level of individual events.

For some purposes, lumping together the violence in a country and reporting overall measures – e.g., the number of deaths, or the mere fact that any violence occurred – makes sense. Yet the aggregation of different categories of violence overlooks important considerations. Existing research shows that those categories can exhibit disparities in terms of causes, dynamics, and impacts. Consider, for example, the cases of Iraq and Mexico. Over the last decade, these two countries exhibited similar numbers of killings from armed violence in many years, which may have resulted in similar fear, corruption, and negative effects on the function of political institutions. Significant distinctions arise, however, with respect to the categories of violence involved. The conventional wisdom holds that Iraq is facing civil war, whereas Mexico is defined by criminal violence. Civil war typically causes much higher numbers of displaced people and more damage to infrastructure than does criminal violence – even when measures of the scale of violence are on par. Therefore, capturing categories of armed violence in datasets is vital to prospects for appropriate analysis and relevant understanding.

Information about the precise locations of violence is equally critical. Knowing whether or not individual countries are affected by violence is worthwhile. In turn, one can evaluate macro-level conditions as risk factors for violence materializing, as well as the consequences of observed violence for those aggregate conditions. Yet these relationships are arguably tenuous, in as much as they treat countries as unitary and homogenous. Violence does not occur everywhere within a country, much less exhibit uniform severity and other characteristics, even at the height of the most intense conflicts. Instead, violence often manifests in some locations, but not others, and events may cluster disproportionately in particular locations. The reasons for the violence, the manner in which the violence unfolds, and the implications of the violence are plausibly connected to the locations where violence is observed, or nearby locations. Decomposing the phenomenon of violence into constituent events, each associated with a location, is vital to assessing these relationships.

Analogous reflections arise with date specificity. Knowing whether or not violence was observed in a given year has utility. Traditionally, data on the factors that one would wish to evaluate as risks for violence, as well as the possible outcomes of observed violence, were available widely only aggregated to years. Again, analysis of these relationships has flaws. Violence does not necessarily occur continuously, much less at uniform severity, over time. Instead, violence often fluctuates, and events may cluster at particular times. For example, it might be crucial for a correct analysis to know whether violence happened before or after elections. The reasons, attributes, and implications of the timing of violence are important to examine empirically. Knowing more precisely when constituent events of violence happen is a constructive lens into these relationships.

Of course, the categories, locations and timings of violence can vary simultaneously within the same conflict-affected setting. Categorized, geocoded, date-specific conflict event data provide an apt means by which to ascertain the nature of this variation. UCDP-GED captures relevant variety, with the necessary specificity. Rather than treating organized armed violence as a broad, aggregate phenomenon, this dataset permits analysis of distinct categories of violence and where and when individual events occur.

Definitions and Data Collection

As indicated earlier, UCDP-GED encompasses three categories of organized armed violence:[2]

- **State-based conflict** takes two primary forms. The first form is inter-state conflict between two governments, which has become increasingly rare (Strand and Buhaug 2016). An example is the conflict between Ethiopia and

Eritrea from 1998–2000. The second form is intra-state conflict between a government and a rebel organization, also known as internal conflict, which has accounted for most cases of state-based conflict since the end of World War II (Melander et al. 2016). An example is the long-running conflict between the government of Colombia and the Revolutionary Armed Forces of Colombia (FARC), which has been ongoing since 1964 – though it appears to be on track to peace with an accord signed in June 2016. Of note, internationalized intra-state conflict can arise with the additional involvement of external actors in support of one or both of the sides of armed actors. Those external actors can be other states, i.e., foreign governments. They can also be non-state actors. The 2014 conflicts in Ukraine, in which Russia played a role, are among the conspicuous recent examples of internationalized internal armed conflicts.

- **Non-state conflict** refers to violence between two organized armed actors, neither of which is an internationally recognized sovereign state. The range of non-state actors includes revolutionary and separatist rebel groups, as well as ethnic and religious militias. An example of non-state conflict is the current violence between the Islamic State (IS) and the Kurdish Democratic Union Party (PYD) in Syria.
- **One-sided violence** involves an organized state or non-state armed actor deliberately killing unarmed civilians.[3] An infamous example is the genocidal violence committed by the Rwandan government and associated militias in Rwanda in 1994. UCDP also includes the violence by Mexican drug cartels in recent years as a case of one-sided violence. (Meanwhile, fighting between Mexican drug cartels is included in non-state conflict.)

To assemble the latest version of UCDP-GED, all killings reflected in the UCDP data, covering the entire world over the period from 1989–2015, are disaggregated to hundreds of thousands of events. Each event represents an instance of organized armed violence, falling into one of the three categories, involving one or more particular actors present at a particular place at a particular time when one or more persons were killed.

With the three categories, UCDP aims to cover most killings from organized armed violence around the world. Very few events of organized lethal armed violence are excluded from the dataset due to not meeting the criteria of any of the categories.[4]

The definitions of the categories are strict and designed to be mutually exclusive. Therefore, the events in the respective categories are salient when reported separately. In practice, violent events falling in different categories can coincide geographically and/or temporally. Therefore, the same location may exhibit multiple categories of violence, even simultaneously. The different categories of events can be pooled to yield an expansive, yet nuanced, profile of organized armed violence. From these pooled data, the numbers of fatalities associated with the events can be added to compute a measure of the total lethal impact of organized armed violence. Equally significant, the definitions of the categories have been consistently applied when compiling the data. As a result, the measurement of events remains fully comparable across the entire dataset, enabling rigorous cross-national and trend analyses.

UCDP-GED records the category of violence, the actors involved, the location and associated coordinates, and the timing of each event, as well as other characteristics. Because the events are the elements that make up the UCDP datasets, the events can also be linked to other constituent datasets. Those datasets provide information, at the level of cases of organized armed conflict or conflict dyads, on dimensions such as the issues being disputed, the primary actors, any secondary actors providing support to the primary actors, negotiations, and peace agreements. UCDP also supplies a descriptive narrative about each conflict, accompanied by a full accounting of all the relevant armed actors. Given events are georeferenced in UCDP-GED, they are easy to display on maps and analyze using Geographic Information Systems (GIS) software.

In the near future, most likely in 2017, UCDP will start to release monthly updates of preliminary versions of these event-data. With this resource, organized armed violence anywhere in the world can be analyzed with data that are at most a few weeks old.

Contributions and Innovations of Research Using UCDP-GED

UCDP has been the source of the most widely used data in academic research on violence committed by organized armed actors (Brzoska 2016). The addition of UCDP-GED, initially released in 2013, has extended the range of applications. This resource introduced prospects for fresh, rigorous exploration of a diverse range of topics related to conflict and peace. The most important usage capitalizes on the potential to study the causes, dynamics, and effects of violence more widely and effectively at a sub-national level. In particular, UCDP-GED provides a means for analyses to test micro-level theories (Sundberg and Melander 2013). A key enabling factor is employing more granular data on violence in conjunction with comparable data on other relevant variables from novel sources, including cell-phone records (Pierskalla and Hollenbach 2013), remote sensing of climate conditions (O'Loughlin et al. 2014; Ide et al. 2014), and surveys (Warren 2015; Wig and Tollefsen 2016). Before the advent of geocoded conflict event datasets with significant cross-national coverage, such research had been infeasible given the limits of available data, most of which was aggregated at the group, conflict or country level. As a result, scholars have begun to more thoroughly unpack long-standing questions, as well as to pursue new lines of inquiry.

At least 40 published articles have already employed UCDP-GED data. Much of this work is concentrated in two areas: (1) the context for conflict onset; and (2) the micro-dynamics of conflict processes.

Studies in the first area demonstrate that the propensity of conflict differs given a diverse range of factors, including economic shocks (Fjelde 2015; Hodler and Raschky 2014; Berman and Couttenier 2015; Koos and Basedau 2013), inequality (Fjelde and Østby 2014), the geographic distribution of ethnic populations (Michalopoulos and Papaioannou 2016), environmental factors (Ide et al. 2014; Fjelde and von Uexkull 2012; Kreutz 2012; O'Loughlin et al. 2014; von Uexkull 2014; von Uexkull et al. 2016), resource endowments (Basedau and Pierskalla 2014), and communication networks (Pierskalla and Hollenbach 2013). All this research revolves around the fundamental proposition that local contexts vary in ways expected to shape patterns of conflict. Therefore, understanding circumstances on the ground, for affected communities and actors, is critical to modeling conflict onset. For example, studies of the climate–conflict link examine the impact of local-level environmental stressors, finding that regions reliant on rain-fed crops face a heightened risk for conflict (von Uexkull 2014), though alternative coping mechanisms (e.g., market transfers) can alleviate these risks (Fjelde and von Uexkull 2012). Studies about economic factors highlight subtleties of local fluctuations in market conditions that shape individuals' opportunity costs for participating in conflict. Among the notable findings are that lower returns on labor-intensive agriculture can increase the likelihood of violence (Fjelde 2015), while economic shocks that have observable impacts on a workforce are positively correlated with conflict occurrence (Hodler and Raschky 2014; Berman and Couttenier 2015).

Studies in the second area have shown that micro-dynamics underpin the strategies of states and rebel groups (Fjelde et al. 2016a; Elfversson 2015; Wood and Kathman 2015), violence committed by these actors against civilians (Wood 2014; Fjelde and Hultman 2013; Wood and Sullivan 2015; Butcher 2014), mediation processes (Ruhe 2015), conflict resolution and termination (Greig 2015; Wood et al. 2014; Tiernay 2013; Ruhe 2015), and peacekeeping operations (Kathman and Wood 2014; Hultman et al. 2013, 2014, 2015). All this research demonstrates that conflict often involves complex interplay among non-unitary actors, operating amid heterogeneous local conditions, which can be properly appreciated only via disaggregation of these processes to spotlight specific mechanisms at play. In particular, this line of work underscores the value of investigating in greater detail where and when conflict occurs, which offers greater leverage in explaining key outcomes. For example, Butcher (2014) demonstrates that the balance of power and the number of actors in a conflict influence how close battlefield activity occurs to a state's capital. Greig (2015) shows that distributions of battle locations and velocities meaningfully influence when peace talks are likely. Thus, the distribution of power can affect where conflict activity occurs, while the distribution of violence can affect the prospects of a resolution. Disaggregate analyses show that the presence of UN peacekeepers can alleviate violence against civilians and reduce battlefield deaths if sufficient military and police personnel are committed (Hultman et al. 2013, 2014). Peacekeepers can themselves become targets, however, when rebels are weakened by battlefield losses and the peacekeepers are perceived as being biased (Fjelde et al. 2016a).

In addition, UCDP-GED has paved the way for methodological advances with a major bearing on substantive contributions to the literature. More granular data offers researchers the chance to implement analytical designs and techniques that improve identification of causal mechanisms theorized to influence sub-national variation in conflict processes. For example, Kreutz (2012) relies on a regression discontinuity design to evaluate whether natural disasters create openings for conflict resolution. O'Loughlin et al. (2014) utilize a multilevel model to assess where effects pool, finding that high temperatures are associated with conflict in the aggregate, but lack explanatory power at a sub-national level. Wig and Tollefsen (2016) employ a matching design to compare similar municipal districts in their study of how local institutions influence the outbreak of civil conflict. Likewise, Wood and Kathman (2015) use a matching design when examining the impact of humanitarian aid on the targeting of civilians.

A further notable avenue is exploring the potential sources of bias in media-based event data, enabled by linking UCDP-GED to other event datasets that rely on different data-generating processes. For example, Weidmann (2014) explores potential reporting bias in news media by comparing conflict events captured in UCDP-GED to the Significant Activities (SIGACTS) data of the US military on conflict incidences in Afghanistan. Weidmann opts to treat SIGACTS as a "ground truth" of conflict. He then detects media reporting bias, relative to the SIGACTS baseline, within a subset of event types: those that take place in remote locations and with a lower number of observers are more likely to be missed or inaccurate in reporting. Weidmann (2016) follows up by outlining a simple diagnostic test for assessing reporting bias in event data. These studies emphasize that even cutting-edge datasets should not be used without reflection. Instead, awareness of how data are compiled – and from what raw source material – remains essential, supplying a foundation for ongoing development and refinement, as well as encouraging researchers to exercise caution and make necessary corrections, accounting for potential bias, when inferring causal relationships (Croicu and Kreutz 2017).

Mapping the Global Impact of Organized Armed Violence

The previous section reviewed existing research that used earlier releases of the UCDP-GED. The latest release is an important evolution in event data on conflict, achieving global coverage for the first time. In this section, we offer some indications – through visualizations and accompanying reflections – of what an upgrade the latest release represents over existing data, as well as of the prospects for illuminating analysis of trends and patterns.

From Conflict Zones to Granular Coverage of Conflict

UCDP-GED was not the first dataset to document locations of armed conflicts around the world at a sub-national level of geographic detail. Instead, this crucial innovation was accomplished by the Conflict Site Dataset (CSD) (Buhaug and Gates 2002; Hallberg 2012), an extension of the UCDP/PRIO Armed Conflict Dataset (Gleditsch et al. 2002; Melander et al. 2016). Coverage in the CSD is limited to state-based armed conflict, from 1989–2008. In the dataset, each observation corresponds to a conflict zone, coded with center-point coordinates plus a radius to denote the spatial extent.

As an example, Figure 4.1 maps the conflict zones in state-based armed conflict from 2006–2008. Some conflict zones comprise small regions of countries. A striking case is Russia, where the conflict zone is confined to the Caucasus. According to the CSD, however, many conflict zones seem to extend over most or all of the countries in which they are located.

Of course, these representations of conflict zones lack a certain degree of precision and can be misleading. The representations make the assumption that conflict zones are (semi-)circular, which is acknowledged to be a limitation, overstating the geographic extent (Hallberg 2011: 3). One by-product is that the zones can extend beyond natural boundaries (e.g., bodies of water) and/or country borders. For practical purposes of analysis, the zones can be clipped to reflect boundaries and borders (Hallberg 2011), resulting in polygons, as reflected in Figure 4.1. Another concern is that the geographic extent of a given zone is largely a function of the greatest distance between known locations of activity and presence, i.e., armed encounters between conflict actors, territories occupied by the conflict actors (strictly rebel groups in the case of intrastate conflicts) and bases of rebel groups. In select cases (seven country-years, across three conflicts), zones have been coded in a manner that excludes extreme outliers of "isolated events of violence occurred at locations very distant from the core conflict area… These events were generally ignored, since they would force the conflict circle to assume an unrealistic size that would cover large amounts of unaffected territory" (Hallberg 2011). Otherwise, nothing in the coding requires that violent activity be pervasive throughout a zone. Yet the resulting representation implies this sort of extensive, uniform, undifferentiated impact of conflict, rather than capturing local variation, including gradations of prevalence and severity and distinctions among types of violence.

The UCDP-GED addresses all these shortcomings, by focusing on conflict events and their specific locations, which are also accompanied by other characteristics. Among the advantages of this approach is the attention devoted to places actually affected by violence, the picture of which is considerably more nuanced than what CSD represents. In the

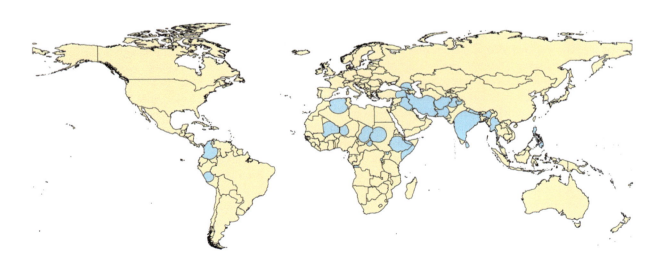

Figure 4.1 Conflict Zones in State-Based Armed Conflict, 2006–2008
Source: Map created on the basis of data from Hallberg (2012). Reproduced with permission of Rowman & Littlefield.

process, UCDP-GED excludes from consideration locations of territories occupied by conflict actors and bases of rebel groups. Obviously, those territories and bases are useful information for those who study conflict. They are simply beyond the scope of what UCDP-GED aims to capture. Other distinct initiatives are actively concentrating on compiling data on territorial control (and other forms of presence, as well as contestation) and rebel (and state) bases. Instead, only violent events are reflected in the UCDP-GED. These events are coded as individual observations, each with their own locations, rather than aggregated, whether to a country-year or to a zone corresponding to a conflict-year. Such aggregations remain feasible, if desired, but the greater value is associated with conducting analysis that is relatively more disaggregate in nature, especially with respect to geography.

Global Trends in Organized Armed Violence

As a simple illustration, Figure 4.2 presents global maps of all organized armed violence coded by UCDP for three different time periods. For these purposes, the numbers of battle-related fatalities from conflict events have been aggregated according to PRIO-GRID (Tollefsen et al. 2012), which provides a lattice of 0.5 x 0.5 decimal degree (approximately 55 km^2) cells covering the entire world. In every period, violence is widespread, spanning significant parts of the world. Yet the locations where violence is most heavily concentrated change to a marked extent from period to period. The maps thereby chart a history of evolving contexts, drivers, and outcomes of conflict activity.

The top map in Figure 4.2 displays organized armed violence from 1989–2000. A prominent factor is an array of conflicts around the world that are at least partly an ongoing legacy of influences of past Cold War rivalry and great power proxy warfare, or that emerge in connection with the end of the Cold War. In particular, the worst warfare in Europe since the end of World War II exploded as the former Yugoslavia fell apart. Substantial violence was also observed in Russia and other successor states to the Soviet Union after its dissolution. In addition, a number of conflicts erupted in Africa, reflecting diverse conditions (e.g., democratization, natural resources, state failure, ethnicity and religion, small arms trafficking). Many of the populated areas of the continent experienced serious violence. Algeria, Angola, several East African countries, Liberia and Sierra Leone in West Africa, and South Africa were severely affected. Also, a rare interstate war between Eritrea and Ethiopia in 1998–2000 claimed many lives. Although the time period pre-dates the era of the so-called War on Terror, substantial violence was already being observed in the Middle East, Central Asia, and South Asia. The civil war in Afghanistan and the First Gulf War stand out. Meanwhile, several serious conflicts remained active in Latin America, though the extent of violence in that region was well below the level of preceding decades. Conflicts in El Salvador, Guatemala, and Peru were already winding down in the early 1990s – and have since concluded. At the time, Colombia was still deep into what has continued on to become a 50-year conflict. Fortunately, a promising peace process is being consummated as we write. Across East Asia, conflicts raged on in Cambodia, Myanmar, and the Philippines, although reduced levels of violence in Cambodia followed the 1991 Paris Peace agreement.

The middle map in Figure 4.2 displays organized armed violence from 2001–2010, a period that is bracketed by the 9/11 attacks and the Arab Spring. A comparison to the prior period discovers important changes, including certain countries around the world that are no longer hot spots like they were during the 1990s. Except for the Caucasus and minor episodes of violence elsewhere, Europe is largely free from organized violence over the decade. The violence associated with the civil wars in the Balkans and the Troubles in Northern Ireland was significantly dampened in the wake of peace agreements. The violence that had been observed in connection with the transition to democracy in South Africa does not persist to any degree. Also, the civil war in Mozambique was terminated. Yet countervailing trends were observed in Africa: violence associated with other civil wars became more pervasive and/or intense, in countries such as Nigeria, Somalia, and Sudan. A mixture of conditions is likewise observed in Latin America. The categories of violence tracked by UCDP disappear from much of Central America – except Guatemala – and also showed signs of abating in parts of South America, especially Peru. At the same time, violence intensified in Colombia and became more extensive in Mexico. In both these countries, the violence includes a prominent criminal element, linked to drug trafficking.[5] No obvious trends are observed in the Middle East. Across Asia, violence worsened markedly in several countries (Afghanistan, India, Pakistan) and persisted in the Philippines and Sri Lanka. On the other hand, Timor-Leste and the Solomon Islands dropped from the list of hot spots.

The bottom map in Figure 4.2 displays organized armed violence from 2011–2015. Europe exhibits almost no violence outside of new conflicts that emerged in Ukraine. The geographic scope of violence in Africa has changed dramatically, with fewer countries experiencing appreciable effects. Instead, most of the violence is concentrated in Central and East Africa and select countries in West Africa (Mali, Nigeria). Libya is rare in exhibiting a surge of new violence, after being spared over the previous 20 years. Mozambique saw a minor recurrence of violence related to the earlier civil war, which had been dormant for over 20 years. In the Middle East, both Syria and Yemen exhibit serious escalations of violence. Less violence is observed across Central America and especially South America, where Colombia is finally making progress

The Geography of Organized Armed Violence

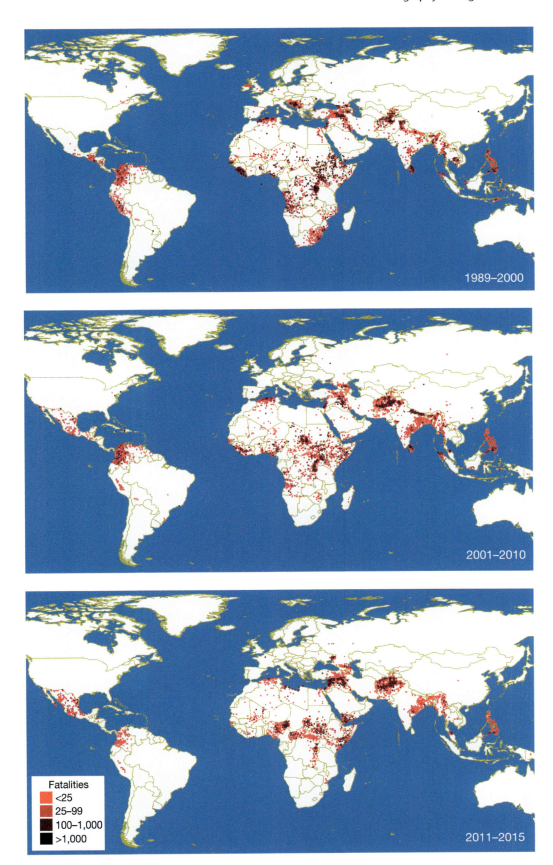

Figure 4.2 Fatalities due to Organized Armed Violence, by PRIO-GRID, 1989–2015
Note: Data are drawn from UCDP-GED, then mapped onto PRIO-GRID.

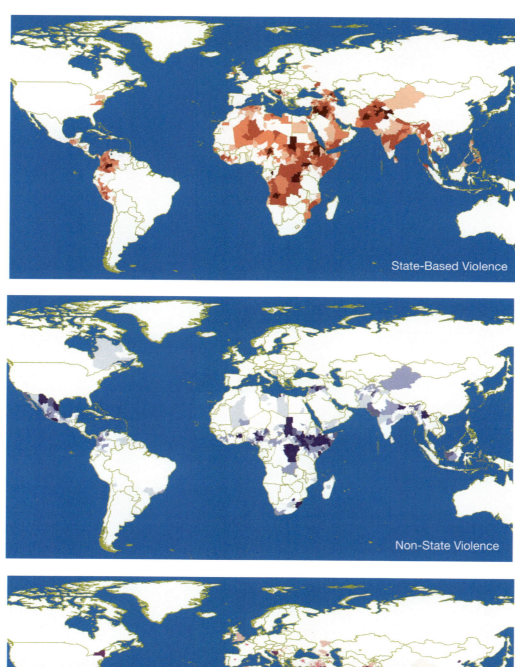
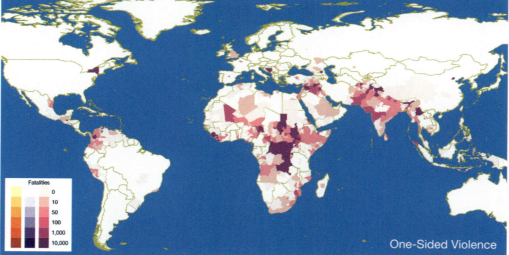

Figure 4.3 Severity of Categories of Organized Armed Violence, by Administrative Division, 1989–2015
Note: Data are drawn from UCDP-GED, then mapped onto first-order administrative divisions.

The Geography of Organized Armed Violence

in negotiating an end to the civil war. In South Asia, the severe civil war in Sri Lanka has ended, while violence in India appears to be on the decline. In East Asia, the extent of violence in Indonesia (Aceh) has dropped drastically and Myanmar is undergoing a transition toward democracy as well as simultaneous peace processes in relation to many long-lasting conflicts. Peace negotiations to end the civil war in the Philippines (Mindanao) are ongoing. A large share of the violence that remains evident around the world is linked to militant Islamic groups, which are active in various countries spanning the Middle East, Africa, and Asia (Melander et al. 2016).

Global Patterns of Categories of Organized Armed Violence

A further feature to highlight is the three different categories of organized armed violence coded by UCDP. Figure 4.3 presents global maps of the severity of violence in each of these categories. Severity is once again measured in terms of fatalities. Darker colors reflect greater numbers of fatalities. To show another option of geographic analysis, fatalities are aggregated to the level of first-order administrative divisions (ADM1s), which are provinces or states in many countries.

This visualization offers a quick means to appreciate contrasts in geographical patterns of the categories of violence. The top map in Figure 4.3 shows that state-based violence is spread across more countries, in Africa, Asia, Latin America, and the Middle East. In many of those countries, the severity of violence has been high or even extreme. As seen from the middle map in Figure 4.3, a smaller set of countries have experienced non-state violence. The regions most affected are Africa and Asia, though with fewer countries exposed, albeit several of them severely. Of note, non-state violence is less pervasive than state-based violence across the Middle East. Yet, some of the most destructive non-state conflict is happening in Syria. In general, the places that exhibit non-state violence have often experienced large-scale state-based violence as well. Mexico and South Africa are among the exceptions, at least as recorded in UCDP data. The bottom map in Figure 4.3 shows that the geographic pattern of one-sided violence – concentrated in Central and East Africa, South Asia and select Middle Eastern countries – largely mirrors that of non-state violence. This finding is consistent with prior research published in *Peace and Conflict 2016* that identifies more cases, a higher rate per conflict, and greater lethality of one-sided violence committed by non-state actors than by state actors (Fjelde et al. 2016b).

Conclusion

This chapter trained a spotlight on progress in georeferenced data of conflict events, which enables innovative sub-national research on the dynamics of political violence, as well as contributing risk factors and resulting outcomes. The latest release of UCDP-GED, which focuses on events involving organized armed actors, has distinguished itself among the available datasets as having the broadest coverage both spatially (global) and temporally (1989–2015). Both aspects of UCDP-GED are outstanding strengths, which permit a better appreciation of patterns and trends, from a long-term, comprehensive cross-national perspective.

Analysis of data confined to select regions and a more recent, shorter time span can easily lead to exaggerated or incorrect conclusions. For instance, a conventional belief holds that violence is at unique levels and more complex than ever before. The severity of organized armed violence observed in several countries – Syria, Yemen, Nigeria, Libya, etc. – over the last five years, as captured by UCDP-GED, could be viewed as consistent with this impression. Yet extending the scope of the analysis by another 10 years reveals that violence was even more pervasive from 2001–2010, with additional countries (e.g., Colombia, Sri Lanka) and sub-regions registering as significant hot spots on par with the contemporary cases. Going back even further, to 1989, reinforces this point. In the early 1990s, more parts of Africa were much more violent than today, with intricate dynamics of actors and issues.

What may be distinctive about recent conflict, however, is that the hub of the recent upsurge in organized armed violence is Syria and Iraq. Neither is among the least developed countries or exhibits the degree of state ineffectiveness, incapacity or outright failure that was frequently associated with the worst conflicts of the 1990s. Therefore, the current conflicts that are drivers of regional instability and international insecurity may require different solutions.

Fortunately, important practical lessons about mediation, peace agreements, and peacekeeping, as well as broad-based strategies of development in multiple domains to address the intersection of conflict-affected settings and fragility in state-society relations, have been learned over the last 25–30 years. Thanks to available data, including new resources that have come online such as UCDP-GED, these lessons are able to reflect a diversity of experiences encompassing periods following the end of the Cold War, the 9/11 attacks, and the Arab Spring, now with global scope.

Notes

1 The UCDP/PRIO Armed Conflict Dataset also provides a list of state-based conflicts from 1946, but the coding of conflict during the period from 1946–1988 does not rely on events in the same manner as UCDP-GED.

2 These definitions are developed and explained in detail at http://www.pcr.uu.se/research/ucdp/definitions/.
3 This definition of one-sided violence excludes killings of civilians as unintentional collateral damage to battles between organized armed actors. Such deaths are included among the battle-related fatalities due to events in the other two categories of violence.
4 For each event included in UCDP data, a reference is provided to at least one source of the information used to code the event in question. All events meet the UCDP's inclusion criteria (Gleditsch et al. 2002; Sundberg et al. 2012; Eck and Hultman 2007). The fact that UCDP requires lethality as an observable criterion of organized armed violence enables the compilation of more reliable, exhaustive lists of events. Lethal events connected to organized armed actors tend to be reported with far greater regularity than other violent events, let alone non-violent events. Yet assessing the exact number of people killed in a violent event can be challenging. No data collection effort with global ambitions can aspire to cover all violent deaths. (The procedures used by UCDP are explained at http://www.pcr.uu.se/research/ucdp/faq/#How_are_UCDP_data_collected.) The numbers provided by UCDP should be considered conservative, meaning that they are minimum numbers or on the low side. When the exact number of fatalities is unknown, UCDP typically reports three estimates (low, best, and high) for fatalities.
5 Criminal violence spiked subsequently across Central America, especially El Salvador, Guatemala and Honduras, leading to the rates of homicide that are among the worst in the world. The gangs involved in this violence are not involved in a traditional civil war, though they share similar features: effectively challenging the authority of the state, often controlling substantial territory, and often having roots – including their leadership and rank and file, areas of influence, and weapons and other resources – in past rebel groups. From UCDP's perspective, none of these considerations are fundamental to decisions about inclusion in the data. Instead, the key criterion is whether a given violent event is attributable to an identifiable organized armed actor engaged in conflict with another identifiable organized armed actor. This criterion excludes many events in Mexico and Central America, thereby understating the true extent of organized armed violence, whereas the impact on the classification of events in Colombia is relatively more limited. In all these countries, UDCP data would need to be augmented with crime statistics in order to achieve a more comprehensive accounting of total armed violence.

References

Basedau, Matthias, and Jan Henryk Pierskalla (2014) "How Ethnicity Conditions the Effect of Oil and Gas on Civil Conflict: A Spatial Analysis of Africa from 1990 to 2010." *Political Geography* 38(2–3): 1–11.
Berman, Nicolas, and Mathieu Couttenier (2015) "External Shocks, Internal Shots: The Geography of Civil Conflicts." *Review of Economics and Statistics* 97(4): 758–776.
Brzoska, Michael (2016) "Progress in the Collection of Quantitative Data on Collective Violence." In Stockholm International Peace Research Institute. *SIPRI Yearbook 2016: Armaments, Disarmament and International Security.* Oxford: Oxford University Press.
Buhaug, Halvard and Scott Gates (2002) "The Geography of Civil War." *Journal of Peace Research* 39(4): 417–433.
Butcher, Charles (2014) "'Capital Punishment' Bargaining and the Geography of Civil War." *Journal of Peace Research* 54(2): 171–186.
Croicu, Mihai and Joakim Kreutz (2017) "Communication Technology and Reports on Political Violence: Cross-National Evidence Using African Events Data." *Political Research Quarterly* 70(1): 19–31.
Croicu, Mihai and Ralph Sundberg (2015) "UCDP GED Codebook version 2.0", Department of Peace and Conflict Research, Uppsala University.
Donnay, Karsten and Ravi Bhavnani (2016) "The Cutting Edge of Research on Peace and Conflict." In David Backer, Ravi Bhavnani and Paul Huth (eds) *Peace and Conflict 2016.* New York: Routledge.
Eck, Kristine and Lisa Hultman (2007) "One-Sided Violence Against Civilians in War: Insights from New Fatality Data." *Journal of Peace Research* 44(2): 233–246.
Elfversson, Emma (2015) "Providing Security or Protecting Interests? Government Interventions in Violent Communal Conflicts in Africa." *Journal of Peace Research* 52(6): 791–805.
Fjelde, Hanne (2015) "Farming or Fighting? Agricultural Price Shocks and Civil War in Africa." *World Development* 67: 525–534,.
Fjelde, Hanne and Lisa Hultman (2013) "Weakening the Enemy: A Disaggregated Study of Violence against Civilians in Africa." *Journal of Conflict Resolution* 58(7): 1230–1257.
Fjelde, Hanne, Lisa Hultman, and Sara Lindberg Bromley (2016a) "Offsetting Losses: Bargaining Power and Rebel Attacks on Peacekeepers." *International Studies Quarterly* 60(4): 611–623.
Fjelde, Hanne, Lisa Hultman, and Margareta Sollenberg (2016b) "Violence against Civilians during Civil War." In David Backer, Ravi Bhavnani and Paul Huth (eds) *Peace and Conflict 2016.* New York: Routledge.
Fjelde, Hanne and Gudrun Østby (2014) "Socioeconomic Inequality and Communal Conflict: A Disaggregated Analysis of Sub-Saharan Africa, 1990–2008." *International Interactions* 40(5): 737–762.
Fjelde, Hanne and Nina von Uexkull (2012) "Climate Triggers: Rainfall Anomalies, Vulnerability and Communal Conflict in Sub-Saharan Africa." *Political Geography* 31(7): 444–453 .
Gleditsch, Nils Petter, Peter Wallensteen, Mikael Eriksson, Margareta Sollenberg, and Håvard Strand (2002) "Armed Conflict 1946–2001: A New Dataset." *Journal of Peace Research* 39(5): 615–637.
Greig, J. Michael (2015) "Rebels at the Gates: Civil War Battle Locations, Movement, and Openings for Diplomacy." *International Studies Quarterly* 59(4): 680–693.
Hallberg, Johan Dittrich (2011) "PRIO Conflict Site 1989–2008 Codebook: A Geo-Referenced Dataset on Armed Conflict Version 3.0." Peace Research Institute Oslo, Center for the Study of Civil War. https://www.prio.org/Data/Armed-Conflict/Conflict-Site/ (accessed on September 29, 2016).
Hallberg, Johan Dittrich (2012) "PRIO Conflict Site 1989–2008: A Geo-Referenced Dataset on Armed Conflict." *Conflict Management and Peace Science* 29(2): 219–232.
Hodler, Roland and Paul A. Raschky (2014) "Economic Shocks and Civil Conflict at the Regional Level." *Economics Letters* 124(3): 530–533.

Hultman, Lisa, Jacob D. Kathman, and Megan Shannon (2013) "United Nations Peacekeeping and Civilian Protection in Civil War." *American Journal of Political Science* 57(4): 875–891.

Hultman, Lisa, Jacob D. Kathman, and Megan Shannon (2015) "United Nations Peacekeeping Dynamics and the Duration of Post-Civil Conflict Peace." *Conflict Management and Peace Science* 33(3): 231–249.

Hultman, Lisa, Jacob D. Kathman, and Megan Shannon (2014) "Beyond Keeping Peace: United Nations Effectiveness in the Midst of Fighting." *American Political Science Review* 108(4): 737–753.

Ide, Tobias, Janpater Schilling, Jasmin S. A. Link, Jürgen Scheffran, Grace Ngaruiya, and Thomas Weinzierl (2014) "On Exposure, Vulnerability and Violence: Spatial Distribution of Risk Factors For Climate Change and Violent Conflict Across Kenya and Uganda." *Political Geography* 43(1): 68–81.

Kathman, Jacob D. and Reed M. Wood (2014) "Stopping the Killing during the 'Peace': Peacekeeping and the Severity of Postconflict Civilian Victimization." *Foreign Policy Analysis* 12: 149–169.

Koos, Carlo and Matthias Basedau (2013) "Does Uranium Mining Increase Civil Conflict Risk? Evidence from a Spatiotemporal Analysis of Africa from 1960 to 2008." *Civil Wars* 15(3): 306–331.

Kreutz, Joakim (2012) "From Tremors to Talks: Do Natural Disasters Produce Ripe Moments for Resolving Separatist Conflicts?" *International Interactions* 38(4): 482–502.

Melander, Erik, Terése Pettersson, and Lotta Themnér (2016) "Organized Violence 1989–2015." *Journal of Peace Research* 53(5): 727–742.

Michalopoulos, Selios and Elias Papaioannou (2016) "The Long-Run Effects of the Scramble for Africa." *American Economic Review* 106(7): 1802–1848.

National Consortium for the Study of Terrorism and Responses to Terrorism (START) (2016) Global Terrorism Database [Data file]. Retrieved from https://www.start.umd.edu/gtd.

O'Loughlin, John, Andrew Martin Linke, and Frank D. Witmer (2014) "Effects of Temperature and Precipitation Variability on the Risk of Violence in Sub-Saharan Africa, 1980–2012." *Proceedings of the National Academy of Sciences* 111(47): 16712–16717.

Pierskalla, Jan H. and Florian M. Hollenbach (2013) "Technology and Collective Action: The Effect of Cell Phone Coverage on Political Violence in Africa." *American Political Science Review* 107(2): 207–224.

Raleigh, Clionadh, Andrew Linke, Håvard Hegre, and Joakim Karlsen. 2010) "Introducing ACLED (Armed Conflict Location and Event Data." *Journal of Peace Research* 47(5): 651–660.

Ruhe, Constantin (2015) "Anticipating Mediated Talks Predicting the Timing of Mediation with Disaggregated Conflict Dynamics." *Journal of Peace Research* 52(2): 243–257.

Salehyan, Idean, Cullen S. Hendrix, Jesse Hamner, Christina Case, Christopher Linebarger, Emily Stull, and Jennifer Williams (2012) "Social Conflict in Africa: A New Database." *International Interactions* 38(4): 503–511.

Strand, Håvard and Halvard Buhaug (2016) "Armed Conflict, 1946-2014." In David Backer, Ravi Bhavnani and Paul Huth (eds) *Peace and Conflict 2016*. New York: Routledge.

Sundberg, Ralph, Kristine Eck, and Joakim Kreutz (2012) "Introducing the UCDP Non-State Conflict Dataset." *Journal of Peace Research* 49(2): 351–362.

Sundberg, R. and E. Melander (2013) "Introducing the UCDP Georeferenced Event Dataset." *Journal of Peace Research* 50(4): 523–532.

Tiernay, Michael (2013) "Killing Kony: Leadership Change and Civil War Termination." *Journal of Conflict Resolution* 59(2): 175–206.

Tollefsen, Andreas Forø, Håvard Strand and Halvard Buhaug (2012) "PRIO-GRID: A Unified Spatial Data Structure." *Journal of Peace Research* 49(2): 363–374.

von Uexkull, Nina (2014) "Sustained Drought, Vulnerability and Civil Conflict in Sub-Saharan Africa." *Political Geography* 43:16–26.

von Uexkull, Nina, Mihai Croicu, Hanne Fjelde, and Halvard Buhaug (2016) "Civil Conflict Sensitivity to Growing-Season Drought." *PNAS* 113(44): 12391–12396.

Warren, T. Camber (2015) "Explosive Connections? Mass Media, Social Media, and the Geography of Collective Violence in African States." *Journal of Peace Research* 52(3): 297–311.

Weidmann, Nils B. (2016) "A Closer Look at Reporting Bias in Conflict Event Data." *American Journal of Political Science* 60(1): 206–218.

Weidmann, Nils B. (2014) "On the Accuracy of Media-Based Conflict Event Data." *Journal of Conflict Resolution* 59(6): 1129–1149.

Wig, Tore and Andreas Forø Tollefsen (2016) "Local Institutional Quality and Conflict Violence in Africa." *Political Geography* 53: 30–42.

Wood, Reed M. (2014) "From Loss to Looting? Battlefield Costs and Rebel incentives for Violence." *International Organization* 68(4): 979–999.

Wood, Reed M. and Christopher Sullivan (2015) "Doing Harm by Doing Good? The Negative Externalities of Humanitarian Aid Provision during Civil Conflict." *Journal of Politics* 77(3): 736–748.

Wood, Reed M. and Jacob D. Kathman (2015) "Competing for the Crown: Inter-Rebel Competition and Civilian Targeting in Civil War." *Political Research Quarterly* 68(1): 167–179.

Wood, Reed M. and Jacob D. Kathman (2014) "Too Much of a Bad Thing? Civilian Victimization and Bargaining in Civil War." *British Journal of Political Science* 44(3): 685–706.

5

Spatial Patterns of Violence against Civilians

Hanne Fjelde, Lisa Hultman, Margareta Sollenberg, and Ralph Sundberg

Introduction

Direct and deliberate violence against civilians is a prevalent phenomenon. Such violence is observed across a large and varied set of countries and perpetrated by a wide range of actors, including state forces, rebel organizations, pro-government militias, and vigilante groups. Previous discussions of civilian targeting have pointed to important patterns, in particular the higher prevalence of civilian victimization in Africa relative to other regions. Examining cross-national variation, violence against civilians is also more common in conjunction with armed conflict (Fjelde, Hultman and Sollenberg 2016). If we are interested in understanding the relationship between civilian victimization and armed conflict, however, sub-national variation should be considered as well. Systematic studies of individual conflicts, such as the Greek civil war (Kalyvas 2006) and the Spanish civil war (Balcells 2010), have highlighted spatial variations within conflicts and demonstrated the usefulness of exploring determinants of violence at the local level. A few studies have explored spatial variation in violence against civilians in an African context (e.g., Fjelde and Hultman 2014; Raleigh 2012). With the recent release by the Uppsala Conflict Data Program (UCDP) of georeferenced event data on the location of violence against civilians, we are now able to examine geographical patterns globally for the period 2005–2013.

Knowledge of locations of one-sided violence (OSV), measured at the sub-national level, enables a more focused examination of the drivers of this behavior at the level where the violence actually unfolds. For example, one explanation links violence against civilians to the extraction of valuable natural resources. Corroborating whether these phenomena actually overlap empirically requires spatial data on the location of violence, as well as spatial data on sites with abundant natural resources. Understanding spatial patterns has value in refining existing theories too. One finding of cross-national studies with a global scope has been that OSV is more frequent in countries with low economic development. We do not know, however, whether such violence occurs in the most poverty-stricken regions of countries, or the national-level correlation is primarily picking up the effect of factors like weak state institutions with limited capacity to uphold societal order. Finally, sub-national spatial data on violence can reveal new, previously unexplored patterns that cannot be identified in aggregate data. For example, more detailed data on OSV may illuminate the existence of hot-spots that are not confined by state borders, attesting to cross-border networks of actors engaged in civilian victimization.

In this chapter, we describe the spatial patterns of violence against civilians in the most recent period, providing more in-depth discussion of some of the relationships mentioned above. In line with UCDP definitions, we use the term *one-sided violence* to refer to violence against civilians by organized armed actors, whether these are state or non-state actors. By definition, civilians are *neither organized nor armed*. Thus, OSV is distinct from the violence that pits organized rebel groups against state militaries in the context of intrastate armed conflicts. Instead, OSV is more fundamentally asymmetric: an armed actor intentionally targets an unarmed civilian population. In addition, the term is reserved for instances involving the direct and deliberate use of violence against civilians. These criteria mean that the definition of OSV does not encompass civilians killed as collateral damage from battle events between organized armed actors. The definition also excludes civilian casualties that occur as an indirect consequence of armed conflict – for example, people starving to death when cut off from livelihoods and food supplies. Finally, the UCDP only reports instances of OSV where an organized armed actor kills at least 25 civilians over the course of a calendar year.[1]

The spatial data on OSV that we use in our analysis are obtained from the UCDP Georeferenced Event Dataset (UCDP-GED, Sundberg and Melander 2013).[2] This dataset has global coverage of events of OSV, corresponding to the definitional criteria outlined above, for the period from 2005–2013.[3] An event of OSV is an incident in which an organized armed actor kills at least 1 civilian in a specific location and at a specific point in time. The dataset provides the geographical location and the date for each of the OSV events that when aggregated surpass the inclusion threshold of 25 deaths in a calendar year (per armed actor). For purposes of our analysis, we link the OSV events reported in the UCDP-GED v4.0 (Croicu and Sundberg 2015) to spatial-temporal units. Specifically, we assigned all of the events to a grid structure, representing units that are 0.5 x 0.5 decimal degrees in size (roughly 55 km x 55 km) and observed annually.[4] The spatial grid is drawn from the PRIO-GRID (Tollefsen, Strand, and Buhaug 2012). We use the exact spatial coordinates of the recorded violence for all maps and the grid structure for all bar charts. Our approach facilitates the discussion of geographical patterns in the prevalence of OSV and its relationship to other phenomena of interest.

We begin our analysis by showing how OSV is distributed spatially in different regions and clusters in some locations. In addition, we illustrate how actors sometimes move across borders and perpetrate OSV in multiple countries. Next, we delve into the relationship between OSV and armed conflict, with a particular focus on how they overlap spatially. The final segment of the analysis takes a closer look at the characteristics of the locations where OSV takes place.

Spatial Patterns of One-Sided Violence

To illustrate interesting inter-regional variation in the spatial patterns of OSV, we zoom in on Asia, Africa and the Middle East, which exhibit the vast majority of OSV events during the period from 2005–2013. Figure 5.1 presents results for South and Southeast Asia. On the map, red circles refer to civilians killed by organized non-state armed actors, while blue circles refer to civilians killed by state actors; the graduated sizes of these circles capture the extent of fatalities. This map suggests three clear patterns.

First, OSV clusters in some countries – in particular, Afghanistan, Pakistan, India, Sri Lanka, Burma, Nepal, and the Philippines. All these countries are experiencing or have previously suffered long-running, severe intra-state armed conflicts (India and Pakistan have also engaged in an inter-state conflict on and off for decades).

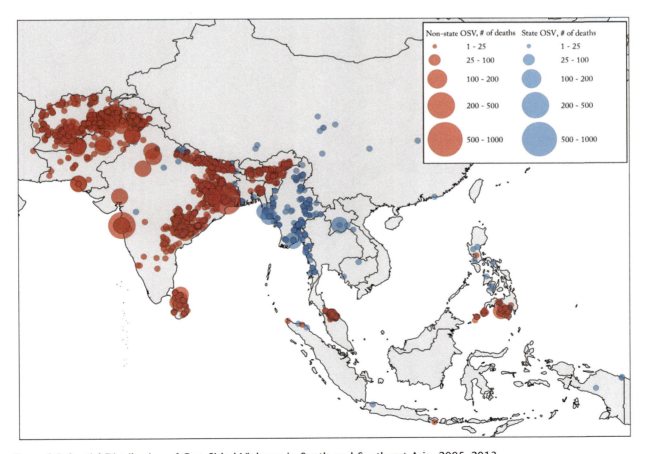

Figure 5.1 Spatial Distribution of One-Sided Violence in South and Southeast Asia, 2005–2013
Source: Data are drawn from UCDP-GED.

Second, OSV is not evenly distributed within countries. In India, for example, certain regions experience more recorded violence against civilians than do other regions. To a certain extent, these within-country variations are linked to population levels: OSV is positively correlated with population density. These variations also reflect that many armed campaigns have goals limited in geographic scope – for instance, concerning a specific piece of territory.

Third, OSV committed by state and non-state actors does not overlap to a great extent across this region. Some countries, such as Myanmar (Burma) exhibit high levels of state-perpetrated OSV. Other countries mainly exhibit OSV by non-state actors, as in the cases of Afghanistan and Pakistan. This relatively low level of overlap implies that state and non-state actors behave differently with respect to the civilian population, depending on factors such as conflict dynamics and local conditions of affinity with and backing from civilian constituencies. In particular, these spatial patterns are consistent with findings that groups will tend to target civilians believed to be supporters of their opponents, as a means of weakening their military and political power (Fjelde and Hultman 2014; Valentino, Huth, and Balch-Lindsay 2004).

Figure 5.2 shows the spatial patterns of OSV in Africa and the Middle East. The recent large-scale violence in Syria is excluded from the map, since UCDP's coding of events in that conflict is still ongoing. Once again, considerable variation is observed, both across and within countries, in terms of where violence takes place and whether the principal perpetrators are state or non-state actors – or both.

The most violence-ridden spots in the Middle East include Iraq, Israel, the Palestinian Territories, Lebanon, and Yemen. Several countries in North Africa are affected to a more modest extent. In Sub-Saharan Africa, major hot-spots are concentrated in Central and East Africa, especially the Great Lakes area, the Central African Republic, the Democratic Republic of the Congo (DRC), Sudan, and Somalia. Various countries in West Africa, especially Nigeria, also exhibited significant levels of OSV. In Southern Africa, Zimbabwe was the lone country to experience any appreciable OSV in this period.

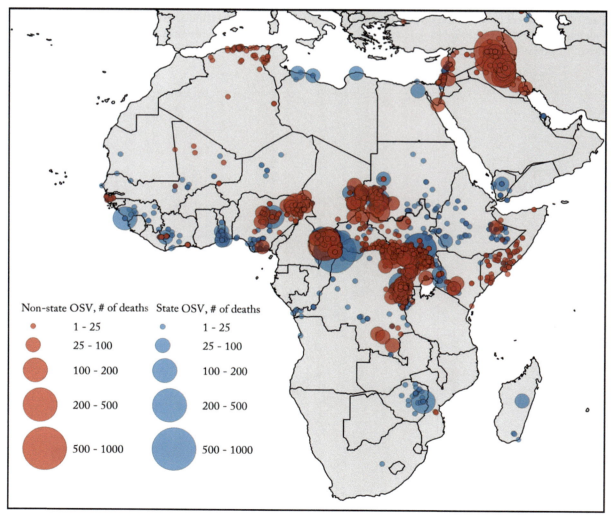

Figure 5.2 Spatial Distribution of One-Sided Violence in Africa and the Middle East, 2005–2013
Source: Data are drawn from UCDP-GED.

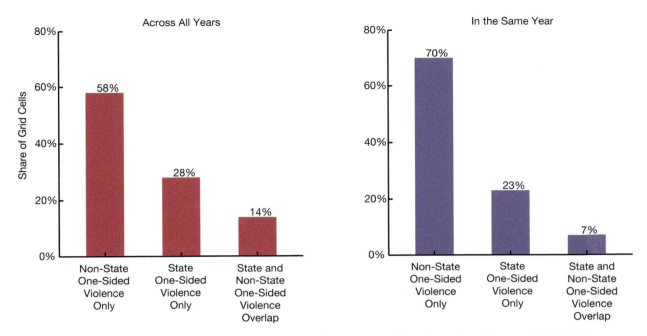

Figure 5.3 Spatial Overlap of One-Sided Violence Committed by State and Non-State Armed Actors, 2005–2013
Source: Data are drawn from UCDP-GED.

As was the case in Asia, OSV tends to cluster in areas of the Middle East and Africa enduring protracted intra-state conflicts. Within-country variation is also observed clearly in some countries. For example, most OSV in the DRC is confined to the eastern part of the country, where the armed conflict is also concentrated. Scattered events of OSV by the state are observed throughout the country as well.

Interestingly, several countries in Africa and the Middle East exhibit far greater spatial overlap in OSV committed by state and non-state armed actors than is found in Asia. We believe this disparity could be related to the types of armed conflicts that are the most prevalent in these regions. While Asia has experienced many territorial conflicts, where boundaries between the warring actors' likely constituencies are readily observable, conflicts in Africa are more often contestations about control over central government authority. The latter circumstances means that actors often operate across larger territories and that violence against civilians follows these fighting patterns (c.f., Beardsley, Gleditsch, and Lo 2015). Moreover, the adversaries' civilian constituencies – which often, but not always, conform to ethnic lines – in Africa and the Middle East may be geographically closer to each other than in Asia. To the extent this is true, one would expect the locations of OSV committed by state and non-state actors to be less differentiated.

Figure 5.3 shows the global shares of grid cells with OSV at any point from 2005–2013, focussing on the extent of overlap between OSV by state and non-state armed actors.[5] Attacks by the two types of actors typically occur in isolation from one another. A majority of the cells exhibited OSV by non-state actors only – more than twice the share that experienced OSV only by state actors. Meanwhile, just one in seven of the locations where OSV was observed exhibited involvement by both types of actors. Disaggregating this analysis by region, we find that the corresponding figures for the overlap of OSV by state and non-state actors are 10% in Asia, 17% in Africa, and 19% in the Middle East. These results confirm the patterns visualized in Figures 5.1 and 5.2. The patterns are accentuated when the analysis focuses on whether state and non-state armed actors target civilians within the same grid cell *during the same calendar year* (as opposed to any year within the period from 2005–2013). Nearly three-quarters of affected grid cells exhibit incidents perpetrated only by non-state actors – more than three times the share that experienced OSV only by state actors. Less than one in ten locations where OSV occurs exhibit incidents perpetrated by both types of actors during the same year. Hence, both state and non-state actors may target civilians in the same location, but not necessarily during the same year.

The spatial data on OSV also allow us to follow specific actors and see where they target civilians at different points in time. In Figure 5.4, we trace the violence perpetrated by the Lord's Resistance Army (LRA), an armed rebel group that emerged in opposition to the Ugandan government in 1987. The spatial patterns of civilian targeting by the LRA closely follow its movements around the region, in addition to developments in its ongoing conflict with the Ugandan government. Over time, the LRA increasingly targeted civilians in northern Uganda, including those who were seen to have failed to support them, as well as groups of civilians perceived to be actively supporting the government. By the early 2000s, killings of civilians were especially widespread across all of northern Uganda. The government progressively pushed

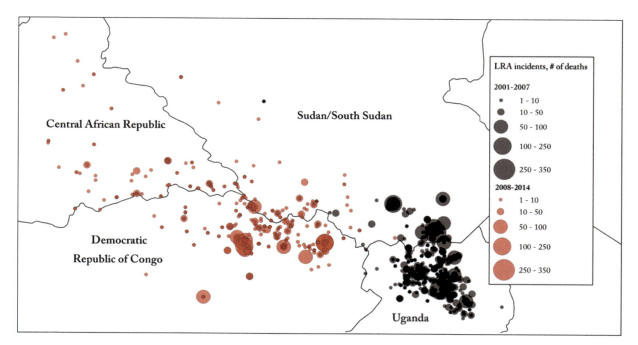

Figure 5.4 One-Sided Violence Committed by the Lord's Resistance Army in Central and East Africa, 2001–2014
Source: Data are drawn from UCDP-GED.

the LRA further and further away from its original bases in northern Uganda, first into southern Sudan in the early 2000s, then into the DRC by 2008, and finally up north from the DRC back across the Sudanese border and into the Central African Republic. The relocation of the LRA across borders was accompanied by a trail of civilian targeting following similar patterns as in northern Uganda: massacres combined with abductions for recruitment.

This example has implications for how to best study OSV. If civilian targeting has significant cross-border dimensions, our inquiries and explanations ought to take that dimension into account. In practical terms, this means that we should not always constrain research to using countries as the unit of analysis, with borders bounding what we observe and measure. The case of the LRA is illustrative: a proper understanding of its activities would be impossible by focusing on Uganda alone. Instead, mapping the LRA's movements and perpetration of violence around the region is crucial to illuminating the full scope of its activities. The LRA is hardly distinctive in its operations across state borders. Armed actors that target civilians in areas outside the country in which the actor was originally based, capitalizing on permeable territorial borders, are a common phenomenon across Africa. Prominent examples from the past couple of decades include the National Patriotic Front of Liberia, which also operated in Côte d'Ivoire and Sierra Leone; Palipehutu FNL, which was active in Burundi and the DRC; and most recently *al-Shabaab*, which is based in Somalia but has extended OSV to Kenya. Moreover, the phenomenon is hardly unique to Africa. A well-known, ongoing case involves *Daesh*/Islamic State, which has committed brutal atrocities across multiple countries, primarily in Syria and Iraq. In addition, we should not lose sight of the fact that cross-border OSV is also perpetrated by state actors. Examples from the past decade include the government of Ethiopia targeting civilians in Somalia, as well as the government of Sudan targeting civilians in Chad and South Sudan.

One-Sided Violence and Armed Conflict

OSV often takes place within a broader context of armed conflict, as in the example of the LRA. In *Peace and Conflict 2016*, we reported that 75% of the country-year observations of OSV (minimum of 25 killings of civilians by a given armed actor) coincide with an active armed conflict (Fjelde, Hultman, and Sollenberg 2016). The country-level correlation need not mean, however, that OSV and armed conflict coincide in the same sub-national locations. We examine this relationship in several ways.

To start, we consider the grid-cells that exhibited OSV at any point during the period from 2005–2013 (approximately 2% of grid-cells globally). Of these cells, 65% also exhibited battle-related deaths due to armed conflict. The other 35% of locations experienced deadly attacks on civilians without suffering lethal violence among the combatants in an armed conflict. Of the cells with OSV, 18% also experienced lethal violence resulting from non-state armed conflict (i.e., an armed conflict between two non-state actors). Thus, in places where OSV is observed, lethal armed conflict is more likely than not to co-occur, but there are many exceptions.

These exceptions can reflect a number of circumstances. OSV may occur against a backdrop of a civil war in which armed groups fight each other in certain spots, while also attacking civilians at different locations within a country. Armed groups sometimes target constituencies of their adversaries, even though these civilians do not reside in the conflict zone (Fjelde and Hultman 2014). One example is the Sri Lankan civil war, which was mainly fought in the northern and eastern parts of the country. During this conflict, the Liberation Tigers of Tamil Eelam (LTTE) attacked civilian targets in the capital of Colombo – located on the southwest coast of the country – notably in 2008–2009. Also, most of the armed violence between the Israeli government and Palestinian insurgent groups occurs in Gaza and the West Bank (including large-scale civilian casualties resulting from Israeli operations in these locations), whereas civilian targeting by the non-state armed actors occurs in otherwise peaceful locations such as Jerusalem and Tel Aviv. In addition, violence against civilians can be associated with actors extracting resources from the civilian population through coercive means, in locations behind the frontlines of a conflict. An example is the 1991–2001 civil war between the government of Sierra Leone and the Revolutionary United Front (RUF), where this pattern was observed for both sides in the conflict. Armed groups may also carry out OSV in locations far away from conflict zones, such as the 9/11 attacks in New York City. A further circumstance is that groups never involved in an armed conflict may carry out terrorist attacks, such as the Tawhid al Jihad in the Sinai Peninsula of Egypt during 2008–2009. In numerous instances, including Zimbabwe in 2008, state repression results in lethal violence against civilians that occurs outside of armed conflict. Another situation is that violence against civilians may be largely criminal in nature: drug-related atrocities in Mexico are a prominent example.

Figure 5.5 reports the spatial relationship between OSV and different types of armed conflict. OSV was observed in 43% of grid-cells also affected by state-based internal armed conflict at any time during the 2005–2013 period.[6] By contrast, OSV was observed in only 1% of cells that did not experience lethal violence due to such armed conflict. Meanwhile, 34% of cells that exhibit lethal violence from armed conflict between two non-state actors, such as rebel groups or ethnic-based militias, also experienced OSV. This share compares to just 2% of the locations without lethal violence from armed conflict between non-state actors. The fact that the correlation is stronger in locations where the state is involved in lethal armed conflict, compared to locations exhibiting violence between non-state actors, is notable. This difference may be indicative of a state's relative superiority to non-state actors in terms of deploying armed force.

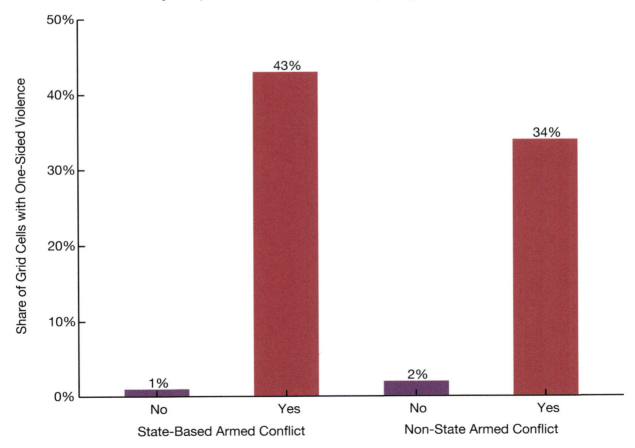

Figure 5.5 Spatial Overlap between One-Sided Violence and Different Types of Armed Conflictm 2005–2013
Source: Data are drawn from UCDP-GED.

These results suggest that armed conflict, regardless of type, is associated with a dramatically higher risk that OSV takes place in the same location. With the descriptive analysis, however, the nature of causation is uncertain. OSV could be spurred by armed conflict. Or OSV may trigger armed conflict. Another possibility is that other factors in those locations increase the risk of both armed conflict and OSV, even in cases where the dynamics of each type of violence are not explicitly related to each other. These potential relationships deserve scrutiny in future research.

The relationship between armed conflict and OSV could be explained by different factors. One category of intrastate armed conflict involves a rebel group contesting with the state for control over territory within a country, seeking autonomy or independent statehood (Toft 2014). Under this circumstance, civilian targeting may be linked to violent displacement or even ethnic cleansing. The alternative scenario of contesting for control of the government can also prompt targeting of supporters of the adversary. In addition, state actors tend to have greater capacity than non-state actors – especially those involved only in non-state conflicts – to extend military operations into areas where civilian supporters of adversaries are located, enhancing the ability to target those civilians more frequently and on a larger scale. Also, actors in state-based conflicts typically have a more hierarchical organizational structure, relative to those in non-state conflicts, which increases the prospects of strategically driven attacks against civilians that require stronger command and control over forces. Another factor relates to a challenge of measurement: in non-state conflicts, distinguishing between civilians and members of armed groups can be difficult. OSV may appear less likely within a non-state conflict as a by-product of how events are reported, to the extent there is a bias toward treating the victims of lethal violence as armed combatants, rather than civilians.

Finally, we take a closer look at OSV perpetrated by state and non-state actors. As shown in Figure 5.6, half of the grid-cells where state actors perpetrated OSV from 2005–2013 also exhibited lethal violence as part of a state-based armed conflict over this same time period. The extent of spatial overlap is reduced if we require that the OSV and armed violence occurred during the same calendar year. By contrast, a large majority of the cells that exhibited OSV by non-state actors from 2005–2013 also experienced lethal violence due to state-based armed conflict over the same time period. The

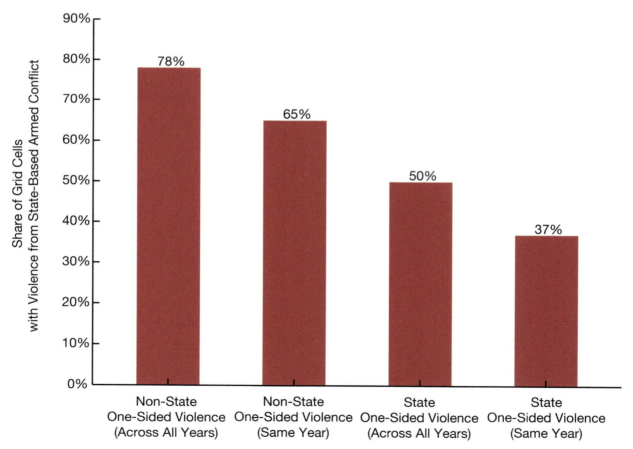

Figure 5.6 Spatial Overlap of State-Based Armed Conflict with One-Sided Violence Committed by State and Non-State Actors, 2005–2013
Source: Data are drawn from UCDP-GED.

extent of spatial overlap is again reduced with the restriction that the OSV and armed violence occurred during the same calendar year. These results are consistent with our proposition above that a state can be expected to have a greater capacity to operate across a large territory and to engage in repressive behavior against the citizenry, even in places without armed conflict. In comparison, non-state actors have more limited capabilities and therefore areas of operation, which largely confines them to engaging in clashes with government forces and attacking civilians in the same locations around the same time.

Characteristics of Locations

Another benefit of disaggregated, georeferenced event data on OSV is the ability to pair with additional spatial data in order to consider other characteristics of locations where this violence takes place. We focus on three characteristics – urban vs. rural, the level of economic development, and the presence of natural resources – that have received significant attention in the literature on political violence.

To classify grid-cells as urban or rural, we use data from *Globcover 2009* (Bontemps et al. 2009).[7] Figure 5.7 shows that OSV is almost twice as prevalent in urban areas compared to rural areas (see also Sundberg and Melander 2013; Höglund et al. 2016). This result conforms to multiple existing theoretical explanations. As a general matter, more populous areas exhibit a higher risk of organized violence. This relationship has been corroborated in studies about the location of civil war battle events conducted at both the national and sub-national levels (Raleigh and Hegre 2009).

One explanation may be that densely populated areas have a higher probability – all else being equal – of supplying the manpower necessary to uphold a viable rebellion, because the recruitment pool is larger. Since urban areas are important hubs for civil war recruitment and activity, the logic follows that urban centers will also be at greater risk of OSV. In addition, urban centers have a higher concentration of economic activity than rural areas. Because armed actors often support their activities by relying on forcible extraction of resources, targeting urban centers with violence may be logical. In as much as violence against civilians serves a strategic purpose in civil war, the value is heightened in areas with greater concentrations of people and resources, since the signaling effects are more pronounced. If a non-state armed actor wants

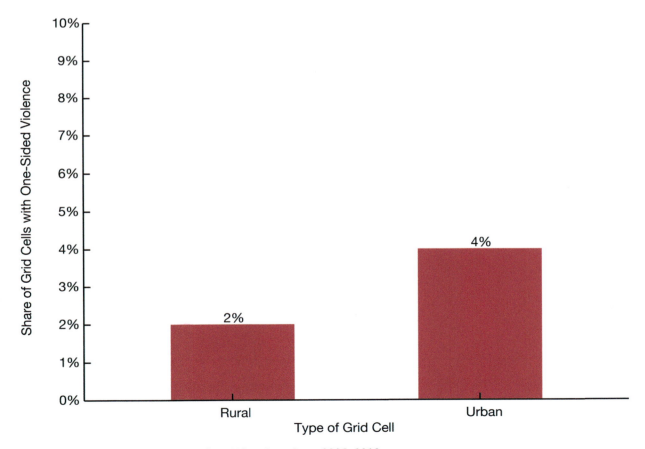

Figure 5.7 One-Sided Violence in Rural vs. Urban Locations, 2005–2013
Source: Data are drawn from UCDP-GED.

to exploit civilian targeting to inflict harm and put political pressure on an incumbent government, attacking populations in the large urban centers may be more effective, compared to low-visibility attacks in less-populated rural locations.

The spatial relationship between the level of economic development and OSV can be examined directly. In many countries, development varies substantially at a local level, with only some areas having a high density of infrastructure, manufacturing industry, natural resources or other factors linked to economic opportunities. As a measure of development, we use the grid-cell equivalent of GDP per capita: the gross cell product (Nordhaus 2006). To reduce this continuous measure to strata of economic development, we group values with respect to standard deviations below and above the global mean.

As Figure 5.8 shows, a positive relationship exists between the share of cells exhibiting OSV and the development strata. High-development locations (i.e., income greater than one standard deviation above the mean) are about 20 times more likely and mid-development locations (between one standard deviation below and one standard deviation above the mean) are eight times more likely to exhibit OSV than poor locations (income more than one standard deviation below the mean), which rarely experience such violence. We would caution, however, that these results probably underreport the prevalence of OSV in the poor locations. Data for the gross cell product indicator are missing for many countries where civilian targeting is frequent. Most of these countries – including Afghanistan, Somalia, and Zimbabwe – are at the bottom of the global income distribution. If the relevant data for those countries was available, we would expect to find that the relationship between economic development and OSV is U-shaped, with greater prevalence of OSV in the richest and the poorest locations, rather than in those that fall in the middle of the income spectrum.

A similar pattern is found when we examine the shares of cells exhibiting OSV that fall in the different income brackets. About 48% of cells with OSV score more than one standard deviation above the global mean of income. This result is partly driven by a handful of medium and high-income countries – Israel and India – that experience repeated incidents of OSV. Another contributing factor is a number of OSV events occurring in relatively richer areas within

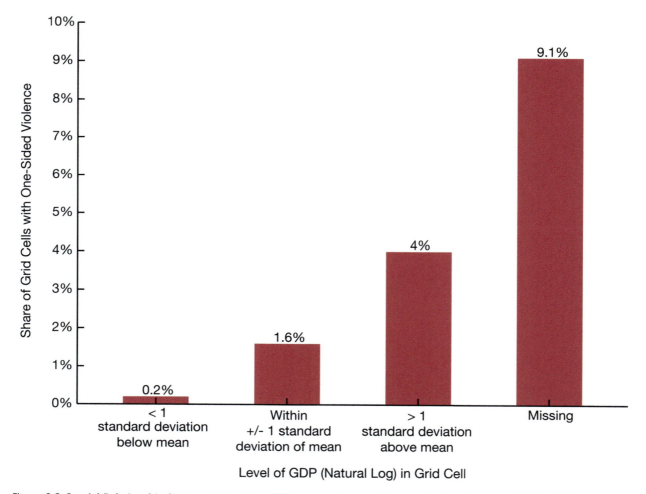

Figure 5.8 Spatial Relationship between One-Sided Violence and Level of Economic Development, 2005–2013
Source: Data are drawn from UCDP-GED.

developing countries, such as urban centers in Nigeria and Kenya. This relationship may be confounded by the higher population density in relatively rich areas. Nevertheless, the results are consistent with studies finding that the risk of terrorist attacks may – at least up to a point – increase with higher levels of income (c.f., Enders et al. 2016). The results are also consistent with sub-national studies of civil war suggesting that pockets of wealth within relatively poor countries may experience a higher risk of violence, since the target values – understood as the resources that can be forcibly extracted by armed actors – are higher in these locations (Hegre, Østby, and Raleigh 2009; Buhaug et al. 2009).

The discussion about how OSV relates to the concentration of wealth hints at the theoretical importance of studying natural resource wealth as well. Figure 5.9 shows the spatial relationship between the presence of natural resources – including gold, diamonds, gems, and petroleum – and the incidence of violence against civilians. The share of cells with resource wealth that exhibit violence against civilians is more than twice that of cells without resource wealth. Existing studies have noted that violence against civilians is more likely in natural resource-rich countries, because rebel groups endowed with resources are more likely to recruit individuals who are more opportunistic and less committed to the cause of the conflict – and therefore more likely to engage in abuses against civilians (c.f., Weinstein 2007). Our spatial analysis indicates, however, that civilian targeting may result not only from indiscipline and lack of control. Instead, OSV may also be a result of strategic efforts to extract resources. In Sierra Leone, for example, many RUF attacks against civilians in the early 1990s occurred in diamond-producing villages, when the RUF sought to establish control over the lucrative resources.

Conclusion

This chapter presented an initial exploration of the spatial patterns of OSV around the world from 2005–2013. The analysis contrasts with a majority of prior research about violence against civilians, which relied on data aggregated to the country level. Turning to the sub-national level reveals interesting variation in where civilian targeting occurs. The spatial correlation with civil war events suggests that OSV may reflect strategic goals of armed actors, such as undermining support

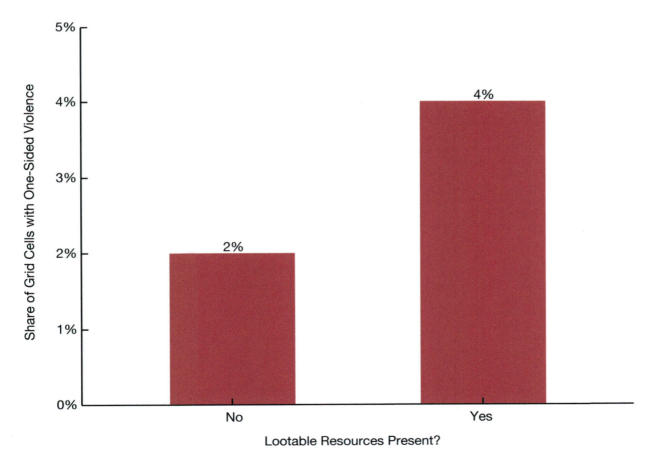

Figure 5.9 One-Sided Violence and Lootable Resources, 2005–2013
Source: Data are drawn from UCDP-GED.

structures and supply lines from civilian populations to the adversary. Yet we also show that considerable violence against civilians takes place in locations with exposure to lethal violence – in particular, killings perpetrated by state actors – from armed conflict. Moreover, most locations exhibit only violence by either states or non-state actors; instances where both states and non-state actors target civilians in the same location are less common. The regional maps suggest that the degree of overlap is very different in Africa relative to Asia and the Middle East. The spatially disaggregated data offers novel opportunities for further investigation of variation in the relationship between OSV and armed conflict, as well as many potential relationships in the involvement of state and non-state actors in targeting civilians and engaging in combat, especially in the same locations. Our analysis also detects signs that relationships between development and violence are much more complex than what has been found when examining aggregate, country-level correlations. OSV appears to be more likely in areas where population density, economic activity or natural resource wealth enhance the strategic value of using violence – whether as a signaling device or to extract assets.

The emergent availability of diverse forms of geographically disaggregated data paves the way for significant advances in our understanding of OSV. The scope of data with clear spatial dimensions is no longer limited to physical and human geography (e.g., terrain, natural resources, population density, etc.). Researchers can now obtain data on political, social, and economic geography (institutions, ethnic demographics, inequality, marginalization, etc.), which regularly vary across a country's territories. These spatial data resources enable a closer look at what influences OSV, amplifying the potential for assessment of the drivers of violence targeting civilians.

Notes

1 There are notable methodological differences and similarities between UCDP's OSV data and the Global Terrorism Database (GTD) and Political Terror Scale (PTS) data used in other chapters in this volume. Some events of violence will overlap across the three data collections. Most notably, both UCDP and GTD data will capture events where non-state actors target and kill unarmed civilians, and UCDP and PTS data will both include direct attacks by state actors on civilians. The GTD excludes, however, attacks on civilians by state actors (so-called "state terrorism"), while PTS data exclude civilian targeting by non-state/sub-national actors. The OSV category includes only fatal outcomes, which is a more limited focus compared to the PTS. The OSV category also excludes attacks on security agents, which may be encompassed in the GTD data, even when such attacks result in civilian casualties, as these fall under the UCDP category of battle-related violence. In terms of theoretical definitions, UCDP OSV data do not use the terms "terrorism" or "repression" and are thus devoid of classifications that differentiate among incidents of fatal violence against civilians.
2 For access to the data and more information on the UCDP, see www.ucdp.uu.se.
3 Since the authoring of this chapter, additional data have been released: UCDP-GED v5.0 is now available covering the 1989–2015 period.
4 We only include grids that have a population greater than 0, since we do not expect to observe political violence in areas that are completely uninhabited (the majority of these uninhabited grid squares are located in northern Canada and northern Russia). We only include events with a precision code of 5 or lower, thus excluding events where there is no more precise location than the country where the violent event takes place.
5 Chi-square tests have been run on all cross-tabulations reported in the chapter, and all results are statistically significant.
6 An intrastate armed conflict is defined as "a contested incompatibility which concerns government and/or territory where the use of armed force between two parties, of which at least one is the government of a state, results in at least 25 battle-related deaths" in a calendar year (Wallensteen and Sollenberg, 2001). Non-state conflicts are defined as "the use of armed force between two organized armed groups, neither of which is the government of a state, which results in at least 25 battle-related deaths" in a calendar year (Sundberg, Eck, and Kreutz 2012).
7 We define a grid-cell as urban if the share of urban land in the cell is higher than the mean in the global sample (>0.212).

References

Balcells, Laia (2010) "Rivalry and Revenge: Violence against Civilians in Conventional Civil Wars," *International Studies Quarterly* 54: 291–313.

Beardsley, Kyle, Kristian Skrede Gleditsch, and Nigel Lo (2015) "Roving Bandits: The Geographical Evolution of African Armed Conflicts," *International Studies Quarterly* 59(3): 503–516.

Bontemps, Sophie, Pierre Defourny, Eric Van Bogaert, Olivier Arino, Vasileios Kalogirou, and Jose Ramos Perez (2009) *GLOBCOVER 2009. Products Description and Validation Report.* Harwell: European Space Agency.

Buhaug, Halvard, Scott Gates, and Päivi Lujala (2009). "Geography, Rebel Capacity, and the Duration of Civil Conflict." *Journal of Conflict Resolution* 53(4): 544–569.

Buhaug, Halvard, Kristian Skrede Gleditsch, Helge Holtermann, Gudrun Østby and Andreas Forø Tollefsen (2011) "It's the Local Economy, Stupid! Geographic Wealth Dispersion and Conflict Outbreak Location," *Journal of Conflict Resolution* 55(5): 814–840.

Croicu, Mihai, and Ralph Sundberg (2015) "UCDP GED Codebook version 2.0," Department of Peace and Conflict Research, Uppsala University.

Enders, Walter, Gary A. Hoover, and Todd Sandler (2016) "The Changing Nonlinear relationship between income and terrorism," *Journal of Conflict Resolution* 60(2): 195–225.

Fjelde, Hanne, and Lisa Hultman (2014) "Weakening the Enemy: A Disaggregated Study of Violence against Civilians in Africa," *Journal of Conflict Resolution* 58(7): 1230–1257.

Fjelde, Hanne, Lisa Hultman, and Margareta Sollenberg (2016) "Violence against Civilians during Civil War." In Backer, David, Ravi Bhavnani, and Paul Huth (eds), *Peace and Conflict 2016*. Abingdon: Routledge.

Hegre, Håvard, Gudrun Østby, and Clionadh Raleigh (2009) "Poverty and Civil War Events: A Disaggregated Study of Liberia," *Journal of Conflict Resolution* 53(4): 598–623.

Höglund, Kristine, Erik Melander, Margareta Sollenberg, and Ralph Sundberg (2016) "Armed Conflict and Space: Exploring Urban-Rural Patterns of Violence." In Björkdahl, Annika and Susanne Buckley-Zistel (eds) *Spatializing Peace and Conflict: Mapping the Production of Place, Sites and Scales of Violence*. Basingstoke: Palgrave Macmillan.

Kalyvas, Stathis (2006) *The Logic of Violence in Civil War*. Cambridge: Cambridge University Press.

Nordhaus, William D. (2006) "Geography and Macroeconomics: New Data and New Findings," *Proceedings of the National Academy of Sciences of the USA*, 103(10): 3510–3517.

Raleigh, Clionadh (2012) "Violence Against Civilians: A Disaggregated Analysis," *International Interactions*, 38(4): 462–481.

Raleigh, Clionadh, and Hegre, Håvard (2009) "Population Size, Concentration, and Civil War: A Geographically Disaggregated Analysis." *Political Geography* 28(4): 224–238.

Sundberg, Ralph, Kristine Eck, and Joakim Kreutz (2012) "Introducing the UCDP Non-State Conflict Dataset." *Journal of Peace Research* 49(2): 523–532.

Sundberg, Ralph, and Erik Melander (2013) "Introducing the UCDP Georeferenced Event Dataset," *Journal of Peace Research* 50(4): 523–532.

Toft, Monica (2014) "Territory and War," *Journal of Peace Research*, 51(2): 185–198.

Tollefsen, Andreas Forø, Håvard Strand, and Halvard Buhaug (2012) "PRIO-GRID: A Unified Spatial Data Structure," *Journal of Peace Research* 49(2): 363–374.

Valentino, Benjamin, Paul Huth, and Dylan Balch-Lindsay (2004) "Draining the Sea: Mass Killing and Guerrilla Warfare." *International Organization* 58(2): 375–407.

Wallensteen, Peter and Margareta Sollenberg (2001) "Armed Conflict 1989–2000." *Journal of Peace Research* 38(5): 629–644.

Weinstein, Jeremy M. (2007) *Inside Rebellion. The Politics of Insurgent Violence*. Cambridge: Cambridge University Press.

6

The Size of Rebel and State Armed Forces in Internal Conflicts

Measurement and Implications

Jacob Aronson and Paul K. Huth

Introduction

Understanding the military capabilities of both rebel groups and state counterinsurgents is fundamental to studying the dynamics of internal conflicts. Such capabilities are expected to influence the ability of rebel groups to sustain fighting and achieve particular outcomes, as well as the types and severity of violence in which those groups engage. In turn, establishing these relationships empirically depends on reliable assessments of the armed strength of rebel groups and state counterinsurgents. Assessments of rebel and state capability divide into two camps. Each camp has a different take on the role that these capabilities play in exerting coercion.

The "information" camp starts from the premise that internal conflicts are quite distinct from interstate armed conflicts because insurgents make use of guerrilla warfare in situations of asymmetry of military forces (Arreguín-Toft 2005). When using guerrilla warfare, the ability of a rebel group to successfully engage in coercion is a function not of the size and strength of armed forces, but rather of whether or not the state has knowledge of vital details such as the location of particular rebel operatives and when and where insurgents are planning to attack (Berman and Matanock 2015; Mikulaschek and Shapiro 2016; Kalyvas 2006). In this setting, a state with access to those details can easily defeat a rebel group – no matter the size. Under these circumstances, the size of a rebel group has little bearing on conflict outcomes and larger forces may even be counterproductive, given the tendency to have a more observable information footprint as a result. Meanwhile, the fact that a state has superior military strength is alone not decisive; rather, information holds the key to outcomes.

By contrast, the "resources" camp posits that the production of coercion, including violence against civilians, is a direct function of military capabilities, which must be sourced through consistent access to new recruits and materiel (Schutte 2015; Wood 2010; Hultman 2007). Yet scholars usually approximate these capabilities in rough terms, often using largely static data (e.g., the Non-State Actor Dataset [Cunningham, Gleditsch, and Salehyan 2009]), or proxies based on the number of battle-related fatalities suffered by states and rebel groups (e.g., UCDP-GED [Sundberg and Melander 2013]). Those measures have shortcomings: the former can be time invariant and is useful mostly for categorical estimates, while the latter is indirect and limits the ability to test hypotheses about group effectiveness. Consequently, existing research does not yet supply a credible basis on which to evaluate how the strength of rebel groups influences various conflict dynamics.

In this chapter, we undertake a fresh set of empirical analyses of the impact of rebel and state forces on conflict outcomes, relying on new annual data on the sizes of forces that we have compiled. Section 2 offers an overview of the new dataset, including the definitions and process that we employed to collect data. Section 3 describes patterns and trends in the sizes of rebel and state forces. Among other things, we show that the on-the-ground balance of forces is not as asymmetric as scholars generally take for granted. Thus, explanations of conflict dynamics that rely on assumptions about extreme military asymmetry may need to be reexamined. Section 4 presents our analysis. We find that the size of a rebel group's military forces is associated with greater numbers of fatalities suffered by state forces in battle and civilians killed, as well as a higher chance of securing more favorable outcomes in both guerrilla and conventional internal conflicts. These

The Size of Forces in Internal Conflicts

results support the arguments of the resources camp, indicating that force size contributes in significant ways to boosting the coercive capacity of a rebel group.

A New Dataset on the Size of Rebel and State Fighting Forces

Several other datasets on force size already exist (e.g., Lawrence 2015; Friedman 2011; Cunningham, Gleditsch, and Salehyan 2009; McGrath 2006). These sources exhibit two important limitations. First, the sources typically estimate group capabilities at the dyad level with either a range of force sizes or a qualitative assessment of the relative balance of power. The imprecision of these estimates is problematic for purposes of quantitative analyses. Second, select studies rely on time-varying estimates of force sizes drawn from raw information available in the database of the Uppsala Conflict Data Program (UCDP). This information is not systematically collected using a consistent protocol, nor has UCDP taken steps to clean and process the information. As a result, the information does not meet the standards of UCDP's officially released datasets.

We have addressed both of these limitations by compiling specific estimates of the sizes of military forces, using a systematic, consistent data-collection protocol. Our new dataset contains two main variables: (1) the number of military forces of each rebel group involved in an internal armed conflict; and (2) the number of military and paramilitary forces a state has deployed to fight rebel groups in each internal armed conflict in which the state is involved. These data are expressed on an annual basis and currently cover the years from 1975–2014. The years for which we collect data, our definition of an internal armed conflict, and the list of rebel groups involved in such conflicts generally correspond to the parameters of the UCDP Armed Conflict Dataset (ACD) (Pettersson and Wallensteen 2015). From the ACD, we exclude a number of cases. One excluded case is the United States vs. al-Qaeda (the day of the attacks of September 11), which is not a conflict fought by an organized group with armed forces in the US. In addition, we exclude cases where the fighting between the relevant actors took the form of a coup launched by a small fraction of the state's armed forces over a short period of time. Our dataset does include, however, any case of a coup that turned into protracted fighting between the state and forces in opposition. After these exclusions, our dataset has 1,927 annual observations corresponding to conflicts between a state and a rebel group that produced at least 25 battle-related fatalities.

Defining Rebel Forces

The size of the military forces of each rebel group is measured at the dyad-year level. For each year in which a rebel group engaged in a conflict that exceeds 25 battle-related fatalities, we seek to identify the number of armed militants that the rebel group commanded. This estimate excludes the forces of other rebel groups, ethnic militias, and external supporters,[1] even when engaged in joint operations, since those forces are not part of the rebel group itself.[2] In addition, the estimate excludes individuals who conduct one-off attacks (e.g., a civilian paid to place an improvised explosive device), as well as supporters who do not take up arms and fight. Our estimate for each group exceeds what could be considered as the rebel vanguard: the hardcore militants who comprise the cadre around which a rebel organization is built. At the same time, the estimate will tend to be far less than the number of supporters, many of whom are unarmed civilians and may be supporters of a rebel group in name only.

Our focus on generating a best estimate of the number of active, full-time militants who are equipped, trained, armed and commanded by the leadership of a rebel group has multiple justifications. From a theoretical perspective, these forces afford a rebel group coercive power and provide the capacity to engage in more sophisticated, costly activities such as holding territory, pressuring civilians, and engaging state forces in sustained, close-quarters combat. From a practical perspective, identifying consistent, reliable figures of the number of temporary fighters a rebel group employs and the size of the group's support base is very difficult. We do not deny that these additional metrics would be valuable to researchers who aim to fully model a group's capabilities. Thus, we welcome efforts to collect this data to supplement our own.

Defining State Forces

Similar to how we gauge rebel forces, we record only the military forces belonging to the state, including the regular army as well as formal paramilitary forces such as armed police or militias who are explicitly under a state's command authority. The figures exclude other sources of military support in the form of armed personnel and allied combatants with their own distinct leadership – such as pro-government militias (PGMs) and external forces.[3]

We take care to identify the number of forces that are actually committed to fighting a rebel group (i.e., mobilized and deployed to a particular conflict area), as opposed to the number of potential forces available. According to our data, the extent of committed forces often differs dramatically from a state's official armed strength. In addition, the ratio of the two

47

numbers varies both within and across cases, as a function of the ability and willingness of a state to commit its forces to internal armed conflict. Consequently, the size of the army can be a poor gauge of the capacity of a state's forces actively implicated in a conflict, which may lead to incorrect findings. Our estimates offer better time-varying data on the size of the forces mobilized for purposes of counterinsurgency than are currently available.

The estimates of the size of state forces are compiled at the conflict-year level, as opposed to the dyad-year (the unit of observation for which data on rebel groups are collected).[4] A conflict may involve fighting between the state and multiple rebel groups that are seeking to accomplish the same goal, whereas a dyad describes the fighting that occurs in the pair comprised of a single state and a single rebel group. A conflict may contain multiple dyads. For example, in Iraq, multiple Sunni groups (nationalist ex-Baathists, al-Qaeda backed radicals, and Kurdish Salafists) fought together in an attempt to take over the government of Iraq. The conflict these rebel groups waged was distinct from the conflict waged by the Mahdi Army, a Shia militia. Thus, for each year of the conflict in Iraq, we identify one number for the size of government forces committed against Sunni insurgents and a separate number for the size of forces committed against Shia insurgents.

Estimating state forces at the conflict-year level makes most sense for two reasons: (1) the rebel groups engaged in the same conflict are likely to coordinate efforts in some fashion, and (2) a state is likely to mobilize forces against this collective threat, rather than against each group individually. For example, al-Qaeda, Baathist and Salafist Kurdish rebels fought together in Iraq and had the same goals and patterns of operation. US-backed Iraqi government forces deployed without distinguishing among these insurgent groups. The government, however, allocated separate military forces and engaged in a distinct set of military operations in the conflict against the Mahdi Army.

Data-Collection Process

In compiling the data, our ultimate goal was point estimates of the size of each combatant's military forces for each year of fighting. A starting point was to generate estimates of force sizes for the first and last years of a conflict. In addition, we paid particular attention to generating estimates for years that likely exhibited meaningful fluctuations in forces. For this purpose, we devoted substantial time to reading through available conflict narratives. In particular, we were interested in accounts that characterize the size of forces and/or events that affect size, e.g., when rebel groups are identified as growing rapidly, incurring substantial losses, or engaging in large-scale fighting. Specific information on force sizes could not be located for about 35% of dyad-years. We generated values on these observations by linearly interpolating between the two estimates in closest proximity within the time series. We believe that this approach should not systematically misrepresent a group's force size, given our efforts to capture instances of substantial variation.

Throughout the process, we relied on multiple data sources wherever available, triangulating among pieces of information as appropriate. In many instances, these sources provided multiple estimates of the size of forces for a given combatant in a given year. These estimates were not always identical. We adjudicated among the varying estimates in several ways. First, we favored the assessments made by more credible third parties (e.g., think-tanks, academic publications, US government) over less reliable sources such as combatant self-reporting and non-retrospective news sources. Second, we prioritized the most recent assessments over prior assessments. Third, when credible sources provided varying estimates for the same year, we used the estimate that was most consistent with the other estimates. This process increases the internal consistency of the data and makes comparisons within the data more accurate. In effect, we gave outliers less weight when choosing the most appropriate point estimate.

The initial sources on which we relied were the UCDP database, the annual military balance reports published by the International Institute for Strategic Studies (IISS), force estimates reported by the Stockholm International Peace Research Institute (SIPRI), and the Non-State Actor Dataset. These sources have certain gaps in coverage. Therefore, we conducted extensive additional research to expand the data, using *Keesings Record of World Events*, reports from various other respected think-tanks and NGOs, and news sources.

Patterns and Trends in the Size of Rebel and State Forces

To orient the analysis, we start by providing an overview of basic patterns and trends in the sizes of military forces derived from our data. First, we present regional trends in the size of rebel forces. Second, we show how the size of rebel forces varies by the "technology of conflict," i.e., symmetric vs. asymmetric (Kalyvas and Balcells 2010).[5] Third, we compare variation in the sizes of rebel and state forces over the duration of conflicts. Fouth, we explore the relative share of state forces committed to fighting against insurgent forces.

Regional Trends in the Size of Rebel Forces

Figure 6.1 shows the trends in the median size of the armed forces of rebel groups, by region. (We exclude Europe in this and subsequent figures because far fewer conflicts occur in that region and the results are dominated by the multiple conflicts in Yugoslavia during the 1990s.) Throughout our analysis, we choose to report the median size of forces, when possible, because of the skewed nature of the underlying data: many smaller groups and a select number of much larger combatants. Each trend line in Figure 6.1 is smoothed over a three-year window to reduce short-term fluctuations and clarify underlying trajectories. The trend lines are accompanied by 90% confidence intervals.

Several interesting results stand out. First, rebel groups in the Middle East have tended to be the largest (median size=5,500), whereas rebel groups in the Americas (primarily Central and Latin America) have been the smallest (median size=2,750).[6] Second, the end of the Cold War, accompanied by the collapse of the Soviet Union, had a significant impact on the size of rebel armed forces in most regions. Comparing the periods from 1975–1991 and 1992–2014, the median force size decreased from 6,750 to 2,500 in Africa, 5,734 to 3,025 in Asia, and 7,357 to 3,750 in the Middle East. Third, the exception is the Americas, where the median size of insurgent forces increased from 2,500 during the Cold War era to 3,217 in the period since. The earlier figure may reflect the ability of the United States to deter overt external support to rebel groups by the Soviet Union and its allies. More recent increases in the size of Latin and Central American insurgent groups are also consistent with increasing profits that result from narcotrafficking (Otis 2014). Fifth, some evidence exists of a recent reversal of the long-run downward trend in the Middle East. After 2011, with the draw-down of US combat forces in the region, an uptick in median force size is observed, due especially to the presence of large, sophisticated insurgent groups such as the Islamic State in Iraq and Syria (ISIS). The median size for 2012–2014 (5,375) is climbing back up substantially closer to the level that had prevailed during the Cold War era.

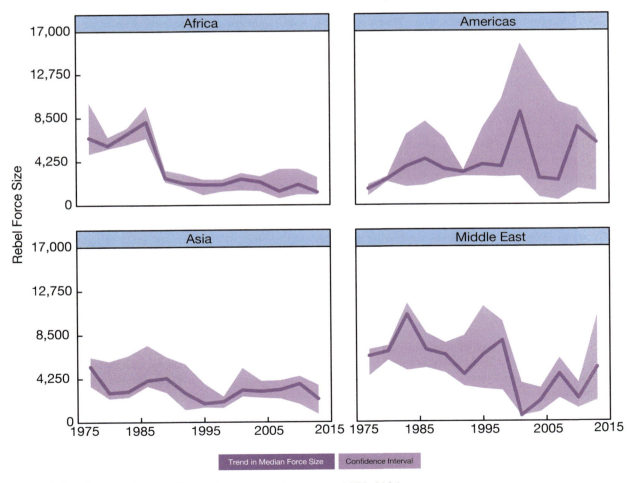

Figure 6.1 Trends in the Median Size of Rebel Forces, by Region, 1975–2014
Note: Data are smoothed over a three-year moving window.

The Technology of Conflict and the Size of Rebel Forces

In addition to the role of external support, another factor that may contribute to regional trends is the nature of how rebel groups fight (Biddle and Friedman 2008; Arreguín-Toft 2005). We place conflicts into two broad categories, based on data from Kalyvas and Balcells (2010). The first category is asymmetric conflict, in which a weaker insurgent wages guerrilla warfare against a conventionally stronger state opponent. Examples include the conflicts in Iraq and Palestine. This type of warfare constitutes 74% of the dyad-years in the dataset. The second category is symmetric conflict, in which combatants on both sides engage in conventional warfare. Examples include the fighting that occurred in select portions of the recent Afghan and Angolan civil wars, as well as the 2006 Hezbollah conflict in Lebanon. The remaining 26% of dyad-years fall into this category.

Figure 6.2 shows the trends in the median size of rebel forces for the two types of warfare. Once more, the trends are smoothed over three-year windows and accompanied by 90% confidence intervals. As expected, insurgents engaged in asymmetric conflicts have smaller forces (median size=3,180) than insurgents in symmetric conflicts (median size=8,000).

The overall results hide the substantial variation over time. For example, the median force size among groups engaged in symmetric warfare dropped from 12,375 during the Cold War era to 5,500 for the period from 1992–2011 – a decline of 56%. Meanwhile, the median force size among groups engaged in asymmetric warfare dropped from 4,740 during the Cold War era to 2,500 for the period from 1992–2011 – a decline of 47%. More recently, symmetric combatants rebounded to a median force size of 10,000 from 2012–2014.

Several factors likely contributed to these historical trends. Following the end of the Cold War, many rebel groups lost their external support. The most direct impact resulted from the loss of sponsorship in proxy wars by the Soviet Union and its allies. The US had no superpower peer to compete against, which also diminished support for insurgencies. As a consequence, numerous groups faced difficulties in sustaining fighting. Some terminated the conflicts in which they were involved. Those that did not frequently suffered a diminished capacity to field armed forces. In addition, the US assumed a more active role in maintaining standing military forces in the Middle East from 2001–2011, which helped to restrain the size of insurgent forces in that region. Groups engaged in both symmetric and asymmetric warfare exhibit the impact of these factors, though the greatest declines were observed among conventional combatants. The more recent bump in the median force size among groups engaged in symmetric warfare coincides with a period of reduced projection of US military power, at least in terms of ground forces based in Iraq and Afghanistan. Also, groups engaged in conventional fighting may have found alternate, reliable forms of funding, such as drugs, oil, and taxing civilian populations.

Comparing Variation in the Size of Rebel and State Forces during Conflicts

Another important consideration is the evolution of the armed forces of rebel groups and the number of counter-insurgency forces committed by states over the duration of each conflict. To analyze this angle, we coded each state-rebel dyad in terms of the number of years that has elapsed since the onset of armed conflict. Figure 6.3 presents the median number of rebel forces (top panel) and state forces (bottom panel), by year of the conflict. For example, the point at a value of "5 Years from Start of Conflict" represents the median force size of all rebel groups that were still fighting five years from when hostilities were first initiated.

The results show that rebel groups tend to be small around the onset of conflicts, but grow as fighting continues, resources are accumulated, and groups focus their attention on recruitment and/or demonstrate their resolve and ability to survive to civilian fence-sitters. The median force size increases from 2,000 in the first year of conflict to 7,700 for groups that are still fighting at the 15-year mark – a 285% increase. Of note, the distribution of force sizes is very nearly bi-modal, with a peak observed around the fourth year of conflict that is not exceeded again until the tenth year of fighting.

Meanwhile, the analysis of the median size of committed state counterinsurgency forces yields two main sets of findings. First, states frequently commit a modest scale of forces to combatting a nascent insurgency. States often face multiple internal security threats, most of which can be handled via the existing security apparatus (e.g., police forces), without needing to undertake the costly activity of mobilizing larger armed forces. As states recognize that they are confronting a real threat, they conduct a steady, sustained build-up of forces through at least the first eight years of conflict. The slope is most pronounced in the first few years of conflict, when a new threat becomes apparent, and then slows down as states identify the number of forces necessary to defeat or contain a threat, and may reflect a point of diminishing returns to mobilization. Second, the size of committed counterinsurgent forces is not overwhelmingly large relative to the size of rebel armed forces (and the size of most states' standing armies). In the median case, states forces outnumber armed insurgents by 10 to 1. If we shift focus from dyads to conflicts – thereby accounting for cases in which multiple groups are probably working together – this advantage falls to just 6 to 1. In nearly 25% of dyads and 35% of conflicts, states do not muster the 3 to 1 advantage in forces that military theorists generally view as necessary to defeat an entrenched opponent. Given the defensive requirements for states in many internal conflicts – the need to distribute soldiers to defend

The Size of Forces in Internal Conflicts

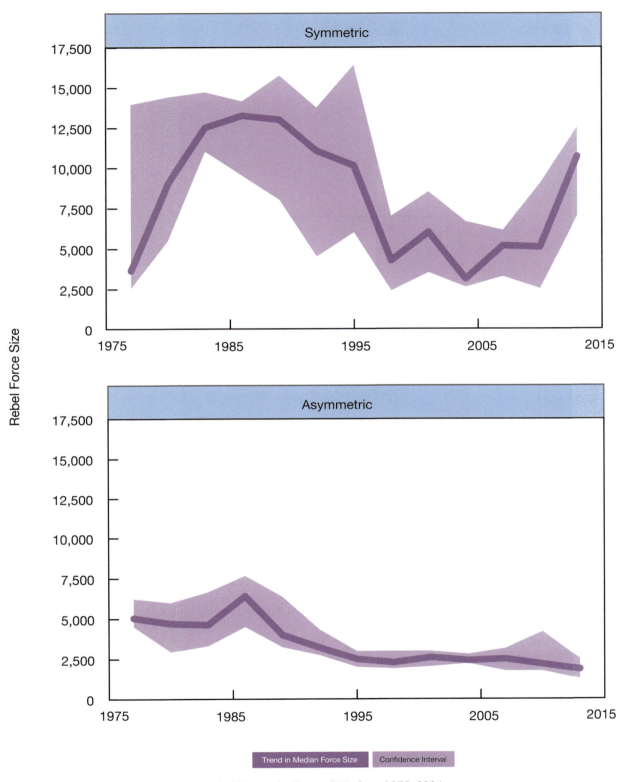

Figure 6.2 Trends in the Median Size of Rebel Forces, by Type of Warfare, 1975–2014
Note: Data are smoothed over a three-year moving window.

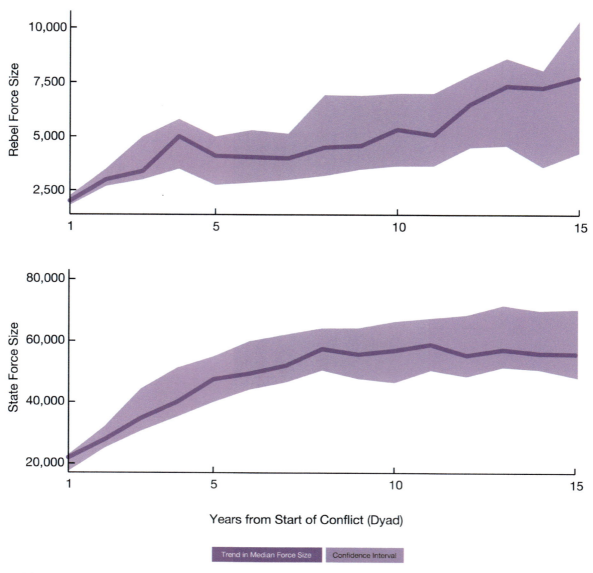

Figure 6.3 Comparing the Median Sizes of Rebel and State Forces, by Conflict Duration

many locations within a conflict zone and thus the inability to concentrate attackers – the battlefield balance of power is likely to be even less asymmetric.

This examination of the extent of military asymmetry has important ramifications for understandings of internal conflicts. A common explanation for the dynamics of internal conflicts, which points to the important role of civilians and the diminished significance of military forces, is that extreme military asymmetry prevents conventional military activity. In so far as rebels are able to field forces sufficient to hold territory or to concentrate those forces enough to consistently win local clashes , both the information and resource theories of internal conflict may prove to be salient simultaneously. Such hybrid dynamics have been observed in recent conflicts. In Afghanistan, for example, insurgents in Helmand province were able to amass enough strength to control large swathes of territory or to contain NATO forces in their forward operating bases (e.g., Ledwidge 2012). Insurgents in Iraq similarly experienced periods of the civil war when they exerted outright control over important cities such as Fallujah, Ramadi, and Mosul (e.g., Ballard 2006).

Variation in the Share of State Forces Committed to Fighting against Insurgency

In the absence of mobilization for total war, states do not commit their full resource or mobilization capacity to defeat an opponent (Reiter 2003). Instead, states weigh the costs of defeating an insurgent versus capitulation to an insurgent's demands. Other factors, such as the number of other threats a state is facing, the varying domestic costs of mobilization (e.g.,

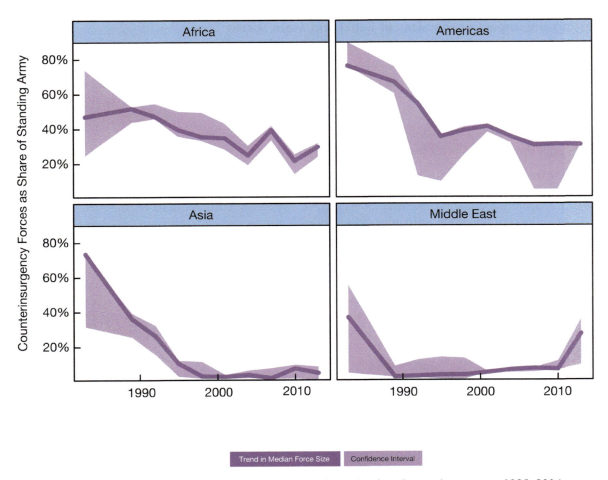

Figure 6.4 Regional Trends in the Median Share of State Forces Committed to Counterinsurgency, 1985–2014

the possibility of a coup), and the technical capacity to sustain forces in the field, weigh on a state's decision to mobilize its soldiers for combat.

In order to examine variation in the amount of force a state commits, Figure 6.4 shows the trends in the median share of a state's total armed forces mobilized to combat an insurgency, by region (once again excluding Europe and with the data smoothed over three-year windows).[7] Two results stand out. First, states in Africa and the Americas have regularly fielded a significant portion of their armies to fight against insurgencies. Second, across Africa, the Americas, and Asia, the share of forces committed to counterinsurgency saw a steady decline during the 1990s, when many of the Cold War-era rebel groups terminated conflicts.

The results for Africa and Latin America likely reflect two factors. The first factor is that most governments in those regions have relatively small armed forces. Across our sample, the median size of armies is 58,400 in Africa and 178,000 in Latin America, compared to 400,000 in both Asia and the Middle East. Thus, African and Latin American governments must field a larger portion of their armed forces to effectively combat insurgencies. The second factor is that the governments in Africa and Latin America chose to commit proportionately large shares of their armies to counterinsurgency activities, which also indicates that they perceive the threats they are facing as more serious. This finding is consistent with the fact that governments in both regions were fighting challenging civil wars – often ethnic conflicts in Africa and leftist insurgencies in Latin America (both of which were also a factor in counterinsurgency mobilization across Asia up through the mid-1990s).

All regions exhibit a post-Cold War effect, with committed forces decreasing as Cold War-era insurgencies won or were defeated, then often stabilizing around a smaller ratio towards the end of the 1990s. The effect is the least substantial and consistent in Africa, which still faced a considerable number of insurgencies that presented serious threats throughout the 1990s and into the 2000s. The small number of state forces committed to counterinsurgency in Asia and the Middle East may reflect a number of different factors, including the need to hold more armed forces in reserve to protect against external threats, fears of rampant disloyalty within armed forces (a problem Syria faced during the 2011 uprisings), or just smaller, more concentrated insurgents that required a smaller commitment of state force.

Assessing the Impact of the Sizes of Rebel and State Forces

Next, our analysis turns to an exploration of two important aspects of the potential impact of the sizes of rebel and state forces. First, we evaluate the relationship between the size of rebel forces and outcomes over the duration of an armed conflict. Second, in order to help understand why there is a relationship between force size and outcomes, we evaluate the associated relationship between the size of rebel forces and their lethality, i.e., the number of government and civilian deaths insurgent groups produce.

Size of Rebel Forces and Outcomes during Internal Armed Conflicts

We characterize outcomes for each rebel group involved within each conflict over the period from 1975–2015. Our coding draws primarily upon the UCDP Conflict Termination Dataset and the UCDP Peace Agreement Dataset, complemented by additional case-study research. Specifically, we differentiate three categories of outcomes.

The first category is **favorable outcomes**, which includes instances where a rebel group captures the state capital, defeats state forces in the field, or secures meaningful concessions (e.g., territorial autonomy), which may result from a peace treaty or a *de facto* agreement followed by a cessation of hostilities. Such favorable outcomes are observed in just 8.7% of internal armed conflicts. The second category is **unfavorable outcomes**, which include outright military defeat of a rebel group or degradation to a point where the group is unable to sustain fighting, falling below the threshold for inclusion in the ACD.[8] Such unfavorable outcomes are observed in 37.5% of internal armed conflicts. The third category is **mixed outcomes**, where insurgents cease fighting without securing a favorable outcome or experiencing an unfavorable outcome. In these cases, a rebel group does not experience success, but still retains the capacity to engage in conflict if desired. These mixed outcomes occur in the remaining 53.8% of cases.

Our coding is designed such that a rebel group may be recorded as experiencing different outcomes at different stages over the course of a given conflict. For example, Hezbollah fought against Israel between 1990 and 1999, at which point Israel withdrew from Southern Lebanon – a favorable outcome for Hezbollah during this initial period of the conflict. In 2006, Israel and Hezbollah returned to fighting, which terminated without Israel providing concessions or defeating the group – a mixed outcome for this second conflict period.

In theory, rebel groups that are able to build and maintain larger armed forces should have a better chance of securing a favorable outcome. This greater likelihood of success is attributable to an increased ability to coerce civilians, control territory and resources, and inflict casualties against the state, which enhances the bargaining position of the rebel group vis-à-vis the state.[9]

Our analysis focuses on observations of force size specific to conflict periods; we use the median size for a given group over a given period. Overall, the results show that the median size of rebel forces during conflict periods in which a favorable outcome was achieved is 15,000, compared to just 3,000 in conflict periods that resulted in an unfavorable outcome. A Monte Carlo simulation confirms that the difference between these two medians of 12,000 is statistically significant, with a 95% confidence interval of 9,000 to 17,125.

Figure 6.5 shows the distribution of outcomes experienced by rebel groups across quintiles of force size. Groups with a median force size during a conflict period that falls in the bottom quintile of the observations (i.e., 600 or fewer armed individuals) were never able to secure a favorable outcome. Instead, 52.0% experienced a mixed outcome, while 48.0% suffered an unfavorable outcome. By contrast, groups in the top quintile (9,437 or more armed individuals) were able to secure a favorable outcome in 20.6% of cases and experienced an unfavorable outcome in only 22.7% of cases. In the remaining 56.7% of cases, groups experienced mixed outcomes. Thus, insurgencies that either started out on a large scale, or built significant forces in the course of fighting, improved their chance of a favorable outcome and reduced their chance of an unfavorable outcome by substantial amounts. Meanwhile, increases in force size have only a minor effect on the likelihood of experiencing a mixed outcome.

Size of Rebel Forces and Lethality in Internal Armed Conflicts

An obvious reason why rebel groups with larger forces should be positioned to secure favorable outcomes more often than rebel groups with smaller forces emanates from the ability to inflict greater damage during the course of a conflict. A state suffering high costs is more likely to fall to defeat or be willing to provide meaningful concessions – potentially under pressure from the population – in order to terminate a conflict.

To determine whether or not this relationship holds, we estimate a linear regression model with several control variables and using fixed effects.[10] We consider two relationships. The dependent variable (DV) in the first regression is the number of battle-related fatalities suffered by state forces. The DV for the second regression is the number of civilian deaths committed by rebel forces. The analysis of civilian targeting drops years during which a rebel group killed no

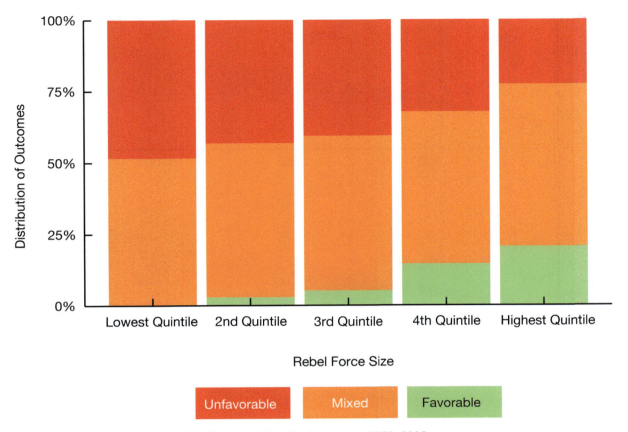

Figure 6.5 Rebel Force Size and the Distribution of Conflict Outcomes, 1975–2005

civilians; not all groups choose to target civilians. This restricted sample allows us to identify how force size influences the ability to kill civilians in years where the rebel chooses to do so. We also rerun both regressions using a subset of the data that removes cases of symmetric fighting, leaving just dyad years when rebel groups waged asymmetric warfare.

In addition to including our main variable of interest, the size of rebel forces, we control for the size of state forces, the balance of power (the total number of rebel forces and their external troop support divided by the total number of state forces and their external troop support), estimates of the number of external troops provided to the state and the rebel group, and the infant mortality rate (a proxy for state capacity). In order to identify if changes in force size across time within the same dyad influence the number of fatalities inflicted, we also include fixed effects at the dyad level.

Figure 6.6 displays the results of our analysis for the sample that includes both symmetric and asymmetric warfare. The top panel shows the relationship between the size of rebel forces and the number of battle-related fatalities suffered by state forces during fighting with this group. The bottom panel shows the relationship between the size of rebel forces and the number of civilian fatalities that a rebel group inflicted. The line in each panel represents the predicted number of fatalities, based on the regression results discussed above.[11] The shaded area reflects the 95% confidence interval of the estimates, generated using a Monte Carlo simulation approach.

This analysis yields a consistent conclusion: larger rebel groups tend to be more lethal – in absolute terms – than smaller rebel groups, killing greater numbers of both state armed forces and, if they choose to turn their violence towards non-combatants, civilians as well. The results indicate that a rebel group with 13,250 fighters active in a year (the 90th percentile) is associated with 74 state battle-related fatalities and 233 civilians killed. By comparison, a rebel group with just 400 active fighters (the 10th percentile) is associated with 19 state battle-related fatalities and 39 civilians killed. Returns to force size exhibit diminishing returns. Rebels seeking to increase their coercive capacity benefit most from adding forces when they are small and benefit less when they are already large. Moving from 400 to 2,400 rebel armed forces increases the number of state fatalities by approximately 21 (from 19 to 40). Adding a further 2,000 rebel armed forces, however, only increases state fatalities by 10 (from 40 to 50).

The results do not differ statistically or substantively when looking at the sub-sample that is confined to dyad-years of asymmetric warfare. This suggests that in both conventional internal conflicts and conflicts featuring less conventional forms of warfare – such as guerrilla activity or terrorism – rebel groups benefit by increasing their force size.

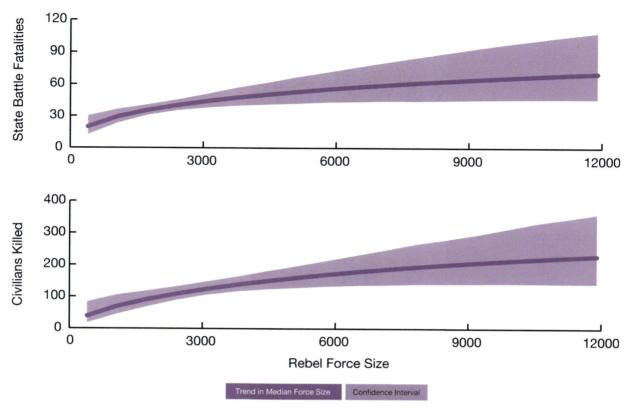

Figure 6.6 Rebel Force Size and Fatalities Inflicted, 1975–2014

Conclusion

This chapter is premised on the argument that the size of rebel forces – in absolute terms and relative to the size of state forces – is an important variable to examine in the context of internal armed conflict. The significance serves as motivation to compile a new dataset, which details the sizes of the forces of conflict actors from 1975–2014. The findings from our subsequent analysis using this novel resource point to the benefits of having these data.

To start, we show how the size of rebel forces varies substantially over time and across regions. Among the suggested factors influencing the variation is differences in state capabilities – including the amount of forces committed to fighting against a particular insurgency – and structural circumstances such as the end of the Cold War. A novel finding is that the balance of power between state and rebel forces tends to vary over the timeline of conflicts, reflecting a potentially endogenous relationship between efforts by rebel groups to mobilize and pursue their ambitions and the responses by states of assessing threats and committing forces to counterinsurgency. In addition, in a substantial portion of insurgencies, states do not hold a clear military advantage.

Our results also reveal that larger rebel groups are more likely to secure favorable outcomes and less likely to experience unfavorable outcomes. This correlation exists across the full set of dyads in our data, as well as the subset of dyads that feature asymmetric warfare. Increasing armed force size matters for rebel groups even when they face stronger states. One reason is that larger rebel groups have a greater capability of producing coercive violence, including killing more state combatants as well as civilians.

The analysis presented here has consequential implications for policy and practice related to ongoing conflicts around the world. In particular, tracking the size of a group's armed forces is vital to understanding the trajectory of an internal conflict, including the expected outcome, the number of casualties likely to be suffered by state forces and civilians, and the possibility of external troop involvement.

Notes

1 We record the number of external troops supporting different combatants, but keep these data distinct from the figures for rebel groups and states.
2 If joint operations involve other rebel groups identified by UCDP, these groups are reflected separately in our dataset. The strength of such joint operations can be computed by aggregating the forces of constituent groups.

3 See Carey, Mitchell, and Lowe (2013) for data identifying pro-government militias.
4 A further limitation of this data is the reduced availability of multiple observations to generate time-varying estimates of state forces committed to conflicts in India and Myanmar (Burma).
5 Kalyvas and Balcells (2010) differentiate insurgencies as conventional, symmetric non-conventional, or irregular fighting. We recast this distinction in military terms: symmetric vs. asymmetric conflict. Conventional and symmetric non-conventional cases count as symmetric fighting in our analysis.
6 Following UCDP, we include North Africa as a part of Africa and not as a part of the Middle East.
7 Data on the size of states' armed forces are obtained from the International Institute for Strategic Studies' annual Military Balance reports. Due to data limitations, we examine the time period from 1985–2014.
8 For each conflict period, we code these outcomes based on source material from UCDP.
9 For initial examinations of the impact of rebel capabilities, see Holtermann 2016 and Clayton 2013.
10 All force sizes are logged to increase the normality of the variable. Confidence intervals are produced using Monte Carlo simulation with 1,000 intervals.
11 These predictions take into account both the absolute size of rebel forces and the observed balance of power between the state and the rebel group. All other variables are also held at their observed values.

References

Arreguín-Toft, Ivan (2005) *How the Weak Win Wars: A Theory of Asymmetric Conflict*. Cambridge: Cambridge University Press.
Ballard, John R. (2006) *Fighting for Fallujah: A New Dawn for Iraq*. Westport, CT: Prager Security International.
Berman, Eli, and Aila M. Matanock (2015) "The Empiricists' Insurgency." *Annual Review of Political Science* 18(1): 443–464.
Biddle, Stephen D., and Jeffrey A. Friedman (2008) "The 2006 Lebanon Campaign and the Future of Warfare: Implications for Army and Defense Policy." *Strategic Studies Institute*. Carlisle, PA: US Army War College.
Carey, Sabine, Neil Mitchell, and Will Lowe (2013) "States, the Security Sector, and the Monopoly of Violence: A New Database on Pro-Government Militias." *Journal of Peace Research* 50(2): 249–245.
Clayton, Govinda (2013) "Relative Rebel Strength and the Onset and Outcome of Civil War Mediation." *Journal of Peace Research* 50(5): 609–622.
Cunningham, David E., Kristian S. Gleditsch, and Idean Salehyan (2009) "It Takes Two: A Dyadic Analysis of Civil War Duration and Outcome." *Journal of Conflict Resolution* 53(4): 570–597.
Friedman, Jeffrey A. (2011) "Manpower and Counterinsurgency: Empirical Foundations for Theory and Doctrine." *Security Studies* 20 (4): 556–591.
Holtermann, Helge (2016) "Relative Capacity and the Spread of Rebellion: Insights from Nepal." *Journal of Conflict Resolution* 60(3): 501–529.
Hultman, Lisa (2007) "Battle Losses and Rebel Violence: Raising the Costs for Fighting." *Terrorism and Political Violence* 19(2): 205–222.
International Institute of Strategic Studies (2015) *The Military Balance 2015*. Abingdon: Routledge.
Kalyvas, Stathis (2006) *The Logic of Violence in Civil War*. Cambridge: Cambridge University Press.
Kalyvas, Stathis N., and Laia Balcells (2010) "International System and Technologies of Rebellion: How the End of the Cold War Shaped Internal Conflict." *American Political Science Review* 104(3): 415–429.
Lawrence, Christopher (2015) *America's Modern Wars: Understanding Iraq, Afghanistan and Vietnam*. Oxford: Casemate.
Ledwidge, Frank (2012) *Losing Small Wars: British Military Failure in Iraq and Afghanistan*. New Haven, CT: Yale University Press.
McGrath, John J. (2006) *Boots on the Ground: Troop Density in Contingency Operations*. Fort Leavenworth: Combat Studies Institute Press.
Mikulaschek, Christoph, and Jacob N. Shapiro (2015) "Lessons on Political Violence from America's Post-9/11 Wars." *Journal of Conflict Resolution*, https://doi.org/10.1177/0022002716669808.
Pettersson, Thérése, and Peter Wallensteen (2015) "Armed Conflicts, 1946–2014." *Journal of Peace Research* 52(4): 536–550.
Otis, John (2014) *The FARC and Colombia's Illegal Drug Trade*. Washington, DC: Wilson Center – Latin American Program.
Reiter, Dan (2003) "Exploring the Bargaining Model of War." *Perspectives on Politics* 1(1): 27–43.
Salehyan, Idean, Kristian S. Gleditsch, and David E. Cunningham (2011) "Explaining External Support for Insurgent Groups." *International Organization* 65(4): 709–744.
Schutte, Sebastian (2015) "Geographic Determinants of Indiscriminate Violence in Civil Wars." *Conflict Management and Peace Science* August: 0738894215593690.
Stockholm International Peace Research Institute (2014) *SIPRI Yearbook 2014*.
Sundberg, Ralph, and Erik Melander (2013) "Introducing the UCDP Georeferenced Event Dataset." *Journal of Peace Research* 50(4): 523–532.
Wood, Reed M. (2010) "Rebel Capability and Strategic Violence against Civilians." *Journal of Peace Research* 47(5): 601–614.

7

The Prevalence of Conflict-Related Sexual Violence

When, Where and By Whom?

Ragnhild Nordås

Introduction

Sexual violence is a grave concern in many of the world's worst crisis situations. For example, such violence has been attributed as a strong driver for why people are fleeing Syria, with their accounts describing grotesque use of rape and sexual slavery. Boko Haram in Nigeria has engaged in massive sexual slavery. All of the major armed conflict actors involved in the wars in eastern Democratic Republic of the Congo (DRC) have been implicated in sexual violence, of various kinds. Extremist Islamist groups and militias are often highlighted as the worst contemporary offenders. Yet sexual violence is committed by numerous armed actors with different characteristics and agendas, including state militaries, some of which are among the most serious offenders.

Empirical research offers useful perspectives about – in certain cases supplementing, in other cases challenging – existing explanations for why sexual violence occurs and how it can be mitigated. Although sexual violence can have many gendered dimensions, gender inequality is not a significant predictor of conflict-wide rape levels (Cohen 2013b). Similarly, sexual violence can be part of a strategy of ethnic cleansing, such as in the Bosnian war, yet ethnic conflict does not predict rape during war (Cohen 2013b). More broadly, sexual violence varies greatly across countries, conflicts, and actors, being neither ubiquitous nor inevitable during war (e.g., Cohen et al. 2013; Wood 2014). One of the most robust findings concerns the role of this form of violence as part of mechanisms of socialization. Sexual violence – gang rape in particular – is employed as a means to foster intra-group cohesion within fighting units (Cohen 2013b, 2016; Cohen and Nordås 2015), akin to how criminal and street gangs use rituals of violence to tie members to the group. This approach is most necessary, and therefore occurs more frequently, among armed groups that rely heavily on forced recruitment. Such groups resort to coercive organization-building to cultivate in-group loyalty among recruits, who are initially unwilling to participate in the conflict and often also strangers to one other.

This chapter examines the phenomenon of conflict-related sexual violence and takes stock of findings from recent statistical studies. To start, I define conflict-related sexual violence. I then discuss how the phenomenon has been placed on the international agenda over recent decades. After being historically overlooked, the topic has now attracted the attention of policymakers worldwide. In parallel with this development, peace and conflict scholars have exhibited increased interest in studying the topic and made significant strides via empirical research (e.g. Baaz and Stern 2013; Cohen 2013a, 2013b, 2016; Sivakumaran 2007; Wood 2006, 2009). A notable recent development, within the last five years, is the collection of more systematic data for quantitative comparative analyses across cases, with the Sexual Violence and Armed Conflict (SVAC) dataset and standing out as a leading example (Cohen and Nordås 2014). I describe central trends and key findings based on cross-national data and analyses. In particular, I highlight where studies have tackled conventional presumptions, including existing explanations for why sexual violence occurs and how it can be mitigated – and especially how new findings have enabled a better understanding of the use of sexual violence by state forces and militia groups. Finally, I consider the current global situation and discuss possible trends in sexual violence and knowledge gaps that should be addressed moving forward.

What is Conflict-Related Sexual Violence?

Sexual violence can be understood as an act of a sexual nature that is committed by force or by a threat of force or other coercion. Conflict-related sexual violence can take many forms, including rape, sexual slavery, sexual mutilation/torture, forced prostitution, and forced sterilization/abortion (Cohen and Nordås 2014). Rape is understood as a form of sexual violence during which "the body of a person is invaded, resulting in penetration, however slight, of any part of the body of the victim, with a sexual organ, or of the anal or genital opening of the victim with any object or other part of the body."[1] This form of sexual violence and many others can be directed and committed by both men and women. A by-product is that the definition of sexual violence is not gender specific. No cases are excluded based strictly on the gender of the perpetrator of the victim. Cases involving female perpetrators and/or male victims are often believed to be less common. Such cases have received less attention and are more likely to be underreported for a number of reasons, including because most organizations working to assist survivors of sexual violence focus on female victims, the stigma associated with rape of males can be particularly pronounced, and views that women are inherently nonviolent remain entrenched (Cohen 2013a; Sivakumaran 2007).

When I write about conflict-related sexual violence in this chapter, I refer to violence perpetrated by armed groups (rebels, militias, state militaries). This definition excludes domestic violence and other sexual violence committed by civilian actors in wars. This restriction is not intended to imply that these other forms of violence are necessarily unrelated to armed conflict or that the civilian sphere is unaffected by conflict-related sexual violence. Indeed, recent research suggests that sexual violence during wartime can influence the risks of intimate partner sexual violence during post-conflict years, as has been found in the case of Peru (Leiby, Østby, and Nordås 2016), and that areas with high exposure to conflict exhibit higher levels of domestic violence as well (Østby 2016).

Sexual violence is a tactic of war used to humiliate and dominate enemy populations, to displace populations from contested territories, and as a tool to generate intra-group cohesion, particularly in armed organizations where the troops are recruited through force (Cohen 2013). This type of violence is rampant in many, but not all, conflicts. When sexual violence occurs, this phenomenon is likely to have detrimental social, psychological and physiological consequences for survivors, their families and affected communities, as well as the perpetrators themselves. These effects can have serious implications for processes of peacebuilding, reconciliation and development after conflict.

Emergence of Conflict-Related Sexual Violence on the International Agenda

Conflict-related sexual violence has become widely recognized as a problem of international security. The practical importance for policy is exemplified not least through various international resolutions. For example, UN Security Council Resolution 1889, adopted in 2009, "emphasizes the responsibility of all States to put an end to impunity and to prosecute those responsible for all forms of violence committed against women and girls in armed conflicts, including rape and other sexual violence." Resolution 1960, adopted in 2010 just after the UN Secretary-General released a major report on the problem, stated a deep concern that "despite its repeated condemnation of violence against women and children in situations of armed conflict, including sexual violence in situations of armed conflict … such acts continue to occur, and in some situations have become systematic and widespread, reaching appalling levels of brutality."[2]

In addition to generating political concern, conflict-related sexual violence is now established as a violation of international humanitarian law. This violence can constitute a crime against humanity and a war crime. This violence can also be a component of genocide, as a tactic that targets the reproductive process of particular groups. Although the International Criminal Court has declared prosecuting sexual violence to be a key goal, few cases have reached the trial stage. Thus, widespread impunity is the norm, rather than the exception. In part, the paucity of prosecutions could be because sexual violence is particularly challenging to investigate: often, evidence of orders to engage in these acts is lacking and victims and witnesses are reluctant to testify.

Among political scientists, especially quantitatively oriented scholars, a strong concern for conflict-related sexual violence is a recent advent. One reason is a lack of useable data. Another likely factor is the marginalization of the problem, which may be rooted in an assumption that sexual violence was an inevitable, but largely irrelevant from a strategic perspective. The first published studies on sexual violence and war, according to the ISI Web of Science, date back only to the mid-1990s. The volume of work on this topic started to rise in the late-2000s. From 1996–2007, fewer than 25 studies per year mentioned both rape and war, compared to more than 60 publications in 2014 and 59 in 2015. The significant increase in scholarship is not a coincidence. A critical influence is increased attention by NGOs and policy-makers, combined with the availablility of new empirical datasets.

The academic debate has been fostered by the seminal research of Elisabeth Wood (2006, 2009), which is instrumental in pointing out the significant variation in sexual violence that warrants explanation. Furthermore, new systematic datasets have been compiled and released on conflict-related rape in civil war (Cohen 2013b), as well as sexual violence during

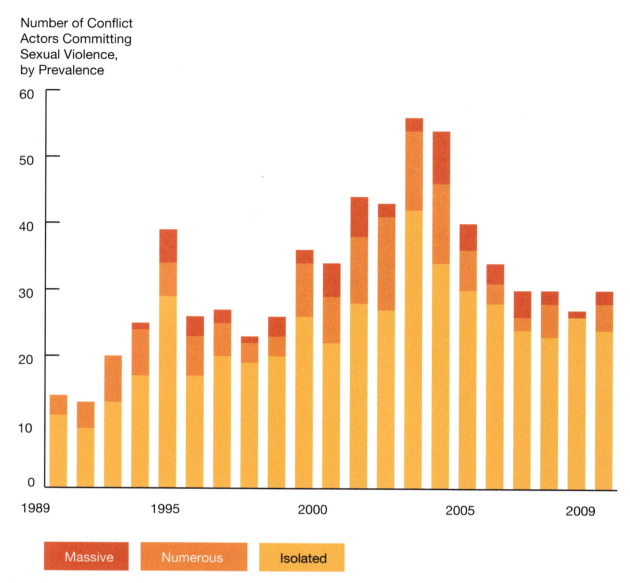

Figure 7.1 Trends in Conflict Actors Perpetrating Sexual Violence, 1989–2009
Source: SVAC dataset (Cohen and Nordås 2014).

both wartime and post-conflict periods (Cohen and Nordås 2014). These datasets enable researchers to document and analyze patterns of sexual violence across actors and time. Many current studies focus on key issues such as the causes and consequences of conflict-related sexual violence. This chapter outlines the current state of knowledge based on studies that draw on these new data sources.

Trends in Conflict-Related Sexual Violence

Figure 7.1 shows the overall trend in the number of armed actors (rebel groups, militias, and state militaries) committing conflict-related sexual violence from 1989–2009 (the period for which systematic data is available as of the time of writing). Involvement increased steadily from 1989 until a peak in 2002, when 57 armed actors reportedly perpetrated sexual violence. Since then, the number of actors reported as perpetrators continued to decrease. In 2009, however, the number was still at 31, more than twice the figure for 1989 (15 groups).

The number of groups at the highest prevalence level (i.e., massive) peaked at eight in 2003. Otherwise, this particular series does not exhibit a clear trend, though such cases were not observed from 1989–1991 and became relatively infrequent from 2007–2009. Instead, the overall trends are driven primarily by the number of groups perpetrating sexual violence at the level of prevalence characterized by isolated incidents. The peak of isolated prevalence was in 2002, when

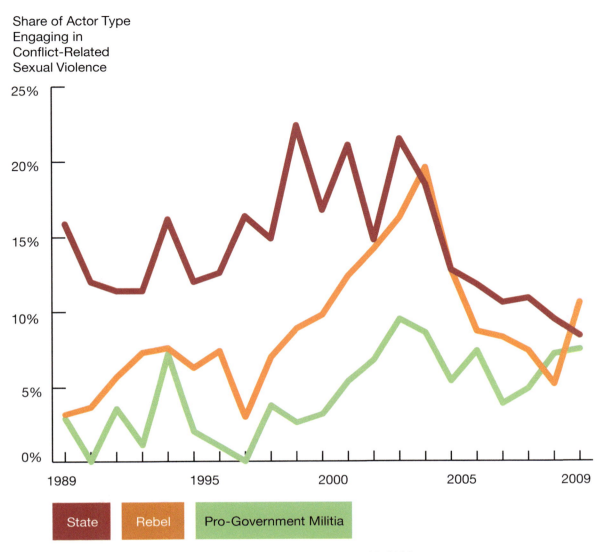

Figure 7.2 Proportions of Conflict Actors Perpetrating Sexual Violence, 1989–2009
Source: SVAC dataset (Cohen and Nordås 2014).

12% (42 of 353) of all actors were reported to have committed sexual violence at this level. These results indicate that sexual violence is more common in recent years, compared to the period right after the end of the Cold War. A word of caution: time trends are notoriously difficult to verify due to potential confounding factors such as increased attention by media and other monitors, which can produce an increase over time in *reporting*, relative to *actual* events. The size of such a possible reporting bias is unknown, as will be discussed further below.

Figure 7.2 shows that the share of state forces reported as perpetrators of sexual violence was higher than the corresponding share among either rebel groups or militias for most of the years over the 1989–2009 time period. During the 1990s, the typical share among state actors was 10–15%. The share reached 20% for several years in the late 1990s and early 2000s. Since 2002, however, the share has trended downwards, reaching the lowest registered level in the time series in 2009 – at just over 8%. The trend in the share of rebel groups reported as perpetrators of sexual violence exhibited a more dramatic upward trajectory, from just around 3% in 1989 up to the peak of nearly 20% in 2003. Subsequently, the share trended downward to a low of about 5% in 2008, before an uptick to 11% in 2009. The share of pro-government militias trended upward from 1989–2009, but with significant fluctuation along the way. After reaching 7% in 1993, the share dropped to zero in 1996, before increasing to a peak of almost 10% in 2002. Over 2003–2009, the share varied between 4 and 9%.

One observation across the three types of actors is they exhibited peaks in shares that were close to simultaneous, occurring in 2002 or 2003. As a result, the year with the highest share of all conflict actors reported to be involved in sexual violence was 2002, with 16.2%. By 2009, however, the share had fallen to 8.8%.

Despite the downward overall trend in 2003–2009, whether or not the problem of wartime sexual violence is lessening remains unclear (Cohen et al. 2013). An important consideration is that the total number of victims of sexual violence per conflict year is unknown, as the relevant data are unavailable. Arriving at precise, credible estimates of the number of individual victims and perpetrators, or events, is currently infeasible in a comprehensive comparative dataset. The challenges to collecting reliable data across many cases include under- and over-reporting, as well as biased accounts in source information (Nordås and Cohen 2011).

Underreporting can be expected for various reasons. Many victims fear stigmatization, a sense of shame, and the risk of retributive violence – all of which discourage them from stepping forward to document their experiences. Medical, social, and legal services are often lacking, as a result of which victims may feel that reporting will not lead to receiving assistance or securing justice. Furthermore, victims may not be able to reach authorities or others to whom violence could be reported. At the extreme, victims may also be killed before they are able to report.

At the same time, the potential for some degree of over-reporting should not be discounted. Individual victims and witnesses, NGOs, and others may estimate numbers that inflate the true extent of the violence. There can be certain incentives to exaggerate the extent of violence, to cast a worse light on the perpetrators. Reporting can even be purposely vindictive – and therefore unfair in the characterization of events. Acts could be attributed to the wrong actors, whether purposefully or due to lack of accurate information. The extent of these issues is unknown.

Similarly, sources of information can be biased. Different categories of sources may be affected by different degrees of bias. Even within the same category, the extent of reliability can vary across specific sources – as research on media bias has demonstrated clearly (e.g., Davenport 2009). In addition, biases can potentially vary over time, which has been suggested to have an impact on aggregate human rights reporting (Fariss 2014) [for a response to this critique, see Chapter 10].

The extent of these issues is probably lessened by using more aggregate measures, such as those that offer a rough gauge of prevalence at the country or group level. Trying instead to establish precise counts and characteristics of individual victims and perpetrators, or of discrete events, imposes requirements on data collection that are often too demanding given the information available (Cohen and Nordås 2014).

Which Conflict Actors Perpetrate Sexual Violence?

Sexual violence is not ubiquitous in war (Wood 2006; 2009). Reports of sexual violence are associated with many conflicts and many armed groups active from 1989–2009, the time period covered by the SVAC data. At the extreme end of the spectrum, 14% of the 129 armed conflicts during this period were characterized by reports of massive sexual violence.

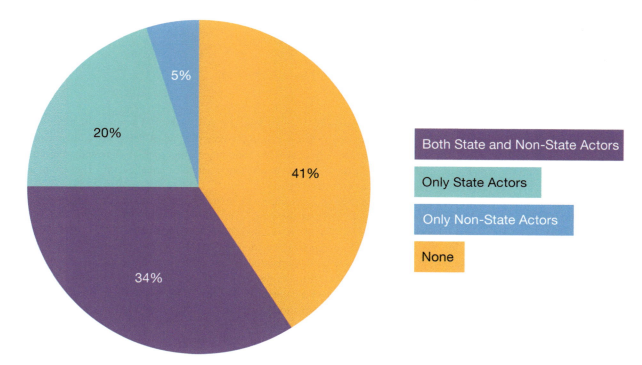

Figure 7.3 Correspondence between Sexual Violence by State and Non-State Forces, 1989–2009
Source: SVAC dataset (Cohen and Nordås 2014).

At the other end of the spectrum, however, 41% of the conflicts lack reports of sexual violence by any of the warring parties. As mentioned above, sexual violence goes unreported in certain cases. Yet we also know, from well-documented cases, that some conflict actors consciously seek to prevent their troops from committing sexual violence and are quite effective in doing so. Hence, we have reason to believe that the absence of reports of sexual violence in a significant number of cases is plausible, rather than simply a reflection of underreporting.

Sexual violence is not an activity that only undisciplined and ruthless non-state actors perpetrate. Quite the contrary: state forces are also implicated regularly (e.g., Cohen et al. 2013; Cohen and Nordås 2014). Figure 7.3 shows the distribution of involvement in sexual violence, by type of actors, in the conflicts that occurred from 1989–2009. Just six conflicts have reports of such violence committed *only* by either rebel groups or pro-government militias. This represents just 5% of the 129 conflicts over this period and 8% of the 76 conflicts for which the SVAC dataset records sexual violence. Instead, the most common pattern is that both state and non-state forces are reported as perpetrators. This outcome was observed in 44 conflicts from 1989–2009, which translates to 34% of all conflicts and 58% of the conflicts with recorded sexual violence. State forces are the *only* armed actors reported as perpetrating sexual violence in 26 conflicts, constituting 20% of all conflicts and 34% of conflicts with recorded sexual violence.

Considering all the armed actors involved in the conflicts during 1989–2009, 42% of state armed forces were reported as perpetrators of sexual violence at some point during the period, compared to 24% of rebel groups and 17% of pro-government militias. The broad comparative finding that state forces engage in sexual violations in war, as part of their wider repertoire of repressive and coercive behaviors, is corroborated by studies with narrower geographical and temporal scope (Leiby 2009; Butler et al. 2007).

In sum, the evidence indicates that state actors are frequent perpetrators of sexual violence – and their involvement actually appears to be more common than among non-state actors. These results raise a question: What is the relationship between the sexual violence committed by state forces and pro-government militias? One common argument is that governments often deliberately outsource or delegate illegal behavior to militia groups, allowing the state to claim plausible deniability for breaking the laws of war (e.g., Ron 2002; Alvarez 2006). Recent research based on the SVAC dataset showed, however, that sexual violence by state armed forces and pro-government militias tended to be complementary over the period from 1989–2009. In fact, the relationship is that state-perpetrated sexual violence tends to increase, not decline, once the militias in an internal armed conflict start using sexual violence (Cohen and Nordås 2015). As Figure 7.4 shows, the extent of sexual violence perpetrated by state forces is typically at the same level or more regularly above the level perpetrated by militias. Also, the limited available information indicates that pro-government militias that have

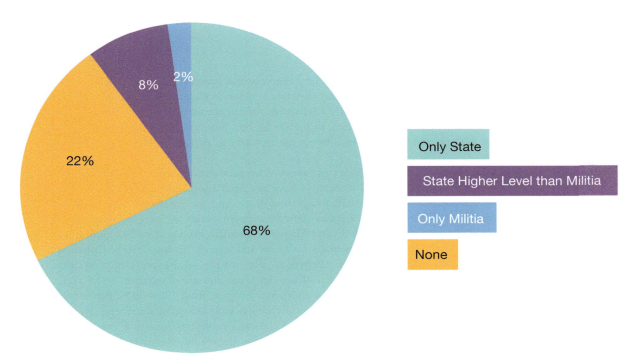

Figure 7.4 Correspondence between Sexual Violence by States and Militias, 1989–2009
Note: Sexual violence committed by rebel groups is excluded from this analysis.
Source: SVAC dataset (Cohen and Nordås 2014).

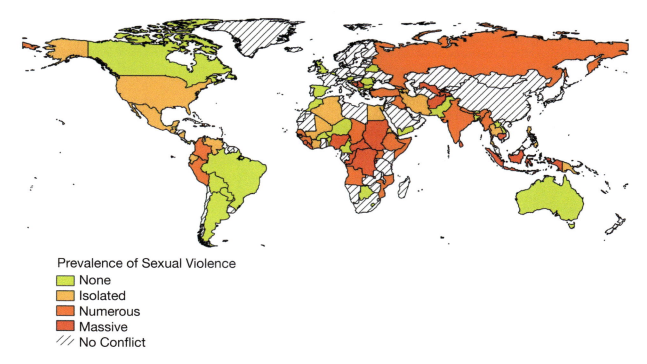

Figure 7.5 Mapping the Prevalence of Conflict-Related Sexual Violence, 1989–2009
Note: Prevalence gauged based on countries of reported perpetrators.
Source: Cohen and Nordås 2014.

received training by the government are more likely to commit sexual violence, compared to militias without training (Cohen and Nordås 2015).

Contrary to conventional wisdom, therefore, no compelling evidence exists that sexual violence by militias consistently substitutes for – as the result of delegation, or for other reasons – similar violence by state forces. Instead, militias are potentially mirroring state behavior or may even be encouraged to engage in this behavior by state officials.

Regional Variation

Two common misunderstandings prevail about where conflict-related sexual violence is expected. One assumption has been that sexual violence is an inevitable fact of war – and therefore a ubiquitous characteristic of all conflicts. Another assumption has been that sexual violence is predominantly a feature of African conflicts. The truth lies in between: sexual violence can be observed in conflicts that occur anywhere in the world, but does not always manifest everywhere. Considerable regional variation is evident, and the problem is by no means solely an African problem (Cohen 2013b; Cohen and Nordås 2014).

The global map in Figure 7.5 clearly demonstrates these conclusions. A substantial number of the countries that participated in the conflicts from 1989–2009 – including several in Africa – have not been associated with reports of conflict-related sexual violence. Yet many more countries were implicated in such violence, and the geographic scope of involvement is broad. Prominent on the list are countries outside of Africa, reflecting recent events in Syria and Iraq, the violence in Bosnia during the 1990s, and notorious cases in Asia and Latin America. Systematic empirical studies confirm that conflict-related rape and sexual violence occur globally, across many countries and regions (Cohen 2013b; Cohen and Nordås 2015). Individual countries and regions are more or less affected, in terms of the relative prevalence of conflict-related violence. Yet no region is subject only to isolated levels of violence, let alone immune altogether.

Figure 7.6 displays the prevalence of conflict-related sexual violence, by region, from 1989–2009. Africa does stand out in terms of having the most conflicts and also the highest shares of conflicts with reports of actors engaging in numerous and massive reports of conflict-related sexual violence. The rest of the cases exhibiting massive levels were confined to Asia (16% of conflicts) and Europe (13% of conflicts). At the same time, these two regions had the highest shares of conflicts with no reports of sexual violence: 50% in Asia and 61% in Europe.

Thus, the picture is more complex than frequently depicted. Conflict-related sexual violence is too pervasive around the world to be considered as exclusively – or even predominantly – an African problem. That said, sexual violence has

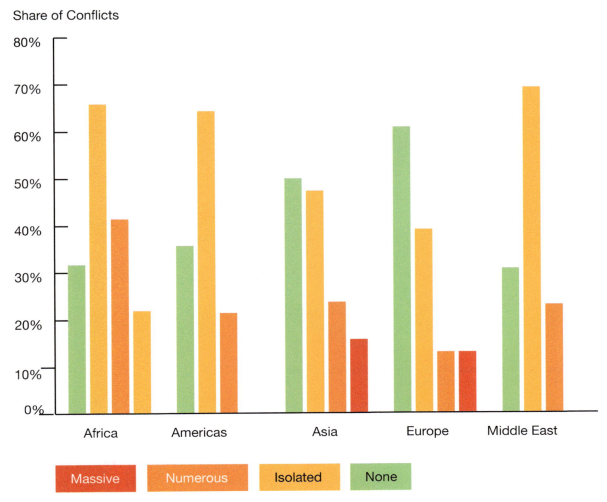

Figure 7.6 Prevalence of Conflict-Related Sexual Violence, by Region, 1989–2009
Source: SVAC dataset (Cohen and Nordås 2014).

been and remains a significant problem in many conflicts across Africa. Given the number of African countries that have experienced armed conflict over the recent decades, this region warrants in-depth examination.

According to SVAC data, Africa conforms to the global patterns whereby reported sexual violence varies by conflict and armed actor. Figure 7.7 shows that no sexual violence was reported among a sizeable majority of the 177 actors engaged in conflict at any point over the period 2000–2009, when sexual violence was more prevalent than in the earlier years of the time series. Yet a significant minority of observations (41%) have at least isolated reports of sexual violence. Of particular concern are the cases of such violence on a massive scale. Although these extreme cases were far from the norm, they have occurred with all too much regularity, affecting large numbers of victims and creating enormous human suffering.

Conclusion

Conflict-related sexual violence has been recognized as a serious problem, with important steps taken to put this problem on the international agenda over the last several years. One of the key measures is the G8 Declaration on Preventing Sexual Violence in Conflict, which was signed by 155 countries in 2013. The most high-profile event to date was the 2014 London Summit, which gathered an unprecedented number of high-level representatives – 1,700 delegates, including 79 ministers, and 123 country delegations – from around the world to discuss the problem of conflict-related sexual violence. The attention to the problem may have a dual effect. On the one hand, the attention increases the focus on prevention and ending impunity for such violence. On the other hand, this form of violence might have become a way for armed actors to gain international attention and to use as a bargaining chip.

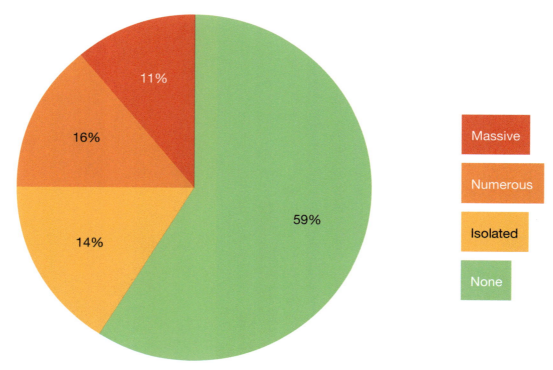

Figure 7.7 Prevalence of Sexual Violence by Conflict Actors in Africa, 2000–2009
Source: SVAC dataset (Cohen and Nordås 2014).

The existing evidence shows that sexual violence occurs in many conflicts around the world, although with significant variation in form and prevalence. At present, we do not know for sure the trajectory of the number of people affected by the violence. The latest data do, however, offer insight into the number of actors reported to be committing such violence, which peaked in 2003, then declined through 2008 before ticking up slightly in 2009 – the last year for which SVAC data are available. Over the years since, stories of massive, brutal sexual violence from the most serious conflict zones of the world have seemingly grown more frequent. The awareness of these cases could simply be a function of increased attention and the proliferation of media around the world. Establishing whether the prominent cases are anomalies or indicative of developing patterns is difficult in the absence of systematic global data from 2010 onwards. What then can we assume about the current situation and the way forward?

In 2015, 50 state-based conflicts were active, compared to 36 in 2009 (Harbom and Wallensteen 2010; Melander et al. 2016). Thus, the number of settings with the potential for experiencing conflict-related sexual violence remains high. Many current conflicts are known to involve the significant use of sexual violence by the armed actors. A limitation in gauging the severity of the problem has been the lack of a systematic comparative dataset that is updated to the last few years. An update to the SVAC dataset, extending the temporal coverage to 2016, is currently underway. The forthcoming release of this resource will enable scholars to answer the question of whether the overall decline in the number and share of conflict actors reported to use conflict-related sexual violence in 2003–2008 has continued, or been reversed, over the recent years.[3] Given what we know anecdotally about the armed actors dominating the conflict scene today, a reasonable expectation is we are more likely to find that the extent of involvement of conflict actors in sexual violence remains at alarming levels and may have even increased.

Despite large strides to better understand conflict-related sexual violence in the last decade, our knowledge gaps are still apparent. Continued, improved data collection and analysis of the dynamics of sexual violence are required to understand temporal developments and to document how, where, and why sexual violence war crimes are being committed. Future research should also focus on studying the relationship between lethal and sexual violence in more detail, as well as uncovering patterns and causes of sexual violence in relation to other forms of political violence beyond state-based conflicts, including one-sided violence and communal conflicts.

Notes

1 From "Definitions of Crimes of Sexual Violence in the ICC": http://www.iccwomen.org/resources/crimesdefinition.html. Last accessed on October 15, 2016.
2 See list and content of Security Council Resolutions: http://www.un.org/en/sc/documents/resolutions/. Last accessed on October 15, 2016.
3 An updated version of the SVAC dataset will be posted on www.sexualviolencedata.org in 2017.

References

Alvarez, Alex (2006) "Militias and Genocide." *War Crimes, Genocide and Crimes against Humanity* 2(1): 1–33.

Baaz, Maria Eriksson, and Maria Stern (2013) *Sexual Violence as a Weapon of War? Perceptions, Prescriptions, Problems in the Congo and Beyond.* London: Zed Books.

Butler, Christopher K., Tali Gluch, and Neil J. Mitchell (2007) "Security Forces and Sexual Violence: A Cross-National Analysis of a Principal – Agent Argument." *Journal of Peace Research* 44(6): 669–687.

Cohen, Dara Kay (2016) *Rape During Civil War.* Ithaca, NY: Cornell University Press.

Cohen, Dara Kay (2013a) "Explaining Rape during Civil War: Cross-National Evidence (1980–2009)." *American Political Science Review* 107(3): 461–477.

Cohen, Dara Kay (2013b) "Female Combatants and the Perpetration of Violence: Wartime Rape in the Sierra Leone Civil War." *World Politics* 65(3): 383–415.

Cohen, Dara Kay, Amelia Hoover Green, and Elisabeth Jean Wood (2013) "Wartime Sexual Violence." USIP Special Report.

Cohen, Dara Kay, and Ragnhild Nordås (2015) "Do States Delegate Shameful Violence to Militias? Patterns of Sexual Violence in Recent Armed Conflicts." *Journal of Conflict Resolution* 59(5): 877–898.

Cohen, Dara Kay, and Ragnhild Nordås (2014) "Sexual Violence in Armed Conflict: Introducing the SVAC Dataset, 1989–2009." *Journal of Peace Research* 51(3): 418–428.

Davenport, Christian (2009) *Media Bias, Perspective, and State Repression: The Black Panther Party.* Cambridge: Cambridge University Press.

Fariss, Christopher J. (2014) "Respect for Human Rights Has Improved over Time: Modeling the Changing Standard of Accountability." *American Political Science Review* 108(2): 297–318.

Harbom, Lotta, and Peter Wallensteen (2010) "Armed Conflicts, 1946–2009." *Journal of Peace Research* 47(4): 501–509.

Leiby, Michele L. (2009) "Wartime Sexual Violence in Guatemala and Peru." *International Studies Quarterly* 53(2): 445–468.

Leiby, Michele L., Gudrun Østby, and Ragnhild Nordås (2016) "The Legacy of Wartime Violence on Intimate Partner Abuse: Micro-Level Evidence from Peru, 1980–2009." Unpublished working paper.

Melander, Erik, Thérése Pettersson, and Lotta Themnér (2016) "Organized Violence, 1989–2015." *Journal of Peace Research* 53(5): 727–742.

Nordås, Ragnhild, and Dara Kay Cohen (2011) "Wartime Sexual Violence: Challenges and Opportunities for Data Collection and Analysis." Centre for the Study of Civil War (CSCW) Report.

Østby, Gudrun (2016) "Violence Begets Violence: Armed Conflict and Domestic Sexual Violence in Sub-Saharan Africa." *HiCN Working Paper* 233.

Ron, James (2002) "Territoriality and Plausible Deniability: Serbian Paramilitaries in the Bosnian War." In Bruce B. Campbell and Arthur D. Brenner (eds) *Death Squads in Global Perspective: Murder with Deniability*, New York: Palgrave McMillan.

Sivakumaran, Sandesh (2007) "Sexual Violence against Men in Armed Conflict." *European Journal of International Law* 18(2): 253–276.

Wood, Elisabeth Jean (2014) "Conflict-Related Sexual Violence and the Policy Implications of Recent Research." *International Review of the Red Cross* 96(894): 457–478.

Wood, Elisabeth Jean (2009) "Armed Groups and Sexual Violence: When is Wartime Rape Rare?" *Politics & Society* 37(1): 131–161.

Wood, Elisabeth Jean (2006) "Variation in Sexual Violence during War." *Politics & Society* 34(3): 307–342.

8

Democracy, Democratization, and Civil War

Suthan Krishnarajan, Jørgen Møller, Lasse Lykke Rørbæk, and Svend-Erik Skaaning

Introduction

In *The Dark Side of Democracy*, Michael Mann (2005) disturbingly claimed that the democratization processes of the nineteenth and twentieth centuries had paved the way for large-scale ethnic cleansing. Mann's book may be said to reflect a more general shift in the literature on democracy and democratization. The 1990s had been democracy's *Belle Époque*, both on the ground and within academia. After a somewhat slow beginning in Southern Europe and Latin America, democracy in this decade spread like wildfire, accompanied by high hopes for progress in terms of peace, freedom, and prosperity (Møller and Skaaning 2013). Alas, the enthusiasm was not to last, neither on the ground nor within academia. The first decades of the 2000s have seen a widespread pessimism about the auspicious effects of democracy and democratization.

Most important for our purposes, an influential research agenda has associated partially democratized regimes and democratization with civil war (see Hegre 2014; Gleditsch and Hegre 2014). At first sight, the notion that intermediate levels of democracy and the process of democratization spark armed conflict seems counterintuitive. Popular discontent should decrease with the level of democracy because political discrimination decreases and public goods provision increases (Bueno de Mesquita et al. 2003). Furthermore, democracy is normally construed as a method for solving societal conflicts in a peaceful way. For instance, scholars have argued that democracy allows effective bargaining among social groups, reduces commitment problems, and infuses decisions with legitimacy (Acemoglu and Robinson 2006; Przeworski 2010). The notion that partial democracy and democratization might trigger armed conflicts is therefore a bold theoretical conjecture with high empirical relevance.

In what follows, we first review this literature, singling out arguments for and against intermediate levels of democracy and changes toward democracy being conducive to civil war. We then enlist new data from the Varieties of Democracy (V-Dem) project to shed light on selected prior findings. More generally, we discuss how these new data can be used to carry out systematic appraisals of how democracy levels and democratization relate to civil war.

The Case against Democracy

The arguments for why democracy may spur armed conflict relate both to the absolute level of democracy and to changes in the direction of democracy. With respect to the first aspect, a number of scholars have identified a curvilinear relationship, where the risk of civil war onset increases at lower rungs of the ladder of democracy, but decreases at higher rungs (e.g., Muller and Weede 1990; Hegre et al. 2001). The result is an inverted-U curve, given the likelihood of civil war onset is higher for partially democratized regimes – also known as anocracies or hybrid regimes – situated in the middle of the spectrum than for either genuine autocracies or genuine democracies.

Theoretically, this relationship is attributed to the lack of steering capacity in partially democratized regimes. Autocracies use repression and cooptation to keep a lid on opposition, whereas democracies deal with societal grievances through political inclusion and public goods provision (Svolik 2012; Bueno de Mesquita et al. 2003). Partially democratized regimes, according to the argument, are less effective in both respects. While they allow oppositional mobilization and expression to a higher extent than autocracies, they are ineffective in addressing popular frustrations and often too weak to crush even minor rebellions. Hence, grievances are not dealt with, but opportunities for airing them are high (Hegre 2014: 163; Gleditsch and Hegre 2014: 146–7).

With respect to democratization, prior scholarship has demonstrated that changes in levels of democracy increase the likelihood of armed conflict (Cederman, Hug, and Krebs 2010; Mansfield and Snyder 2012). Democratization can spur civil war in several ways. Invoking seminal work on political order by Huntington (1968), Mansfield and Snyder (1995, 2005) argue that democratization tends to create mass mobilization that weak institutions cannot channel. In this situation, elites are wont to drum up nationalist sentiments, something that increases the risk of both interstate war and civil war.

Other scholarship has focused more directly on the instability wrought by changes in political institutions (Gleditsch and Ruggeri 2010). The introduction of elections gives incumbents an incentive to use fraud and losers an avenue to dispute outcomes. This "sore loser" effect is likely to be aggravated in winner-takes-all systems, where minority groups, which are bound to lose in democratic contests, may see fighting as their best means for maintaining or gaining power. On top of this, initial democratic reforms are normally only partial and therefore tend to create demand for more reforms. If powerholders resist these demands, the result may be a descent into violence (Gleditsch and Hegre 2014: 149–150; see also Cederman, Gleditsch, and Hug 2013; Collier, Hoeffler, and Söderbom 2008). To make matters worse, many countries contain latent social conflicts that have been suppressed by authoritarian control. Competitive politics often serve to politicize such conflicts, including most notoriously antagonisms revolving around ethnic divides (Eifert, Miguel, and Posner 2010; Horowitz 1985). This cocktail of conditions is inherently conflict prone – and sometimes causes the onset of civil war.

Problems with Prior Research

Although these claims have won wide acceptance, the literature contains a number of objections against the notion that democracy and democratization are conducive to armed conflict.

First, confounding factors might affect the nature of democratic institutions, changes in these institutions, and the risk of civil war (Hegre 2014: 163; Gleditsch and Hegre 2014: 146). For instance, political instability, rather than specific regime characteristics, might lead to armed conflict. Hybrid regimes can be seen as failed attempts to preserve power firmly in the hands of either the people or a strong, uncontested leader, and regime change by definition entails instability. In this context, elections can serve as a concession, made because of the precarious position of those in power (Hegre 2014: 164–165). Also, socio-economic development may drive both regime changes and armed conflict through, for example, the impact of development on factors such as rates of inequality and the mobility of economic assets, both of which have been associated with regime change and civil war (see, e.g., Boix 2003, 2008). In addition, deeper historical processes, centered on the distinction between inclusive and extractive political institutions, can create virtuous and vicious circles, respectively, which might affect both regime type and conflict propensity (Acemoglu and Robinson 2012).

Second, the inverted-U curve might reflect reverse causality, given that armed conflicts are apt to weaken state institutions, at least in the short run (Gleditsch and Hegre 2014: 147–48). Similar objections can be made against the democratization–conflict nexus. If Acemoglu and Robinson (2006) are correct that democratization is a concession elites give when they fear revolution, then democratization signals weakness – and, more generally, democratization is endogenous to armed conflict.

Third, shortcomings of data might produce misleading conclusions. Most of the prominent statistical findings over the past decades are based on the well-known Polity index, a composite measure (ranging from −10 to 10) that includes indicators related to the openness and competitiveness of executive recruitment, constraints on the chief executive, and the regulation and openness of political participation (Marshall, Gurr, and Jaggers 2014). As Vreeland (2008) has convincingly argued, the Polity index can create biased results in analyses of the relationship between democracy levels, democratization, and civil war because two of the components of the index – "Regulation of Participation" and "Competitiveness of Participation" – are expressly coded with reference to political violence. Indeed, the values for these components that fall in the middle of the range, corresponding to partial democracies that may be in a transitional phase, are precisely those that can be considered "political violence-contaminated" (Vreeland 2008: 2).

Disaggregating Regime Categories with New Data

As our review indicates, the findings regarding the influence of democracy and democratization on civil war onset are inconclusive (see also Bartusevicius and Skaaning 2016; Cederman, Gleditsch, and Hug 2013). To shed new light on the issue, recent studies have begun disaggregating the explanatory variable (Goldstone et al. 2010; see also Fjelde 2010). This approach is in line with the call by Gleditsch and Hegre (2014: 146) to unpack regime categories to investigate "how the specific characteristics of political institutions" affect the likelihood of armed conflict. Gleditsch and Hegre (2014: 148) illustrate this entreaty by pointing out that the inverted-U curve is in itself a very poor – or at least overly general – measurement of the way political regimes are associated with armed conflict. Furthermore, by disaggregating characteristics of political regimes and looking into which specific institutions of democracy are actually driving the conflict propensity that prior scholarship has identified, we might be able to work out distinctive empirical implications of competing theories, which right now – on the aggregate level – predict similar outcomes (Hegre 2014: 168).

The literature has already moved in this direction by, for example, using the disaggregated Polity indicators, rather than the general index. To genuinely push this research agenda forward, nuanced indicators of particular aspects of political regimes are required. First, we need to ensure that analytical results are not driven by indicators contaminated by political violence. The reassessment along these lines must be performed in a more systematic manner than Vreeland was able to achieve with the Polity data. Second, we need to go to a level of disaggregation that allows us to probe the theoretical mechanisms used to explain why partially democratized regimes and democratization may increase the risk of civil war.

Fortunately, the V-Dem Project has recently released this kind of data. V-Dem is a large-scale data collection effort that includes more than 350 new, disaggregated indicators of regime characteristics, covering most sovereign and semi-sovereign polities from 1900 until the present. The indicators capture various conceptions of democracy and their components in a detailed fashion. About half of the indicators, typically of a more factual nature, have been coded by research assistants. The other half of the indicators, typically of a more evaluative nature, are assigned scores on the basis of expert surveys, normally five country experts per indicator. The expert assessments are combined into point estimates with uncertainty levels. This processing is performed via a sophisticated Bayesian item response measurement model that takes into account varying levels of reliability, bias, and standards ("thresholds") among coders (Coppedge et al. 2016a).

In what follows, we use these new data to carry out a rather simple replication of the analysis of the inverted-U curve at different levels of aggregation. Our aim is to assess whether a similar pattern is produced when using different components and sub-components of democracy. Subsequently, we discuss further possibilities the new dataset gives scholars interested in investigating the relationship between democracy, democratization, and civil war onset.

Specifically, we concentrate on the V-Dem electoral democracy index (see Teorell et al. 2016). This index is based on Dahl's (1998) seminal conception of polyarchy. As illustrated in Figure 8.1, the electoral democracy index subsumes the following five attributes: clean elections, elected executive, suffrage, freedom of association, and freedom of expression. The measurement of these five attributes aggregates the scores of 38 indicators. For instance, as illustrated in Figure 8.1, the clean elections sub-index is based on nine indicators (more on this below).

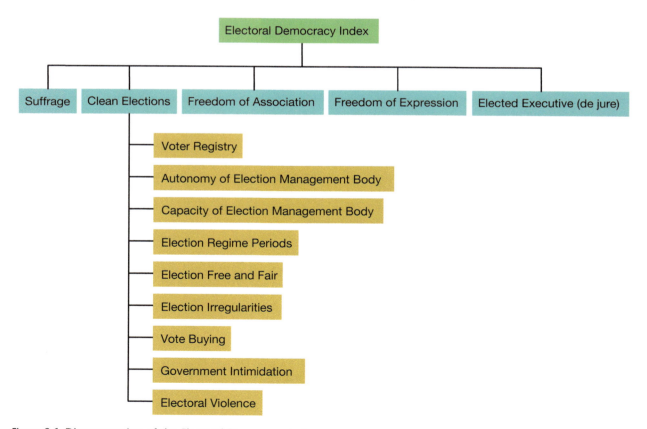

Figure 8.1 Disaggregation of the Electoral Democracy Index

Empirical Analysis

We designed a statistical model that includes the most basic confounders of civil war onset identified in the literature: GDP per capita (logged, from the Maddison Database; Bolt and van Zanden 2014), population size (logged, from Haber and Menaldo 2011), and prior war (time polynomials capturing peace years). Civil war onset is measured using the Uppsala/PRIO Armed Conflict Dataset (v. 3.0; Gleditsch et al. 2002). This dataset includes every armed conflict between a government and a rebel organization known to have caused at least 25 annual battle-related deaths in the period 1946–2014.[1]

Figure 8.2 reports the results of a regression of civil war onset against the V-Dem electoral democracy index, accounting for the confounders listed above, over the period from 1946–2010. At this level of aggregation, the new data clearly corroborates the inverted-U curve relationship.

What drives the relationship between levels of electoral democracy and civil war onset? To delve deeper, we ran the same model with three of the attribute-level indices: clean elections, freedom of association, and freedom of expression. The two remaining attribute-level indices, universal suffrage and elected executive, tend towards a bimodal distribution and therefore cannot explain – or be meaningfully used to assess – the inverted-U curve.[2]

Figure 8.3 shows that the freedom of association and freedom of expression attributes sustain the finding of partially democratized regimes being the most conflict prone: intermediate scores on these indices exhibit the highest probability of civil war onset. By contrast, the cleanness of elections is consistently associated with decreasing probabilities of armed conflict, except for the lowest scores on the index. Thus, the inverted-U curve seems to be driven by partially granted freedom rights, rather than the electoral core of democracy, here measured by the attribute of clean elections. This finding is interesting because the implication is that liberal – rather than electoral – aspects of democracy underpin the inverted-U curve relationship.

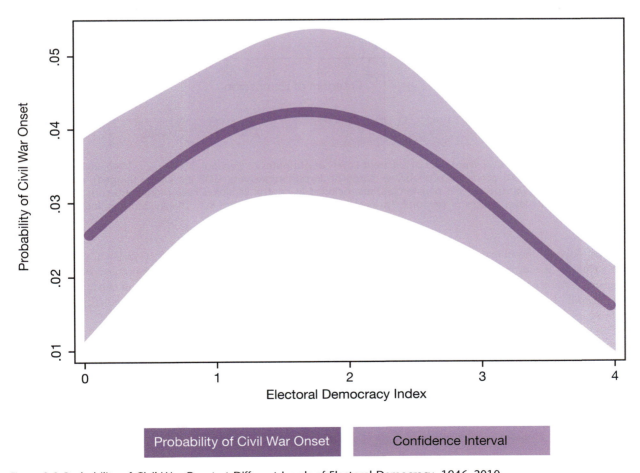

Figure 8.2 Probability of Civil War Onset at Different Levels of Electoral Democracy, 1946–2010
Note: The figure reports predicted probabilities based on logistic regression. GDP per capita (logged), population size (logged), and prior war (peace-year polynomials) are included as control variables. The shaded area indicates the 90% confidence interval.

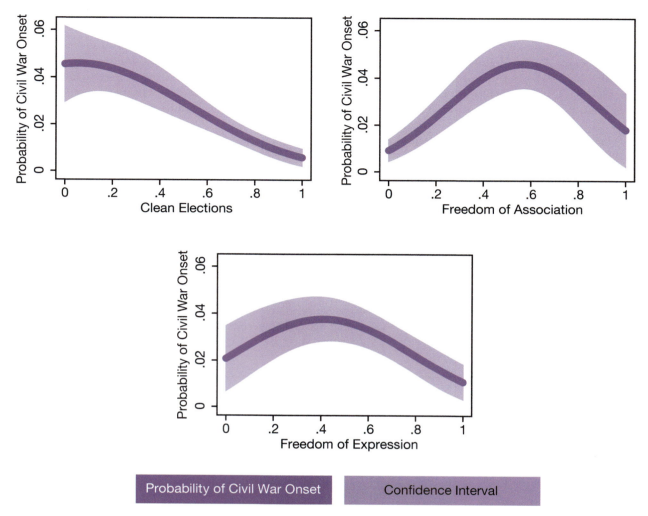

Figure 8.3 Probability of Civil War Onset at Different Levels of Attributes of Electoral Democracy, 1946–2010
Note: The figure reports predicted probabilities based on logistic regression. GDP per capita (logged), population size (logged), and prior war (peace-year polynomials) are included as control variables. Each model also controls for the four remaining attribute-level indices of electoral democracy, as illustrated in Figure 8.1. The shaded area indicates the 90% confidence interval.

These findings prevail even though two of the nine indicators of clean elections – electoral violence and government intimidation – directly capture the presence of armed conflict, raising the potential for the same problem of tautology that Vreeland (2008) has identified regarding analyses relying on the Polity index. In contrast, the indices of freedom of association and freedom of expression, which demonstrate inverted-U curve relationships, do not contain such violence-contaminated indicators.

This finding seems puzzling. Therefore, we pursue the analysis down to the indicator level for the clean elections index. Performing analysis at such a further level of disaggregation also serves to show some of the possibilities of using the V-Dem data. An advantage of analysis at the indicator level is that we can assign substantial meaning to the different scores, something that is not possible at the higher levels of measurement employed in Figures 8.2 and 8.3, where a particular aggregate score can reflect very different combinations of indicator scores.

Figure 8.4 reports results for seven out of nine of the clean elections indicators.[3] The results show that two of the indicators of clean elections – electoral violence and government intimidation – produce an inverted-U curve. Three other indicators – voter registry, EMB autonomy,[4] and election irregularities – produce a very flat curve. Finally, two of the indicators each behave quite differently from the rest. Vote buying produces a negative but relatively flat linear relationship. EMB capacity is approximately convex, meaning that the likelihood of civil war onset decreases more with the first improvements in the capacity of election management bodies. The most interesting result is that the indicators exhibiting the inverted-U curve relationships are exactly those contaminated by violence. If we put these aside, on the

Democracy, Democratization, and Civil War

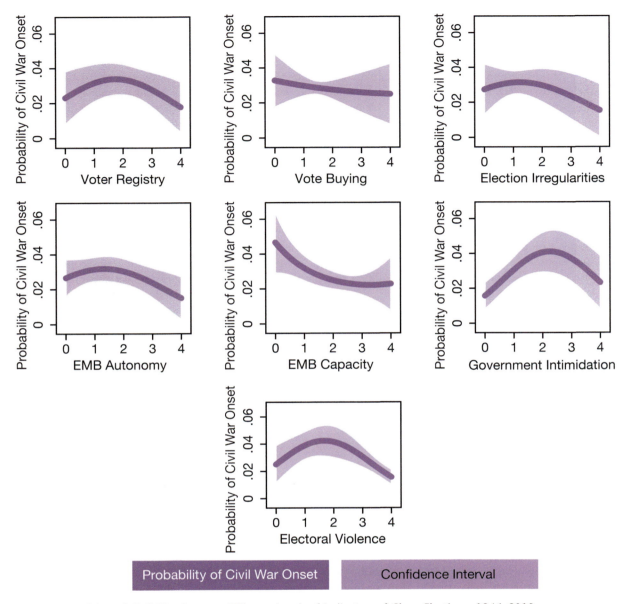

Figure 8.4 Probability of Civil War Onset at Different Levels of Indicators of Clean Elections, 1946–2010
Note: The figure reports predicted possibilities based on logistic regression. GDP per capita (logged), population size (logged), and prior war (peace-year polynomials) are included as control variables. Each model also controls for the four remaining attribute-level indices of electoral democracy, as well as the remaining indicators of clean elections (see Figure 8.1). The shaded area indicates the 90% confidence interval. EMB is an abbreviation for "electoral management body".

basis of the objection raised by Vreeland (2008), no other evidence exists of electoral aspects of democracy producing anything like an inverted-U curve relationship.

What can we say about the risk of civil war onset in relation to particular levels of the indicators of clean elections? For the indicators producing a concave relationship, conflict propensity generally seems to be the highest somewhere between the scores of 1 and 2. If we take election irregularities as an example, the codebook descriptions of these scores are "non-systematic, but common" (the score 1) and "sporadic" (the score 2) irregularities. Concerning government intimidation, the risk of armed conflict is markedly higher at the score 2, indicating "non-systematic" intimidation of the opposition, compared to the score 1, indicating "systematic" intimidation of the opposition (Coppedge et al. 2016b).

We have run similar large-N analyses to assess the relationship between democratization and civil war onset. Generally speaking, these results go a long way towards corroborating the finding of Cederman, Hug, and Krebs (2010) that democratization is more conducive to civil war than autocratization. Space limitations prevent us from presenting and interpreting these findings in greater detail.[5]

The Way Forward

The results presented here demonstrate some of the potential of the new V-Dem data. We can think of other ways that these data facilitate the advancement of scholarship about how democracy and democratization relate to civil war. To achieve this, the turn toward disaggregating the measurement of political regimes should be backed up by two other analytical moves.

First, the existing literature has not adequately studied the specific conditions that could potentially moderate the democracy–conflict relationship. For example, democratization and the introduction of multiparty elections during an economic crisis could increase zero-sum conflicts and ethnic-divisionary sentiments much more than is the case during periods of rapid economic growth. Hence, democratization during economic downturns might enhance the risk of armed conflicts, whereas democratization during periods of rapid economic growth may be much more peaceful. Other potential conditioning factors include levels of political or socio-economic exclusion and levels of state capacity (Cederman, Gleditsch, and Buhaug 2013; Sobek 2010).

Second, long-term historical analysis is warranted. In particular, Hegre (2014: 168) advocates examining the dynamics between socio-economic processes, regime change, and conflict. Proper studies of these dimensions would require analyses of longer time-series, as well as historical investigations of critical events and periods.

On both accounts, the V-Dem data can be of assistance. The new dataset includes a number of other indicators that can be seen as capturing of potential conditioning factors. Coupled with additional new datasets on socio-economic factors, systematic inquiry into how other factors condition the effects of regime characteristics on civil war onset should be possible. With respect to historical investigations, the V-Dem data go back to 1900. Analyses using the full extent of this long time-series are therefore less vulnerable to the objection that the regime-conflict nexus may have been suppressed in certain periods, such as during the Cold War (see Møller 2016). Furthermore, an offshoot of the V-Dem project, the so-called Historical V-Dem, is currently coding selected indicators all the way back to 1789. This dataset, once available, will open new possibilities for analyzing how sequences of democratization and autocratization have historically affected the propensity for civil war. Here, we stand to benefit from the fact that very different sequences of democratization occurred in the nineteenth century (see Ziblatt 2006; Knutsen, Møller, and Skaaning 2016). Historical analysis of these processes presents a way to address, among other things, the issues raised in the "sequencing debate" about whether electoral democratization should be postponed until effective, political institutions have been constructed (see Mansfield and Snyder 2007; Carothers 2007).

Conclusions

The new scholarship that has associated democracy and democratization with civil war onset is highly relevant both theoretically and empirically. The findings of this literature, however, have been challenged by a number of scholars, often with reference to the aggregate nature of the analyses and the poor quality of existing data used for key variables. An emerging consensus favors enlisting new data and further disaggregating regime characteristics to genuinely probe these relationships. In this chapter, we reviewed the relevant literature and illustrated empirically how the new V-Dem data is suited to heed the calls for in-depth analysis.

Our results show that the inverted-U curve relationship is much more pronounced for some attributes of democracy, namely freedom of speech and assembly, than for other attributes, most notably clean elections. Furthermore, when we drill down to the indicator level of the electoral attribute of democracy, the association with civil war onset evaporates completely, with the exception of those indicators encompassing violence by definition. A similar disaggregation could be performed in analyses of how democratization and autocratization relate to armed conflict. Furthermore, the new data enable more systematic analysis of the extent to which these relationships are conditioned by other factors, as well as historical investigation of processes of regime change, including the historical sequencing of regime characteristics.

The upshot of this study is that democracy does not serve as a magic wand of peace – at least not in situations where a genuine fulfillment of democratic criteria is still beckoning. Instead, the evidence indicates that partial democracy can spark armed conflict. Does this mean that democracy has a dark side? In a sense, the answer to this question depends very much on the baseline. Democratization inherently has a violent potential, in the sense that the process can be seen as a means for deprived groups to get their say – and hence their piece of the pie. At the same time, well-functioning democracy affords a means for peacefully solving social conflicts. Such is the Janus-faced reality of the democratization-conflict nexus in a real-world context.

Notes

1 The onset variable indicates the year in which an armed conflict started, and observations with ongoing conflict are dropped.
2 The bimodal distributions arise because fulfillment of the formal requirements for having an elected executive or universal suffrage is very much an "either/or" question in the post-WWII period that we investigate.

3 One of the excluded indicators, free and fair elections, is too general for our purpose, while the other, capturing electoral interruptions, is dichotomous.
4 "EMB" is an abbreviation for electoral management body.
5 Likewise, we do not have space to explain the way we have modelled this, including the way to measure democratization and autocratization. Interested readers can contact the authors to receive the results of these analyses.

References

Acemoglu, Daron, and James Robinson (2006) *Economic Origins of Dictatorship and Democracy*. New York: Cambridge University Press.

Acemoglu, Daron, and James Robinson (2012) *Why Nations Fail*. New York: Crown Publishers.

Bartusevicius, Henrikas and Svend-Erik Skaaning (2016) *Electoral Democracy and Civil War*. Manuscript.

Boix, Carles (2008) "Economic Roots of Civil Wars and Revolutions in the Contemporary World." *World Politics* 60(2): 390–437.

Boix, Carles (2003) *Democracy and Redistribution*. New York: Cambridge University Press.

Bolt, Jutta, and Jan van Zanden (2014) "The Maddison Project." *The Economic History Review* 67(3): 627–651.

Bueno de Mesquita, Bruce, Alastair Smith, Randolph M. Siverson and James M. Morrow (2003) *The Logic of Political Survival*. Cambridge, MA: MIT Press.

Carothers, Thomas (2007) "The 'Sequencing' Fallacy." *Journal of Democracy* 18(1): 12–27.

Cederman, Lars-Erik, Kristian Gleditsch, and Simon Hug (2013) "Elections and Ethnic Civil War." *Comparative Political Studies* 46(3): 387–417.

Cederman, Lars-Erik, Kristian Gleditsch, and Halvard Buhaug (2013) *Inequality, Grievances, and Civil War*. Cambridge: Cambridge University Press.

Cederman, Lars-Erik, Simon Hug, and Lutz Krebs (2010) "Democratization and Civil War – Empirical Evidence." *Journal of Peace Research* 47(4): 377–394.

Collier, Paul, Anke Hoeffler, and Måns Söderbom (2008) "Post-Conflict Risks." *Journal of Peace Research* 45(4): 461–478.

Coppedge, Michael, John Gerring, Staffan I. Lindberg, Daniel Pemstein, Svend-Erik Skaaning, Jan Teorell, Eitan Tzelgov, Yi-ting Wang, David Altman, Michael Bernhard, M. Steven Fish, Adam Glynn, Allen Hicken, Carl Henrik Knutsen, Kelly McMann, Megan Reif, Jeffrey Staton, and Brigitte Zimmerman (2016a) *Varieties of Democracy: Methodology v6*. Varieties of Democracy (V-Dem) Project.

Coppedge, Michael, John Gerring, Staffan I. Lindberg, Svend-Erik Skaaning, Jan Teorell, with David Altman, Michael Bernhard, M. Steven Fish, Adam Glynn, Allen Hicken, Carl Henrik Knutsen, Kelly McMann, Pamela Paxton, Daniel Pemstein, Jeffrey Staton, Brigitte Zimmerman, Frida Andersson, Valeriya Mechkova, and Farhad Miri (2016b) *V-Dem Codebook v6*. Varieties of Democracy (V-Dem) Project.

Dahl, Robert (1998) *On Democracy*. New Haven, CT: Yale University Press.

Eifert, Benn, Edward Miguel, and Daniel N. Posner (2010) "Political Competition and Ethnic Identification in Africa." *American Journal of Political Science* 54(2): 494–510.

Fjelde, Hanne (2010) "Generals, Dictators and Kings: Authoritarian Regimes and Civil Conflict 1973–2004." *Conflict Management and Peace Science* 27(3): 195–218.

Gleditsch, Kristian, and Håvard Hegre (2014) "Regime Type and Political Transition in Civil War." In Karl DeRoen and Edward Newman (eds) *Routledge Handbook of Civil War*. London: Routledge.

Gleditsch, Kristian Skrede, and Andrea Ruggeri (2010) "Political Opportunity Structures, Democracy, and Civil War." *Journal of Peace Research* 47(3): 299–310.

Gleditsch, Nils Petter, Peter Wallensteen, Mikael Eriksson, Margareta Sollenberg, and Håvard Strand (2002) "Armed Conflict 1946–2001: A New Dataset." *Journal of Peace Research* 39(5): 615–637.

Goldstone, Jack, Robert Bates, David Epstein, Ted Gurr, Michael Lustik, Monty Marshall, Jay Ulfelder, and Mark Woodward (2010) "A Global Model for Forecasting Political Instability." *American Journal of Political Science* 54(1): 190–208.

Haber, Stephen, and Victor Menaldo (2011) "Do Natural Resources Fuel Authoritarianism? A Reappraisal of the Resource Curse." *American Political Science Review* 105(1): 1–26.

Hegre, Håvard (2014) "Democracy and Armed Conflict." *Journal of Peace Research* 51(2): 159–172.

Hegre, Håvard, Tanja Ellingsen, Scott Gates, and Nils Petter Gleditsch (2001) "Toward a Democratic Civil Peace? Democracy, Political Change and Civil War 1816–1992." *American Political Science Review* 95(1): 33–48.

Horowitz, Donald (1985) *Ethnic Groups in Conflict*. Berkeley: University of California Press.

Huntington, Samuel P. (1968) *Political Order in Changing Societies*. New Haven, CT: Yale University Press.

Knutsen, Carl Henrik, Jørgen Møller, and Svend-Erik Skaaning (2016) "Going Historical: Measuring Democraticness before the Age of Mass Democracy." *International Political Science Review* 37(5): 679–689.

Mann, Michael (2005) *The Dark Side of Democracy*. New York: Cambridge University Press.

Mansfield, Edward, and Jack Snyder (2012) "Democratization and Civil War." In Jack Snyder, *Power and Progress*. London: Routledge.

Mansfield, Edward, and Jack Snyder (2007) "The Sequencing 'Fallacy'." *Journal of Democracy* 18(3): 5–10.

Mansfield, Edward, and Jack Snyder (2005) *Electing to Fight: Why Emerging Democracies go to War*. Cambridge, MA: MIT Press.

Mansfield, Edward, and Jack Snyder (1995) "Democratization and the Danger of War." *International Security* 20(1): 5–38.

Marshall, Monty; Ted Gurr, and Keith Jaggers (2014) *Polity IV project: Dataset users' manual*. http://www.systemicpeace.org/inscr/p4manualv2013.pdf.

Møller, Jørgen (2016) "Putting the Conflict-Regime Nexus in Historical Perspective". *Comparative Democratization Newsletter*.

Møller, Jørgen, and Svend-Erik Skaaning (2013) *Democracy and Democratization in Comparative Perspective*. London: Routledge.

Muller, Edward, and Erich Weede (1990) "Cross-National Variation in Political Violence: A Rational Action Approach." *Journal of Conflict Resolution* 34(4): 43–59.

Przeworski, Adam (2010) *Democracy and the Limits of Self-Government*. New York: Cambridge University Press.

Sobek, David (2010) "Masters of their Domains: The Role of State Capacity in Civil Wars." *Journal of Peace Research* 47(3): 267–273.

Svolik, Milan (2012) *The Politics of Authoritarian Rule*. New York: Cambridge University Press

Teorell, Jan, Michael Coppedge, Staffan Lindberg, and Svend-Erik Skaaning (2016) *Measuring Electoral Democracy with V-Dem Data*. Varieties of Democracy (V-Dem) Working Paper Series: 25.

Vreeland, James (2008) "The Effects of Political Regime on Civil War: Unpacking Anocracy." *Journal of Conflict Resolution* 52(3): 401–425.

Ziblatt, Daniel (2006) *The Third Wave: Democratization in the Late Twentieth Century*. Norman: University of Oklahoma Press.

9

Evolution of Global Terrorism
The Growing Lethality of Attacks

Gary LaFree and Laura Dugan[1]

Introduction

This chapter reports results from the latest available version of the Global Terrorism Database (GTD), which includes data on the characteristics of more than 141,000 terrorist attacks that occurred worldwide between 1970 and 2014. We provide an update of baseline information about the trends and regional patterns of terrorist attacks. In addition, our analysis concentrates on the associated fatalities and how they are distributed across attacks, regions, countries, cities, targets, tactics, and weapons. Of note, total attacks and fatal attacks worldwide were at their highest level in 2014 since the GTD data series began in 1970. A major contributing factor is the recent rapid rise of the Islamic State of Iraq on the Levant (ISIL), which accounted for five of the 20 deadliest terrorist attacks over the entire time period.

Background on GTD

The GTD is maintained by the National Consortium for the Study of Terrorism and Responses to Terrorism (START) at the University of Maryland. The database is currently complete through 2014,[2] with the exception of 1993 data, which were misplaced prior to the transfer of the records to START and are treated as missing in this chapter. The dataset is updated annually and made available to policymakers, analysts, scholars, and the general public through START's website (www.start.umd.edu/gtd). Data collection for 2015 was well underway as this chapter was being prepared. Under a contract with the US State Department, an abridged version of the GTD will support the statistical annex for the US State Department's *2015 Country Reports on Terrorism*.

For purposes of the GTD, our operational definition of terrorism is *the threatened or actual use of illegal force by non-state actors, in order to attain a political, economic, religious or social goal, through fear, coercion or intimidation*. In practice, we require that incidents are intentional, entail some level of violence or threat of violence, and have been carried out by sub-national actors (for a complete description, see http://www.start.umd.edu/gtd/downloads/Codebook.pdf). In the process, the GTD excludes state terrorism and genocide, topics that are important and complex enough to warrant separate attention and data collection.

To compile the GTD, including identifying and systematically recording details of terrorist attacks, START relies entirely on unclassified sources, primarily print and electronic media articles. At present, this process begins with a universe of over 1.6 million articles published daily worldwide, within which a relatively small subset of articles describe terrorist attacks. We use customized search strings to isolate an initial pool of potentially relevant articles, followed by more sophisticated machine learning techniques to further refine the search results. For this subset of articles, additional manual review is required to identify the unique events that satisfy the GTD inclusion criteria and are subsequently researched and coded according to the specifications of the GTD Codebook. For each month of data collection, about 18,000 articles are manually reviewed and about 1,500 attacks are typically identified and coded.

Worldwide Trends in Terrorism

One of the most striking features of worldwide terrorism during the past half century is how much it has changed over time and across regions. This evolution is clearly illustrated by considering total attacks worldwide since 1970.

As Figure 9.1 shows, total attacks were relatively infrequent during the early 1970s, with fewer than 1,000 incidents each year until 1977. We observe steady increases, however, throughout the decade: between 1970 and 1979, the number of attacks increased by more than 300%, from 651 to 2,661. This rise is associated especially with high levels of activity in Western Europe and the United States. In particular, 47% of all attacks during the 1970s occurred in Western Europe. Within Western Europe, more than three quarters of the attacks occurred in just three countries: the United Kingdom (35%); Italy (22%); and Spain (19%). These numbers are driven by organizations involved in the so-called "Troubles" related to the republic–unionist conflict in Northern Ireland, such as the Irish Republican Army; leftist groups like the Red Brigades in Italy; and the Basque separatists, Basque Fatherland and Freedom (ETA), in Spain. Meanwhile, 15% of all terrorist attacks during the 1970s occurred in the United States. Many of those attacks were perpetrated by left-wing militant groups (e.g., Weather Underground) and other leftists (e.g., student radicals), black nationalists (e.g., Black Panthers), and Puerto Rican nationalists (e.g., Fuerzas Armadas de Liberación Nacional [FALN]).

During the 1980s, the trends and locations of terrorism changed considerably. The annual frequency continued to increase throughout the 1980s until a distinct peak in 1992 (5,077 attacks), with smaller peaks in 1984 (3,494 attacks) and 1989 (4,322 attacks). This steady rise in attacks was due in large part to a surge of attacks in Latin America. More than 55% of all terrorist attacks in the 1980s took place in South America (31%) and Central America and the Caribbean (24%).

After 1992, the number of terrorist attacks worldwide dropped dramatically, falling to a 20-year low in 1998. Likely the main reason for this drop-off was the collapse of the Soviet Union in 1991. Many of the organizations most active in committing terrorist attacks in Latin America during the 1980s were left-wing groups with strong Marxist-Leninist or Maoist sympathies, including the Sendero Luminoso (Shining Path) in Peru, the Fuerzas Armadas Revolucionarias de Colombia (FARC) in Colombia, and the Frente Farabundo Martí para la Liberación Nacional (FMLN) in El Salvador. Declines in attacks after 1990 were especially pronounced in El Salvador, where total attacks dropped by 82% from the 1980s to the 1990s, and Guatemala, where attacks dropped by 71% over the same period.

Figure 9.1 shows another major transition that occurred during the 2000s. Total attacks in 2000 (1,814), the year prior to the 9/11 attacks, were just a few hundred more than the corresponding figure for 1978 (1,526). Total attacks rose sharply in the aftermath of the United States and its allies invading Iraq in 2003. By 2011, total attacks reached 5,065 – nearly the

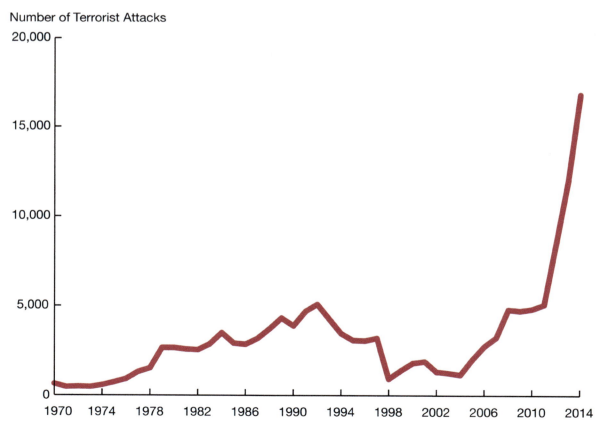

Figure 9.1 Annual Number of Terrorist Attacks, 1970–2014
Note: Total attacks=141,966.

same as the record level experienced in 1992. Since 2011, total attacks have shattered all previous records. In 2013, total attacks stood at 11,999, or 136% higher than the peak in 1992. Another record was set in 2014: total attacks increased by 40% from 2013, reaching the highest level in the entire time period covered by the GTD. These rapid increases in attacks since the late 1990s have produced a strong J-shaped curve in the trend line.

Worldwide Trends in Fatalities

In total, the attacks reported in the GTD resulted in 706,044 casualties, comprised of 310,017 fatalities (44%) and 396,027 injuries (56%). Of the nearly 142,000 attacks from 1970–2014, 63,321 (50.4%) resulted in at least one fatality. Fatalities include all victims and perpetrators who died as a direct result of the incident. In general, the GTD picks up fatalities more reliably than injuries because of their relative newsworthiness. The relative likelihood of fatalities and injuries is often a function of factors independent of the nature of the attack, other than location, which brings into play considerations like the distance to an emergency medical facility and the quality of the medical system. While the metrics are quite different, the underlying trends between attacks and injuries are highly correlated (r = 0.87; p < 0.001). Likewise, total fatalities and injuries are also highly correlated (also r = 0.87; p < 0.001).

Figure 9.2 shows annual terrorism-related casualties from 1970–2014. Casualties during the 1970s were a small fraction of what they have been in recent years: for example, fatalities in 2014 were 254 times greater than they were in 1970. Casualties broke 10,000 for the first time in 1983. They fluctuated a great deal during the 1980s and 1990s and did not pass 20,000 per year until 1995. Casualties hit another peak in 2007, then declined slightly for a few years before increasing precipitously over the last four years of the data series. In 2014, the GTD reported 43,501 fatalities and 40,986 injuries. The average number of casualties from an attack was 2.59 deaths and 2.44 injuries in 2014, compared to averages of 0.71 deaths and 0.73 injuries during the 1970s.

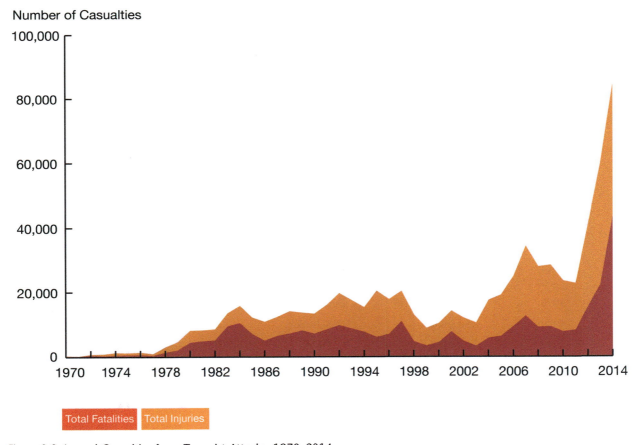

Figure 9.2 Annual Casualties from Terrorist Attacks, 1970–2014
Note: Total reported fatalities=310,017; total reported injuries=396,027.

The Deadliest Attacks in the World between 1970 and 2014

Table 9.1 shows the 20 most lethal terrorist attacks recorded in the GTD from 1970–2014. Each of these attacks resulted in at least 298 deaths. Together, the 20 incidents were responsible for a total of 12,054 reported deaths. Of note, the attacks ranked second and third in Table 9.1 were coded as a "multiple category risk." This coding indicates that GTD analysts conclude there is sufficient information to include each case in the dataset, but questions whether these cases uniquely qualifies as terrorism, which arises when cases share characteristics with non-terrorist events or lack incomplete information. Here, the second-ranked attack shares characteristics of an insurgency, while the third-ranked attack shares characteristics of ethnic cleansing.

Table 9.1 Twenty Most Lethal Terrorist Attacks, 1970–2014

Rank	Year	Location	Country	Attributed Perpetrator	Total Fatalities
1	2001	New York City	United States	al-Qaeda	2,763
2	2014	Tikrit	Iraq	Islamic State of Iraq and the Levant (ISIL)	1,500
3	1994	Gikoro	Rwanda	Hutu Extremists	1,180
4	2014	Badush	Iraq	Islamic State of Iraq and the Levant (ISIL)	670
5	2004	Bedi	Nepal	Communist Party of Nepal-Maoist (CPN-M)	518
6	2014	Raqqah	Syria	Islamic State of Iraq and the Levant (ISIL)	517
7	2014	Sinjar	Iraq	Islamic State of Iraq and the Levant (ISIL)	500
8	1978	Abadan	Iran	Mujahedin-e Khalq (MEK)	422
9	1987	Homoine	Mozambique	Mozambique National Resistance Movement (MNR)	388
10	1996	Kivyuka	Burundi	Tutsi Extremists	375
11	2004	Beslan	Russia	Riyadus-Salikhin Reconnaissance and Sabotage Battalion of Chechen Martyrs	344
12	1985	Toronto	Canada	Sikh Extremists	329
13	1998	Kilinochchi	Sri Lanka	Liberation Tigers of Tamil Eelam (LTTE)	320
14	2014	Gamboru Ngala	Nigeria	Boko Haram	315
15	2014	Palmyra district	Syria	Islamic State of Iraq and the Levant (ISIL)	310
16	1996	Central Burundi	Burundi	Hutu Extremists	304
17	1980	Suchitoto	El Salvador	Unknown	300
18	1984	Uaskeing	Sudan	Christian Extremists	300
19	1997	Gisenyi	Rwanda	Hutu Extremists	300
20	2014	Hrabove	Ukraine	Donetsk People's Republic	298

Note: Certain of the original sources provide only an approximate number of fatalities (e.g., at least 500 persons killed). In these instances, the lowest number is reported in the GTD.

The 9/11 attack by al-Qaeda on the World Trade Center in New York still ranks at the top of the list.[3] The next two deadliest incidents were a 2014 attack in Tikrit, Iraq and a 1994 attack in Gikoro, Rwanda. In the 2014 ISIL attack, 1,686 soldiers were kidnapped from an encampment. Two soldiers reportedly escaped, but the remainder are presumed dead. ISIL claimed responsibility, saying that the attack was perpetrated in revenge for the killing of their leader, Abdul-Rahman al Beilawy. In the Rwandan attack, a Hutu paramilitary organization, the Interahamwe, murdered more than 1,100 Tutsis who were hiding in a Catholic church, in one of the more notorious incidents amid the Rwandan genocide.

Four other attacks resulted in at least 500 fatalities. Three were perpetrated by ISIL during 2014. On 10 June, 2014, ISIL militants stormed Badush prison in Iraq, freeing all of the Sunni prisoners while killing the 670 Shiite prisoners. Another attack began when ISIL abducted a large number of Syrian soldiers at an airbase. The pitched battle with Syrian forces that followed resulted in 517 fatalities, two-thirds of which were the perpetrators. In the third attack, ISIL perpetrators kidnapped an estimated 300 women and killed at least 500 Yazidi civilians in Sinjar, Iraq. They reportedly sold the women into forced "marriages." The fourth attack that killed more than 500 was perpetrated by the Communist Party of Nepal-Maoist (CPN-M) during 2004. The CPN-M robbed a state bank, freed prisoners, and bombed a bridge, local administrative offices, and the airport in Bedi, Nepal. Government forces fought back. In the end, an estimated 500 perpetrators and 18 security personnel were killed.

Consistent with the recent rapid rise in the number of fatalities discussed in connection with Figure 9.2, five of the 20 deadliest attacks happened in 2014. The list includes only one attack from the 1970s (Abadan, Iran) and four attacks from the 1980s (Suchitoto, El Salvador; Uaskeing, Sudan; Toronto, Canada; and Homoine, Mozambique).

The country locations of the 20 deadliest attacks are widely dispersed, though Iraq (3), Syria (2), Rwanda (2) and Burundi (2) each exhibited multiple large-scale incidents. ISIL perpetrated five of the 20 deadliest attacks – the most of any group. Ongoing inter-ethnic violence between Hutus and Tutsis, observed in Rwanda and Burundi, account for four of the attacks in the top 20.

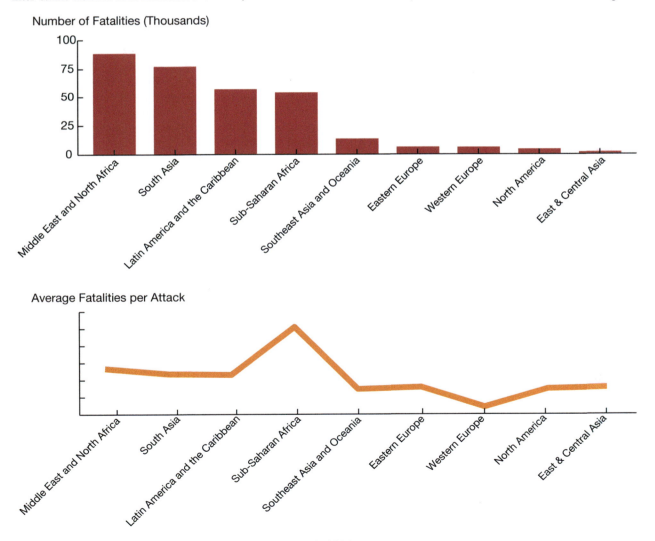

Figure 9.3 Fatalities from Terrorist Attacks, by Region, 1970–2014

Fatalities and Average Fatalities by Region

Figure 9.3 shows total fatalities and average fatalities per attack for nine regions of the world (see Appendix 9.1 [pp. 85–6] for a list of the countries in each region). The largest shares of terrorism-related fatalities since 1970 have been shouldered by four regions: (1) the Middle East and North Africa, (2) South Asia, (3) Latin America and the Caribbean, and (4) Sub-Saharan Africa. Together, these regions have suffered over 277,000 fatalities from terrorism – over eight times more than the 33,000 fatalities suffered by the remaining five regions. The Middle East and North Africa region has suffered the highest number of fatalities, nearly 90,000, followed closely by South Asia. Latin America and the Caribbean and Sub-Saharan Africa have experienced considerably fewer fatalities, but still many more than the remaining five regions.

Figure 9.3 indicates a complex relationship at the regional level between average fatalities per attack and total fatalities. We identify three roughly distinct categories. In the first category, comprised of three regions (Middle East and North Africa, South Asia, and Latin America and the Caribbean), terrorist-related fatalities were high, but the average fatalities per attack were at an intermediate level. This pattern likely reflects the extreme number of attacks in those regions, not all of which were lethal. The second category is comprised of Sub-Saharan Africa, where total fatalities were at an intermediate level, but the average rate of fatalities per attack was very high. This pattern implies a greater concentration of attacks that resulted in mass casualties. As we reported in Table 9.1, seven of the 20 most lethal attacks recorded in the GTD occurred in Sub-Saharan Africa, which is disproportionate to the region's share of total attacks (8.1%). In the third category, comprised of the other regions (Southeast Asia and Oceania, Eastern Europe, Western Europe, North America, East and Central Asia), both total fatalities and average fatalities per attack were relatively low. Therefore, these regions had less overall exposure to terrorism and also tended to avoid mass-casualty attacks. The contrast across categories is best illustrated by the comparison between Sub-Saharan Africa, which averaged more than five fatalities per attack, and Western Europe, which averaged one fatality per 2.5 attacks.

Targets

Table 9.2 presents the total number of fatalities, the average fatalities per attack, and the share and number of attacks for a range of target types. Not surprisingly, private citizens and property account for the largest numbers of attacks and total fatalities. Yet these purely civilian targets – those without a more specific institutional or organizational affiliation – account for only about one-quarter of all the attacks. The next most common targets are the military and the police. Taken together, these three types of targets account for 54% of the total attacks.

Table 9.2 Fatalities from Terrorist Attacks, by Target, 1970–2014

Type of Target	Total Fatalities	Average Fatalities per Attack	Share of Attacks	Number of Attacks
Private Citizens and Property	120,955	3.57	25.0%	35,421
Military	78,398	4.16	14.5%	20,612
Police	43,234	2.24	14.0%	19,919
Government (General)	22,625	1.29	13.0%	18,410
Business	22,253	1.33	12.8%	18,183
Transportation	12,800	2.24	4.3%	6,108
Religious Figures/Institutions	10,777	3.11	2.5%	3,568
Terrorists	6,878	2.99	1.7%	2,347
Airports and Airlines	6,365	5.28	0.9%	1,314
Educational Institutions	3,514	0.96	2.7%	3,799
Violent Political Party	2,987	2.16	1.0%	1,400
Government (Diplomatic)	2,533	0.82	2.3%	3,267
Other	2,522	7.40	0.3%	359
Utilities	1,956	0.42	3.7%	5,292
Journalists and Media	1,403	0.60	1.8%	2,535
Maritime	1,067	3.89	0.2%	315

Table 9.2 Fatalities from Terrorist Attacks, by Target, 1970–2014 – continued

Type of Target	Total Fatalities	Average Fatalities per Attack	Share of Attacks	Number of Attacks
Tourists	1,018	2.42	0.3%	443
NGOs	880	1.10	0.6%	847
Food or Water Supply	265	1.08	0.2%	284
Telecommunication	209	0.25	0.6%	910
Abortion Related	9	0.04	0.2%	253

Note: Attacks can be directed toward multiple targets. Consequently, some attacks are represented more than once in this table. Also, 2,872 attacks resulting in 3,033 fatalities had unknown targets.

Across targets, the lethality of attacks varies considerably. Interestingly, the highest average is for the "other" category of targets. This result is largely due to attacks on refugees and internally displaced persons (IDPs), especially by Hutu paramilitaries, the Lord's Resistance Army, and Bodo militants. Refugee and IDP camps face a heightened risk, especially of mass-casualty attacks, because of the concentration of large numbers of potential victims, many of whom have fled conflict and are in a vulnerable position. Attacks on airports and airlines tend to be highly lethal because of the possibility of mass-casualty attacks on crowded terminals and planes in flight. Attacks on military targets may be characterized by high fatality rates in so far as perpetrators are focused on maximizing impact and thus attack bases and other places were soldiers are stationed. Also, the defenses on military targets present a challenge that can be expected to attract mainly the most serious, well-trained, well-resourced attackers. Maritime attacks may be especially lethal because attacks at sea make rescue more complex and less effective. On the other side of the spectrum, several types of targets result in less than one fatality per attack.

Tactics

Table 9.3 shows the tactics used by terrorists, which are grouped into eight categories. Bombings are attacks that use explosive devices, including bombs detonated manually or by remote timer and suicide bombings. Armed assaults are in-person attacks whose primary objective is to cause physical harm or death directly on human targets by any means other than explosives. Hence, we would classify the use of an explosive or an incendiary device as a bombing, but the use of a projectile grenade in the hands of an attacker as an armed assault. Assassinations are attacks that kill or attempt to kill specific prominent figures. Such attacks are considered assassinations even if they are accomplished by implementing another tactic (e.g., bombing or armed assault). A recent example occurred in October 2011, when suspected members of al-Qaeda in the Arabian Peninsula placed a bomb in the car of an Air Force Colonel in Yemen, killing the Colonel and two passengers. This attack was classified as an assassination, rather than a bombing, given the Colonel's prominent position. Facility or infrastructure attacks are those whose primary objective is to cause damage to non-human targets, such as buildings or monuments. Kidnappings involve hostage taking of persons or groups of persons distinguished by the intention to move and hold the hostages in a clandestine location. Barricade/hostage attacks are those whose primary objective is to obtain political or other concessions in return for the release of the hostages. Such attacks are distinguished from kidnappings because the incident is initiated and usually plays out at the target location, without holding the hostages in a separate clandestine location. Hijackings are attacks that involve the forcible takeover of vehicles, including airplanes, buses, and ships, for the purpose of obtaining some concession, such as the payment of a ransom or the release of political prisoners. Hijackings are different from barricade/hostage attacks because the target is the vehicle, regardless of whether there are people in the vehicle.

Table 9.3 Fatalities from Terrorist Attacks, by Tactic, 1970–2014

Type of Tactic	Total Fatalities	Average Fatalities per Attack	Share of Attacks	Number of Attacks
Armed Assault	151,076	4.39	25.7%	36,497
Bombing/Explosion	116,302	1.78	48.5%	68,779
Assassination	22,333	1.33	11.9%	16,831
Hostage Taking (Kidnapping)	16,533	2.35	6.0%	8,465
Facility/Infrastructure Attack	7,837	0.93	6.4%	9,018

Table 9.3 Fatalities from Terrorist Attacks, by Tactic, 1970–2014 – continued

Type of Tactic	Total Fatalities	Average Fatalities per Attack	Share of Attacks	Number of Attacks
Hijacking	3,675	7.32	0.4%	535
Hostage Taking (Barricade Incident)	2,360	3.46	0.5%	770
Unarmed Assault	717	0.97	0.5%	752

Note: Attacks can rely upon multiple tactics. Consequently, some attacks are represented more than once in this table. Also, 4,714 attacks resulting in 19,741 fatalities had unknown attack types.

As shown in Table 9.3, bombings and armed assaults account for the largest numbers of attacks – jointly responsible for over 74% of all cases included in the GTD. Assassinations, hostage taking (kidnapping), and facility attacks are far less common, each accounting for between 6% and 12% of all attacks. Hijackings, hostage taking involving barricades, and unarmed assaults are even less common, each accounting for less than 1% of the total. While bombings and armed assaults are the most common tactics, they differ greatly in terms of lethality: on average, armed assaults are more than twice as deadly as bombings. While hijacking is among the least common terrorist tactic, it produces the highest average number of fatalities per attack. Hostage taking involving barricades is also a relatively lethal tactic. By contrast, facility attacks and unarmed assaults produce less than one fatality per attack on average.

Weapons

Because of how terrorism is typically depicted by the media and in popular entertainment, there is an understandable tendency to think that most attacks are complex, carefully orchestrated events that rely heavily on sophisticated weaponry. As we have explained elsewhere (LaFree, Dugan, and Miller 2015), however, the vast majority of terrorist attacks instead rely on rather ordinary, relatively accessible weapons – mostly explosives and firearms.

Table 9.4 Fatalities from Terrorist Attacks, by Weapon, 1970–2014

Type of Weapon	Total Fatalities	Average Fatalities per Attack	Share of Attacks	Number of Attacks
Firearms	164,499	3.40	36.1%	51,173
Explosives/Bombs/Dynamite	129,495	1.89	50.8%	72,162
Melee	18,870	5.42	2.5%	3,542
Incendiary	15,503	1.53	7.6%	10,813
Vehicle	3,256	28.31	0.1%	115
Chemical	746	2.90	0.2%	264
Other	571	3.28	0.1%	178
Sabotage Equipment	127	0.69	0.1%	185
Biological	9	0.26	0.03%	36
Fake Weapons	7	0.14	0.04%	51
Radiological	0	0.00	0.01%	13

Note: Attacks can rely upon multiple types of weapons. Consequently, some attacks are represented more than once in this table. Also, 11,046 attacks resulting in 26,602 fatalities had unknown weapon types.

Table 9.4 shows the total fatalities associated with different types of weapons, as well as their average lethality. Explosives and firearms were, by far, the most common weapons used by terrorists, jointly accounting for more than 87% of all attacks where a weapon was recorded. The next most common were incendiary and melee attacks. Incendiaries are weapons that are capable of catching fire, causing fire, or burning readily when exploded. Melee attacks are those where the perpetrator comes into direct contact with the target, using low-technology weapons such as fists or knives. All other weapon types account for less than 1% of attacks in total. Vehicle attacks are those in which people are killed using a vehicle, including airplanes, cars and trucks. Sabotage equipment refers to situations where perpetrators create a weapon by demolishing or destroying property (e.g., removing bolts from train tracks). The "other" category here includes rocks, smoke flares, and fire crackers. Reliance on more complex weapons such as chemical, biological, radiological and nuclear (CBRN) agents remains rare. Within this group, chemical weapons are the most common, accounting for 84% of all CBRN attacks. To this point in time, the GTD does not include a single nuclear attack. Use of fake weapons, where perpetrators claim to have a weapon at the time of the incident, but it is later discovered that the weapon is either non-existent or incapable of producing the threatened effects, are very uncommon in the GTD.

While explosives are the most common weapon used, firearms cause more fatalities. On average, firearms claim nearly twice as many deaths per attack on average as bombings. Table 9.4 also shows that vehicles used as weapons are especially lethal. This result is largely attributable to including airplanes in this category. The confusion and chaos engendered by melee-style attacks are key reasons why this type of weapon is the second-most lethal on the list.

Conclusions

In this chapter, we examined the latest available data on terrorist activity from the GTD, with a special focus on the lethality of attacks over time and across characteristics of attacks. Our review suggests that both total terrorist attacks and lethal attacks increased dramatically from 1970 to the early 1990s, declined up until about 2002, and then increased rapidly during the past decade. In 2014, total attacks and total fatal attacks worldwide were at their highest levels since the data series began in 1970.

Among the most striking trends in global terrorism over the past half century is the shift away from attacks being concentrated in Western Europe and North America during the 1970s, to Latin America during the 1980s, and then to South Asia, the Middle East/North Africa and Sub-Saharan Africa beginning during the 1990s and intensifying in recent years. This shift across regions also had consequences for the lethality of terrorism. Most notably, terrorist attacks during the 1970s were characterized by relatively few fatalities. In contrast, the terrorist attacks during the past decade have been far deadlier. The rapid rise of ISIL in recent years is emblematic of this shift and accounts for five of the 20 deadliest terrorist attacks since 1970.

Appendix 9.1 Countries Listed under Each Region

Region	Countries/Territories		
East and Central Asia	China	Kyrgyzstan	Taiwan
	Hong Kong	Macao	Tajikistan
	Japan	North Korea	Turkmenistan
	Kazakhstan	South Korea	Uzbekistan
Eastern Europe	Albania	Georgia	Russia
	Armenia	Hungary	Serbia
	Azerbaijan	Latvia	Serbia-Montenegro
	Bosnia-Herzegovina	Lithuania	Slovak Republic
	Bulgaria	Kosovo	Slovenia
	Belarus	Macedonia	Soviet Union
	Croatia	Moldova	Ukraine
	Czechoslovakia	Montenegro	Yugoslavia
	Czech Republic	Poland	
	Estonia	Romania	
Latin America and the Caribbean	Antigua and Barbuda	Dominica	Martinique
	Argentina	Dominican Republic	Nicaragua
	Bahamas	Ecuador	Panama
	Barbados	El Salvador	Paraguay
	Belize	Falkland Islands	Peru
	Bermuda	French Guiana	Puerto Rico

Appendix 9.1 Countries Listed under Each Region – continued

Region	Countries/Territories		
	Bolivia	Grenada	St. Kitts and Nevis
	Brazil	Guadeloupe	Suriname
	Cayman Islands	Guatemala	Trinidad and Tobago
	Chile	Guyana	Uruguay
	Colombia	Haiti	Venezuela
	Costa Rica	Honduras	Virgin Islands (US)
	Cuba	Jamaica	
Middle East and North Africa	Algeria	Kuwait	South Yemen
	Bahrain	Lebanon	Syria
	Cyprus	Libya	Tunisia
	Egypt	Morocco	Turkey
	Iran	North Yemen	United Arab Emirates
	Iraq	Oman	West Bank and Gaza Strip
	Israel	Qatar	Western Sahara
	Jordan	Saudi Arabia	Yemen
North America	Canada	Mexico	United States
South Asia	Afghanistan	Kashmir	Pakistan
	Bangladesh	Maldives	Seychelles
	Bhutan	Mauritius	Sri Lanka
	India	Nepal	
Southeast Asia and Oceania	Australia	Myanmar	South Vietnam
	Brunei	New Caledonia	Thailand
	Cambodia	New Hebrides	Timor-Leste
	Fiji	New Zealand	Tonga
	French Polynesia	Papua New Guinea	Vanuatu
	Guam	Philippines	Vietnam
	Indonesia	Samoa (Western Samoa)	Wallis and Futuna
	Laos	Solomon Islands	
	Malaysia	Singapore	
Sub-Saharan Africa	Angola	Gambia	Nigeria
	Benin	Ghana	Rwanda
	Botswana	Guinea	Senegal
	Burkina Faso	Guinea-Bissau	Sierra Leone
	Burundi	Ivory Coast	Somalia
	Cameroon	Kenya	South Africa
	Central African Republic	Lesotho	South Sudan
	Chad	Liberia	Sudan
	Comoros	Madagascar	Swaziland
	Congo (Brazzaville)	Malawi	Tanzania

Appendix 9.1 Countries Listed under Each Region – continued

Region	Countries/Territories		
	Congo (Kinshasa)	Mali	Togo
	Djibouti	Mauritania	Uganda
	Equatorial Guinea	Mauritius	Zaire
	Eritrea	Mozambique	Zambia
	Ethiopia	Namibia	Zimbabwe
	Gabon	Niger	
Western Europe	Andorra	Gibraltar	Netherlands
	Austria	Great Britain	Northern Ireland
	Belgium	Greece	Norway
	Corsica	Iceland	Portugal
	Denmark	Ireland	San Marino
	East Germany	Italy	Spain
	Finland	Luxembourg	Sweden
	France	Malta	Switzerland
	Germany	Isle of Man	West Germany

Notes

1 Address correspondence to Gary LaFree (glafree@umd.edu) or Laura Dugan (ldugan@umd.edu). Support for this work was provided by the Department of Homeland Security (DHS) through the National Center for the Study of Terrorism and Responses to Terrorism (START), grant number N00140510629. Any opinions, findings, or recommendations in this document are those of the authors and do not necessarily reflect the views of DHS.

2 The GTD has gone through four different data collection periods: (1) 1970–1997, (2) 1998–2007, (3) 2008–2011, and (4) 2012–present. While we have made every effort to preserve continuity across these periods, the resources available for data collection, the methods used to prepare the database, and the extensiveness of the world-wide media have changed over time. Most notably, much of the data collected during the second period noted above was collected retrospectively. By the time we had completed the original GTD, covering 1970 to 1997, it was already 2005, meaning our data collection was eight years behind real time. As we worked to extend the data forward, we were forced to rely on older sources for the initial years beyond 1997, whereas we approached real-time data collection, using current sources, for more recent years. To the extent that newspaper and electronic media are not archived, availability of original sources may erode over time, causing underreporting or missing data. These issues are likely to be especially problematic in regards to small, regional and local newspapers. We also initiated major changes in the data collection process during the fourth period. For a detailed discussion of the strengths and weaknesses of the GTD, see LaFree, Dugan and Miller (2015).

3 We have chosen to treat the coordinated attacks on the twin towers of the World Trade Center as one event here – in part because to this day we do not know exactly how many lives were lost in each tower. If the attacks are instead treated as two separate events, the 2014 attack by ISIL in Tikrit would be the deadliest attack in the GTD.

Reference

LaFree, Gary, Laura Dugan, and Erin Miller (2015) *Putting Terrorism in Context: Lessons from the Global Terrorism Database*. London: Routledge.

10

Are Global Human Rights Conditions Static or Improving?

Peter Haschke and Mark Gibney

Introduction

Human rights conditions around the world remain a high-priority issue for the international community. One of the primary needs in this regard is reliable data that tracks practices. Such data facilitates understanding of patterns and trends within and across countries, as well as the identification of countries, regions and contexts that exhibit different outcomes – improvement, stagnation, or regression in human rights conditions. With those purposes in mind, multiple existing dataset projects are devoted to gauging the extent of citizen security, in the past and on an ongoing basis.

The two leading datasets are the Political Terror Scale (PTS) and the Cingranelli and Richards Physical Integrity Rights Index (CIRI), both of which provide ordinal measures coding physical integrity violations. The PTS (www. politicalterrorscale.org) employs a five-point scale, with higher scores indicating worse levels of human rights conditions. Separate scores are provided based on the information from the annual human rights reports of the US State Department, Amnesty International, and more recently, Human Rights Watch. The CIRI (www.humanrightsdata.com) provides disaggregate scores for four physical integrity violations – political imprisonment, summary executions, disappearances, and torture – as well as a total score for each country. The scores are based primarily on information from the US State Department annual human rights reports. Although the PTS and CIRI essentially measure the same thing, their approaches also exhibit important differences (Wood and Gibney 2010; Cingranelli and Richards 2010).

Lately, these datasets have been subject to critiques by scholars. A primary concern the critiques raise is a perceived inconsistency, over time, in the source material on which these datasets rely. In particular, the critics represent the nature of reporting as having changed in such a way that more violations ought to be detected in recent years than would be detected in earlier years, all else being equal. For the same actual level of violations, therefore, measures based on available reporting would tend to be more accurate for recent years, whereas the measures for earlier years would understate the true extent of violations. Of note, evaluations of human rights conditions globally have remained relatively static according to both the PTS and CIRI. In turn, the implication of the critiques is that conditions may actually be improving, in as much as accurate measures for earlier years ought to reveal higher numbers of violations than have been reported.

In this chapter, we address the critiques by systematically analyzing the sources of the PTS data. Our results ultimately show that the critiques are largely unfounded: the basis of the claims cannot be substantiated. This analysis reinforces the reliability and significance of the evaluations of global human rights conditions using the PTS data. We certainly would like to identify an improvement in these conditions. Yet we are confident that the PTS data, unfortunately, indicate otherwise: conditions are not improving to an appreciable degree.

Background

Recently, a number of scholars have raised concerns that the nature of the State Department and Amnesty International reports has changed fundamentally and consequentially over time. Therefore, these scholars question the validity of at least some of the scores – especially those from earlier years – that PTS and CIRI derive from the reports.

Clark and Sikkink (2013) maintain that the quantity and quality of information in the reports have improved considerably. A key reason they cite is increased resources being devoted to the assembly of the reports. They further argue that what constitutes a violation of international human rights standards has become less exacting, as a result of which

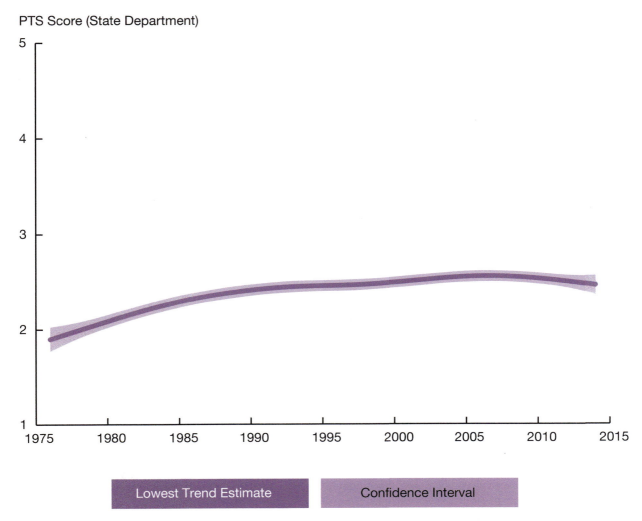

Figure 10.1 Global Annual Average PTS (State Department) Scores, 1976–2014
Note: This figure shows the smoothed global annual average PTS scores, compiled based on the State Department reports (N=6,399). On the PTS scale, a score of "1" corresponds to very few violations during the year, whereas a score of "5" indicates gross and systematic human rights violations.

violations are more likely to be identified in recent years than before. Fariss (2014) makes many of the same arguments. He describes a "changing standard of accountability," arising as a result of better information, more access to governmental practices (especially through the increased involvement of nongovernmental organizations), and changes in what are considered to be "good" human rights practices. Consequently, monitors have evolved in the direction where they "look harder for abuse, look in more places for abuse and classify more acts as abuse" (Fariss 2014: 299). He goes even further by claiming that since the overall global scores from both the PTS and CIRI have been relatively unchanged over time (the trend in PTS scores is reflected in Figure 10.1), this is tantamount to showing an improvement of human rights practices. In essence, if much more information about human rights violations exists now than before, but global average scores are remaining static, signs actually point to the world becoming safer.

We take these critiques seriously. Without hesitation, we accept that characteristics of source materials could change and that those changes can indeed affect resulting data products. Significant evolution in source materials presents a plausible reason to examine closely the validity of the data, especially the expectation of comparability of measures across a long-term time series.

That said, we have concerns of our own about the foundations of the critiques. Clark and Sikkink (2013) and Fariss (2014) root their arguments primarily in the notion that recent reporting is fundamentally different from prior reporting. Yet they never identify when this change occurred. Was the change paradigmatic, associated with some specific point and explicit decisions, or the result of an accumulation of progressive shifts without obvious intentionality? Also, they repeatedly assert that the annual reports are now longer and more detailed – and presumably more accurate – than they had been in the past. Yet the evidence that they marshal in this regard is selective and does not constitute compelling proof.

In support of their argument, Clark and Sikkink (2013) focus heavily on the information about Latin America during the 1980s. It is a known fact that the State Department annual reports exhibit evident bias, understating the extent of violations committed by governments in the region during the time period (Poe, Carey, and Vazquez 2001). We accept this as a limitation of the measures based on the State Department reports for that region at that time (Wood and Gibney 2010). Clark and Sikkink (2013) fail to demonstrate, however, that the problem is more pervasive, or to establish the general trend that the length and depth of reporting have increased over time, let alone in a manner that improves accuracy. Meanwhile, Fariss (2014) presents a table that examines a single country (Guatemala) and one particular type of human rights violation (torture) at three intervals: 1981, 1991 and 2001. He focuses on a metric of length – the total number of words in the reports – and consistent with his thesis, at least in certain respects, shows increases over time. In 1981, the torture section in the State Department Report was 329 words, while the word count for the entire report for Guatemala was 3,930; in 1991, the torture section was 562 words and the entire report was 5,768; and in 2001, the torture section alone was 3,669 words and the total report for Guatemala was 32,064 words. Yet Fariss does not mention that Guatemala's PTS scores were actually lowest when the word count was the highest (2001) and highest when the word count was the lowest (1981). Thus, the relationship between word count and PTS score appears to run entirely contrary to the claim that more extensive reporting necessarily tends to lead to identifying worse conditions.

Analytical Design

Given the importance of validating the measurement of human rights conditions, and our reservations about the critiques of the PTS, a systematic assessment is warranted. Specifically, we analyze two sets of claims. The first set of claims is descriptive in orientation: recent human rights reports are longer (and implicitly more detailed, thorough and comprehensive) than earlier reports. The second set of claims attributes an impact in measurement to these changes: the expanding content of the reports biases trends in PTS scores toward finding more violations.

Our analysis involves examining word counts in the State Department annual reports for the period from 1999–2015. Ideally, the analysis would have covered the entire time series of PTS, which starts in 1976. Unfortunately, the State Department annual reports were first posted on the internet only in 1999 (while 2015 is the latest year for which annual reports are available). Having access to this electronic resource makes the analysis tractable. Extending the analysis to cover the years without this available resource would have entailed reliably digitizing large volumes of material – estimated to be in the order of 1,500 pages per year, or approximately 35,000 pages in total from 1976–1998. Undertaking such an effort was beyond the scope of this study. We recognize that our analysis excludes more than 20 years of potential data, which would have afforded a fuller picture of trends in reporting and measurement. Nonetheless, the 17 years covered by the analysis offer a long-term perspective that we think should still be sufficient to detect meaningful trends and patterns of association.

To conduct the analysis, we downloaded all the annual reports as plain text files from the State Department's website (http://www.state.gov/j/drl/rls/hrrpt/). In total, we compiled 3,281 separate reports for 196 countries and territories. We pre-processed these full reports by removing spaces, mark-up, and typos. In practice, the coding of PTS using the State Department material focuses primarily on the executive summary and Section 1 (Respect for the Integrity of the Person) of each of the reports. Therefore, we generated additional text files containing only those two segments of each report, drawing on the pre-processed full version. In the end, our database consists of 3,281 text files containing the text of the full reports and 3,281 text files containing the text of the reports' executive summaries and Section 1s (hereafter referred to as Section 1s, for sake of simplicity).

Table 10.1 Summary Statistics for Word Counts in State Department Human Rights Reports, 1999–2015

Measure	Minimum	Maximum	Mean	Median	Standard Deviation
Words in Full Report	1,610	76,840	10,920	9,620	6,867
Words in Section 1	348	21,840	3,550	2,927	2,567

Note: This analysis covers State Department Human Rights Reports from 1999–2015 (N = 3,281).

Table 10.1 provides summary statistics for the word counts,[1] differentiating between full reports and Section 1s. On average, full reports contain about 11,000 words and Section 1s about 3,500 words. The counts vary widely. San Marino 2000 is the shortest full report (1,610 words), while China 2010 is the longest (76,840 words). The longest Section 1 belongs to the 2000 report for Colombia (21,840 words), the shortest to the 1999 report for Denmark (348 words).

Results

Here, we present the results of the analysis related to the two sets of claims made by critics. We begin by examining report length, finding no clear, strong trends. Next, we evaluate the relationship between report length and PTS scores, finding no appreciable impact.

Report Length over Time

Figure 10.2 displays the word counts of the full reports, by year. These results provide limited evidence to suggest that reports have increased modestly in length. The median count was 8,133 words in 1999 and 10,462 words in 2015. In between, the annual medians fluctuated, generally remaining within a few hundred words of the overall median for the period of 9,620 words. Thus, the trend is neither monotonic nor substantial.

Figure 10.3 reveals no upward trend in the word counts for Section 1s. The median count was 2,817 words in 1999 and 2,761 in 2015. Both these counts were below the overall median of 2,927. Consequently, even if the full reports may have grown slightly longer over time, Section 1s – arguably more relevant for coding the PTS – have gotten shorter.

Another way to approach the critics' claim is to examine the trend in annual growth rates of report lengths. Figure 10.4 displays the growth rates for full reports, by year. The results do not indicate that reports are growing cumulatively longer year after year. For the entire period, the median growth rate is 1.5%. Yet this does not reflect a consistent upward trend. For example, the median report length grew by 14.3% from 1999 to 2000, but shrank by 3.8% from 2014 to 2015. Report lengths tend to follow a cyclical pattern of years with increases followed by years of reductions. No country maintained a positive growth rate over the entire period.

We observe much the same pattern in growth rates for Section 1s, as captured in Figure 10.5. The median growth rate of Section 1s is not increasing over time. The median rate is 0.38% for the entire period, with cyclical variation between years of increases and years of reductions. Not a single country maintained a positive growth rate over the entire period.

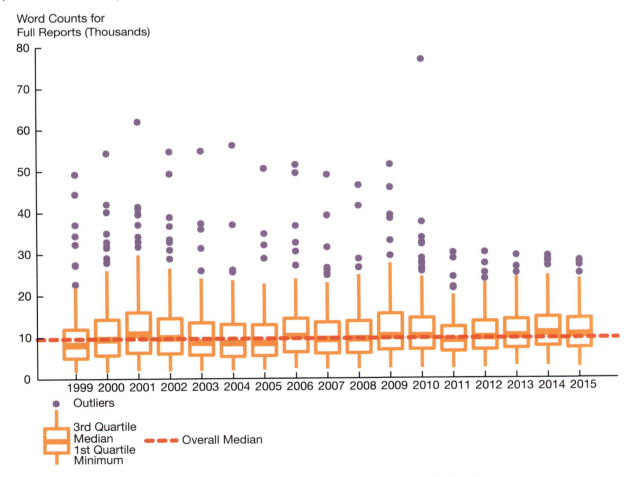

Figure 10.2 Word Counts in State Department Human Rights Reports, by Year, 1999–2015
Note: This figure shows boxplots for the word counts of the State Department Human Rights Reports (N=3,281).

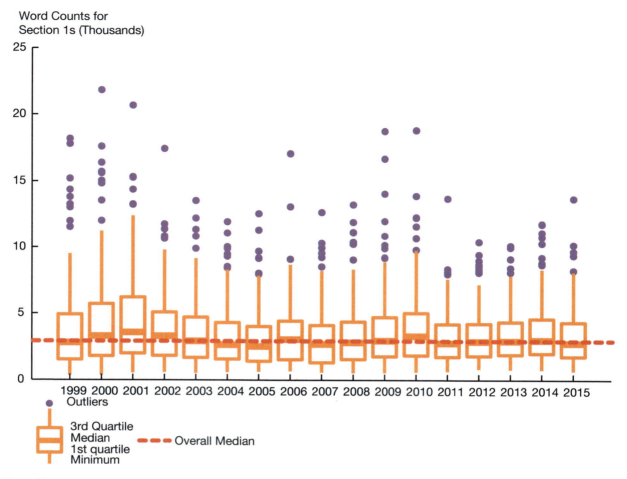

Figure 10.3 Word Counts in Section 1s of State Department Human Rights Reports, by Year, 1999–2015
Note: This figure shows boxplots for the word counts of Section 1s of the State Department Human Rights Reports (N=3,281).

To examine the country-level trends, Table 10.2 reports the results of three specifications to estimate the effect of time (years) on word counts. Columns 1 and 4 present estimates of pooled OLS regressions. Columns 2 and 5 account for within-country variation by including country fixed effects. Columns 3 and 6 represent average marginal effects obtained from kernel regularized least squares (KRLS) regressions.[2]

Table 10.2 Time Effects for Word Counts, 1999–2015

Dependent Variable: Word Count (thousands)						
Regressor	OLS full report	OLS full report	KRLS full report	OLS Section 1	OLS Section 1	KRLS Section 1
Intercept	−40.897	−29.633		79.439*	86.706*	
	(49.122)	(21.967)		(18.317)	(9.396)	
Year	0.025	0.023	0.005	−0.037*	−0.040*	−0.027*
	(0.003)	(0.011)	(0.006)	(0.009)	(0.005)	(0.006)
N	3,281	3,281	3,281	3,281	3,281	3,281
R2	0.00	0.81	0.00	0.01	0.81	0.01
Fixed effects	no	yes	no	no	yes	no

Note: This table shows the coefficients (OLS) or average marginal effects (KRLS), with standard errors in parentheses, of regressions of word counts on year. * indicates significance at $p < 0.05$.

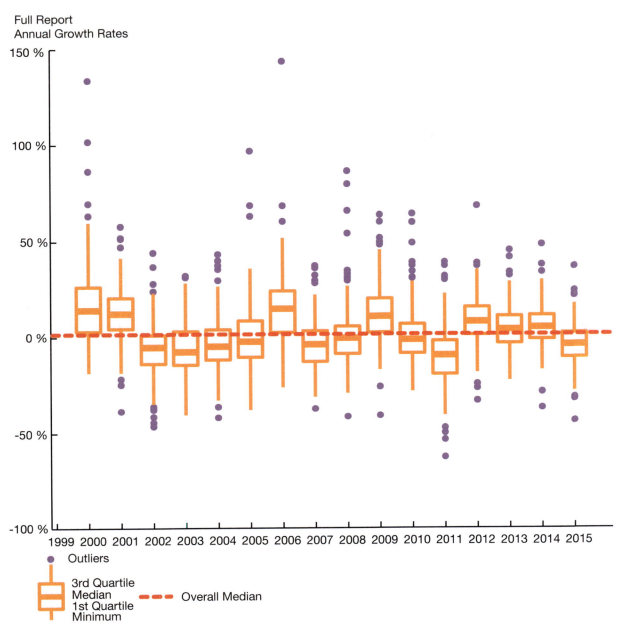

Figure 10.4 Annual Growth Rates of State Department Human Rights Reports, 1999–2015
Note: This figure shows boxplots for the annual growth rates of the State Department Human Rights Reports (N=3,092).

According to the basic specification, full reports grew by about 25 words per year, though this effect is not statistically discernible from zero (Column 1). The fixed effects specification yields a statistically significant estimate of an increase of 23 words per year (Column 2). The effect shrinks to about five words per year when accounting for potential non-linearities, though the effect is again not statistically significant (Column 3). Over the entire period, therefore, the estimations suggest that full reports may have grown by an average of between 85 and 425 words. In our view, the extent of the growth is negligible, taking into account the length of reports. The increase amounts to 1–5%, which is of a scale that would not be expected to have a marked impact on PTS scores. In fact, we show later that the extent of the increase is substantively unimportant in terms of the effect.

Meanwhile, the estimations indicate that Section 1s have actually become slightly shorter over time, by an average of 37 words per year according to the basic specification (Column 4), 40 words with the fixed effects specification (Column 5), and 27 words when accounting for potential non-linearities (Column 6). All of these estimates are statistically significant. Yet, the downward trend is modest, with an average decline of between 459 and 680 words over the period, or 5–8% relative to the typical length of Section 1s. We show later that this scale of change is also substantively unimportant.

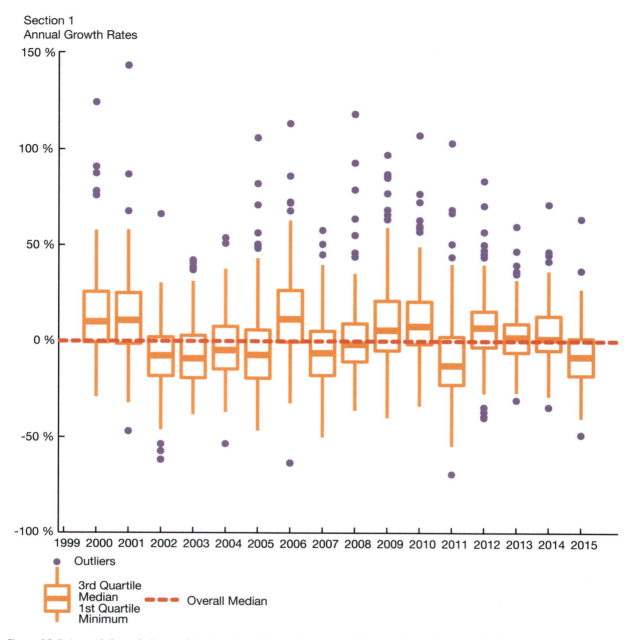

Figure 10.5 Annual Growth Rates of Section 1s of State Department Human Rights Reports, 1999–2015
Note: This figure shows boxplots for the annual growth rates of Section 1s of the State Department Human Rights Reports (N=3,092).

These same conclusions hold when estimating separate models for each country. Overall, the average marginal effects of time on word count are positive for full reports (Figure 10.6) and negative for Section 1s (Figure 10.7). Yet most of the effects cluster around zero, within +/− 250 words per year.

In sum, the temporal trends in report length that we detect are slight – and not necessarily in the direction that supports the claims of the critics. Far from growing by large amounts, the relevant content may actually be shrinking.

Report Length and the PTS

The question remains whether any relationship exists between the length of reports and PTS scores. If Clark and Sikkink (2013) and Fariss (2014) are correct, longer reports are more likely to document, and in greater detail, violations of physical integrity rights than shorter reports. Consequently, longer reports are expected to be coded with higher PTS scores, on average. The claims focus on changes in report length over time. We already demonstrated, however, that reports have

Are Human Rights Conditions Improving?

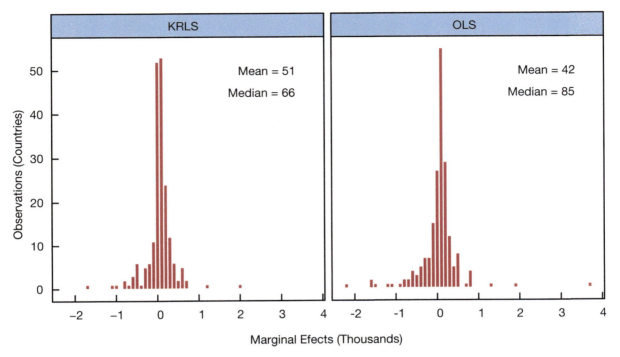

Figure 10.6 Within-Country Time Effects on Full Report Word Counts, 1999–2015
Note: This figure shows histograms of (average) marginal effects for KRLS regressions (left panel) and OLS regressions (right panel) of full report word counts on year.

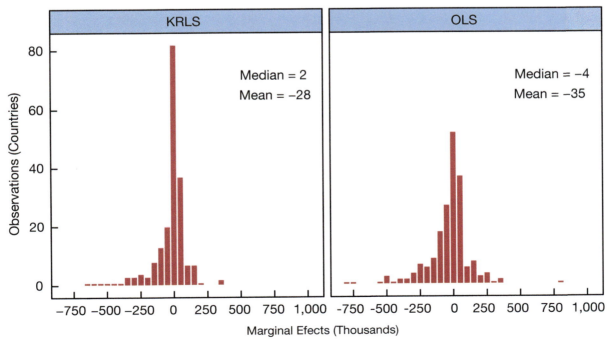

Figure 10.7 Within-Country Time Effects on Section 1 Word Counts, 1999–2015
Note: This figure shows histograms of (average) marginal effects for KRLS regressions (left panel) and OLS regressions (right panel) of Section 1 word counts on year.

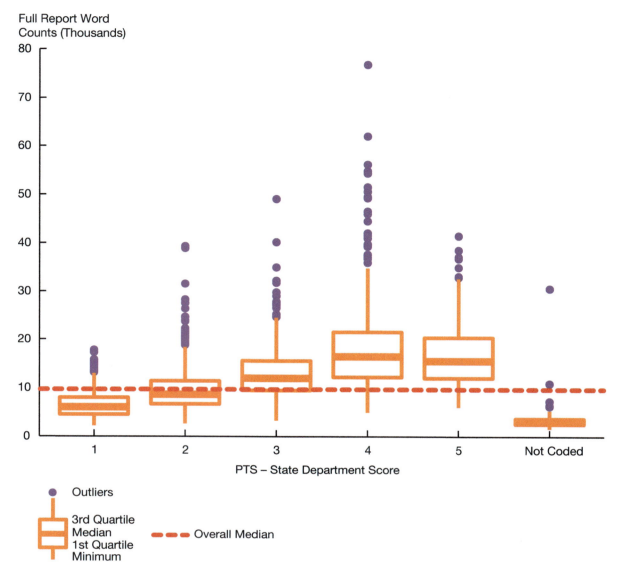

Figure 10.8 Full Report Word Counts by PTS Scores, 1999–2014
Note: This figure shows boxplots for the word counts of the State Department Human Rights Reports (N = 3,086; 232 reports were not coded).

not trended toward substantially greater lengths. In any event, the underlying logic – that report length introduces bias – can still be examined.

Figure 10.8 illustrates the relationship between the word counts of full reports and PTS scores from 1999–2014 (the last year for which PTS scores were available when the analysis was conducted). The median word count of reports that are coded with a score of 5 is almost 2.5 times greater than the median word count of reports that are coded 1.[3] Figure 10.9 presents the analogous results for Section 1s. Here, the relationship between word count and PTS scores is even more pronounced. The median word count of Section 1s of reports coded with a score of 5 is more than 4.5 times greater than the median count of Section 1s of reports coded with a score of 1.

On an aggregate basis, therefore, report length appears to be a strong predictor of PTS scores. The worst PTS scores tend to be associated with longer reports, whereas the best PTS scores are associated with shorter reports, consistent with the claims advanced by Clark and Sikkink (2013) and Fariss (2014).

To be thorough, examining relationships at a country level is crucial. Table 10.3 reports the results of three specifications to estimate the effect of word counts (in thousands) on PTS scores. Columns 1 and 4 present estimates of pooled

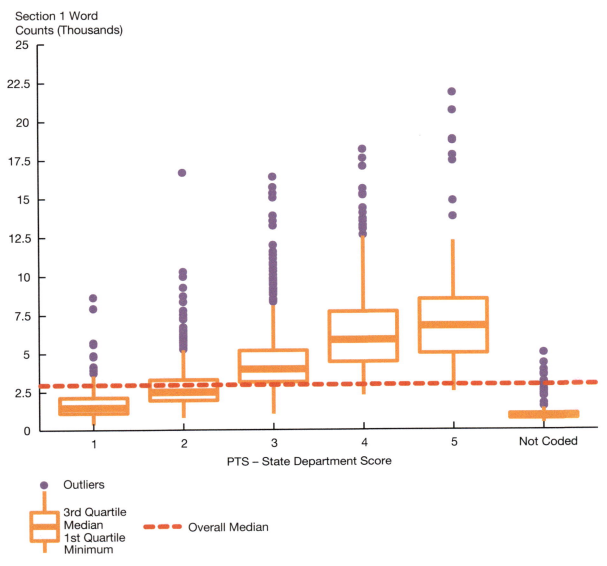

Figure 10.9 Section 1 Word Counts by PTS Scores, 1999–2014
Note: This figure shows boxplots for the Section 1 word counts of the State Department Human Rights Reports (N = 3,086; 232 reports were not coded).

OLS regressions. Columns 2 and 5 account for within-country variation by including country-fixed effects. Columns 3 and 6 represent average marginal effects obtained from KRLS regressions.

According to the basic specification, a 1,000-word increase in the length of a full report is associated, on average, with a 0.09-point increase on the five-point PTS scale (Column 1). This means that a one-point increase in the PTS score would be expected only with an increase of over 11,000 words, which is a large amount considering that the median length of a full report is less than 10,000 words and the standard deviation is less than 7,000 words (see Table 10.1, p. 90). Meanwhile, a one-point increase in the PTS score would be expected only with nearly a 3,500-word increase of the length of Section 1 (Column 4 in Table 10.3). Consider here that the median length of a Section 1 is around 3,000 words and the standard deviation is around 2,600 words (see Table 10.1). When accounting for potential non-linearities, the estimated average marginal effects are substantively larger. On average, a 1,000-word increase in a full report is associated with a 0.14-point increase in the PTS score (Column 3 in Table 10.3), meaning that about 7,000 words equates to a one-point increase in the score. Meanwhile a 1,000-word increase in Section 1 is associated with a 0.44-point increase in the PTS score (Column 6 in Table 10.3), so about 2,250 words equates to a one-point increase in the score. All these results are statistically significant.

Table 10.3 Relationship between Word Count Estimates and PTS Scores, 1999–2014

Dependent Variable: PTS Score						
Regressor	OLS Full Report	OLS Full Report	KRLS Full Report	OLS Section 1	OLS Section 1	KRLS Section 1
Intercept	1.422*	4.430*		1.397*	4.347*	
	(0.034)	(0.133)		(0.027)	(0.130)	
Words/1000	0.093*	0.020*	0.142*	0.292*	0.064*	0.443*
	(0.003)	(0.003)	(0.004)	(0.006)	(0.007)	(0.010)
N	2,854	2,854	2,854	2,854	2,854	2,854
R2	0.32	0.81	0.42	0.45	0.81	0.57
Fixed effects	no	yes	no	no	yes	no

Note: This table shows the coefficients (OLS) or average marginal effects (KRLS), with standard errors in parentheses, for regressions of PTS scores on word counts (in thousands) from 1999–2014; * indicates significance at p

One aspect these analyses overlook is the nature of within-country variability of report lengths. Figure 10.10 presents histograms of the within-country standard deviations of word counts for full reports and Section 1s. The median standard deviations are less than 2,000 words and 1,000 words, respectively. Thus, the standard deviations for the full sample are misleading: within-country variation is more modest. The estimates that take account of within-country variation show that the associations between word counts and PTS scores are exceedingly small (Columns 2 and 5 in Table 10.3). An increase of 1,000 words in a full report corresponds to a 0.02-point increase in the PTS score, so a full report would have to be 50,000 words longer to expect a one-point increase in the score. Meanwhile, an increase of 1,000 words in Section 1 corresponds to a 0.06 increase in the PTS score, so a Section 1 would have to be more than 16,000 words longer to expect a one-point increase in the score.

Figure 10.11 presents histograms of average marginal effects for 162 separate KRLS regressions of PTS scores on word counts (in thousands) – one regression for each country with non-constant PTS scores. For the full reports, the average marginal effects cluster around zero, with a median average marginal effect of 0.007 points per 1,000 words. For Section 1s, the average marginal effects also cluster around zero, with a median average marginal effect of 0.031 points per 1,000 words. Needless to say, these effect sizes are miniscule.

We believe the findings from the analysis conducted at a country level demonstrate that report length is ultimately a substantively weak predictor of PTS scores. Only unusually large changes of the length of the reports will be expected to have a meaningful effect on PTS scores. Within countries, however, these reports are virtually constant in length over time: for example, the report on China has always been long, whereas the report on Nauru has always been short.

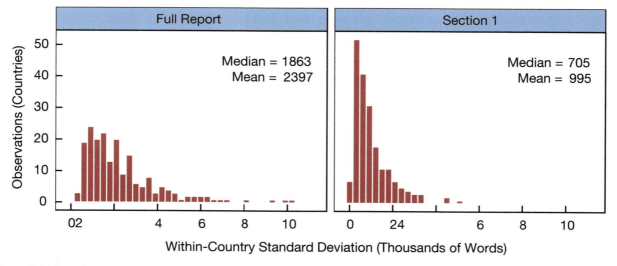

Figure 10.10 Within-Country Variability of Report Word Counts, 1999–2015
Note: This figure shows histograms of the within-country standard deviations of word counts for full reports (left panel) and Section 1s (right panel).

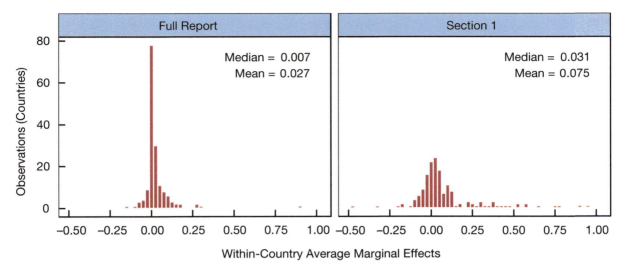

Figure 10.11 Within-Country Effects of Word Counts on PTS Scores, 1999–2014
Note: This figure shows histograms of average marginal effects from KRLS regressions of PTS scores on word counts (in thousands) for full reports (left panel) and Section 1s (right panel). Each regression corresponds to a single country. The analysis drops observations for countries with only one coded report, as well as countries with constant PTS scores over the period.

Applying the results, the trend toward a slight increase in the length of full reports from 1999–2015 (see Table 10.2) may bias PTS scores upward by no more than 0.01 points on the five-point scale over the entire time period, while the trend toward a modest decrease in the length of Section 1s from 1999–2015 (see again Table 10.2) may bias PTS scores downward by 0.03–0.05 points over this time period.

In sum, we feel secure in concluding that the estimated effects of report lengths on PTS scores are far too inconsequential to support the critiques raised by Clark and Sikkink (2013) and Fariss (2014). Any effects are vanishingly small, in both absolute and relative terms. Of crucial importance, the scale of the effects is not of a degree that would alter findings about long-term trends. In addition, the results for the analysis of Section 1s indicate that any measurable bias is actually in the opposite direction of what the critics claim.

Conclusion

Critics argue that measures of human rights conditions – including PTS scores – are biased. They maintain that reporting practices have changed, yielding reports that continue to grow longer and more detailed over time. In their view, additional length and depth is entirely an artifact of the evolution of monitoring capacity, rather than indicative of greater evidence unearthed by human rights monitors that documents deteriorating human rights practices. As a result, they believe that measurement is prone to inflate scores for recent years and/or to understate scores for earlier years, as a function of the nature of reporting. The upshot of the purported biases is to diminish the extent of changes in global human rights conditions over time, when the true trend is going in a positive direction.

In this chapter, we showed that the length of human rights reports published by the US State Department did not increase significantly, if at all, during the 1999–2015 time period. Our analysis also indicates that report length does serve as a useful predictor of PTS scores – longer reports are associated with worse PTS scores. Yet, the explanatory power serves only as a means to distinguish among the entire pool of country reports. The effect is washed out when we account for within-country variation in report lengths, which is relatively small and not predictive of PTS scores. Another way of stating this conclusion is that we are able to differentiate China's PTS scores from Liechtenstein's scores based on the lengths of their respective reports, but report length does not help to differentiate China's 1999 report from China's 2007 report. Thus, report lengths have a negligible impact on trends in conditions both within and across countries.

Our analysis is not definitive, since we covered just the most recent 17 years, PTS scores, the State Department reports, and the metric of word counts. Conducting a more complete assessment, to address the full spirit of the critiques of Clark and Sikkink (2013) and Fariss (2014), would require extending the analysis back in time, examining CIRI scores and considering Amnesty International reports as well, and evaluating other meaningful indicators of report content. In this regard, we encourage scholars to think carefully about alternative mechanisms that might shape human rights reports and bias measures of human rights conditions.

Notes

1 Word counts include all section headers, numbers, abbreviations, and stop words.
2 KRLS flexibly fits the response surface and finds the best-fitting functional form from a large space of smooth functions, rather than assuming a particular functional form and relying on linearity or additivity (Hainmueller and Hazlett 2014). The technique produces estimates of partial derivatives characterizing the marginal effects of each regressor at each data point, thus combining the versatility of generalized additive models with the interpretability of OLS estimates (Hainmueller and Hazlett 2014: 144). Using KRLS is appropriate in this context to allow for the estimation of quantities of interest that are readily interpretable, while at the same time guarding against misspecification bias.
3 Uncoded reports – typically those of small or micro-states (e.g., Andorra, Liechtenstein, Nauru) – tend to be significantly shorter than coded reports. As such, missingness of PTS scores is not random.

References

Cingranelli, David, and David Richards (2010) "The Cingranelli and Richards (CIRI) Human Rights Data Project." *Human Rights Quarterly* 32(3): 401–424.

Clark, Ann Marie, and Kathryn Sikkink (2013) "Information Effects and Human Rights Data: Is the Good News about Increased Human Rights Information Bad News for Human Rights Measures?" *Human Rights Quarterly* 35(3): 539–568.

Fariss, Christopher J. (2014) "Respect for Human Rights Has Improved Over Time: Modeling the Changing Standard of Accountability." *American Political Science Review* 108(2): 297–318.

Hainmueller, Jens, and Chad Hazlett (2014) "Kernel Regularized Least Squares: Moving Beyond Linearity and Additivity with a Flexible and Interpretable Machine Learning Approach." *Political Analysis* 22(2): 143–168.

Poe, Steven C., Sabine C. Carey, and Tonya C. Vazquez (2001) "How are These Pictures Different: A Qualitative Comparison of the US State Department and Amnesty International Human Rights Reports, 1976–1995." *Human Rights Quarterly* 23(3): 650–677.

Wood, Reed, and Mark Gibney (2010) "The Political Terror Scale (PTS): A Re-Introduction and a Comparison to CIRI." *Human Rights Quarterly* 32(3): 367–400.

11

The Peace and Conflict Instability Ledger 2017

A New Methodology and Ranking of Countries on Forecasted Risks

David A. Backer, Jacob Aronson, and Paul K. Huth

Introduction

The Peace and Conflict Instability Ledger (PCIL) consists of country-level assessments of the likelihood of observing phenomena with significant potential to disrupt governmental functions, including the ability to exercise meaningful authority and to deliver core services. The Center for International Development and Conflict Management (CIDCM) at the University of Maryland developed the original version of the PCIL in 2008 (Hewitt 2008).[1] Ever since, CIDCM has compiled the PCIL on an annual basis. In 2015, CIDCM redesigned the PCIL methodology, markedly improving the quality and utility of this resource. The new methodology was enhanced in 2016. The analysis now yields separate forecasts of the risk of adverse regime change, internal war, state-based mass killing, and non-state mass killing, as well as the overall risk of observing any of these phenomena. The forecasts are based on estimations of models tailored to account for the particular nature of each of these types of instability, using the most recent available empirical data and state-of-the art statistical techniques.

This chapter presents the latest results of the PCIL, which forecast risks for the three-year period of 2015–2017. Before discussing those results, we describe the motivations for the redesign initiated in 2015, highlighting the strengths and limitations of the previous methodology, then detail the new methodology. The findings once again reveal that the worst vulnerabilities to serious instability are concentrated in countries across Sub-Saharan Africa and South Asia. These forecasts provide important guidance for major stakeholders with concerns about conflict preparedness and management.

Previous Methodology

The original PCIL had several strengths. The methodology reflected a synthesis of leading research on conceptualizing, explaining, and forecasting political instability. In particular, the analysis employed the definition established by the Political Instability Task Force (PITF) of state failure events, which encompassed a wide variety of types, including adverse regime changes, revolutionary wars, ethnic wars, genocides and politicides. While the set of events is heterogeneous, they share a fundamental similarity: their occurrence signals a disruption of the normal capacity of a government to exercise authority and to deliver services. In addition, these events are of clear interest to multiple stakeholders who work on issues related to conflicts and crises, including influential governmental and intergovernmental agencies, as well as leading non-governmental organizations, around the world. For purposes of the PCIL, forecasts of instability outcomes were generated via a theoretically-driven statistical model. The specification of this model involved identifying factors for which agreement about their relative importance was consistent among researchers. Empirical analysis confirmed historical associations between instability and five factors: regime characteristics (especially inconsistent institutions and factionalism), infant mortality, economic openness, the level of militarization, and civil war in a neighboring country. Using this parsimonious list of factors, the model was able to forecast instability outcomes with a strong degree of accuracy: generally around 80%. The analysis afforded global coverage, spanning more than 160 countries (all of those with populations of at least 500,000), and relied on data that are publicly available, readily accessible, and regularly updated for these countries. The approach was designed and implemented by leading scholars and vetted through an academic peer-review process.

Though the PCIL functioned well over several years, certain concerns arose in the wake of the Arab Spring about the reliability of the methodology. Several countries in the Middle East and North African region were not classified according to the PCIL as being at a heightened risk of instability, yet experienced adverse regime change and/or serious violence, within the 2011–2013 timeframe. In particular, the PCIL methodology tended to discount the prospects of upheaval materializing in long-standing, seemingly entrenched autocracies like those in Egypt, Libya, Syria, and Tunisia.

These concerns prompted CIDCM to revisit the PCIL methodology, with the aim of considering appropriate modifications to make improvements where warranted. This review identified a number of shortcomings, which contributed to the deficiencies in anticipating the Arab Spring cases and more broadly constrained the quality and utility of results that the methodology yielded.

The most prominent shortcoming was the reliance on a single model in the statistical estimation of risk. This model employed an amalgamated binary dependent variable, reflecting the occurrence of any of three types of instability: adverse regime change, internal war (ethnic or revolutionary), and genocide/politicide. Resulting forecasts could not indicate which of these types of instability was projected to occur, since the dependent variable lacked those delineations.

Also, the statistical estimation was restricted to a subset of the country-year observations, excluding those that exhibited active internal wars. Projecting outcomes in countries already experiencing such conflict was nominally outside the scope of the analysis. Consequently, the estimations did not contemplate vital questions: Are internal wars expected to continue? Are countries experiencing internal war susceptible to other types of instability? Despite these gaps in the design, forecasts of the risk of instability were actually calculated for all country-years, without regard for their status in terms of active internal war. Such an application goes well beyond the design of the methodology and the cases for which the results are valid.

Further shortcomings were evident in the model specification, which omits factors that are potentially prominent drivers of instability. The model specification in the original PCIL methodology was not fully faithful to PITF's final results: among other things, variables for regime characteristics were not implemented in the exact same way. In addition, the original PCIL model specification lacked a number of types of variables with solid theoretical rationales that have been demonstrated empirically to influence instability. Some of these variables were tested previously by PITF, using data available at the time, and not found to be statistically significant. Yet certain variables were never evaluated. Of note, the PCIL methodology ignored conceivable relationships among the several different types of instability.

Finally, the original PCIL methodology had remained static since the initial implementation in 2008. Risk estimates continued to be based on results from the same training model, using the same specification and run on a dataset spanning 1950–2003. Among the reasons for the static foundation were understandable preferences for continuity in the analysis and comparability in the results across cycles of forecasts. Yet a thorough process for reassessment and updating had been lacking. Whether the training model still performs effectively to capture contemporary risks – or gains in forecasting could be made by altering the methodology – warrants periodic verification.

Updated Methodology

The new PCIL addresses each of these shortcomings. The essential aim remains the same: to forecast the risk of serious instability. A key improvement is to produce separate forecasts of the risks of adverse regime change, internal war, state-based mass killing, and non-state mass killing. In addition, distinct estimations are performed for the risk of onset of internal war and the risk of ongoing internal war. The individual models are tailored with factors suited to the respective dependent variables, accounting for influences among types of instability as well. The risk analysis appropriately encompasses all relevant country-years, regardless of whether or not they exhibited active conflict. The period of the data used in the analysis is extended to be as current as possible, feeding into the re-estimation of the models, to be updated with each cycle.

This section presents a technical description of the new methodology, including the measures of instability, the analytical framework, the model specifications, the estimation procedures and results, the model diagnostics, and the process of calculating risk scores and generating risk classifications.

Measures of Instability

Table 11.1 presents the definitions and data sources for the four types of instability that are forecast. The new PCIL preserves the measurement of adverse regime change, based on the PITF definition and data. Measurement of internal war now employs data obtained from the Uppsala Conflict Data Program (UCDP), with an adjusted definition. State-based mass killing was substituted in place of genocide/politicide as part of the 2015 redesign of the PCIL, then non-state mass killing was added in the 2016 enhancement of the methodology. Both outcome measures rely again on UCDP for definitions and data. All these choices reflect the best available country-level indicators of instability, in terms of accessibility, broad geographic and temporal coverage, quality, empirical relevance, and analytical value.

Table 11.1 Types of Instability: Definitions and Data Sources

Type of Instability	Definition	Data Source
Adverse Regime Change	Significant, negative alteration to the pattern of governance in a given country-year, including: major, abrupt shifts from more open, electoral systems to more closed, authoritarian systems; revolutionary overhaul in political elites and the mode of governance; contested dissolution of federated states or secession of a substantial area of a state by extrajudicial means; or complete or near-total collapse of central state authority and the ability to govern	Political Instability Task Force
Internal War	Contested incompatibility, concerning control of government and/or territory, between organized non-state armed group(s) and the government of a state, where these actors use force that has resulted in at least 25 battle-related deaths in a given country-year and at least 1,000 conflict-related deaths for any group-state dyad over the course of the conflict	Uppsala Conflict Data Program
State-Based Mass Killing	Internationally recognized government of a state uses armed force that intentionally kills at least 100 civilians in a given country-year	Uppsala Conflict Data Program
Non-State Mass Killing	Organized rebel group uses armed force that intentionally kills at least 100 civilians in a given country-year	Uppsala Conflict Data Program

Separate statistical estimations are conducted to forecast the future risks of each of the four types of instability. The results are subsequently aggregated into an overall forecast that one or more of these types will be observed in the future. Thus, the results now have five main elements, in contrast to the single element that comprised the original PCIL. These five elements offer a rich, nuanced perspective on understanding the extent and nature of vulnerability to instability.

Framework of Analysis

The new PCIL methodology retains the basic approach used in the past, which relies on establishing the relationship between instability outcomes and relevant risk factors according to comparative historical data. This objective is accomplished by conducting statistical estimations of "training" models for each of the four types of instability; the original PCIL methodology was limited to a single training model. The sequence of steps is outlined in Figure 11.1.

The models of adverse regime change (Step 1), state-based mass killing (Step 3) and non-state mass killing (Step 4) do not distinguish between new advents and cases with histories of similar events that carry over from the previous year (i.e., ongoing instability) or were observed in prior years (i.e., recurring instability). A simplified approach was favored for a

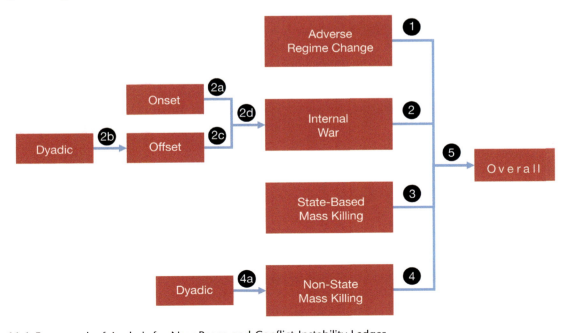

Figure 11.1 Framework of Analysis for New Peace and Conflict Instability Ledger

number of reasons. Datasets tend to record an adverse regime change in the year when this outcome was consummated. A subsequent adverse regime change is recorded as a discrete event, rather than a continuation of the prior event, even if related. Since adverse regime change is not generally treated as a prolonged episode extending over multiple years, modeling the persistence of such instability from year to year is superfluous. At most, the analysis could account for any prior – especially recent – adverse regime change as a potential risk factor for further instability of this sort. In contrast, both state-based mass killing and non-state mass killing can be episodes sustained over multiple years. Thus, the notion of separately modeling the onset and persistence of mass killing is plausible. In theory, certain factors (e.g., international sanctions) may influence whether mass killing persists that do not necessarily affect the onset of mass killing. Our explorations along those lines, however, yielded no appreciable gains in terms of reliably forecasting these particular types of instability. Therefore, the models of both state-based mass killing and non-state mass killing simply consider whether these types of instability transpire, not whether they continue from previous years.

Internal war is approached in a different manner. Some internal wars are brief, but many last multiple years and even decades. Consequently, forecasts of internal war ought to address both onset (i.e., whether war begins) and offset (whether war ends, or persists). As mentioned earlier, the latter aspect was a gap in the original PCIL methodology. Addressing the gap appropriately in the analysis requires taking into account a well-established literature that identifies divergent sets of factors influencing onset and offset. Another key consideration is the numerous instances where multiple organized armed rebel groups are engaged simultaneously in fighting against the government within the same country, as part of one or more active internal wars. The offset of internal war in a country requires the termination of every active dyad, each comprised of a single rebel group and the government against which the group is fighting. Certain dyads – and wars – may be more likely to persist than others, because of their respective characteristics. As a result of this variation, a country with multiple dyads could remain in active conflict even if a given dyad terminates. At the same time, the outcome of one dyad could affect outcomes of any other dyads in a country. While the risk of internal war is ultimately forecast at the country level, taking into account these dimensions of individual wars, down to the dyadic level, is important to ensure comprehensive, incisive forecasts.

With these aspects in mind, we analyze internal war via a multi-stage process. To start, a model of onset, covering country-years not exhibiting active internal wars, is estimated (Step 2a). Next, a model of offset at the dyadic level is estimated for country-years with active internal wars (Step 2b). By doing so, new data on rebel capabilities – some compiled by CIDCM – can also be leveraged. Based on the results, the dyad in a given country-year that is least likely to experience offset (i.e., drop and stay below a threshold of 25 battle-related deaths in all three subsequent years) can be identified. The corresponding probabilities for those dyads are then used as a factor in a model of offset of internal war at the country-year level (Step 2c). At this stage, offset requires every dyad active in a given country-year to drop and stay below a threshold of 25 battle-related deaths in all three subsequent years. The forecasted probabilities of onset (for country-years without active internal war) and offset (for country-years with active internal war) are combined to produce forecasts of the future risk of observing internal war (Step 2d).

The analysis of non-state mass killing has an analogous aspect, in order to reflect circumstances where multiple rebel groups are active and the potential for the violence that one group commits to affect the actions of another group. Existing literature articulates reasons why the influence could be unfavorable ("outbidding," i.e., groups compete to demonstrate coercive power) or favorable (reputational advantages of exhibiting distinction from groups that violate norms of affording civilians protection from violence) in terms of the association with the potential of engaging mass killing. Therefore, non-state mass killing is initially analyzed at a dyadic level (Step 4a). Based on the results, the dyad in a given country-year that is most likely to engage in mass killing is identified. The corresponding probability is incorporated as a risk factor in an analysis conducted at the country-year level, to assess the risk of any rebel group committing such large-scale atrocities.

Finally, the separate estimated probabilities of the four types of instability are combined to give an overall estimate of the probability of observing at least one of the types of instability (Step 5).

Model Specification

In each training model, the value of the dependent variable for an observation on a country or dyad in year t reflects whether or not a particular instability outcome transpired during the subsequent three-year period from year $t+1$ to year $t+3$. Adverse regime change, onset of internal war, state-based mass killing, and non-state mass killing are each considered to have transpired if the outcome happened in any of the three subsequent years. For example, an observation for Country A in 2007 would reflect whether the given type of instability occurred during 2008, 2009 and/or 2010. Offset of internal war requires that rebel-state dyads active in year t terminate in year $t+1$ and remain terminated through year $t+3$.[2]

The final specifications of the several country-year and dyad-year training models include a total of over 40 risk factors, as summarized in Table 11.2. For this purpose, we draw on indicators at the international, country, regime, conflict, and actor levels, as well as our forecasts of instability outcomes. In contrast, the previous PCIL methodology only considered a small number of factors at the international, country, and regime levels. Incorporating more layers of factors is consistent with the latest trends in empirical research on instability. Studies still acknowledge structural conditions as background influences, but increasingly delve into specific contexts, events, and agents and examine relationships among processes. The additional layers also accomplish a priority of ensuring that the analysis sufficiently reflects the levels at which pertinent dynamics actually unfold in practice. Each risk factor was selected based on theoretical relevance and the availability of empirical data with the requisite temporal and geographic scope. Table 11.2 lists key literature that serves as justification of the risk factors, as well as the sources of data used in the analysis. The final specifications take into account the theoretical importance and statistical significance of each indicator evaluated in the estimations, as well as their contributions to model performance. Additional risk factors were considered in the analysis, but omitted from the final model specifications on those grounds.

Estimation Procedure

All the statistical estimations of the models employ the same basic approach, which involves a series of tasks repeated in 3,000 runs. First, two samples of observations are drawn at random, with replacement (i.e., allowing duplicates), from the full data. The sample used as training data corresponds to 85% of the full data, while the sample used as test data corresponds to the remaining 15%. The full data for the models of adverse regime change and internal war cover 1975–2010.[3] In this cycle of analysis, the full data for the models of state-based mass killing and non-state mass killing cover 1989–2010, since the UCDP dataset on one-sided violence only goes back to 1989. Second, the training model is estimated on the random set of training data, using logit regression. Third, the coefficient estimates from the training model are applied to the random set of test data to forecast outcomes. Fourth, performance metrics are gathered for both the training model estimation and the forecasts using the test data. The runs yield distributions of results and performance metrics, which are averaged across the runs. This bootstrapping approach mitigates against generating results that hinge on arbitrary choices of which country-years to use as training or test data. Instead, the reported results are composites using a diversity of many samples of country-years and dyad-years.

Results of Estimations of Training Models

Table 11.3 presents the results of the estimations of the several training models.

The **model of adverse regime change** includes 10 risk factors, from four categories. The results of the estimation indicate that the expected prospect of observing such a change was higher during the Cold War, as well as in countries with greater levels of infant mortality, partial or factionalized democracy or a failed state, a new onset of armed conflict, and longer exposures to armed conflict. The expected probability was lower in countries with greater levels of economic growth and judicial independence, as well as those experiencing low-level conflict. All the results are consistent with theoretical logic, in terms of directions of effects.

The **model of the onset of internal war** includes 10 risk factors, spanning all six categories. The expected prospect of observing onset was higher during the Cold War and in countries with greater levels of infant mortality, larger populations, partial democracy or a failed state, low-level conflict, bigger aggrieved ethnic groups with affinities favoring a rebel group, and a higher likelihood of adverse regime change. The expected prospect of onset was lower in countries facing civil war in neighboring countries, as well as countries with democratic regimes. Most of the results are consistent with theoretical logic, in terms of directions of effects. The lone exception is the negative association between the risk of onset of internal war and existing civil war(s) in neighboring countries, whereas a positive relationship could be hypothesized due to spillover effects.

The **dyad-year model of the offset of internal war** includes 15 risk factors, from two categories. The expected prospect of observing offset was higher in conventional and semi-conventional conflicts, as well as when battle-related deaths have dropped, an irregular change of the leader of the government or a rebel group has occurred, the size of rebel forces declined substantially, other rebel groups are active, and negotiations occur between governments and rebel groups. The expected prospect of offset was lower when a conflict had lasted over five years, the government had been supported by external forces or had greater forces relative to the other conflict actors, and rebel groups had more secure shelter within the country. Also, the size of rebel forces has a negative but diminishing association with the expected prospect of offset. All the results are consistent with theoretical logic, in terms of directions of effects.

Table 11.2 Factors in Models of Instability Risk

Category Indicator	Description	Theoretical Relevance	Data Source(s)	Adverse Regime Change	Internal War		State-Based Mass Killing	Non-State Mass Killing
					Onset	Offset		
INTERNATIONAL CONTEXT FACTORS								
Cold War	Whether or not year is before 1990	Kalyvas and Balcells (2010)	Created for PCIL	■	■	■	■	
Neighboring civil war	Number of countries with shared borders that are experiencing active internal armed conflict	Salehyan and Gleditsch (2006)	Melander et al. (2016)		■	■		
COUNTRY-LEVEL (STRUCTURAL) FACTORS								
Infant mortality	Normalized rate	Fearon and Laitin (2003)	World Bank (2016)	■	■		■	■
GDP per capita growth	Annual rate	Gassebne et al. (2016)	World Bank (2016)	■				
Population	Number of people in country	Hegre et al. (2013)	World Bank (2016)		■	■	■	■
Population density	Number of people in country per square mile	Hegre et al. (2013)	World Bank (2016)					▣
REGIME-LEVEL (INSTITUTIONAL) FACTORS								
Partial democracy	Some executive restraints and non-polarized party competition	Goldstone et al. (2010)	Marshall (2011)	■	■			
Factionalized democracy	Some executive restraints; polarized parties	Goldstone et al. (2010)	Marshall (2011)	■			■	
Democracy	Full executive restraints; competitive parties	Goldstone et al. (2010)	Marshall (2011)		■			
State failure	Country lacks functioning government	Hegre et al. (2013)	Marshall (2011)	■	■			
Judicial independence	Extent of undue influence and implementation of decisions	Linzer and Staton (2015)	Linzer and Staton (2015)	■			■	
CONFLICT-LEVEL FACTORS								
Conflict type	Conventional vs. semi-conventional vs. guerilla	Balcells and Kalyvas (2014)	Balcells and Kalyvas (2014)			▣		
New conflict onset	Internal armed conflict started in current year	Collier et al. (2004)	Melander et al. (2016)	■				
Ongoing conflict	Any internal armed conflict in previous year	Collier et al. (2004)	Melander et al. (2016)					■
Low-level conflict	Dyad ≥25 battle-related deaths in country-year but <1,000 deaths to date	Findley and Young (2012)	Melander et al. (2016)	■	■			

Table 11.2 Factors in Models of Instability Risk – continued

Category Indicator	Description	Theoretical Relevance	Data Source(s)	Adverse Regime Change	Internal War		State-Based Mass Killing	Non-State Mass Killing
					Onset	Offset		
Duration of conflict	Number of years internal armed conflict has been ongoing	Walter (2009)	Melander et al. (2016)	■		▣		▣
Drop in conflict severity	Decline in battle-related deaths of ≥2/3 relative to previous year	Hultman (2007)	Melander et al. (2016)			▣		
Lootable resources	Gems or diamonds available to actors engaged in internal armed conflict	Buhaug et al. (2009)	Lujala (2009) Lujala et al. (2005); Buhaug and Lujala (2005)			■	■	
Peace negotiations	Government and rebel group in dyad conduct negotiations	Slantchev (2003)	UCDP (2016)			▣		
ACTOR-LEVEL FACTORS								
Government leader loss	Irregular change of head of government	Prorok (2016)	Aronson et al. (2016)			▣		
Government force balance	Number of government forces relative to number of other forces	McGrath (2006)	Aronson et al. (2016)			▣		
External support to government	Number of external military forces supporting government	Sullivan and Karreth (2015)	Aronson et al. (2016)			▣		▣
Government mass killing	Government committed large-scale deliberate killings of civilians during previous year	Linke et al. (2012)	Eck and Hultman (2007)					▣
Rebel leader loss	Irregular change of head of rebel group	Johnston (2012)	Aronson et al. (2016)			▣		▣
Rebel founding leader loss	Irregular change of founder of rebel group	Johnston (2012)	Aronson et al. (2016)					▣
Rebel founding leader killed	Founder of rebel group was killed	Johnston (2012)	Aronson et al. (2016)					▣
Rebel group count	Number of rebel groups involved in internal armed conflict	Cunningham (2006)	Melander et al. (2016)			■		▣
Rebel force size	Number of rebel forces in dyad	Aronson and Huth (2017)	Aronson and Huth (2017)			▣		▣
Large drop in rebel force size	Number of rebel forces in dyad fell by ≥50% relative to previous year	Aronson and Huth (2017)	Aronson and Huth (2017)			▣		▣
Other rebel forces	Number of forces of all other rebel groups engaged in internal armed conflict	Aronson and Huth (2017)	Aronson and Huth (2017)			▣		

Table 11.2 **Factors in Models of Instability Risk – continued**

Category Indicator	Description	Theoretical Relevance	Data Source(s)	Adverse Regime Change	Internal War Onset	Internal War Offset	State-Based Mass Killing	Non-State Mass Killing
Rebel shelter	Extent of access to shelter by rebel group in dyad	Aronson et al. (2016)	Aronson et al. (2016)				■	
Rebel internal shelter	Access to shelter within country by rebel group in dyad	Aronson et al. (2016)	Aronson et al. (2016)			▣		▣
Ethnic support count	Number of aggrieved ethnic groups aligned to rebels in conflict	Cederman et al. (2011)	Vogt et al. (2015)	■			■	
Ethnic support size	Ethnic groups aligned to rebels are ≥5% of population	Cederman et al. (2011)	Vogt et al. (2015)				■	
External support to rebels	Number of external military forces supporting rebel group in dyad	Lyall and Wilson (2009); Fearon and Laitin (2007)	Aronson et al. (2016); Högbladh et al. (2011)					▣
Rebel group reliance on lootable resources	Rebels engaged in internal armed conflict traffic in gems or diamonds	Humphreys and Weinstein (2006)	Tollefson et al. (2012)					▣
Rebel mass killing	Rebel group committed large-scale deliberate killings of civilians during previous year	Konstanz et al. (2012); Avdan adn Uzonyi (2017)	Eck and Hultman (2007)				■	
Peacekeeping presence	Nature of peacekeeping forces	Hultman (2014)	Cil (2017); IPI (2016)			■		
OTHER FORECASTED INSTABILITY								
Risk of adverse regime change	Probability of adverse regime change within next three years		PCIL model of adverse regime change	■	■		■	■
Dyadic risk of internal war offset	Lowest probability of end to active conflict sustained for next three years in any existing dyad		PCIL dyadic model of internal war offset			■		
Risk of internal war	Probability of internal war within next three years		PCIL model of internal war				■	■
State-based mass killing risk	Probability of state-based mass killing within next three years		PCIL model of state-based mass killing					■
Dyadic risk of non-state mass killing	Greatest probability of large-scale deliberate killings of civilians by rebel group in any existing dyad over next three years		PCIL dyadic model of non-state mass killing					■

Note: ■ indicates factor in country-year model   ▣ indicates factor in dyad-year model

The **country-year model of the offset of internal war** includes eight risk factors from five categories. The expected prospect of observing offset was lower during the Cold War, as well as in countries with civil wars in neighboring countries, larger populations, lootable resources, and risk factors that forecast a higher likelihood of adverse regime change (though statistical significance is marginal). The expected prospect of offset was associated positively with a stronger peacekeeping presence and the lowest likelihood of offset in an existing state-rebel conflict dyad. The latter variable capitalizes on the estimation of the dyadic model. All the results are consistent with theoretical logic, in terms of directions of effects.

The **model of state-based mass killing** includes 11 risk factors, from five categories. The expected prospect of observing such atrocities was higher during the Cold War, as well as in countries with greater levels of infant mortality, larger populations, factionalized democracy, rebels that have access to shelter, higher numbers and population shares of aggrieved ethnic groups with affinities favoring a rebel group, and rebel groups that engage in mass killing. The expected prospect of state-based mass killing was lower in countries with greater judicial independence and risk factors that forecast higher likelihoods of adverse regime change (though statistical significance is marginal) and internal war. All the results are consistent with theoretical logic, in terms of directions of effects.

The **dyad-year model of non-state mass killing** includes 15 risk factors, from three categories. The expected prospect of observing such atrocities was higher in countries with denser populations, as well as in armed conflicts that had a government backed by external military forces and/or a rebel group that was larger in size (with diminishing returns reflected in the negative size-related squared term), had experienced a recent large drop in forces, enjoyed internal shelter, received external support or relied on lootable resources. The expected prospect of non-state mass killing was lower in lengthier armed conflicts (due to the effect of the duration-related squared term) and when the government had committed mass killing, the total number of rebel groups engaged in active conflict was smaller and the leader of a given rebel group was killed. The results generally conform to theoretical logic, in terms of directions of effects.

The **country-year model of non-state mass killing** includes seven risk factors, from three categories. The expected prospect of such atrocities was higher in countries with greater levels of infant mortality, larger populations, ongoing armed conflict, and risk factors that forecast higher likelihoods of adverse regime change and internal war (though statistical significance is lacking on the last two variables), as well as a higher likelihood that at least one rebel group would engage in mass killing of civilians (incorporating the information on probabilities from the dyad-year model). The results generally conform to theoretical logic, in terms of the direction of effects.

Model Diagnostics

The new PCIL methodology produces forecasts with consistently better fits to observed instability outcomes than the forecasts produced by the original PCIL methodology. The improvement in performance is a function of differences in both what is being forecast (i.e., choices and definitions of instability outcomes) and how the forecasts are conducted (i.e., structure of analysis, model specifications, variables, data, and statistical techniques). The new methodology does a better job of forecasting instability, as now measured, than the original methodology did in forecasting the amalgamated measure of instability. This improvement is demonstrated by several standard metrics for evaluating the performance of forecasting models. A comparison of results for these metrics is presented in Table 11.4.

The **AUC score** gauges how effective a forecasting methodology is in distinguishing between the conditions more conducive to observing an outcome and the conditions less likely to produce such an outcome. In technical terms, an AUC score represents the probability that a particular binary classifier system (e.g., a model forecasting whether or not instability will be observed in the future) ranks a randomly chosen positive instance (instability) higher than a randomly chosen negative instance (no instability). AUC scores are normalized to a scale from 0 to 1. A score of 0.5 means that a model does no better than a coin flip in making distinctions, while a score of 1 means perfect prediction. Most models fall somewhere in between. Scores above 0.8 are generally considered to be excellent. For example, a score of 0.9 means that 90% of the time a randomly selected positive instance had a higher predicted probability than a randomly selected negative instance. In terms of this metric, the results indicate that the new PCIL methodology clearly outperforms the original PCIL methodology. Each of the new models has an AUC score well above the 0.8 level, whereas the previous model was just below this level. The performance of the set of models that comprise the new methodology was equally strong in sample (i.e., within the training data) and out of sample (i.e., within the test data). In contrast, the original methodology exhibited a substantial drop in out-of-sample performance. Also, the AUC score for the overall risk of observing any instability using the new methodology is 0.94, representing a huge improvement over the original methodology.

True positives are cases where an instability outcome was projected to occur, based on results of the training model estimation as applied to observed values for the risk factors, and did occur in practice. **False positives** are cases where an

Table 11.3 Estimations of Models of Instability Risk

STEP 1

Adverse Regime Change [N=5,524 country-years]	
CATEGORY *Variable*	Coefficient (95% Confidence Interval)
INTERNATIONAL CONTEXT FACTORS	
Cold War	0.18 (−0.33, 0.65)
COUNTRY-LEVEL (STRUCTURAL) FACTORS	
Infant mortality	1.31*** (0.75, 1.84)
GDP per capita growth	−4.47*** (−7.16, −1.7)
REGIME-LEVEL (INSTITUTIONAL) FACTORS	
Partial democracy	1.25** (0.48, 1.97)
Factionalized democracy	2.56*** (1.93, 3.15)
State failure	3.15*** (2.52, 3.78)
Judicial independence	−2.28*** (−3.71, −1.02)
CONFLICT-LEVEL FACTORS	
New conflict onset	1.01* (0.24, 1.90)
Low-level conflict	−0.55 (−1.38, 0.12)
Duration of conflict	0.20* (0.00, 0.41)
Constant	−4.76*** (−5.80, −3.86)

STEP 2

Onset of Internal War [N=4,719 country-years]	
CATEGORY *Variable*	Coefficient (95% Confidence Interval)
INTERNATIONAL CONTEXT FACTORS	
Cold War	0.15 (−0.37, 0.66)
Neighboring civil war	−0.05 (−0.30, 0.17)
COUNTRY-LEVEL (STRUCTURAL) FACTORS	
Infant mortality	0.35 (−0.25, 0.91)
Population	0.22** (0.06, 0.36)
REGIME-LEVEL (INSTITUTIONAL) FACTORS	
Partial democracy	−0.47 (−1.18, 0.18)
Democracy	−16.40*** (−17.07, −15.40)
State failure	0.87 (−0.61, 2.04)
CONFLICT-LEVEL FACTORS	
Low-level conflict	2.62*** (2.08, 3.20)
ACTOR-LEVEL FACTORS	
Rebel ethnic support count	0.99*** (0.55, 1.42)
OTHER FORECASTED INSTABILITY	
Adverse regime change risk	1.20 (−1.30, 3.44)
Constant	−8.02*** (−10.51, −5.57)

Dyadic Offset of Internal War [N=1,118 dyad-years]	
CATEGORY *Variable*	Coefficient (95% Confidence Interval)
CONFLICT-LEVEL FACTORS	
Conventional conflict	0.70** (0.06, 1.35)
Semi-conventional conflict	0.45 (−0.29, 1.18)
Conflict duration	−0.62* (−1.28, 0.04)
Conflict duration squared	0.69*** (0.08, 1.29)
Drop in conflict severity	0.28*** (0.10, 0.46)
Peace negotiations	0.35*** (0.13, 0.56)
ACTOR-LEVEL FACTORS	
Government leader loss	0.27*** (0.10, 0.44)
Government external forces	−0.19 (−0.50, 0.12)
Government force balance	−0.33** (−0.58, −0.07)
Rebel leader loss	0.12 (−0.04, 0.28)
Rebel force size	−0.66*** (−1.12, −0.20)
Rebel force size squared	0.16*** (0.06, 0.26)
Rebel force size large drop	0.20*** (0.05, 0.35)
Other rebel forces	0.08 (−0.11, 0.27)
Rebel internal shelter	−0.30** (−0.56, −0.04)
Constant	−2.92*** (−3.28, −2.57)

Offset of Internal War [N=710 country-years]	
INTERNATIONAL CONTEXT FACTORS	
Cold War	−0.68 (−2.10, 0.54)
Neighboring civil war	−0.37 (−0.96, 0.06)
COUNTRY-LEVEL (STRUCTURAL) FACTORS	
Population	−0.56* (−1.36, 0.01)
CONFLICT-LEVEL FACTORS	
Lootable resources	−0.80 (−2.51, 0.56)
ACTOR-LEVEL FACTORS	
Rebel count	−1.05** (−2.35, −0.25)
Peacekeeping presence	0.43 (−0.14, 0.97)
OTHER FORECASTED INSTABILITY	
Adverse regime change risk	−0.86 (−5.51, 1.64)
Dyadic internal war offset risk	4.48 (0.46, 9.92)
Constant	8.32* (−1.59, 21.74)

Two-tailed *p*-value: * $p < 0.1$ ** $p < 0.05$ *** $p < 0.01$

Table 11.3 Estimations of Models of Instability Risk - continued

STEP 3

State-Based Mass Killing [N=3,529]		
CATEGORY *Variable*	Coefficient (95% Confidence Interval)	
INTERNATIONAL CONTEXT FACTORS		
Cold War	0.81	(−0.48, 1.76)
COUNTRY-LEVEL (STRUCTURAL) FACTORS		
Infant mortality	1.52***	(0.72, 2.35)
Population	0.32**	(0.12, 0.50)
REGIME-LEVEL (INSTITUTIONAL) FACTORS		
Factionalized democracy	0.91*	(−0.01, 1.69)
Judicial independence	−6.15***	(−8.15, −4.30)
ACTOR-LEVEL FACTORS		
Rebel shelter	0.43	(−0.08, 0.96)
Rebel ethnic support count	0.88***	(0.45, 1.39)
Rebel ethnic support size	1.38*	(0.08, 2.45)
Rebel mass killing	0.11*	(−0.01, 0.24)
OTHER FORECASTED INSTABILITY		
Adverse regime change risk	−1.04	(−3.16, 0.66)
Internal war risk	−0.14	(−1.51, 1.14)
Constant	−9.40***	(−12.68, −5.96)

STEP 4

Dyadic Non-State Mass Killing [N=1,147 dyad-years]		
Variable	Coefficient (95% Confidence Interval)	
COUNTRY-LEVEL (STRUCTURAL) FACTORS		
Population density	0.19	(−0.15, 0.53)
CONFLICT-LEVEL FACTORS		
Conflict duration	1.62**	(0.26, 2.98)
Conflict duration squared	−2.45**	(−4.61, −0.29)
ACTOR-LEVEL FACTORS		
External support to government	0.32**	(0.06, 0.58)
Government mass killing	−0.14***	(−0.22, −0.05)
Rebel leader loss	−1.40***	(−1.55, −1.26)
Rebel founding leader loss	−0.06	(−0.42, 0.31)
Rebel founding leader killed	−1.40***	(−1.57, −1.24)
Rebel group count	−0.56***	(−0.87, −0.24)
Rebel force size	1.11***	(0.46, 1.75)
Rebel force size squared	−0.30***	(−0.47, −0.12)
Large drop in rebel force size	0.23***	(0.07, 0.40)
Rebel internal shelter	0.22	(−0.07, 0.51)
Rebel external support	0.27*	(−0.00, 0.53)
Rebel reliance on lootable resources	0.15	(−0.17, 0.47)
Constant	−2.11***	(−2.59, −1.64)

Non-State Mass Killing [N=3,529 country-years]		
Structural (country-level) factors		
Infant mortality	1.02***	(0.43, 1.65)
Population	0.23***	(0.10, 0.36)
CONFLICT-LEVEL FACTORS		
Ongoing conflict	2.47***	(1.78, 3.12)
OTHER FORECASTED INSTABILITY		
Adverse regime change risk	0.60	(−0.88, 2.19)
Internal war risk	−0.07	(−1.05, 0.88)
State-based mass killing risk	0.85	(−0.42, 2.02)
Dyadic non-state mass killing risk	2.81***	(1.17, 4.57)
Constant	−8.64***	(−10.96, -6.60)

Two-tailed *p*-value: * $p < 0.1$ ** $p < 0.05$ *** $p < 0.01$

Table 11.4 Diagnostics for Models of Instability Risk

Performance Metric	Original PCIL Methodology		New PCIL Methodology					
			Adverse Regime Change	Internal War		State-Based Mass Killing	Non-State Mass Killing	Overall (Any Instability)
				Onset	Offset			
	1950–2003 Training Data	1975–2010 Training Data						1975–2010 Data
			1975–2010 Data			1989–2010 Data		
IN SAMPLE								
AUC Score	0.78	0.77	0.88	0.89	0.85	0.93	0.92	0.94
True/False Positives	172/1,307	645/1,452	230/2,116	173/1,831	40/260	178/1,320	248/1,250	1,100/1,662
True/False Negatives	2,180/39	1,966/133	2,326/23	1,998/8	299/4	1,500/0	1,492/9	2,701/61
OUT OF SAMPLE								
AUC Score	0.66	0.77	0.88	0.88	0.82	0.92	0.93	Not applicable
True/False Positives	2/32	113/258	40/374	30/324	7/46	31/233	43/221	Not applicable
True/False Negatives	102/3	346/24	409/4	353/1	53/1	266/0	264/1	Not applicable

outcome was projected to occur, but did not. **True negatives** are cases where an outcome was projected not to occur and did not occur. **False negatives** are cases where an outcome was not projected to occur, but did occur.

False negatives, in particular, present a vital concern when forecasting instability, since unexpected events can mean that prevention measures were not deployed. Instead, alternatives have to be activated in response, which tend to be more costly than prevention measures and are not necessarily as effective at reducing harms associated with instability. The consequences can be dire, in so far as serious upheaval, large-scale violence and/or mass atrocities ensue. Thus, limiting false negatives and maintaining a high ratio of true to false negatives are essential to avoid the damage associated with not anticipating instability outcomes. Other common rules of thumb are keeping false positives low and the ratio of true to false positives high. Such indicators stand out as important in this context because of the typical treatment of cases deemed at a heightened risk of instability. What if those forecasts do not consistently materialize? In particular, suppose instability is forecast to occur in a sizeable number of cases, but only a fraction actually exhibit instability. This situation undermines the efficiencies of allocations of resources (e.g., attention, personnel, funds, materiel), which are valuable and constrained. A natural reaction might be that resources were not allocated wisely when false positives are observed, especially with regularity. Yet a share of false positives might be due to an awareness that certain cases are vulnerable, warranting allocation of resources, which could contribute to mitigating risks of instability. Thus, the downside of false positives is arguably less severe than what arises with false negatives.

For purposes of the PCIL methodology, each predicted probability was classified based on the median prediction for the model: for values above the threshold, the instability outcome was expected (i.e., a positive prediction), whereas below the threshold the outcome was not expected (i.e., a negative prediction). As the results show, the new PCIL methodology is superior to the previous PCIL methodology with respect to the metrics of true and false positives and true and false negatives. The new methodology is better able to forecast instances where particular types of instability occur, while minimizing instances where these types of instability occur unexpectedly.

In addition, the new PCIL methodology accomplishes a priority of producing better retrospective forecasts for 13 crucial cases identified by USAID as having unexpected instability outcomes in 2011, around the time of the Arab Spring. Of note, 10 of these crucial cases exhibited active internal wars as of 2010. Out of those cases, seven were evaluated by the PCIL offset model as being at *highest risk* of ongoing internal war during 2011–2013, two at *high risk*, and one at *moderate risk*. Meanwhile, the onset model evaluated Syria as *high risk*, Egypt as *moderate risk*, and Libya as *some risk* of internal war during 2011–2013.[4] Similar results were obtained using 2009 data, forecasting the risk of internal war during 2010–2012. For both time periods, the new PCIL methodology placed each crucial case in a more serious risk classification than was found with the original methodology. According to the new methodology, all these cases ought to have warranted at least a degree of scrutiny, often heightened, whereas the previous methodology conspicuously discounted their risks of instability.

Calculation of Risk Scores

Instability risk scores are calculated via a multi-step process. The starting place is the coefficients for the various risk factors from the estimations of the training models. These coefficients amount to weights on the factors, which can be used to forecast probabilities of future instability in a given country as of a given year. The coefficient weights are applied to the latest available data to produce the most current set of forecasts possible. In the current cycle of analysis, forecasts of instability risk for 165 countries during the 2015–2017 period are generated using data from 2014, the most recent year for which complete information on every indicator is available across all the countries (due to lags in data reporting).

The forecasts for the different types of instability can be combined into an overall probability of observing any of these types of instability. Specifically, the overall risk of instability for a given country in year t is computed, relying on basic probability theory, via the following equation:

$$P_{overall,t} = 1 - (1 - P_{adverseregimechange,t})(1 - P_{internalwar,t})x$$

$$(1 - P_{state-basedmasskilling,t})(1 - P_{non-statemasskilling,t})$$

where:

$P_{adverseregimechange,t}$ is the forecast probability of observing adverse regime change in years $t+1$ through $t+3$;
$P_{internalwar,t}$ is the forecast probability of observing internal war in years $t+1$ through $t+3$, which is the forecast probability of either the onset of internal war $(1 - P_{onsetofinternalwar,t})$ or ongoing internal war $(1 - P_{offsetofinternalwar,t})$, depending on the conflict status of the country;
$P_{state-basedmasskilling,t}$ is the forecast probability of observing state-based mass killing in years $t+1$ through $t+3$; and
$P_{non-statemasskilling,t}$ is the forecast probability of observing non-state mass killing in years $t+1$ through $t+3$.

To make the forecasts more comprehensible, the probabilities are transformed and presented as risk scores, which reflect relative likelihoods of observing instability. Specifically, a risk score is computed as the ratio of the probability for a given country to the historical mean probability among the countries that are members of the Organisation for Economic Co-operation and Development (OECD).[5] For example, a risk score of 20.0 would indicate that the forecast likelihood of instability being observed in a given country is estimated to be 20 times greater than the likelihood for OECD countries on average over time. The relative risk scores place the forecasts in a long-term comparative context, highlighting risks that stand out. The OECD member-countries are used as a reference point because they tend to exhibit limited exposure to serious instability of the types considered in this analysis.

Each risk score is accompanied by a confidence range, comprised of an upper bound and a lower bound. The reason is that the results of nearly any statistical estimation reflect a degree of uncertainty in the evaluated relationship; perfect association between outcome and predictor variables is rare. Here, the inclusion of the confidence range is an acknowledgement of the uncertainty inherent in the forecasts of instability risk. A 95% confidence range is reported. In essence, there is a 95% probability that the true risk estimate lies somewhere within the confidence range.

Generation of Risk Classifications

The risk scores and their corresponding upper and lower bounds are also assigned classifications, following the same procedure traditionally employed as part of the PCIL methodology.[6] The procedure is applied separately to the results for each type of instability and for overall instability. Countries are initially grouped based on their estimated risk scores and confidence ranges: generally speaking, those countries with significant overlaps are placed in the same group, whereas those with little or no overlap are placed in different groups. At this stage, 10–15 groups are typically formed. These groups are then combined as necessary to reduce all countries to five classifications: *highest risk, high risk, moderate risk, some risk,* and *low risk.* Some of these classifications correspond to a single group, while other classifications encompass multiple groups. The goal is an appropriate, meaningful distribution of countries among the classifications, with targets of approximately 10–15% of countries being classified as highest risk, 10–15% high risk, 10–15% moderate risk, 10–15% some risk, and 40–60% low risk. The distributions remain roughly comparable – but can vary to an extent – across types of instability and the annual cycles of analysis.

In select cases, a country's confidence range may encompass multiple risk classifications. Such results suggest the need for greater caution in making assessments about those countries, given uncertainty about the precise level of risk they face.

Instability Risk Forecasts

Over the upcoming pages, global maps of risk classifications, by type of instability and overall, are presented. Full results of the risk scores and classifications appear in the Appendix (pp. 119–139).

Adverse Regime Change

Of the countries with the 25 highest forecast risks of adverse regime change from 2015–2017, 13 are located in Africa, six in Asia, four in Latin America and the Caribbean, and two in Europe. The countries near the top of the top 25 list face huge risks relative to OECD countries. This finding is intuitive given the latter countries are entrenched democracies where such a change would be unconventional and unexpected. In total, 79 countries are classified with at least *some risk*, including notable ones outside the top 25 list such as Burundi, Colombia, Egypt, India, Indonesia, Kenya, Lebanon, Nigeria, North Korea, the Philippines, Russia, Sudan, and Turkey (Figure 11.2).

Internal War

Of the countries with the 25 highest forecast risks of internal war from 2015–2017, 12 are located in Asia, including four in the Middle East, and 10 are in Africa. Most of these countries were already engaged in active armed conflict as of 2014. Their rankings ought to come as little surprise. Existing conflict is among the main vulnerabilities for future conflict. Outside of countries with active conflict, the estimated risks of internal war tend to drop off precipitously, even for most of the countries exposed to conflict within the previous 10 years. The implication is that the risk of conflict recurrence is elevated relative to the risk of an entirely new onset of conflict, but hardly on par with the risk of ongoing conflict. In total, 72 countries are classified with at least *some risk*, including notable ones outside the top 25 list, but with risk scores above the long-term OECD mean, such as China, Indonesia, Iran, Mali, Saudi Arabia, and Venezuela (Figure 11.3).

State-Based Mass Killing

Of the countries with the 25 highest forecast risks of state-based mass killing from 2015–2017, 15 are located in Africa and 10 are in Asia, including four in the Middle East. Here again, the countries near the top of the list face huge risks relative to OECD countries. These findings are logical given that OECD countries are well-established democracies in which large-scale, deliberate atrocities against civilians tend to be abnormal (as would be the potential contributing context of armed conflict). In total, 81 countries are classified with at least *some risk*, including notable ones outside the top 25 list such as Cambodia, China, Colombia, Egypt, Haiti, India, Indonesia, Mali, Mexico, North Korea, the Philippines, Russia, Rwanda, Saudi Arabia, Ukraine, Venezuela, and Zimbabwe (Figure 11.4).

Non-State Mass Killing

Of the countries with the 25 highest forecast risks of non-state mass killing from 2015–2017, 11 are located in Asia, including four in the Middle East, and 10 are in Africa. Countries near the top of the list face substantial risks relative to OECD countries, where conditions under which non-state actors are prone to target civilians tend to be absent, given the political, security, and social context. In total, 81 countries are classified with at least *some risk*, including notable ones outside the top 25 list, but with risk scores above the long-term OECD mean, such as Algeria, Brazil, Burundi, Ethiopia, Ghana, Haiti, Indonesia, Kenya, South Africa, Yemen, and Zimbabwe (Figure 11.5).

Overall Instability

Of the countries with the 25 highest forecast overall risks of instability from 2015–2017, 11 are located in Africa and 11 are in Asia, including four in the Middle East. In total, 74 countries are classified with at least *some risk*, including notable ones outside the top 25 list such as Burundi, China, Egypt, Haiti, Indonesia, Iran, Kenya, Lebanon, Mexico, North Korea, Turkey, Saudi Arabia, Venezuela, and Zimbabwe (Figure 11.6).

Discussion

A persistent pattern is that more countries confront significant risks of instability in Africa than in any other region. Out of 29 countries classified in the *highest risk* or *high risk* categories for their overall scores, 14 (48%) are located in Africa. Asia also has a concentration of states exhibiting at least *high risk*, with Pakistan, India, and Afghanistan appearing atop the rankings and Burma, Iraq, the Philippines, and Syria also in the top 25. These two regions have consistently been the most vulnerable to instability, as the PCIL has shown dating back to 2008.

A further finding to emphasize is that overlaps are observed among the sets of countries ranked in the top 25 for the distinct types of instability and for the overall risk score, but these sets exhibit some consequential differences. Seven countries – Afghanistan, the Democratic Republic of the Congo, Iraq, Libya, Pakistan, Somalia, and South Sudan – rank in the top 25 for all four types of instability and their overall risk scores likewise rank near the top of the list. Yet other countries face selective vulnerabilities, ranking in the top 25 only for certain types of instability, and therefore can have overall risk scores that do not rank near the top of the list.

As a consequence, 51 countries rank in a top 25 for the risk of at least one type of instability (Table 11.5). Among these countries are 23 located in Africa and 19 in Asia, including seven in the Middle East. Of note, 11 countries are ranked in the top 25 only for the risk of adverse regime change,[7] two countries in the top 25 only for the risk of internal war,[8] six countries in the top 25 only for the risk of state-based mass killing,[9] and four countries in the top 25 only for the risk of non-state mass killing.[10] Each of these 23 countries is ranked outside the top 25 – even well outside – for the risks of all

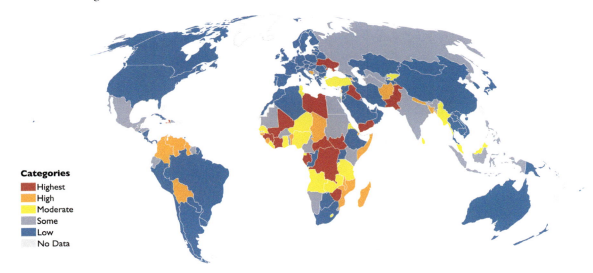

Figure 11.2 Global Map of Classifications for Risk of Adverse Regime Change, 2015–2017

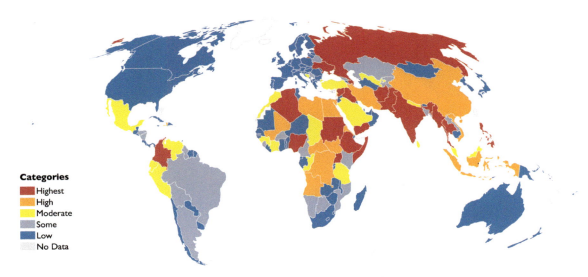

Figure 11.3 Global Map of Classifications for Risk of Internal War, 2015–2017

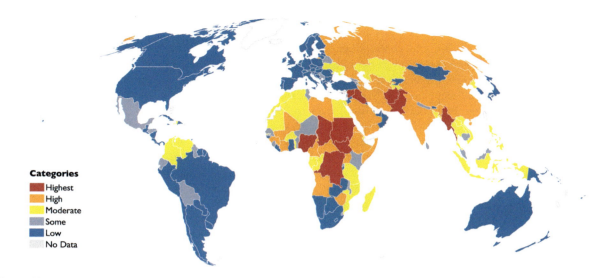

Figure 11.4 Global Map of Classifications for Risk of State-Based Mass Killing, 2015–2017

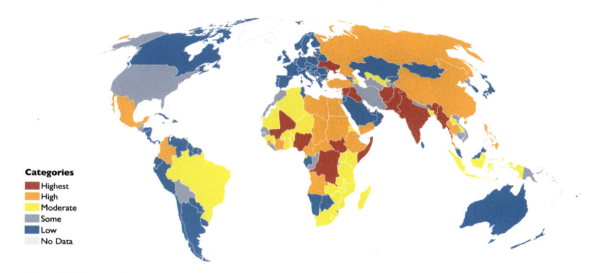

Figure 11.5 Global Map of Classifications for Risk of Non-State Mass Killing, 2015–2017

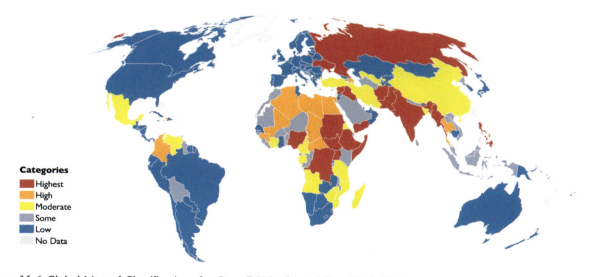

Figure 11.6 Global Map of Classifications for Overall Risk of Instability, 2015–2017

The Peace and Conflict Instability Ledger

the other types of instability. These findings reinforce the merits of evaluating the risk factors for the distinct types of instability in separate model estimations, as well as the informational value of the results for identifying the particular vulnerabilities to instability that countries face.

Another important point to highlight is that the separate models for estimating the risk of the four distinct types of instability reflect certain interdependencies among the types. The results of the analysis showed that countries subject to adverse regime change are more likely to experience internal war, while countries subject to adverse regime change and/or state-based mass killing are more likely to experience non-state mass killing. Thus, a country may not currently exhibit an extreme risk of internal war, but this type of instability could emerge as a more pressing concern in the event of an adverse regime change. Similarly, a country may not currently exhibit an extreme risk of non-state mass killing, but the prospect of such atrocities could be elevated if an existing regime is susceptible to serious upheaval or to engaging in atrocities. These links among the distinct types of instability hold the potential for countries to quickly rise in the global rankings due to the effects that one type of instability can have on the risk of exhibiting another type.

Conclusion

This chapter presented the latest results of the Peace and Conflict Instability Ledger, ranking countries around the world according to their estimated risk of experiencing significant political instability during the three-year period of 2015–2017. Once again, the findings establish a concentration of serious vulnerabilities in Sub-Saharan Africa and South Asia.

The analysis reflects major advances in the PCIL methodology. A notable change is to offer more complete and specific insight into the risks of instability. The scope of the forecasts is enhanced by disaggregating instability into four distinct types and accounting for both the onset and offset of internal war – crucial dimensions absent from the original PCIL methodology. This approach generates separate risk estimates for the four types of instability, from which an overall estimate of risk is also derived. Risk estimates are still obtained using statistical forecasting models. The results of observed historical relationships between instability outcomes and relevant risk factors are then applied to the latest data to project the prospects of future instability. In the process, the models are tailored to include different risk factors, including interdependencies among the types of instability. The tailoring is based on established theory and the latest findings, while still remaining relatively parsimonious. Overlaps are observed among the risk factors of the distinct types of instability. Yet the dynamics contributing to each type differ in material respects. Peer-reviewed empirical research conducted by leading scholars clearly demonstrates the differences. Likewise, our analyses conducted confirm that the distinct types of instability outcomes have characteristic risk factors.

All data continue to be obtained from reliable sources and satisfy essential criteria of substantive merits and comprehensive coverage. Many of the independent variables are fresh to the analysis. A number of factors are evaluated using indicators from recently developed and novel data sources, including ones compiled by the authors and others at the CIDCM. Some of these sources were unavailable when the original PCIL methodology was devised. Certain of the added independent variables have the necessary data available for fewer years than those used in the previous methodology, which necessitates shifting the start date of the training data. Meanwhile, the period covered by the training data has been extended to be more current, affording greater salience to the recent state of the world and observed patterns and trends. Another benefit is data on key factors that boost the performance of forecasts can thereby be included.

The new methodology significantly improves the rankings and classification of countries. At the same time, coverage is maintained and accuracy is increased across the full set of forecasts. Individually and collectively, the models with the disaggregate dependent variables produce stronger results, in terms of the fit of predictions to observed outcomes, than the original PCIL. These improvements are directly attributable to tailoring model specifications. The new independent variables increase the accuracy of the forecasts, partly by providing greater context and nuance than the independent variables in the original PCIL. Once the new independent variables are included, several independent variables in the original PCIL no longer register as statistically significant or vary in significance across models. All these requirements are achieved in a manner that is feasible to sustain in the future. We employed cutting-edge statistical techniques to conduct the estimations, assess performance, and check the robustness of the results. In addition, we instituted regular consultations with an advisory group of other experts who specialize in forecasting instability, to strengthen mechanisms for periodic reevaluation and refinement of the methodology, further bolstering the credibility of the analysis.

Table 11.5 Countries Ranked in Top 25 for Any Type of Instability Risk, 2015–2017

Country	Adverse Regime Change	Internal War	State-Based Mass Killing	Non-State Mass Killing	Overall
Pakistan	8 ★	1 ★	9 ★	4 ★	1
India	75	2 ★	51	1 ★	2
Afghanistan	16 ★	15 ★	1 ★	3 ★	3
South Sudan	3 ★	21 ★	3 ★	2 ★	4
Sudan	83	4 ★	6 ★	21 ★	5
Nigeria	55	6 ★	10 ★	6 ★	6
Philippines	70	3 ★	50	14 ★	7
Congo, Dem. Rep.	7 ★	22 ★	2 ★	5 ★	8
Iraq	5 ★	16 ★	4 ★	10 ★	9
Myanmar	48	14 ★	7 ★	9 ★	10
Uganda	105	5 ★	21 ★	32	11
Ukraine	12 ★	12 ★	57	7 ★	12
Yemen	13 ★	7 ★	24 ★	28	13
Russia	78	8 ★	32	18 ★	14
Ethiopia	115	9 ★	13 ★	27	15
Syria	119	18 ★	8 ★	11 ★	16
Thailand	129	11 ★	65	17 ★	17
Somalia	21 ★	19 ★	11 ★	8 ★	18
Israel	61	10 ★	117	24 ★	19
Algeria	126	13 ★	46	54	20
Libya	2 ★	23 ★	20 ★	23 ★	21
Azerbaijan	98	17 ★	15 ★	49	22
Central African Republic	1 ★	43	22 ★	13 ★	23
Colombia	30	20 ★	49	22 ★	24
Mali	14 ★	26	31	12 ★	25
Egypt	62	24 ★	30	16 ★	26
Chad	32	40	5 ★	25 ★	27
Guinea	6 ★	48	18 ★	34	28
Haiti	4 ★	42	43	48	29
Côte d'Ivoire	9 ★	38	19 ★	29	30
China	114	31	33	15 ★	31
Angola	42	30	14 ★	26	32
Zimbabwe	10 ★	77	29	44	33
Uzbekistan	71	32	12 ★	42	34
Eritrea	43	29	17 ★	41	35
Lebanon	33	25 ★	109	133	36
Turkey	36	46	100	20 ★	37
Cameroon	53	68	16 ★	30	38
Mexico	69	44	79	19 ★	39
Gabon	11 ★	107	55	89	40
Madagascar	15 ★	74	53	55	41
Venezuela	17 ★	36	37	84	42
Iran	104	28	23 ★	69	43
Bangladesh	19 ★	58	42	36	44
Malawi	18 ★	76	80	51	47
Nepal	24 ★	49	60	60	48
Bolivia	22 ★	54	66	71	49
Guyana	20 ★	62	72	105	50
Turkmenistan	63	89	25 ★	63	56
Djibouti	25 ★	125	54	78	58
Bosnia and Herzegovina	23 ★	66	114	149	60

Risk Category
- Highest
- High
- Moderate
- Some
- Low

★ Country ranks in top 25 for type of instability

Appendix

For each country, the relevant risk score and confidence range are provided in numerical form and displayed visually, with color codings to indicate corresponding risk classifications. In addition, rankings of countries in both the current analysis and the analysis using the prior year's data are provided for the forecasts of adverse regime change, internal war, and state-based mass killing. Only the rankings in the current analysis are provided for the forecast of non-state mass killing, which is a new element, and the overall risk of instability, which incorporates this new element.

Table 11.6 Country Rankings of Risk of Adverse Regime Change, 2015–2017

2016 Rank	2015 Rank	Country	Lower Bound	Risk Ratio	Upper Bound
1	1	Central African Republic	103.3	130.2	151.3
2	3	Libya	83.6	122.6	157.4
3	4	South Sudan	88.6	110.1	130.5
4	6	Haiti	53.7	77.2	101.4
5	5	Iraq	41.2	66.6	97.5
6	8	Guinea	42.2	62.3	83.6
7	12	Congo, Dem. Rep.	22.9	52.7	96.5
8	7	Pakistan	31.2	52.6	81.5
9	11	Côte d'Ivoire	31.0	47.3	67.2
10	16	Zimbabwe	30.1	45.6	62.8
11	13	Gabon	22.8	34.9	49.1
12	26	Ukraine	14.2	33.7	68.4
13	91	Yemen	14.3	30.9	58.6
14	9	Mali	12.1	30.7	60.0
15	88	Madagascar	20.5	30.2	41.3
16	2	Afghanistan	10.9	24.6	47.3
17	17	Venezuela	13.2	22.7	35.7
18	14	Malawi	13.9	22.6	32.9
19	15	Bangladesh	15.1	22.3	31.7
20	20	Guyana	14.0	20.7	29.1
21	28	Somalia	8.1	18.4	36.9
22	21	Bolivia	11.9	18.2	25.8
23	22	Bosnia and Herzegovina	8.2	17.7	32.6
24	18	Nepal	11.0	16.9	24.2
25	29	Djibouti	8.6	15.6	26.2
26	46	Sierra Leone	6.9	15.2	27.5
27	44	Guinea-Bissau	7.8	14.6	24.0
28	25	Armenia	8.3	14.0	21.0
29	42	Mozambique	7.4	14.0	23.0
30	26	Colombia	6.6	13.2	24.2
31	38	Benin	6.3	12.5	21.3
32	30	Chad	7.2	12.5	20.8
33	36	Lebanon	5.4	12.5	26.8
34	36	Liberia	6.5	12.4	20.4
35	24	Niger	6.1	11.8	19.5
36	93	Turkey	5.7	11.2	19.8
37	19	Equatorial Guinea	6.7	11.2	17.7
38	38	Burundi	5.7	11.1	18.3
39	38	Kyrgyzstan	6.6	10.8	16.2
40	32	Senegal	5.7	10.2	16.2
41	38	Tanzania	5.5	10.1	17.1
42	51	Angola	5.2	9.8	17.6
43	63	Eritrea	5.0	9.4	16.0
44	32	Zambia	4.6	8.7	14.0
45	22	Malaysia	4.5	8.6	13.9

Risk Ratio Category
- Highest
- High
- Moderate
- Some
- Low

Upper and Lower Bounds Category
- Low
- Some
- Moderate
- High
- Highest

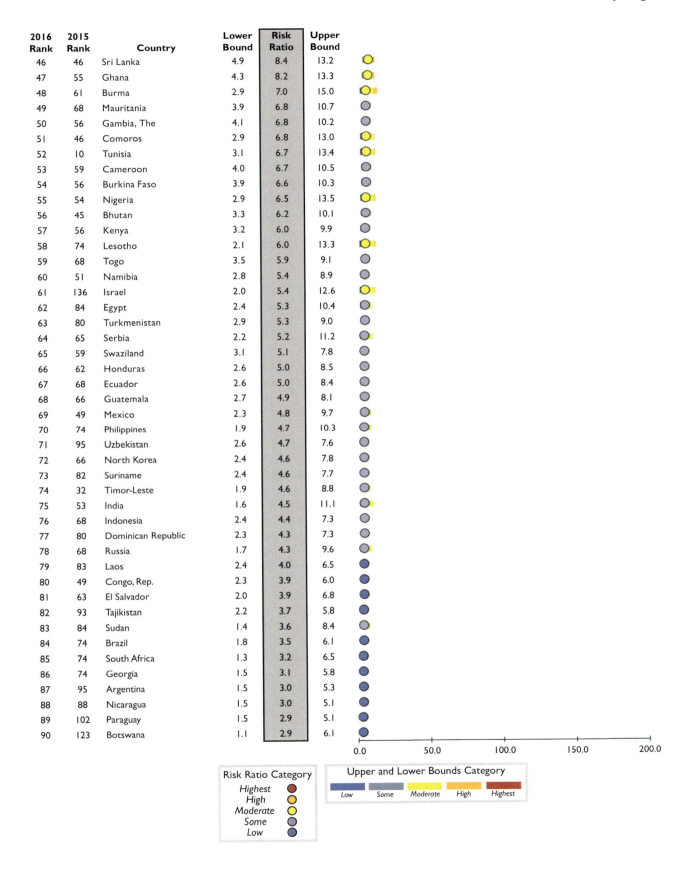

The Peace and Conflict Instability Ledger

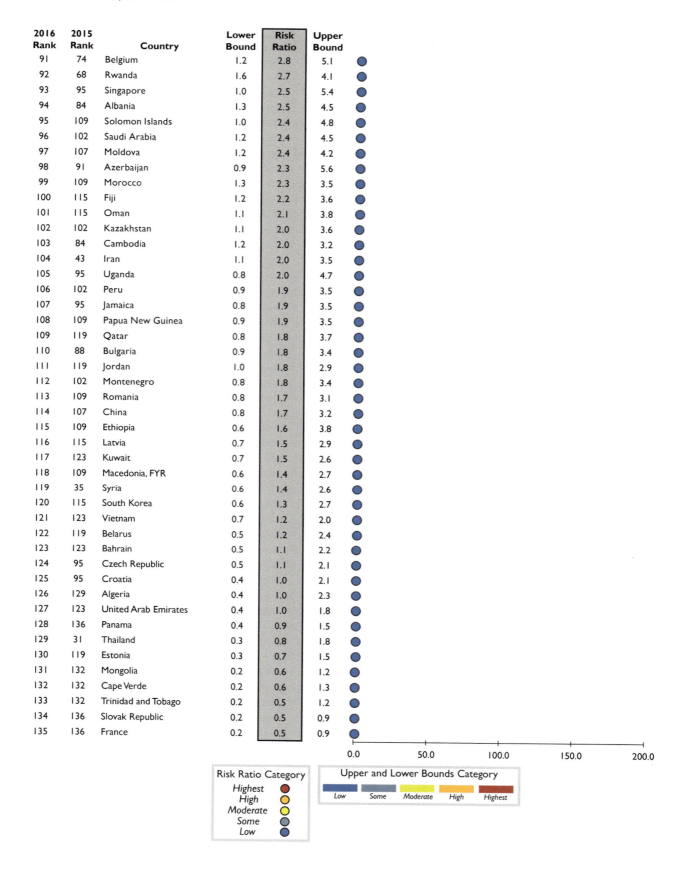

The Peace and Conflict Instability Ledger

2016 Rank	2015 Rank	Country	Lower Bound	Risk Ratio	Upper Bound	
136	123	Cuba	0.1	0.4	1.0	●
137	132	Italy	0.1	0.4	0.8	●
138	143	Mauritius	0.1	0.4	0.8	●
139	143	Uruguay	0.1	0.3	0.7	●
140	143	Chile	0.1	0.3	0.7	●
141	129	Greece	0.1	0.3	0.7	●
142	143	Costa Rica	0.1	0.3	0.7	●
143	143	Lithuania	0.1	0.3	0.5	●
144	143	Poland	0.1	0.3	0.5	●
145	143	Hungary	0.1	0.2	0.6	●
146	136	Spain	0.1	0.2	0.5	●
147	129	Cyprus	0.1	0.2	0.5	●
148	136	Portugal	0.1	0.2	0.5	●
149	155	New Zealand	0.1	0.2	0.5	●
150	155	United States	0.1	0.2	0.5	●
150	143	Austria	0.1	0.2	0.5	●
152	143	Netherlands	0.1	0.2	0.5	●
153	155	Switzerland	0.1	0.2	0.5	●
154	155	Canada	0.1	0.2	0.5	●
155	155	United Kingdom	0.1	0.2	0.5	●
156	143	Denmark	0.1	0.2	0.5	●
157	143	Finland	0.1	0.2	0.5	●
158	155	Australia	0.1	0.2	0.5	●
159	155	Sweden	0.1	0.2	0.5	●
160	155	Norway	0.1	0.2	0.4	●
161	155	Japan	0.1	0.2	0.4	●
161	136	Slovenia	0.1	0.2	0.4	●
163	155	Germany	0.1	0.2	0.4	●
164	143	Ireland	0.1	0.2	0.4	●
165	155	Luxembourg	0.0	0.2	0.4	●

Risk Ratio Category: Highest, High, Moderate, Some, Low

Upper and Lower Bounds Category: Low, Some, Moderate, High, Highest

Backer, Aronson, and Huth

Table 11.7 Country Rankings of Risk of Internal War, 2015–2017

2016 Rank	2015 Rank	Country	Lower Bound	Risk Ratio	Upper Bound
1	5	Pakistan	20.1	20.5	20.5
2	2	India	18.7	20.3	20.5
3	1	Philippines	19.5	20.2	20.5
4	19	Sudan	18.8	20.2	20.5
5	7	Uganda	19.0	19.9	20.4
6	8	Nigeria	17.9	19.7	20.4
7	18	Yemen	18.5	19.7	20.4
8	10	Russia	17.7	19.6	20.4
9	9	Ethiopia	17.6	19.4	20.3
10	130	Israel	15.9	19.0	20.2
11	12	Thailand	16.8	19.0	20.1
12	78	Ukraine	16.7	18.9	20.1
13	13	Algeria	16.5	18.7	20.0
14	6	Burma	16.4	18.7	20.0
15	4	Afghanistan	16.2	18.6	20.0
16	15	Iraq	16.3	18.6	20.0
17	43	Azerbaijan	11.6	16.7	19.6
18	17	Syria	12.2	16.5	19.2
19	20	Somalia	11.4	16.3	19.4
20	3	Colombia	8.9	16.2	19.5
21	13	South Sudan	9.7	15.1	18.6
22	16	Congo, Dem. Rep.	8.9	14.9	18.2
23	26	Libya	3.9	11.2	17.0
24	41	Egypt	4.9	8.1	11.8
25	64	Lebanon	2.5	4.8	7.8
26	23	Mali	1.4	3.4	7.3
27	25	Vietnam	1.0	2.1	3.7
28	24	Iran	0.9	2.0	3.6
29	31	Eritrea	0.9	1.7	2.8
30	29	Angola	0.7	1.6	3.1
31	28	China	0.5	1.5	3.2
32	34	Uzbekistan	0.7	1.2	2.0
33	32	Morocco	0.6	1.2	1.9
34	33	Sri Lanka	0.6	1.2	2.0
35	37	Indonesia	0.4	1.1	2.4
36	35	Venezuela	0.6	1.0	1.7
37	37	Saudi Arabia	0.6	1.0	1.7
38	42	Côte d'Ivoire	0.5	0.9	1.8
39	22	Malaysia	0.5	0.9	1.6
40	39	Chad	0.4	0.9	1.8
41	45	Tanzania	0.4	0.9	1.7
42	30	Haiti	0.2	0.9	3.1
43	21	Central African Republic	0.1	0.9	3.5
44	49	Mexico	0.3	0.9	1.7
45	47	Peru	0.4	0.9	1.6

Risk Ratio Category
- Highest
- High
- Moderate
- Some
- Low

Upper and Lower Bounds Category: Low, Some, Moderate, High, Highest

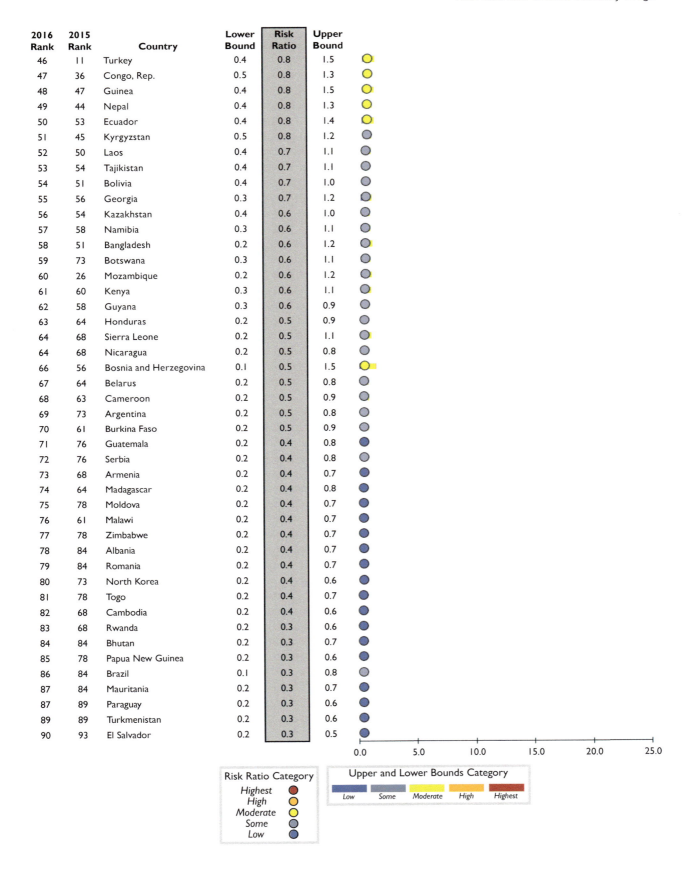

The Peace and Conflict Instability Ledger

2016 Rank	2015 Rank	Country	Lower Bound	Risk Ratio	Upper Bound
91	93	South Africa	0.1	0.3	0.7
92	93	Bulgaria	0.1	0.3	0.5
93	89	Niger	0.1	0.3	0.7
94	102	Ghana	0.1	0.3	0.6
95	96	Jordan	0.1	0.3	0.5
96	89	Gambia, The	0.1	0.3	0.5
97	106	Benin	0.1	0.3	0.6
98	96	Zambia	0.1	0.3	0.5
99	102	Cuba	0.1	0.3	0.5
100	96	United Arab Emirates	0.1	0.3	0.5
100	106	Croatia	0.1	0.3	0.4
102	102	Belgium	0.1	0.2	0.5
103	102	Senegal	0.1	0.2	0.5
103	106	Montenegro	0.1	0.2	0.5
105	106	Burundi	0.1	0.2	0.6
106	96	Equatorial Guinea	0.1	0.2	0.5
107	96	Gabon	0.1	0.2	0.4
107	96	Swaziland	0.1	0.2	0.4
109	112	Latvia	0.1	0.2	0.4
110	106	Oman	0.1	0.2	0.4
111	112	Macedonia, FYR	0.1	0.2	0.4
112	116	South Korea	0.1	0.2	0.5
113	112	Kuwait	0.1	0.2	0.4
114	119	Dominican Republic	0.1	0.2	0.4
115	112	Liberia	0.1	0.2	0.4
116	119	Suriname	0.1	0.2	0.4
117	119	Lesotho	0.1	0.2	0.4
118	116	Qatar	0.1	0.2	0.3
119	39	Tunisia	0.1	0.2	0.3
120	119	Fiji	0.1	0.2	0.3
121	78	Guinea-Bissau	0.1	0.2	0.4
122	116	Bahrain	0.1	0.2	0.3
123	123	Czech Republic	0.1	0.2	0.3
124	106	Timor-Leste	0.1	0.1	0.3
125	123	Djibouti	0.1	0.1	0.3
126	123	Comoros	0.1	0.1	0.3
127	127	Jamaica	0.1	0.1	0.3
128	127	Singapore	0.1	0.1	0.3
129	130	Solomon Islands	0.0	0.1	0.2
130	130	Estonia	0.0	0.1	0.2
131	142	Australia	0.0	0.0	0.0
131	150	Austria	0.0	0.0	0.0
131	130	Canada	0.0	0.0	0.0
131	150	Cape Verde	0.0	0.0	0.0
131	137	Chile	0.0	0.0	0.0

0.0   5.0   10.0   15.0   20.0   25.0

Risk Ratio Category
- Highest
- High
- Moderate
- Some
- Low

Upper and Lower Bounds Category

Low	Some	Moderate	High	Highest

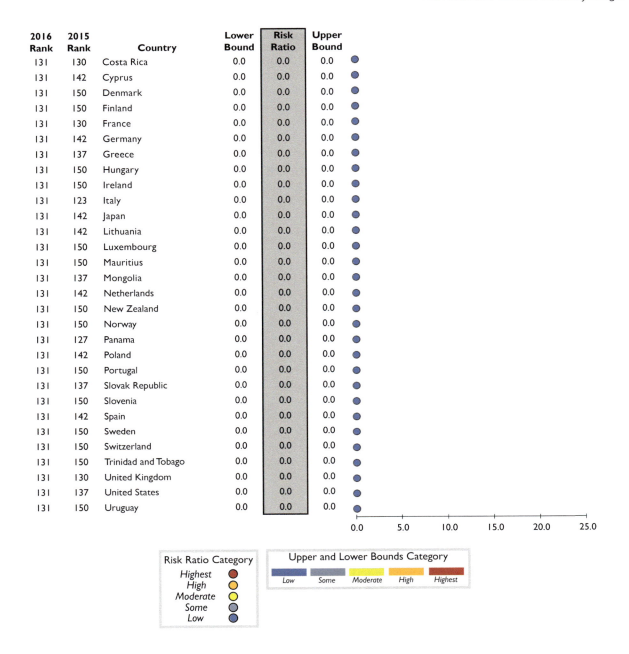

Table 11.8 Country Rankings of Risk of State-Based Mass Killing, 2015–2017

2016 Rank	2015 Rank	Country	Lower Bound	Risk Ratio	Upper Bound
1	1	Afghanistan	481.4	824.0	903.0
2	2	Congo, Dem. Rep.	427.1	746.4	882.9
3	5	South Sudan	311.9	637.0	843.4
4	8	Iraq	162.5	492.6	800.5
5	11	Chad	241.1	482.1	726.7
6	4	Sudan	214.4	477.7	730.5
7	3	Burma	174.5	439.5	719.3
8	6	Syria	72.4	429.0	801.3
9	13	Pakistan	61.2	275.4	657.2
10	14	Nigeria	59.4	239.9	604.8
11	15	Somalia	86.6	214.5	451.6
12	19	Uzbekistan	137.7	211.8	293.4
13	6	Ethiopia	69.8	208.3	452.6
14	12	Angola	84.6	183.7	346.9
15	32	Azerbaijan	62.9	171.4	370.3
16	36	Cameroon	60.6	163.7	360.6
17	25	Eritrea	96.8	152.8	221.8
18	23	Guinea	57.0	148.1	299.5
19	21	Côte d'Ivoire	53.8	146.4	308.1
20	46	Libya	35.9	115.8	304.9
21	10	Uganda	51.5	112.0	213.0
22	24	Central African Republic	34.5	107.7	280.5
23	9	Iran	52.4	103.9	175.8
24	18	Yemen	29.3	90.0	227.3
25	48	Turkmenistan	37.9	75.3	128.2
26	27	Saudi Arabia	40.9	74.4	125.4
27	17	Congo, Rep.	42.7	68.0	104.3
28	21	Tanzania	38.9	67.5	105.5
29	57	Zimbabwe	25.8	66.8	143.4
30	39	Egypt	28.9	59.5	111.6
31	29	Mali	13.4	55.8	180.5
32	20	Russia	17.3	55.5	167.1
33	16	China	19.0	54.2	122.5
34	26	Mozambique	27.3	53.4	92.7
35	44	North Korea	24.3	52.0	95.8
36	37	Burkina Faso	23.1	50.6	91.8
37	33	Venezuela	20.9	49.0	98.6
38	52	Togo	23.1	43.4	73.4
39	48	Tajikistan	27.1	42.8	61.9
40	61	Equatorial Guinea	18.5	41.1	82.3
41	44	Laos	22.5	39.5	63.1
42	34	Bangladesh	13.1	38.1	85.0
43	52	Haiti	18.8	36.5	64.7
44	64	Mauritania	15.5	32.4	58.9
45	43	Morocco	17.9	31.0	51.2

Risk Ratio Category
Highest
High
Moderate
Some
Low

Upper and Lower Bounds Category
Low — Some — Moderate — High — Highest

The Peace and Conflict Instability Ledger

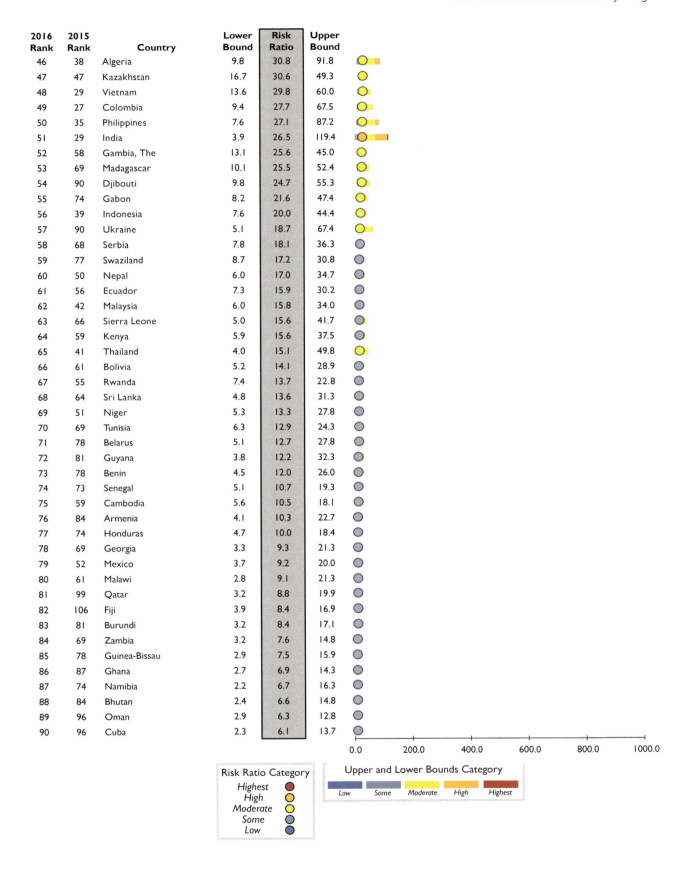

129

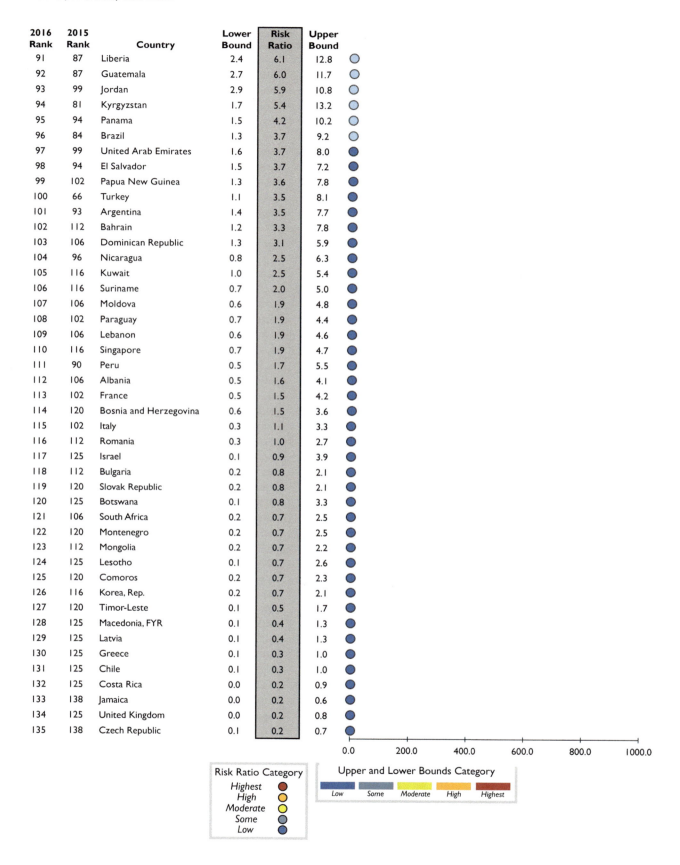

The Peace and Conflict Instability Ledger

2016 Rank	2015 Rank	Country	Lower Bound	Risk Ratio	Upper Bound	
136	125	Croatia	0.0	0.2	0.7	
137	138	Lithuania	0.0	0.2	0.6	
138	125	United States	0.0	0.2	0.7	
139	125	Poland	0.0	0.2	0.6	
140	138	Belgium	0.0	0.2	0.5	
141	138	Spain	0.0	0.2	0.5	
142	125	Canada	0.0	0.2	0.7	
143	138	Solomon Islands	0.0	0.1	0.5	
144	138	Hungary	0.0	0.1	0.4	
145	138	Trinidad and Tobago	0.0	0.1	0.4	
146	138	Germany	0.0	0.1	0.4	
147	138	Uruguay	0.0	0.1	0.3	
148	138	Cape Verde	0.0	0.1	0.4	
149	138	Japan	0.0	0.1	0.4	
150	138	Mauritius	0.0	0.1	0.3	
151	138	Portugal	0.0	0.1	0.3	
152	138	Netherlands	0.0	0.1	0.3	
153	138	Cyprus	0.0	0.1	0.3	
154	138	Australia	0.0	0.1	0.3	
155	138	Austria	0.0	0.1	0.2	
155	138	Switzerland	0.0	0.1	0.2	
157	138	Sweden	0.0	0.1	0.2	
158	138	New Zealand	0.0	0.0	0.2	
159	160	Estonia	0.0	0.0	0.2	
160	160	Ireland	0.0	0.0	0.2	
161	138	Denmark	0.0	0.0	0.2	
162	160	Norway	0.0	0.0	0.2	
163	160	Finland	0.0	0.0	0.2	
164	160	Slovenia	0.0	0.0	0.2	
165	160	Luxembourg	0.0	0.0	0.1	

0.0   200.0   400.0   600.0   800.0   1000.0

Risk Ratio Category
Highest
High
Moderate
Some
Low

Upper and Lower Bounds Category
Low   Some   Moderate   High   Highest

Table 11.9 Country Rankings of Risk of Non-State Mass Killing, 2015–2017

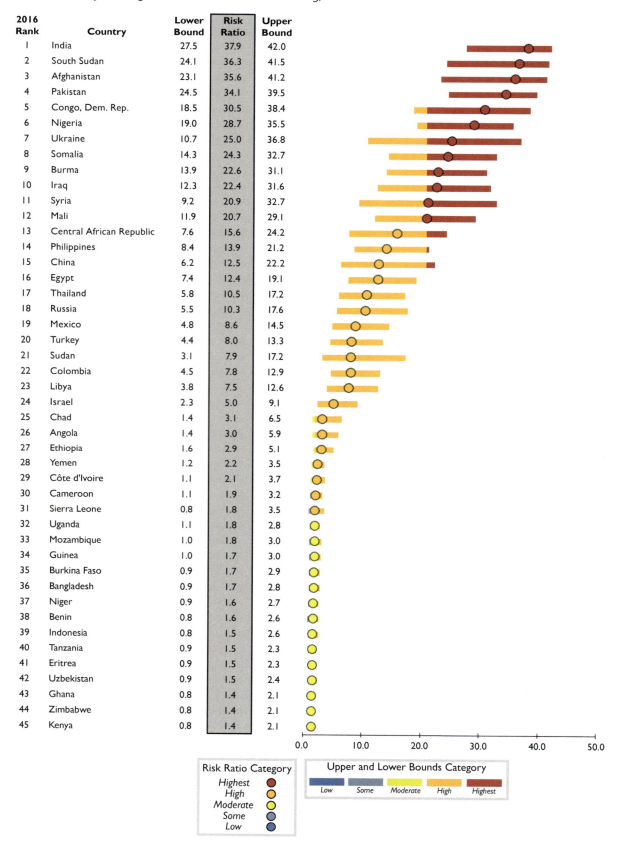

The Peace and Conflict Instability Ledger

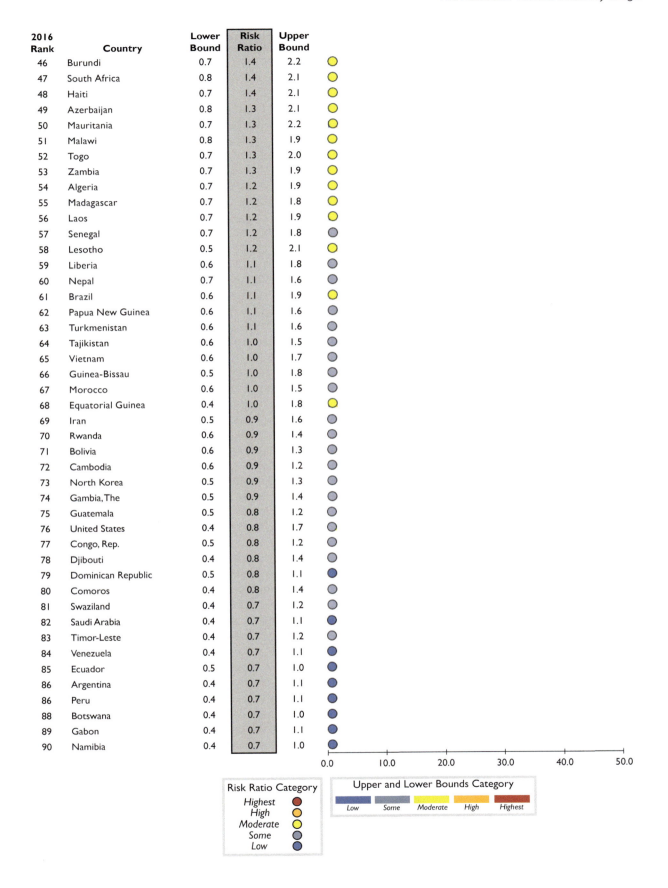

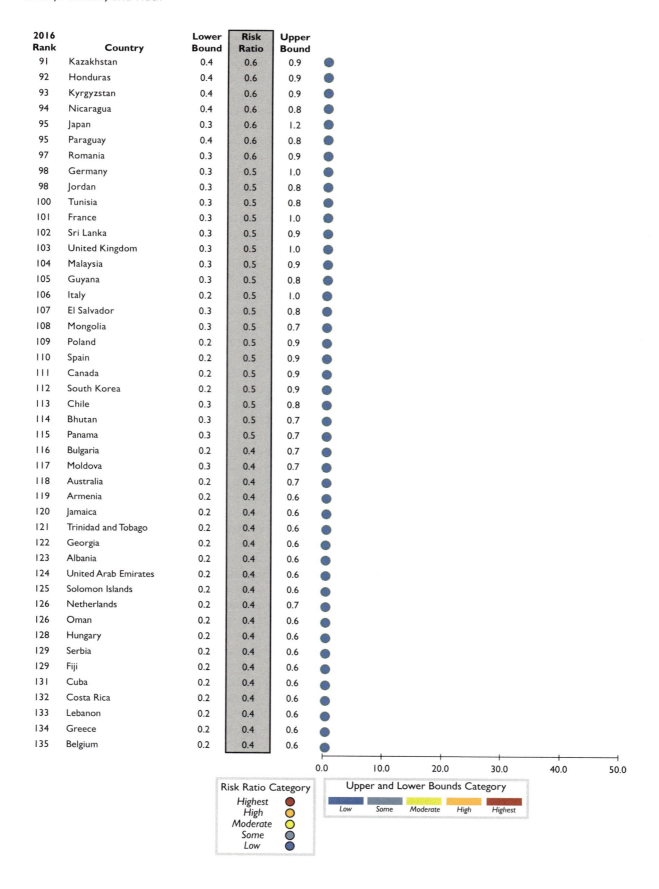

The Peace and Conflict Instability Ledger

2016 Rank	Country	Lower Bound	Risk Ratio	Upper Bound	
136	Uruguay	0.2	0.4	0.6	●
137	Belarus	0.2	0.4	0.6	●
138	Cape Verde	0.2	0.4	0.6	●
139	Slovak Republic	0.2	0.4	0.6	●
140	Portugal	0.2	0.3	0.6	●
141	Czech Republic	0.2	0.3	0.6	●
142	Kuwait	0.2	0.3	0.6	●
143	Suriname	0.2	0.3	0.6	●
144	Switzerland	0.2	0.3	0.6	●
145	Austria	0.2	0.3	0.6	●
146	Sweden	0.2	0.3	0.6	●
147	Mauritius	0.2	0.3	0.5	●
148	New Zealand	0.2	0.3	0.5	●
149	Bosnia and Herzegovina	0.2	0.3	0.5	●
150	Denmark	0.1	0.3	0.5	●
151	Qatar	0.2	0.3	0.5	●
152	Croatia	0.1	0.3	0.5	●
153	Latvia	0.2	0.3	0.5	●
154	Ireland	0.1	0.3	0.5	●
155	Singapore	0.1	0.3	0.5	●
156	Finland	0.1	0.3	0.5	●
157	Norway	0.1	0.3	0.5	●
158	Macedonia, FYR	0.1	0.3	0.5	●
159	Lithuania	0.1	0.3	0.5	●
160	Bahrain	0.1	0.3	0.4	●
161	Slovenia	0.1	0.2	0.4	●
162	Estonia	0.1	0.2	0.4	●
163	Cyprus	0.1	0.2	0.4	●
164	Montenegro	0.1	0.2	0.4	●
165	Luxembourg	0.1	0.2	0.3	●

Table 11.10 Country Rankings of Overall Forecast Risk of Instability, 2015–2017

2016 Rank	Country	Lower Bound	Risk Ratio	Upper Bound
1	Pakistan	15.0	15.2	15.2
2	India	14.7	15.1	15.2
3	Afghanistan	14.5	15.1	15.2
4	South Sudan	14.0	15.1	15.2
5	Sudan	14.2	15.1	15.2
6	Nigeria	14.2	15.0	15.2
7	Philippines	14.6	15.0	15.1
8	Congo, Dem. Rep.	12.9	15.0	15.2
9	Iraq	13.7	15.0	15.2
10	Burma	13.5	14.8	15.1
11	Uganda	14.1	14.8	15.1
12	Ukraine	13.2	14.8	15.1
13	Yemen	13.9	14.7	15.1
14	Russia	13.4	14.7	15.1
15	Ethiopia	13.2	14.6	15.1
16	Syria	10.7	14.4	15.1
17	Thailand	12.8	14.3	15.0
18	Somalia	11.3	14.2	15.1
19	Israel	12.0	14.2	15.0
20	Algeria	12.3	13.9	14.8
21	Libya	9.4	13.6	15.0
22	Azerbaijan	9.2	13.0	14.8
23	Central African Republic	10.1	12.9	14.6
24	Colombia	7.8	12.8	14.7
25	Mali	5.7	10.0	13.4
26	Egypt	6.0	9.2	12.2
27	Chad	5.0	9.2	13.0
28	Guinea	4.7	7.5	10.4
29	Haiti	5.0	7.5	10.2
30	Côte d'Ivoire	3.9	6.6	9.9
31	China	2.8	5.8	9.9
32	Angola	2.7	5.3	8.9
33	Zimbabwe	3.2	5.2	7.5
34	Uzbekistan	3.1	4.8	6.7
35	Eritrea	2.8	4.5	6.6
36	Lebanon	2.3	4.5	7.3
37	Turkey	2.3	4.1	6.6
38	Cameroon	1.8	4.0	7.5
39	Mexico	2.1	3.9	6.6
40	Gabon	2.2	3.6	5.2
41	Madagascar	2.2	3.5	5.0
42	Venezuela	1.9	3.5	5.5
43	Iran	1.8	3.4	5.6
44	Bangladesh	1.9	3.3	5.2
45	Tanzania	1.6	2.9	4.6

Risk Ratio Category
- Highest
- High
- Moderate
- Some
- Low

Upper and Lower Bounds Category: Low, Some, Moderate, High, Highest

The Peace and Conflict Instability Ledger

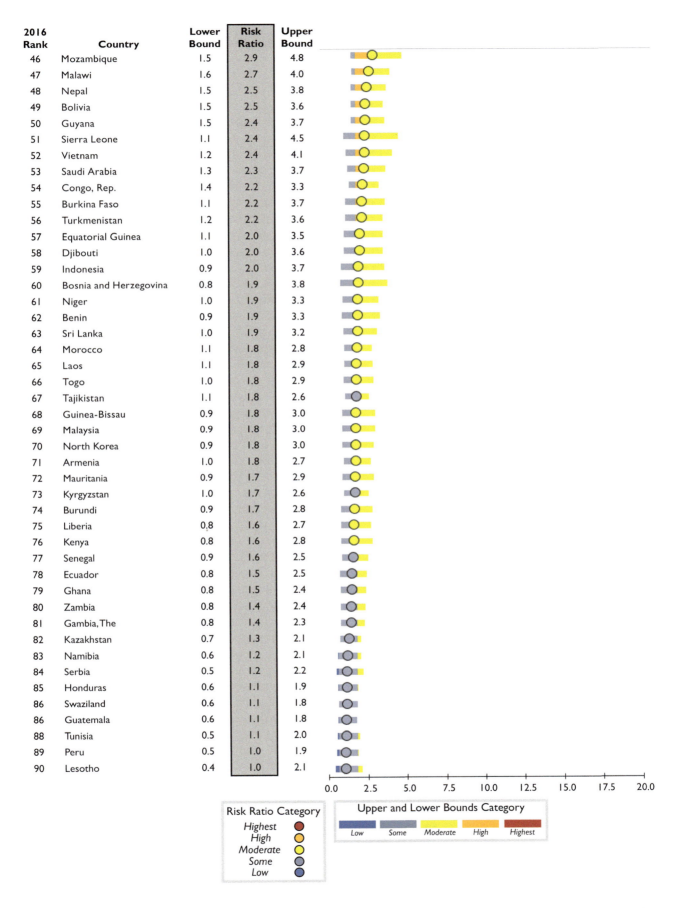

2016 Rank	Country	Lower Bound	Risk Ratio	Upper Bound
91	Bhutan	0.5	1.0	1.8
92	Georgia	0.5	1.0	1.9
93	Rwanda	0.6	1.0	1.6
94	Brazil	0.5	1.0	1.8
95	South Africa	0.5	1.0	1.8
95	Comoros	0.4	0.9	1.8
97	Botswana	0.4	0.9	1.7
98	Cambodia	0.5	0.9	1.4
98	Argentina	0.4	0.9	1.5
100	Nicaragua	0.4	0.8	1.4
101	Papua New Guinea	0.4	0.8	1.4
102	Dominican Republic	0.5	0.8	1.4
103	El Salvador	0.4	0.8	1.3
104	Belarus	0.4	0.8	1.4
105	Timor-Leste	0.3	0.7	1.4
106	Paraguay	0.4	0.7	1.2
107	Suriname	0.3	0.7	1.2
108	Moldova	0.3	0.7	1.2
109	Albania	0.3	0.7	1.1
110	Romania	0.3	0.6	1.1
111	Jordan	0.4	0.6	1.0
112	Oman	0.3	0.6	1.0
113	Fiji	0.3	0.6	1.0
114	Bulgaria	0.3	0.5	0.9
115	Belgium	0.2	0.5	1.0
116	Qatar	0.2	0.5	1.0
117	United Arab Emirates	0.2	0.5	0.8
118	South Korea	0.2	0.5	0.9
119	Cuba	0.2	0.4	0.9
120	Singapore	0.2	0.4	0.9
121	Kuwait	0.2	0.4	0.8
122	Solomon Islands	0.2	0.4	0.8
123	Montenegro	0.2	0.4	0.8
124	Jamaica	0.2	0.4	0.7
125	Latvia	0.2	0.4	0.7
126	Macedonia, FYR	0.2	0.4	0.7
126	Croatia	0.2	0.4	0.7
128	Bahrain	0.2	0.4	0.7
129	Czech Republic	0.1	0.3	0.6
129	United States	0.1	0.3	0.7
131	Panama	0.2	0.3	0.5
132	France	0.1	0.3	0.5
133	Mongolia	0.1	0.2	0.4
134	Italy	0.1	0.2	0.5
135	Japan	0.1	0.2	0.4

Risk Ratio Category
Highest
High
Moderate
Some
Low

Upper and Lower Bounds Category
Low — Some — Moderate — High — Highest

The Peace and Conflict Instability Ledger

2016 Rank	Country	Lower Bound	Risk Ratio	Upper Bound	
136	Germany	0.1	0.2	0.4	
137	Estonia	0.1	0.2	0.4	
138	United Kingdom	0.1	0.2	0.4	
139	Chile	0.1	0.2	0.3	
140	Poland	0.1	0.2	0.4	
141	Spain	0.1	0.2	0.4	
142	Canada	0.1	0.2	0.4	
143	Trinidad and Tobago	0.1	0.2	0.3	
144	Slovak Republic	0.1	0.2	0.3	
145	Cape Verde	0.1	0.2	0.3	
146	Australia	0.1	0.2	0.3	
147	Costa Rica	0.1	0.2	0.3	
148	Greece	0.1	0.2	0.3	
149	Hungary	0.1	0.2	0.3	
150	Netherlands	0.1	0.2	0.3	
151	Uruguay	0.1	0.2	0.3	
152	Mauritius	0.1	0.1	0.3	
153	Portugal	0.1	0.1	0.3	
154	Switzerland	0.1	0.1	0.2	
155	Austria	0.1	0.1	0.2	
156	Sweden	0.1	0.1	0.2	
157	New Zealand	0.1	0.1	0.2	
158	Denmark	0.1	0.1	0.2	
159	Lithuania	0.1	0.1	0.2	
160	Ireland	0.1	0.1	0.2	
161	Finland	0.1	0.1	0.2	
162	Norway	0.1	0.1	0.2	
163	Slovenia	0.0	0.1	0.2	
164	Cyprus	0.0	0.1	0.2	
165	Luxembourg	0.0	0.1	0.1	

0.0   2.5   5.0   7.5   10.0   12.5   15.0   17.5   20.0

Risk Ratio Category
Highest
High
Moderate
Some
Low

Upper and Lower Bounds Category
Low   Some   Moderate   High   Highest

Notes

1 CIDCM developed the predecessor to the PCIL – the Peace and Conflict Ledger (PCL) – in 2001. The PCL differs from the original PCIL in several respects. First, the PCL was intended to gauge the peacebuilding capacity of countries, whereas the PCIL was designed to assess the risk of instability events. Second, the PCL is constructed as an index reflecting the integration of several factors, whereas the PCIL is a forecast that leverages analysis of the historical relationship between several factors and instability outcomes of interest. Third, the PCL uses indicators of seven factors (human security, self-determination, discrimination, regime type, durability, societal capacity, neighborhood conditions), while the PCIL uses a distinct but overlapping set of five factors (institutional consistency, economic openness, infant mortality, militarization, neighborhood conditions).

2 This definition institutes a stricter standard of conflict offset, which must be immediate (i.e., occur in year $t+1$) and sustained (i.e., last continuously through year $t+3$). Less stringent alternative definitions would merely require conflict offset in any of the subsequent three years.

3 The endpoint of 2010 was chosen to maximize the extent of the data used in the training models while ensuring no overlap between the period covered by the dependent variables (latest observations reflect outcomes for 2011–2013) and the year for which the latest forecasts are generated (2014).

4 The risks facing a number of these cases, especially Libya, might have been evaluated as more serious with the inclusion of additional risk factors. One candidate is factionalism within militaries; however, data on this indicator are not currently available on a comprehensive basis.

5 The historical means reflect the extent of the data: 1975–2014 for both adverse regime change and internal war and 1989–2014 for both state-based mass killing and non-state mass killing.

6 For more details of the mechanics of the classification procedure, see David A. Backer and Paul K. Huth (2016). "The Peace and Conflict Instability Ledger: Ranking States on Future Risks." In David A. Backer, Ravi Bhavnani, and Paul K. Huth. *Peace and Conflict 2016*. New York, NY: Routledge.

7 Bangladesh, Bosnia and Herzegovina, Djibouti, Gabon, Guyana, Haiti, Madagascar, Malawi, Nepal, Venezuela, and Zimbabwe.

8 Algeria and Lebanon.

9 Angola, Cameroon, Eritrea, Iran, Turkmenistan, and Uzbekistan.

10 China, Colombia, Mexico, and Turkey.

References

Aronson, Jacob, and Paul Huth (2017) "The Size of Rebel and State Armed Forces in Internal Conflicts: Measurement and Implications." In David Backer, Ravi Bhavnani, and Paul Huth (eds). *Peace and Conflict 2017*. New York: Routledge.

Aronson, Jacob, Paul Huth, Mark Lichbach, and Kiyoung Chang (2016) "How Rebels Win (and Why They Lose)." Unpublished manuscript.

Avdan, Nazli, and Gary Uzonyi (2017) "V for Vendetta: Government Mass Killing and Domestic Terrorism." *Studies in Conflict & Terrorism* 40(11): 934–965.

Balcells, Laia, and Stathis Kalyvas (2014) "Does Warfare Matter? Severity, Duration, and Outcomes of Civil Wars." *Journal of Conflict Resolution* 58(8): 1390–1418.

Buhaug, Halvard, Scot Gates, and Pavi Lujala (2009) "Geography, Rebel Capability, and the Duration of Civil Conflict." *Journal of Conflict Resolution* 53(4): 544–569.

Buhaug, Halvard, and Päivi Lujala (2005) "Accounting for Scale: Measuring Geography in Quantitative Studies of Civil War." *Political Geography* 24(4): 399–418.

Cederman, Lars-Erik, Nils B. Weidmann, and Kristian Skrede Gleditsch (2011) "Horizontal Inequalities and Ethnonationalist Civil War: A Global Comparison." *American Political Science Review* 105(3): 478–495.

Cil, Deniz (2017) "Multilateral Peacekeeping Operations Active in 2015." In David Backer, Ravi Bhavnani, and Paul Huth (eds) *Peace and Conflict 2017*. New York: Routledge.

Collier, Paul, Anke Hoeffler, and Måns Söderbom (2004) "On the Duration of Civil War." *Journal of Peace Research* 41(3): 253–273.

Cunningham, David (2006) "Veto Players and Civil War Duration." *American Journal of Political Science* 50(4): 875–892.

Eck, Kristine, and Lisa Hultman (2007) "One-Sided Violence against Civilians in War: Insights from New Fatality Data." *Journal of Peace Research* 44(2): 233–246.

Fearon, James, and David Laitin (2007) "Civil War Termination." Paper presented at the Annual Meeting of the American Political Science Association, Chicago, IL, 30 August–2 September.

Fearon, James, and David Laitin (2003) "Ethnicity, Insurgency, and Civil War." *American Political Science Review* 97(1): 75–90.

Findley, Michael, and Joseph Young (2012) "Terrorism and Civil War: A Spatial and Temporal Approach to a Conceptual Problem." *Perspectives on Politics* 10(2): 285–305.

Gassebne, Martin, Jerg Gutmann, and Stefan Voigt (2016) "When to Expect a Coup d'État? An Extreme Bounds Analysis of Coup Determinants." *Public Choice* 169(3): 293–313.

Goldstone, Jack A., Robert H. Bates, David L. Epstein, Ted R. Gurr, Michael B. Lustik, Monty G. Marshall, Jay Ulfelder, and Mark Woodward (2010) "A Global Model for Forecasting Political Instability." *American Journal of Political Science* 54(1): 190–208.

Hegre, Håvard (2014) "Democracy and Armed Conflict." *Journal of Peace Research* 51(2): 159–172.

Hegre, Håvard, Joakim Karlsen, Håvard Nygård, Håvard Strand, and Henrik Urdal (2013) "Predicting Armed Conflict, 2010–2050." *International Studies Quarterly* 57(2): 250–270.

Hewitt, J. Joseph (2008) "The Peace and Conflict Instability Ledger: Ranking States on Future Risk." In J. Joseph Hewitt, Jonathan Wilkenfeld, and Ted R. Gurr (eds) *Peace and Conflict 2008*. Boulder, CO: Paradigm Publishers.

Högbladh, Stina, Therése Pettersson, and Lotta Themnér (2011) "External Support in Armed Conflict 1975–2009. Presenting new data." Paper presented at the Annual Convention of the International Studies Association, Montreal, Canada, 16–19 March.

Hultman, Lisa (2014) "Beyond Keeping Peace: United Nations Effectiveness in the Midst of Fighting." *American Political Science Review* 108(4): 737–754.

Hultman, Lisa (2007) "Battle Losses and Rebel Violence: Raising the Costs for Fighting." *Terrorism and Political Violence* 19(2): 205–222.

Humphreys, Macartan, and Jeremy Weinstein (2006) "Handling and Manhandling Civilians in Civil War." *American Political Science Review* 100(3): 429–447.

International Peace Institute (IPI) (2016) "IPI Peacekeeping Database." Available at www.providingforpeacekeeping.org (accessed in December 2016).

Johnston, Patrick (2012) "Does Decapitation Work? Assessing the Effectiveness of Leadership Targeting in Counterinsurgency Campaigns." *International Security* 36(4): 47–79.

Kalyvas, Stathis, and Laia Balcells (2010) "International System and Technologies of Rebellion: How the End of the Cold War Shaped Internal Conflict." *American Political Science Review* 104(3): 415–429.

Konstanz, Gerald, Margit Bussmann, and Constantin Ruhe (2012) "The Dynamics of Mass Killings: Testing Time-Series Models of One-Sided Violence in the Bosnian Civil War." *International Interactions* 38(4): 443–561.

Linke, Andrew, Frank Witmer, and John O'Loughlin (2012) "Space-Time Granger Analysis of the War in Iraq: A Study of Coalition and Insurgent Action-Reaction." *International Interactions* 38(4): 402–425.

Linzer, Drew, and Jeffrey Staton (2015) "A Global Measure of Judicial Independence, 1948–2012." *Journal of Law and Courts* 3(2): 223–256.

Lujala, Päivi (2009) "Deadly Combat Over Natural Resources: Gems, Petroleum, Drugs, and the Severity of Armed Civil Conflict." *Journal of Conflict Resolution* 53(1): 50–71.

Lujala, Päivi, Nils Petter Gleditsch, and Elisabeth Gilmore (2005) "A Diamond Curse? Civil War and a Lootable Resource." *Journal of Conflict Resolution* 49(4): 538–562.

Lyall, Jason, and Isaiah Wilson (2009) "Rage Against the Machines: Explaining Outcomes in Counterinsurgency Wars." *International Organization* 63(1): 67–106.

Marshall, Monty (2011) "Polity IV Project: Political Regime Characteristics and Transitions, 1800–2010." Available at www.systemicpeace.org/polity/polity4.htm (accessed in December 2016).

McGrath, John (2006) *Boots on the Ground: Troop Density in Contingency Operations.* Fort Leavenworth: Combat Studies Institute Press.

Melander, Erik, Therése Pettersson, and Lotta Themnér (2016) "Organized Violence, 1989–2015." *Journal of Peace Research* 53(5): 727–742.

Prorok, Alyssa (2016) "Leader Incentives and Civil War Outcomes." *American Journal of Political Science* 60(1): 70–84.

Salehyan, Idean, and Kristian Skrede Gleditsch (2006) "Refugees and the Spread of Civil War." *International Organization* 60(2): 335–366.

Slantchev, Branislav (2003) "The Principle of Convergence in Wartime Negotiations." The *American Political Science Review* 97(4): 621–632.

Sullivan, Patricia, and Johannes Karreth (2015) "The Conditional Impact of Military Intervention on Internal Armed Conflict Outcomes." *Conflict Management and Peace Science* 32(3): 269–288.

Tollefsen, Andreas Forø, Håvard Strand, and Halvard Buhaug (2012) "PRIO-GRID: A Unified Spatial Data Structure." *Journal of Peace Research* 49(2): 363–374.

Uppsala Conflict Data Program (UCDP) (2016) *UCDP Conflict Encyclopedia.* Available at http://ucdp.uu.se/ (accessed in December 2016).

Vogt, Manuel, Nils-Christian Bormann, Seraina Rüegger, Lars-Erik Cederman, Philipp Hunziker, and Luc Girardin (2015) "Integrating Data on Ethnicity, Geography, and Conflict: The Ethnic Power Relations Dataset Family." *Journal of Conflict Resolution* 59(7): 1327–1342.

Walter, Barbara (2009) "Bargaining Failures and Civil War." *Annual Review of Political Science* 12(1): 243–261.

World Bank (2016) "World Development Indicators." Washington, DC: The World Bank (producer and distributor). http://data.worldbank.org (accessed in December 2016).

12

Refugees and Conflict Diffusion

Seraina Rüegger

Introduction

Forced displacement is currently at an all-time recorded high. The latest statistics show global totals of 21.3 million refugees and 65.3 million internally displaced persons as of December 2015 (UNHCR 2016a). These uprooted people suffer immensely, in terms of both their exposure to the circumstances that prompt displacement and what they face as a result of displacement. At the same time, displaced populations pose major challenges for sending and receiving countries, as well as for the international community.

Governments, political parties and others in some countries, especially across Europe, have reacted harshly to sharp increases in irregular migration of people from places such as Syria, Afghanistan, and Somalia. Many of the responses are restrictive, including intensifying border control, building fences, barring access, and refusing to provide asylum. Those restrictions are premised on risks of negative externalities associated with refugees, despite their displacement being involuntary, their resulting vulnerability, and the internationally recognized humanitarian interests and responsibilities to ensure their protection. Critics of accepting refugees claim an assortment of risks, often highlighting the burden on the economy, social services, and state budgets and threats to cultural identity, public health, law and order, and security. In particular, refugees have been portrayed as a consequence *and* a cause of conflict. Examples of positing the latter relationship are numerous, with notable past examples including the Palestinians in Lebanon during the 1970s and Rwandan refugees in Uganda and Zaire (now the Democratic Republic of the Congo) during the 1990s.

Fundamental connections exist between forced displacement and political violence. The strong link is reflected in the 1951 UN Convention relating to the Status of Refugees, according to which a refugee is:

> a person who owing to a well-founded fear of being persecuted for reasons of race, religion, nationality, membership of a particular social group or political opinion, is outside the country of his nationality and is unable or, owing to such fear, is unwilling to avail himself of the protection of that country [...]

(UNHCR 2007: 17)

The language in the Refugee Convention is not just notional – it aligns closely with ongoing empirical realities of political violence, which are drivers of forced displacement. Figure 12.1 illustrates the relationship at a global level between the count of active armed conflicts, as recorded in the UCDP/PRIO Dataset (Gleditsch et al. 2002), and the numbers of refugees from 1960–2015 (UNHCR 2016b). The correlation between conflict incidence and refugee counts for this time period is statistically significant ($p=0.000$, $R^2=0.64$, $N=56$). More detailed studies have found that various forms of political violence, including wars and state repression, are major causes of refugee outflows (e.g., Davenport, Moore, and Poe 2003; Melander and Öberg 2006; Schmeidl 1997; Weiner 1993; Wood 1994; Zolberg, Suhrke, and Aguayo 1986). Yet systematic analysis of whether – and if so, when and why – refugee inflows have an unfavorable impact on conflict remains limited.

This chapter aims to advance understanding of the empirical relationship between refugees and political violence in the country of asylum (CoA). I begin by reviewing existing research on refugees and conflict diffusion. My empirical analysis focuses on the argument that refugees can disturb the ethnic balance in the CoA. For instance, the ethnic Macedonian majority government on several occasions expressed its concern that the fragile balance between ethnic Macedonians and ethnic Albanians at a local level would be adversely affected by Kosovar Albanian refugees arriving in 1999 (Milner 2000: 29).

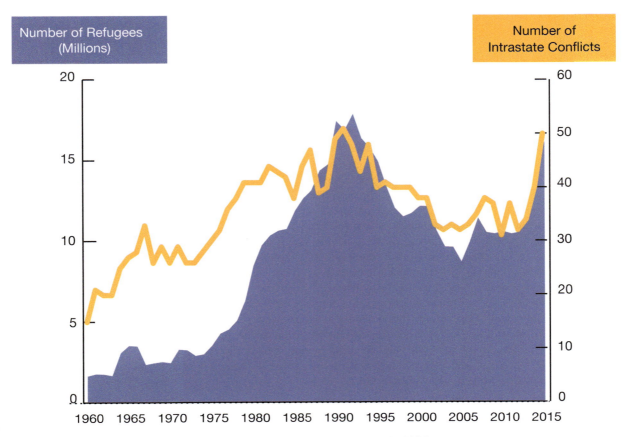

Figure 12.1 Annual Refugee Count and Prevalence of Armed Conflicts, 1960–2015

I use novel data on the ethnicity of refugees, which enables me to distinguish between refugees who have ethnic ties to the population in the CoA and refugees without such kin. Results of my statistical estimations indicate that refugees do not cause conflict directly. They can, however, exacerbate already existing political tensions, especially when transborder ethnic kin (TEK) groups suffer from political marginalization. A suggested policy implication of the findings is that governments often wrongfully blame refugees for internal tensions and thereby overstate the security threats that refugees pose.

The Spread of Civil Conflict

The geographic clustering of civil conflicts in some regions of the world is undisputed in the literature (Hegre and Sambanis 2006; Most and Starr 1980; Tavares 2009; Wallensteen and Sollenberg 1998; Ward and Gleditsch 2002). A lively debate exists, however, about the causes for this geographic concentration of political violence. Some scholars argue the concentration is due to systemic factors, such as poverty, which increase the risk of intrastate conflict and also cluster regionally (Fearon and Laitin 2003; Murdoch and Sandler 2002). Other scholars contend that conflicts cluster geographically because the impact of civil conflicts is not necessarily confined within the borders of individual states where violence is initiated. Instead, these conflicts often have cross-border dimensions (e.g., Buhaug and Gleditsch 2008; Cederman et al. 2013; Gleditsch 2007; Lake and Rothchild 1998; Sambanis 2001). Among the relevant dimensions are ethnic ties of warring groups, refugee movements, arms flows, and regional economic disruptions. As a result of such factors, conflicts can be contagious, with violence diffusing geographically, particularly to neighboring countries (Buhaug and Gleditsch 2008; Forsberg 2014; Gleditsch 2007; Hill and Rothchild 1986; Sambanis 2001).

Building on previous research (Elkins and Simmons 2005; Lake and Rothchild 1998; Most and Starr 1980), I define a conflict as involving geographical diffusion if the outbreak of intrastate conflict in one country is influenced by a temporally prior intrastate conflict in another country. Forsberg (2014) distinguishes between direct and indirect mechanisms of conflict diffusion. Direct mechanisms reflect tangible things – for example, conflict actors, refugees, and arms – that physically flow from one country to another. As a result of such influxes, a new conflict can be precipitated, potentially due to an extension or relocation of conflict occurring elsewhere. A primary indirect mechanism is demonstration effects, whereby the conflict in one country may serve as inspiration for conflict in another country. In some cases, the issues are mirrored and actors have similar interests. Forsberg (2014) is also among the latest contributions to the literature that highlights the limited knowledge about conflict diffusion processes involving these indirect factors, partially owing to the lack of systematic data.

Refugee-Related Conflict Diffusion

Refugees have been identified as the basis of one form of spillover mechanism that contributes to conflict diffusion (Lischer 2005; Salehyan and Gleditsch 2006; Stedman and Tanner 2003; Whitaker 1998; Zolberg, Suhrke, and Aguayo 1986). Research on refugee militarization makes clear that refugees can become active agents in violent events (e.g., Adelman 1998; Lebson 2013; Muggah and Mogire 2006; Zolberg, Suhrke, and Aguayo 1989). Some refugee flows are associated with the expansion of rebel or terrorist networks (Choi and Salehyan 2013; Harpviken et al. 2013; Lebson 2013; Milton, Spencer, and Findley 2013; Salehyan 2007). In this respect, distinguishing voluntary rebel–refugee collaboration from involuntary refugee manipulation and instrumentalization by insurgent or governmental groups is important. Refugees have mobilized militarily in the form of new insurgent movements, such as the Rwandan Patriotic Front that was founded by Tutsi refugees in Uganda (Khan 2001: 5). Also, refugees may import ideologies that encourage the opposition in the host country (Salehyan and Gleditsch 2006: 343). During the late-1970s, the Thai government feared that refugees from Cambodia "were predominantly Khmer Rouge who might be a subversive element in the Thai border provinces" (Stein 1979: 717). Meanwhile, insurgent groups can use refugee camps as sanctuaries, affording them vital protection and even bases of operations, and as venues to recruit fighters (Barber 1997; Lischer 2003; Terry 2002). For example, in 2008, armed members of the Justice and Equality Movement (JEM), fighting against the Sudanese government, infiltrated refugee camps in Chad and recruited heavily among the ethnic Zaghawa refugee population (US Committee for Refugees and Immigrants 2009). Furthermore, refugee camps can be used for the storage and trafficking of small arms (Muggah and Mogire 2006; Weiner 1993).

In addition, analysts and policymakers posit other mechanisms whereby refugees present security concerns that heighten the potential for diffusion of armed conflict. Large refugee influxes are especially likely to lead to economic disruptions for host states (Goldstone 2002; Martin, 2005). For instance, the Jordanian government has been concerned that the massive influx of refugees from Syria is exacerbating Jordan's already severe economic problems (Phillips 2013). Refugee flows often engender economic pressures because of the needs of refugees in regards to space, shelter, food, and health services (Weiner 1993; Gomez et al. 2010). In many – particularly poorer – countries, an influx of refugees can result in competition over scarce resources between refugees and the host population, which can have subsequent negative effects such as increased crime (Baez 2011: 391), as well as other forms of violence. For example, refugees from Rwanda and Burundi chopped down thousands of trees in the Kagera region of Tanzania for personal and commercial purposes, resulting in environmental degradation and causing local people to travel further and in dangerous terrain in search of wood (Baez 2011: 406). Thus, sudden population growth associated with large refugee caseloads can destabilize the host country (Raleigh and Urdal 2007). In the event of economic decline, the asylum state faces a higher risk of experiencing conflict (Collier and Hoeffler 2002; Miguel, Satyanath, and Sergenti 2004).

If these arguments hold consistently, countries and regions that host refugees in a given year should tend to be more likely to exhibit conflict in subsequent years. On the surface, the evidence is suggestive. Conflicts cluster in certain regions, especially Africa, Asia, and the Middle East. These conflicts are drivers of a large share of the refugee population, most of which is concentrated in neighboring countries within the same regions (UNHCR 2016a). According to the theoretical claims, these neighboring countries have a greater potential to be conflict affected as well, which tends to be true empirically. The question, however, is whether a systematic relationship exists in which refugee populations actually contribute to conflict diffusion, by influencing the incidence of violence in the countries to which they flee. Alternative explanations exist. In particular, refugees fleeing conflict may happen to migrate to other conflict-affected areas, especially in transborder regions, in which case the presence of refugees is coincidental to the violence observed in the places where they relocate, rather than a contributing factor.

Select comparative studies examine refugee-related security problems for the asylum country. Lischer (2001) reports that approximately 15% of the refugee populations between 1987 and 1998 experienced violence, including attacks between governments and refugees or attacks among refugees. She highlights the capability and willingness of the host state to accommodate the refugees and to prevent their militarization as key determinants of security threats related to refugees (Lischer 2005: 29). Analyzing a global sample over 50 years, Salehyan and Gleditsch (2006: 360) found that only refugees from neighboring countries increase the risk of intrastate conflict. This finding is noteworthy considering that the majority of refugees worldwide reside in states that are contiguous to their country of origin (CoO) (UNHCR 2016a).

The Role of Refugees' Ethnic Linkages to the Host Population

A line of argument that has attracted significant attention is the socio-demographic impact of refugee inflows, in relation to the host society, which can have significant political implications. Refugees are not "an undifferentiated mass" (Lischer 2007: 134). Instead, individual refugees have their own characteristics. Refugee populations may share the same characteristics, or be diverse. The extent to which those characteristics coincide with those of a host country could be a critical factor influencing the prospects of conflict diffusion. Certain refugee inflows can change the composition of the asylum country's population in ways that are destabilizing and liable to trigger conflict (Lake and Rothchild 1998: 25). For instance, during the late 1970s, "Malaysia was upset by the high percentage of ethnic Chinese from Vietnam amongst the recent boat [refugees], the acceptance of whom could disturb Malaysia's delicate internal ethnic balance between Malays and Chinese" (Stein 1979: 717).

Consequently, information about demographic characteristics of refugees is crucial for assessing the role of refugees in conflict diffusion dynamics. The example from Malaysia illustrates that knowing the ethnicity of refugees, in addition to their country of origin, is important.

Ethnic group membership is based on a shared belief in a putative descent and marked by a common language, religion or physical features (Cederman, Wimmer, and Min 2010: 13). The ethnicity of refugees is expected to influence where they flee, as well as how they are perceived in the asylum country and especially their relationship with a host population. As illustrated in Figure 12.2, many refugees flee along TEK linkages (Rüegger and Bohnet 2015). For instance, Iraqi Shia refugees fled to Iran, Serbs to Serbia, Hutus to Zaire, and Afghani Pashtuns to Pakistan during the 1990s (Ogata 2005: 327). In general, governments and populations in asylum countries tend to be more receptive to co-ethnic refugees, who can more effectively integrate due to similar language, religion, and cultural norms, as well as being less likely to cause conflict (Jacobsen 1996: 669; Newland 1993: 86).

The risk of refugee-related conflict diffusion is elevated in ethnically or religiously divided societies with existing intergroup tensions. Among the key reasons are that a significant influx of refugees can alter the ethnic/religious balance, imperil a political equilibrium among ethnic/religious groups, and threaten cultural identity within the asylum state,

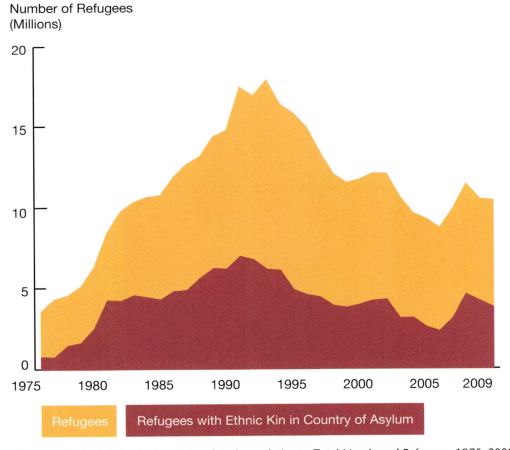

Figure 12.2 Refugees with Co-Ethnics in Countries of Asylum relative to Total Number of Refugees, 1975–2009

which might ultimately end in civil violence (Adamson 2006; Goldstone 2002; Krcmaric 2014; Loescher and Milner 2004; Newland 1993; Salehyan and Gleditsch 2006; Weiner 1993). In particular, refugees who are kin of a minority may shift the power balance by raising the number of people belonging to that ethnic group, thereby strengthening the group's demographic weight and putative claims upon political, social, and economic status. Such a refugee influx can therefore embolden dissatisfied minority groups and threaten the majority group's predominance. In response, the incumbent group(s) might undertake to reinforce the exclusion and repression of such challenging minorities – a backlash that increases the risk of violence. In addition, existing conflicts between local ethnic groups may be transmitted to refugees, as in the case of Somali refugees in Kenya, who suffered from the same discrimination as the local ethnic Somali population. Meanwhile, the large influx of Somali refugees to Kenya also increased resentments and hostilities of other Kenyans against ethnic Somalis (Kagwanja and Juma 2008: 223). Furthermore, refugees who are co-ethnics of a minority group usually receive less support than refugees with links to the majority, who do not challenge the political status quo. The lack of assistance and protection can be a major source of insecurity in refugee settlements, which increases the potential of refugees exhibiting grievances and being subject to militarization and manipulation by rebel groups (Crisp 2000).

In sum, the impact of refugees on inter-ethnic relations in an asylum state can be expected to depend on how the ethnic composition of refugees intersects with ethnic dynamics in the asylum state. Figure 12.3 illustrates different scenarios of refugee inflows. The central distinction is whether refugees have ties to governmental or marginalized ethnic groups. I expect the risk of refugees triggering violence to be higher in the latter case. Therefore, I state the following hypothesis: *Refugee-related conflict diffusion is conditional on TEK ties to a politically marginalized group* in the CoA.

Evaluating these claims statistically has presented a challenge, owing to a scarcity of systematic data, beyond case-based evidence. In the absence of disaggregated cross-national data on characteristics of refugee populations, existing large-N studies struggle to assess the impact of refugees on local ethnic demographics, as part of the equation of refugee-related conflict diffusion. Consequently, the claim that refugees diffuse conflict by disturbing the ethnic balance in the country of asylum has never been analyzed quantitatively as a global phenomenon. Further, no study on refugees has distinguished different cross-border linkages, including ties to governmental and powerless groups, which have been identified as crucial structural factors in conflict processes (Cederman et al. 2013; Forsberg 2014). Little is known about the causal mechanisms of how refugees may contribute to conflict diffusion, besides the strong intuition that refugees are involved in transnational dimensions of conflict dynamics.

Testing the Ethnic Balance Argument Using New Refugee Data

Fortunately, refugee data has improved greatly in recent years, sufficient to enable more in-depth analysis. In particular, the Office of the United Nations High Commissioner for Refugees publishes annual data on the numbers of refugees for each country in the world UNHCR (2016b). The advances in these data include demographic breakdowns covering age and sex, as well as monthly data on asylum seekers. The available data have shortcomings, however, so they must be used with caution and may not be suitable for purposes of all analyses. Many displaced individuals never register with the relevant authorities. As a result, reported statistics of the counts of refugees and their demographic composition should be viewed as incomplete and imprecise. Moreover, the UNHCR does not disaggregate the data with respect to the causes of flight – key details that are pertinent to studies of refugee-related conflict diffusion. Furthermore, the ethnic background of a refugee can be a very sensitive issue. Many refugees can be afraid to share this information. In addition, the UNHCR

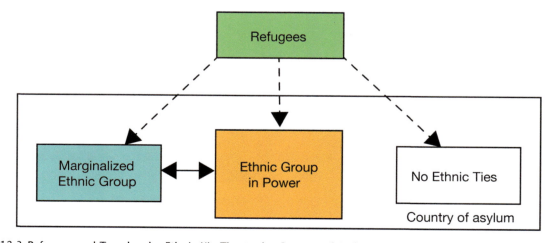

Figure 12.3 Refugees and Transborder Ethnic Kin Ties to the Country of Asylum

is often unwilling to record and publish ethnicity data, with the end product being that such data is neither collected nor reported on a systematic basis.

To address this gap, I have collaborated in assembling cross-national data, with global coverage, on the ethnicity of refugees from 1975–2009 (Rüegger and Bohnet 2015). The dataset encompasses stocks of at least 2,000 refugees for a given pair of a country of origin and a country of asylum – which are, at most, 950 km away from each other – in a given year. This set of cases is defined based on statistics provided by the UNHCR. Because the data focus on stocks of refugees, no distinctions are made between those who are new arrivals and those who have been displaced for a longer period of time. Of course, these distinctions are pertinent to various angles of analysis, but documenting such specifics was beyond the bounds of the data compilation. The data reflect the fact that the ethnic composition of refugees who flee from one country to another is often heterogeneous: simultaneously, members of multiple ethnic groups leave the same country of origin for the same country of asylum. A good example is Kenya, which in 2009 hosted Ethiopian refugees who were of at least three ethnicities: Amhara, Oromo, and Tigre. The dataset indicates whether each ethnic refugee group is dominant (> 75%), a majority (50–75%), or a minority (< 50%) within the flow corresponding to a country pair for a given year. We adopted these discrete thresholds as a basis of categorization of cases, to enable certain gradations while taking account of the lack of precise counts of the ethnic composition of refugees.

The dataset has several applications of high relevance to research, policies, and programming related to refugees. Here, knowledge of the ethnicity of refugees will be employed to study mechanisms of conflict diffusion. In addition, this same information is essential to examine other topics, including: (1) the risks that and reasons why a given person becomes a forced migrant, especially in conflicts where certain ethnic identity groups are persecuted, (2) the direction of flight by refugees, which may be influenced by the existence of ethnic kin in neighboring countries, and (3) how refugees are received in a country of asylum, since cultural similarities facilitate integration and authorities often grant refugee status to asylum seekers belonging to particular ethnic groups.

Analytical Framework

My empirical analysis of refugee-related conflict diffusion encompasses 154 countries from 1975–2009, reflecting the scope of availability of the data on the ethnic composition of refugee stocks. The unit of analysis is the country-year. In all of the model specifications that I estimate, the dependent variable (DV) measures the onset of intrastate conflict. If at least one conflict began during a country-year, I coded the DV as 1; if not, I coded the DV as 0. Any country-year immediately subsequent to one exhibiting an active conflict is dropped, which means that the estimation reflects the risk of observing a new conflict onset, as opposed to encompassing the continuation of an existing conflict as well. As the primary means to capture the diffusion of intrastate conflict, I included in all the model specifications an independent variable (IV) that indicates whether or not a civil conflict was active in a neighboring country – one that shares a common border – during the preceding year. I derived all variables related to intrastate conflict from the UCDP/PRIO Armed Conflict Dataset (Version4_2015), which defines an armed conflict "as a contested incompatibility that concerns government or territory or both where the use of armed force between two parties results in at least 25 battle-related deaths... Of these two parties, at least one is the government of a state" (Gleditsch et al. 2002: 618–619).

I evaluated four model specifications, the results of which are displayed in Table 12.1. A base specification omits all variables related to refugees and is estimated with only the control variables (CVs). Three subsequent model specifications test different versions of how conflict onset may be affected by the extent and nature of refugee presence, which are reflected by different IVs.

Model 2 includes a binary measure of whether or not any refugees were present in the CoA in the previous year, as indicated by the UNHCR (2016b). Previous research has substantiated that the mere presence of refugees from neighboring countries increases the risk of conflict in the CoA (Salehyan and Gleditsch 2006).

Model 3 distinguishes between refugees who have co-ethnics in the CoA and refugees who have no kin in the CoA. To assemble this IV, I linked the data on the ethnicity of refugees (Rüegger and Bohnet 2015) to the TEK data (Vogt et al. 2015), which identifies all ethnic groups that are politically relevant in more than one state. The typical circumstance is that the population of such an ethnic group resides in neighboring states. The ethnic kin refugee variable is lagged one year. I expect refugee-related conflict diffusion to be more likely in cases where the ethnic balance is affected by a refugee influx owing to ethnic kinship between refugees and the host population.

Rüegger

Table 12.1 Estimations of Models of Impact of Refugees on Conflict Onset

Dependent Variable: Onset of Intrastate Conflict	Model 1	Model 2	Model 3	Model 4
Independent Variables				
Refugees (lagged)		0.150		
		(0.195)		
Kin refugees (lagged)			0.209	
			(0.240)	
Kin refugees of marginalized ethnic group (lagged)				0.523*
				(0.299)
Kin refugees of ethnic group in power (lagged)				−0.095
				(0.296)
Non-kin refugees (lagged)			−0.006	0.021
			(0.258)	(0.254)
Conflict in neighbor (lagged)	0.761***	0.751***	0.761***	0.762***
	(0.224)	(0.217)	(0.217)	(0.218)
Excluded population %	0.282	0.324	0.313	0.054
	(0.354)	(0.379)	(0.378)	(0.435)
Population (logged, lagged)	0.138**	0.123*	0.128*	0.115*
	(0.066)	(0.069)	(0.067)	(0.070)
GDP (logged, lagged)	−0.366***	−0.347***	−0.356***	−0.367***
	(0.000)	(0.000)	(0.000)	(0.000)
Elevation	-0.000	-0.000	-0.000	-0.000
	(0.000)	(0.000)	(0.000)	(0.000)
War history	0.080	0.086	0.082	0.067
	(0.062)	(0.062)	(0.062)	(0.061)
Peace years	−0.223***	−0.228***	−0.226***	−0.218***
	(0.054)	(0.058)	(0.058)	(0.057)
Peace years (squared)	0.009***	0.009***	0.009***	0.009***
	(0.003)	(0.003)	(0.003)	(0.003)
Peace years (cubed)	−0.000***	−0.000***	−0.000***	−0.000***
	(0.000)	(0.000)	(0.000)	(0.000)
Constant	−1.001	−1.110	−1.072	−0.851
	(0.965)	(1.009)	(1.027)	(1.043)
Observations	3,880	3,768	3,768	3,768
χ^2	129.297	120.560	124.808	122.706

Note: Country-clustered standard errors in parentheses. * $p<0.1$, ** $p<0.05$, *** $p<0.01$.

Model 4 distinguishes between refugees whose ethnic kin groups have access to state decision-making in the CoA and refugees whose ethnic kin groups are politically excluded in the CoA. The political power status of ethnic groups is obtained from the Ethnic Power Relations (EPR) dataset (Vogt et al., 2015). Governmental groups are coded in EPR as monopoly, dominant, senior partner, or junior partner, while excluded groups are coded as powerless, discriminated, or self-exclusionist. Given the majority of TEK groups are peaceful, simple measures of ethnic connection that neglect power relations might bear little significance to assessments of refugee-related conflict diffusion. Instead, I theorize that refugees who are ethnic kin of a politically dissatisfied group are more likely to increase existing inter-group tensions, possibly escalating to violence, than groups without such kin in a CoA.

All the model specifications include the same set of CVs, to account for alternative explanations of the onset of intrastate conflict. The *share of excluded population* reflects findings that political marginalization of large proportions of society is a major cause of civil violence (Cederman, Wimmer, and Min 2010). Following Salehyan and Gleditsch (2006), I include *GDP per capita (logged)* and *population (logged)* (Heston, Summers, and Aten 2011). Wealthy countries typically have a lower risk of conflict (Blattman and Miguel 2010) and better capacities to cope with refugee inflows. More populous states tend to be associated with a higher risk of civil conflict, though they might also have better capacities to absorb large refugee caseloads. *Elevation* accounts for the fact that refugee flows are deterred by mountainous terrain. This measure uses data downloaded from the GROWup online platform (Girardin et al. 2015), which are based on various sources. Finally, I control for the *war history* and *peace years* – with linear, squared, and cubed terms – of the CoA, to reflect how duration influences the impact of conflict legacy on conflict onset and to capture the potential for conflict recurrence (Carter and Signorino, 2010).

Results

The results of the estimation of Model 1 confirm the claim that conflicts cluster because the risk of onset in any given country is strongly influenced by the existence of recent conflict in neighboring countries. This finding offers compelling evidence that civil conflicts are inherently contagious and prone to diffuse to nearby countries. Furthermore, the results show that poor and populous states face a higher risk of experiencing intrastate violence.

The results for Model 2 indicate that the presence of refugees, by itself, is not consistently associated with the onset of intrastate conflict in countries of asylum. The coefficient on the key IV is positive, matching theoretical expectations, but not statistically significant.

The results for Model 3 suggest that only refugees with ethnic kin among the population in the countries of asylum may appreciably influence their susceptibility to conflict onset, though the coefficient estimate is again not statistically significant. Hence, the simple indicator of ethnic ties, which neglects power relations of co-ethnics, does not improve understanding of whether and how refugees might contribute to the diffusion of conflict to countries hosting refugees.

The results for Model 4 reveal that only refugees who are kin of politically excluded groups in countries of asylum increase their risk of experiencing the onset of intrastate conflict. The variable capturing this factor is statistically significant. Meanwhile, the coefficient estimate for the variable reflecting refugees whose kin are ethnic groups in control of governments in countries of asylum is negative, hinting at a dampening effect on conflict onset, though this result is not statistically significant.

Two other aspects of the results are worth noting.

First, the coefficient on the neighborhood conflict IV hardly budges when any of the refugee variables are included in the model estimations. Thus, refugees affect conflict dynamics in the CoA, particularly in circumstances with existing inter-group issues, but do not alter the intrinsic risk of conflict diffusion from neighboring countries. Another way of saying this is that refugees do not appear to be the mechanism that transmits conflict from one country to another, but they can intensify already volatile conditions in receiving states. Therefore, a reasonable conclusion is that refugees do not present an inherent threat to stability in countries of asylum – they pose an additional risk only in so far as conditions in those countries are such that refugees tilt the balance over a threshold of conflict initiation.

Second, the IV for the presence of refugees with excluded TEK is a binary indicator, not a count of the number of these refugees. The implication is that the effect is observed without respect to the size of the refugee group, whether in absolute terms or relative to the size of the kin group and its share of the population in the CoA. A variable effect associated with size is plausible, to take more precise account of the impact on local demographics, and warrants analysis in future research.

Figure 12.4 displays the substantive effects and 90% confidence intervals implied by the estimation of Model 4. I computed the predicted probability of the onset of intrastate conflict by moving the values of the three key IVs related to refugees from "0" to "1" using the observed-value approach for analyzing marginal effects (Hanmer and Kalkan 2013).

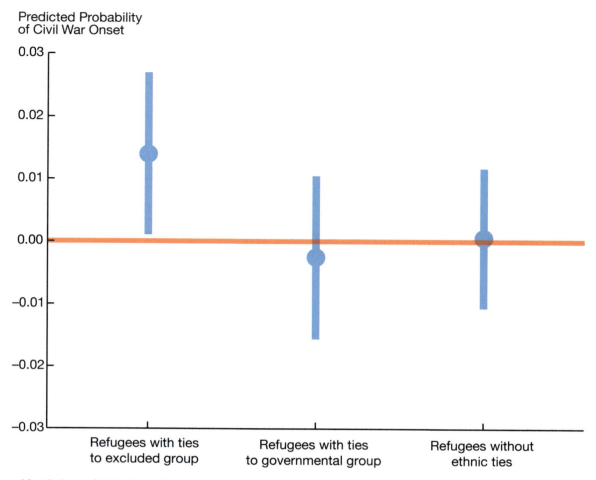

Figure 12.4 Estimated Risk of Conflict Onset for Countries with Refugees, 1975–2009

The results show that refugees with ties to an excluded group increase the likelihood of conflict in the CoA by 1.4%, relative to not having refugees at all. This difference may appear small in absolute terms. Yet the baseline risk of conflict onset for the sample of country-years used in the analysis, over the period from 1975–2009, was 3.5%. Thus, the marginal impact of refugees with excluded TEK in the CoA is quite large in proportional terms – nearly a 40% difference relative to the baseline probability. Clearly, this effect qualifies as noteworthy. Conflict onset is a rare event. Under select circumstances, influxes of refugees tend to heighten the vulnerability substantially.

The finding corroborates that the ethno-political context in the CoA is a key determinant of the risk of refugee-induced violence (Adamson 2006; Lischer 2005; Stedman and Tanner 2003). The results provide evidence consistent with the argument that instances where a refugee population affects the ethnic equilibrium in an asylum state, intensifying pressures in settings where part of the population suffers from political exclusion and consequent grievances, are associated with a heightened risk of onset of intrastate conflict.

Conclusion

The current extreme situation of forced displacement poses a major, political challenge. The common understanding that political violence, including civil wars, produces refugees is undisputed. A more controversial claim is that refugees can contribute to the diffusion of conflict to neighboring countries where they seek asylum. This claim reflects the potential repercussions of negative externalities associated with refugees. Understanding whether or not and how refugees could destabilize CoAs is vital for governments and the international community.

The analysis presented in this chapter focuses on the claim that refugees can disrupt the ethnic balance in receiving countries. I find that the impact of refugees on the risk of the onset of intrastate conflict depends on ethno-politics in the asylum state. The presence of refugees alone does not have a consistent influence on conflict. Refugees with ethnic kin in an asylum state can increase the risk of conflict, but only in already tense situations where the TEK group is politically excluded. By testing the argument that refugees diffuse violence to the CoA when they affect the ethnic balance, this analysis contributes to the emerging literature on transnational actors and their impact on intrastate conflict dynamics.

Closing borders based on fears of negative consequences of refugees – an argument often raised in debates – is neither a sustainable nor a secure solution. A key policy implication of this study is that potential host governments that accuse refugees of spreading conflict by threatening the cultural balance have no reason to refuse hosting or assisting refugees. Conflict in neighboring countries increases the risk of civil conflict, but refugees are not responsible for its diffusion. Refugees only intensify the risk of conflict when they enter already uneasy settings and their presence exacerbates the demographics of contentious inter-ethnic group relations. The proper response is not for potential host governments to resist such inflows of refugees who share ethnic kinship with a local minority, which in reality is unenforceable due to porous borders and international norms. Instead, I suggest that by providing security to refugees, as well as the local community, and pursuing inclusionary policies towards minorities, governing elites can minimize the risk of grievances and rebellions among the population. The lack of protection for refugees without powerful patrons in the CoA is what increases insecurity and facilitates refugee manipulation by warring parties. The onus is on key stakeholders, including the international community, NGOs and humanitarian organizations, to provide adequate refugee relief and support and protection – and to pressure host governments to do the same. The need for all these efforts is amplified by settings that present a heightened risk of refugee-related conflict, owing to co-ethnicity between refugees and politically excluded groups and consequent reluctance among governing groups in countries of asylum to accept refugees.

References

Adamson, Fiona B. (2006) "Crossing Borders: International Migration and National Security." *International Security* 31(1): 165–199.

Adelman, Howard (1998) "Why Refugee Warriors are Threats." *Journal of Conflict Studies* 18(1): 49–69.

Baez, Javier E. (2011) "Civil Wars Beyond Their Borders: The Human Capital and Health Consequences of Hosting Refugees." *Journal of Development Economics* 96(2): 391–408.

Barber, Ben (1997) "Feeding Refugees, or War." *Foreign Affairs* 76(4): 8–14.

Blattman, Christopher, and Edward Miguel (2010) "Civil War." *Journal of Economic literature* 48(1): 3–57.

Buhaug, Halvard, and Kristian Skrede Gleditsch (2008) "Contagion or Confusion? Why Conflicts Cluster in Space." *International Studies Quarterly* 52(2): 215–233.

Carter, David B., and Curtis S. Signorino (2010) "Back to the Future: Modeling Time Dependence in Binary Data." *Political Analysis* 18(3): 271–292.

Cederman, Lars-Erik, Kristian Skrede Gleditsch, Idean Salehyan, and Julian Wucherpfennig (2013) "Transborder Ethnic Kin and Civil War." *International Organizations* 67(2): 389–410.

Cederman, Lars-Erik, Andreas Wimmer, and Brian Min (2010) "Why Do Ethnic Groups Rebel? New Data and Analysis." *World Politics* 62(1): 87–119.

Choi, Seung-Whan, and Idean Salehyan (2013) "No Good Deed Goes Unpunished: Refugees, Humanitarian Aid, and Terrorism." *Conflict Management and Peace Science* 30(1): 53–75.

Collier, Paul, and Anke Hoeffler (2002) "On the Incidence of Civil War in Africa." *Journal of Conflict Resolution* 46(1): 13–28.

Crisp, Jeff (2000) "Forms and Sources of Violence in Kenya's Refugee Camps." *Refugee Survey Quarterly* 19(1): 54–70.

Davenport, Christian A., Will H. Moore, and Steven C. Poe (2003) "Sometimes You Just Have to Leave: Domestic Threats and Forced Migration, 1964–1989." *International Interactions* 29(1): 27–55.

Elkins, Zachary, and Beth Simmons (2005) "On Waves, Clusters, and Diffusion: A Conceptual Framework." *Annals of the American Academy of Political and Social Science* 598(1): 33–51.

Fearon, James D., and David D. Laitin (2003) "Ethnicity, Insurgency, and Civil War." *American Political Science Review* 97(1):75–90.

Forsberg, Erika (2014) "Transnational Transmitters: Ethnic Kinship Ties and Conflict Contagion 1946–2009." *International Interactions* 40(2): 143–165.

Girardin, Luc, Philipp Hunziker, Lars-Erik Cederman, Nils-Christian Bormann, and Manuel Vogt (2015) "GROWup: Geographical Research On War, Unified Platform." Online: http://growup.ethz.ch/. Accessed 16 May 2016.

Gleditsch, Kristian Skrede (2007) "Transnational Dimensions of Civil War." *Journal of Peace Research* 44(3): 54–66.

Gleditsch, Nils Petter, Peter Wallensteen, Mikael Eriksson, Margareta Sollenberg, and Håvard Strand (2002) "Armed Conflict 1946–2001: A New Dataset." *Journal of Peace Research* 39(5): 615–637.

Goldstone, Jack A. (2002) "Population and Security: How Demographic Change Can Lead to Violent Conflict." *Journal of International Affairs* 56(1): 3–21.

Gomez, Margarita Puerto, Asger Christensen, Yonatan Yehdego Araya, and Niels Harild (2010) "The Impacts of Refugees on Neighboring Countries: A Development Challenge." *World Development Report background papers.* Washington, DC: World Bank. Online: http://documents.worldbank.org/curated/en/459601468337158089/The-impacts-of-refugees-on-neighboring-countries-a-development-challenge. Accessed 4 June 2013.

Hanmer, Michael J., and Kerem Ozan Kalkan (2013) "Behind the Curve: Clarifying the Best Approach to Calculating Predicted Probabilities and Marginal Effects from Limited Dependent Variable Models." *American Journal of Political Science* 57(1): 263–277.

Harpviken, Kristian Berg, and Sarah Kenyon Lischer (2013) "Refugee Militancy in Exile and upon Return in Afghanistan and Rwanda." In *Transnational Dynamics of Civil War,* ed. Jeffrey T. Checkel. Cambridge: Cambridge University Press, pp. 89–119.

Hegre, Havard, and Nicholas Sambanis (2006) "Sensitivity Analysis of Empirical Results on Civil War Onset." *Journal of Conflict Resolution* 50(4): 508–535.

Heston, Alan, Robert Summers, and Bettina Aten (2011) "Penn World Table, Version 7.0." Online: http://pwt.econ.upenn.edu/php_site/pwt_index.php. Accessed 14 March 2012.

Hill, Stuart, and Donald Rothchild (1986) "The Contagion of Political Conflict in Africa and the World." *Journal of Conflict Resolution* 30(4): 716–735.

Jacobsen, Karen (1996) "Factors Influencing the Policy Responses of Host Governments to Mass Refugee Influxes." *International Migration Review* 30(3): 655–678.

Kagwanja, Peter, and Monica Juma (2008) "Somali Refugees: Protracted Exile and Shifting Security Frontiers." In *Protracted Refugee Situations: Political, Human Rights, and Security Implications*, ed. Edward Newman, Gil Loescher, James Milner, and Gary Troeller. Tokyo and New York: United Nations University Press.

Khan, Shaharyan (2001) *The Shallow Graves of Rwanda*. London: I.B. Tauris.

Krcmaric, Daniel (2014) "Refugee Flows, Ethnic Power Relations, and the Spread of Conflict." *Security Studies* 23(1): 182–216.

Lake, David, and Donald Rothchild (1998) *The International Spread of Ethnic Conflict: Fear, Diffusion and Escalation*. Princeton, NJ: Princeton University Press.

Lebson, Mike (2013) "Why Refugees Rebel: Towards a Comprehensive Theory of Refugee Militarization." *International Migration* 51(5): 1–16.

Lischer, Sarah Kenyon (2007) "Causes and Consequences of Conflict-Induced Displacement." *Civil Wars* 9(2): 142–155.

Lischer, Sarah Kenyon (2005) *Dangerous Sanctuaries: Refugee Camps, Civil War, and the Dilemmas of Humanitarian Aid*. Ithaca, NY: Cornell University Press.

Lischer, Sarah Kenyon (2003) "Collateral Damage, Humanitarian Assistance as a Cause of Conflict." *International Security* 28(1): 79–109.

Lischer, Sarah Kenyon (2001) "Refugee-Related Political Violence: When? Where? How Much?" Online: http://web.mit.edu/cis/www/migration/pubs/rrwp/10_lischer.html. Accessed 22 October 2010.

Loescher, Gil, and James Milner (2004) "Protracted Refugee Situations and State and Regional Insecurity." *Conflict, Security & Development* 4(1): 3–20.

Martin, Adrian (2005) "Environmental Conflict between Refugee and Host Communities." *Journal of Peace Research* 42(3): 329–346.

Melander, Erik, and Magnus Öberg (2006) "Time to Go? Duration Dependence in Forced Migration." *International Interactions* 32(2): 129–152.

Miguel, Edward, Shanker Satyanath, and Ernest Sergenti (2004) "Economic Shocks and Civil Conflict: An Instrumental Variables Approach." *Journal of Political Economy* 112(4): 725–753.

Milner, James (2000) "Sharing the Security Burden: Towards the Convergence of Refugee Protection and State Security." Refugee Studies Centre Working Paper #4.

Milton, Daniel, Megan Spencer, and Michael Findley (2013) "Radicalism of the Hopeless: Refugee Flows and Transnational Terrorism." *International Interactions* 39(5): 621–645.

Most, Benjamin A., and Harvey Starr (1980) "Diffusion, Reinforcement, Geopolitics, and the Spread of War." *American Political Science Review* 74(4): 932–946.

Muggah, Robert, and Edward Mogire (2006) "Arms Availability and Refugee Militarization in Africa: Conceptualizing Issues." In *No Refuge: The Crisis of Refugee Militarization in Africa*, ed. Robert Muggah. London and New York: Zed Books.

Murdoch, James C., and Todd Sandler (2002) "Economic Growth, Civil Wars, and Spatial Spillovers." *Journal of Conflict Resolution* 46 (1): 91–110.

Newland, Kathrin (1993) "Ethnic Conflict and Refugees." *Survival* 35(1): 81–101.

Office of the United Nations High Commissioner for Refugees (UNHCR) (2007) "Convention and Protocol Relating to the Status of Refugees." Online: http://www.unhcr.org/protect/PROTECTION/3b66c2aa10.pdf. Accessed 2 December 2010.

Ogata, Sadako (2005) *The Turbulent Decade, Confronting the Refugee Crises of the 1990s*. New York, London: W.W. Norton & Company.

Phillips, Christopher (2013) "The Impact of Syrian Refugees on Turkey and Jordan." Online: http://www.chathamhouse.org/publications/twt/archive/view/186289. Accessed 4 August 2013.

Raleigh, Clionadh, and Henrik Urdal (2007) "Climate Change, Environmental Degradation and Armed Conflict." *Political Geography* 26(6): 674–694.

Rüegger, Seraina, and Heidrun Bohnet (2015) "The Ethnicity of Refugees (ER): A New Dataset for Understanding Flight Patterns." *Conflict Management and Peace Science*. DOI: doi:10.1177/0738894215611865.

Salehyan, Idean (2008) "The Externalities of Civil Strife: Refugees as a Source of Inter- national Conflict." *American Journal of Political Science* 52(4): 787–801.

Salehyan, Idean (2007) "Transnational Rebels, Neighboring States as Sanctuary for Rebel Groups." *World Politics* 59(1): 217–242.

Salehyan, Idean, and Kristian Skrede Gleditsch (2006) "Refugees and the Spread of Civil War." *International Organization* 60(2): 335–366.

Sambanis, Nicholas (2001) "Do Ethnic and Nonethnic Civil Wars Have the Same Causes?" *Journal of Conflict Resolution* 45(3): 259–282.

Schmeidl, Susanne (1997) "Exploring the Causes of Forced Migration: A Pooled Time Series Analysis, 1971–1990." *Social Science Quarterly* 78(2): 284–308.

Stedman, S. J., and F. Tanner (2003) *Refugee Manipulation: War, Politics, and the Abuse of Human Suffering*. Washington, DC: Brookings Institution Press.

Stein, Barry N. (1979) "The Geneva Conferences and the Indochinese Refugee Crisis." *International Migration Review* 13(4): 716–723.

Tavares, Rodrigo (2009) "Regional Clustering of Peace and Security." *Global Change, Peace & Security* 21(2): 153–164.

Terry, Fiona (2002) *Condemned to Repeat? The Paradox of Humanitarian Action*. Ithaca, NY: Cornell University Press.

UNHCR (2016a) "Global Trends 2015." Online: http://www.unhcr.org/global-trends-2015.html. Accessed on August 16, 2016.

UNHCR (2016b) "Population Statistics Database." Online: popstats.unhcr.org/. Accessed 16 August 2016.

US Committee for Refugees and Immigrants (2009) "World Refugee Survey 2008." Online: http://www.refugees.org/article.aspx?id=2114&subm=19&ssm=29&area=About%20Refugees. Accessed 1 October 2010.

Vogt, Manuel, Nils-Christian Bormann, Seraina Rüegger, Lars-Erik Cederman, Philipp Hunziker, and Luc Girardin (2015) "Integrating Data on Ethnicity, Geography, and Conflict: The Ethnic Power Relations Dataset Family." *Journal of Conflict Resolution* 59(7): 1327–1342.

Wallensteen, Peter, and Margareta Sollenberg (1998) "Armed Conflict and Regional Conflict Complexes, 1989–1997." *Journal of Peace Research* 35(5): 621–634.

Ward, Michael D., and Kristian Skrede Gleditsch (2002) "Location, Location, Location: An MCMC Approach to Modeling the Spatial Context of War and Peace." *Political Analysis* 10(3): 244–260.

Weiner, Myron (1993) "Security, Stability, and International Migration." *International Security* 17(3): 91–126.

Whitaker, Reg (1998) "Refugees: The Security Dimension." *Citizenship Studies* 2(3): 413–434.

Wood, William (1994) "Forced Migration: Local Conflicts and International Dilemmas." *Annals of the Association of American Geographers* 84(4): 607–634.

Zolberg, Aristide R., Astri Suhrke, and Sergio Aguayo (1989) *Escape from Violence, Conflict and the Refugee Crisis in the Developing World*. Oxford: Oxford University Press.

Zolberg, Aristide R., Astri Suhrke, and Sergio Aguayo (1986) "International Factors in the Formation of Refugee Movements." *International Migration Review* 20(2): 151–169.

13
Armed Conflicts Active in 2015

Margareta Sollenberg

Introduction

This chapter summarizes the origins and evolution of armed conflicts active in 2015, as recorded by the Uppsala Conflict Data Program (UCDP). Descriptive profiles are provided of active armed conflicts that reached the level of war either in 2015 or in one or more previous years.[1] War is defined as an armed conflict that resulted in at least 1,000 battle-related deaths within a calendar year. This chapter is compiled based on information published on the UCDP website and included in various UCDP datasets (www.ucdp.uu.se). The details about armed conflict activity in 2015 also draw on the most recent publications about UCDP data (Melander, Pettersson, and Themnér 2016).

UCDP Definitions and Data

The UCDP defines armed conflict as a contested incompatibility that concerns control over government or territory, or both, where the use of armed force between two parties results in at least 25 battle-related deaths in a calendar year. The profiles presented in this chapter have been limited to state-based armed conflicts in which, at least one of the parties has to be the government of a state.[2] Conflicts are differentiated by type:

- *Interstate armed conflict:* conflict between two or more states.
- *Internationalized intrastate armed conflict:* conflict between the government of a state and at least one internal opposition group, with intervention from at least one other state, in the form of troops, on behalf of either side.
- *Intrastate armed conflict:* conflict between the government of a state and at least one internal opposition group.

Conflicts are also divided into two categories according to their intensity:

- *War:* at least 1,000 battle-related deaths in a calendar year.
- *Minor armed conflict:* at least 25 – but fewer than 1,000 – battle-related deaths in a calendar year.

Countries may have more than one armed conflict active in the same year, fought over different incompatibilities. Therefore, the number of conflicts may exceed the number of country locations.

UCDP data are compiled mainly using secondary written sources, including reports by news media as well as human rights institutions and organizations. The fatality estimates reported in the data are conservative best estimates. This characterization means that data are not likely to be exhaustive depictions of all violence that may have occurred in a conflict. Some violence goes unreported, or the perpetrators remain unknown. The figures for battle-related deaths do not include deaths in non-state conflict (i.e., conflict between non-state actors, where no government armed force is involved) or from one-sided violence (i.e., deliberate targeting of unarmed civilians by state or non-state armed actors).[3]

Summary

In 2015, 50 armed conflicts were active. Of these conflicts, 25 have never been recorded as wars involving the current combatant parties. This chapter covers the remaining 25 conflicts, which were active in 21 countries across the world. Among the pertinent details of these 25 conflicts are the following:

- Two of the conflicts are new on the list for 2015, one in Syria,[4] the other in Nigeria, with both cases evolving from previous conflicts in these countries.
- Three conflicts restarted in 2015 after having been inactive in 2014: Ethiopia (Oromiya), Pakistan (Balochistan), and Turkey (Kurdistan).
- 11 of the conflicts were wars – causing more than 1,000 deaths – in 2015 itself, the same number as in 2014.
- 14 of the conflicts were over control of government, compared to 11 over territory.
- Only one case was an interstate conflict (India vs. Pakistan), whereas all the others were intrastate conflicts.
- 14 of the intrastate conflicts were internationalized, with one or both warring sides receiving troop support from other states.
- Overall, the conflicts resulted in 92,794 battle-related deaths (compared to 99,027 in 2014), ranging from a low of 25 (Ethiopia vs. OLF) to a high of 33,966 (Syria vs. Syrian insurgents).
- Seven of the conflicts escalated (> 25% increase in the number of battle-related deaths compared to the previous year) in terms of severity of the violence, five deescalated (> 25% decrease), and nine remained relatively stable (< 25% increase/decrease) in 2015 (ther remaining four conflicts were not active in the previous year).

Meanwhile, armed conflicts in three countries that were active in 2014, and which at some point had been recorded as wars, terminated by 2015: Democratic Republic of Congo, Israel (Palestine), and Ukraine (Donetsk).

Profiles of Active Armed Conflicts

Box 13.1 Afghanistan, et al. vs. Taliban	
Side A	Government of Afghanistan, Pakistan, USA
Side B	Taliban
Incompatibility	Government
Type of Conflict	Internationalized intrastate
First Year of Conflict	1978
Status in 2015	Ongoing
Intensity in 2015	War
Battle-Related Deaths in 2015	16,581
Trajectory of Conflict in 2015	Escalating

Afghanistan has been embroiled in continuous civil war since 1978. The civil war has involved a number of different warring parties and changing alliances after the Soviet invasion of 1979 and even more so after the Soviet Union withdrew in 1989. The *Mujahideen*, which had constituted the opposition against the Soviet forces, ultimately took power in 1992 after the collapse of the communist Najibullah government. Civil war continued, however, pitting new constellations of *Mujahideen* forces against each other.

The current civil war involves the *Taliban*, which first surfaced in 1994 and later assumed power in September 1996, proclaiming the Islamic Emirate of Afghanistan. Groups that had been part of, or at least loyal to, the overthrown government united against the *Taliban*, under the banner of the Northern Alliance. After September 11, 2001, when the US-led multinational coalition entered Afghanistan, the Northern Alliance – heavily backed by its international allies – rapidly overthrew the *Taliban* government. Since late-2001, the *Taliban* have been battling the government of Afghanistan, as well as the US-led multinational coalition.

The conflict against the *Taliban* escalated in 2013 and continued to escalate in 2014, when over 12,000 battle-related deaths occurred – the highest number that had been recorded since 1989. The Afghan security forces suffered an increasing burden of fatalities, as they assumed the full responsibility for security in Afghanistan. International forces continued their planned withdrawal and the International Security Assistance Force (ISAF) mission was officially terminated in December 2014. As part of the new mission, Operation Resolute Support, security agreements with the United States (US) and NATO allowed for 12,000 soldiers to remain in the country in 2015.

During that year, the conflict escalated even further, resulting in over 16,000 battle-related deaths, making this the second most deadly case of the year, after the Syrian war. Indirect and informal talks between the conflict's parties during the first half of the year resulted in direct peace talks in early July. With the late-July announcement of the death of the Taliban leader, Mullah Omar, and a subsequent leadership dispute, negotiations stalled. Instead of talks, the new *Taliban* leadership opted for a military offensive. The *Taliban* took control of the city of Kunduz in late-September, the group's biggest military achievement since its forces were pushed out of Kabul in 2001. Despite the termination of the ISAF mission in 2014, the conflict continued to be internationalized in 2015. The government of Afghanistan received direct troop support during 2015 from the US – though only the US contribution to Operation Resolute Support was mandated for combat – as well as from Pakistan.

Box 13.2 Algeria vs. AQIM	
Side A	Government of Algeria
Side B	AQIM (al-Qaeda Organization in the Islamic Maghreb)
Incompatibility	Government
Type of Conflict	Intrastate
First Year of Conflict	1991
Status in 2015	Ongoing
Intensity in 2015	Minor
Battle-Related Deaths in 2015	84
Trajectory of Conflict in 2015	Stable

Algeria gained independence from France in 1962, after a bloody war of independence. Following 27 years of socialist one-party rule, Algeria held its first multiparty local elections in 1990, in response to growing public unrest. By then, an Islamist political party, the Islamic Salvation Front (FIS), had surfaced as the main opposition force in the country. FIS won the first round of parliamentary elections in 1991, in response to which the army cancelled the second round of the elections. Amid increasing political violence, FIS was outlawed in March 1992. These events marked the beginning of the plunge into a civil war that remains ongoing, as well as a period characterized by military rule and a series of successive army-backed regimes. The conflict in Algeria has involved a number of different armed Islamist groups, each with its own strategies and religious beliefs, but all sharing the goal of establishing an Islamic state.

One of the first Islamist groups to take up arms was the Armed Islamic Movement (MIA), via its Islamic Salvation Army (AIS) wing, which emerged in 1992. FIS realized it had lost the initiative, in favor of groups choosing to engage in armed struggle, and opted to endorse MIA in 1993. The Armed Islamic Group (GIA), which was later the major insurgent force in the civil war, also formed in 1992. GIA's radical political agenda – rejecting democracy and pluralism and viewing *jihad* as an end in itself – contrasted sharply with that of FIS. GIA subsequently splintered into even more extremist factions, most notably the Salafist Group for Preaching and Combat (GSPC), which appeared in 1998. In January 2007, the group changed its name to AQIM (*al-Qaida* Organization in the Islamic Maghreb), in the process confirming its allegiance to *al-Qaida*.

The Algerian conflict escalated to war in 1993, exhibiting increasing brutality over time. The army's counter-measures also became more and more ruthless, resulting in gross human rights abuses. In the latter half of the 1990s, GIA engaged in extensive targeting of civilians, which came to be a dominant feature of the armed struggle. The AIS declared a unilateral ceasefire in 1997 and later disbanded. The intensity of the violence decreased in 2002. By 2004, the main armed group fighting against the Algerian government was the GSPC.

Conflict activity involving the GSPC has been fairly consistent over the years. The largest numbers of deaths were observed in 2000 and 2003, after which fatalities decreased each time. This trend reversed in 2007, with an increase in attacks by what had become AQIM. This group also changed tactics to favor high-impact attacks, notably suicide bombings. In 2008, the conflict continued along the same lines, but by 2009 suicide attacks diminished, presumably due to their costs in terms of popular support. Battle-related fatalities still rose in 2009, almost reaching the level recorded in 2003. Since then, fatalities from the violence have consistently declined.

The conflict in Algeria remained active during 2015, though with the lowest number of battle-related fatalities since the early 1990s. The majority of the violence over the last few years has taken place in the mountainous Kabylie region separating the coastal areas from the Saharan desert. Violence has also been observed on the Tunisian border, as well as in the Saharan desert. The tactics of AQIM remained the same in 2015 as in previous years, with small-scale attacks on security forces and widespread use of improvised explosive devices (IED).

Box 13.3 Azerbaijan vs. Nagorno-Karabakh and Armenia

Side A	Government of Azerbaijan
Side B	Republic of Nagorno-Karabakh, Armenia
Incompatibility	Territory (Nagorno-Karabakh)
Type of Conflict	Internationalized intrastate
First Year of Conflict	1991
Status in 2015	Ongoing
Intensity in 2015	Minor
Battle-Related Deaths in 2015	72
Trajectory of Conflict in 2015	Escalating

The region of Nagorno-Karabakh in Azerbaijan is mainly populated by Armenians, and its territorial status has long been disputed. Nagorno-Karabakh was part of Armenia at the beginning of the 20th century, but the area was transferred to Azerbaijan in the 1920s. During the Soviet era, the underlying conflict in the area was suppressed. With new Soviet policies in the late-1980s, the conflict re-emerged. In 1988, the regional council in Nagorno-Karabakh voted for the integration of the region into Armenia. In late-1989, Armenia declared the enclave to be part of a unified Armenian republic, which neither the Soviet central government nor the Azerbaijani Republic accepted as legal. These moves were followed by a two-year war between Armenia and the Soviet Union over Nagorno-Karabakh.

After the dissolution of the Soviet Union and Azeri independence in 1991, the conflict continued and intensified, with fighting between the Armenia-supported Republic of Nagorno-Karabakh and the government of Azerbaijan. The fighting had resulted in several thousand deaths by the point that a ceasefire agreement was finally concluded in 1994. At the time of the agreement, the Nagorno-Karabakh authorities had *de facto* control over the Nagorno-Karabakh region, as well as substantial Azeri territories, including most of the strategic heights around Nagorno-Karabakh. Despite the truce, which had effectively ended large-scale fighting, sporadic clashes along the border continued.

The first peace talks were initiated in 1992. Subsequently, numerous rounds of talks between the two parties have taken place. Since 2004, talks have been organized under a framework known as the Prague Process, with meetings between the Armenian and Azerbaijani presidents and the Minsk Group of the Organization for Security and Co-operation in Europe (OSCE). Yet no formal negotiations on the core conflict issues have been initiated. Thus, the process has left unresolved several key questions, including the return of refugees, Nagorno-Karabakh's interim status, and the process for determining the final status of the region.

In 2014, tensions between Azerbaijan and Nagorno-Karabakh increased significantly. Skirmishes escalated on the ceasefire line, the so-called Line of Contact, particularly during the summer of 2014. The fighting was far from the level of intensity observed in the early 1990s, but still produced more fatalities than in any year since the 1994 ceasefire. Russian-led talks between the Presidents of Armenia and Azerbaijan were held in September, followed by OSCE-sponsored talks in October. Neither of these interactions managed to relieve tensions.

Throughout 2015, skirmishes continued on the Line of Contact, following the same pattern as in the previous year, but with slight increases in the numbers of clashes and battle-related deaths. No progress was reported in resolving the long-standing conflict through talks or third-party diplomatic efforts during the year.

Box 13.4 Colombia vs. FARC and ELN

Side A	Government of Colombia
Side B	FARC (Fuerzas Armadas Revolucionarias de Colombia: Revolutionary Armed Forces of Colombia), ELN (Ejército de Liberación Nacional: National Liberation Army)
Incompatibility	Government
Type of Conflict	Intrastate
First Year of Conflict	1964
Status in 2015	Ongoing
Intensity in 2015	Minor
Battle-Related Deaths in 2015	134
Trajectory of Conflict in 2015	Stable

Colombia has been plagued by large-scale political violence along the left–right spectrum since the initiation of *La Violencia* in 1948, which turned into a decade of widespread violence pitting numerous non-state armed groups against each other. Most of the violence took place in rural areas, involving land owners and peasants.

In the mid-1960s, left-wing guerrilla groups began forming; some were based on rural self-defense groups formed during *La Violencia*. The most important of these groups was the Revolutionary Armed Forces of Colombia (FARC), which has remained the largest insurgent organization up until today. Other groups followed suit, notably the National Liberation Army (ELN), which unlike FARC had more of an urban-based profile. In the late-1970s, guerrillas had begun financing their armed struggle with income from coca cultivation and violence spread also to urban areas. By the 1980s, the government of Colombia was fighting several left-wing groups and violence intensified. Some smaller rebel groups subsequently signed agreements with the government, leaving FARC and ELN as the main parties at war with the government from the 1990s onwards.

The conflict became more complex with the involvement of a number of right-wing paramilitary groups targeting left-wing guerrillas and civilians allegedly sympathizing with the guerrillas. The United Self-Defense Forces of Colombia (AUC) was formed in 1997 as an umbrella organization for local paramilitary groups and was later revealed to have links with government officials. All parties involved in the war in Colombia have extensively targeted civilians whom they claim support the other side.

Up through 2015, attempts at resolving the conflict and ending the violence had failed. Some agreements were signed with both FARC and ELN in the late-1990s. Yet none of these agreements was associated with an observable decline in violence. Instead, conflict further intensified up until the mid-2000s. Negotiations initiated in 2005 began to have an effect on the intensity of the conflict. Although the talks were interrupted intermittently by outbursts of violence, the trend of decreasing violence has been consistent since 2006. The demobilization of the AUC, which was completed by 2006, also played a role in reducing tensions. Peace talks involving FARC, with the express aim of dealing with political issues such as land reform as well, began in Oslo in 2012 and have continued since then. Some agreements were reached in 2015, including on reparations for war victims and the establishment of special tribunals for all ex-combatants. A ceasefire between the government and FARC was also reached in early 2015, but was subsequently terminated by FARC in May, citing government ceasefire violations. Negotiations with ELN also took place during 2015.

Despite the ongoing peace process, violence still continued during the 2013–2015 period, but at a significantly lower level than in previous decades, likely due to the ongoing peace process. The intensity of the conflict rose slightly in 2015 compared to 2014 as ELN, which had not been active in the previous year, again engaged the government in battle.

Armed Conflicts Active in 2015

Box 13.5 Ethiopia vs. OLF	
Side A	Government of Ethiopia
Side B	OLF (Oromo Liberation Front)
Incompatibility	Territory (Oromiya)
Type of Conflict	Intrastate
First Year of Conflict	1977
Status in 2015	Recurring
Intensity in 2015	Minor
Battle-Related Deaths in 2015	25
Trajectory of Conflict in 2015	Not applicable (inactive in 2014)

Ethiopia's population consists of around 70 different ethnic groups. In connection, the country has faced a long history of separatist sentiments. Oromiya is the largest Ethiopian state and the Oromo people make up over a third of Ethiopia's population. The territory that today constitutes the Oromiya region came under Ethiopian control during the 1890s. Since then, the Oromo have had little political influence and representation in the country. This circumstance, together with numerous unpopular government policies, has led to widespread discontent among the Oromo.

In late-1973, Oromo representatives met clandestinely in Addis Ababa. The Oromo Liberation Front (OLF) was formed in January 1974. Three months later, in April 1974, OLF initiated the armed struggle for independence. The conflict first surpassed the 25 battle-related deaths threshold in 1977.

When OLF launched its armed struggle, the country was already involved in upheaval linked to widespread dissatisfaction with Haile Selassie, the ruling Emperor. In September 1974, Selassie was ousted in a military coup. He was succeeded by a pro-Soviet military junta, the Derg, led by Mengistu Haile Mariam. The new government failed to gain support in the country. Numerous armed groups, some aiming to overthrow the government and others primarily fighting for independence, joined forces. During the war against the Derg, the OLF cooperated militarily with both the Tigray People's Liberation Front (TPLF), which was fighting to overthrow the Derg regime, and the Eritrea People's Liberation Front (EPLF), which was fighting for an independent Eritrea.

During the 1970s, the Derg regime initiated various policies, including resettlement, to contain the OLF. At the time, the OLF was relatively weak and its zone of operation was limited to eastern Oromiya. By the mid-1980s, however, the Derg's policies had backfired. In this context, OLF was able to rally an increasing number of followers and spread its operations to western Oromiya. In spite of this, the Ethiopian army was still superior to OLF in both organization and equipment.

The Derg came under increasing military pressure in the late-1980s, due to developments in the conflicts with TPLF and EPLF, rather than OLF activity. In mid-1991, TPLF forces seized the capital, Addis Ababa, and defeated the Derg regime. The transitional council that assumed power was led by the Ethiopian People's Revolutionary Democratic Front (EPRDF) umbrella group, in which TPLF was the dominant force. EPRDF also included the OLF, among others.

With Tigrayans only making up around 10% of the population, other ethnic groups soon became disillusioned with the TPLF-led government. In the run-up to the June 1992 elections, the OLF left the government. Fierce fighting erupted when OLF forces left their camps and the conflict reignited. The OLF suffered major losses in face of superior EPRDF military forces, forcing many rebels to flee to Kenya.

In subsequent years, fighting continued intermittently. After a period of very low activity, the conflict between the EPRDF government and the OLF escalated in 1999. Taking advantage of the fact that Ethiopian forces were occupied with the interstate war against neighboring Eritrea at the time, OLF launched an invasion from Somalia, leading to intense fighting with the government. Numerous reports surfaced of Eritrea supplying the OLF with weapons, support that continued even after 1999.

The government launched a large-scale offensive on rebel positions in 2006. Due to an extreme drought, however, the offensive lost momentum. Since then, the conflict has continued, albeit on a low scale. Because of a lack of independent reporting, few details are known about the fighting. In 2009, a Kenyan TV crew revealed that fighting was still taking place, with OLF rebels admitting to monthly losses of between 10 and 20 fighters. From 2010 and onwards, Ethiopia has been cooperating increasingly with the Kenyan government, which clamped down against the presence of the OLF. From 2010–2015, fighting between Ethiopian forces and the OLF led to at least 25 battle-related deaths on an annual basis, with the exception of 2014. Over the years, various attempts to reach a negotiated settlement to the conflict have been made, without success.

Sollenberg

Box 13.6 India vs. Kashmir Insurgents	
Side A	Government of India
Side B	Kashmir insurgents
Incompatibility	Territory (Kashmir)
Type of Conflict	Intrastate
First Year of Conflict	1990
Status in 2015	Ongoing
Intensity in 2015	Minor
Battle-Related Deaths in 2015	162
Trajectory of Conflict in 2015	Stable

The insurgency in the Indian part of Kashmir, formally known as Jammu and Kashmir, originates in the state's disputed accession to India following partition in 1947. The so-called Line of Control (LoC), the ceasefire line agreed upon through UN mediation in 1949 after the first war over Kashmir, has effectively defined the *de facto* borders of Kashmir, dividing it between Indian- and Pakistani-controlled sections.

In the 1970s, a militant opposition movement emerged with secessionist demands for Indian Kashmir. Dissent was temporarily mitigated by democratic policies implemented in the early 1980s. By 1988, however, progress was reversed and non-violent channels for expressing discontent became more limited. Support for militant groups advocating violent secession from India increased dramatically. A series of anti-government demonstrations and strikes, as well as violent attacks on government targets, launched in July 1988, marked the onset of the Kashmir insurgency, which first reached 25 deaths in a year in 1989 and escalated into war in 1990. Since then, the insurgency in Kashmir has been the most important internal security issue in India. The conflict has involved a range of groups and factions, collectively referred to as Kashmir insurgents, fighting against the Indian government. Although the insurgents originally included movements advocating Kashmiri independence from both India and Pakistan, groups favoring union with Pakistan have since emerged as dominant. India has repeatedly accused Pakistan of fueling the insurgency. More broadly, the matter of Kashmir has been intertwined continuously and closely with the interstate conflict between India and Pakistan (see below).

The conflict over Kashmir has deescalated significantly since 2005. Nevertheless, the conflict remained active in 2015, at intensity levels similar to those in previous years and affecting a large number of districts within the state. Fighting occurred along the LoC, as well as in other areas. Indian security forces continued to engage insurgents attempting to cross the LoC. Kashmiri insurgents also carried out several attacks within Jammu and Kashmir, notably on police stations and military encampments and outposts, causing further fatalities.

Box 13.7 India vs. Pakistan	
Side A	Government of India
Side B	Government of Pakistan
Incompatibility	Territory (Kashmir)
Type of Conflict	Interstate
First Year of Conflict	1948
Status in 2015	Ongoing
Intensity in 2015	Minor
Battle-Related Deaths in 2015	29
Trajectory of Conflict in 2015	Stable

India and Pakistan have fought a series of wars since independence from Britain and partition in 1947. Large-scale wars were fought immediately after independence in 1947–48 and again in 1965, 1971 and 1999.

The unsettled territorial status of the strategically and symbolically important state of Kashmir has remained at the core of the incompatibility between India and Pakistan up until today (see further under the profile of "India vs. Kashmiri Insurgents" above). In particular, the interstate conflict between India and Pakistan over Kashmir has become increasingly intertwined with the Kashmir insurgency that has been ongoing since the late-1980s. A number of Kashmiri rebel groups have allegedly been supported by Pakistan. Increased tension in the interstate conflict has often tended to spill over into increased tension in the intrastate conflict, and vice versa. A clear illustration of this dynamic is the Kargil war of 1999, which was triggered by the large-scale movement of Kashmiri militants into Kashmir, allegedly under the auspices of Pakistan. Tensions were reduced in 2003, when a formal truce between the two parties came into effect and dialogue was initiated. The continuing dialogue has resulted in little substantive change, but both parties have continually reaffirmed their commitment to dialogue and peaceful relations. Despite this, sporadic fighting between the respective armed forces, the Indian Border Security Force and the Pakistan Army, has continued across the disputed LoC.

Fighting in 2014 surpassed the 25 battle-related deaths threshold for the first year since 2003. Skirmishes on the LoC escalated in the summer of 2014, accompanied by increasingly hostile political rhetoric between the newly elected Indian Prime Minister Modi and the Pakistani government. As in previous years, each side blamed the other for having initiated the skirmishes.

Occasional shelling across the LoC, as well as sniper fire between Pakistani and Indian forces, continued on the same intensity level in 2015. While casualty levels in 2014 and 2015 were the highest since the early 2000s, fighting still remained sporadic. Some signs of reduced tension were seen in the form of unannounced talks held between India and Pakistan in Bangkok in December 2015. These talks were followed by a visit to Islamabad by the Indian Foreign Minister. Discussions included the issue of Jammu and Kashmir and the ceasefire line.

Box 13.8 Iraq, et al. vs. IS	
Side A	Government of Iraq, Australia, Bahrain, Belgium, Canada, Denmark, France, Jordan, the Netherlands, Saudi Arabia, United Arab Emirates, United Kingdom, United States of America
Side B	IS (Islamic State)
Incompatibility	Government
Type of Conflict	Internationalized intrastate
First Year of Conflict	2004
Status in 2015	Ongoing
Intensity in 2015	War
Battle-Related Deaths in 2015	11,547
Trajectory of Conflict in 2015	Stable

Iraq has been involved in a number of different wars over the past decades. The latest is a civil war that has engulfed most of the country since 2003.

Following the victory by the US, the UK and Australia against Iraq in the 2003 military intervention, Saddam Hussein's regime was replaced by a new Iraqi government. Forces from a coalition of countries remained in Iraq to support the new government. Violence soon commenced and subsequently involved a number of different groups, most of which had religious agendas. Fighting in Iraq has been fierce since 2004, though the intensity of violence declined after 2006. A new phase of escalation began in 2013, which culminated in unprecedented levels of violence in 2014 and 2015. In addition to the war with the government, various conflicts between armed groups have occurred throughout the war, as have extensive killings of civilians.

During the first years of the conflict, the main opposition armed forces were the Sunni group *Ansar al-Islam*, the Shi'ite group *Al-Mahdi* Army, and an al-Qaeda-affiliated organization that later became known as the Islamic State of Iraq (ISI) and is known today as the Islamic State (IS). The government of Iraq has engaged in heavy fighting with several armed groups, particularly the *Al-Mahdi* Army in southern Iraq during 2004. Since the onset of war, however, the bulk of the violence has involved the ISI.

ISI was formed as the *Jama'at al-Tawhid wa'al-Jihad*, led by Abu Mus'ab al-Zarqawi. The group changed its name to *Tanzim Qa'idat al-Jihad fi Bilad al-Rafidayn* (TQJBR) in the fall of 2004, when it also pledged allegiance to *al-Qaida* (see p. 176, "United States of America, et al. vs. Al-Qaida"). On October 15, 2006, the official formation of ISI was declared. Al-Zarqawi was killed in June 2006. Thereafter, the leadership of ISI was formed by representatives from several different factions.

From 2004–2009, the Iraqi government was supported by troops from a US-led multinational coalition. During these years, the foreign troops provided the majority of the armed forces on the government side. On June 30, 2009, responsibility for security in Iraq was handed over to the Iraqi government and by the end of July, only US forces remained.

With the official termination of Operation Iraqi Freedom on August 31, 2010, the US combat mission in Iraq ended. The last US troops were withdrawn from Iraq in December 2011.

In April 2013, ISI changed its name to the Islamic State in Iraq and al-Sham (ISIS), signaling the group's widened territorial claims, which also included Syria (see p. 171, "Syria, et al. vs. IS"). The violence between the Iraqi government and ISIS escalated in 2013, with ISIS increasing its attacks on both military and civilian targets, especially during the second half of the year.

Fighting escalated dramatically in 2014. At least 12,000 people were killed. ISIS carried out large-scale attacks and seized vast areas, including Mosul, Iraq's second-largest city. A dispute with *al-Qaida* caused the expulsion of ISIS from the larger *al-Qaida* network in 2014. The group also changed its name to IS (Islamic State) and announced that it had established a caliphate in parts of Iraq and Syria.

The conflict continued largely unabated in 2015. Thousands of people were killed as IS carried out large-scale attacks and clashed with Iraqi security forces and the Peshmerga, the military forces of the autonomous region of Iraqi Kurdistan. Heavy clashes occurred over control of Ramadi in Anbar province. The city was captured by IS in May 2015 and remained under its full control until December 2015, when Iraqi government forces retook parts of the city. In response to IS advances and in face of mounting reports of various types of atrocities, the US and a number of other countries commenced air strikes against the group in 2014, which continued in 2015.

Box 13.9 Myanmar vs. KIO	
Side A	Government of Myanmar
Side B	KIO (Kachin Independence Organization)
Incompatibility	Territory (Kachin)
Type of Conflict	Intrastate
First Year of Conflict	1961
Status in 2015	Ongoing
Intensity in 2015	Minor
Battle-Related Deaths in 2015	140
Trajectory of Conflict in 2015	Escalating

A number of ethnic groups have been in conflict with the government of Myanmar (previously Burma) since independence in 1948. The Kachin ethnic group, based in the far north in an area straddling the border with China and India, had already been involved in discussions about autonomy for Kachin areas prior to independence. Autonomy did not materialize, however, once the country gained independence. As a result, discontent grew among the Kachin population, which saw few resources being allocated to the development of Kachin-dominated areas.

Mobilization for armed struggle among the mainly Christian Kachin population was finally triggered in 1960 by new government policies, which included a campaign for "Burmanisation" and an explicit goal of making Buddhism the state religion. In 1961, the Kachin Independence Organization (KIO) was formed and commenced its armed campaign for independence.

In 1989, the ageing leadership of KIO decided to change their goal from independence to greater autonomy within Myanmar. After several failed attempts at ceasefires and negotiations, a permanent ceasefire between the government and KIO was announced in October 1993. KIO was given formal authority over the territory it controlled, with the right to create a local civil administration.

While the ceasefire held for almost two decades, little integration occurred between the KIO-controlled areas and the rest of Myanmar. The Kachin Independence Army (KIA), the armed wing of KIO, remained in place. Meanwhile, the government and local police forces rejected any attempts at political settlement. After the new constitution came into force in 2007, several ethnic representatives that had participated in the drafting process, including KIO, declared their disappointment with the contents. KIO was meant to reform its armed force into an army-controlled Border Guard Force, but refused and tensions between the two sides increased.

The government eventually sent forces into the area in 2011, which led to the breakdown of the 1993 ceasefire agreement and the renewal of fighting. Several rounds of Chinese-sponsored talks occurred during 2011 and 2012, but these failed to produce a new ceasefire agreement. In 2012, the fighting between the government and KIA escalated across both Kachin and Shan states. Government forces used heavy weapons and occasionally airstrikes against the rebels. The fighting resulted in the deaths of hundreds of government soldiers and rebels, as well as the displacement of tens of thousands of civilians. Several rebel organizations representing other ethnic groups joined in the fighting on the KIO side. Fighting continued in 2013 and 2014, though on a lower level of intensity than in 2011 and 2012. Talks also took place in 2013 and 2014, but failed to produce an end to the fighting.

Clashes between the government and KIO continued throughout 2015 in the Kachin and Shan states, resulting in more deaths than in 2014, but still lower numbers than in 2011 or 2012. In November 2015, a KIA spokesman reported that the fighting was exceptionally fierce in the southern region of the Kachin state. During the year, the government attempted to conclude a nationwide ceasefire with non-state armed groups, but KIO refused to sign the agreement.

Box 13.10 Nigeria, et al. vs. Boko Haram	
Side A	Government of Nigeria, Chad, Niger
Side B	Jama'atu Ahlis Sunna Lidda'awati wal-Jihad (or, Boko Haram)
Incompatibility	Government
Type of Conflict	Internationalized intrastate
First Year of Conflict	2009
Status in 2015	Ongoing
Intensity in 2015	War
Battle-Related Deaths in 2015	1,916
Trajectory of Conflict in 2015	Deescalating

Since independence, Nigeria has experienced different forms of conflict, especially related to divisions between Muslims and Christians. The Muslim population is mainly concentrated in the north, and a number of northern states have adopted Sharia law since 1999.

Jama'atu Ahlis Sunna Lidda'awati wal-Jihad, commonly known as *Boko Haram*, was formed in 2002 in Maiduguri of Borno state in northern Nigeria. The founders of the group were reportedly inspired by the *Taliban* of Afghanistan. *Boko Haram* seeks to topple the government and set up strict Islamic rule. Until 2009, *Boko Haram* was relatively unknown. In late-July of that year, the group launched an attack on a police station, marking the beginning of armed conflict with the government. The violence culminated as the security forces lay siege to the *Boko Haram* base in Maiduguri, in the course of which the rebel leader Mohammed Yussuf was captured and killed. The government reported that most of the group's members had been killed or captured. Yet some managed to escape and later made threats of renewed violence. After the death of Yussuf, the leadership and cohesion of the group became unclear, with indications that the group had split into different factions. Many believe the main faction of the group since Yussuf's death has been led by Abubakar Shekau, who was Yussuf's deputy leader.

Boko Haram resurfaced in late-2010 and intensified its attacks on state targets in 2011. The geographical scope of attacks soon widened beyond Maiduguri and the group's tactics became increasingly deadly. The government responded by strengthening its security force presence in Maiduguri and surrounding areas and declaring a state of emergency for parts of northern Nigeria bordering Cameroon, Chad, and Niger. The conflict escalated throughout 2012, in terms of both geographical scope and the number of people killed. In particular, *Boko Haram* stepped up its attacks on civilians. The group's operations expanded to cover all of northern Nigeria. Security forces carried out a number of offensives and were able to inflict serious losses on *Boko Haram*. Nevertheless, the group was able to establish control over some areas of Borno state by early 2013, in connection with which violence continued to escalate. In May 2013, the government declared a state of emergency for the three northeastern states of Nigeria and launched a large-scale military offensive, involving ground troops as well as fighter jets. The army forced the rebels to retreat to the border areas with Cameroon and Niger, in the immediate aftermath of which violence declined. *Boko Haram* soon managed to stage new attacks and killings intensified again.

Fighting further escalated in 2014, with the security situation in the north and northeastern parts of the country deteriorating. *Boko Haram* made rapid territorial gains in August and September 2014, then announced the establishment of an Islamic caliphate in areas under the group's control in November 2014. The group persisted in its fight against the Nigerian military and its large-scale attacks against civilians. In October, the Nigerian government announced that a ceasefire deal had been signed, which was denied by *Boko Haram* leader Abubakar Shekau, and attacks continued thereafter.

In late-January 2015, a loose coalition of military forces from Nigeria, Chad, and Niger launched an offensive and managed to push *Boko Haram* from most of its territory. On March 7, 2015, *Boko Haram* leader Shekau pledged allegiance to IS and its leader al-Baghdadi (see p. 161 "Iraq, et al. vs. IS"). The gesture was reciprocated on March 12, 2015, when the pledge was accepted. *Boko Haram* changed its name to Wilayat West Africa and became part of the IS. With that, the conflict over government power was terminated, replaced by the onset of a territorial conflict (see further below in the profile of "Nigeria, et al. vs. IS").

Box 13.11 Nigeria, et al. vs. IS	
Side A	Government of Nigeria, Chad, Niger
Side B	IS (Islamic State)
Incompatibility	Territory (Islamic State)
Type of Conflict	Internationalized intrastate
First Year of Conflict	2015
Status in 2015	New
Intensity in 2015	War
Battle-Related Deaths in 2015	2,548
Trajectory of Conflict in 2015	Not applicable (inactive in 2014)

The territorial conflict between the Nigerian government and IS commenced in March 2015. In several ways, this conflict represents a continuation of the conflict fought between the government and *Boko Haram* (see the profile of "Nigeria, et al. vs. *Boko Haram*" above). One key difference concerns the nature of the incompatibility.

Beginning in 2009, *Boko Haram* had sought to overthrow the government of Nigeria and establish strict Islamic rule throughout the country. In March 2015, the group pledged allegiance to IS, which accepted the pledge several days later. In the process, the rebel group previously known as *Boko Haram* integrated into IS and was renamed Wilayat West Africa. The group subsequently changed its goal to the more wide-reaching one stated by IS: the creation of a global Islamic State.

At the time of the March 2015 pledge, *Boko Haram* was in the midst of being pushed from the vast territory it had controlled in northeastern Nigeria. A coalition of troops from Chad, Niger and Nigeria was on the offensive. By mid-2015, IS in Nigeria was reverting to guerrilla tactics. In May 2015, the newly elected Nigerian president Muhammadu Buhari declared that the group would soon be forced to its knees. By the end of 2015, IS in Nigeria had lost almost all the territory it had occupied in 2014, and president Buhari declared that the group was "technically defeated". IS in Nigeria demonstrated throughout the year, however, that it was far from defeated, launching a wave of suicide attacks, bombings and massacres throughout the northeast of Nigeria. The combined number of battle-related deaths in 2015, from this new conflict in Nigeria and the previous *Boko Haram* conflict, roughly equals the number of battle-related deaths reported for 2014, which had exhibited the highest intensity level since the beginning of the conflict.

Box 13.12 Pakistan and Afghanistan vs. TTP	
Side A	Government of Pakistan, Afghanistan
Side B	TTP (Tehrik-i-Taleban Pakistan: Taliban Movement of Pakistan)
Incompatibility	Government
Type of Conflict	Internationalized intrastate
First Year of Conflict	2007
Status in 2015	Ongoing
Intensity in 2015	War
Battle-Related Deaths in 2015	1,954
Trajectory of Conflict in 2015	Deescalating

Pakistan has experienced years of political instability and several shifts between military dictatorship and democracy since independence in 1947. After an insurgency involving the Mohajirs – Urdu-speaking settlers who left India after partition – in the 1990s, Pakistan has been involved in conflict with Islamist groups since 2007. The role of religion in

Pakistan had been a contested issue since independence, with segments of society favoring a more Islamist-oriented system of governance. By the time conflict erupted in 2007, groups pressing for such reforms had become increasingly prominent, as well as militant. This tendency was particularly evident in the areas along the Afghan border: the Khyber Pakhtunkhwa (KP) province, previously known as the North-West Frontier Province, and the Federally Administered Tribal Areas (FATA).

The main Islamist organization, the Taliban Movement of Pakistan (TTP), was established on December 14, 2007. The goals of the TTP were to enforce Sharia law, unite against NATO forces in Afghanistan, and perform defensive jihad against the Pakistani army. Since then, TTP has engaged the Pakistani military in battles primarily in northwestern Pakistan. Areas under TTP control have long been a sanctuary for *al-Qaida*, the Afghan *Taliban*, and a number of other Islamist groups from across Asia. TTP militants have also been involved in operations in Afghanistan and maintain close ties with the Afghan *Taliban*.

Heavy fighting between the government and the TTP took place throughout 2008, followed by further escalation in 2009. The Pakistani government launched several offensives across KP province and FATA, which dislodged TTP from controlling territory in most regions. TTP responded by committing bomb attacks in population centers in the south of the country. Throughout 2009, US mounted air attacks on *al-Qaida* (see also the profile of "United States of America, et al. vs. Al-Qaida", p. 176). As *al-Qaida* hideouts often coincided with TTP camps, these attacks also struck hard on TTP. Meanwhile, another Islamist group, the *Lashkar-e-Islam* (Army of Islam), became active in 2009. Although this group remained active in the following years, the vast majority of fatalities in the conflict resulted from fighting involving the TTP.

High-intensity conflict continued throughout 2010 and fighting was particularly heavy along the Afghan border. Despite a relative decline in fatalities compared to 2009, terrorist attacks spread beyond FATA and KP and were increasingly carried out in major cities and in the Punjab province of Pakistan. The TTP also claimed responsibility for a number of attacks against NATO supply convoys. Conflict continued in the same areas during 2011 and 2012, but the level of intensity declined slightly. By 2012, the TTP had split and the TTP-Tariq Afridi faction joined the conflict as a separate organization. The conflict further deescalated in 2013, when TTP seemed to have been weakened by US drone attacks.

In 2014, violence increased again. During the first half of the year, peace talks were held with the TTP, which led to a reduction in hostilities. These talks created rifts in the organization, however, leading to the emergence of a TTP splinter group, the *Jamaat-ul-Ahrar*. Peace talks collapsed in June when TTP and the Islamic Movement of Uzbekistan (IMU) – a group that has challenged the governments in both Uzbekistan and Tajikistan and is fighting alongside the *Taliban* in Afghanistan – carried out an attack against Karachi International Airport. Despite serious infighting and a massive government offensive, the TTP carried out a terrorist attack against a school in Peshawar in December 2014, severely damaging the prospects for future negotiations.

In 2015, the Pakistani government continued the military operation, *Zarb-e-Azb*, which had commenced in June 2014, targeting militants mainly in North Waziristan and the Khyber Agency. *Lashkar-e-Islam* and *Jamaat-ul-Ahrar* claimed allegiance to TTP in March 2015 to jointly target Pakistani security forces. After this move, very few clashes were reported involving these two groups, leaving TTP as the only active armed group in this conflict. In spite of the alliance, the intensity of the conflict decreased significantly relative to 2014, though still surpassing the threshold of a war.

Box 13.13 Pakistan vs. BLA, et al.	
Side A	Government of Pakistan
Side B	BLA (Balochistan Liberation Army), BRA (Balochistan Republican Army), BLF (Baloch Liberation Front)
Incompatibility	Territory (Balochistan)
Type of Conflict	Intrastate
First Year of Conflict	1974
Status in 2015	Recurring
Intensity in 2015	Minor
Battle-Related Deaths in 2015	89
Trajectory of Conflict in 2015	Not applicable (inactive in 2014)

The conflict in Balochistan (or Baluchistan), the largest province in Pakistan, dates back to precolonial times, when the Baloch Khanate of Kalat extended across areas in Pakistan, as well as Afghanistan and Iran, where significant numbers of ethnic Balochis also reside. When the state of Pakistan was established in 1947, the Khanate of Kalat declared independence for the central parts of Balochistan, but later acceded into Pakistan.

A combination of neglect and marginalization by the highly centralized Pakistani government resulted in Balochistan becoming Pakistan's least developed province. Another source of grievance was the domination of the Balochistan bureaucracy by non-local Punjabis and Bengalis. In 1971, when Zulfikar Bhutto became president of Pakistan, a Baloch nationalist government came to power in the province. Ethno-nationalist rule in Balochistan was only temporary, however, and the provincial government was disbanded in 1974.

In response, an insurgency led by the Baloch Liberation Front (BLF) was launched in 1974. Throughout the conflict, the BLF received considerable military and logistical support from neighboring Afghanistan. The insurgency, characterized by guerrilla warfare with few major battles, was met with harsh counter-insurgency tactics by the Pakistani government. The fighting was at its fiercest in 1974, when it reached the level of a war. This first phase of the Baloch insurgency ended with a ceasefire on July 5, 1977. The ceasefire was closely related to the overthrow of President Bhutto in a military coup led by Zia ul-Haq, who released jailed separatist leaders and granted amnesty for insurgents.

Baloch nationalism later resurfaced, with the emergence of several new groups that culminated in 2004, when an insurgency was launched to challenge the Pakistani government over Baloch territory. All these groups have employed similar tactics, mainly focusing on guerrilla warfare. The Pakistani government has responded with counter-insurgency offensives. Despite the presence of an armed Baloch group, the *Jondollah*, fighting the government in neighboring Iran, there is no evidence of cooperation with Baloch militants in Pakistan.

In June 2004, the Balochistan Liberation Army (BLA) declared it was fighting for independence, initiating a conflict that has continued since then. BLA was dominated by tribes that had been involved in the 1974–1977 insurgency. The *Baloch Ittehad* (Baloch Unity), which also had links to the 1970s insurgency, was formed in 2003. By August 2005, the *Baloch Ittehad* leader demanded autonomy and large-scale fighting erupted towards the end of the year. The group was defeated a year later. In August 2007, the Balochistan Republican Army (BRA) initiated armed struggle for independence. Following a period of limited activity, fighting escalated quickly in July 2008, when the government launched a counter-offensive on BRA bases.

The Pakistani parliament has made some attempts at finding a negotiated resolution to the conflict, but none have led to a lasting solution. BLA and BRA announced a unilateral ceasefire in 2008, but this led to no progress towards settling the conflict.

In 2010, the violence did not pass the threshold of active conflict. The frequency of Baloch attacks increased sharply in 2012, the first year that BLA, BRA, and BLF engaged in significant attacks against the government forces – with BRA claiming responsibility for the majority.

In 2015, the Balochistan conflict continued with the same intensity as the previous years. The Frontier Corps, the auxiliary military forces of Balochistan, continued to target armed militants in the region. BLA, BLF, and BRA were all active in violence during the year. Because of BLF's involvement once more and the conflict's earlier status as a war, this case is profiled here.

Box 13.14 The Philippines vs. ASG, et al.	
Side A	Government of the Philippines
Side B	ASG (Abu Sayyaf Group), BIFM (Bangsamoro Islamic Freedom Movement), MILF (Moro Islamic Liberation Front)
Incompatibility	Territory (Mindanao)
Type of Conflict	Intrastate
First Year of Conflict	1972
Status in 2015	Ongoing
Intensity in 2015	Minor
Battle-Related Deaths in 2015	404
Trajectory of Conflict in 2015	Escalating

The conflict in Mindanao dates back to colonial times, with the formation of the Moro identity and the idea of an independent Moro homeland in southern Philippines. Not until the late-1960s, however, did Moro nationalists begin organizing an Islamist-oriented independence struggle.

In May 1968, the Mindanao Independence Movement (MIM) was created in the province of Maguindanao. The group's aim was the creation of an independent state in Mindanao. Parts of the youth section of MIM later established the Moro National Liberation Front (MNLF), under the leadership of Nur Misuari. The first MNLF offensive was staged in 1972. MNLF was the main rebel group fighting the government in Mindanao throughout the 1970s and 1980s. In some years, the fighting was intense.

By 1976, the MNLF had dropped its demands for independence in favor of seeking autonomy. This shift led to splits within the organization and the birth of the more radical Islamist Moro Islamic Liberation Front (MILF), which took up arms in 1986, developed into the main Moro rebel group, and still remains active. Other groups also formed, including the Abu Sayyaf Group (ASG), based on the islands of Basilan and Jolo. ASG has been fighting the government since 1993 and has become infamous for targeting civilians, including foreigners.

Negotiations between the government and MNLF commenced in the 1970s. A four-year round of talks, initiated in 1992, ultimately resulted in the Final Peace Agreement signed by the government and MNLF on September 2, 1996. MILF did not participate in the 1996 agreement, but had committed not to obstruct peace.

Fighting decreased in subsequent years, as low-level talks between MILF and the government were held. Despite the start of formal negotiations in 1999, the government declared all-out war against the Moro groups in 2000. Government offensives during the first half of the year resulted in MILF leaving the negotiations in June 2000. Fighting spiraled in 2000, resulting in heavy death tolls. The remainder of the 2000s then oscillated between periods of negotiations, de-escalation, and ceasefires, and periods of escalation. Particularly intense conflict activity was recorded in 2003.

After MILF proclaimed a unilateral ceasefire in 2009, which coincided with ongoing negotiations, fighting between MILF and the government dropped off markedly. ASG remained active and a splinter from MILF, the Bangsamoro Islamic Freedom Movement (BIFM), took up arms in August 2012. The BIFM had been formed in response to MILF dropping the demand for full independence; BIFM vowed to continue the fight for a fully separate Moro homeland. The government and MILF finally signed the Comprehensive Agreement on the Bangsamoro (CAB) in March 2014, seemingly ending their conflict.

In spite of the agreement, fighting between the government and MILF erupted in January 2015, shattering the three-year ceasefire. The passage of the Bangsamoro Basic Law in the Philippine Congress, which was meant to implement the 2014 agreement, was delayed several times during 2015. By the end of the year, the peace agreement still had not been implemented. Moreover, both ASG and BIFM continued to fight the government in 2015. Overall, the conflict in Mindanao escalated in 2015, resulting in the highest death toll since 2009.

Box 13.15 The Philippines vs. CPP	
Side A	Government of the Philippines
Side B	CPP (Communist Party of the Philippines)
Incompatibility	Government
Type of Conflict	Intrastate
First Year of Conflict	1969
Status in 2015	Ongoing
Intensity in 2015	Minor
Battle-Related Deaths in 2015	168
Trajectory of Conflict in 2015	Stable

The origins of the conflict with the Communist Party of the Philippines (CPP) can be traced to the Huk Rebellion of 1946–54, which was led by activists from the Filipino Communist Party (PKP). Inspired by the successful revolutions in China and Cuba and fueled by reactions to increasing US involvement in the Philippines, PKP members led by Jose Maria Sison set out to revive armed struggle in the 1960s. Consequently, the Maoist Communist Party of Philippines (CPP) was established in 1968 and its military wing, New People's Army (NPA), has engaged in armed rebellion since 1969.

Over the following years, NPA kept expanding. In 1972, President Ferdinand Marcos declared countrywide martial law to suppress the "state of rebellion." By the mid-1980s, CPP mustered more than 25,000 fighters, who were active in 80 percent of the country's 73 provinces.

In the early 1990s, fighting decreased. The military was preoccupied with internal struggles, the CPP was also weakened by internal divisions and diminishing international support, and several peace initiatives were launched. Conflict activity kept decreasing as formal peace negotiations were held in the mid-1990s and general amnesties led to a decline in CPP military strength.

After Joseph Estrada became President in 1998 and the economic crisis of 1998–99, criticism of the government increased and the different factions of CPP united. These circumstances led to another escalation of the conflict in the early 2000s. After several rounds of failed negotiations in 2004, President Gloria Arroyo ordered an all-out war against CPP in 2006, with the stated aim of wiping out the group by 2010. The rebels responded with an intensification of the struggle. Despite a decrease in rebel troop size, due to battle casualties and surrenders, NPA continued to inflict losses on the Philippine Armed Forces, as well as on civilians. By the end of the 2000s, however, NPA had been severely weakened and the group's troop size was at its lowest since the mid-1990s.

Formal talks resumed in 2011, for the first time since 2004. Talks broke down in early 2013, over the release of detained CPP members, and have not resumed since. During the second half of 2014, however, back-channel communications to prepare for future peace talks were conducted in the Netherlands. Despite renewed calls from both sides to go back to the negotiating table, peace talks did not resume in 2015. A traditional Christmas ceasefire was announced in December 2015, but during the rest of the year, fighting continued unabated. The annual number of battle-related deaths has remained largely unchanged since 2011.

Box 13.16 Somalia, et al. vs. Al-Shabaab	
Side A	Government of Somalia, Burundi, Djibouti, Ethiopia, Ghana, Kenya, Nigeria, Sierra Leone and Uganda
Side B	Al-Shabaab (The Youth)
Incompatibility	Government
Type of Conflict	Internationalized intrastate
First Year of Conflict	2006
Status in 2015	Ongoing
Intensity in 2015	War
Battle-Related Deaths in 2015	1,161
Trajectory of Conflict in 2015	Stable

The armed conflict in Somalia dates back to the beginning of the 1980s, when armed clan-based opposition groups were formed to overthrow the increasingly repressive regime of President Siad Barre. In January 1991, President Barre was ousted from power. Amid the power vacuum after Barre's fall, various clan-based militias began to compete violently for control of government. This conflict pushed Somalia towards state collapse. Fighting has raged almost non-stop since 1991, with numerous armed groups involved. UN and US troops were deployed in Somalia from 1992–1995, but failed to stem the violence. During several periods, Somalia has lacked a functioning government, particularly during the second half of the 1990s.

Multiple attempts at forging a central administration have been made, such as the 2000 Transitional National Government (TNG). In response to the establishment of the TNG, several opposition factions united in the Somali Reconciliation and Restoration Council (SRRC) in 2001. Another attempt at a central administration came in the form of the 2004 Transitional Federal Government (TFG), which resulted from negotiations led by the Intergovernmental Authority on Development (IGAD), a multinational body representing the trade bloc of eight East African countries.

The Mogadishu-based part of the TFG was soon pushed out of the city by an expanding network of local Islamic courts, which became the Supreme Islamic Council of Somalia (SICS). SICS declared its opposition to the government and its ally, Ethiopia. Most of the territory of southern Somalia was soon controlled by SICS. Worried by developments, Ethiopia sent troops in 2006 to aid the Somali government and together they pushed SICS back towards Mogadishu. SICS later retreated further to the south, where fighting continued. By January 2007, there were reports of *al-Qaida* operatives fighting alongside SICS, which prompted US air strikes. During the spring of 2007, attacks on government targets and Ethiopian troops in Mogadishu occurred on almost a daily basis. Later in 2007, SICS was absorbed into the Alliance for the Re-Liberation of Somalia (ARS), a new anti-Ethiopian and anti-TFG umbrella group launched in Eritrea.

Armed Conflicts Active in 2015

The security situation in Somalia deteriorated further in 2008, when the insurgency grew in scope, intensity, and complexity. UN-hosted talks in mid-2008 brought promise, but eventually proved fruitless. The presence of Ethiopian troops in Somalia remained the most divisive issue, eventually prompting a split in the ARS. The worsening security situation, political infighting in the TFG, and the announced intention of Ethiopia to withdraw its troops left the TFG significantly weakened.

By 2008, *Al-Shabaab* had become the main insurgent actor fighting government troops and its Ethiopian ally. *Al-Shabaab* emerged from the Islamist camp as an independent organization in 2007. Since then, much of the territory in southern and central Somalia has fallen under the control of *Al-Shabaab*, which imposed strict Sharia law. This organization has the most far-reaching aims of any of the Islamist opposition organizations in Somalia, seeking to establish a global Islamic caliphate. *Al-Shabaab* initially enjoyed popularity for reestablishing order after years of chaos. The organization's harsh policies, however, reduced public support. During 2012–2013, *Al-Shabaab*'s power declined, partly because of increased pressure from the African Union Mission in Somalia (AMISOM), but also due to internal struggles. The military pressure forced *Al-Shabaab* to change tactics from holding territory to guerrilla warfare. This shift also led to an increase in attacks on civilians. In 2013, the Somali National Army was able to push *Al-Shabaab* from many of its previous strongholds.

In 2014 and 2015, a similar pattern continued, though with slightly higher levels of fatalities. The pressure on *Al-Shabaab* intensified further in 2015. The Somali army, together with AMISOM troops, drove *Al-Shabaab* out of strongholds in central Somalia, where significant areas had previously been under the group's control, and forced the group to relocate toward the north and south. The mobilization against *Al-Shabaab* has not led, however, to an improved security situation. For example, numerous guerrilla-style attacks were launched during 2015, including suicide bombs targeting the UN staff in Mogadishu, signifying a shift towards an urban insurgency.

Box 13.17 South Sudan and Uganda vs. SPLM/A–In Opposition

Side A	Government of South Sudan, Uganda
Side B	SPLM/A-In Opposition (Sudan People's Liberation Movement/Army–In Opposition)
Incompatibility	Government
Type of Conflict	Internationalized intrastate
First Year of Conflict	2011
Status in 2015	Ongoing
Intensity in 2015	Minor
Battle-Related Deaths in 2015	480
Trajectory of Conflict in 2015	Deescalating

South Sudan became an independent state on July 9, 2011, after a referendum on the status of the territory was held in January 2011. The referendum was stipulated in the Comprehensive Peace Agreement of 2005, which ended the conflict between the government of Sudan and the Sudan People's Liberation Movement (SPLM) (see further below in the profile of "Sudan vs. SRF and Darfur Joint Resistance Forces", p. 170).

From the outset, the new government of South Sudan was challenged by two rebel groups: the South Sudan Democratic Movement/Army (SSDM/A) and the South Sudan Liberation Movement/Army (SSLM/A), both of which were supported by the government of Sudan. Civil war has been ongoing in South Sudan ever since. The country has also experienced an interstate conflict (thus far, below the level of war) with Sudan over its common border, as well as various conflicts between non-state actors.

The fighting with SSDM/A mainly took place in Jonglei state, with some clashes also in the neighboring Upper Nile state. Negotiations held with the SSDM/A resulted in a peace agreement in February 2012, which ended the fighting with this group. The SSLM/A continued to fight until 2013. In late-April 2013, a presidential pardon to all rebels active in South Sudan was announced, an offer that the SSLM/A accepted.

Although the fighting between the government and the SSDM/A and the SSLM/A formally terminated, violence did not end. Instead, two new groups entered the stage: the SSDM/A-Cobra faction and the Sudan People's Liberation Movement/Army-In Opposition (SPLM/A-In Opposition). The SSDM/A-Cobra faction was involved in fighting in Jonglei state in 2013, after which clashes subsided. A far higher intensity of violence was recorded in fighting involving the SPLM/A-In Opposition. This conflict started in mid-December 2013 with a battle between different factions of the presidential guard. One of the factions was loyal to the sitting president, Salva Kiir, while the other faction was loyal to

169

the former vice-president Riek Machar, who had been ousted from the government in July 2013. The fighting started in the capital city of Juba, but quickly spread to other areas of South Sudan. Battles were particularly fierce in the strategically important states of Bor, Malakal, and Unity. The fighting started only in mid-December 2013, but over 1,100 people were recorded as being killed by the end of the year.

The conflict continued in 2014, when fighting between the government and SPLM/A-In Opposition reached the level of a war. Much of the fighting was concentrated in three key cities with oil resources, Bor, Malakal and Bentiu, which changed hands multiple times during the year. Both sides retaliated by targeting civilians, often along ethnic lines. Attempts at negotiations, led by the Intergovernmental Authority on Development (IGAD), took place in Addis Ababa throughout the year. Several ceasefires were declared, only to be breached by the conflict parties.

The conflict continued throughout 2015, but deescalated sharply compared to the previous year. The largest offensives took place during April and October 2015 in the Greater Upper Nile region. Negotiations between the parties were held in Addis Ababa and Arusha and resulted in the signing of a comprehensive peace agreement in August 2015. As in 2014, Ugandan troops provided support to the South Sudanese government in 2015. Following the signing of the August agreement, however, Uganda began to withdraw its troops in October 2015, a process that was completed by early November 2015. These developments did not mark the end of fighting, but did help lower the intensity of armed clashes between the parties.

Box 13.18 Sudan vs. SRF and Darfur Joint Resistance Forces	
Side A	Government of Sudan
Side B	SRF (Sudanese Revolutionary Front), DJRF (Darfur Joint Resistance Forces)
Incompatibility	Government
Type of Conflict	Intrastate
First Year of Conflict	1983
Status in 2015	Ongoing
Intensity in 2015	War
Battle-Related Deaths in 2015	1,258
Trajectory of Conflict in 2015	Escalating

Sudan has suffered from civil war, involving a variety of rebel groups, for over 30 years. The conflict is primarily rooted in the centralization of economic and political power in the capital, Khartoum, and the marginalization of peripheral areas. Religious and cultural divisions, as well as access to natural resources, have also played important roles in fueling the conflict.

The violence began in the south, where the main rebel organization was the SPLM. This phase was ended with a peace agreement in 2005 and subsequent independence for South Sudan in 2011. Since 2003, the civil war has mainly centered on Darfur, in the western part of the country.

In Darfur, the government initially faced challenges from two rebel groups: the Sudan Liberation Movement/Army (SLM/A) and the Justice and Equality Movement (JEM). Both of these groups were striving to change the political system in the direction of democracy, equality, and decentralization. Aside from the fighting between the rebel groups and the army, a government-aligned Arab militia known as the *Janjaweed* has been wreaking havoc since 2003, killing large numbers of civilians and precipitating a massive refugee crisis in the Sudan–Chad border area.

Both the SLM/A and the JEM negotiated with the government in 2003–05. These negotiations resulted in the establishment of an African Union (AU) peacekeeping force, although efforts to conclude power-sharing and security arrangements stalled. Fighting deescalated significantly in 2005. Violence increased again in 2006, amid a deteriorating humanitarian situation, intra-rebel fighting, and rebel group fragmentation. The most important contributing factor was discontent with the Darfur Peace Agreement (DPA), signed by the government of Sudan and a faction of the SLM/A in May 2006. Further fragmentation – particularly of the SLM/A, but also of the JEM – continued in 2007. Despite the numerous splits, the different groups often cooperated militarily against government troops. An umbrella movement called the United Resistance Front (URF) was later formed, unifying some of the SLM/A factions. The deteriorating situation led to an international response in 2007. Joint UN/AU mediation had little success during the year, but a hybrid UN/AU peacekeeping force began to deploy in Darfur.

The impending referendum about independence for southern Sudan meant a risk of war between the north and the south. Given the ongoing conflict in Darfur, the government of Sudan wanted to avoid a two-front war. Consequently, the government set out to crush the Darfurian rebel resistance in 2010, which resulted in the highest levels of violence since 2006.

In late-2011, the Sudan Revolutionary Front (SRF) was formed as an alliance between the SLM/A, the JEM, and other groups based in South Kordofan and Blue Nile states, which border with South Sudan. The SRF has since fought in Darfur in the west, as well as in the southern states.

The SRF coalition continued to fight the government in 2014. A new alliance of rebel groups, the Darfur Joint Resistance Forces (DJRF), also emerged. A former *Janjaweed* leader established a new political movement called Sudanese Awakening Revolutionary Council (SARC), which fought the government in 2014. Negotiations took place between the government and the SRF, producing a framework agreement for future dialogue.

The conflict in Sudan escalated during 2015, when the government initiated a large-scale offensive against the SRF coalition. Major clashes took place in Darfur, Blue Nile, and South Kordofan states. The DJRF also fought the government in early 2015. No conflict activity involving SARC, was recorded during the year. Negotiations between the government and the SRF, facilitated by the AU High-Level Implementation Panel (AUHIP), took place in 2015, but no progress was made in resolving the conflict.

Box 13.19 Syria, et al. vs. IS

Side A	Government of Syria, Iran, Russia
Side B	IS (Islamic State)
Incompatibility	Territory (Islamic State)
Type of Conflict	Internationalized intrastate
First Year of Conflict	2013
Status in 2015	Ongoing
Intensity in 2015	War
Battle-Related Deaths in 2015	11,075
Trajectory of Conflict in 2015	Escalating

In April 2013, the group that had formerly been known as the Islamic State of Iraq (ISI), originally an Iraqi organization active in the Iraqi war (see the profile of "Iraq, et al. vs. IS", p. 161), changed its name to the Islamic State in Iraq and al-Sham (ISIS). This change reflected the group's greater territorial claims, which included not only Iraqi territory, but also Syrian territory, as the basis for an Islamic caliphate. ISIS subsequently changed names again to Islamic State (IS) in June 2014. The goals of ISIS differ from those of other rebel groups in Syria, which mainly aim for the overthrow of the Assad regime (see below in the profile of "Syria, et al. vs. Syrian Insurgents"). Therefore, the conflict between the government of Syria and ISIS/IS is recorded separately by UCDP. Much of the fighting involving ISIS/IS has occurred distinct from the conflict concerning government power. ISIS/IS has, however, fought many of the other Syrian insurgent groups.

During the early stages of conflict in 2013, ISIS quickly advanced through Syria, taking control over large swaths of territory, mainly in the north, and becoming one of the major insurgent groups presenting a challenge to the Syrian government. In the process, ISIS eventually clashed with other rebel groups, adding to the number of conflicts among non-state armed groups that were active in Syria, which occurred parallel to the main conflicts with the Assad government. Around this same time, Sunni–Shia sectarian divisions in Syria became increasingly significant, a development reinforced by the actions of ISIS. The group has also become notorious for its widespread human rights violations, especially the targeting of civilians.

During 2014, the conflict between the Syrian government and IS first reached the level of war, with over 1,500 reported battle-related deaths. In addition, severe fighting took place between IS and other rebel groups throughout the year. Meanwhile, IS made large territorial advances, including taking control of government bases in the Aleppo, Raqqa, and al-Hasakah provinces. The city of Raqqa was made the *de facto* capital of IS-held territory.

In 2015, IS continued to make territorial advances, including in central and southern Syria. Of note, after taking the ancient city of Palmyra in May and al-Qaryatayn in August, IS increased its presence in the Homs province, which is strategically located for access to Damascus. In total, the fighting between the government of Syria and IS resulted in at least 11,000 battle-related deaths in 2015, with the important caveat that conflict in Syria is complex and fatality figures are difficult to estimate (see further below in the profile of "Syria, et al. vs. Syrian Insurgents").

Box 13.20 Syria, et al. vs. Syrian Insurgents	
Side A	Government of Syria, Iran, Russia
Side B	Syrian insurgents
Incompatibility	Government
Type of Conflict	Internationalized intrastate
First Year of Conflict	2011
Status in 2015	Ongoing
Intensity in 2015	War
Battle-Related Deaths in 2015	33,966
Trajectory of Conflict in 2015	Stable

The conflict in Syria began after a popular uprising in March 2011 as part of the Arab Spring. The Syrian government, led by Bashar al-Assad, lashed out against the largely peaceful protests with gunfire, mass arrests, and torture. As brutality increased, so too did the number of defectors from the army. These army defectors formed the basis for the creation of the Free Syrian Army (FSA) in July 2011, a loosely organized umbrella organization composed of various recently formed militia groups. FSA began engaging in battles in September 2011 and was already posing a considerable challenge to the government in the fall of 2011.

Fragmentation of the opposition was soon evident, however, as new groups continuously formed. In 2012, radical Sunni Islamist groups such as *Jabhat al-Nusra li al-Sham* and *Ahrar al-Sham* emerged. These groups grew in strength, and reports surfaced of foreign fighters joining, notably from the war in Iraq. By this time, the Syrian regime was fighting several rebel groups, ranging from separatist Kurdish groups to jihadist groups seeking to establish an Islamic caliphate. The proliferation of many small armed groups has since continued, with the result that identifying all the armed actors operating on the battlefield is virtually impossible. The groups vary greatly in size and ideology, and their relationships to one another are frequently fluid.

As the war in Syria progressed, the Sunni–Shia sectarian dimension became increasingly significant, with the mainly Sunni rebels pitted against the Shia-supported government. Furthermore, the regional dimension of the war became more pronounced, with several neighboring countries providing support to one or more of the warring sides. Much of the fighting in the conflict has been confined to urban areas and key towns across Syria. Government forces have indiscriminately shelled cities and towns associated with rebel groups, causing large numbers of civilian deaths.

Violence continued on a massive scale throughout 2013 and affected many areas of the country. The government lost its first provincial capital, Raqqa, in early March 2013. Aided by Lebanese-based Hezbollah, government forces later retook the strategically located town of al-Qusayr. The military has relied heavily on aerial bombardment, as seen in the massive assault of Aleppo in late-2013. Another important development during 2013 was the advance into Syria of the Islamic State in Iraq and al-Sham (ISIS) (see above, p. 161, in the profile of "Iraq, et al. vs. IS").

The conflict in Syria continued at exceptionally high levels of intensity throughout 2014 and 2015, including continual aerial bombardments. Reports of chemical warfare in the northern part of the country also surfaced during this period.

An important shift in the Syrian war in 2015 was the direct involvement of Russia and Iran in support of the Syrian government. This substantially tipped the balance in favor of the Assad regime. On September 30, 2015, Russian airstrikes against rebel forces were initiated. The Russian government stated that IS was the main target, but most of the air strikes were reported to have targeted other anti-Assad groups. Around the same time, Iran sent troops to reinforce ground offensives by the Syrian government. Previously, the Iranian government was reported to have provided troops only for intelligence and combat training, rather than for direct combat. By the end of 2015, the Syrian government had retaken some territory lost during the war, including strategically important mountain areas in northern Latakia Governorate near the border with Turkey, as well as in the Qalamoun region in southern Syria. The government also regained control over most areas of Homs, Syria's third-largest city.

A number of unsuccessful peace initiatives to end the Syrian war have been launched since the beginning of the war. New attempts were made in 2015. The Vienna Process, involving a number of states and supported by the endorsement of a UN Security Council resolution in December 2015, led to a proposal for formal talks to begin in early 2016. This process, however, lacked Syrian representation. At the time, which rebel groups would be invited to participate in the talks also remained unclear.

The complexity of the Syrian war, with a multitude of warring parties engaged in conflict with the government and each other, combined with the relative lack of independent reporting, has complicated efforts to reliably estimate death tolls. The number provided by UCDP for 2014 was an estimate calculated by triangulating various summary figures. The number for 2015 was calculated by using event reports and summary figures from the Syrian Observatory for Human Rights (SOHR) – and is therefore not fully comparable with the 2014 figure. Thus, the seemingly lower death toll reported for 2015 (~34,000), compared to the figure for 2014 (~54,000), may not reflect a real change in severity of violence. Moreover, UCDP listed only one active conflict in 2014, whereas this war was divided into two separate conflicts in 2015. The total estimated number of battle-related deaths across both Syrian conflicts (see further above in the profile of "Syria, et al. vs. IS") was about 45,000 in 2015. Little evidence was observed of major changes on the battlefield that would indicate a substantially lower number of deaths in 2015, which works against a conclusion that the conflict has deescalated.

Regardless, the level of battle-related deaths in the Syrian war during both 2014 and 2015 was the highest of any civil war since the end of the Cold War. In addition, the refugee crisis continued in 2015, with half of Syria's population being displaced, either internally or externally as refugees.

Box 13.21 Turkey vs. PKK

Side A	Government of Turkey
Side B	PKK (Partiya Karkeren Kurdistan: Kurdistan Workers' Party)
Incompatibility	Territory (Kurdistan)
Type of Conflict	Intrastate
First Year of Conflict	1983
Status in 2015	Recurring
Intensity in 2015	Minor
Battle-Related Deaths in 2015	903
Trajectory of Conflict in 2015	Not applicable (inactive in 2014)

Turkey became an independent state in 1918, following the dissolution of the Ottoman Empire. In 1923, the Republic of Turkey was established. After a period of authoritarian rule under Mustafa Kemal, multi-party elections were held in 1950. Since then, the Turkish democracy has experienced periods of instability, as well as multiple military takeovers of government. Turkey's population is predominantly ethnically Turkish, but includes a substantial Kurdish minority (about 20%).

Kurdish resentment of discriminatory policies and human rights abuses by the Turkish government led to the formation in 1974 of the Kurdistan Workers' Party (PKK), a Marxist-Leninist group aiming for an independent and socialist Kurdish state. Under the leadership of Abdullah Öcalan, PKK initially turned against other Kurdish groups and Kurdish landlords in order to consolidate its position among the Kurds. In August 1984, PKK forces began ambushing Turkish troops on Kurdish territory, marking the beginning of over three decades of armed conflict between PKK and the Turkish government.

The conflict began as a low-level urban guerrilla campaign in southeastern Turkey, but developed into a full-fledged war in 1992. The conflict was most violent during the 1990s, when PKK also engaged in large-scale one-sided violence. After several years of war, violence consistently declined from 1998 to 2002. High rates of PKK fatalities during the mid-1990s and the capture of Öcalan in 1999 weakened the group, which pivoted its goals to autonomy for the Kurdish minority in Turkey.

Clashes between Turkish security forces and PKK became more frequent after the group officially renewed its struggle in June 2004. In 2005, the number of clashes sharply increased, as PKK forces increasingly found refuge in and conducted operations from bases in the Kurdish-controlled parts of northern Iraq. After a decline in deaths in 2006, the Turkish government stepped up its military action against PKK and the number of deaths rose again in 2007 and 2008. Violence dropped in 2009 and 2010, only to escalate again in 2011 and 2012. PKK declared several unilateral ceasefires during this period, but continued clashes indicated that the ceasefires were often ignored by one or both sides.

Despite continued escalation of the conflict in 2012, talks between the Turkish government and the imprisoned PKK leader Öcalan were initiated in December of that year. The main topic was reported to have been the question of PKK's disarmament. Ongoing talks led to a dramatic deescalation of the conflict in early 2013, culminating in a ceasefire announced by Öcalan on March 21, and the withdrawal into northern Iraq of all PKK forces on Turkish soil. The ceasefire largely held throughout the remainder of 2013, 2014, and the first half of 2015.

The increasingly fragile ceasefire was abandoned in late-July 2015, effectively ending the peace process. Tensions had been building over a number of issues, one of which was the PKK blaming the Turkish government for not preventing IS attacks on Kurds in Turkey. Immediately after an IS suicide bombing in Suruc on July 20, 2015, the conflict quickly escalated to a level not seen since the 1990s. The remainder of the year was marked by daily attacks by PKK on security forces, as well as large army and police operations in the Kurdish-dominated southeastern parts of Turkey. The government also regularly conducted air raids on Kurdish areas in southeastern Turkey, as well as on PKK bases in the Qandil mountains in northern Iraq. Both sides experienced heavy battle-related casualties and civilian casualities mounted as well, particularly in key towns placed under curfew.

Box 13.22 Uganda and DRC vs. ADF	
Side A	Government of Uganda, DRC
Side B	ADF (Alliance of Democratic Forces)
Incompatibility	Government
Type of Conflict	Internationalized intrastate
First Year of Conflict	1980
Status in 2015	Ongoing
Intensity in 2015	Minor
Battle-Related Deaths in 2015	197
Trajectory of Conflict in 2015	Deescalating

A large portion of Uganda's post-independence history has been characterized by violence. Rebel groups have been involved in continuous warfare against successive regimes since 1978. The 1970s and 1980s witnessed a number of violent regime changes, with Milton Obote (president from 1966–1971 and 1980–1985) and Idi Amin (president from 1971–1979) among the main principals. This period ended when the National Resistance Movement (NRM) took power in 1986, after a five-year guerrilla war. Since then, NRM leader Yoweri Museveni has been the president of Uganda.

The Museveni regime was soon challenged by remnants of the former Obote regime. In addition, a new rebellion erupted in 1986, with the emergence of the Holy Spirit Movement (HSM), a group driven by its own version of Christian ideology, in northern Uganda. HSM's lack of success on the battlefield led to the formation of a related but competing group led by Joseph Kony in 1987. This group eventually became the Lord's Resistance Army (LRA). After initial military setbacks, the LRA was able to take its armed struggle to a new level in the 1990s with the support of the government of Sudan, which led to a regionalization of the conflict. Boosted with resources provided by Sudan, but short on manpower, LRA resorted to a tactic that has made the group infamous: forced recruitment of children. Relations between Uganda and Sudan improved from 2000 onwards, effectively ending Sudanese support for LRA. The LRA ultimately returned to northern Uganda, where violence surged in 2002.

Meanwhile, the Alliance of Democratic Forces (ADF) emerged in western Uganda in late 1996, also vowing to fight against the government. Like the LRA, the ADF attacked indiscriminately, killing and abducting large numbers of civilians. The ADF has had access to rear bases in the Democratic Republic of the Congo (DRC) throughout its armed struggle. In 1998, Uganda intervened in the conflict in DRC in pursuit of the ADF. The main outcome was the dispersion of ADF forces and a geographical spread of the conflict. Beginning in 2000, the government destroyed several ADF bases in eastern DRC and the activity of the group subsequently diminished.

Negotiations with the LRA were initiated in 2006, but the peace process was ultimately a failure. The LRA launched new attacks toward the end of 2008. The government, supported by forces from the DRC and southern Sudan, responded by launching Operation Lightning Thunder into the DRC. After the offensive, LRA forces scattered over the Central African Republic (CAR), DRC and southern Sudan and fighting decreased. The LRA still remained a regional threat. In 2013, troops operating under AU command carried out a number of operations against LRA targets, but these efforts were hampered by the chaos engulfing the CAR and South Sudan. Nevertheless, the LRA seems to have become weakened and few battles involving its forces were reported in 2014. In 2015, even fewer attacks involving LRA were reported, with the death toll falling below the 25 battle-related deaths threshold.

By contrast, violence involving the ADF surged in 2014. The ADF had stepped up its attacks in North Kivu in 2013. DRC armed forces responded by launching an offensive against ADF in December 2013. With the aid of the UN Force Intervention Brigade, a multinational force set up in 2013 to fight the various rebel groups active in the DRC, several hundred ADF troops were killed and a number of the group's bases were destroyed. Operations by DRC troops, reinforced by the UN Force Intervention Brigade, continued throughout 2015 in North Kivu. The stated aim was to wipe out the ADF. Fighting was mainly reported from the area around the city of Beni, where the ADF had committed large-scale attacks on civilians. The fighting resulted in substantially fewer battle-related deaths in 2015 than in 2014.

Box 13.23 Ukraine vs. United Armed Forces of Novorossiya and Russia	
Side A	Government of Ukraine
Side B	United Armed Forces of Novorossiya, Russia
Incompatibility	Territory (Novorossiya)
Type of Conflict	Internationalized intrastate
First Year of Conflict	2014
Status in 2015	Ongoing
Intensity in 2015	War
Battle-Related Deaths in 2015	1,304
Trajectory of Conflict in 2015	Stable

The ongoing conflict between the government of Ukraine and the United Armed Forces of Novorossiya, supported by Russia, has evolved from a series of events that commenced in 2013. In November 2013, President Viktor Yanukovych cancelled the planned signing of a Ukraine association agreement with the European Union (EU), and instead chose to deepen ties with Russia. As a result, mass protests unfolded in Kiev and the Maidan military opposition, calling for the resignation of the government, was formed. A brief minor armed conflict followed. In late-February 2014, Yanukovych fled to Russia, after having been dismissed by the parliament.

The pro-Western change in government resulting from these events, combined with Russia's annexation of Crimea in March 2014, triggered the mobilization of a pro-Russian movement in the eastern parts of Ukraine. This process escalated into a series of territorial conflicts. One of the organizations formed by pro-Russian elements was the Donetsk People's Republic (DPR), which demanded sovereignty over the Donetsk Oblast in April 2014. Military confrontations with Ukrainian armed forces followed, resulting in large numbers of deaths. Both sides undertook extensive military operations, including tank offensives and heavy shelling. By early May 2014, the DPR had secured sufficient territory to run a referendum on independence for the region. The DPR subsequently declared independence from Ukraine on May 12. The Ukrainian army, however, had regrouped, was back on the offensive by mid-May, and subsequently retook about half of the territory lost to the rebels. The Ukrainian government, the US, and the EU consistently accused Russia of providing extensive support, including arms and troops, to the separatists throughout this period.

The Organization for Security and Co-operation in Europe (OSCE) negotiated a ceasefire agreement, beginning on September 5, 2014, between the government of Ukraine and DPR, as well as another separatist group, the Luhansk People's Republic (LPR). The agreement, however, soon fell apart. On September 16, a union between the DPR and the LPR was announced. The new group, the United Armed Forces of Novorossiya, claimed a territory larger than the Donetsk and Luhansk Oblast combined: Novorossiya. Since these territorial claims differ in specific ways from those of the DPR and the LPR, this situation was considered to be the onset of a new conflict as of 2014, rather than a continuation of the previous conflict.

A ceasefire signed with the Ukrainian government on September 19, 2014 did not end fighting. Warfare included heavy shelling of towns in Donetsk and Luhansk by both sides, resulting in daily casualties among both fighting forces and civilians. Bloody clashes also occurred near government-held areas, such as the Donetsk airport, and in the important communications node of Debaltseve. By December 2014, the ceasefire had completely collapsed.

Fighting intensified further in early 2015. By this time, negotiations over a new ceasefire and peace plan had been initiated in Minsk. On February 11, 2015, a draft agreement was reached. The draft agreement included a withdrawal from the front line, return of control over the state border to Ukraine, and a path to self-governance for the rebel areas. Novorossiya troops, however, stalled a final decision on the draft until their army had captured two strategic points: Donetsk airport and Debaltseve. Following this, both parties agreed to the ceasefire terms, which largely held throughout the remainder of the year, reducing violence significantly. Continued sporadic clashes led to further talks in August and September 2015, which contributed to deescalation.

Box 13.24 United States of America, et al. vs. Al-Qaida	
Side A	Government of USA, Afghanistan, Pakistan
Side B	al-Qaeda (The Base)
Incompatibility	Government
Type of Conflict	Internationalized intrastate
First Year of Conflict	2001
Status in 2015	Ongoing
Intensity in 2015	Minor
Battle-Related Deaths in 2015	65
Trajectory of Conflict in 2015	Deescalating

Starting in 2001, the United States (US) has engaged the *al-Qaida* network in an intrastate conflict with foreign involvement. This conflict constitutes an non-traditional case of internal armed conflict, where most of the violent activity has taken place outside of the US. Troops from over 20 different countries have been involved.

The conflict began on September 11, 2001, when *al-Qaeda* operatives attacked US civilian and military targets in New York City and Washington DC. Except for the 9/11 attacks, no violence has taken place on US soil. Instead, fighting has mainly been located in Afghanistan and Pakistan, but also Saudi Arabia, Somalia, Yemen and most recently Syria. In some of these locations, the bulk of fighting has been carried out by US allies, as opposed to US forces. The conflict already reached the level of war in 2001, as a result of the attacks in the US and subsequent operations against *al-Qaeda* in Afghanistan.

Al-Qaeda was formed in 1988 by volunteer forces fighting alongside the rebels in Afghanistan. After the withdrawal of Soviet troops in 1989, *al-Qaida* declared continued jihad in defense of Islamic movements. *Al-Qaeda*'s founder, Usama bin Laden, became increasingly critical of the US, focusing particularly on its presence in the Islamic world. A stated goal in connection with the 9/11 attacks was to force the US to abandon its overseas involvement, specifically in the Middle East.

US President George W. Bush responded to the 9/11 attacks by declaring the War on Terror and specifically a war on *al-Qaeda*. Several other countries soon joined the US government in their fight against terrorism. On October 7, 2001, the US launched Operation Enduring Freedom, targeting suspected *al-Qaida* bases in Afghanistan, after the *Taliban* government had rejected the request of extradition of *al-Qaeda* leaders based in the country. The operation also included troops from Australia, Canada, France, Germany, Italy, Poland, Turkey, and the United Kingdom, while other countries offered additional support.

After the *Taliban* government of Afghanistan was defeated in November 2001, US attacks on *al-Qaeda* intensified. Most surviving *al-Qaeda* operatives fled across the Pakistani border in 2002–2003, while others regrouped in Saudi Arabia. The dispersion of the *al-Qaeda* network resulted in a temporary lull in conflict activity in 2003. When the conflict resumed in 2004, almost all the activity took place in the Pakistani tribal areas and in Saudi Arabia. In particular, the border region between Afghanistan and Pakistan was the scene of most of the activity from 2005–2008. Also, a limited number of missile strikes were launched against targets in Somalia. In September 2008, a new front was opened as *al-Qaeda* operatives launched attacks on the US embassy in Yemen. These attacks later evolved into a battle between *al-Qaeda* in the Arabian Peninsula (AQAP) and the government of Yemen (see further below in the profile of "Yemen vs. AQAP, et al.").

Fatalities rose in 2009 due to an increasing use of US drone attacks targeting *al-Qaeda* operatives in the tribal areas of Pakistan. In May 2011, Usama bin Laden was killed by US special forces in his hideout in Pakistan. In 2013, conflict activity – the majority of which was again US drone attacks – remained clustered in Afghanistan, Pakistan, and Somalia. In 2014, however, most activity took place in Syria, with only a lesser share in Afghanistan and Pakistan. By 2014, core *al-Qaeda* operatives had established a presence in Syria. In response, US military forces conducted a number of air strikes in September and November 2014 on *al-Qaeda*'s Khorasan group, which is closely cooperating with *Jabhat al-Nusra li al-Sham*, one of the rebel groups active in the Syrian civil war (see the profile of "Syria, et al. vs. Syrian Insurgents", p. 172).

In 2015, attacks on *al-Qaeda* by US forces decreased and the conflict deescalated compared to 2014. Conflict activity was concentrated in Pakistan and Afghanistan and to a lesser extent in Syria, where only a few US strikes on the Khorasan group were reported. In Pakistan, deaths were mainly incurred in Pakistani security operations, cooperating with US forces, and a small number of US drone attacks. In Afghanistan, deaths resulted from drone attacks, as well as combined US–Afghan operations.

Armed Conflicts Active in 2015

Box 13.25 Yemen vs. AQAP, et al.	
Side A	Government of Yemen
Side B	AQAP (al-Qaeda in the Arabian Peninsula), Ansarallah (Supporters of God), Forces of Hadi and Bahrain, Egypt, Jordan, Kuwait, Morocco, Qatar, Saudi Arabia, Sudan, United Arab Emirates
Incompatibility	Government
Type of Conflict	Internationalized intrastate
First Year of Conflict	2009
Status in 2015	Ongoing
Intensity in 2015	War
Battle-Related Deaths in 2015	6,532
Trajectory of Conflict in 2015	Escalating

Throughout the 1990s and the beginning of the 2000s, *al-Qaeda* (see the profile of "United States of America, et al. vs. Al-Qaeda", p. 176) had been active at a low level in both Saudi Arabia and Yemen. *Al-Qaida* in Yemen was considerably strengthened in February 2006, when key *al-Qaeda* members escaped from Sana'a prison. The group recruited new members and set up new bases in Yemen.

In January 2009, local *al-Qaeda* branches in Saudi Arabia and Yemen merged and formed *al-Qaeda* in the Arabian Peninsula (AQAP), with the aim of establishing an Islamic State in the Arabian Peninsula. After the creation of AQAP, the Yemeni government came under increased pressure from neighboring countries, as well as the US, to prevent AQAP from gaining further ground. The first battles between the government and AQAP took place in 2009. The US launched its first missile strikes on AQAP strongholds in Yemen toward the end of that year.

In 2010, battles between Yemeni government forces and AQAP became more frequent. The group also conducted several attacks on foreign targets. Fears that AQAP posed a threat also outside Yemen led to an increase in international involvement, with various states pledging to support the government of Yemen's efforts to fight AQAP.

In 2011, the armed conflict escalated dramatically. Demonstrations in Sana'a during the Arab Spring had weakened the government and kept it preoccupied with responding to public unrest. AQAP launched a large-scale offensive in March 2011, resulting in the capture of vast territory in the Abyan governorate in southern Yemen. AQAP encountered resistance, however, from the Yemeni military in the Abyan capital of Zinjibar, where fighting raged for the remainder of 2011. In the meantime, calls for the resignation of President Saleh, which were reinforced by US pressure, finally resulted in Saleh stepping down in November 2012. An interim president, Mansour al-Hadi, took over in early 2012.

The conflict escalated even further in 2012. The government intensified its efforts to retake territory in the south. AQAP responded with large-scale bombings, striking even in the capital of Sana'a. As a result of AQAP advances in Abyan, many local tribes had joined the weakened and deeply divided Yemeni army, which proved decisive for eventually pushing back the militants. By the end of the summer, AQAP had lost most of its strongholds. Following these setbacks, AQAP shifted tactics to high-profile assassinations and suicide attacks. Violence escalated again in 2014, with a number of deadly attacks, though the conflict was not as intense as in 2012. As in previous years, the US continued to carry out drone strikes against AQAP.

In 2014, the Yemeni government was also challenged by an additional actor: *Ansarallah* (Supporters of God), commonly referred to as The Huthis. This group, which had been formed in the mid-1990s by the northern Huthi tribe, initially strived for socioeconomic justice and an end to Huthi discrimination. The group had been involved in intermittent clashes in northwestern Yemen since 2004. In March 2014, *Ansarallah* called for the government's resignation. Over the course of the early spring of 2014, *Ansarallah* advanced south toward Sana'a, where armed clashes eventually erupted on September 18. Three days later, *Ansarallah* took control of most of the capital. A peace agreement, which included provisions for the formation of a new government and a ceasefire, was later concluded.

Subsequent developments culminated in a considerable escalation of the war in 2015, in terms of both battle intensity and the degree of internationalization. A new phase began in January 2015, when *Ansarallah* ousted the government led by President al-Hadi and took full control over the capital and effectively became the new government. Armed forces loyal to al-Hadi struck back militarily from February 2015 onwards. On March 26, 2015, a Saudi-led coalition initiated air strikes against the new government, in support of the forces of al-Hadi. The airstrikes continued throughout the year, causing very high death tolls. As a result, a massive humanitarian crisis, with millions of Yemenis displaced, unfolded during the year. Clashes between the government of Yemen and AQAP continued in 2015, but were largely overshadowed by the war between the new government and the forces of al-Hadi and their regional allies.

Notes

1 This case selection criterion differs from the one used in corresponding chapters of editions of *Peace and Conflict* up until 2014. In those chapters, the profiles covered all conflicts that had accumulated a total of at least 1,000 battle-related deaths, whether in a single calendar year (war) or over time (what UCDP had labeled to that point as intermediate armed conflict).
2 For in-depth definitions of key concepts, see www.pcr.uu.se/research/ucdp/definitions/.
3 Please see the UCDP website (www.ucdp.uu.se) for separate data on these types of violence.
4 This conflict occurred between the Syrian government and the Islamic State (IS). In *Peace and Conflict 2014*, the conflict was coded as part of the main war in Syria. The UCDP has since recoded the Syrian war, and the separate conflict with IS should have been included as a war already for 2014.

Reference

Melander, Erik, Therése Pettersson, and Lotta Themnér (2016) "Organized Violence 1989–2015," *Journal of Peace Research* 53(5): 727–742.

14

Multilateral Peacekeeping Operations Active in 2015

Deniz Cil

Introduction

The United Nations (UN) has been deploying peacekeeping missions since 1948, soon after its founding in the wake of World War II. Over the decades, a total of 69 missions have been conducted in 42 countries around the world.

The missions deployed from 1948–1989, during the Cold War era, mostly consisted of unarmed observers with mandates limited to monitoring ceasefires and investigating claims of violations, following interstate wars. In addition to being smaller in scope, these missions tended to be smaller in scale and uncommon – just 18 missions in 42 years. The first mission, the United Nations Truce Supervision Organization (UNTSO), was established in order to observe a ceasefire between Israel and the Arab States. The first armed mission, UN Emergency Force (UNEF I), was deployed in 1956 in response to the Suez Crisis.

By contrast, post–Cold War era missions increasingly became more multidimensional and frequent (51 missions in 25 years). The evolution reflects the needs and challenges that arise in addressing different security environments associated with a larger number of internal conflicts, which progressively shifted the geographical deployment of missions from Europe to Africa and Asia (Figure 14.1). This second generation of peacekeeping missions undertook various new tasks, such as election monitoring; providing support for creating and improving institutions of governance; monitoring programs for the demobilization, disarmament and reintegration (DDR) of ex-combatants; providing training to national police forces as part of security sector reforms and generally to improve the rule of law; and protecting civilians in conflict zones.

The UN is not the only international organization that conducts peacekeeping operations. Among the first non-UN operations were the International Commissions for Supervision and Control in Vietnam (ICSC-Vietnam), Cambodia (ICSC-Cambodia) and Laos (ICSC-Laos). These operations were established in August 1954 to oversee the implementation of the Geneva Agreements on the Cessation of Hostilities in what had been the French colony of Indochina, accompanied by a transition to three independent countries. Over subsequent years, several other international organizations, including the European Union (EU), the African Union (AU), the Organization of American States (OAS), the Organization for Security and Co-operation in Europe (OSCE), and the Economic Community of West African States (ECOWAS), established peacekeeping operations. In addition, several multilateral monitoring operations, such as the International Monitoring Team (IMT) in the Philippines and the Joint Monitoring Mission/Joint Military Commission (JMM/JMC) addressing conflict in Sudan, assumed peacekeeping roles.

At any given point since 1945, the number of UN missions has always exceeded the number of non-UN missions. Since 2000, however, the number of non-UN missions has increased steadily and overall more new non-UN missions have been initiated than new UN missions (Heldt and Wallensteen 2011). Otherwise, the long-term historical patterns in UN and non-UN peacekeeping missions are similar: the post-World War II missions were deployed mainly to address interstate conflicts with more traditional mandates, whereas the majority of post-Cold War missions were deployed to address intrastate conflicts with multidimensional mandates.

The academic literature on peacekeeping operations has also evolved. Initial work mostly focused on providing a historical account of UN practices in a mission or a comparison of a group of missions in a region (e.g., Burns and Heathcote 1963; Cox 1967; Pelcovits 1984; Mackinlay 1989; Higgins 1996). Early empirical analyses yielded mixed results on the effectiveness of peacekeeping in addressing interstate conflicts (Haas et al. 1972; Wilkenfeld and Brecher 1984). Research

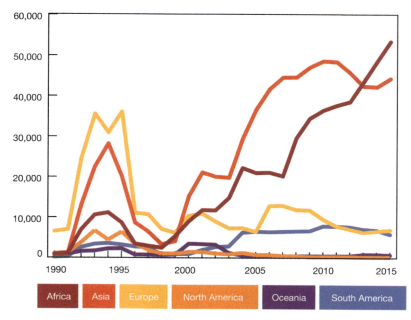

Figure 14.1 Regional Trends in Deployment of UN Mission Personnel, 1990–2015

in the 1990s focused on case studies of peacekeeping failures, highlighting high-profile examples in Somalia, Rwanda, and Bosnia (e.g., Jett 1999; Boulden 2001; Fleitz 2002).[1] In the 2000s, scholars continued to exhibit interest in evaluating whether or not peacekeeping missions are effective in achieving their various goals. Increasing attention was paid to assessing explanations for the outcomes (Diehl and Druckman 2010). Studies were conducted with greater breadth and depth, often utilizing quantitative methods and addressing threats to inference by taking into account the non-random deployment of peacekeepers (Mullenbach 2005; Kathman 2013). Among the key findings were that peacekeeping missions increase the duration of peace following civil wars (Doyle and Sambanis 2006; Fortna 2008), especially those missions with more robust and multilateral operations (Doyle and Sambanis 2000). An important reason why peacekeepers improve the chances that conflicts end at the negotiating table, and prolong the duration of peace, is the provision of security guarantees to combatants in the post-conflict period (Walter 2002). These insights are noteworthy given that peacekeepers are actually deployed in contexts of more severe conflicts with higher risk of recurrence (Fortna 2008; Gilligan and Stedman 2003; Gilligan and Sergenti 2008).

More recent studies have revealed an association between higher numbers of peacekeeping troops and lower numbers of battle-related and civilian deaths in ongoing conflicts (Hultman et al. 2013, 2014). These results are significant because peacekeeping missions deployed to ongoing conflicts have been increasingly common over the past two decades. Another important line of research focuses on disaggregating the types of personnel, differentiating between troops, police, and observers. Multiple studies have revealed that a larger troop presence in post-conflict countries is associated not only with longer durations of peace, but also with less civilian victimization (Hultman et al. 2016; Kathman and Wood 2016). Another emergent angle in the literature is the supply side of peacekeeping missions, including budgets of UN missions (Selway 2013), the patterns of personnel contributions to UN and non-UN missions (Shimizu and Sandler 2002; Gaibulloev, Sandler and Shimizu 2009; Bove and Elia 2011; Gaibulloev et al. 2015; Uzonyi 2015; Ward and Dorussen 2016), and the duration of peacekeeping missions (Wright and Greig 2012).

Consistent with the leading edge in peace and conflict studies, the latest work on peacekeeping operations examines where peacekeepers are deployed sub-nationally, in the process testing different mechanisms to explain deployment patterns (e.g., convenience vs. instrumental). The results demonstrate that peacekeepers are deployed to frontlines of conflict and reduce the duration of conflict on a local level (Ruggeri et al. 2016, 2017).

All this research is advancing understanding of how peacekeeping operates in practice, contributing especially to our knowledge of how and when peacekeeping works. The findings have concrete implications for the design and conduct of future missions, informing ways to use resources more effectively and achieve better results. Several issue areas remain, however, to be investigated in greater depth, including varying strategies employed by different peacekeeping units, military and infrastructural capabilities available to peacekeepers, and the effects of these factors on peace and conflict outcomes at both national and sub-national levels. Sustaining inquiry into peacekeeping is vital, given the number of missions currently active and the expectation that the need for ongoing conflict resolution will persist.

The rest of this chapter provides profiles of 23 multilateral peacekeeping operations conducted by international organizations and/or a set of states that were active as of December 2015.[2] The profiles are organized in chronological order, based on the date of establishment. Each profile presents an historical overview of the establishment, mandate, operations, and deployment of the mission. In addition, charts provide information, where available, on the personnel contributions from the top five countries; the rest of the personnel are aggregated in the "Other" category, with the number of contributing states presented in parenthesis.[3] In 2015, 123 countries contributed a total of 106,830 uniformed personnel (91,140 troops, 13,854 police and 1,836 observers) to the 16 UN missions profiled in this chapter. The approved budget for these missions for the July 2015–June 2016 fiscal year was about $8.27 billion.[4] In 2015, 71 states contributed a total of 26,609 personnel to the seven non-UN missions profiled in this chapter. Table 14.1 offers a summary of the UN and non-UN missions, including the year of establishment and average number of deployed personnel, by type, in 2015.

Table 14.1 Overview of Multilateral Peacekeeping Missions Active in 2015

Type (Sponsor)	Name of Mission	Location	Year Established	Average Personnel in 2015		
				Observers	Police	Troops
UN	UNTSO	Middle East	1948	147	0	0
UN	UNMOGIP	India and Pakistan	1949	44	0	0
UN	UNFICYP	Cyprus	1964	0	63	861
UN	UNDOF	Golan	1974	0	0	809
UN	UNIFIL	Lebanon	1978	0	0	10,463
UN	MINURSO	Western Sahara	1991	187	5	28
UN	UNMIK	Kosovo	1999	8	8	0
UN	UNMIL	Liberia	2003	116	1,396	3,885
UN	UNOCI	Côte d'Ivoire	2004	179	1,456	5,443
UN	MINUSTAH	Haiti	2004	0	2,319	3,158
UN	UNAMID	Sudan (Darfur)	2007	183	3,178	13,948
UN	MONUSCO	Dem. Rep. of the Congo	2010	476	1,137	18,210
UN	UNISFA	Sudan (Abeyi)	2011	116	23	4,186
UN	UNMISS	South Sudan	2011	184	1,070	11,143
UN	MINUSMA	Mali	2013	10	1,058	9,768
UN	MINUSCA	Central African Republic	2014	138	1,560	8,917
Non-UN (Egypt and Israel)	MFO	Egypt (Sinai)	1981	0	0	1,682
Non-UN (several)	JCC	Moldova (Trans-Dniestr)	1992	0	0	1,121
Non-UN (IMT)	IMT	Philippines (Mindanao)	2004	0	3	25
Non-UN (EU)	EUFOR-Althea	Bosnia and Herzegovina	2004	0	0	796
Non-UN (AU)	AMISOM	Somalia	2007	0	481	21,645
Non-UN (ECOWAS)	ECOMIB	Guinea-Bissau	2012	0	145	398
Non-UN (EU)	EUFOR-RCA	Central African Republic	2014	0	0	313

UNTSO, Middle East, May 1948

The first UN peacekeeping operation, the United Nations Truce Supervision Organization (UNTSO), was established in May 1948 and is still in operation. In November 1947, the UN General Assembly endorsed a plan for the partition of Palestine into an Arab state and a Jewish state, which was not accepted by the Palestinian Arabs and the Arab states. After the United Kingdom relinquished its mandate over Palestine and the State of Israel was proclaimed, the Arab states reneged on the plan and hostilities broke out. In response, the UN Security Council decided that the UN Mediator would supervise a truce and be provided with a sufficient number of military observers.[5] Ever since, UNTSO military observers have remained in the area.

In response to changes in the security situation, especially after the 1956, 1967 and 1973 Arab–Israeli wars, the composition and functions of the mission were periodically adjusted. In 1956, the Chief of Staff of UNTSO became the Commander of the UN Emergency International Force. He was tasked to recruit officers from among UNTSO observers and from various UN member states, excluding the permanent members of the UN Security Council, to establish the Emergency International Force.[6] In December 1967, the observation posts on each side of the Suez Canal increased from nine to 18 and the observer strength increased to 90 in order to monitor the ceasefire.[7] In 1973, several contingents from the UN Peacekeeping Force in Cyprus transferred to Egypt as the UN Emergency Force and the UNTSO Chief of Staff became the interim Commander of the Emergency International Force.[8]

The headquarters of UNTSO is located in Jerusalem. As of December 2015, UNTSO maintains two observer groups. Observer Group Golan (OGG) supports the United Nations Disengagement Observer Force (UNDOF) in the Golan Heights. While most of the UNDOF observers were withdrawn from the area in September 2014, UNTSO observers continued to work with OGG and supported observer positions of UNDOF on the Israeli side of the separation line. OGG-T is deployed in Teverya (Tiberias) and OGG-D is located in Camp Ziouani. Observer Group Lebanon (OGL) supports the United Nations Interim Force in Lebanon (UNIFIL) in Southern Lebanon. OGL has its headquarters in An Naqurah and maintains two patrol bases in Qiryat and Shemona, in northern Israel. The UNTSO also has liaison offices in Beirut (Lebanon), Ismailia (Egypt), and Damascus (Syria).

By the late-1990s, the total number of UNTSO personnel had dropped by roughly half from the levels observed in the early 1990s, remaining nearly steady ever since. Between 1991 and 1993, the composition of personnel shifted from exclusively troops to exclusively observers. As of December 2015, UNTSO had 147 observers from 26 countries (Figure 14.2). The mission is financed through the UN Regular Biennial Budget. Total appropriations for 2014–2015 were $74,291,900.

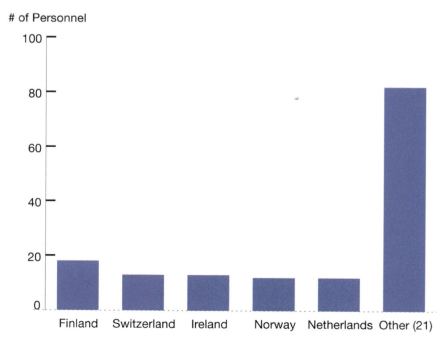

Figure 14.2 Contributors of Personnel to UNTSO in 2015

UNMOGIP, India and Pakistan, January 1949

Under the scheme of partition provided by the Indian Independence Act of 1947, Kashmir was free to accede to either India or Pakistan. Kashmir's subsequent accession to India initated a dispute between the two countries, which later turned into an armed conflict. In January 1948, the UN Security Council established the UN Commission for India and Pakistan (UNCIP), composed of representatives of three UN members – one selected by India, a second selected by Pakistan, and the third chosen by the selected representatives – to investigate and mediate the dispute.[9] In April 1948, the UN Security Council decided to expand the commission and include military observers to stop the fighting.[10]

The first team of observers arrived in the area in January 1949. The observers helped the local authorities in their investigations, while avoiding any direct intervention between the opposing parties until the Karachi Agreement was signed in July 1949. According to the agreement, UNCIP would deploy units when deemed necessary in order to help local commanders verify the ceasefire line. Any disagreement over the ceasefire line would be referred to UNCIP. The UN Military Observer Group in India and Pakistan (UNMOGIP) replaced the UNCIP in 1951 and continued to observe the ceasefire and investigate reports of violations.

In 1971, hostilities broke out along the border of East Pakistan over the independence movement that led to the creation of Bangladesh. India and Pakistan signed another ceasefire in December 1971 and later an agreement in July 1972 defining the Line of Control (LoC) in Kashmir. India took the position that the UNMOGIP is no longer relevant since its mandate to observe the line established by the Karachi Agreement has been altered with this new agreement; Pakistan did not accept this position. The mission continued to observe the 1971 ceasefire line. Since 1972, Pakistani officials have filed regular complaints about ceasefire violations to UNMOGIP, while Indian officials stopped filing complaints and restricted the activities of the UN personnel on the Indian side of the LoC. In July 2014, India hardened its position and closed the Liaison Office of UNMOGIP located in New Delhi. The tensions along the LoC escalated in 2014 and 2015, most recently in August 2015, which reportedly resulted in several casualties to forces on both sides as well as to civilians. The parties initiated a new round of peace talks in September 2015, followed by the Pakistani proposal to expand the UNMOGIP's mandate to observe a formalized version of the 2003 ceasefire agreement.

UNMOGIP's headquarters is located in Srinagar and the rear headquarters in Islamabad. In addition, 11 field stations are distributed across the LoC. Since 1993, the mission has been composed exclusively of observers. As of December 2015, the mission had 44 observers, contributed by 10 countries (Figure 14.3). The mission is financed through the UN Regular Biennial Budget. Total appropriations for 2014–2015 were $19,647,100.

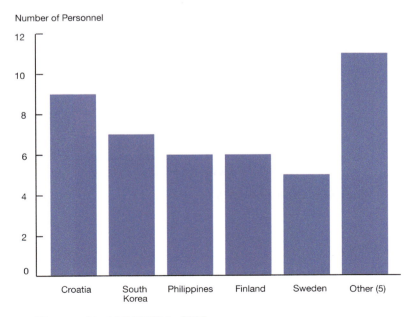

Figure 14.3 Contributors of Personnel to UNMOGIP in 2015

UNFICYP, Cyprus, March 1964

The UN Peacekeeping Force in Cyprus (UNFICYP) was deployed in March 1964, after the outbreak of violence in December 1963 and the failed attempts to solve the constitutional crisis and restore peace.[11] UNFICYP's initial mandate was to prevent the recurrence of fighting and to contribute to the restoration and maintenance of law and order.

The July 1974 coup in Cyprus, by Greek Cypriots favoring union with Greece, was followed by an intervention of the Turkish military, which occupied the northern part of the island. The UN Security Council called for a ceasefire and requested the withdrawal of Turkish troops.[12] A *de facto* ceasefire came into effect in August 1974. At this point, the new mandate of UNFICYP became to monitor the ceasefire in the buffer zone that separates Cyprus National Guard forces and the Turkish and the Turkish Cypriot forces, which extends 180 kilometers (111.8 miles) across the island. UNFIYCP troops are deployed along the ceasefire line. A police component of the mission was introduced in 2003, after the Turkish Cypriot authorities opened several crossing points for visits.

Under the leadership of the office of the UN Secretary-General, the parties agreed to a foundation agreement for the Comprehensive Settlement of the Cyprus Problem, which was submitted to simultaneous referenda on April 24, 2004. The solution plan was approved by the Turkish Cypriots, but rejected by the Greek Cypriot electorate, and therefore did not enter into force.[13] In the subsequent years, the UN Secretary-General's Special Representative continued efforts to solve the incompatibility. In February 2014, the parties agreed to re-launch high-level negotiations and hold talks in May and June 2014.[14] In October 2014, the talks were suspended due to a disagreement concerning Turkey's attempt to conduct a seismic survey in an exclusive economic zone.[15] In May 2015, talks were reinitiated and several confidence-building measures followed, including several demining activities that were led by UNFICYP and working towards opening two additional crossing points. UNFICYP continued its regular patrols along the ceasefire line and to facilitate civilians' daily activities in the buffer zone.

The mission and police headquarters are located in Nicosia. Sector headquarters are located in Skouriotissa, Nicosia, and Famagusta. Troop and police units are deployed in a total of 12 locations throughout the buffer zone and in Leonarisso. As of December 2015, 19 countries were contributing a total of 924 personnel to the mission (Figure 14.4). The approved budget for the 2015–2016 fiscal year was $52,538,500.

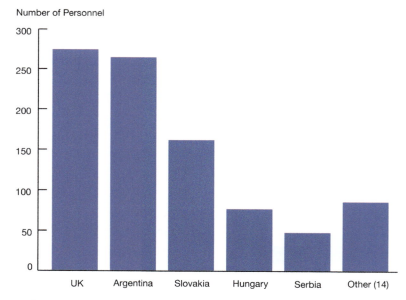

Figure 14.4 Contributors of Personnel to UNFICYP in 2015

UNDOF, Golan, June 1974

Following the 1973 outbreak of conflict between Egypt and Israel in the areas of the Suez Canal and the Sinai, as well as between Israel and Syria in the Golan, the UN Security Council deployed the United Nations Emergency Force II in October 1974. While the situation was stabilized in the Suez Canal area, the Golan area became increasingly unstable in early 1974. By May 1974, the UN Security Council authorized the UN Disengagement Observer Force (UNDOF) to enforce the Agreement on Disengagement between Israeli and Syrian forces.[16]

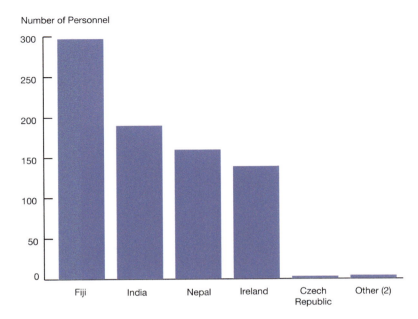

Figure 14.5 Contributors of Personnel to UNDOF in 2015

UNDOF maintains a separation area, which is 75 kilometers (46.6 miles) long and 10 kilometers (6.2 miles) wide in the center before narrowing down to 200 meters (0.12 miles) in the south. In addition to patrolling the area, UNDOF has also supported mine clearance activities and assisted the International Committee of the Red Cross (ICRC) in the passage of mail, goods, and persons through the area of separation.

The situation in the separation area has remained relatively quiet up until the recent outbreak of war in Syria, which started to affect the UNDOF area in 2012. The use of heavy weapons by the Syrian government and opposition groups, as well as air operations in close proximity to the area of separation, continue to undermine the Disengagement Agreement.

In August 2014, UNDOF personnel came in direct contact with several armed groups, including the *al-Nusra* Front, which resulted in the abduction of 45 peacekeepers and the confinement of 72 others to two UN positions. On September 11, the abducted peacekeepers were released. Due to continued heavy fighting, the mission headquarters in Camp Faouar – seven positions and two observer posts – were temporarily relocated to the Alpha (Israeli) side in mid-September, limiting the movement of UNDOF personnel on the Bravo (Syrian) Line. Since then, UNDOF has remained on the Alpha side, while maintaining positions in Mount Hermon in the northern part of Bravo Line and position 80 in the south along the Jordanian border.

The ceasefire between Israel and Syria was maintained throughout 2015, yet the situation in the separation area remained volatile due to ongoing conflict in Syria. Repeated rocket and artillery fire was launched by armed groups operating in proximity to the separation area. Meanwhile, the presence of Syrian Armed Forces around Al Baath, Khan Arnabah, and Al Wisiyah, along the road connecting Quneitra to Damascus, and in Hadar, violates the Disengagement of Forces Agreement.[17] UNDOF is planning to expand its position in the north in 2016.[18]

As of December 2015, the mission had a total of 809 troops, contributed by seven countries (Figure 14.5). The approved budget for the 2015–2016 fiscal year was $51,706,200.

UNIFIL, Lebanon, March 1978

In response to the attacks by the Palestine Liberation Organization (PLO), Israeli forces invaded and occupied the southern part of Lebanon, except the city of Tyre and its surrounding area, in March 1978. Four days after the invasion, the UN Security Council adopted two resolutions calling for an immediate ceasefire, the withdrawal of Israeli forces, and the establishment of the UN Interim Force in Lebanon (UNIFIL), at the request of the Government of Lebanon.[19] The original mandate of UNIFIL was to confirm the withdrawal of Israeli forces, restore international peace, and assist the Government of Lebanon in establishing its authority in the area.

In 1985, Israel partially withdrew from parts of Lebanon it occupied in 1982, while retaining control of the southern part manned by the Israeli Defense Force (IDF), De Facto Forces (DFF), and the South Lebanon Army (SLA) until May 2000. In June 2000, UNIFIL confirmed the withdrawal of Israel forces in compliance with the SC Resolution 425 (1978).

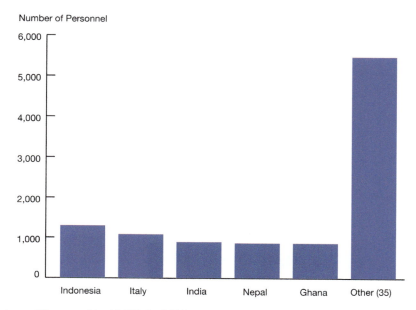

Figure 14.6 Contributors of Personnel to UNIFIL in 2015

The Government of Lebanon started to deploy police and army personnel and re-establish local administration in the occupied areas in August 2000. In July 2006, however, heavy fighting erupted between Israel and Hezbollah, operating from Lebanese territory. In response, the UN Security Council increased the size of the mission to a maximum of 15,000 troops to monitor ceasefire and continue to implement its mandate.[20]

In July and August 2014, the outbreak of the Gaza conflict threatened the stability along the Blue Line (a border demarcation between Lebanon and Israel, delineated by the UN on June 7, 2000 to confirm Israeli withdrawal) and in the area of UNIFIL operations. In the wake of rocket attacks launched from Lebanon, UNIFIL continued its close contact with both sides in an effort to deescalate the situation and restore the cessation of hostilities. An UNIFIL investigation claimed that the attacks were individual initiatives to express solidarity with Gaza during Israel's military operations.[21]

Serious violations of the ceasefire were observed during 2015. A prominent example was the January 28 incident during which Hezbollah launched anti-tank guided missiles from the UNIFIL area of operations towards an Israeli military convoy, which was followed by Israeli retaliation and the death of one UNIFIL peacekeeper during retaliatory fire.[22] Israeli unarmed vehicles also engaged in numerous violations of Lebanese airspace, reflecting escalating tensions between Hezbollah and Israel.[23] In addition, civilians with unauthorized weapons in the area of operations committed various breaches.

UNIFIL's headquarters is located in Naqoura, while the East Sector Headquarters is located near Marjayoun and the West Sector Headquarters is located near Al Bayyadah. UNIFIL maintains 53 positions throughout southern Lebanon. As of December 2015, UNIFIL had a total of 10,463 troops contributed by 40 countries (Figure 14.6). The approved budget for the 2015–2016 fiscal year was $506,346,400.

MFO, Egypt (Sinai), August 1981

The Multinational Force and Observers (MFO) was established based on the March 1979 Treaty of Peace signed between Egypt and Israel, following the 1973 conflict. The UN has maintained several observer missions in the region, but did not renew a Sinai peacekeeping mission after the mandate of the UN Emergency Force II expired in July 1979. Following the failure of the UN Security Council to reach an agreement to establish a UN Force and Observers in May 1981, Egypt and Israel, with the support of the United States, started to work on a framework to establish an observer force outside the UN framework. These efforts led to the establishment of the MFO in August 1981. The mandate of the new force was to observe and verify compliance with the military personnel and equipment limitations specified in the Treaty of Peace, especially in four zones identified in the Annex 1, i.e., Zones A, B, and C in the Sinai Peninsula in Egypt and Zone D in Israel.[24]

In 2005, after the Israeli withdrawal from Gaza, Egypt agreed to deploy border security guards to the region. To observe Egyptian deployment, the MFO mandate was expanded. Since then, the mandate has remained unchanged.

In the wake of the overthrow of Egyptian President Mubarak in January 2011 and subsequent events, MFO faced several logistical and security challenges, especially in the northern Sinai.[25] Since 2011, the situation in the Sinai has

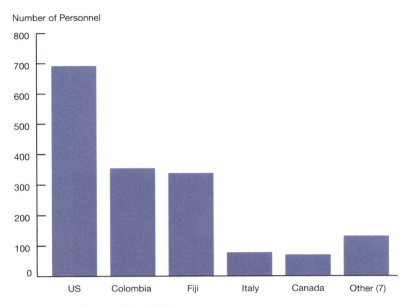

Figure 14.7 Contributors of Personnel to MFO in 2015

remained volatile with the emergence of multiple non-state armed actors fighting against Egyptian security forces. This upheaval continued to affect operations of the MFO. Key incidents included the blockade of all MFO movements by armed elements in northeast Sinai during late-April and early May 2012, as well as the September 2012 attack against the MFO's North Camp.[26] Also, missions of the Civilian Observer Unit (COU) are frequently interrupted by operations of the Egyptian military and activity of other armed actors. After militants shot down an Egyptian military helicopter in January 2014, COU ceased all aerial reconnaissance missions and instead continued verification on the ground.[27] On September 6, 2015, MFO removed its personnel from Checkpoint 1-F located in the northeast Sinai, 5 kilometers from North Camp in El Gorah, due to an inability to resupply the area safely.

Currently, MFO operates from two major camps. The largest one is the North Camp, which houses the mission headquarters and is the base of activities in the northern and central sectors of Zone C. Operations in the southern sector of Zone C are based from the South Camp, which is located near Sharm el Sheikh. MFO has two liaison offices in Cairo and Tel Aviv, while its international headquarters is located in Rome, Italy. In addition, MFO has one Coastal Protection Unit (CPU) stationed at the port of Sharm close to South Camp and 23 remote operational sites composed of Sector Control Centers (SCCs), Observation Posts (OPs), and Checkpoints (CPs) deployed throughout Zone C. As of December 2015, MFO had a total of 1,682 troops contributed by 12 countries (Figure 14.7).

MINURSO, Western Sahara, April 1991

After efforts by the Organization of African Unity (OAU) and the UN Secretary-General in the late 1980s to solve the conflict over Western Sahara between Morocco and POLISARIO (*Frente popular de liberación de Saguia el Hamra y Rio de Oro*; Popular Front for the Liberation of Saguia el Hamra and Rio de Oro), the UN Security Council established the UN Mission for the Referendum in Western Sahara (MINURSO) on April 26, 1991.[28] The initial mandate included monitoring the ceasefire; verifying the reduction of Moroccan troops; monitoring confinement of Moroccan and POLISARIO troops; taking steps towards ensuring the release of all Western Sahara political prisoners; overseeing the exchange of prisoners; implementing the repatriation; identifying and registering voters; and organizing and ensuring a free and fair referendum.[29] Many aspects of the mandate were successfully implemented, with the referendum being a notable exception.

Identification of voters was finalized in December 1999, after issues about registering the members of the three contested tribes were resolved. Yet differences concerning the repatriation of refugees and the appeals process endured. Two rounds of UN-sponsored talks in June and August 2007, followed by a third round in January 2008 and informal meetings in August 2009 and February 2010, did not lead to substantive progress on resolving core issues. After the failed direct negotiations, the Secretary-General's Special Envoy has continued to hold bilateral talks with the parties and neighboring states since 2013, seeking to work towards a solution for self-determination of the Western Sahara.

MINURSO continues to monitor the ceasefire, work to reduce the threat of mines, support confidence-building mechanisms between the parties, assist the UN High Commissioner for Refugees in its activities in the refugee camps near Tindouf, and cooperate with the observer delegation of the African Union in Laayoune. During 2015, the mission

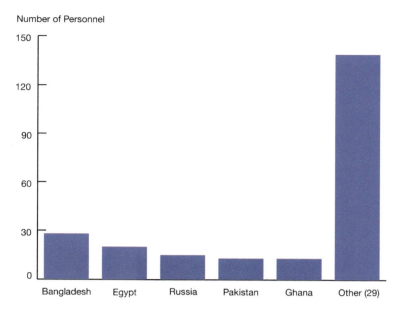

Figure 14.8 Contributors of Personnel to MINURSO in 2015

regularly monitored 570 units, 29 training areas, 316 observation posts, and 355 notified operational activities by the Moroccan Army on the West side of the berm (a sand wall structure that separates the two sides), as well as 93 units, eight training areas, 38 observation posts, and four operational activities of POLISARIO armed forces on the East side of the berm.

MINURSO's headquarters is located in Laayoune. Two liaison offices are located in Tindouf and Ad Dakhla. The mission also maintains nine team sites on both sides of the berm. As of December 2015, 34 countries were contributing a total of 220 uniformed personnel to the mission (Figure 14.8). The approved budget for the 2015–2016 fiscal year was $53,190,000.

JCC, Moldova (Trans-Dniestr Region), July 1992

Tensions in the Trans-Dniestr region started after Moldova declared independence in 1991 and escalated after the clashes between Moldovan soldiers and the Slavic minority of the Trans-Dniestr region, which sought independence. A July 1992 ceasefire agreement, brokered by Russia, ended the conflict. The agreement created a security zone along both sides of the Dniestr River and a tripartite peacekeeping force constituted with Russian, Moldovan and Trans-Dniestrian units.

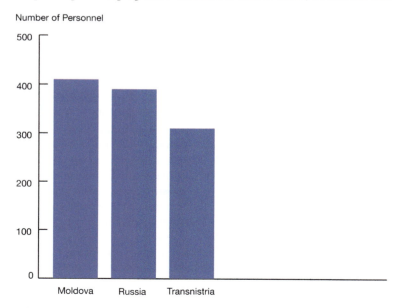

Figure 14.9 Contributors of Personnel to JCC in 2015

The Joint Control Commission (JCC), composed of delegates from the three parties as well as Ukraine and the Organization for Security and Co–operation in Europe (OSCE), was established to oversee the operations of the peacekeeping force and the return of refugees, while working towards a political solution in the region. In September 2005, US and EU representatives joined the JCC.

Although some progress was made by the new JCC (5+2), the negotiations broke down in 2006 and remained deadlocked until 2010.[30] In the meantime, the presence of Russian troops in the region also became a contentious issue. Moldova called for the replacement of Russian troops with international observers, whereas Trans-Dniestria called for an increase in Russian troops. New talks brokered by the JCC commenced in November 2011. The sides came to an agreement on common principles and mechanisms for negotiations in April 2012.[31] Tensions were heightened in the region during 2013, however, with a new border extension decree issued by Trans-Dniestria.[32] In December 2015, JCC's work on solving the dispute restarted, as both sides started to discuss the new agenda, including an increase in the number of Russian peacekeepers.[33] As of December 2015, three countries were contributing a total of 1,121 troops to the mission (Figure 14.9).

UNMIK, Kosovo, June 1999

In June 1999, the UN Security Council decided to deploy both a civil and a security presence in Kosovo. The civil presence, the UN Interim Administration Mission in Kosovo (UNMIK), was tasked with ensuring that the people of Kosovo could enjoy substantial autonomy until a final settlement is reached, including performing basic civilian administrative functions and facilitating a political process to determine the future status of Kosovo. The security presence, the NATO-led Kosovo Force (KFOR), was tasked with deterring renewed hostilities; maintaining the ceasefire; preventing the return of the Federal and Republic military, police and paramilitary forces; demilitarizing the Kosovo Liberation Army (KLA) forces; and establishing a secure environment for the return of refugees.[34]

UNMIK was the first mission of its kind in two respects. One was assuming a wide range of administrative responsibilities. Another was to have a civil peacekeeping mission under UN leadership that brought together different intergovernmental organizations, namely UNHCR, the Organization for Security and Co-operation in Europe (OSCE), and the European Union (EU), which were responsible for humanitarian assistance, democratization and economic development, respectively.

In early 2006, the UN Secretary-General's Special Envoy, Martti Ahtisaari, initiated direct talks between Kosovo's Albanian community and Serbia. In August 2007, a new mediation effort was initiated by the "Troika": the EU, the Russian Federation and the United States of America.[35] Following the failure to reach an agreement on the status of Kosovo, the Assembly of Kosovo declared independence in February 2008.[36] In response, the mandate and the size of UNMIK were adjusted accordingly. The mission successfully concluded its gradual reconfiguration and reached the

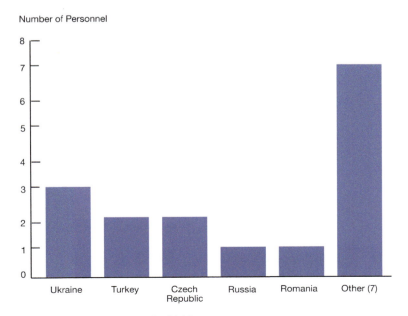

Figure 14.10 Contributors of Personnel to UNMIK in 2015

authorized strength of 510 personnel by July 2009, factoring in the deployment of the EU Rule of Law Mission (EULEX).[37]

A political stalemate following the June 2014 elections came to an end with the formation of the new Kosovo government in December 2014. High-level talks between Kosovo and Serbia started in February 2015.[38] UNMIK continues its regular engagement with the governments of Serbia and Kosovo, all communities and relevant stakeholders in Kosovo, and regional and international actors to promote security, stability, rule of law and respect for human rights in Kosovo and across the region.

The mission headquarters is located in Pristina and the regional headquarters is located in Kosovska Mitrovica. As of December 2015, 12 countries were contributing a total of 16 personnel to the mission (Figure 14.10). The approved budget for the 2015–2016 fiscal year was $40,031,000.

UNMIL, Liberia, September 2003

Liberia's second major civil conflict ended when President Charles Taylor (who as a rebel leader played a primary role in initiating the first civil war in 1990) stepped down in August 2003 and the vice-president signed an agreement with the Movement for Democracy in Liberia (MODEL) and the Liberians United for Reconciliation and Democracy (LURD). The National Transitional Government of Liberia (NTGL) was subsequently established in October 2003. In order to monitor the implementation of a ceasefire, assist the development of cantonment sites, ensure security in these sites and support the work of the Joint Monitoring Committee, and provide humanitarian assistance, the UN Security Council established the UN Mission in Liberia (UNMIL) on September 19, 2003.[39] UNMIL formally assumed responsibilities from the ECOWAS Mission in Liberia (ECOMIL) in October 2003, and all troops of ECOMIL were reassigned to UNMIL as UN peacekeepers.[40]

In October 2004, the disarmament of MODEL, LURD and former government forces was completed. UNMIL assumed a wide range of roles in the demobalization, disarmament and reintegration program, including central coordination, mobilization of resources, preparation and security of cantonment sites, and the collection and destruction of weapons.[41]

In September 2005, the UN Security Council expanded the mandate of the mission to deploy 250 UN personnel to Sierra Leone in order to provide security and logistical support to the Special Court for Sierra Leone (SCSL), after the mandate of the UN Mission in Sierra Leone ended.[42] The Special Court was established in 2002 to address serious crimes against humanity committed during the 1991–2002 civil war in Sierra Leone. Charles Taylor was eventually arrested and prosecuted by the SCSL (though the trial proceedings occurred at the facilities of the International Criminal Court in The Hague, the Netherlands) for his involvement in the Sierra Leone conflict. UNMIL troops operated only within the premises of the SCSL and worked together with the UN Integrated Office in Sierra Leone. In June 2009, after significant delays, Liberia's Truth and Reconciliation Commission submitted its report to the legislature and the President. The Commission recommended that an extraordinary criminal tribunal should be established to prosecute those who committed gross violations of human rights, including the former President, Charles Taylor. In May 2012, Charles Taylor was

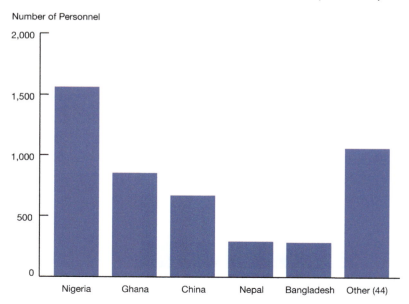

Figure 14.11 Contributors of Personnel to UNMIL in 2015

sentenced to 50 years in prison by the SCSL for "aiding and abetting" war crimes and crimes against humanity committed in Sierra Leone.

In October 2005, national elections were held in Liberia. UNMIL supported the Liberian National Police at the polling stations on the Election Day and provided logistical support for transporting ballots, while the UNMIL Election Unit assisted the National Elections Commission (NEC) in planning and organizing the elections.[43] UNMIL later assisted the NEC with the 2011 general and 2014 senatorial elections.

During the 2014–2015 Ebola outbreak, UNMIL provided humanitarian assistance, along with the local and regional organizations, as a part of the UN Mission for Ebola Emergency Response (UNMEER). Meanwhile, UNMIL continued its main activities, such as monitoring human rights violations, but certain activities, such as police training, were suspended.[44]

As the Ebola outbreak came to end, the UN Security Council reauthorized the drawdown of UNMIL, which was suspended in December 2014.[45] The new deadline for the Government of Liberia to assume full security responsibilities from UNMIL was set as June 30, 2016.

UNMIL's headquarters is located in Monrovia, while military and police units are deployed in 20 locations throughout Liberia. As of December 2015, 49 countries were contributing a total of 5,397 personnel to the mission (Figure 14.11). The approved budget for the 2015–2016 fiscal year was $344,712,200.

UNOCI, Côte d'Ivoire, April 2004

In April 2004, the United Nations Security Council established the UN Operation in Côte d'Ivoire (UNOCI), replacing the smaller political mission – the UN Mission in Côte d'Ivoire – that had been deployed since May 2003. UNOCI's mandate was extensive: to monitor the ceasefire agreement of May 3, 2003; to help the Government of National Reconciliation in implementing the national demobilization, disarmament and reintegration program; to protect UN personnel and civilians; to provide assistance, in cooperation with ECOWAS, in the conduct of free and fair elections, as envisioned in Linas-Marcoussis Agreement of January 2003; and to facilitate the delivery of humanitarian assistance.[46]

Over the next four years, the Government of Côte d'Ivoire and New Forces (FN) signed several peace agreements regulating the different issue areas and/or reaffirming previous agreements. The security situation stayed calm after the Ouagadougou Agreement was signed in March 2007. An integrated command center was established in April 2007. Cantonment of ex-combatants and disarmament were delayed until mid- to late-2008, due to disagreements over the reintegration arrangements.[47] The presidential elections, originally planned for November 2008, were postponed several times because of delays in voter registration. In February 2010, reports alleged a fraudulent registration process. In response, the president dissolved both the government and the Independent Electoral Commission (IEC). A new government and a new IEC were formed in February 2010.[48]

In the wake of the disputed presidential elections held in October-November 2010, UNOCI and a peacekeeping mission (*Opération Licorne*) of the French Armed Forces undertook military operations to protect their own personnel and

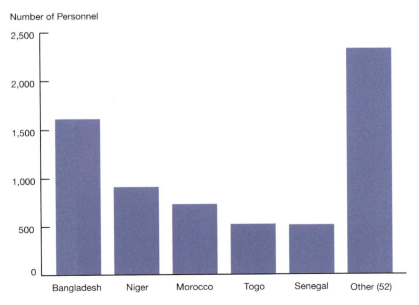

Figure 14.12 Contributors of Personnel to UNOCI in 2015

civilian populations, who came under attack on April 6, 2011. Opposition candidate Alassane Ouattara had been announced as the winner by the IEC, while the Constitutional Council announced that the winner was incumbent President Gbagbo, who then refused to step down.[49] Fighting between the *Forces Républicaines de Côte d'Ivoire* (FRCI), established by Outtara, and the pro-Gbagbo forces commenced in mid-March.

Gbagbo and his wife, Simone, were arrested on April 11, 2011.[50] In October 2011, the International Criminal Court (ICC) opened an investigation into acts of violence committed during the conflict after the election, between December 2010 and April 2011. On November 23, 2011, the ICC issued an arrest warrant for Laurent Gbagbo, charging him with four counts of crimes against humanity: murder, rape and other forms of sexual violence, persecution, and other inhuman acts. He was transferred to ICC custody on November 29, 2011. Subsequently, the ICC issued arrest warrants for Simone Gbagbo, on November 22, 2012, and for Charles Blé Goudé, former Minister for Sports and Youth, on October 1, 2013. After multiple delays, the trial of Laurent Gbagbo and Goudé before the ICC began on January 29, 2016. Simone Gbagbo was tried by an Ivoirian court, convicted, and sentenced on March 10, 2015 to 20 years in jail for crimes against humanity.

As the security situation improved over the next couple of years, the UN Security Council gradually reduced the size of UNOCI, while extending the mission until June 2016.[51] UNOCI helped local authorities and the IEC in the preparation and conduct of the 2015 presidential elections, in which Ouattara was elected for his second and final term. UNOCI also provided technical expertise to improve the functioning of law enforcement and security institutions as a part of larger security sector reform.[52]

The military headquarters of UNOCI is located in Abidjan. The mission has two sector headquarters, in Daloa (West) and Abidjan (East), and 40 military, police and observer unit locations. As of December 2015, 57 countries were contributing a total of 7,078 personnel to the mission (Figure 14.12). The approved budget for the 2015–2016 fiscal year was $402,794,300.

MINUSTAH, Haiti, June 2004

The first UN mission in Haiti, the UN Observer Group for the Verification of the Elections in Haiti (ONUVEH), was established to observe the elections of 1990–1991. After the 1991 coup, the situation in Haiti deteriorated, which led the UN Security Council to authorize a multi-national force in July 1994, followed by several missions between 1994 and 2000. Once the conflict restarted in February 2004, the UN Security Council authorized the Multinational Interim Force (MIF) and declared its readiness to deploy a stabilization force.[53] The UN Stabilization Mission in Haiti (MINUSTAH) was established in April 2004 and then assumed authority from MIF on June 1, 2004.[54] MINUSTAH's mandate included supporting the transitional government to ensure security, assisting the national police with demobilization, disarmament and reintegration programs, supporting political processes that were underway, and monitoring and reporting on the human rights situation to the United Nations High Commissioner for Human Rights (UNHCHR).

In the aftermath of the earthquake in January 2010, the UN Security Council authorized additional troop and police deployments to support the recovery efforts.[55] The capacity of the mission was further increased in June 2010.[56]

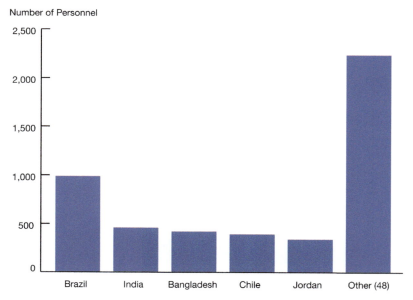

Figure 14.13 Contributors of Personnel to MINUSTAH in 2015

MINUSTAH also provided technical and logistical support during the 2010–2011 legislative and presidential elections. More recently, MINUSTAH provided transportation for mobile teams, helped to develop the communications plan for the voter registration campaign of the National Identification Office and held pre-electoral forums for civic education in relation to the October 2014 presidential elections, then helped the Electoral Council and the government with addressing the political impasse that led to the cancellation of the election. First-round legislative elections were finally held in August 2015. Second-round legislative elections were conducted together with the presidential and local elections in October 2015. MINUSTAH partnered with the UN Development Program (UNDP) and the UN Office for Project Services to provide technical and logistical support to the Provisional Electoral Council. The second round of the presidential elections, originally planned for December 2015, was postponed to April 2016. MINUSTAH police and military units continued their joint patrols and operations of crime prevention and reduction, community policing, and crowd control training throughout 2015.[57]

The headquarters of MINUSTAH is located in Port-au-Prince. Military and police units are deployed in locations throughout Haiti. As of December 2015, 53 countries were contributing a total of 5,477 personnel to the mission (Figure 14.13). The approved budget for the 2015–2016 fiscal year was $380,355,700.

IMT, Philippines (Mindanao), October 2004

After a nearly three-decade-long conflict between the Government of the Philippines and the Moro Islamic Liberation Front (MILF) over the independence of Moros in the Mindanao region, both sides agreed to reinitiate negotiations in 2004. In light of the progress in negotiations brokered by Malaysia on behalf of the Organization of the Islamic Conference (OIC), the International Monitoring Team (IMT) was deployed to Mindanao region to monitor the ceasefire. Deployed in areas of heavy MILF presence, the mandate of the IMT is to verify the cessation of hostilities and to ensure that the peace process moves forward.

The presence of the IMT facilitated the negotiation process. Both sides cooperated with the observers and ensured their freedom of movement in the initial years of the IMT. The negotiation process continued until mid-2006, and the ceasefire violation claims decreased significantly between late 2004 and mid-2006, with IMT helping both sides to maintain the ceasefire. The negotiations halted in May 2006, however, as heavy fighting broke out, then continued until March 2008. Finally, the parties signed a new ceasefire agreement in July 2008 and agreed to extend the mandate of IMT until November 2008. At the end of 2008, IMT temporarily withdrew its observers because of operational difficulties due to continued fighting and a unilateral request from the Government of the Philippines, only returning once both sides agreed to the new mandate of IMT.[58]

After the negotiations were restarted in 2009, the mandate of the IMT was renewed in 2010. A civilian protection unit was added to ensure the compliance of the parties with international humanitarian law. Following several setbacks, the Government of Philippines and MILF finally signed a framework agreement in April 2012.[59] Over the course of the next few years, the Government and MILF signed several additional framework agreements that ultimately resulted in the

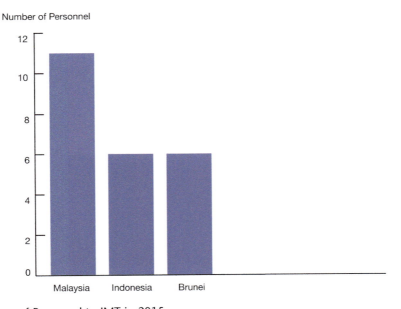

Figure 14.14 Contributors of Personnel to IMT in 2015

Comprehensive Agreement on the Bangsamoro in March 2014, ending the conflict. Throughout the peace process, the IMT continued to monitor the ceasefire and investigate the violations. The mission will continue until full demobilization of MILF.[60]

The IMT's main office is located inside the Southern Command Headquarters of the Armed Forces of the Philippines in Zamboanga City. IMT is deployed in four sectors that cover the conflict-affected region: Iligan City, General Santos City, Davao City, and Cotabato City. As of December 2015, three countries were contributing a total of 28 uniformed personnel to the mission (Figure 14.14).

EUFOR-Althea, Bosnia and Herzegovina, December 2004

Althea, launched in December 2004, is the third and largest peacekeeping operation undertaken by the European Union Military Force (EUFOR), under the European Security and Defense Policy (ESDP). In November 2004, the UN Security Council adopted Resolution 1575, which welcomed EUFOR operations and authorized UN Member States to establish multinational stabilization forces as legal successors to the NATO-led Stabilization Force (SFOR) in Bosnia and Herzegovina.[61] The initial mandate of the mission was to ensure compliance with the Annexes 1A (Military Aspects of the Peace Settlement) and 2 (Inter-Entity Boundary Line and Related Issues) of the Dayton Agreement, which call for the cessation of hostilities, establishment of an implementation force, withdrawal of foreign forces, and delimitation of an inter-entity border, in order to contribute to a safe environment in Bosnia and Herzegovina (BiH).

Over the years, EUFOR-Althea underwent several transformations. In February 2007, troop levels decreased to around 1,600 from around 6,000 in the previous years, and Liaison and Observation Teams (LOTs) were integrated. The general mission of LOTs is to liaise with local authorities and the population to monitor the overall situation across BiH and to be aware of local conditions that might affect the security situation. In 2012, troop levels were further reduced to 600.

The mission currently focuses on providing capacity building and training to the Armed Forces for BiH.[62] Some examples of activities undertaken during 2015 include crowd control, disaster relief, and bridge rehabilitation and construction projects. In March 2015, the Armed Forces of BiH and EUFOR signed a Road Map Agreement (RMA15) to coordinate planning and training for the next two years and to improve capacity-building activities. In the document, both sides agreed that BiH will assume greater responsibility and EUFOR will continue to monitor and assist the activities of the Armed Forces. New areas of cooperation (e.g., training of military police on forensic techniques and mountain techniques for natural disaster relief operations) were also identified in the road map.

Initially, the mission was deployed in three main regions in the country: the Multi-National Task Force (North) in Tuzla, the Multi-National Task Force (North West) in Banja Luka, and the Multi-National Task Force (South East) in Mostar. Currently, EUFOR has a Multinational Battalion in order to support BiH authorities as they maintain a safe and secure environment, an Explosives and Ordinance Disposal Team, 17 LOTs across BiH, and a LOTs Coordination Center (LCC) in Sarajevo. As of December 2015, 22 countries were contributing a total of 796 troops to the mission (Figure 14.15).

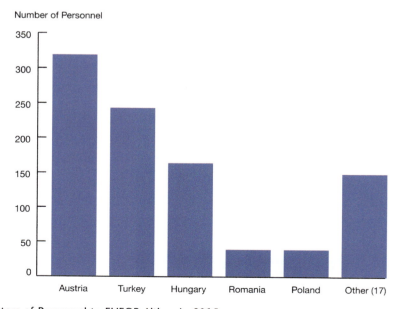

Figure 14.15 Contributors of Personnel to EUFOR-Althea in 2015

AMISOM, Somalia, January 2007

The armed conflict in Somalia started in the early 1980s, when several armed groups emerged with the goal of overthrowing President Barre, who had been in power since 1969. The government of Barre was overthrown in 1991, followed by declarations of new governments by two rival factions in different parts of the country – one in Mogadishu, the other in the Republic of Somaliland, the northern region of the country where one of the armed groups was based. The main opposition group, the United Somali Congress (USC) led by Mohammad Farrah Aidid, continued to fight against the government in Mogadishu as well as international forces deployed in the early 1990s, namely the United Nations Operation in Somalia (UNOSOM I), UNOSOM II, and the US-led United Task Force (UNITAF). The USC signed several failed agreements with the Government of Somalia. The last of these agreements, brokered by the UN, was signed in March 1994. This agreement did not last, eventually leading to the withdrawal of all UN and US troops in 1995. The fighting between armed factions continued, with periodic attempts made to restart negotiations and form a functioning Transitional National Government.

Against this backdrop and an escalation of violence in 2007, the African Union Mission in Somalia (AMISOM) was created by the African Union's Peace and Security Council in January 2007. The original mandate of AMISOM was (1) to support dialogue and reconciliation by providing safety and freedom of movement to all parties involved in the formation of Transitional Federal Institutions and in the national reconciliation conference to be convened including all stakeholders; (2) to provide protection to Transitional Federal Institutions, helping them to carry out functions of government; (3) to assist with the National Security and Stabilization Plan, especially the effective re-establishment and training of all-inclusive Somali forces; and (4) to contribute to the creation of the necessary security conditions for the provision of humanitarian assistance.[63] As the *Al-Shabaab* threat increased in Somalia, the mandate of the mission expanded in October 2013 to authorize AMISOM to take all necessary actions in cooperation with Somalia National Defense and Public Safety Institutions to reduce the security threat posed by *Al-Shabaab* and assist consolidating the control of Federal Government of Somalia over its territory.[64] The troop presence of AMISOM was also increased accordingly.[65]

Throughout 2014 and 2015, AMISOM conducted joint military operations with the Somali National Army to recover territory from *al-Shabaab*. In March 2015, AMISOM and Jubba Administration forces recaptured Kudhaa Island in the Juba Hoose region, located in the southern part of the country, while joint offensives against *al-Shabaab* continued in Puntland, in the northern part of the country.[66] On June 11, 2015, an AMISOM convoy was ambushed by *al-Shabaab* at Jama'a village, in the Bay region; a reinforcement of troops was ambushed twice the following day. On June 26, *al-Shabaab* fighters attacked an AMISOM base in Leego, also in the Bay region, detonating a car-bomb and causing heavy AMISOM casualties. On July 15, AMISOM, Somali security forces, and Ethiopian and Kenyan Defense Forces launched Operation Juba Corridor to expel *al-Shabaab* from its remaining strongholds. Baardheere, Gedo region, Diinsoor, and Bay region were seized on July 23 and 24, respectively. Meanwhile, AMISOM continued to target suspected *al-Shabaab* positions in the Hiraan and Galguduud regions.[67]

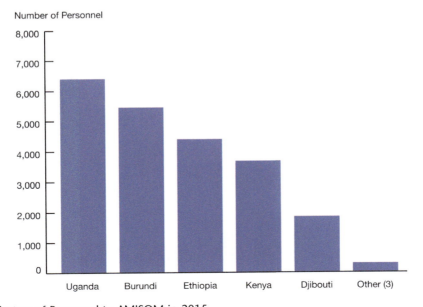

Figure 14.16 Contributors of Personnel to AMISOM in 2015

AMISOM has military, police and civilian components. The military component, the largest of the three, is deployed across five sectors: Sector 1 covers the regions of Banadir and Lower Shabelle; Sector 2 covers the Lower and Middle Jubba regions; Sector 3 covers the Bay and Bakool regions, as well as Gedo (Sub-Sector 3); Sector 4 covers the Hiiraan and Galgaduud regions; and Sector 5 covers the Middle Shabelle region. The military component conducts armed operations, together with an additional maritime component, effective since December 2011. The civilian and police components, deployed in Mogadishu since 2011 and 2014, respectively, continue to support the Federal Government to re-establish a functioning state and to provide services, through several units (e.g., Political, Humanitarian Liaison, Public Information, Formed Police). As of December 2015, eight countries were contributing a total of 22,126 uniformed personnel to the mission (Figure 14.16).

UNAMID, Sudan (Darfur), July 2007

The conflict in the Darfur region of Sudan, between the Government of Sudan and the Sudan Liberation Movement/ Army (SLM/A) and the Justice and Equality Movement (JEM), started in 2003. In July 2004, the African Union Mission in Sudan (AMIS) was deployed with just 60 troops. The size of the mission increased quickly to 3,320 personnel in October 2004. AMIS was replaced by the AU/UN Hybrid operation in Darfur (UNAMID) in July 2007.[68] UNAMID is authorized to take the necessary action, in areas of deployment, to protect its personnel, civilians, and humanitarian workers, to support the implementation of the Darfur Peace Agreement (signed on May 5, 2006 by one of the factions of SLM/A), to assist with the restoration of security conditions, and to facilitate the joint UN-AU mediation process.

In 2009–2010, several attempts at resolving the conflict were made by the UN-AU mediation team and UNAMID that resulted in the Doha Framework Agreement in February 2010. Negotiations continued throughout 2011 to include the non-signatory groups in the Agreement. The security and humanitarian situations remained significant concerns, with ongoing fighting between government forces and various armed groups during 2012–2013, particularly in Northern Darfur, in addition to ongoing inter-communal conflict over resources (arable land, lucrative minerals, and hydrocarbons). UNAMID facilitated several conferences bringing together civil society representatives and community leaders to address the root causes of resource-based conflict in late-2013.

In April 2014, the UN Security Council prioritized three tasks for UNAMID: facilitation of high-level mediation between the Sudanese Government and armed groups, the protection of civilians and facilitation of delivery of humanitarian assistance, and the provision of support toward the mediation of communal conflict.[69] The security crisis in Darfur persisted, despite the direct talks held in November 2014 between the government and non-signatory groups to the Doha Framework Agreement, namely the Sudan Liberation Army/Minni Minawi and the Justice and Equality Movement – Gibril Ibrahim factions. These efforts quickly failed in December 2014, and the conflict between these factions, the Sudan Liberation Army/Abdul Wahid faction, and the Sudanese Armed Forces and Rapid Support Forces restarted.

Throughout 2015, the conflict between the Government of Sudan and armed groups rapidly escalated in Northern and Western Darfur, while the inter-communal conflict over resources continued in Southern and Central Darfur.[70]

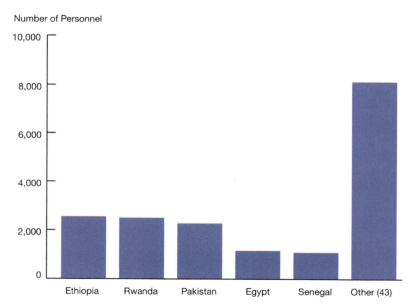

Figure 14.17 Contributors of Personnel to UNAMID in 2015

Approximately 150 criminal incidents against UNAMID personnel and assets were observed, including attacks against UNAMID convoys, shootings at UNAMID sites, abductions and armed robberies. Meanwhile, no tangible progress was made in high-level mediation efforts aside from preparatory talks to launch negotiations. UNAMID did provide financial and logistical support for inter-communal mediation efforts, convened numerous meetings to facilitate coexistence between farmers and pastoralists and to promote intergroup dialogue, and engaged local authorities and communal leaders to facilitate conflict resolution. In addition, UNAMID continued to protect civilians, especially in internally displaced people camps, by conducting routine and long-range patrols, as well as by increasing the number of integrated field protection teams to identify early warning indicators and to provide preventive measures. UNAMID also provided protection for emergency relief convoys of the UN Children's Fund (UNICEF) and the World Food Program (WFP).[71]

The mission headquarters is located in El Fasher. Sector headquarters are located in Zam Zam (North), Nyala (South), El Geneina (West) and Zallingei (Central). UNAMID peacekeepers are deployed at 30 other locations throughout Darfur. As of December 2015, 48 countries were contributing a total of 17,309 personnel to the mission (Figure 14.17). The approved budget for the 2015–2016 fiscal year was $1,102,164,700.

MONUSCO, Democratic Republic of the Congo, July 2010

After the July 1999 Lusaka agreement, signed between the Governments of the Democratic Republic of the Congo (DRC) and Angola, Namibia, Rwanda, Uganda, and Zimbabwe, the UN Security Council established the UN Organization Mission in the Democratic Republic of the Congo (MONUC). The initial mandate of MONUC was to monitor the ceasefire, to facilitate coordination among signatories, and to provide technical assistance for the disengagement of forces.[72] Later in 2006, MONUC assisted with the organization of legislative and presidential elections. In 2010, the UN Security Council renamed the mission as the UN Organization Stabilization Mission in the Democratic Republic of the Congo (MONUSCO).[73] In conjunction, the updated mandate included the protection of civilians and support for government military operations against the *Forces Démocratiques de Libération du Rwanda* (FDLR) and the Lord's Resistance Army (LRA), demobilization activities, reformation of DRC armed forces and police, and the Government of the DRC's continued efforts to combat the illegal trade of natural resources in North and South Kivu.

In response to renewed conflict in 2012, the UN Security Council decided in March 2013 to introduce an "Intervention Brigade" in order to neutralize armed groups.[74] This measure was also undertaken in furtherance of the Peace, Security and Cooperation Framework for the DRC, which had been signed by the 11 countries in the region, as well as the African Union (AU), the International Conference on the Great Lakes Region, the Southern African Development Community (SADC), and the UN Secretary-General. The brigade, with headquarters in Goma and acting under the direct command of MONUSCO, was composed of three infantry battalions, an artillery company, and a special-forces and reconnaissance company. In November 2013, the rebel group M23 was defeated. Yet FDLR, the Allied Democratic Forces (ADF), and Mayi-Mayi groups remain active in the eastern DRC.

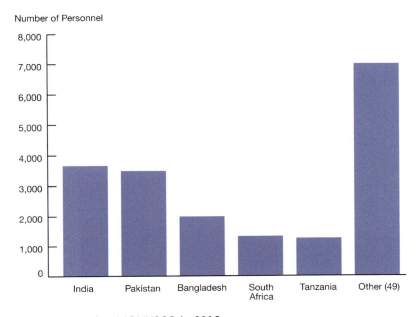

Figure 14.18 Contributors of Personnel to MONUSCO in 2015

During the first half of 2015, MONUSCO undertook the Sukola I Operation, supporting the operations of the Armed Forces of the Democratic Republic of the Congo (FARDC) against ADF in the North and South Kivu regions. This action led to the clearing of one of the main ADF camps.[75] FARDC actions against FDLR, including the Sukola II Operation, continued throughout 2015, without support from MONUSCO. In June 2015, new FARDC operations, with ground and air support from MONUSCO, were launched against the *Force de Résistance Patriotiques de l'Ituri* (FRPI) in the Ituri district of Orientale Province. Joint MONUSCO, FARDC and United States Africa Command operations continued against LRA areas in Haut-Uélé and Bas-Uélé provinces.[76] MONUSCO also provided support to the Electoral Commission for local and gubernatorial elections, which were scheduled for October 2015, but later postponed due to delays in voter registration and other logistical problems. In addition, MONUSCO continued to support efforts to reform the security sector (by providing expertise and training), as well as the implementation of the national disarmament, demobilization and reintegration program (by managing transit camps and funding construction for reinsertion centers).

The mission's headquarters is located in Kinshasa. Five brigade headquarters are distributed across the eastern part of the country, in Bunia, Goma, Buvaku, Lubumbashi and Kisingani. Peacekeepers are deployed to 17 other locations. As of December 2015, 54 countries were contributing a total of 19,823 personnel to the mission (Figure 14.18). The approved budget for the 2015–2016 fiscal year was $1,332,178,600.

UNISFA, Sudan (Abyei), June 2011

The Government of Sudan and the Sudan People's Liberation Movement (SPLM) signed an agreement in June 2011 that called for the demilitarization of the Abyei Area. The UN Security Council authorized the UN Interim Security Force for Abyei (UNISFA) in July 2011 to monitor and verify the redeployment of the military forces of both sides, to assist with de-mining activities, to facilitate the delivery of humanitarian aid, and to strengthen the capacity of the Abyei Police Service.[77] The UN Security Council later expanded the mandate of UNISFA to include activities such as assisting the parties in establishing the Demilitarized Border Zone, and supporting operational activities of the Joint Border Verification and Monitoring Mechanism (JBVMM), in order to accommodate demands from parties for help in implementing two additional agreements concerning border security signed on June 29 and July 30, 2011.[78]

In the following years, the mission engaged community leaders to prevent communal conflicts over resources in the area; supported African Union attempts to solve the incompatibility; assisted the activities of JBVMM, which was operationalized in December 2012 after delays in appointing monitors by both sides; and continued its cooperation with UNMISS and UNAMID on border security and other joint operations. In October 2013, the Ngok Dinka community held a unilateral referendum, which heightened tension in the area due to a large influx of people from South Sudan in advance of the referendum. On October 31, the Ngok Dinka leadership announced that 99.99% of eligible voters had opted for the Abyei Area to become part of South Sudan. The Government of Sudan and the Misseriya community called the referendum illegitimate, while the African Union condemned the referendum, noting that it would complicate the resolution of the Abyei dispute; the Government of South Sudan refrained from making comments.[79] Among the people

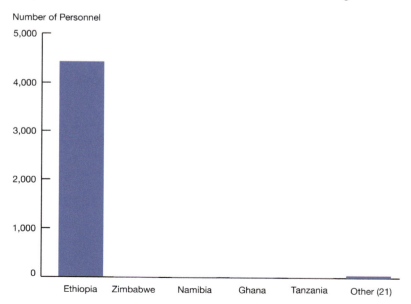

Figure 14.19 Contributors of Personnel to UNISFA in 2015

who arrived in the Abyei area for the referendum, UNISFA observed up to 1,000 SPLA and South Sudan police personnel, which deteriorated relations between Sudan and South Sudan and caused active fighting between Sudan People's Liberation Army (SPLA), the South Sudan police and the Misseriya militia in the first half of 2014.

During the first half of 2015, throughout the migration season of Misseriya nomads, UNISFA continued to employ conflict prevention and mitigation strategies by establishing an area of disengagement, deploying troops to flashpoint areas, monitoring and assessing the respective locations and movements of communities. Aside from a few incidents, the security situation remained calm. UNISFA also trained unarmed community protection units in an effort to establish protection committees composed of volunteers from both communities, as well as to support JBVMM activities.[80] Meanwhile, the Government of Sudan continued to maintain 120–150 police personnel inside the Diffra oil complex in northern Abyei, in direct violation of the 2011 Agreement.[81]

The headquarters of UNISFA is located in Abyei. Sector headquarters are located in Diffra (North), Dokura (Center), and Athony (South). Peacekeepers are deployed to six additional locations in the Abyei area. As of December 2015, 26 countries were contributing a total of 4,325 personnel to the mission (Figure 14.19). The approved budget for the 2015–2016 fiscal year was $268,256,700.

UNMISS, South Sudan, July 2011

As a part of the Comprehensive Peace Agreement signed between the Government of Sudan and the Sudan People's Liberation Movement/Army (SPLM/A), a referendum was held in January 2011 to determine the future of South Sudan. Following the vote, South Sudan became independent in July 2011. The UN Mission in the Republic of South Sudan (UNMISS) was established to support peace consolidation, state-building and economic development, including providing advice to the Government of South Sudan on the political transition, governance, and establishment of state authority and rule of law.[82]

Throughout much of 2012, a border dispute between South Sudan and Sudan appeared to unify all the political parties in South Sudan in their support for the policies of the Government of South Sudan towards Sudan. At the same time, the security situation progressively deteriorated. In addition to inter-communal conflicts in Jonglei, between December 2011 and January 2012 two rebel groups emerged: the South Sudan Democratic Movement/Army (SSDM/A) and the South Sudan Liberation Movement/Army (SSLM/A). SSDM/A signed an agreement terminating conflict in February 2012.[83] In April 2013, President Salva Kiir declared amnesty for six leaders of the armed groups. SSLM/A accepted the offer and integrated its force into SPLA. Yet the Yau Yau group, which splintered off from SSDM/A, continued fighting. In March and April 2013, UNMISS convoys were ambushed in Jonglei state by unidentified armed elements.[84]

In July 2013, President Kiir dismissed the national cabinet and Vice-President Riek Machar. He also suspended the Secretary-General of the Sudan People's Liberation Movement (SPLM), Pagan Amum, who was under investigation for alleged mismanagement of party affairs. In December 2013, fighting broke out in the meeting of the SPLM National Liberation Council. UNMISS could not identify the cause of fighting, while the government announced that there had

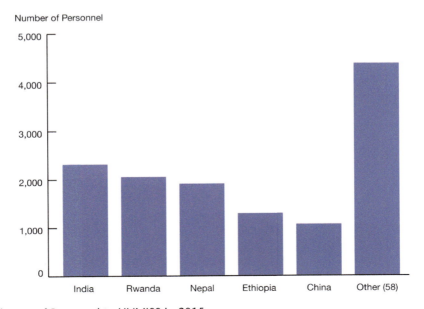

Figure 14.20 Contributors of Personnel to UNMISS in 2015

been a coup attempt. Thereafter, tensions arose between the executive and the legislative branches in 10 state governments and several units defected from the SPLA. Many civilians sought refuge in UNMISS bases as the fighting escalated across the country in late-2013.[85] Subsequently, the security situation remained unstable. Throughout 2014, negotiations continued under the auspices of the Intergovernmental Authority on Development (IGAD).

In response to the crises, the UN Security Council realigned the UNMISS mandate to prioritize the protection of civilians in May 2014.[86] During the first months of 2015, an ongoing IGAD peace initiative led to a preliminary agreement between President Kiir and the leader of the Sudan People's Liberation Movement/Army in Opposition, Riek Machar, to form a transitional government by July. Talks broke down in March 2015.[87] The following four months were dominated by various attempts to bring parties to the negotiating table, even as the conflict escalated in Upper Nile, Unity, Jonglei, Western Bahr el-Ghazal and Eastern Equatoria States.[88] Negotiations restarted in July, resulting in a 16-point Agreement on the Resolution of the Conflict in the Republic of South Sudan in August 2015. While the agreement included a ceasefire, opposition forces and splinter groups continued fighting in Upper Nile, Unity, Western and Eastern Equatoria States. UNMISS persisted in investigating the alleged ceasefire violations, in addition to implementing its mandate to protect civilians by hosting them in six UNMISS sites, helping to resolve intercommunal conflicts through engaging local community leaders, and investigating human rights and international humanitarian law violations.[89]

The mission headquarters is located in Juba, while sector headquarters are located in Wau (West), Bor (East), and Malakal (North). UNMISS troops are deployed in 10 additional locations. As of December 2015, 63 countries were contributing a total of 12,397 personnel to the mission (Figure 14.20). The approved budget for the 2015–2016 fiscal year was $1,085,769,200.

ECOMIB, Guinea-Bissau, May 2012

Following the death of President Malam Bacai Sanhá on January 9, 2012, the Angolan Military Mission to Guinea-Bissau (MISSANG) averted a coup attempt, after which relations between the military and MISSANG deteriorated. MISSANG had been deployed in 2011 as a replacement for the EU Security Sector Reform (SSR) mission to help reform the Armed Forces of Guinea-Bissau.

On March 18, 2012, Guinea-Bissau held a presidential election, which was tainted by the assassination of the former chief of military intelligence, Samba Diallo, and accusations of vote fraud by the opposition, especially the front runner, who decided to boycott the second round of elections scheduled for April 29. The Economic Community of West African States (ECOWAS), the African Union (AU) and the United Nations (UN) established a joint fact-finding mission to investigate the fraud claims. On April 12, the army imprisoned the interim president (Raimundo Pereira), the prime minister (Adiato Djaló Nandigna), and several other senior officials. During the days leading up to the coup, reports from Guinea-Bissauan and ECOWAS officials about rising tensions with the military prompted ECOWAS to deploy the Economic Community Mission in Bissau (ECOMIB) on April 26, with a mandate to facilitate the withdrawal of MISSANG and facilitate the transitional process.

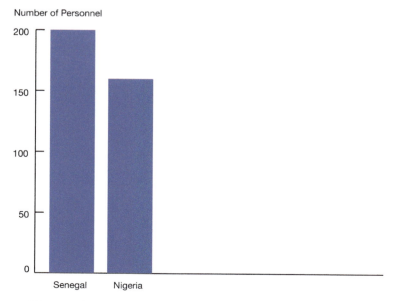

Figure 14.21 Contributors of Personnel to ECOMIB in 2015

In its early months of deployment, ECOMIB conducted daily patrols with the Public Order Police, to facilitate restoration of the constitutional order. In May, the military junta ceded power to a civilian transitional authority.[90] ECOMIB's mandate was later expanded to help the Guinea-Bissauan authorities along with more than 400 international monitors with the preparations for the first national elections after the 2012 coup. In April and May 2014, parliamentary and presidential elections were held and the constitutional order fully restored. Guinea-Bissau's suspension from the AU, as a result of the coup, ended on June 17, 2014, following the successful elections and inauguration of the National Assembly. The newly elected president, José Mário Vaz, dismissed the chief of general staff of the armed forces, Mamadu Ture Kuruma, who had launched the 2012 coup, and appointed his replacement on September 2014.[91] ECOMIB has been working with Guinea-Bissauan authorities and the Security Sector Reform Steering Committee to restructure and improve the armed forces. In January 2015, ECOMIB handed over four refurbished barracks along with other military infrastructure and assets, which were funded by the Defense and Security Sector Reform Program (DSSRP) with the support of regional organizations, including ECOWAS and AU.

As of December 2015, two countries, Nigeria and Senegal, were contributing a total of 543 uniformed personnel to the mission (Figure 14.21). The Nigerian contingent is located in Bissau, while the Senegalese contingent is located in Cumere.

MINUSMA, Mali, April 2013

In early-2012, a conflict commenced in the north of Mali between three sets of actors: government forces, a Tuareg rebel group called the *Mouvement national pour la libération de l'Azawad* (MNLA), and several Islamic armed groups called *Ansar Dine*, al-Qaeda in the Islamic Maghreb (AQIM) and the *Mouvement pour l'unicité et le jihad en Afrique de l'Ouest* (MUJAO). In response, the UN Security Council deployed the UN Office in Mali (UNOM), which was tasked with providing support for the ongoing process of resolving conflict, initiated by ECOWAS, and the planning and organization of the African-led International Support Mission in Mali (AFISMA).[92] As the situation deteriorated in January 2013 in the northern areas, France intervened and AFISMA accelerated its deployment. Subsequently, the UN Security Council established the UN Multidimensional Integrated Stabilization Mission in Mali (MINUSMA) in April 2013.[93] The mandate of the mission includes the stabilization of population centers, supporting the reestablishment of state authority, the implementation of the transitional road map, provision of humanitarian assistance, protection of civilians and UN personnel, promotion of human rights, and supporting national and international justice.

Four rounds of negotiations were held in July–November 2014, supported by a mediation team that included representatives of the UN/MINUSMA, the AU, the Economic Community of West African States (ECOWAS), the European Union (EU), the Organization of Islamic Cooperation (OIC), and the governments of Burkina Faso, Chad, Mauritania and Niger. These negotiations generated a draft document that includes provisions on greater regionalization, strengthening local governments, and an internationally financed development package for the northern region. Bilateral

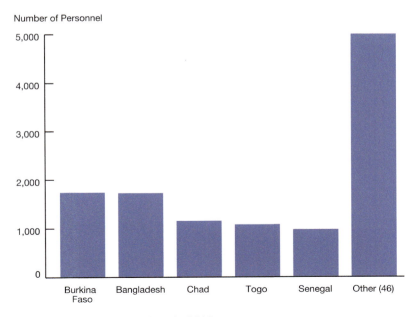

Figure 14.22 Contributors of Personnel to MINUSMA in 2015

consultations continued between the Coordination – comprised of MNLA and two Azawad groups, the *Haut Conseil pour l'Unité de l'Azawad* (HCUA) and the *Mouvement Arabe de l'Azawad* (MAA), the *Coordination des Mouvements et Fronts Patriotiques de Résistance* II (CMFPR-II), and a faction of the *Coalition du Peuple pour l'Azawad* (CPA) – and the Platform, composed mainly of CMFPR-I, CPA, a faction of MAA and the *Groupe d'autodéfense touareg Imghad et alliés* (GATIA). These consultations contributed to drafting a peace agreement with the lead mediator in a fifth round held during February 2015. This dialogue finally resulted in the Agreement on Peace and Reconciliation in Mali, which was signed in May 2015 by the Government of Mali, two elements of the Coordination – the CMFPR-II and a faction of CPA – and the Platform; other parties did not sign the agreement.

In late-April 2015, two elements of the Platform, GATIA and MAA-Platform, attacked the Coordination positions to take over Ménaka. MINUSMA organized a meeting with the representatives of the Government, the Platform and the Coordination to review the findings of two joint verification teams as to the violations of ceasefire. Following the intervention of the joint mediation team, the Platform agreed to withdraw from Ménaka. In addition, the remaining non-signatories from the Coordination announced intentions to sign the peace agreement in June 2015.[94] Meanwhile, MINUSMA continued to monitor the ceasefire in the Timbuktu, Gao, and Kidal regions, as well as in Ménaka, in addition to helping with the organization of intra- and inter-communal dialogues between Tuareg and Arab communities and the development of a national disarmament and security sector reform strategy.[95] Although progress in the peace process was observed, Islamist extremist violence in the Mopti, Ségou, and Timbuktu regions and in Bamako escalated during the second half of 2015. MINUSMA convoys remained the primary target of direct attacks and improvised explosive devices.

The main headquarters of MINUSMA is located in Bamako. Three regional headquarters are located in Timbuktu (West), Kidal (North) and Gao (East). Nine other troop and police units are spread across the country. As of December 2015, 51 countries were contributing a total of 10,836 personnel to the mission (Figure 14.22). The approved budget for the 2015–2016 fiscal year was $923,305,800.

EUFOR-RCA, Central African Republic, February 2014

In December 2012, Séléka – a predominantly Muslim alliance of rebel groups involved in previous conflict – initiated a series of violent attacks in the Central African Republic (CAR) that ultimately led to the fall of President Bozizé's government in March 2013. In August 2013, the leader of Séléka, Michel Djotodia, became the head of the transitional government. Inter-communal conflict subsequently continued, however, when the Christian and animist militias of the anti-balaka movement immediately took up arms and engaged in an increasing cycle of violence with Séléka militias, which had yet to disband. Attacks in December 2013 led to extreme civilian casualties, internal displacement of thousands, and an overall worsening of humanitarian crises.[96] President Djotodia then resigned under pressure from regional leaders in January 2014.

The European Union Military Force–*République Centrafricaine* (EUFOR-RCA) was established in February 2014, with the authorization of the UN Security Council, to provide security in the capital of Bangui.[97] The force also contributed

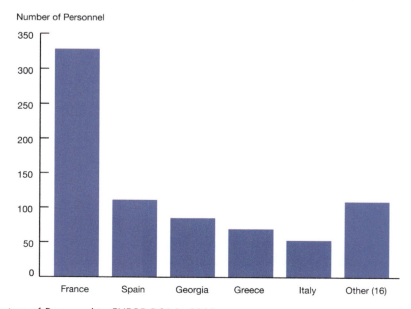

Figure 14.23 Contributors of Personnel to EUFOR-RCA in 2015

to the efforts to protect civilians at risk and provided security for delivery of humanitarian aid. The initial six-month mandate of the operation was subsequently extended until March 2015.[98] The mission completed its mandate and was terminated on March 15, 2015. As of March 2015, 21 countries were contributing a total of 313 troops to the mission (Figure 14.23).

MINUSCA, Central African Republic, April 2014

In addition to playing a role in the establishment of EUFOR-RCA, the UN Security Council took several other steps to respond to the developments in the CAR during 2012–2013. First, the mandate of the UN Integrated Peacebuilding Office in the Central African Republic (BINUCA) was changed in October 2013 to support the implementation of the transition process.[99] BINUCA had originally deployed in January 2010. Second, the International Support Mission to the CAR (MISCA) and a French–led peacekeeping force (Operation Sangaris) were authorized in December 2013 to be deployed. At the same time, plans for the transformation of MISCA into a UN peacekeeping operation were initiated.[100] Third, the United Nations Multidimensional Integrated Stabilization Mission in the Central African Republic (MINUSCA) was established in April 2014. The mandate of the mission includes protecting civilians and UN personnel, facilitating the delivery of humanitarian assistance, protecting and promoting human rights, providing support for national and international justice and disarmament, demobilization and reintegration programs, and coordinating international assistance as appropriate. MINUSCA assumed the authority from MISCA as planned on September 15, 2014.

During the early months of 2015, fighting continued between anti-balaka and ex-Séléka members, especially in the central part of the country. In February 2015, MINUSCA launched a joint operation with French Sangaris Forces in Bria, Haute-Kotto, to take over administrative buildings occupied by ex-Séléka members, which enabled the redeployment of national gendarmes in the area.[101] The Group of Eight (G-8) – France, the Republic of the Congo, the US, the Economic Community of Central African States (ECCAS), the Mediator's team, MINUSCA, the World Bank and the EU – and the UN Secretary-General's Special Representatives for Central Africa and the Central African Republic continued their efforts to reach a political solution with the secretariat support from MINUSCA. Key activities included weekly meetings and regular visits to Transitional Authorities. These efforts eventually led to the Bangui Forum on National Reconciliation in May 2015, during which participants discussed issues related to peace and security, governance, justice and reconciliation, and economic and social development. At the end of the Forum, the Transitional Government and nine armed groups signed an agreement on the principles of demobilization, disarmament and reintegration.[102] Progress following the Bangui Forum was hampered by eruption of fighting in September 2015, after the discovery of the body of a young Muslim man in Bangui. This event triggered reprisal attacks by ex-Séléka members, which escalated to clashes with MINUSCA and French Sangaris forces. In November 2015, MINUSCA launched a joint operation with French forces to secure several neighborhoods in Bangui.[103] After several delays, the presidential and legislative elections, along with a constitutional referendum, were held in December 2015, with the support of MINUSCA. In addition, MINUSCA continued to protect civilians, investigate human rights violations, co-lead the task force on monitoring violations against

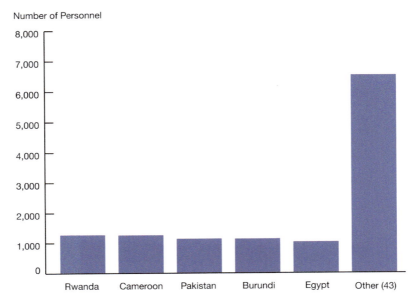

Figure 14.24 Contributors of Personnel to MINUSCA in 2015

Cil

children with UNICEF, provide protection to humanitarian aid convoys, and support the demobilization efforts logistically and technically.[104]

The mission headquarters is located in Bangui and three sector headquarters are located in Bouar (West), Kaga Bandoro (Center), and Bria (East). In addition, MINUSCA has four troop locations in the western and central regions. As of December 2015, a total of 10,615 uniformed personnel were deployed, contributed by 48 countries (Figure 14.24). The approved budget for the 2015–2016 fiscal year was $814,066,800.

Notes

1 See Fortna and Howard (2008) for more detailed discussion of early research on peacekeeping.
2 The profiles exclude several types of missions: (1) unilateral military operations (e.g., France's Operation Sangaris in the Central African Republic); (2) political, advisory, or training missions (e.g., UN Assistance Mission in Afghanistan [UNAMA], European Union Training Mission in Somalia [EUTM-Somalia]; and (3) multilateral military operations (e.g., the NATO-led International Security Assistance Force [ISAF] in Afghanistan and Kosovo Force [KFOR])), which are tasked to maintain security without exhibiting the main features (e.g., confidence building, consent and neutrality), core functions (e.g., monitoring ceasefires and maintaining buffer zones) or second-generation elements (e.g., election monitoring, humanitarian support, and training) of peacekeeping (Heldt and Wallensteen 2011).
3 Information on the number of personnel and regional trends for UN missions is obtained from the International Peace Institute's Peacekeeping Database, which records total uniformed personnel contributions by type and contributing country for each mission from November 1990 to the present. Information on the number of personnel and contributing states for non-UN missions is obtained from the *Yearbook* and *Military Balance* of the Stockholm International Peace Research Institute (SIPRI).
4 United Nations Peacekeeping Operations, Fact Sheet: 31 December 2015.
5 United Nations Security Council, Resolution 50, May 29, 1948.
6 United Nations General Assembly, Resolution A/RES/1000 (ES-I), "Resolution 1000 (ES-I)," November 5, 1956.
7 United Nations Security Council, "Report by the Secretary-General on the Observation of the Cease-Fire in the Suez Canal Sector," S/8035/Add.3, October 31, 1967.
8 United Nations Security Council, Resolution 339, October 25, 1973.
9 United Nations Security Council, Resolution 39, January 20, 1948.
10 United Nations Security Council, Resolution 47, April 21, 1948.
11 United Nations Security Council, Resolution 186, March 4, 1964.
12 United Nations Security Council, Resolution 353, July 20, 1974.
13 United Nations Security Council, "Report of the Secretary-General on His Mission of Good Offices in Cyprus," S/2004/437, May 28, 2004.
14 United Nations Security Council, "Report of the Secretary-General on the United Nations Operation in Cyprus," S/2014/461, July 9, 2014.
15 United Nations Security Council, "Report of the Secretary-General on the United Nations Operation in Cyprus," S/2015/17, January 9, 2015.
16 United Nations Security Council, Resolution 350, May 1974.
17 United Nations Security Council, "Report of the Secretary-General on the UN Disengagement Observer Force for the Period from 29 May to 28 August 2015," S/2015/699, September 10, 2015.
18 United Nations Security Council, "Report of the Secretary-General on the UN Disengagement Observer Force for the Period from 29 August to 18 November 2015," S/2015/930, December 3, 2015.
19 United Nations Security Council, Resolution 425, March 19, 1978.
20 United Nations Security Council, Resolution 1701, August 11, 2006.
21 United Nations Security Council, "Report of the Secretary-General on the Implementation of Security Council Resolution 1701 (2006)," S/2014/784, November 5, 2014.
22 United Nations Security Council, "Report of the Secretary-General on the Implementation of Security Council Resolution 1701 (2006)," S/2015/147, February 27, 2015.
23 United Nations Security Council, "Report of the Secretary-General on the Implementation of Security Council Resolution 1701 (2006)," S/2015/837, November 4, 2015.
24 Global Peace Operations Review, Annual Review of Global Peace Operations, Mission Notes: Middle East, Non-UN Operations (MFO Sinai, TIPH 2), 2006.
25 Multinational Force and Observers Director General's Report to the 2011 Trilateral Meeting, Plenary Meeting 17 November 2011, Rome, Italy.
26 Multinational Force and Observers Director General's Report to the 2012 Trilateral Meeting, Plenary Meeting 15 November 2012, Rome, Italy.
27 Multinational Force and Observers Director General's Report to the 2014 Trilateral Meeting, Plenary Meeting 20 November 2014, Rome, Italy.
28 United Nations Security Council, Resolution 690, "The Situation Concerning Western Sahara," April 29, 1991.
29 United Nations Security Council, "The Situation concerning Western Sahara: Report of the Secretary-General," S/21360, June 18, 1990.
30 Global Peace Operations Review, Annual Review of Global Peace Operations, Mission Notes: Moldova–Trans-Dniester, 2006, 2007 and 2011.
31 Global Peace Operations Review, Annual Review of Global Peace Operations, Mission Notes: Moldova–Trans-Dniester, 2013.
32 Agnieszka Tomczyk, "The New (Old) Moldovan-Transnistrian Border Conflict," *New Eastern Europe*, October 30, 2013.

Peacekeeping Operations Active in 2015

33 *Eurasia Daily,* "Moldova and Transnistria Unblock Joint Control Commission," December 4, 2015.
34 United Nations Security Council, Resolution 1244, June 10, 1999.
35 United Nations Security Council, "Report of the Secretary-General on the United Nations Interim Administration Mission in Kosovo," S/2007/582, September 28, 2007.
36 United Nations Security Council, "Report of the Secretary-General on the United Nations Interim Administration Mission in Kosovo," S/2008/211, March 28, 2008.
37 United Nations Security Council, "Report of the Secretary-General on the United Nations Interim Administration Mission in Kosovo," S/2009/497, September 30, 2009.
38 United Nations Security Council, "Report of the Secretary-General on the United Nations Interim Administration Mission in Kosovo," S/2015/303, April 27, 2015.
39 United Nations Security Council, Resolution 1509, September 19, 2003.
40 United Nations Security Council, "First Progress Report of the Secretary-General on the United Nations Mission in Liberia," S/2003/1175, December 15, 2003.
41 United Nations Security Council, "Fifth Progress Report of the Secretary-General on the United Nations Mission in Liberia," S/2004/972, December 17, 2004.
42 United Nations Security Council, Resolution 1629, September 19, 2005.
43 United Nations Security Council, "Ninth Progress Report of the Secretary-General on the United Nations Mission in Liberia," S/2005/764, December 7, 2005.
44 United Nations Security Council, "Twenty-Ninth Progress Report of the Secretary-General on the United Nations Mission in Liberia," S/2015/275, April 23, 2015.
45 United Nations Security Council, Resolution 2215, April 2, 2015.
46 United Nations Security Council, Resolution 1528, February 27, 2004.
47 United Nations Security Council, "Eighteenth Progress Report of the Secretary-General on the United Nations Operation in Côte d'Ivoire," S/2008/645, October 13, 2008.
48 United Nations Security Council, "Twenty-Fourth Progress Report of the Secretary-General on the United Nations Operation in Côte d'Ivoire," S/2010/245, May 20, 2010.
49 United Nations Security Council, "Twenty-Seventh Progress Report of the Secretary-General on the United Nations Operation in Côte d'Ivoire," S/2011/211, March 30, 2011.
50 United Nations Security Council, "Twenty-Eighth Report of the Secretary-General on the United Nations Operation in Côte d'Ivoire," S/2011/387, June 24, 2011.
51 United Nations Security Council, Resolution 2226, June 25, 2015.
52 United Nations Security Council, "Thirty-Seventh Report of the Secretary-General on the United Nations Operation in Côte d'Ivoire," S/2015/940, December 8, 2015.
53 United Nations Security Council, Resolution 1529, February 29, 2004.
54 United Nations Security Council, Resolution 1542, April 30, 2004.
55 United Nations Security Council, Resolution 1908, January 19, 2010.
56 United Nations Security Council, Resolution 1927, June 4, 2010.
57 United Nations Security Council, "Report of the Secretary-General on the UN Stabilization Mission in Haiti," S/2015/667 and S/2016/225, August 31, 2015 and March 8, 2016.
58 Global Peace Operations Review, Annual Review of Global Peace Operations, Mission Notes: Mindanao Philippines, 2008 and 2009.
59 Global Peace Operations Review, Annual Review of Global Peace Operations, Mission Notes: Asia-Pacific, 2013.
60 Global Peace Operations Review, Annual Review of Global Peace Operations, Mission Notes: Asia-Pacific, 2015.
61 United Nations Security Council, Resolution 1575, November 22, 2004.
62 Global Peace Operations Review, Annual Review of Global Peace Operations, Mission Notes: Europe and The Western Balkans, 2013.
63 United Nations Security Council, Resolution 1744, February 20, 2007.
64 African Union Peace and Security Council 399th Meeting, PSC/PR/COMM.(CCCXCIX), October 10, 2013, Addis Ababa, Ethiopia.
65 United Nations Security Council, Resolution 2124, November 12, 2013.
66 United Nations Security Council, "Report of the Secretary-General on Somalia," S/2015/331, May 12, 2015.
67 United Nations Security Council, "Report of the Secretary-General on Somalia," S/2015/702, September 11, 2015.
68 United Nations Security Council, Resolution 1769, July 31, 2007.
69 United Nations Security Council, Resolution 2148, April 3, 2014.
70 United Nations Security Council, "Report of the Secretary-General on the African Union–United Nations Hybrid Operation in Darfur," S/2015/729, September 25, 2015.
71 United Nations Security Council, "Report of the Secretary-General on the African Union–United Nations Hybrid Operation in Darfur," S/2015/378 and S/2015/1027, May 26, 2015 and December 24, 2015.
72 United Nations Security Council, Resolution 1279, November 30, 1999.
73 United Nations Security Council, Resolution 1925, May 28, 2010.
74 United Nations Security Council (SC), Resolution 2098, March 28, 2013.
75 United Nations Security Council, "Report of the Secretary-General on the United Nations Organization Stabilization Mission in the Democratic Republic of the Congo," S/2015/486, June 26, 2015.
76 United Nations Security Council, "Report of the Secretary-General on the United Nations Organization Stabilization Mission in the Democratic Republic of the Congo," S/2015/741 and S/2015/1031, September 28, 2015 and December 24, 2015.
77 United Nations Security Council, Resolution 1990, June 27, 2011.
78 United Nations Security Council, Resolution 2024, December 14, 2011.

79 United Nations Security Council, "Report of the Secretary-General on the Situation in Abyei," S/2013/706, November 27, 2013.

80 United Nations Security Council, "Report of the Secretary-General on the Situation in Abyei," S/2015/439, June 16, 2015.

81 United Nations Security Council, "Report of the Secretary-General on the Situation in Abyei," S/2015/302, April 29, 2015.

82 United Nations Security Council, Resolution 1996, July 8, 2011.

83 United Nations Security Council, "Report of the Secretary-General on South Sudan," S/2012/486, June 26, 2012.

84 United Nations Security Council, "Report of the Secretary-General on South Sudan," S/2013/366, June 20, 2013.

85 United Nations Security Council, "Report of the Secretary-General on South Sudan," S/2014/158, March 6, 2014.

86 United Nations Security Council, Resolution 2155, May 29, 2014.

87 United Nations Security Council, "Report of the Secretary-General on South Sudan," S/2015/296, April 29, 2015.

88 United Nations Security Council, "Report of the Secretary-General on South Sudan," S/2015/655, August 21, 2015.

89 United Nations Security Council, "Report of the Secretary-General on South Sudan," S/2015/902, November 23, 2015.

90 United Nations Security Council, "Report of the Secretary-General on the Restoration of Constitutional Order in Guinea-Bissau," S/2012/704, September 12, 2012.

91 United Nations Security Council, "Report of the Secretary-General on the Restoration of and Respect for Constitutional Order in Guinea-Bissau," S/2014/603, August 18, 2014.

92 United Nations Security Council, Resolution 2085, December 20, 2012.

93 United Nations Security Council, Resolution 2100, April 25, 2013.

94 United Nations Security Council, "Report of the Secretary-General on the Situation in Mali," S/2015/732, September 22, 2015.

95 United Nations Security Council, "Report of the Secretary-General on the Situation in Mali," S/2015/1030, December 24, 2015.

96 Council of the European Union (EU), "Council Conclusions on the Central African Republic," Foreign Affairs Council Meeting, January 20, 2014.

97 United Nations Security Council, Resolution 2134, January 28, 2014.

98 European Union Council Decision 2014/775/CFSP, extending Decision 2014/73/CFSP on a European Union military operation in the Central African Republic (EUFOR RCA).

99 United Nations Security Council, Resolution 2121, October 10, 2013.

100 United Nations Security Council, Resolution 2127, December 5, 2013.

101 United Nations Security Council, "Report of the Secretary-General on the Situation in the Central African Republic," S/2015/227, April 1, 2015.

102 United Nations Security Council, "Report of the Secretary-General on the Situation in the Central African Republic," S/2015/576, July 29, 2015.

103 United Nations Security Council, "Report of the Secretary-General on the Situation in the Central African Republic," S/2015/918, November 30, 2015.

104 United Nations Security Council, "Report of theSecretary-General on the Situation in the Central African Republic," S/2015/918, November 30, 2015.

References

Benson, Michelle, and Jacob D. Kathman (2014) "United Nations Bias and Force Commitments in Civil Conflicts." *Journal of Politics* 76(2): 350–363.

Boulden, Jane (2001) *Peace Enforcement: The United Nations Experience in Congo, Somalia, and Bosnia.* Westport, CT: Greenwood Publishing Group.

Bove, Vincenzo, and Leandro Elia (2011) "Supplying Peace: Participation in and Troop Contribution to Peacekeeping Missions." *Journal of Peace Research* 48(6): 699–714.

Burns, Arthur Lee, and Nina Heathcote (1963) "Peace-Keeping by UN Forces, from Suez to the Congo." New York: The Center of International Studies, Princeton University.

Cox, Arthur M. (1967) *Prospects for Peacekeeping.* Washington, DC: Brookings Institution.

Diehl, Paul F., and Daniel Druckman (2010) *Evaluating Peace Operations.* Boulder, CO: Lynne Rienner Publishers.

Doyle, Michael W., and Nicholas Sambanis (2006) *Making War and Building Peace: United Nations Peace Operations.* Princeton, NJ: Princeton University Press.

Doyle, Michael W., and Nicholas Sambanis (2000) "International Peacebuilding: A Theoretical and Quantitative Analysis." *American Political Science Review* 94(4): 779–801.

Fleitz, Frederick H. (2002) *Peacekeeping Fiascoes of the 1990s: Causes, Solutions, and US Interests.* Westport, CT: Greenwood Publishing Group.

Fortna, Virginia Page (2008) *Does Peacekeeping Work? Shaping Belligerents' Choices after Civil War.* Princeton, NJ: Princeton University Press.

Fortna, Virginia Page, and Lise Morjé Howard (2008) "Pitfalls and Prospects in the Peacekeeping Literature." *Annual Review of Political Science* 11(1): 283–301.

Gaibulloev, Khusrav, Justin George, Todd Sandler, and Hirofumi Shimizu (2015) "Personnel Contributions to UN and Non-UN Peacekeeping Missions: A Public Goods Approach." *Journal of Peace Research* 52(6): 727–742.

Gaibulloev, Khusrav, Todd Sandler, and Hirofumi Shimizu (2009) "Demands for UN and Non-UN Peacekeeping Nonvoluntary versus Voluntary Contributions to a Public Good." *Journal of Conflict Resolution* 53(6): 827–852.

Gilligan, Michael J., and Ernest J. Sergenti (2008) "Do UN Interventions Cause Peace? Using Matching to Improve Causal Inference." *Quarterly Journal of Political Science* 3(2): 89–122.

Gilligan, Michael, and Stephen John Stedman (2003) "Where Do the Peacekeepers Go?" *International Studies Review* 5(4): 37–54.

Haas, Ernst B., Robert Lyle Butterworth, and Joseph S. Nye (1972) *Conflict Management by International Organizations*. New York: General Learning Press.

Heldt, Birger, and Peter Wallensteen (2011) "Peacekeeping Operations: Global Patterns of Intervention and Success, 1948–2004." SSRN Scholarly Paper ID 1899505. Rochester, NY: Social Science Research Network.

Higgins, Rosalyn (1996) "The United Nations Role in Maintaining International Peace: The Lessons of the First Fifty Years." *New York Law School Journal of International and Comparative Law* 16(1): 135–149.

Hultman, Lisa, Jacob D. Kathman, and Megan Shannon (2016) "United Nations Peacekeeping Dynamics and the Duration of Post-Civil Conflict Peace." *Conflict Management and Peace Science* 33(3): 231–249.

Hultman, Lisa, Jacob Kathman, and Megan Shannon (2013) "United Nations Peacekeeping and Civilian Protection in Civil War." *American Journal of Political Science* 57(4): 875–891.

Hultman, Lisa, Jacob Kathman, and Megan Shannon (2014) "Beyond Keeping Peace: United Nations Effectiveness in the Midst of Fighting." *American Political Science Review* 108(4): 737–753.

Jett, Dennis C. (1999) *Why Peacekeeping Fails: A Comparative Assessment of Angola*. New York: St. Martin's Press.

Kathman, Jacob D. (2013) "United Nations Peacekeeping Personnel Commitments, 1990–2011." *Conflict Management and Peace Science* 30(5): 532–549.

Kathman, Jacob D., and Reed M. Wood (2016) "Stopping the Killing during the 'Peace': Peacekeeping and the Severity of Postconflict Civilian Victimization." *Foreign Policy Analysis* 12(2): 149–169.

Mackinlay, John (1989) *The Peacekeepers: An Assessment of Peacekeeping Operations at the Arab-Israel Interface*. Boston, MA: Unwin Hyman.

Mullenbach, Mark J. (2005) "Deciding to Keep Peace: An Analysis of International Influences on the Establishment of Third-Party Peacekeeping Missions." *International Studies Quarterly* 49(3): 529–555.

Pelcovits, Nathan Albert (1984) *Peacekeeping on Arab-Israeli Fronts: Lessons from the Sinai and Lebanon* Vol. 3. Boulder, CO: Westview Press.

Ruggeri, Andrea, Han Dorussen, and Theodora-Ismene Gizelis (2016) "On the Frontline Every Day? Subnational Deployment of United Nations Peacekeepers." *British Journal of Political Science* doi: https://doi.org/10.1017/S000712341600017X.

Ruggeri, Andrea, Han Dorussen, and Theodora-Ismene Gizelis (2017) "Winning the Peace Locally: UN Peacekeeping and Local Conflict." *International Organization* 71(10): 163–185.

Selway, Bianca (2013) "Who Pays for Peace?" IPI Global Observatory. http://theglobalobservatory.org/2013/11/who-pays-for-peace/ Accessed April 8, 2016.

Shimizu, Hirofumi, and Todd Sandler (2002) "Peacekeeping and Burden-Sharing, 1994–2000." *Journal of Peace Research* 39(6): 651–668.

Uzonyi, Gary (2015) "Refugee Flows and State Contributions to Post-Cold War UN Peacekeeping Missions." *Journal of Peace Research* 52(6): 743–757.

Walter, Barbara F. (2002) *Committing to Peace the Successful Settlement of Civil Wars*. Princeton, NJ: Princeton University Press.

Ward, Hugh, and Han Dorussen (2016) "Standing alongside Your Friends Network Centrality and Providing Troops to UN Peacekeeping Operations." *Journal of Peace Research* 53(3): 392–408.

Wilkenfeld, Jonathan, and Michael Brecher (1984) "International Crises, 1945–1975: The UN Dimension." *International Studies Quarterly* 28(1): 45–67.

Wright, Thorin M., and J. Michael Greig (2012) "Staying the Course: Assessing the Durability of Peacekeeping Operations." *Conflict Management and Peace Science* 29(2): 127–147.

15

Criminal Justice for Conflict-Related Violations

Developments during 2015

Anupma L. Kulkarni

Introduction

In recent decades, criminal investigations and prosecutions for conflict-related violations have increased. Cases have been pursued in international institutional venues such as ad hoc war crimes tribunals, hybrid courts and the International Criminal Court (ICC), as well as by ordinary and specialized national courts, some domestic and others in foreign countries.[1] These cases vary on several key dimensions, including the types of conflicts involved; the length of time that has passed between when violations were allegedly perpetrated and criminal cases are initiated; the ranks of the individuals being prosecuted; the authorities undertaking the prosecution or investigation of these acts; and the outcomes. This chapter profiles legal activity during 2015 (as well as certain key developments in 2016) in the context of cases involving crimes under international conventions – i.e., war crimes, crimes against humanity, genocide and/or torture – that were ongoing or concluded, plus situations in which such crimes were being investigated by a prosecuting authority.[2] At least 60 countries are involved in cases profiled below, as locations where violations occurred and/or those responsible are being prosecuted.

The global picture reveals continuing progress on opening legal avenues to criminal accountability, enabled by evolving norms and legal decisions that continue to weaken provisions that have historically blocked criminal trials, such as amnesties, statutes of limitations and sovereign immunity.[3] Of note, developments occurred at the international, regional and national levels on four fronts.

First, new legal applications of war crimes set precedents for prosecuting the destruction of antiquities, historical monuments, sites of religious significance, and cultural heritage more broadly. The destruction of intellectual and cultural heritage has long been recognized as an act of targeted violence against groups and their mode of existence. Yet these types of actions have not previously formed part of the charges in the context of prosecuting crimes under international conventions, where such destructive acts are specifically enumerated due to the existential threat they pose to the survival of the targeted groups and communities. The prosecution of such crimes by the ICC in the case of Mali, profiled below, opens the door to more effectively protecting the cultural foundations of groups and their identities using international law.

Second, the ICC's examination of the situation in Palestine sets an important precedent for less powerful entities to leverage the international justice system, when other avenues of pursuing accountability and redress may be prohibitive. Following the recognition of Palestine as an Observer State by the United Nations (UN) General Assembly, a pathway emerged for Palestine to become a signatory of the Rome Statute and thereby accept the jurisdiction of the ICC. In 2015, the Office of the Prosecutor accepted a request to commence a preliminary examination of the Israel–Palestine situation.

Third, efforts are evolving towards the investigation and criminal prosecution of actions during the communist era, as well as in the course of the transitions from communism, across Eastern Europe. Romania, profiled below, stands out in this regard. A broader initiative has emerged to create a regional consortium of countries facing the challenges of investigating and prosecuting communist-era crimes under international conventions. In 2015, Romania and Bulgaria were added to the existing list of countries backing the initiative. One of its aims is to establish a regional mechanism – such as a tribunal – to conduct the investigations and prosecutions.[4] Such a body has not yet been created. Nonetheless, support for national- and regional-level processes to seek accountability for, preserve the memory of, and make public communist-era crimes is evident elsewhere. Steps include national-level prosecutions; regional-level meetings to promote and discuss the potential for a tribunal or specialized court; and the formation of a consortium of Members of European Parliament and institutions involved in investigations and prosecutions.[5]

Fourth, progress has been made on gender-based violence as a violation of international humanitarian law at the national level, highlighted by the case of Guatemala. The first international legal precedents recognizing and prosecuting rape and sexual violence as war crimes were established via cases tried in the International Criminal Tribunal for Rwanda (ICTR), the International Criminal Tribunal for Former Yugoslavia (ICTY)[6] and the Special Court for Sierra Leone (SCSL).[7] These tribunals held individuals criminally responsible for acts of sexual violence, including rape, sexual slavery and forced marriage. The verdicts concerned violence against both individuals, in cases involving war crimes and crimes against humanity, and groups, in cases involving genocide and ethnic cleansing. Building on these international precedents, the grave crimes court in Guatemala, profiled below, achieved progress in this area through the successful prosecution of gender-based crimes at the national level.

At the same time, blockages, challenges, and other potential setbacks continue to be observed at the national and international levels. The cases of Kenya and the Sudan, profiled below, are particularly instructive regarding the limits of criminal prosecution for international crimes in which top officials are accused, in the face of resistance and a lack of compliance by states and powerful political actors. In a significant move to reject the authority of the ICC, several countries announced and took steps towards their withdrawal from the Rome Statute, citing concerns about bias against African states. Burundi was the first to advance down this path; the decision was confirmed by a vote in the legislature on October 12, 2016.[8] South Africa announced its intentions to withdraw on October 21,[9] followed by Gambia on October 26.[10] In November 2016, Russia announced plans to withdraw its signature from the Rome Statute.[11] That announcement was made subsequent to the ICC Office of the Prosecutor (OTP) issuing the 2016 report on preliminary examinations. In the report, the OTP determined the situation in Crimea, following its annexation by Russia, as constituting a "state of ongoing occupation" to which the laws of armed conflict would apply.[12] While the respective decisions of these states to withdraw are not yet final as of the time of writing, the precedent set by their moves to exit the Rome Statute raises numerous concerns for the viability of the ICC and the protection of human rights and prosecution of violations at the national and international levels, particularly when prospects for holding heads of state accountable are at issue. In all the instances, the decision to withdraw has been met with criticism from domestic constituencies that challenge the legality and ethics of these decisions.

In several difficult situations, progress has been facilitated by a combination of efforts by different types of actors. Important examples include the opinion of the Inter-American Commission for Human Rights in the CREOMPAZ case in Guatemala, the ruling of the International Court of Justice ordering the government of Senegal to fulfill its obligations under international law, and the decision of the European Court of Human Rights articulating the expectation that Romania should move forward with prosecuting human rights violations. These actions by regional and international institutions, often reflecting tireless efforts by domestic and international civil society, pushed the respective states to move forward with legal cases at the national level.

Country Profiles

Box 15.1 Argentina	
Conflict:	Military dictatorship (1976–1983)
Charges:	Torture; crimes against humanity; forced disappearance
Accused:	Members of the military junta, military officers, and collaborating civilians
Prosecuting Authority:	Argentine Courts
Location:	Argentina
Legal Activity during 2015:	Plan Condor trial ongoing; La Perla trial ongoing

From 1976–1983, approximately 30,000 people were killed, disappeared or tortured as the result of the "dirty war" conducted by the Argentine military government. These acts targeted leftists, students, and other perceived members of the opposition. The violence was focused domestically, but also extended to neighboring countries with *Plan Condor*, a joint enterprise with the military regimes of other countries in the region (Bolivia, Brazil, Chile, Paraguay, and Uruguay) to eliminate their respective political opponents.

Soon after the government collapsed, actions were taken to investigate these atrocities and hold those responsible to account. A truth commission was organized and completed its work in 1984. In addition, between 1984 and 1987 prosecutions were undertaken against the nine top members of the junta, leading to five convictions. During the years immediately thereafter, under a threat of backlash, the pursuit of justice was halted and even rolled back by a series of measures: the "full-stop" law (1986), which established a deadline for initiating prosecutions; the "due-obedience" law (1987), which effectively absolved low-ranking members of the military of criminal responsibility, on the basis that they were following orders; and pardons issued by President Menem for those individuals who had been convicted of crimes.

In 2003, President Kirchner had the 1986 and 1987 amnesty laws repealed. In 2005, the Argentine Supreme Court declared the amnesty laws unconstitutional and recognized states' obligations to investigate, prosecute and punish serious violations of human rights conventions.[13] Subsequently, key criminal trials have involved the prosecution of senior members of the military junta and civilian officials for notorious policies of kidnapping, hiding and changing the identities of the children of political opponents (*Plan Sistemático*); detention, torture, and killing in clandestine prison sites; and *Plan Condor*.[14]

As of 2014, 121 trials had been conducted for crimes against humanity, with 503 convictions.[15] In addition, 1,611 suspects were reportedly being investigated for their involvement in similar crimes.[16] In 2014, several high-profile cases involving numerous military officers and civilians were completed. Among these was the Case of the Abducted Babies, concerning newborn babies born in the clandestine birthing center of Campo de Mayo who were abducted and hidden by the military dictatorship. The defendants, including two military officers and two civilians, were convicted and sentenced to prison terms. Meanwhile, the trial of two officers for the killing of Bishop Enrique Angelelli also ended in conviction. In addition, 16 military officers and other officials were convicted and sentenced for the murder, detention and torture of 128 people in La Cacha camp in La Plata province.

In 2015, the La Perla – La Ribera trial continued. This joint trial involved 43 defendants on charges of enforced disappearances, torture and unlawful detention. Chief among these was General Luciano Benjamín Menéndez, who had been in charge of state terrorism operations in 12 Argentinian provinces, as well as the La Perla and La Ribera clandestine detention camps in Córdoba province, where an estimated 2,000–3,000 people disappeared. The prosecution represented 720 victims. In April 2016, the verdict, convicting 38 "repressors" and acquitting five accused, was issued. Of those found guilty, 28 received life sentences and 10 received prison sentences from 2–14 years. For General Menéndez, the highest-ranking officer on trial, this was his 12th life sentence and 14th conviction for the commission of crimes against humanity.[17] Other high-profile defendants include Héctor Pedro Vergez, a former paramilitary commander, and Ernesto Guillermo Barreiro, a former lieutenant.[18] In anticipation of the pronouncement of sentence, 10,000 people reportedly waited outside the courthouse in Córdoba. This landmark conviction is the first to confirm that crimes of this magnitude began prior to the official start of the military dictatorship, with the activities of paramilitary groups like the *Comando Libertadores de América*.

In May 2016, the Plan Condor trial was completed. The trial, which started in 2013 in Buenos Aires, charged 25 high-ranking military officers (including one from Uruguay) with crimes committed as part of the conspiracy to kidnap, torture and murder political opponents of military dictatorship in the Southern Cone. Among those on trial were Generals Jorge Videla (deceased) and Reynaldo Bignone. Both had headed the military dictatorship, with Bignone the last one holding this position before the return to civilian rule in 1983. The charges identify 171 victims from Argentina, Bolivia, Chile, Cuba, Ecuador, Paraguay, Peru and Uruguay. Ultimately, 18 of the military officers received guilty verdicts, including Bignone.[19]

As of August 2016, 600 people have been tried and convicted of atrocities perpetrated during the military dictatorship.[20]

Box 15.2 Bangladesh	
Conflict:	Civil war between West and East Pakistan (1971)
Charges:	Crimes against humanity; war crimes; genocide
Accused:	Members of pro-Pakistan groups and militias
Prosecuting Authority:	International Crimes Tribunal (ICT)
Location:	Bangladesh
Legal Activity during 2015:	Proceedings in 11 cases continued; appeals to the Supreme Court were in progress; investigations are continuing

In the 1970 elections in Pakistan, which at the time was composed of West Pakistan (now Pakistan) and East Pakistan (now Bangladesh), the Awami League in East Pakistan won the majority (167 of 169) seats in the parliament, concentrating power in the eastern portion of the country for the first time. Unwilling to accept this outcome, General Yahya Khan took repressive military action in East Pakistan. The military campaign caused an estimated 1–3 million deaths; a massive humanitarian crisis, sending approximately 10 million refugees across borders, primarily into India; and an armed insurgency against the repressive actions of West Pakistan.[21] Ultimately, two states were formed: Pakistan in the west and Bangladesh in the east.

The International Crimes Tribunal (ICT) was established to prosecute atrocities allegedly perpetrated by 195 Pakistani military officers in the 1971 conflict. None of these officers were remanded to newly independent Bangladesh to face prosecution and remain beyond the reach of the Tribunal as currently configured.[22] Though the law creating the ICT was adopted in 1973, soon after the independence of Bangladesh, the Tribunal was not actually formed until 2010, following an amendment to the original law in 2009. The law was initially written to prosecute members of the Pakistani military, but all of the 27 individuals pursued by the ICT allegedly belonged to groups that were opposed to Bangladesh's secession from Pakistan, including the Razakar and Al Badr (militias) among others, and all are affiliated with the political opposition.[23] They are charged with committing war crimes, crimes against humanity and genocide, in conjunction with repressive military actions by West Pakistani forces.

As of 2014, the ICT had completed 19 prosecutions (including six *in absentia*). All trials have ended in convictions. Fourteen of the convicted individuals have been sentenced to death, while the remainder received life imprisonment sentences. One death sentence was commuted to life imprisonment. In 2014, four trials were prosecuted and judgments in six cases were issued. Eight cases were ongoing at various stages, and several ongoing appeals processes remained in progress.[24]

In 2015, the Tribunal carried on with proceedings connected to at least 11 cases, concerning a total of 35 accused individuals. A total of 16 defendants, across three of the cases, were not present (listed as "absconded") and thus were tried *in absentia*. Since the beginning of 2015 to September 2016, the ICT sentenced at least 15 persons to death.[25] In May 2016, Motiur Rahman Nizami, leader of Bangladesh's largest Islamist party, Jamaat-e-Islami, was executed. Nizami's execution, carried out in a tense political and security situation, is the fifth death sentence ordered by the ICT that has been carried out since 2013.[26]

The ICT continues its work in a politically contentious and sensitive environment. The Tribunal has come under serious criticism for not conforming to standards of international law and procedures, while simultaneously setting up a separate standard of justice within Bangladesh, most notably depriving defendants of rights that would be afforded them if they were to be prosecuted according to existing Bangladeshi criminal procedures.[27] The ICT adoption and application of the death penalty have drawn opprobrium from the international human rights community and been a barrier to working with international institutions, jurists and legal advisors. The ICT has been accused of serving the political interests of the Awami League – the current political party in power – and its trials have been characterized as a means to eliminate opponents of the ruling party.[28] The executions have been polarizing issues domestically, evoking visible public support and celebrations, as well as public condemnation and protests. Over 500 people have reportedly been killed in such demonstrations, as of the beginning of 2015.[29]

Box 15.3 Cambodia	
Conflict:	Khmer Rouge dictatorship (1975–1979)
Charges:	Genocide; crimes against humanity; war crimes
Accused:	Nuon Chea, Khieu Samphan (002/02); Meas Muth (003); Ao An, Yim Tith (004); Im Chaem (004/01)
Prosecuting Authority:	Extraordinary Chambers in the Courts of Cambodia (ECCC)
Location:	Cambodia
Legal Activity during 2015:	Cases 002/02, 003 and 004 ongoing; 004/01 severed appeals in case 002/01

In 1975, the Khmer Rouge, led by Pol Pot, captured control of Phnom Penh, the capital of Cambodia, and established Democratic Kampuchea. The new government undertook a massive campaign of forcible social reorganization. The ensuing reign of terror is estimated to have caused the deaths of 1.2–2.8 million people.[30] The government was toppled in 1978 by neighboring Vietnam, which occupied the country until 1989. This period was marked by repression and violent resistance.

Following a 1991 peace agreement, the United Nations Transitional Authority for Cambodia facilitated the transition and restoration of the Cambodian government in 1993. The hurdles to prosecuting the individuals responsible for the massive violence perpetrated by the Khmer Rouge were not overcome until 2005, when the United Nations and the government of Cambodia reached an agreement on establishing and funding a special court for that purpose. In 2007, the

Extraordinary Chambers in the Courts of Cambodia (ECCC) began investigating atrocities committed in Democratic Kampuchea.

As of 2014, the Court had completed the prosecution of two cases (001 and 002/01), involving three individuals. In 2014, the first high-ranking Khmer Rouge officials, Nuon Chea and Khieu Samphan, were found guilty of crimes against humanity and sentenced to life imprisonment. They are also being tried in a second case (002/02) on a different set of charges, including genocide against the Cham and the Vietnamese; forced marriages and rape; and atrocities committed at the notorious S-21 detention site. The original case (002) against Nuon Chea and Khieu Samphan was split; the charges were severed in order to limit the scope of each trial. The proceedings in their second trial are ongoing. Two additional cases, designated 003 and 004, were still in preliminary and investigative stages. In Case 003, Meas Muth was charged (in absentia) in March 2015 with homicide, crimes against humanity and war crimes allegedly committed at the S-21 and Wat Enta Nhien detention centers, in Kampong Som and Kratie, and against Vietnamese, Thai and other foreigners.[31] The identities of two additional suspects in Case 003 remain under seal.[32] In Case 004, Ao An and Im Chaem (in absentia) are charged with homicide and crimes against humanity for their alleged role in the running of a forced labor camp and the deaths of thousands of Cambodians.[33] Cases 003 and 004 have proceeded in an environment of reported political pressure and tension between the Cambodian and international investigative judges, as well as reports of non-cooperation by the judicial police.[34]

Part of the charges in Case 002/02 include inhumane acts of sexual violence, with particular attention to two contexts in which rape was perpetrated. In the formulation of charges, investigators concluded that rape was widely perpetrated against victims in detention at numerous locations (S-21, Kraing Ta Chan, North Zone, Prey Damrei Srot, Sang, Tram Kok Cooperatives), but the official policy of the Communist Party of Kampuchea (CPK) was to prevent and punish rape in this setting. In contrast, rape in the context of forced marriage was pursued as part of the CPK policy, meant as a targeted attack against the civilian population. In August 2016, the trial chamber heard evidence on the "regulation of marriage" policy of the CPK.[35]

In 2015, Meas Muth was charged and appeared before the international co-investigating judge to hear charges.[36] The case against Im Chaem was severed, creating a separate case file 004/01 in February 2016. Chaem faces several charges: (1) homicide, as a violation of the 1956 Cambodian Penal Code, allegedly committed at Phnom Trayoung security center and Spean Sreng worksite; (2) the crimes against humanity of murder, extermination, enslavement, imprisonment, persecution on political grounds, and other inhumane acts allegedly committed at the Phnom Trayoung security center; and (3) the crimes against humanity of murder, enslavement, imprisonment, and other inhumane acts allegedly committed at the Spean Sreng worksite. Case 004/01 is due to proceed in 2016–2017.

Box 15.4 Central African Republic	
Conflict:	Armed conflict following attempted coup d'état (2002–03)
Charges:	War crimes; crimes against humanity; offences against administration of justice
Accused:	Jean-Pierre Bemba Gombo; Aimé Kilolo Musamba; Jean-Jacques Mangenda Kabongo; Fidèle Babala Wandu; Narcisse Arido
Prosecuting Authority:	International Criminal Court (ICC)
Location:	The Hague, Netherlands
Legal Activity during 2015:	Decision in the Bemba case pending; Bemba, et al. case commenced and trial ongoing

In 2004, the government of the Central African Republic (CAR) referred its own situation to the ICC with respect to war crimes and crimes against humanity perpetrated in a period following a failed coup attempt in 2002. In the ensuing armed conflict, widespread sexual violence and civilian targeting were reported.

In May 2008, the ICC Prosecutor requested an arrest warrant for Jean-Pierre Bemba Gombo, a national of the Democratic Republic of the Congo (DRC) and the President and Commander-in-Chief of the *Mouvement de libération du Congo* (MLC). The MLC allegedly allied with a segment of the CAR national armed forces loyal to President Ange-Félix Patassé, to confront the forces of Francois Bozizé, a former leader of the CAR armed forces who led a rebellion against the Patassé regime. Bemba was charged with three war crimes (murder, rape, and pillaging) and two crimes against humanity (murder and rape) for acts perpetrated during the conflict in 2002–2003. He was apprehended by Belgian authorities and surrendered to the ICC in July 2008. His trial commenced in 2010. In 2014, closing oral statements were concluded. Bemba was convicted of war crimes and crimes against humanity on March 21, 2016, then sentenced to 18 years of imprisonment on June 22, 2016.[37] Bemba subsequently filed an appeal.

In 2013, the ICC Prosecutor initiated a second related case, charging Bemba along with four others (Aimé Kilolo Musamba, Jean-Jacques Mangenda Kabongo, Fidèle Babala Wandu and Narcisse Arido), with "offences against the administration of justice." This was the first case brought by the ICC Prosecutor for actions involving interference with witnesses and their testimony. Given the challenges the ICC faces in protecting witnesses, who often remain vulnerable in the aftermath of the conflict, this case can be expected to set an important precedent in signaling the Court's commitment to ensuring the security of potential witnesses and victims of the serious crimes being prosecuted and the integrity of the evidence presented at trial. The governments of Belgium, the DRC, France and the Netherlands undertook the arrest and surrender of the four additional defendants in this case in 2013. In October 2014, the four defendants were ordered to be released based on a determination by the Pre-Trial Chamber that their detention prior to the start of trial was for an unreasonable length of time. The defendants have been released on an interim basis pending additional developments in the Prosecution's case that might warrant their re-arrest. The Prosecutor appealed this decision and preparations for this trial continued. In November 2014, the Court confirmed the charges against the defendants.[38]

In September 2015, the trial against Jean-Pierre Bemba Gombo, Aimé Kilolo Musamba, Jean-Jacques Mangenda Kabongo, Fidèle Babala Wandu and Narcisse Arido opened, with all defendants present. Closing arguments were concluded in May 2016.[39] The verdict, reached on October 21, 2016, found the five defendants guilty of various charges, including corruptly influencing witnesses, presenting false evidence, soliciting false testimony, and aiding and abetting in false testimony. Kabongo, Wandu, and Arido were acquitted for aiding and abetting in false testimony by select witnesses.[40]

Box 15.5 Chad	
Conflict:	Dictatorship of Hissène Habré (1982–1990)
Charges:	Crimes against humanity; torture; war crimes
Accused:	Hissène Habré
Prosecuting Authority:	Extraordinary African Chambers
Location:	Senegal
Legal Activity during 2015:	Habré trial commenced; verdict issued 2016

Hissène Habré became the president of Chad through a coup d'état in 1982. During his rule, approximately 40,000 people were reportedly killed, and many detained, tortured and disappeared. In 1990, he was ousted in another coup and went into exile in Senegal.

In 2000, the first complaints were filed in Senegal and Belgium accusing Habré of committing crimes against humanity, torture, and genocide. Although calls for his prosecution were persistently put forward by victims of his policies, there was little movement in that direction in Senegal. The government initially asserted that it could not prosecute him for lack of jurisdiction, but simultaneously refused to extradite him to Belgium, which might have prosecuted him based on the principle of universal jurisdiction. Belgium then brought the matter to the International Court of Justice (ICJ). In July 2012, the ICJ found that the government of Senegal had not fulfilled its obligations under the Convention against Torture and ordered that it either submit Habré's case to the proper authorities for prosecution or else extradite him to Belgium.[41] Following this ruling, in August 2012, a formal agreement between the government of Senegal and the African Union (AU) was reached establishing the Extraordinary African Chambers (Chambers) in Senegal to prosecute international crimes committed in Chad from 1982–1990. In February 2013, the Chambers were inaugurated. In July, charges of crimes against humanity, war crimes and torture were filed against Habré, who was then detained, pending trial. It was announced that the Habré trial would commence in mid-2015. In 2014, an additional agreement between the AU and Senegal established a Defence Office within the Chambers and investigations in Habré's case continued.[42]

In January 2015, the trial of Hissène Habré commenced. He was charged with murder, torture, enforced disappearance and unlawful confinement as crimes against humanity and war crimes. Evidence in this case was assembled from multiple sources, including prior investigations into allegations of human rights violations by the Chadian Truth Commission (1992), Belgian case files, an extensive probe by the investigating judges from the Extraordinary Chambers (2013–2014) that involved interviewing approximately 2,500 direct and indirect victims of the Habré regime, and documents recovered by Human Rights Watch, pertaining to the activities of the Directorate of Documentation and Chadian Security (DDS), the Chadian secret police.[43] During September–December 2015, the Chambers interviewed 96 victims, witnesses, and experts.

In February 2016, trial proceedings concluded. In a summary of its decision, the court concluded that following the assumption of power through force in June 1982, a campaign of repression ensued against political opponents, primarily undertaken by the DDS, the Special Rapid Intervention Brigade (BSIR), and the armed forces under Habré (the FANT), until December 1990. Opponents and members of their families were arrested, detained and tortured in a network of seven clandestine prisons in N'Djamena. Additional categories of crimes include sexual violence and violence against prisoners of war. Habré was found guilty of the following crimes against humanity: rape, sexual enslavement, murder, torture, massive and systematic executions, abduction, and enforced disappearances. He was also found guilty of war crimes, including murder, torture, inhumane treatment and illegal detention, on the basis of command responsibility. In May 2016, Habré was convicted of the abovementioned crimes and sentenced to life imprisonment.[44]

Box 15.6 Chile

Conflict:	Military dictatorship under Augusto Pinochet (1973–1990)
Charges:	Crimes against humanity; torture
Accused:	Pedro Ramón Cáceres Jorquera; Edgar Cevallos Jones; Rosauro Martinez; Sergio Víctor Arellano Stark; Pedro Octavio Espinoza Bravo; and others
Prosecuting Authority:	Chilean national courts
Location:	Chile
Legal Activity during 2015:	Cáceres Jorquera and Cevallos Jones convicted of torture; Martinez charged and arrested

In 1973, Augusto Pinochet came to power through a military coup. Repressive actions perpetrated by the military regime resulted in over 3,000 deaths and disappearances and an estimated 30,000 cases of torture. Amnesty decrees adopted by the former military leadership remained in effect until 1994, precluding the possibility of pursuing prosecutions against officers and officials serving the military dictatorship. Over time, however, the effectiveness and legality of the amnesty provisions began to progressively weaken. Allowances for investigations into disappearances – considered as ongoing crimes – were made. In addition, cases involving the recognition of international law in matters of crimes against humanity and genocide were accepted as binding precedents.

As of 2015, a total of 1,056 cases of human rights violations were under investigation, including 112 for torture. The human rights program in the Ministry of the Interior reported 344 persons had received final sentences and 117 were serving prison sentences.[45] In July 2015, the case of "Los Quemados" progressed with the arrest of seven army officers in connection to the 1986 killing of 19-year old Rodrigo Rojas de Negri and the disfigurement of 18-year old Carmen Gloria Quintana during a protest against the Pinochet dictatorship.[46] Multiple other investigations and trials are also ongoing.

Box 15.7 Côte d'Ivoire

Conflict:	Post-election violence (2010–2011)
Charges:	Crimes against humanity
Accused:	Laurent Gbagbo; Simone Gbagbo; Charles Blé Goudé
Prosecuting Authorities:	International Criminal Court (ICC); Côte d'Ivoire national courts
Locations:	The Hague, Netherlands, and Abidjan, Côte d'Ivoire
Legal Activity during 2015:	Laurent Gbagbo and Charles Blé Goudé cases joined; trial commenced in January 2016 and ongoing; Simone Gbagbo trial commenced in Côte d'Ivoire

In the aftermath of Côte d'Ivoire's 2010 presidential election, contention and confusion regarding the outcome were prevalent. Opposition candidate Alassane Ouattara was eventually recognized by the Ivoirian election body, the United Nations and the African Union as the victor. Supporters of incumbent Laurent Gbagbo, claiming he was the rightful winner, carried out violent attacks against individuals and communities that supported Ouattara. The resulting violence, concentrated mostly in the western region of the country, caused approximately 3,000 deaths and 150 reported cases of rape, as well as population displacement that precipitated a humanitarian crisis, which threatened to destabilize Côte d'Ivoire, with potential spillover into bordering Liberia. In 2011, the United Nations created an emergency mission to help bring conditions under control and ensure that Ouattara could form his government and pacify the situation.

In the same year, Côte d'Ivoire recognized the authority of the ICC and referred the matter to the Prosecutor, who requested arrest warrants for the former president and the first lady, Simone Gbagbo. The couple was apprehended by UN and French troops in late 2011. Laurent Ggagbo was arrested and surrendered to the ICC. In 2014, the ICC pre-trial chamber confirmed the charges against Laurent Gbagbo, which consist of multiple counts of crimes against humanity. Simone Gbagbo was taken into custody in Côte d'Ivoire, where she was tried for "undermining state security" and sentenced to a 20-year prison sentence in March 2015. Her trial took place alongside 82 other supporters of Laurent Gbagbo. Many of these trials are continuing.[47] Meanwhile, the ICC arrest warrant for Simone Gbagbo remained active, but had not been acted upon by the Ivoirian government. In addition, Charles Blé Goudé, Minister for Sports and Youth in Gbagbo's government, was arrested and in 2014 charged by the ICC with committing crimes against humanity. He remains in custody. In 2015, his case was joined with that of Laurent Gbagbo. The charges of crimes against humanity specifically include: murder, rape, other inhumane acts and persecution, allegedly committed during 2010–2011 in the context of post-election violence.[48] The trial began in January 2016 and was ongoing as of the time of writing.

In April 2015, President Ouattara announced that future trials pertaining to post-election violence would be held in national courts. In May 2015, the ICC maintained its request that Simone Gbagbo be remanded to ICC custody and rejected the government's request to retain jurisdiction over her case. Thus far, the government has refused to surrender her to the ICC for trial, opting instead to prosecute her in national courts. In May 2016, a second trial of Simone Gbagbo, in which she was charged with war crimes and crimes against humanity, began in Côte d'Ivoire's High Court.[49]

Box 15.8 Democratic Republic of the Congo	
Conflict:	Armed conflict between the DRC government and rebel groups (1997–present)
Charges:	War crimes; crimes against humanity
Accused:	Thomas Lubanga Dyilo; Bosco Ntaganda; Germain Katanga; Sylvestre Mudacumura; Mathieu Ngudjolo Chui
Prosecuting Authority:	International Criminal Court (ICC)
Location:	The Hague, Netherlands
Legal Activity during 2015:	Ntaganda trial opened and ongoing

The conflict in the Democratic Republic of the Congo (DRC) stretches back several decades. The allegations of war crimes and crimes against humanity being prosecuted by the ICC have roots in the armed conflict for power after the ouster of Mobutu Sese Seko, who was President of what was then Zaire, in 1997. The establishment of the government of Laurent Kabila, via armed takeover, was soon followed by the creation of multiple armed groups. The violent rebellion continued even after Laurent Kabila was assassinated in 2001 and succeed by his son, Joseph. The civil war, which has involved at least six other nations and cost the country an estimated five million lives, is still being fought in areas, despite peace accords, elections and a UN mission to help stabilize the country and to facilitate a transition to democratic governance.

In 2004, the DRC government referred its own situation to the ICC to investigate and prosecute individuals responsible for war crimes and crimes against humanity committed since 2002. The Prosecutor issued indictments against six senior commanders of four distinct groups involved in the DRC conflicts: Lubanga Dyilo, Commander of the *Forces Patriotiques pour la Libération du Congo* (FPLC); Bosco Ntaganda, Deputy Chief of the Staff and Commander of Operations of the FPLC; Germain Katanga, Commander of the *Force de Résistance Patriotique en Ituri* (FRPI); Callixte Mbarushimana, Executive Secretary of the *Forces Démocratiques pour la Libération du Rwanda – Forces Combattantes Abacunguzi* (FDLR-FCA, FDLR); Sylvestre Mudacumura, Supreme Commander of the *Forces Démocratiques pour la Libération du Rwanda* (FDLR); and Mathieu Ngudjolo Chui, former leader of the *Front des Nationalistes et Intégrationnistes* (FNI). The charges against Mbarushimana were dismissed and he was released from ICC custody in 2011.[50]

Lubanga Dyilo was found guilty in 2012 of conscripting children to fight; this verdict was upheld after appeal in 2014.[51] He was sentenced and remains in ICC custody. Chui was acquitted and released from ICC custody in 2012, but that verdict was appealed by the Prosecutor. The acquittal was upheld in February 2015.[52] In 2014, Germain Katanga's trial was completed. He was found guilty as an accessory to war crimes and crimes against humanity and has been sentenced; all appeals have been discontinued. He remains in ICC custody.[53]

The trial against Bosco Ntaganda opened in September 2015 and remains ongoing. The charges, confirmed in June 2014, include 13 counts of war crimes: murder and attempted murder, attacking civilians, rape, sexual slavery of civilians, pillaging, displacement of civilians, attacking protected objects, destroying the enemy's property, and rape, sexual slavery, enlistment and conscription of child soldiers under the age of 15 years and using them to participate actively in hostilities. Additionally, he is charged with five counts of crimes against humanity: murder and attempted murder, rape, sexual slavery, persecution, and forcible transfer of population. The alleged crimes were committed in Ituri province from 2002–2003 directed against civilians thought to be "non-Hema."[54] Meanwhile, the arrest warrant for Mudacumura continues to be active and he is still at large.[55]

Box 15.9 Former Yugoslavia	
Conflict:	Wars in the Former Yugoslavia (1991–1999)
Charges:	War crimes; crimes against humanity; genocide
Accused:	Political and military leaders; military personnel; others
Prosecuting Authorities:	International Criminal Tribunal for the Former Yugoslavia (ICTY); national courts in Serbia, Croatia, Bosnia and Herzegovina, and Kosovo
Locations:	The Netherlands, Serbia, Croatia, Bosnia and Herzegovina, and Kosovo
Legal Activity during 2015:	Multiple trials and appeals ongoing

During the 1990s, a set of brutal wars were fought among the republics that emerged out of the breakdown of the former Yugoslavia. In the midst of the wars, the United Nations established the International Criminal Tribunal for the Former Yugoslavia (ICTY) in 1996. At the time, the prospects for pursuing prosecutions for war crimes and crimes against humanity in the courts of the constituent nations of the Former Yugoslavia were complex and remote. Armed conflict was still active, and suspected war criminals had consolidated power in the changing political geography of the region. In lieu of domestic legal actions, the ICTY pursued numerous cases, resulting in 80 convictions (out of 161 total indictments) from 1993 to 2015.[56] Over the past several years, the work of the ICTY has wound down. Meanwhile, judicial activity in national courts has been increasing.

In 2015, the ICTY had only four active trials and appeals concerning 14 accused in three cases on its dockets.[57] All four of the active trials involved prominent individuals.

Radovan Karadžic is charged with genocide, war crimes and crimes against humanity for his role in a joint criminal enterprise (JCE) to permanently remove Bosnian Muslim and Bosnian Croat populations from territory in Bosnia and Herzegovina, as well as the siege of Sarajevo and the Srebrenica massacre. In 2014, his defense team finished presenting its case and closing arguments in the trial were concluded, with a judgment expected in December 2015.[58] In March 2016, Karadžic was convicted of genocide, crimes against humanity and war crimes, for which he was sentenced to 40 years' imprisonment.[59] He is appealing the court's decision through the United Nations Mechanism for International Criminal Tribunals (MICT).

Ratko Mladić is charged with crimes against humanity and war crimes for his participation in a JCE to permanently remove Bosnian Muslims from the territory of Bosnia and Herzegovina and the siege of Sarajevo. In 2014, the prosecution concluded its case and the defense started to present its case. In 2015, Mladić's trial was ongoing. The judgment is expected in 2017.[60]

Goran Hadžic, former President of the Government of the self-proclaimed Serbian Autonomous District Slavonia, Baranja and Western Srem and later President of the Republic of Serbian Krajina (RSK) in Croatia, is charged with crimes against humanity and war crimes for his participation in a JCE whose aim was the forcible removal of the Croat and non-Serb populations from the area in Croatia to create a new Serb dominated state.[61] In July 2016, Hadžic died before the ICTY decision was reached.[62]

Vojislav Šešelj, founder of the Serbian National Renewal Party, is charged with crimes against humanity and war crimes for his role in "forcible removal of a majority of the Croat, Muslim and other non-Serb civilian populations from parts of Croatia, [Bosnia and Herzegovina] and from the province of Vojvodina in the Republic of Serbia." In 2014, the Trial Chamber ordered Seselj released on grounds of his worsening health.[63] He returned to Serbia in 2014, while awaiting the verdict in his case, expected towards the end of 2015.[64] In March 2015, the ICTY revoked his release, finding that Šešelj had violated its terms.[65] Afterwards, Šešelj publicly declared that he would not return to ICTY custody.[66] In March 2016, he was acquitted by the ICTY. The decision is being appealed by the prosecutor in the MICT.[67]

Developments in other significant cases were also observed in 2015. The 2013 ICTY decision to acquit former Serbian state security officers Jovica Stanišić and Franko Simatović was overturned by the ICTY Appeals Chamber. In December 2015, the re-trial of Stanisic and Simatovic, who are charged with the perpetration of war crimes in Bosnia and Croatia, began. The re-trial will be held in the MICT.[68] Jadranko Prlić, Bruno Stojić, Slobodan Praljak, Milivoj Petković,

Valentin Ćorić and Berislav Pušić, high-ranking officials of the Croatian Defence Council (HVO), filed an appeal against the 2013 verdict finding them guilty of war crimes and crimes against humanity. In 2015, the Appeals Chamber began consideration of the matter; a decision is expected in 2017.[69]

Meanwhile, national-level prosecutions continued during 2015. As of September 2016, at least 646 people have been convicted in local courts across Bosnia and Herzegovina, Croatia, Serbia, and Kosovo.[70] The greatest activity took place in Bosnia and Herzegovina, where prosecuting authorities aimed to charge as many as 100 individuals for war crimes in 2014. In one prominent example, 15 individuals were charged with war crimes for their alleged role in the Zecovi Massacre.[71] In Croatia, charges were filed against two Croatian soldiers in two separate cases, relating to war crimes associated with Operation Storm, a Croatian offensive to retake Krajina.[72] In 2015, Serbia's war crimes prosecutor charged eight former members of the Bosnian-Serb special police for the killing of 1,300 people in the village of Kravica, near Srebrenica.[73] In Kosovo, a case against the Drenica Group, a unit of the Kosovo Liberation Army accused of detainee abuse and torture, is being prosecuted, among others.[74] Montenegro has been less active in pursuing domestic war crimes prosecutions, but debates about doing so continued in 2014.[75]

In August 2015, Kosovo lawmakers voted to change the constitution to establish a special court outside Kosovo to try senior members of the Kosovo Liberation Army (KLA) for war crimes and crimes against humanity. The decision to create an extra-territorial body to prosecute allegations against high-ranking KLA fighters for abuses allegedly perpetrated from 1998–2000, to be set up in The Hague in 2016, has drawn criticism and resistance from opposition politicians and former fighters. Part of the impetus for this approach has been the difficulties of prosecuting war crimes within Kosovo, undertaken by international community administration for the past 17 years.[76] The Kosovo Specialist Chambers is a culmination of a process stemming from allegations that the KLA had trafficked ethnic Serbs from Kosovo to Albania for organ harvesting from 1999–2000. Those abuses were first brought to light in 2003 by American investigative journalists and were further investigated by the ICTY and the United Nations Mission in Kosovo (UNMIK). Additional concerns were raised in 2009 after the discovery of illegal detention centers in Albania, where Kosovo Albanian, Serb and Roma civilians were allegedly held, tortured and murdered. Subsequently, a Special Investigative Task Force (SITF) was set up by the European Union in 2011. The SITF findings supported the indictment of senior KLA members for crimes against humanity and other abuses in 2014.[77] The Kosovo special court will have international judges, but operate according to the Kosovo legal code. It is distinct from an international court or tribunal model in that it is a Kosovo court, which operates outside the territory of Kosovo.[78]

In some instances, the pursuit of justice has gone hand-in-hand with continuing political tensions in the region. For instance, Croatia indicted and sought the extradition from Australia of Dragan Vasijlković for crimes committed by him and under his command in the Benkovac and Knin areas of Croatia.[79] Serbia also requested his extradition, on the grounds that he is a national of Serbia and fought for the country. The matter has been submitted before the International Court of Justice (ICJ), which has not yet issued a decision. In May 2015, the Australian High Court approved his extradition to Croatia.[80] In July 2015, Vasijlkovic was transferred to Croatia. He was charged with war crimes in January 2016.[81] These disputes have compounded tensions between Croatia and Serbia, evidenced by their mutual accusations of genocide filed with the ICJ.[82]

Box 15.10 Guatemala	
Conflict:	Guatemalan civil war (1960–2000)
Charges:	Genocide; crimes against humanity; murder; enforced disappearances; sexual violence; domestic and sexual slavery; torture
Accused:	Efraín Ríos Montt; José Mauricio Rodríguez Sánchez; Pedro Garcia Arredondo; Esteelmer Reyes Girón; Heriberto Valdez Asig; Manuel Benedicto Lucas García; and other military officers
Prosecuting Authority:	Guatemalan national courts
Location:	Guatemala
Legal Activity during 2015:	Trial of Ríos Montt and Rodríguez Sánchez remained suspended pending resolution of legal challenges to its resumption; Garcia Arredondo convicted; Sepur Zarco investigation and pre-trial hearings; CREOMPAZ investigation ongoing; investigations into additional cases ongoing

In 1982, Efraín Ríos Montt seized power in a military coup d'état and assumed the presidency of Guatemala. Though armed conflict dated back to 1960, under the 17-month leadership of Ríos Montt, the war entered a new phase of increased intensity and brutality. By the time the war ended in 2000, approximately 200,000 people had been killed and 40,000 disappeared. The majority of the victims of this state terror were the indigenous Maya.

In 2012, Ríos Montt and his chief of military intelligence, José Mauricio Rodríguez Sánchez, were indicted for the massacre of 1,771 Mayan Ixils, the forcible displacement of 29,000, sexual violations, and torture. Genocide and crimes against humanity were subsequently added to the indictment. The remarkable step of prosecuting these two individuals in Guatemalan courts is rendered even more extraordinary given that Ríos Montt was the sitting President of the Congress at the time charges were brought against him. Moreover, previous efforts to document the casualties of the conflict and seek accountability resulted in a backlash.

Among the noteworthy examples of this was the 1998 assassination of Bishop Gerardi, two days after the release of a report on human rights violations in Guatemala, compiled by the non-governmental Recovery of Historical Memory (REHMI) Project that he headed. In 1999, the UN's Historical Clarification Commission (*Comisión para el Esclarecimiento Histórico*, or CEH) released a separate report about human rights violations during the armed conflict. Though the impact of this investigation was not immediately perceived, it helped to provide a basis for a number of political and judicial decisions that would eventually remove barriers to prosecuting cases of human rights violations. Key steps along this path included the creation of the International Commission against Impunity in Guatemala (*Comisión Internacional contra la Impunidad en Guatemala*, or CICIG) in 2007 by the United Nations and the State of Guatemala; the creation of a special prosecution unit dealing with violations of human rights; a decision by the Constitutional Court that amnesty did not apply in certain cases of grave crimes; and the establishment of a so-called "high-risk" court to try cases of a politically sensitive nature.

On May 10, 2013, Ríos Montt was found guilty of genocide, while Rodriguez Sánchez was acquitted.[83] Yet this historic judgment was overturned 10 days later by the Constitutional Court, which reasoned that Ríos Montt had been deprived of legal representation when his attorney was temporarily expelled from the courtroom. The court vacated the decision and ordered that the retrial resume from that point in the proceedings. Since then, however, the resumption of the trial has been frustrated by a series of issues. A partial list of the most serious matters causing delays includes:

- A re-consideration by the Constitutional Court of whether the 1986 amnesty could apply in this case.[84] In October 2015, the Guatemalan Constitutional Court issued a ruling that the amnesty did not apply.[85]
- Problems experienced by judges facing reprisals.[86]
- A recent and widening corruption scandal that led to the resignation of Guatemala's Vice-President and implicated Judge Patricia Flores, the pre-trial judge who originally changed the charges against Ríos Montt from murder to genocide and then ruled that the verdict convicting Ríos Montt and Rodriguez Sánchez of genocide should be annulled and returned to the investigative stage. Flores is now facing calls for her impeachment.[87]
- The assassination of Ríos Montt's defense attorney.[88]
- Accusations of bias brought by Ríos Montt's legal team against the President of the Court with a motion for recusal.
- A travel ban against the lead prosecutor, resulting from a complaint filed against him by an affiliate of Ríos Montt.[89] This ban was rejected in June 2015.
- Ríos Montt being declared unfit for trial due to dementia, rendering him incapable of understanding the charges.

In December 2014, the Constitutional Court made it possible for the retrial to go forward in January 2015 by ordering Judge Patricia Flores to annul her decision to set the trial back to the investigative stage. Despite this ruling, which attempted to settle one aspect of the question regarding the stage at which the trial should resume, the trial remained held up by scheduling problems.[90] After multiple efforts at establishing dates for the trial to resume, including accommodations for holding the trial *in camera* following the declaration that Ríos Montt was mentally unfit, the trial did not resume in 2015. The trial finally resumed behind closed doors on March 28, 2016. In June 2016, the court decided that the trial would be suspended indefinitely.[91]

In October 2014, the trial of Pedro Garcia Arredondo, former head of the National Police Special Investigation Unit "Command Six," began.[92] Garcia Arredondo is charged with murder, attempted murder and crimes against humanity for the killing of 37 people during a siege on the Spanish Embassy compound in Guatemala City in January 1980 carried out by Guatemalan security forces, and the killing of two protesters at the funeral for those killed in the siege.[93] In January 2015, Garcia Arredondo was found guilty of murder and crimes against humanity.[94]

Two other high-profile cases progressed in 2015. The first case involved Lieutenant Colonel Esteelmer Reyes Girón, former commander of Sepur Zarco military base, and former military commissioner Heriberto Valdez Asig. In June 2015, parties presented evidence about charges of mass sexual violence and slavery on Sepur Zarco military base from 1982–1988.[95]

On February 1, 2016, the trial opened. On February 23, 2016, the accused were convicted of sexual violence, domestic and sexual slavery against 15 Maya Q'eqchi' women, several enforced disappearances and homicides. This was the first case of crimes against humanity with a specific focus on sexual violence and sexual slavery to be tried in a Guatemalan court. In addition to the legal significance of the trial and convictions in this case, the deliberate and systematic use of sexual violence as a means of dominating, degrading and destroying individuals, families and communities in the Guatemalan civil war was brought to light, substantiated and made part of the public record.[96]

The second case concerned atrocities perpetrated at Military Zone 21 (MZ21), also known as CREOMPAZ. Over 550 bodies have been exhumed in CREOMPAZ, which was a central military and intelligence base for counterinsurgency operations.[97] In 2015, investigations into this case continued. In January 2016, 14 military officers were arrested. Eight of those arrested have been charged with multiple counts of enforced disappearance, torture, sexual violence, and extra-judicial execution carried out between 1981 and 1987.[98] Among the accused are Manuel Benedicto Lucas García, head of the General High Command of the Guatemalan Army during the military regime led by his brother, Fernando Romeo Lucas García (1978–82). Several appeals and objections have been filed and trial proceedings have been delayed until these are resolved. A major concern in this case, as in others before the High Risk court, has been serious threats to the safety and independence of prosecutors and justices. Some of these challenges have been brought to the fore by justices in an effort to secure the judicial independence necessary for the integrity of the legal process. These efforts have been partially addressed by the Constitutional Court of Guatemala, as well as heard by the Inter-American Commission on Human Rights.[99]

Investigations, the development of cases, and associated trials connected to the 36-year civil war continued in a climate of political crisis in Guatemala. In 2015, the question of renewing the mandate of the International Commission against Impunity in Guatemala (CICIG), which is backed by the UN, arose. On April 23, 2015, President Otto Pérez Molina announced that he would request the UN Secretary-General to renew CICIG's mandate for another two years despite his initial reluctance to do so.[100] The CICIG mandate was renewed by the UN in June 2015. Contemporaneous with these developments, 17 officials were arrested and accused of involvement in widespread corruption. Public protests resulted, continuing for several months and culminating in the resignation of the President and Vice-President, both of whom await trial on corruption charges. Following these resignations, the scheduled presidential elections were conducted in September 2015.

Box 15.11 **Kenya**	
Conflict:	Post-election violence (2007–2008)
Charges:	Crimes against humanity
Accused:	Uhuru Muigai Kenyatta; William Samoei Ruto; Joshua Arap Sang; Francis Kirimi Muthaura; Mohammed Hussein Ali; Walter Osapiri Barasa
Prosecuting Authority:	International Criminal Court (ICC)
Location:	The Hague, Netherlands
Legal Activity during 2015:	Charges against Kenyatta withdrawn; Ruto and Sang trial continued, but the case was vacated in 2016; arrest warrant for Barasa remains active

The 2007 presidential elections in Kenya were followed by a wave of violence, precipitated in part by disputed results and largely involving members of rival political parties, with a significant ethnic dimension. In the violence, an estimated 1,300 people were killed.

In 2010, the ICC Prosecutor initiated an investigation into the situation based on authority granted under Article 15 of the Rome Statute, which allows such investigation even if a case was not referred to the ICC by a State government or the United Nations Security Council. Following these preliminary investigations, the Prosecutor requested that summonses to appear be issued for five individuals, including Uhuru Mugai Kenyatta, the President of Kenya; William Ruto, Deputy President of Kenya; and Joshua Arap Sang, Head of Operations at Kass FM in Nairobi, Kenya. In 2012, charges of multiple counts of crimes against humanity were confirmed against Kenyatta, Ruto and Sang, but charges against one individual (Ali) were not confirmed and those against another individual (Muthaura) were eventually withdrawn.[101] In 2013, a new case was initiated, against Walter Osapiri Barasa, charging him with offences against the administration of justice for allegedly attempting to influence ICC witnesses. In December 2014, following two vacated attempts to start the trial of Uhuru Kenyatta, all charges were withdrawn by the Prosecutor.[102]

In 2015, the case against Ruto and Sang progressed with the prosecution concluding its presentation of evidence in September. After this, however, the trial stalled. In February 2016, the trial chamber decided to vacate the case altogether. In a statement issued by the Prosecutor, she asserts that Kenya had exhibited a

> relentless campaign to identify individuals who could serve as Prosecution witnesses in this case and ensure that they would not testify. This project of intimidation preceded the start of our investigation in Kenya, intensified in the weeks leading up to the beginning of the trial, and continued throughout the life of the case. As a result, potential witnesses told us they were too afraid to commit to testifying against the Accused. Others, who initially gave us accounts of what they saw during the post-election period, subsequently recanted their evidence, and declined to continue cooperating with the Court.

In her statement, she goes on to describe the ways in which a climate of fear was created by vilifying prosecution witnesses at public rallies and in social media.[103] Meanwhile, an arrest warrant remains active for Barasa, who remains at large.[104]

Box 15.12 Libya	
Conflict:	Repression by Libyan forces against Libyan population and protesters (2011)
Charges:	Crimes against humanity
Accused:	Saif Al-Islam Gaddafi
Prosecuting Authority:	International Criminal Court (ICC)
Location:	The Hague, Netherlands
Legal Activity during 2015:	Efforts to secure cooperation of the Libyan government in the apprehension and surrender of Saif Al-Islam Gaddafi continued

In 2011, following uprisings in Tunisia and Egypt, similar movements emerged in Libya to protest the regime of Muammar Gaddafi. In February 2011, the security apparatus of the Libyan government is alleged to have targeted several civilian demonstrators, resulting in deaths, detentions, and displacement. Over the subsequent six months, the situation in Libya rapidly deteriorated, as a result of the government's actions plunging the country into a civil war. Benefiting from a NATO enforced no-fly zone, Libyan rebel groups succeeded in overtaking the Gaddafi regime in Tripoli and formed an interim National Transitional Council government, which was internationally recognized, in August 2011.

Meanwhile, in early 2011, prior to the fall of the Gaddafi regime, the United Nation's Security Council adopted Resolution 1970, which referred the Libyan situation to the ICC Prosecutor. Following preliminary investigations, the Prosecutor requested arrest warrants for Muammar Gaddafi; Saif Al-Islam Gaddafi, honorary chairman of the Gaddafi International Charity and Development Foundation and *de facto* Prime Minister; and Abdullah Al-Senussi, Colonel in the Libyan Armed Forces and Head of Military Intelligence. The charges against these three individuals included multiple counts of crimes against humanity. Muammar Gaddafi was killed by rebel fighters in October 2011. Saif Gaddafi and Al-Senussi were captured in November 2011.

In May 2014, the ICC determined that Libyan authorities would not be able to carry out the requisite proceedings in regards to the charges against Saif Al-Islam Gaddafi and confirmed that his case was therefore admissible.[105] The ICC also ruled that the Government of Libya was in non-compliance due to the refusal to surrender Saif Gaddafi to ICC custody.[106] In July 2014, the Appeals Chamber of the ICC declared Al-Senussi's case inadmissible before the ICC, accepting he was being subjected to competent proceedings in Libya for the actions that gave rise to the charges by the ICC.[107]

In 2015, the Office of the Prosecutor (OTP) maintained its request for cooperation from the Government of National Accord in the arrest and surrender of Saif Al-Islam Gaddafi. The Libyan government has said that it does not have access to Al-Islam Gaddafi, due to his detention by a Libyan militia faction.[108] In July 2015, Al-Senussi was convicted and sentenced to death by the Tripoli Court of Assize. The decision is being appealed. The OTP continues to monitor the situation in Libya and compile information on the ongoing commission of human rights violations by various factions in the conflict.[109]

Justice for Conflict Violations during 2015

Box 15.13 Mali

Conflict:	Armed conflict and coup d'état by Islamist groups (2012–2013)
Charges:	War crimes; destruction of historic and religious monuments
Accused:	Ahmad Al Faqi Al Mahdi
Prosecuting Authority:	International Criminal Court (ICC)
Location:	The Hague, Netherlands
Legal Activity during 2015:	Arrest warrant issued; suspect arrested and transferred to ICC; verdict and sentencing in 2016

In January 2012, the Malian armed forces and several non-state armed groups, including the *Mouvement National de Libération d'l'Azawad* (MNLA), al-Qaeda in the Islamic Maghreb (AQIM), *Ansar Dine*, and the *Mouvement pour l'Unicité, et le Jihad en Afrique de l'Ouest* (MUJAO), clashed over control of the northern territories of Mali. In March 2012, just before the presidential election, the government of President Touré fell in a military coup d'état led by Amadou Haya Sanogo. In April 2012, Malian forces were pushed out of the northern region by rebel groups. The ensuing period was characterized by fighting among various armed actors to establish territorial control. Concurrently, the Economic Community of West African States (ECOWAS), the African Union (AU) and the United Nations (UN) sought to establish a transitional government, create a new timeline for elections, and discuss plans for an intervention force to assist the government in quelling the developing violence in northern Mali. In May 2012, the government approached the ICC Prosecutor to request an investigation into the situation in the regions of Kidal, Gao and Timbuktu, which were under the control of rebel groups. In July 2012, the UN Security Council adopted resolution 2056, expressing concern for the destruction of religious and historic cultural monuments, acts that constitute war crimes. In that period, ECOWAS also requested that the ICC Prosecutor investigate war crimes allegations.[110]

In 2015, the Office of the Prosecutor requested that the ICC issue an arrest warrant for Ahmad Al Faqi Al Mahdi, who was allegedly a member of *Ansar Dine* and headed the "Hisbah" – a body created to uphold "public morals and prevent vice" – during the occupation of Timbuktu. He is charged with directing the destruction of historic and religious monuments, including nine mausoleums and one mosque in Timbuktu, between about June 30, 2012 and July 10, 2012.[111] In September 2015, Al Mahdi was surrendered to ICC custody in The Hague, Netherlands, by the government of Niger. Though the destruction of cultural heritage and artifacts was recognized as a war crime and an act of genocide, this is the first indictment and trial in an international war crimes court for acts of cultural destruction. Charges were confirmed in this case in March 2016. Al Mahdi's trial was held in August 2016. He pled guilty to the charges,[112] then was sentenced to a nine-year prison term.[113]

Box 15.14 Nepal

Conflict:	Civil war (1996–2006)
Charges:	War crimes; crimes against humanity, genocide
Accused:	Pending investigation
Prosecuting Authority:	National courts in Nepal and the United Kingdom
Location:	Nepal; United Kingdom
Legal Activity during 2015:	Creation of commissions to investigate

During 1996–2006, an armed conflict between the Communist Party of Nepal-Maoist (CPN-M) People's Liberation Army (PLA) and the armed forces of Nepal claimed approximately 13,000 lives and approximately 1,300 persons were disappeared. In 2008, a Comprehensive Peace Agreement was reached.

In 2014, the Commission on Investigation into Disappeared Persons, Truth and Reconciliation Act (CoID-TR Act) established the Truth and Reconciliation Commission (TRC) and a Commission of Inquiry on the Disappearances (CoID). The legislation drew criticism from the United Nations High Commissioner for Human Rights for being inconsistent with international legal standards.[114] One of the key provisions of concern pertains to the power of the Commissions to recommend amnesty for grave violations. This provision was also challenged domestically by a legal action brought on behalf of victims of the conflict.

In February 2015, the Supreme Court of Nepal ruled that the war crimes commission could not grant amnesties to government forces or Maoist rebels.[115] Despite the Court's judgment that the Act's amnesty provisions violated the country's constitution, efforts to retain this provision continue in the form of a "nine-point deal" between the two key political parties that comprise the Communist Party of Nepal-Unified Marxist Leninist (CPN-UML) coalition government of Prime Minister K.P. Sharma Oli.[116] The legislature has moved forward with the law, which still contains a provision for amnesty.[117] While there has been movement towards establishing the mechanisms that would potentially enable the pursuit of prosecutions for grave crimes committed during the course of the conflict, the persistent efforts to institute amnesty and the current tension between the divergent positions taken by the Supreme Court and the ruling coalition and legislature present concerns for whether and how the justice process will unfold.

Also in 2015, the first trial of a Nepalese army officer for torture allegedly committed during the civil war was prosecuted on the basis of universal jurisdiction in the United Kingdom. The defendant, Colonel Kumar Lama, was charged with torturing two detainees at an army barracks under his command in 2005. He was acquitted of all charges in September 2016.[118]

Box 15.15 Romania	
Conflict:	Communist-era repression (1948–1989) and post-transition violence
Charges:	Crimes against humanity
Accused:	Alexandru Visinescu; Ion Iliescu; Tudor Postelnicu; George Homosteanu; Marian Parvulescu; Vasile Hodis
Prosecuting Authority:	National courts of Romania
Location:	Romania
Legal Activity during 2015:	Investigation and trials ongoing

During 1948–1989, Romania was under communist rule. Following the overthrow of the regime of Nicolae Ceauşescu in 1989, Romania ushered in a new government under the leadership of Ion Iliescu. In 2005, the Investigation of Communist Crimes and Memory of the Romanian Exile (ICCMER) was formed, under the auspices of the Romanian government. This body has pursued the investigation of and accountability for communist-era crimes.[119] In 2014, the first trial of a communist-era prison official charged with crimes against humanity began. Alexandru Visinescu, the prison commander of Râmnicu Sărat Prison from 1956–1963, was charged with crimes against humanity for the torture, abuse and deaths of political prisoners in the prison under his command. In 2015, he was convicted and sentenced to 20 years in prison.[120] This trial has set a precedent for future trials that are expected to come from ongoing investigations of communist-era officials and crimes committed during that repressive period. Râmnicu Sărat Prison has now been converted into a site of memory.[121]

The impetus for pursuing prosecutions for grave crimes was enhanced by the 2014 judgment of the European Court of Human Rights (ECHR) faulting Romania for its failure to prosecute human rights violations for injuries caused by a violent crackdown on anti-government protests in 1990, when Ion Iliescu was President.[122] In 2015, Iliescu was formally charged with the violent suppression of anti-government protests in which six persons reportedly died and hundreds injured. He is charged with the deaths of three people and injury to four.[123]

In 2014–15, an investigation into the death of Gheorghe Ursu in 1985, while in detention by the Secret police, progressed. This investigation led to criminal charges against four high-ranking security officials: Tudor Postelnicu, who headed the Securitate from 1978 to 1987, former Interior Minister George Homosteanu, and retired Securitate secret police officers Marian Parvulescu and Vasile Hodis. Their trial opened in August 2016. The decision to prosecute, issued by the Prosecutor's Office in the High Court of Cassation and Justice, was long-awaited and pursued by Ursu's kin and the ICCMER. This trial constitutes the second of high-ranking political and security officials in the Ceauşescu regime.[124]

Box 15.16 Rwanda	
Conflict:	Genocide in Rwanda (1994)
Charges:	Genocide; crimes against humanity
Accused:	Multiple across locations
Prosecuting Authorities:	International Criminal Tribunal for Rwanda (ICTR); national courts of Rwanda; foreign country national courts
Locations:	Rwanda; Tanzania; Belgium; Canada; France; Germany; Norway; Sweden
Legal Activity during 2015:	Multiple trials and appeals ongoing

During the 1994 genocide in Rwanda, an estimated 500,000–800,000 people were killed, with a significant segment of the population involved in the perpetration of the violence. Criminal prosecutions related to these atrocities have gone through several stages over the past 20 years and still continue.

Parallel processes in the ICTR, located in Tanzania, and in Rwandan national courts began in 1994. The ICTR was established by the United Nations to try individuals responsible for the most serious offenses, including genocide, war crimes and crimes against humanity. Many of those indicted by the ICTR had fled Rwanda when the Rwandan Patriotric Front defeated the Rwandan army and overtook the government. Among these suspects were those thought to have planned and instigated the genocide, including key figures such as the former Prime Minister Jean Kambanda, former Army Chief of Staff General Augustin Bizimungu and former Ministry of Defence Chief of Staff Colonel Bagosora.[125] Within Rwanda, individuals accused of involvement in the mass killings were subject to arrest and prosecution within the national justice system. At one point early in this process, the population of those incarcerated pending trial on genocide charges swelled to 130,000.

Recognizing the infeasibility of trying in national courts all those suspected of having participated in the genocide, the Rwandan government established the *gacaca* system of local tribunals in 2000. This system was tasked with expediting the handling of the bulk of those incarcerated for lower-order offenses. More than 40,000 panels of *inyangamugayo* convened local hearings, through which they gathered information regarding the acts that occurred and rendered judgments in individual cases in a process that combined aspects of a court, alternative dispute resolution, and a truth-seeking process. In just the first five years of the *gacaca* process, starting with the 2002 piloting of the tribunals, the information gathered generated approximately one million new case files. In 2012, as the *gacaca* process came to a close, the government reported that nearly two million cases were adjudicated via this system.[126]

Those alleged to have planned and instigated the genocide continued to be prosecuted by conventional courts. As of 2014, approximately 10,000 individuals had been tried for genocide in the national court system of Rwanda.[127] During 2014, genocide prosecutions continued in Rwanda, including such cases as that of Charles Bandora, who was the first genocide suspect to be extradited to Rwanda from a European country (Norway). His trial began in Kigali in September 2014. In May 2015, he was convicted of conspiracy, genocide and murders as crimes against humanity.[128] A number of other investigations, indictments, arrest and extradition requests were actively pursued by the Rwandan government in 2015.[129] In 2016, the United States (US) extradited Leopold Munyakazi, a Rwandan living in the US, to Rwanda to stand trial on charges relating to his alleged part in the commission of genocide and crimes against humanity. This is the fourth extradition from the US, which reportedly received 21 arrest warrants for genocide suspects in the US. The Rwandan government continues to pursue suspects globally and has issued a reported 600 warrants worldwide, as of September 2016.[130]

As of 2015, the ICTR had indicted 93 individuals of genocide and other serious violations of international humanitarian law. Of these, 61 individuals were convicted and sentenced, 14 were acquitted, 10 were referred to national jurisdictions for trial, and three fugitives had been referred to the Mechanism for International Criminal Tribunals (MICT).[131] During 2014, the ICTR was in the process of transferring the remaining cases to the Rwandan government, completing the appeals processes with only one remaining appeals judgment expected in 2015, and setting up the MICT, which will process matters relating to outstanding arrest warrants and administrative needs relating to the work of the ICTR once its trial and appeals chambers are closed.[132] The ICTR was officially closed on December 31, 2015.

In addition to prosecutions by the national judicial system of Rwanda and the ICTR, a number of cases have been brought on the basis of universal jurisdiction against accused individuals who reside outside of Rwanda. In 2015, such cases were active in Belgium, Canada, France, Germany, Norway and Sweden.[133]

Box 15.17 Sudan	
Conflict:	Armed insurgency against Sudanese Government (2002–present)
Charges:	War crimes; crimes against humanity; genocide
Accused:	Ahmad Muhammad Harun ("Ahmad Harun"); Ali Muhammad Ali Abd-Al-Rahman ("Ali Kushayb"); Omar Hassan Ahmad Al-Bashir; Bahar Idriss Abu Garda; Abdallah Banda Abakaer Nourain; Abdel Raheem Muhammad Hussein
Prosecuting Authority:	International Criminal Court (ICC)
Location:	The Hague, Netherlands
Legal Activity during 2015:	Arrest warrants are active and open; ICC Pre-Trial Chamber found that the Democratic Republic of the Congo (DRC) failed to cooperate with the Court in the execution of the arrest warrant for Al Bashir while he was in their territory and the matter was referred to the United Nations Security Council; in 2016, ICC Pre-Trial Chamber found Uganda and Djibouti to be in non-compliance as well

Following a protracted armed conflict between the north and south of Sudan dating back to the 1980s, an armed insurgency led by the Sudan Liberation Movement/Army (SLM/A) and the Justice Equality Movement (JEM) against the Sudanese government began in 2002, contemporaneous with the signing of a Comprehensive Peace Agreement. This insurgency was met with force by the Sudanese government, which engaged local groups in the form of the Popular Defense Force (PDF) and *Janjaweed* militias to fight the rebels. Estimates of the casualties resulting from the conflict are in the vicinity of 400,000 killed and 2.5 million displaced persons.

In 2005, the United Nations Security Council, acting under Chapter VII of the Charter of the United Nations, adopted Resolution 1593, which referred the situation in Darfur to the Prosecutor of the ICC. Following preliminary investigations, the ICC Prosecutor requested warrants of arrest for seven individuals accused of bearing criminal responsibility for war crimes and crimes against humanity and Genocide in Darfur. These indictments were particularly controversial, as they called for the arrest of the sitting head of state, Omar al-Bashir,[134] along with senior members of his government, including Ahmad Harun, Minister of State for the Interior of the Government of Sudan and Minister of State for Humanitarian Affairs,[135] and Abdel Raheem Muhammed Hussein, Current Minister of National Defence and former Minister of the Interior and former Sudanese President's Special Representative in Darfur.[136] In addition, charges of war crimes and crimes against humanity were brought against leaders of militarized groups, including Ali Muhammad Ali Abd-Al-Rahman ("Ali Kushayb"), leader of the *Janjaweed* militia,[137] Abdallah Banda Abakaer Nourain, Commander-in-Chief of JEM, who is now thought to be deceased,[138] and Bahar Idriss Abu Garda, Chairman and General Coordinator of Military Operations of the United Resistance Front. Of those for whom arrest warrants were issued, only Garda appeared before the ICC, whereupon the Pre-Trial Chamber did not confirm the Prosecutor's charges.[139]

As of 2014, the arrest warrants for President al-Bashir, his ministers and Rahman remained open, with no movement on the stalemate between the government of the Sudan and the ICC apparent in this matter. In 2014, Pre-Trial Chamber II of the ICC found that the DRC had failed to cooperate in the arrest and surrender of President al-Bashir during a February 2014 visit.[140] The Pre-Trial Chamber referred the matter to the United Nations Security Council (UNSC). Subsequently, in March 2015, the ICC Pre-Trial Chamber II issued a finding that the government of Sudan had failed to cooperate with the ICC in its request to arrest President al-Bashir and surrender him to the Court and referring the matter to the UNSC.[141] The ICC Prosecutor's report submitted in December 2015 documented al-Bashir's travel to multiple countries in 2015, including Algeria, China, Ethiopia, India, Mauritania, Pakistan, Saudi Arabia, South Africa, South Sudan and the United Arab Emirates. According to the OTP report, none of these countries acted to prevent al-Bashir from entering or exiting their territory or to cooperate with the ICC in accordance with the UNSC Resolution. The OTP also reported that in October 2015, eight victims who had "participatory rights" withdrew from the case.[142] In 2016, the Pre-Trial Chamber found Uganda and Djibouti to be in non-compliance with the request to arrest and surrender al-Bashir.

Though the States where al-Bashir travelled have certain obligations to cooperate based on the UN Security Council Resolution 1593, many of them are not signatories of the Rome Statute. In contrast, South Africa is a signatory and serves as an important example of the tensions between a state's obligation to cooperate with the ICC and the political and legal norms with respect to immunity for sitting heads of state. In June 2015, al-Bashir traveled to South Africa, where he attended an African Union meeting. Despite South Africa's obligations as a member-state to cooperate with the ICC in regards to the request to arrest and surrender al-Bashir, the South African government did not do so, instead choosing to allow him to leave the country unimpeded.[143] Not only did this decision constitute a blow to the ongoing efforts to arrest and try al-Bashir a decade after the original indictments were issued against him and the other accused, it was seemingly in contravention of South Africa's legal obligations, both domestic and international. The decision gave rise to a legal challenge, brought by the Southern African Litigation Centre (SALC) against the South African Government in South African courts. The Gauteng Division of the High Court, Pretoria, concluded that not taking steps to arrest and detain al-Bashir, for surrender to the ICC, was inconsistent with South Africa's obligations in terms of the Rome Statute and the South African Implementation of the Rome Statute of the International Criminal Court Act 27 of 2002, and therefore unlawful.[144] This decision was then reviewed by the Supreme Court of Appeals which confirmed, in March 2016, that although head-of-state immunity continued to be a norm supported by customary international law, by signing the Rome Statute and incorporating the terms of the Statute into domestic South African law in the form of the Implementation of the Rome Statute of the International Criminal Court Act 27 of 2002 passed by Parliament, such immunity was specifically removed in the case of international crimes. Thus, the Supreme Court of Appeal dismissed the appeal and allowed the High Court's order to stand.[145] In 2016, al-Bashir traveled to Mauritania, Morocco, Ethiopia and Chad.[146] The arrest warrants for the accused remain active; the investigation in the case is ongoing. In October 2016, South Africa announced its intention to withdraw from the Rome Statute and the ICC, becoming the second country – after Burundi – to do so.

Box 15.18 Uganda	
Conflict:	Armed conflict between Lord's Resistance Army (LRA) and the Ugandan Government (1987–present)
Charges:	War crimes; crimes against humanity
Accused:	Joseph Kony; Vincent Otti; Okot Odhiambo; Raska Lukwiya; Dominic Ongwen
Prosecuting Authority:	International Criminal Court (ICC)
Location:	The Hague, Netherlands
Legal Activity during 2015:	Ongwen arrested and surrendered to ICC, charges confirmed, trial preparations underway; arrest warrants for Kony and Otti remain active

The armed rebellion by the Lord's Resistance Army (LRA) against the Ugandan government began in 1987 and is estimated to have caused close to 100,000 deaths, involved nearly 100,000 abductions – nearly half of children – across four countries, and displaced approximately 1.7 million people. The LRA is especially notorious for the abduction of children, who have been used for labor, sex and war fighting. The protracted length and nature of this conflict have taken a profound humanitarian toll. Its resolution and the progress towards recovery are greatly complicated by the coerced involvement in the hostilities of a significant share of the population in northern Uganda.

In 2003, Ugandan President Yoweri Musuveni referred the actions of the LRA to the ICC. In 2005, the ICC Office of the Prosecutor issued indictments against five senior figures of the LRA for alleged war crimes and crimes against humanity. Arrest warrants were subsequently issued against Joseph Kony, LRA Commander-in-Chief; Vincent Otti, Vice-Chairman and Second-in-Command; Okot Odiambo, LRA Army Commander;[147] Raska Lukwiya, LRA Army Commander;[148] and Dominic Ongwen, Commander of the LRA's Sinia Brigade.[149] In 2011, the United States deployed approximately 100 special forces troops to aid Uganda and the African Union in the search for LRA commanders, who have reportedly moved into areas of the Sudan, the DRC and the CAR. In 2013, the United States offered a monetary reward for information leading to the accused. The US military procured additional air support for the search in 2014.

Of the accused, only Dominic Ongwen has been arrested, surrendering to US troops in the CAR in January 2015 and subsequently remanded to ICC custody. In February 2015, Ongwen's case was severed from the other accused who remain at large. The charges against Ongwen, which comprise a range of crimes against humanity and war crimes, including rape, sexual slavery, attacks upon a civilian population and the conscription and use of children in active hostilities, were confirmed in March 2016. His trial is scheduled to begin in December 2016 in The Hague.[150]

Kony and Otti remain at large and the search for them continues.

Other Major ICC Activity

Full Investigations

In addition to the cases profiled above, the ICC Office of the Prosecutor (OTP) engaged in full investigations about two countries during 2015. Following preliminary investigations, the Office of the Prosecutor may seek authorization from the Court to pursue a full investigation if, based on the result of preliminary examinations, the Court determines that the evidence collected is sufficient to support a "reasonable basis to believe that a crime within the jurisdiction of the Court has been or is being committed" and it is therefore reasonable to proceed with a full investigation.[151]

Central African Republic II: After a coup d'état through which Michel Djotodia, leader of the Seleka group, ousted President François Bozizé, Seleka forces continued to pursue an offensive against populations in the north of the country. The targeted areas were associated with support for Bozizé. In response to the armed attacks of Seleka, "anti-Balaka" groups emerged to resist the assaults. Though Djotodia ostensibly disbanded Seleka, its fighters have reportedly continued an armed campaign. In December 2013, as the African Union was deploying its peacekeeping mission with support of French troops, anti-balaka forces attacked Seleka's position in Bangui. In the ensuing conflict, anti-balaka and Seleka forces reportedly targeted geographic areas with large Muslim populations, in a campaign of ethnic cleansing. In May 2014, CAR authorities referred the situation to the ICC Prosecutor, who has determined that there is reasonable basis to believe that both Seleka and anti-balaka forces committed crimes against humanity and war crimes. Accordingly, the Prosecutor's second investigation into the CAR situation was undertaken and is ongoing.[152]

Georgia: This examination focuses on alleged war crimes and crimes against humanity perpetrated during the armed conflict between South Ossetia and Georgia in 2008. Allegations under investigation include forcible transfer of ethnic Georgians, attacks on Georgian civilians by South Ossetian forces, and an attack on Russian peacekeepers. In October 2015, the OTP requested authorization from the pre-trial chamber to launch an investigation with respect to war crimes and crimes against humanity allegedly committed in South Ossetia between July 1 and October 10, 2008.[153]

Preliminary Examinations Initiated or Continued

The ICC Office of the Prosecutor engaged in "preliminary" investigations about nine countries during 2015. Preliminary examinations focus on whether the allegations presented constitute crimes within the jurisdiction of the ICC, such as war crimes, crimes against humanity or genocide; the matter is admissible; and the interests of justice would be served by pursuing further investigation and prosecution of any cases that might arise.[154]

Afghanistan: This examination focuses on alleged war crimes and crimes against humanity committed from 2003–2015 by members of three categories of armed actors: anti-government groups (*Taliban* and their affiliates), Afghan government forces, and members of international forces. Alleged violations include attacks against civilians, including women, children, and aid workers, torture of detainees, and attacks on humanitarian facilities, such as the October 2015 bombing that struck the *Médecins sans Frontières* hospital in Kunduz.

Burundi: This examination, formally opened in April 2016, focuses on alleged crimes against humanity committed since the onset of an escalating political crisis, which was precipitated in April 2015 by the incumbent President's decision to run for a third term of office, in contravention of the Constitution. President Nkurunziza, head of the Council for the Defence of Democracy – Forces for the Defence of Democracy (CNDD-FDD), was re-elected in July 2015. Since April 2015, a reported 430 people have been killed and over 230,000 displaced and approximately 3,400 persons have been arrested. Reported crimes being examined include killing, imprisonment, torture, rape, and other forms of sexual violence, as well as cases of forced disappearances.[155] In October 2016, the Burundian legislature voted to withdraw from the Rome Statute, which it signed in 2004, and the ICC. It is the first country to vote domestically to withdraw from the treaty establishing the ICC. The ICC has urged Burundi to reconsider this choice.[156]

Colombia: This examination focuses on alleged crimes against humanity and war crimes perpetrated by the government and paramilitary groups since 2002 in the context of a 50-year armed conflict. Crimes under investigation include murder, abduction, forced displacement, torture, sexual violence, conscription of children, and assaults on civilian populations. In June 2015, the Government of Colombia and the Armed Revolutionary Forces of Colombia – Popular Army (FARC-EP) agreed to the creation of a Commission for the Clarification of the Truth, Coexistence and Non-repetition. In September 2015, the Government of Colombia and FARC-EP announced the "New Agreement" that would establish a "Special Jurisdiction for Peace," a discrete judicial mechanism to prosecute which will have jurisdiction over war crimes, crimes against humanity and genocide. The review and evaluation of the provisions agreed upon form part of the OTP's preliminary examination.[157]

Gabon: This examination, opened in September 2016 after the OTP received a referral from the government of Gabon, focuses on alleged crimes perpetrated in the context of violence committed following disputes over the August

2016 presidential election outcome, in which Ali Bongo was re-elected.[158] Several people have been killed in post-election clashes between civilians and security forces; approximately 1,000 people have reportedly been arrested.[159]

Guinea: This examination focuses on alleged crimes against humanity during a violent military action against a gathering of the political opposition in September 2009 at Conakry Stadium. Allegations under investigation include the killing of nearly 160 protesters, sexual violence and rape, disappearances, and torture of detainees. In 2015, the OTP continued to monitor the progress of the three-judge panel created by the Government of Guinea to investigate and prosecute those criminally responsible for the 2009 events. The Panel has so far indicted several high-ranking officials, including the former president and vice-president.[160]

Iraq/United Kingdom: This examination focuses on alleged war crimes, including mistreatment, torture and killings of Iraqi detainees and civilians by United Kingdom (UK) officials in Iraq from 2003–2008. The examination into these allegations was initiated on January 10, 2014 by the European Center for Constitutional and Human Rights (ECCHR) and Public Interest Lawyers (PIL), who submitted a communication alleging the responsibility of UK officials for war crimes involving systematic detainee abuse in Iraq. Iraq is not a State Party to the Rome Statute. Since the UK has ratified the Statute, however, the ICC has jurisdiction over war crimes and crimes against humanity committed in the UK and/or by nationals of the UK. In 2015, the UK responded to the allegations under ICC investigation, which is ongoing.[161]

Nigeria: This examination focuses on alleged crimes against humanity and war crimes perpetrated in the armed conflict between Boko Haram and security forces of the Nigerian government. Allegations under investigation include armed attacks against civilians, abductions of women and girls, sexual violence and gender-based abuses, forcing women and children to carry out deadly attacks by Boko Haram, and torture and mass civilian executions by the Nigerian military. In 2015, examination of the Nigerian situation continued. Thus far, the OTP has identified at least eight potential cases: six pertain to conduct by Boko Haram and two relate to the conduct of the Nigerian security forces.[162]

Palestine: This examination focuses on allegations of war crimes committed by all sides, including Palestinian armed groups and the Israeli Defense Force (IDF) during the Israel–Gaza conflict between July 7 and August 26, 2014. The OTP is also looking at alleged settlement-related violations in the West Bank and East Jerusalem. The pathway for investigations into this situation was opened after Palestine was granted Observer State status by the United Nations General Assembly in 2014. In January 2015, Palestine acceded to the Rome Statute, thereby accepting the jurisdiction of the ICC.[163]

Ukraine: This examination focuses on alleged injury and killing of protestors, disappearances and torture during the Maidan protest events of 2013–2014. In 2015, the OTP extended the timeframe of the examination to include events that occurred through September 2015. These events include the armed conflict within Ukraine following the change of government in 2014, annexation of Crimea into the Russian Federation, and hostilities in Eastern Ukraine between government forces and separatist groups in Donbas.[164]

Preliminary Examinations Closed

In 2015, the ICC also closed one preliminary examination. The Office of the Prosecutor determined that there is not a basis to seek authorization to proceed with further investigation in the following situation.[165]

Honduras: This examination focuses on alleged crimes against humanity following the 2009 coup d'état removing President José Manuel Zelaya from office. In 2015, the OTP determined that while serious violations have been perpetrated, the information available does not support the conclusion that the crimes within the jurisdiction of the ICC have occurred in this situation, therefore leaving no reasonable basis to proceed with the investigation, prompting the examination to be closed.[166]

Universal Jurisdiction Cases

Below is a list of countries where legal activity occurred in 2015 to pursue or undertake prosecutions of non-nationals for violations committed outside the territory of the national prosecuting authority and involving victims who are not nationals of that country. The basis for bringing these legal actions is the concept of universal jurisdiction for *jus cogens* violations, such as crimes against humanity, war crimes, and genocide. The countries where the legal actions occurred are listed first, followed in parentheses by the countries whose conflicts were the subject of such legal activity. Of note, investigations pertaining to detainee treatment in United States facilities were active in three countries during 2015.[167]

Argentina (Paraguay, Spain)
Belgium (Liberia, Rwanda, Sierra Leone)
Chile (Venezuela)
Finland (Iraq)

France (Algeria, Congo, Libya, Rwanda, Syria, United States [Guantanamo])
Germany (DRC, Rwanda, Syria, United States [various detention facilities])
Netherlands (Afghanistan)
Norway (Rwanda)
Senegal (Chad, DRC)
South Africa (Madagascar, Zimbabwe)
Spain (China, DRC, El Salvador, Guatemala, Iraq, Morocco, Nigeria, United States [Guantanamo])
Sweden (Rwanda)
Switzerland (Bahrain, Guatemala, Liberia)
United Kingdom (Nepal)
United States (Somalia)[168]

Notes

1 Additional cases have been pursued for civil violations, through courts and human rights commissions. These cases are outside the scope of this chapter.

2 This chapter focuses on cases in which violations of international criminal conventions are alleged. Each of these legal categories of crimes incorporates numerous types of possible violations. Particular situations and cases often involve allegations of multiple types of violations and may include specific charges, such as rape, enslavement, deportation, killing, enforced disappearances, kidnapping, use of children as combatants, and so forth. For brevity, the charges referred to in these profiles designate the broad categories of crimes. When possible, references to full case summaries are made where specific charges are completely and precisely elaborated.

3 Anupma Kulkarni, "Criminal Justice for Conflict-Related Violations: Developments during 2014," in David Backer, Ravi Bhavnani and Paul Huth (eds) *Peace and Conflict 2016*, New York: Routledge, 2016.

4 "Bulgaria, Romania Join Estonian Initiative to Investigate Crimes of Communism", *The Baltic Times* (August 12, 2015). Led by Estonia, to date Latvia, Lithuania, Poland, the Czech Republic, Slovakia, Hungary, Ukraine and Georgia have joined the initiative. http://www.baltictimes.com/bulgaria__romania_join_estonian_initiative_to_investigate_crimes_of_communism/#.

5 See Reconciliation of European Histories, https://eureconciliation.eu/about/.

6 Richard J. Goldstone Hon., "Prosecuting Rape as a War Crime," 34 *Case W. Res. J. Int'l L.* 277 (2002).

7 Valerie Oosterveld, "The Gender Jurisprudence of the Special Court for Sierra Leone: Progress in the Revolutionary United Front Judgments," *Cornell Int'l L.J.* 49 (2011): 49–74.

8 Associated Press, "Burundi Lawmakers Vote to Withdraw from ICC; Would Be 1st," *The New York Times* (October 12, 2016).

9 Sewell Chan and Marlise Simmons, "South Africa to Withdraw from International Criminal Court," *The New York Times* (October 21, 2016).

10 Al Jazeera, "Gambia Withdraws from International Criminal Court" (October 25, 2016), http://www.aljazeera.com/news/2016/10/gambia-withdraws-international-criminal-court-161026041436188.html.

11 Shaun Walker and Owen Bowcott, "Russia Withdraws Signature from International Court Statute," *The Guardian* (November 16, 2016).

12 OTP, "Report on Preliminary Examination Activities 2016" (November 14, 2016), p. 35.

13 TRIAL, http://www.trial-ch.org/en/resources/trial-watch/trial-watch/profiles/profile/844/action/show/controller/Profile/tab/context.html.

14 See National Security Archive declassified documents, briefs and books on *Operation Condor* at http://nsarchive.gwu.edu/NSAEBB/NSAEBB514/.

15 Human Rights Watch, *World Report 2015: Events of 2014* (2015), p. 65.

16 Ibid., p. 65. Human Rights Watch's source for this number was the Centro de Estudios Legales y Sociales (CELS).

17 "Argentine General and 28 Others Sentenced to Life for Crimes against Humanity", Telesurtv.net (August 25, 2016). "La Perla Trial Delivers Justice for Córdoba" (August 26, 2016), http://www.buenosairesherald.com/article/220593/la-perla-trial-delivers-justice-for-córdoba.

18 Jonathan Gilbert, "Ex-Military Officers Convicted of Human Rights Crimes during Argentina Dictatorship," *New York Times* (August 25, 2016), http://www.nytimes.com/2016/08/26/world/americas/argentina-trial-cordoba.html?_r=0.

19 Carlos Osorio, ed., "Operation Condor on Trial: Legal Proceedings on Latin American Rendition and Assassination Program open in Buenos Aires," National Security Archive (March 8, 2013). See also, National Security Archive Electronic Briefing Book No. 416 for supporting declassified documents. Carlos Osorio, ed., "Operation Condor Verdict: Guilty!", National Security Archive (May 27, 2016). See National Security Archive Electronic Briefing Book No. 514, to access declassified government documents and communications regarding Operation Condor. These documents were also presented in evidence during the trial in 2015.

20 See, Centro de Estudio Legales y Sociales (CELS) "Juicios: Proceso de justicia por crímenes de lesa humanidad," http://www.cels.org.ar/blogs/estadisticas/.

21 See Sajit Gandhi, ed., "The Tilt: The US and the South Asian Crisis of 1971" (National Security Archives Electronic Briefing Book No. 79, 16 December 2002), as well as accompanying declassified documents, http://nsarchive.gwu.edu/NSAEBB/NSAEBB79/#docs, pertaining to the 1971 crisis.

22 See International Crimes Tribunal Bangladesh, http://www.ict-bd.org. Charges against the 195 Pakistani officers were dropped and they were repatriated to Pakistan as part of a 1974 Tripartite Agreement. For discussion, see Geoffrey Roberts, Q.C., "Report on the International Crimes Tribunal of Bangladesh" (International Forum for Democracy and Human Rights, February 2015), p. 50.

23 This figure is derived from multiple sources, including trial monitoring by TRIAL and judgments and decisions handed down from the ICT.

24 While the website for the ICT has provided documents relating to judgments and decisions, it does not yet provide specific case information.

25 See ICT decisions, http://www.ict-bd.org/ict1/judgments.php and http://www.ict-bd.org/ict2/judgments.php.

26 BBC News, "Motiur Rahman Nizami: Bangladeshi Islamist Leader Hanged" (May 11, 2016), http://www.bbc.com/news/world-asia-36261197.

27 See Roberts, "Report" on the ICT. The Roberts report provides a methodical analysis of the 1973 law creating the original Tribunal, as well as subsequent legal adaptations when it was implemented starting in 2009. His analysis finds the ICT, in its present form, in breach of a number of legal standards now accepted and developed through the experiences of international criminal tribunals, including those for the former Yugoslavia (1993); Rwanda (1992); Sierra Leone (2002); and the International Criminal Court (2002).

28 "Islamist Opposition Leader Executed for War Crimes in Bangladesh," *The Guardian* (April 11, 2015), see http://www.theguardian.com/world/2015/apr/11/islamist-opposition-leader-executed-war-crimes-bangladesh-muhammad-kamaruzzaman.

29 Geoffrey Roberts, "Report", p. 108.

30 Patrick Hueveline, "Between One and Three Million: Towards the Demographic Reconstruction of a Decade of Cambodian History (1970–79)," *Population Studies: A Journal of Demography* 52(1) (1998): 49–65.

31 For a full description of charges and case status, see ECCC, http://www.eccc.gov.kh/en/case/topic/286 The charges against Muth were brought in absentia reportedly due to a lack of cooperation by the Cambodian judicial police (TRIAL, http://www.trial-ch.org/en/resources/trial-watch/trial-watch/profiles/profile/4269/action/show/controller/Profile/tab/legal-procedure.html)

32 Extraordinary Chambers in the Courts of Cambodia (ECCC), http://www.eccc.gov.kh/en.

33 For a full description of charges and case status, see ECCC, http://www.eccc.gov.kh/en/case/topic/98.

34 Open Society Justice Initiative, "Recent Developments at the Extraordinary Chambers in the Courts of Cambodia: March 2015" (Briefing Paper).

35 See EEEC statement in the *Closing Order* (Case 002), https://www.eccc.gov.kh/en/topic/1506.

36 EEEC, Case 003 summary, https://www.eccc.gov.kh/en/case/topic/286.

37 *The Prosecutor v. Jean-Pierre Bemba Gombo, Aimé Kilolo Musamba, Jean-Jacques Mangenda Kabongo, Fidèle Babala Wandu and Narcisse Arido*, "Summary of the Judgment," https://www.icc-cpi.int/iccdocs/PIDS/publications/2016.03.21_Summary_of_the_Judgment-Eng.pdf (updated March 21, 2016).

38 *The Prosecutor v. Jean-Pierre Bemba Gombo, Aimé Kilolo Musamba, Jean-Jacques Mangenda Kabongo, Fidèle Babala Wandu and Narcisse Arido*, Case Information Sheet, ICC-PIDS-CIS-CAR-02–009/15_Eng (updated May 29, 2015).

39 Ibid. (updated June 2016).

40 *The Prosecutor v. Jean-Pierre Bemba Gombo, Aimé Kilolo Musamba, Jean-Jacques Mangenda Kabongo, Fidèle Babala Wandu and Narcisse Arido*, Summary of the Judgment, https://www.icc-cpi.int/itemsDocuments/Bemba-et-al_Article_70_Judgment_Summary_ENG.pdf (updated October 19, 2016).

41 International Court of Justice, "Questions relating to the Obligation to Prosecute or Extradite (Belgium v. Senegal)" (Judgment of July 20, 2012), http://www.icj-cij.org/docket/files/144/17064.pdf.

42 See also, Chambres africaines extraordinaire, http://www.chambresafricaines.org.

43 Human Rights Watch, "Q&A: The Case of Hissène Habré before the Extraordinary African Chambers in Senegal" (March 3, 2016).

44 Dionne Searcey, "Hissène Habré, Ex-President of Chad, Convicted of War Crimes.," *New York Times* (May 30, 2016).

45 Human Rights Watch, "World Report 2016" (Chile).

46 Pascale Bonnefoy, "Officers Arrested in 1986 Burning Death of US Student in Chile," *New York Times* (July 21, 2015). See also National Security Archive documents pertaining to the case at "Los Quemados: Chile's Pinochet Covered up Human Rights Atrocity" (July 31, 2015), http://nsarchive.gwu.edu/NSAEBB/NSAEBB523-Los-Quemados-Chiles-Pinochet-Covered-up-Human-Rights-Atrocity/.

47 Case of Simone Gbagbo reported by TRIAL, http://www.trial-ch.org/en/resources/trial-watch/trial-watch/profiles/profile/3875/action/show/controller/Profile.html.

48 *The Prosecutor v. Laurent Gbagbo and Charles Blé Goudé*, ICC-PIDS-CIS-CI-04–02/15_Eng (updated March 31, 2015); *The Prosecutor v. Simone Gbagbo*, Case Information Sheet, ICC-PIDS-CIS-CI-02–004/15_Eng (updated March 23, 2015).

49 Human Rights Watch, "Côte d'Ivoire: Simone Gbagbo Trial Begins: Needs to Be Fair, Followed by Trials of Pro-Ouattara Commanders" (May 30, 2016), https://www.hrw.org/news/2016/05/30/cote-divoire-simone-gbagbo-trial-begins.

50 *The Prosecutor v. Callixte Mbarushimana*, Case Information Sheet, ICC-PIDS-CIS-DRC-04–003/11_Eng (updated March 27, 2012).

51 *The Prosecutor v. Thomas Lubanga Dyilo*, Case Information Sheet, ICC-PIDS-CIS-DRC-01–012/15_Eng (updated March 25, 2015).

52 *The Prosecutor v. Mathieu Ngudjolo Chui*, Case Information Sheet, ICC-PIDS-CIS-DRC2–06–006/15_Eng (updated February 27, 2015).

53 *The Prosecutor v. Germain Katanga*, Case Information Sheet, ICC-PIDS-CIS-DRC-03–011/15_Eng (updated March 25, 2015).

54 *The Prosecutor v. Bosco Ntaganda*, Case Information Sheet, ICC-PIDS-CIS-DRC-02–008/15_Eng (updated April 22, 2015).

55 *The Prosecutor v. Sylvestre Mudacumura*, Case Information Sheet, ICC-PIDS-CIS-DRC-05–003/15_Eng (updated March 25, 2015).

56 The ICTY has acquitted 18 individuals, referred 13 to a national jurisdiction and withdrawn indictments against 36. For summary, see http://www.icty.org/sections/TheCases/KeyFiguresoftheCases.

57 For details and documents related to ICTY trials and appeals cases, see http://www.icty.org/action/cases/4.

58 *Prosecutor v. Radovan Karadžić* (IT-95–5/18). http://www.icty.org/case/karadzic/4.

59 Julian Borger and Owen Bowcottt, "Radovan Karadžić Sentenced to 40 Years for Srebrenica Genocide," *The Guardian* (March 24, 2016), https://www.theguardian.com/world/2016/mar/24/radovan-karadzic-criminally-responsible-for-genocide-at-srebenica.

60 *Prosecutor v. Ratko Mladić* (IT-09–92), http://www.icty.org/x/cases/mladic/cis/en/cis_mladic_en.pdf.

61 *Prosecutor v. Goran Hadžić* (IT-04–75), http://www.icty.org/x/cases/hadzic/cis/en/cis_hadzic_en.pdf.

62 Sven Milekic, "Croat War Victims Regret Hadzic's Death before Verdict," *Balkan Insight* (July 13, 2016), http://www.balkanin sight.com/en/article/victims-complain-on-serb-wartime-leader-non-prosecution-07-13-2016.

63 Milka Domanovic and Marija Ristic, "Vojislav Seselj Returns to Serbia after 11 Years," *Balkan Insight* (November 12, 2014), http://www.balkaninsight.com/en/article/vojislav-seselj-arrives-to-serbia-after-11-years.

64 *Prosecutor v. Vojislav Šešelj (IT-03–67)*, http://www.icty.org/x/cases/seselj/cis/en/cis_seselj_en.pdf.

65 Thomas Escritt and Matt Robinson, "War Crimes Court Revokes Serb Nationalist Seselj's Compassionate Release," *Reuters*, (March 30, 2015).

66 "Serbian Nationalist Rebuffs Order to Return to War Crimes Court," *Reuters*, (March 30, 2015).

67 Mechanism for International Criminal Tribunals: Vojislav Šešelj (MICT-16–99).

68 See *The Prosecutor v. Jovica Stanišić & Franko Simatović (IT-03–69)* Case Information Sheet, http://www.icty.org/x/cases/stanisic_simatovic/cis/en/cis_stanisic_simatovic_en.pdf. See also, Marija Ristic, Denis Dzidic, "Serbian Security Chiefs Plead Not Guilty at Retrial," *Balkan Insight* (December 15, 2015), http://www.balkaninsight.com/en/article/simatovic-stanisic-plead-not-guilty-12-18-2015.

69 See *The Prosecutor v. Jadranko Prlić, Bruno Stojić, Slobodan Praljak, Milivoj Petković, Valentin Ćorić & Berislav Pušić*, Case Information Sheet, (IT-04–74), http://www.icty.org/x/cases/prlic/cis/en/cis_prlic_al_en.pdf.

70 See "BIRN Launches Interactive War Crimes Verdict Map," *Balkan Insight* (September 22, 2016), http://www.balkaninsight.com/en/article/birn-launches-interactive-war-crimes-verdict-map-09-20-2016.

71 Denis Dzidic, "Bosnia Charges 15 Serbs for Zecovi Massacre," *Balkan Insight* (December 12, 2014), http://www.balkaninsight.com/en/article/zecovi-massacre-indictment-raised.

72 Sven Milekic, "Croatia Indicts Soldier for Operation Storm Killings," *Balkan Insight* (November 26, 2014), http://www.balka ninsight.com/en/article/indictment-for-operation-storm-killings-1.

73 Associated Press, "Serbia: Eight Former Officers Charged in 1995 Massacre Near Srebrenica," *New York Times* (September 10, 2015).

74 Marija Ristic, "The Troubled Trial of Kosovo's 'Drenica Group,'" *Balkan Insight* (May 27, 2015) http://www.balkaninsight.com/en/article/kosovo-awaits-kla-guerilla-verdict.

75 Dusica Tomovic, "Montenegro Must Tackle War Crimes, Chief Prosecutor Says," (May 20, 2015), http://www.balkaninsight.com/en/article/montenegro-needs-to-tackle-war-crimes-chief-prosecutor-says.

76 Marija Ristic, "New Kosovo Court Confronts Witness Protection Fears," *Balkan Insight* (October 3, 2016), http://www.balka ninsight.com/en/article/new-kosovo-court-confronts-witness-protection-fears-10-02-2016.

77 Marija Ristic, "From Kosovo's Organ-Harvesting Controversy to Special Court," *Balkan Insight*, http://www.balkaninsight.com/en/article/timeline-kosovo-organ-harvesting.

78 Petrit Collaku, "Kosovo President Signs War Court Agreement with Holland," *Balkan Insight* (February 29, 2016), http://www.balkaninsight.com/en/article/kosovo-president-gives-green-light-for-the-start-of-the-special-court-02-29-2016.

79 Marija Ristic, "Serb Paramilitary 'Captain Dragan' Pleads for Release," *Balkan Insight* (16 May 2014), http://www.balkaninsight.com/en/article/captain-dragan-asks-for-his-release.

80 Rick Wallace, "'Captain Dragan' Looks Set to Be Extradited to Croatia," *The Australian* (May 15, 2015), http://www.theaustralia n.com.au/news/nation/captain-dragan-looks-set-to-be-extradited-to-croatia/story-e6frg6nf-1227356356814.

81 Sven Milekic, "Croatia Indicts Serb Paramilitary 'Captain Dragan'," *Balkan Insight* (January 8, 2016), http://www.balkaninsight.com/en/article/croatian-state-attorney-office-indicts-captain-dragan–01-08-2016.

82 ICC, "Application of the Convention on the Prevention and Punishment of the Crime of Genocide (Croatia v. Serbia)" (Judgment, February 3, 2015).

83 Emi MacLean, *Judging a Dictator: The Trial of Guatemala's Ríos Montt* (Open Society Foundation, 2013).

84 Emi MacLean, "Renewed Amnesty Threat to Rios Montt Prosecution," *International Justice Monitor* (December 28, 2014), www.ijmonitor.org/2014/12/renewed-amnesty-threat-to-rios-montt-prosecution/.

85 Sophie Beaudoin, "Guatemalan Court Rules Out Amnesty for Genocide and Crimes against Humanity," *International Justice Monitor* (October 15, 2015), www.ijmonitor.org/2015/10/guatemalan-court-rules-out-amnesty-for-genocide-and-crimes-aga inst-humanity/.

86 Emi MacLean and Sophie Beaudoin, "Guatemalan Judges Reportedly Facing Retaliation for Judicial Independence," *International Justice Monitor* (March 6, 2015), www.ijmonitor.org/2015/03/guatemalan-judges-reportedly-facing-retaliation-for-judicial-indep endence/.

87 Sophie Beaudoin, "Impeachment Request Filed against Judge Carol Patricia Flores," *International Justice Monitor* (May 4, 2015), www.ijmonitor.org/2015/05/impeachment-request-filed-against-judge-carol-patricia-flores/.

88 Emi MacLean and Sophie Beaudoin, "Ríos Montt's Defense Attorney Killed by Hitmen in Guatemala City," *International Justice Monitor* (June 4, 2015), www.ijmonitor.org/2015/06/rios-montts-defense-attorney-killed-by-hitmen-in-guatemala-city/.

89 Emi MacLean, "Judge Imposes Travel Ban on Prosecutor following His Public Statements about Historic Genocide Trial," *International Justice Monitor* (April 14, 2015).

90 Emi MacLean and Sophie Beaudoin, "Guatemala Court May Block Resumption of Rios Montt Genocide Trial," *International Justice Monitor* (December 12, 2014), www.ijmonitor.org/2014/12/guatemala-court-may-blog-resumption-of-rios-montt-genoci de-trial/.

91 Jo-Marie Burt, "Appeals Court Upholds Suspension of Ríos Montt Genocide Trial," *International Justice Monitor* (June 3, 2016), www.ijmonitor.org/2016/06/appeals-court-upholds-suspension-of-rios-montt-genocide-trial/.

92   Emi MacLean and Sophie Beaudoin, "More Than 30 Years Later, Guatemala's Deadly Spanish Embassy Siege IS on Trial in a Guatemalan Courtroom," *International Justice Monitor* (November 25, 2014), www.ijmonitor.org/2014/11/more-than-thirty-yea rs-later-guatemalas-deadly-spanish-embassy-siege-is-on-trial-in-a-guatemalan-courtroom/.

93   Sophie Beaudoin, "In Closing Arguments, Prosecution Seeks Life in Prison for Former Guatemalan National Police Official for Spanish Embassy Fire" *International Justice Monitor* (January 15, 2015), www.ijmonitor.org/2015/01/in-closing-arguments-prose cution-seeks-1240-years-against-former-guatemalan-national-police-official-for-spanish-embassy-fire/.

94   Emi MacLean and Sophie Beaudoin, "Guatemalan Police Official Found Guilty of Homicide and Crimes against Humanity," *International Justice Monitor* (January 20, 2015), www.ijmonitor.org/2015/01/guatemalan-police-official-found-guilty-of-hom icide-and-crimes-against-humanity/.

95   Sophie Beaudoin, "Parties Present Evidence in Case of Sexual Violence at Sepur Zarco Military Base," *International Justice Monitor* (June 15, 2015), www.ijmonitor.org/2015/06/parties-present-evidence-in-case-of-sexual-violence-at-sepur-zarco-military-base/.

96   Jo-Marie Burt, "Military Officers Convicted in Landmark Sepur Zarco Sexual Violence Case," *International Justice Monitor* (March 4, 2016), www.ijmonitor.org/2016/03/military-officers-convicted-in-landmark-sepur-zarco-sexual-violence-case/.

97   Jo-Marie Burt, "Guatemala Grave Crimes Cases Delayed," *International Justice Monitor* (July 13, 2016), www.ijmonitor.org/2016/ 07/guatemala-grave-crimes-cases-delayed/.

98   Jo-Marie Burt, "War Crimes Prosecutions Update: The CREOMPAZ Case," *International Justice Monitor* (September 20, 2016), www.ijmonitor.org/2016/09/war-crimes-prosecutions-update-the-creompaz-case/.

99   Sophie Beaudoin, "Guatemala Transitional Justice Update: Judges Continue to Challenge Threats to Judicial Independence," *International Justice Monitor* (March 23, 2015) www.ijmonitor.org/2015/03/guatemala-transitional-justice-update-judges-conti nue-to-challenge-threats-to-judicial-independence/.

100   Sophie Beaudoin, "Guatemala's President Gives CICIG Extension a Green Light," *International Justice Monitor* (April 23, 2015), www.ijmonitor.org/2015/04/guatemalas-president-gives-cicig-extension-a-green-light/.

101   Francis Kirimi Muthaura and Mohammed Hussein Ali were initially summoned and charged, along with Kenyatta, Ruto and Sang (http://www.icc-cpi.int/iccdocs/doc/doc985621.pdf#search=Prosecutor%20v%2E%20Muthaura%20and%20Ali).

102   *The Prosecutor v. Uhuru Muigai Kenyatta*, Case Information Sheet, ICC-PIDS-CIS-KEN-02–014/15_Eng (updated March 13, 2015).

103   "Statement of the Prosecutor of the International Criminal Court, Fatou Bensouda, Regarding Trial Chamber's Decision to Vacate Charges against Messrs William Samoei Ruto and Joshua Arap Sang without Prejudice to their Prosecution in the Future" (April 6, 2016).

104   *The Prosecutor v. Walter Osapiri Barasa*, Warrant of Arrest, ICC-01/09–01/13–1-Red2 (August 2, 2013).

105   *The Prosecutor v. Saif Al-Islam Gaddafi*, Case Information Sheet, ICC-PIDS-CIS-LIB-01–011/15_Eng (March 26, 2015).

106   ICC Pre-Trial Chamber I, "Decision on the Non-compliance by Libya with Requests for Cooperation by the Court and Referring the Matter to the United Nations Security Council," ICC-01/11–01/11 (December 10, 2014).

107   ICC Appeals Chamber, "Judgment on the Appeal of Mr Abdullah Al-Senussi against the Decision of Pre-Trial Chamber I of 11 October 2013 Entitled 'Decision on the Admissibility of the Case against Abdullah Al-Senussi'" ICC-OI/II-OI/IIOA6 (July 24, 2014).

108   Fatou Bensouda, "Statement to the United Nations Security Council on the Situation in Libya, Pursuant to UNSCR 1970 (2011)" (May 26, 2016).

109   "Eleventh Report of the Prosecutor of the International Criminal Court to the United Nations Security Council Pursuant to UNSCR 1970 (2011)," https://www.icc-cpi.int/itemsDocuments/otp_report_lib_26052016-eng.pdf.

110   The Office of the Prosecutor, International Criminal Court, "Situation in Mali: Article 53.1 Report" (January 16, 2013).

111   The specific sites include the following mausoleums: Sidi Mahmoud Ben Omar Mohamed Aquit; Sheikh Mohamed Mahmoud Al Arawani; Sheikh Sidi Mokhtar Ben Sidi Muhammad Ben Sheikh Alkabir, Alpha Moya; Sheikh Sidi Ahmed Ben Amar Arra- gadi; Sheikh Muhammad El Micky; Cheick Abdoul Kassim Attouaty; Ahamed Fulane; Bahaber Babadié and, Sidi Yahia mosque. *The Prosecutor v. Ahmad Al Faqi Al Mahdi*, Case Information Sheet, ICC-PIDS-CIS-MAL-01–06/16_Eng (August 24, 2016).

112   Ibid.

113   ICC Press Release, "ICC Trial Chamber VIII Declares Mr Al Mahdi Guilty of the War Crime of Attacking Historic and Religious Buildings in Timbuktu and Sentences Him to Nine Years' Imprisonment" (September 27, 2016), https://www.icc-cpi.int/pa ges/item.aspx?name=pr1242.

114   UN Office of the High Commissioner for Human Rights, "The Nepal Act on the Commission on Investigation of Disappeared Persons, Truth and Reconciliation, 2071 (2014) – as Gazetted 21 May 2014," OHCHR Technical Note, http://www.ohchr. org/Documents/Countries/NP/OHCHRTechnical_Note_Nepal_CIDP_TRC_Act2014.pdf.

115   Ross Adkin, "Nepal Supreme Court Rejects Amnesty for War Crimes," *Reuters* (February 27, 2015).

116   Human Rights Watch, "Nepal: 9-Point Deal Undermines Transitional Justice" (May 12, 2016).

117   International Center for Transitional Justice, "Ten Years after Peace, Is Nepal Finally Serious about Finding Its Disappeared?" Human Rights Watch (August 29, 2016), https://www.ictj.org/news/nepal-disappeared-search.

118   Owen Bowcott, "Nepalese Officer Cleared of Torturing Suspected Maoist Detainee," *The Guardian* (September 6, 2016), https:// www.theguardian.com/law/2016/sep/06/nepalese-officer-col-kumar-lama-cleared-torturing-maoist-detainees.

119   See ICCMER, http://www.iiccr.ro/en/.

120   Associated Press, "Communist-era Romanian Prison Commander Jailed for 20 Years," *The Guardian* (July 24, 2015).

121   Râmincu Sărat (1945–1963), http://memorialulramnicusarat.ro.

122   ECHR, Grand Chamber Judgment in *Case of Mocanu and Others v. Romania*, Applications nos. 10865/09, 45886/07 and 32431/ 08 (September 14, 2014), http://hudoc.echr.coe.int/eng?i=001-146540#.

123   Associated Press, "Romanian Ex-President Ion Iliescu Prosecuted for Crimes against Humanity," *The Wall Street Journal* (October 21, 2015), http://www.wsj.com/articles/romanian-ex-president-ion-iliescu-prosecuted-for-crimes-against-humanity-1445423822.

124 ICCMER, "The Gheorghe URSU Case: The Military Prosecutors Sent Four People to Trial for the Murder by Torture of the Former Engineer" (August 1, 2016), http://www.iiccr.ro/en/gheorghe-ursu-case-military-prosecutors-sent-trial-four-people-murder-torture-former-engineer/.

125 For a complete list of indictees, see ICTR, http://www.unictr.org/sites/unictr.org/files/publications/ictr-key-figures-en.pdf.

126 Ibid.

127 Human Rights Watch, "Rwanda: Justice after Genocide, 20 Years On" (March 28, 2014), http://www.hrw.org/sites/default/files/related_material/2014_March_Rwanda_0.pdf.

128 Charles Bandora case reported by TRIAL, http://www.trial-ch.org/en/resources/trial-watch/trial-watch/profiles/profile/905/action/show/controller/Profile/tab/fact.html.

129 See TRIAL, http://www.trial-ch.org/en/resources/trial-watch/search/action/search/controller/Profile.html?jf=61&tx_wetwdb_profile%5BjudgementPlace%5D=61&cHash=85f7cf1fa8c3e38acb3448a57b4f029d.

130 *Reuters*, "Professor Arrives in Rwanda from US to Face Genocide Trial," *The New York Times* (September 28, 2016).

131 ICTR, http://www.unictr.org/en/tribunal

132 See ICTR, "Report on the Completion Strategy of the International Criminal Tribunal for Rwanda as at 5 May 2015" (S/2015/340). See also, MICT, "Assessment and Progress Report of the President of the International Residual Mechanism for Criminal Tribunals, Judge Theodor Meron, for the Period from 16 November 2014 to 15 May 2015" (S/2015/341) and ICTR, "Nineteenth Annual Report of the International Criminal Tribunal for the Prosecution of Persons Responsible for Genocide and Other Serious Violations of International Humanitarian Law Committed in the Territory of Rwanda and Rwandan Citizens Responsible for Genocide and Other Such Violations Committed in the Territory of Neighbouring States between 1 January and 31 December 1994" (A/69/206; S/2014/546).

133 TRIAL, European Center for Constitutional and Human Rights (ECCHR) and International Federation for Human Rights (FIDH), "Universal Jurisdiction Annual Review 2015" (2015).

134 *The Prosecutor v. Omar Hassan Ahmad Al Bashir*, "Case Information Sheet" ICC-PIDS-CIS-SUD-02–004/15_Eng (updated March 26, 2015).

135 *The Prosecutor v. Ahmad Muhammad Harun ("Ahmad Harun") and Ali Muhammad Ali Abd-Al-Rahman ("Ali Kushayb"),* Case Information Sheet, ICC-PIDS-CIS-SUD-001–004/15_Eng (updated March 25, 2015).

136 *The Prosecutor v. Abdel Raheem Muhammad Hussein*, Case Information Sheet, ICC-PIDS-CIS-SUD-05–003/15_Eng (updated March 25, 2015).

137 *The Prosecutor v. Ahmad Muhammad Harun ("Ahmad Harun") and Ali Muhammad Ali Abd-Al-Rahman ("Ali Kushayb")* Case Information Sheet, ICC-PIDS-CIS-SUD-001–004/15_Eng (updated March 25, 2015).

138 *The Prosecutor v. Abdallah Banda Abakaer Nourain* Case Information Sheet, ICC-PIDS-CIS-SUD-04–006/15_Eng (updated March 23, 2015).

139 *The Prosecutor v. Bahar Idriss Abu Garda*, Case Information Sheet, ICC-PIDS-CIS-SUD-03–002/11_Eng (updated June 15, 2012).

140 ICC Pre-Trial Chamber II, "Decision on the Cooperation of the Democratic Republic of the Congo regarding Omar Al Bashir's Arrest and Surrender to the Court," ICC-02/05–01/09, (April 9, 2014), http://www.icc-cpi.int/iccdocs/doc/doc1919142.pdf.

141 ICC Pre-Trial Chamber II, "Decision on the Prosecutor's Request for a Finding of Non-Compliance against the Republic of the Sudan," ICC-02/05–01/09, (March 9, 2015), http://www.icc-cpi.int/iccdocs/doc/doc1919142.pdf.

142 ICC Pre-Trial Chamber II, "Decision on the Non-compliance by the Republic of Uganda with the Request to Arrest and Surrender Omar Al-Bashir to the Court and Referring the Matter to the United Nations Security Council and the Assembly of State Parties to the Rome Statute," ICC-02/05–01/09–267 (July 11, 2016); ICC Pre-Trial Chamber II, "Decision on the Non-compliance by the Republic of Djibouti with the Request to Arrest and Surrender Omar Al-Bashir to the Court and Referring the Matter to the United Nations Security Council and the Assembly of the State Parties to the Rome Statute," ICC-02/05–01/09–266 (11 July 2016). See, ICC OTP, "Twenty-Second Report of the Prosecutor of the International Criminal Court to the United Nations Security Council Pursuant to UNSCR 1593 (2005)" (December 15, 2015).

143 Norimitsu Onishi, "Omar al-Bashir, Leaving South Africa, Eludes Arrest Again," *The New York Times* (June 15, 2015).

144 Gauteng Division of the High Court, *Southern Africa Litigation Centre v. Minister of Justice and Constitutional Development & Others* 2015 (5) SA 1 (GP).

145 Supreme Court of Appeal, South Africa, Judgment in *The Minister of Justice and Constitutional Development v. The Southern African Litigation Centre* (867/15) [2016] ZASCA 17 (March 15, 2016).

146 ICC Registrar, "Report of the Registry on Information Received Regarding Omar Al Bashir's Travels to States and Non-States Parties from 22 July 2016 to 8 August 2016," (September 9, 2016) ICC-02/05–01/09.

147 *The Prosecutor v. Joseph Kony, Vincent Otti and Okot Odhiambo*, "Case Information Sheet," ICC-PIDS-CIS-UGA-001–004/15_Eng (updated March 26, 2015).

148 ICC Pre-Trial Chamber II, "Decision to Terminate Proceedings against Raska Lukwiya," ICC-02/04–01/05 (July 11, 2007), http://www.icc-cpi.int/iccdocs/doc/doc297945.pdf.

149 *The Prosecutor v. Dominic Ongwen*, Case Information Sheet, ICC-PIDS-CIS-UGA-02–003/15_Eng (updated June 2016).

150 Ibid.

151 Article 53(1)(a)-(c) of the Rome Statute, http://www.icc-cpi.int/NR/rdonlyres/ADD16852-AEE9-4757-ABE7-9CDC7CF02886/283503/RomeStatutEng1.pdf.

152 ICC, "Situation in the Central African Republic II: Article 53(1) Report Executive Summary" (September 24, 2014), http://www.icc-cpi.int/iccdocs/otp/SAS-CARII-Art53-1-Executive-Summary-24Sept2014-Eng.pdf.

153 Pre-trial Chamber 1, International Criminal Court, "Situation in Georgia: Decision on the Prosecutor's Request for Authorization of an Investigation" (January 27, 2016).

154 OTP, International Criminal Court, "Report on Preliminary Examination Activities 2014" (December 2, 2014).

155 OTP, "Statement of the Prosecutor of the International Criminal Court, Fatou Bensouda, on Opening a Preliminary Examination into the Situation in Burundi" (April 25, 2016).

156 ICC President's Office, "Statement of the President of the Assembly of States Parties on the Process of Withdrawal from the Rome Statute by Burundi" (October 18, 2016).

157 OTP, "Report on Preliminary Examination Activities 2015"; Hector Olasolo, "The Special Jurisdiction for Peace and the Cautious Optimism of the Prosecutor of the International Criminal Court," *Peace Processes and Human Dignity*, Summer Autumn 2015, http://www.peaceprocesses.it/journal/third-quarter-2015/notes/25-the-special-jurisdiction-for-peace-in-colombia.

158 OTP, "Statement of the Prosecutor of the International Criminal Court, Fatou Bensouda, concerning Referral from the Gabonese Republic" (September 29, 2016).

159 Ruth Maclean, "Gabon Court Rules President Ali Bongo Rightful Winner of September Election," *The Guardian* (September 24, 2016).

160 UN News Centre, "UN Envoy Welcomes Indictment of Former Guinean Leader over 2009 Stadium Deaths" (July 9, 2015), http://www.un.org/apps/news/story.asp?NewsID=51370#.V-LGhDvgKlI.

161 OTP, "Report on Preliminary Examination Activities" (November 12, 2015).

162 Ibid.

163 Ibid.

164 Ibid. See also OTP, "Report on Preliminary Examination Activities" (November 14, 2016).

165 Ibid.

166 Fatou Bensouda, "Statement of the Prosecutor of the International Criminal Court, Fatou Bensouda, on the Conclusion of the Preliminary Examination into the Situation in Honduras" (October 28, 2015).

167 TRIAL, European Center for Constitutional and Human Rights (ECCHR) and FIDH, "Universal Jurisdiction Annual Review 2016" (2016).

168 Case of Samantar Mohammed Ali, (former General in the Somali National Army (SNA), Minister of Defence, First Vice President and Prime Minister of Somalia) facing allegations of torture brought in US courts, see case report by TRIAL, http://www.trial-ch.org/en/resources/trial-watch/trial-watch/profiles/profile/1067/action/show/controller/Profile/tab/legal-procedure.html.

Index

Abadan, fatalities in 80

Abd-Al-Rahman, Ali Muhammad Ali ("Ali Kushayb") 224

Abu Garda, Bahar Idriss 224

accountability, changing standard of 89

Acemoglu, Daron, and James Robinson 68, 69

active armed conflicts (2015) 2, 154–78; ADF (Alliance of Democratic Forces), Congo Democratic Republic and 174–5; ADF (Alliance of Democratic Forces), Uganda and 174–5; Afghanistan, Taliban and 155–6; Afghanistan, Tehrik-i-Taleban Pakistan (TTP) and 164–5; al-Qaida, United States and 176; Al-Shabaab (The Youth), Somaliland 168–9; Algeria, AQIM (al-Qaeda Organization in the Islamic Maghreb) and 156–7; Ansarallah (Supporters of God), Yemen and 177–8; AQAP (al-Qaeda in the Arabian Peninsula), Yemen and 177–8; AQIM (al-Qaeda Organization in the Islamic Maghreb), Algeria and 156–7; Armenia, Azerbaijan and 157; ASG (Abu Sayyaf Group), Philippines and 166–7; Azerbaijan, Armenia and 157; Azerbaijan, Nagorno-Karabakh and 157; BIFM (Bangsamoro Islamic Freedom Movement), Philippines and 166–7; BLA (Balochistan Liberation Army), Pakistan and 165–6; BLF (Baloch Liberation Front), Pakistan and 165–6; Boko Haram, Nigeria and 163–4; BRA (Balochistan Republican Army), Pakistan and 165–6; Colombia, ELN (Ejército de Liberación Nacional) and 158; Colombia, FARC (Fuerzas Armadas Revolucionarias de Colombia) and 158; Congo Democratic Republic, ADF (Alliance of Democratic Forces) and 174–5; CPP (Communist Party of the Philippines), Philippines and 167–8; DJRF (Darfur Joint Resistance Forces), Sudan and 170–71; ELN (Ejército de Liberación Nacional), Colombia and 158; Ethiopia, OLF (Oromo Liberation Front) and 159; FARC (Fuerzas Armadas Revolucionarias de Colombia), Colombia and 158; India, Kashmir insurgents and 160; India, Pakistan and 160–61; internationalized interstate armed conflict 154; interstate armed conflict 154; intrastate armed conflict 154; Iraq, IS (Islamic State) and 161–2; IS (Islamic State), Iraq and 161–2; IS (Islamic State), Nigeria and 164; IS (Islamic State), Syria and 171; Kashmir insurgents, India and 160; KIO (Kachin Independence Organization), Myanmar and 162–3; MILF (Moro Islamic Liberation Front), Philippines and 166–7; minor armed conflict 154; Myanmar, KIO (Kachin Independence Organization) and 162–3; Nagorno-Karabakh, Azerbaijan and 157; Nigeria, Boko Haram and 163–4; Nigeria, IS (Islamic State) and 164; OLF (Oromo Liberation Front), Ethiopia and 159; Pakistan, BLA (Balochistan Liberation Army) and 165–6; Pakistan, BLF (Baloch Liberation Front) and 165–6; Pakistan, BRA (Balochistan Republican Army) and 165–6; Pakistan, India and 160–61; Pakistan, Tehrik-i-Taleban Pakistan (TTP) and 164–5; Philippines, ASG (Abu Sayyaf Group) and 166–7; Philippines, BIFM (Bangsamoro Islamic Freedom Movement) and 166–7; Philippines, CPP (Communist Party of the Philippines) and 167–8; Philippines, MILF (Moro Islamic Liberation Front) and 166–7; PKK (Partiya Karkeren Kurdistan: Kurdistan Workers' Party), Turkey and 173–4; profiles of 155–78; Somalia, Al-Shabaab (The Youth) and 168–9; South Sudan, SPLM/A-In Opposition (Sudan People's Liberation Movement/Army-In Opposition) and 169–70; SPLM/A-In Opposition (Sudan People's Liberation Movement/Army-In Opposition), South Sudan and 169–70; SPLM/A-In Opposition (Sudan People's Liberation Movement/Army-In Opposition), Uganda and 169–70; SRF (Sudanese Revolutionary Front), Sudan and 170–71; Sudan, DJRF (Darfur Joint Resistance Forces) and 170–71; Sudan, SRF (Sudanese Revolutionary Front) and 170–71; summary 155; Syria, IS (Islamic State) and 171; Syria, Syrian insurgents and 172–3; Syrian insurgents, Syria and 172–3; Taliban, Afghanistan and 155–6; Tehrik-i-Taleban Pakistan (TTP), Afghanistan and 164–5; Tehrik-i-Taleban Pakistan (TTP), Pakistan and 164–5; Turkey, PKK (Partiya Karkeren Kurdistan: Kurdistan Workers' Party) and 173–4; Uganda, ADF (Alliance of Democratic Forces) and 174–5; Uganda, SPLM/A-In Opposition (Sudan People's Liberation Movement/Army-In Opposition) and 169–70; Ukraine, United Armed Forces of Novorossiya and 175; United Armed Forces of Novorossiya, Ukraine and 175; United States, al-Qaida and 176; Uppsala Conflict Data Program (UCDP) 154; Uppsala Conflict Data Program (UCDP), compilation of data 154; Uppsala Conflict Data Program (UCDP), definitions and data 154; war, category of 154; Yemen, Ansarallah (Supporters of God) and 177–8; Yemen, AQAP (al-Qaeda in the Arabian Peninsula) and 177–8

actor-level instability risk factors 107–8

Adamson, Fiona B. 146, 150

Adelman, Howard 144

ADF (Alliance of Democratic Forces), Congo Democratic Republic, Uganda and 174–5

adverse regime change: data sources on 103, 104; global map of risk of 115; model of 105; risk factors 114

Afghanistan: adverse regime change, risk for (2015–2017) 120; conflict-related violations (2015), criminal justice for 226; instability risk (2015–2017) 118; instability risk forecast for (2015–2017) 136; integrating conflict event data in (2008) 10; internal war, risk for (2015–2017) 124; non-state mass killing, risk for (2015–2017) 132; state-based mass killing, risk for (2015–2017) 128; Taliban and 155–6; Tehrik-i-Taleban Pakistan (TTP) and 164–5

Africa: African-led International Support Mission in Mali (AFISMA) 201; prevalence of sexual violence by conflict actors in (2000–2009) 66; risks on instability in 115; spatial distribution of OSV in 36

African Union (AU) 179, 200

African Union Mission in Somalia (AMISOM) 181, 195–6

African Union Mission in Sudan (AMIS) 196

Al Mahdi, Ahmad Al Faqi 221

al-Qaeda 48, 83, 156, 162, 165, 168, 177; armed conflict over time 16; global terrorism, evolution of 80, 81; United States and 47, 176

Al-Shabaab (The Youth) 16, 19, 21, 38, 168–9, 195

al-Zarqawi, Abu Mus'ab 161

Albania: adverse regime change, risk for (2015–2017) 122; instability risk forecast for (2015–2017) 138; internal war, risk for (2015–2017) 125; non-state mass killing, risk for (2015–2017) 134; state-based mass killing, risk for (2015–2017) 130

Algeria: adverse regime change, risk for (2015–2017) 122; AQIM (al-Qaeda Organization in the Islamic Maghreb) and 156–7; instability risk (2015–2017) 118; instability risk forecast for (2015–2017) 136; internal war, risk for (2015–2017) 124; non-state mass killing, risk for (2015–2017) 133; state-based mass killing, risk for (2015–2017) 129

Alvarez, Alex 63

Amin, Idi 174

Amnesty International 88, 99

An, Ao 212

Angelelli, Bishop Enrique 210

Angola: adverse regime change, risk for (2015–2017) 120; Angolan Military Mission to Guinea-Bissau (MISSANG) 200; instability risk (2015–2017) 118; instability risk forecast for (2015–2017) 136; internal war, risk for (2015–2017) 124; non-state mass killing, risk for (2015–2017) 132; state-based mass killing, risk for (2015–2017) 128

Ansar Dine, al-Qaeda in the Islamic Maghreb (AQIM) 19, 156–7, 201, 221

Ansarallah (Supporters of God) 177–8

AQAP (al-Qaeda in the Arabian Peninsula), Yemen and 177–8

Argentina: adverse regime change, risk for (2015–2017) 121; conflict-related violations (2015), criminal justice for 209–10, 227; instability risk forecast for (2015–2017) 138; internal war, risk for (2015–2017) 125; non-state mass killing, risk for (2015–2017) 133; state-based mass killing, risk for (2015–2017) 130

Arido, Narcisse 213

armed conflict: armed assault 83–4; Armed Conflict Location and Event Data (ACLED) Project 23; attack concentration, shift in 85–7; extent o 16; internationalization of 19–20; internationalized interstate conflict 154; one-sided violence (OSV) and 38–41; relationship between civilian victimization and 34; spatial overlap between OSV and type of conflict 39

armed conflict over time 1, 16–22; al-Qaeda 16; annual frequency of types of organized armed conflict, global trends (1946–2015) 17; civil wars in Muslim countries or with Islamic insurgents 22; extent of armed conflict 16; internationalization of armed conflict 19–20; internationalization of armed conflict (1946–2015) 19; Islamic State (IS) 16; Islamism, role in internationalized internal conflict (1991–2015) 20; lethality of armed conflict 16; militant Islam, increase in dominance of 20–22; number of active armed conflicts (2015) 16; severity of organized armed conflict, global trends (1989–2015) 18; spatial trends in armed conflicts (1989–2015) 21; Uppsala Conflict Data Program (UCDP) 16; worrying trend, entrenchment of 16–19

Armenia: adverse regime change, risk for (2015–2017) 120; Azerbaijan and 157; instability risk forecast for (2015–2017) 137; internal war, risk for (2015–2017) 125; non-state mass killing, risk for (2015–2017) 134; state-based mass killing, risk for (2015–2017) 129

Aronson, Jacob xi, 2, 46–57, 101–41

Aronson, Jacob, and Paul Huth 107

Aronson, Jacob, Paul Huth, Mark Lichbach, and Kiyoung Chang 107, 108

Arreguín-Toft, Ivan 46, 50

Arroyo, Gloria 168

ASG (Abu Sayyaf Group), Philippines and 166–7

Asia: East and Central Asia, countries in 85; South Asia, countries in 86; Southeast Asia, countries in 86; spatial distribution of OSV in South Asia 35; spatial distribution of OSV in Southeast Asia 35

al-Assad, Bashar 172

assassination 83–4

association, freedom of 70, 71, 72

AU/UN Hybrid operation in Darfur (UNAMID) 181, 196–7

AUC score 109, 112

Australia: adverse regime change, risk for (2015–2017) 123; instability risk forecast for (2015–2017) 139; internal war, risk for (2015–2017) 126; non-state mass killing, risk for (2015–2017) 134; state-based mass killing, risk for (2015–2017) 131

Austria: adverse regime change, risk for (2015–2017) 123; instability risk forecast for (2015–2017) 139; internal war, risk for (2015–2017) 126; non-state mass killing, risk for (2015–2017) 135; state-based mass killing, risk for (2015–2017) 131

autocracies 68–9

Azerbaijan: adverse regime change, risk for (2015–2017) 122; Armenia and 157; instability risk (2015–2017) 118; instability risk forecast for (2015–2017) 136; internal war, risk for (2015–2017) 124; Nagorno-Karabakh and 157; non-state mass killing, risk for (2015–2017) 133; state-based mass killing, risk for (2015–2017) 128

Baaz, Maria Eriksson, and Maria Stern 58

Babala Wandu, Fidèle 213

Backer, David A. xi, 1–3, 23–33, 101–41

Badush, fatalities in 80

Baez, Javier E. 144

al-Baghdadi, Abu Bakr 164

Bagosora, Colonel Théonesta 223

Bahrain: adverse regime change, risk for (2015–2017) 122; instability risk forecast for (2015–2017) 138; internal war, risk for (2015–2017) 126; non-state mass killing, risk for (2015–2017) 135; state-based mass killing, risk for (2015–2017) 130

Balcells, Laia 34

Balcells, Laia, and Stathis Kalyvas 106

Ball, Patrick, Jana Asher, David Sulmont, and Daniel Manrique 11

Ball, Patrick, Paul Kobrak, and Herbert F. Spirer 8

Ballard, John R. 52

Bandora, Charles 223

Bangladesh: adverse regime change, risk for (2015–2017) 120; conflict-related violations (2015), criminal justice for 210–11; instability risk (2015–2017) 118; instability risk forecast for (2015–2017) 136; internal war, risk for (2015–2017) 125; non-state mass killing, risk for (2015–2017) 132; state-based mass killing, risk for (2015–2017) 128

Barasa, Walter Osapiri 219

Barber, Ben 144

Barre, Siad 168

Bartusevicius, Henrikas and Svend-Erik Skaaning 69

Basedau, Matthias, and Jan Henryk Pierskalla 26

al-Bashir, Omar 224–5

Beardsley, Kyle, Kristian Skrede Gleditsch, and Nigel Lo 37

Bedi, fatalities in 80

al Beilawy, Abdul-Rahman 81

Belarus: adverse regime change, risk for (2015–2017) 122; instability risk forecast for (2015–2017) 138; internal war, risk for (2015–2017) 125; non-state mass killing, risk for (2015–2017) 135; state-based mass killing, risk for (2015–2017) 129

Belgium: adverse regime change, risk for (2015–2017) 122; conflict-related violations (2015), criminal justice for 227; instability risk forecast for (2015–2017) 138; internal war, risk for (2015–2017) 126; non-state mass killing, risk for (2015–2017) 134; state-based mass killing, risk for (2015–2017) 131

Index

Bemba Gombo, Jean-Pierre 212–13
Benin: adverse regime change, risk for (2015–2017) 120; instability risk forecast for (2015–2017) 137; internal war, risk for (2015–2017) 126; non-state mass killing, risk for (2015–2017) 132; state-based mass killing, risk for (2015–2017) 129
Berman, Eli, and Aila M. Matanock 46
Berman, Nicolas, and Mathieu Couttenier 26
Beslan, fatalities in 80
Bhavnani, Ravi xi, 1–3, 4–15
Bhutan: adverse regime change, risk for (2015–2017) 121; instability risk forecast for (2015–2017) 138; internal war, risk for (2015–2017) 125; non-state mass killing, risk for (2015–2017) 134; state-based mass killing, risk for (2015–2017) 129
Bhutto, Zulfikar 166
Biddle, Stephen D., and Jeffrey A. Friedman 50
BIFM (Bangsamoro Islamic Freedom Movement), Philippines and 166–7
Bignone, General Reynaldo 210
bin Laden, Usama 176
Bivand, Roger S., Edzer Pebesma, and Virgilio Gómez-Rubio 12
Bizimungu, Augustin 223
BLA (Balochistan Liberation Army), Pakistan and 165–6
Blattman, Christopher, and Edward Miguel 149
Blé Goudé, Charles 215
BLF (Baloch Liberation Front), Pakistan and 165–6
Boix, Carles 69
Boko Haram 58, 227; global terrorism, evolution of 80; Nigeria and 163–4
Bolivia: adverse regime change, risk for (2015–2017) 120; instability risk (2015–2017) 118; instability risk forecast for (2015–2017) 137; internal war, risk for (2015–2017) 125; non-state mass killing, risk for (2015–2017) 133; state-based mass killing, risk for (2015–2017) 129
Bolt, Jutta, and Jan van Zanden 71
bombings 83–4
Bongo, Ali 227
Bontemps, Sophie, Pierre Defourny, Eric Van Bogaert, Olivier Arino, Vasileios Kalogirou, and Jose Ramos Perez 41
Bosnia and Herzegovina: adverse regime change, risk for (2015–2017) 120; instability risk (2015–2017) 118; instability risk forecast for (2015–2017) 137; internal war, risk for (2015–2017) 125; multilateral peacekeeping missions in 181; NATO-led Stabilization Force (SFOR) in Bosnia 194; non-state mass killing, risk for (2015–2017) 135; state-based mass killing, risk for (2015–2017) 130
Botswana: adverse regime change, risk for (2015–2017) 121; instability risk forecast for (2015–2017) 138; internal war, risk for (2015–2017) 125; non-state mass killing, risk for (2015–2017) 133; state-based mass killing, risk for (2015–2017) 130
Boulden, Jane 180
Bove, Vincenzo, and Leandro Elia 180
Bozizé, François 121, 226
BRA (Balochistan Republican Army), Pakistan and 165–6
Brazil: adverse regime change, risk for (2015–2017) 121; instability risk forecast for (2015–2017) 138; internal war, risk for (2015–2017) 125; non-state mass killing, risk for (2015–2017) 133; state-based mass killing, risk for (2015–2017) 130
Brunsdon, Chris, and Lex Comber 12
Brzoska, Michael 25
Bueno de Mesquita, Bruce, Alastair Smith, Randolph M. Siverson and James M. Morrow 68
Buhari, Muhammadu 164
Buhaug, Halvard xi, 1, 16–22
Buhaug, Halvard, and Kristian Skrede Gleditsch 143
Buhaug, Halvard, and Päivi Lujala 107
Buhaug, Halvard, Scott Gates, and Päivi Lujala 43, 107

Buhaug, Halvard and Scott Gates 27
Bulgaria: adverse regime change, risk for (2015–2017) 122; conflict-related violations (2015), criminal justice for 208; instability risk forecast for (2015–2017) 138; internal war, risk for (2015–2017) 126; non-state mass killing, risk for (2015–2017) 134; state-based mass killing, risk for (2015–2017) 130
Burkina Faso: adverse regime change, risk for (2015–2017) 121; instability risk forecast for (2015–2017) 137; internal war, risk for (2015–2017) 125; non-state mass killing, risk for (2015–2017) 132; state-based mass killing, risk for (2015–2017) 128
Burns, Arthur Lee, and Nina Heathcote 179
Burundi: adverse regime change, risk for (2015–2017) 120; conflict-related violations (2015), criminal justice for 226; fatalities in 80; instability risk forecast for (2015–2017) 137; internal war, risk for (2015–2017) 126; non-state mass killing, risk for (2015–2017) 133; state-based mass killing, risk for (2015–2017) 129; terrorist attacks (1970–2014) 80
Bush, George W. 176
Butcher, Charles 26
Butler, Christopher K., Tali Gluch, and Neil J. Mitchell 63

Cambodia: adverse regime change, risk for (2015–2017) 122; conflict-related violations (2015), criminal justice for 211–12; ICSC-Cambodia (International Commissions for Supervision and Control in Cambodia) 179; instability risk forecast for (2015–2017) 138; internal war, risk for (2015–2017) 125; non-state mass killing, risk for (2015–2017) 133; state-based mass killing, risk for (2015–2017) 129
Cameroon: adverse regime change, risk for (2015–2017) 121; instability risk (2015–2017) 118; instability risk forecast for (2015–2017) 136; internal war, risk for (2015–2017) 125; non-state mass killing, risk for (2015–2017) 132; state-based mass killing, risk for (2015–2017) 128
Canada: adverse regime change, risk for (2015–2017) 123; instability risk forecast for (2015–2017) 139; internal war, risk for (2015–2017) 126; non-state mass killing, risk for (2015–2017) 134; Sikh extremists in 80; state-based mass killing, risk for (2015–2017) 131; terrorist attacks (1970–2014) 80
Cape Verde: adverse regime change, risk for (2015–2017) 122; instability risk forecast for (2015–2017) 139; internal war, risk for (2015–2017) 126; non-state mass killing, risk for (2015–2017) 135; state-based mass killing, risk for (2015–2017) 131
Carey, Sabine, Neil Mitchell, and Will Lowe 57n3
Caribbean, terrorism in 85–6
Carothers, Thomas 74
Carter, David B., and Curtis S. Signorino 149
Ceaușescu, Nicolae 222
Cederman, Lars-Erik, Andreas Wimmer, and Brian Min 145, 149
Cederman, Lars-Erik, Kristian Gleditsch, and Halvard Buhaug 74
Cederman, Lars-Erik, Kristian Gleditsch, and Simon Hug 69
Cederman, Lars-Erik, Kristian Skrede Gleditsch, Idean Salehyan, and Julian Wucherpfennig 143, 146
Cederman, Lars-Erik, Nils B. Weidmann, and Kristian Skrede Gleditsch 108
Cederman, Lars-Erik, Simon Hug, and Lutz Krebs 69, 73
Center for International Development and Conflict Management (CIDCM) 1; Peace and Conflict Instability Ledger (2017) 101, 102, 104, 117, 140n1
Central African Republic: adverse regime change, risk for (2015–2017) 120; conflict-related violations (2015), criminal justice for 212–13, 226; instability risk (2015–2017) 118; instability risk forecast for (2015–2017) 136; internal war, risk for (2015–2017) 124; multilateral peacekeeping missions in 181; non-state mass killing, risk for (2015–2017) 132; state-based mass killing, risk for (2015–2017) 128

Chad: adverse regime change, risk for (2015–2017) 120; conflict-related violations (2015), criminal justice for 213–14; instability risk (2015–2017) 118; instability risk forecast for (2015–2017) 136; internal war, risk for (2015–2017) 124; non-state mass killing, risk for (2015–2017) 132; state-based mass killing, risk for (2015–2017) 128

Chaem, Im 212

Chechen Martyrs 80

chemical, biological, radiological and nuclear (CBRN) agents 84–5

Chile: adverse regime change, risk for (2015–2017) 123; conflict-related violations (2015), criminal justice for 214, 227; instability risk forecast for (2015–2017) 139; internal war, risk for (2015–2017) 126; non-state mass killing, risk for (2015–2017) 134; state-based mass killing, risk for (2015–2017) 130

China: adverse regime change, risk for (2015–2017) 122; instability risk (2015–2017) 118; instability risk forecast for (2015–2017) 136; internal war, risk for (2015–2017) 124; non-state mass killing, risk for (2015–2017) 132; state-based mass killing, risk for (2015–2017) 128

Choi, Seung-Whan, and Idean Salehyan 144

Chojnacki, Sven, Christian Ickler, Michael Spies, and John Wiesel 6

Christian Extremists in Sudan 80

Chui, Mathieu Ngudjolo 215

CIAT (Centro Internacional de Agricultura Tropical) 12

CIESIN (Center for International Earth Science Information Network) 12, 13

Cil, Deniz xi, 2, 108, 179–207

Cingranelli, David, and David Richards 88

Cingranelli and Richards Physical Integrity Rights Index (CIRI) 88, 89, 99

civil conflict, spread of 143–4

civil war onset: democratization and 70, 71, 74; probability of (1946–2010) 71, 72

Clark, Ann Marie, and Kathryn Sikkink 88–90, 94, 96, 99

Clayton, Govinda 57n9

clean elections 70, 71, 72, 73, 74

closing borders 151

coercion, engagement in 46

Cohen, Dara Kay 58, 59, 64

Cohen, Dara Kay, Amelia Hoover Green, and Elisabeth Jean Wood 58, 62, 63

Cohen, Dara Kay, and Ragnhild Nordås 58, 59, 60, 61, 62, 63, 64, 65, 66

Cold War era peacekeeping missions 179

Collier, Paul, and Hoeffler, Anke 144

Collier, Paul, Anke Hoeffler, and Måns Söderbom 69, 106

Colombia: adverse regime change, risk for (2015–2017) 120; conflict-related violations (2015), criminal justice for 226; ELN (Ejército de Liberación Nacional) and 158; FARC (Fuerzas Armadas Revolucionarias de Colombia) and 158; instability risk (2015–2017) 118; instability risk forecast for (2015–2017) 136; internal war, risk for (2015–2017) 124; non-state mass killing, risk for (2015–2017) 132; state-based mass killing, risk for (2015–2017) 129

Communist Party of Nepal-Maoist (CPN-M) 80, 81

Comoros: adverse regime change, risk for (2015–2017) 121; instability risk forecast for (2015–2017) 138; internal war, risk for (2015–2017) 126; non-state mass killing, risk for (2015–2017) 133; state-based mass killing, risk for (2015–2017) 130

conflict-related sexual violence, prevalence of 2, 58–67; Africa, prevalence of sexual violence by conflict actors in (2000–2009) 66; conflict actors perpetrating sexual violence: proportions of (1989–2009) 61; trends in (1989–2009) 60; conflict actors perpetrating sexual violence, mapping prevalence of (1989–2009) 64; conflict-related sexual violence: definition of 59;

emergence of 59–60; knowledge gap on 66; phenomenon of 58; prevalence by region (1989–2009) 65; trends in 60–62; gender inequality, sexual violence and 58; International Criminal Court (ICT) 59; media proliferation and 66; phenomenon of conflict-related sexual violence 58; rituals of violence 58; sexual violence: concern about 58; conflict actors' perpetration of 62–4; occurrence in many conflicts 66; regional variation in 64–5; Sexual Violence and Armed Conflict (SVAC) dataset 58, 62, 66; by state and non-state forces, correspondence between (1989–2009) 62; by states and militias, correspondence between (1989–2009) 62; stigmatization, fear of 62; UN Security Council Resolution 1889 (2009) 59

conflict-related violations (2015), criminal justice for 2–3, 208–33; Afghanistan 226; Argentina 209–10, 227; Bangladesh 210–11; Belgium 227; Bulgaria 208; Burundi 226; Cambodia 211–12; Central African Republic 212–13, 226; Chad 213–14; Chile 214, 227; closed preliminary examinations 227; Colombia 226; communist era in Eastern Europe 208–9; Congo Democratic Republic 215–16; Côte d'Ivoire 214–15; country profiles 209–25; European Court of Human Rights (ECHR) 209; Finland 227; France 228; Gabon 226–7; Georgia 226; Germany 228; Guatemala 209, 217–19; Guinea 227; Honduras 227; ICC Office of the Prosecutor (OTP) 209, 220, 224, 226, 227; Inter-American Commission for Human Rights 209; International Criminal Court (ICC) 208–9, 212–15, 219, 220, 221, 224–5, 226, 227; International Criminal Tribunal for Former Yugoslavia (ICTY) 209; International Criminal Tribunal for Rwanda (ICTR) 209; investigations 226–7; Israel-Palestine 208; Kenya 209, 219–20; Libya 220; Mali 208, 221; Nepal 221–2; Netherlands 228; Nigeria 227; Norway 228; Palestine 227; Palestine, situation in 208; Romania 208, 222; Rome Statute (2004) 208, 209, 224–5, 226, 227, 232n142; Rwanda 222–3; Senegal 228; South Africa 228; Spain 228; Special Court for Sierra Leone (SCSL) 209; Sudan 209, 224–5; Sweden 228; Switzerland 228; Uganda 225; Ukraine 227; United Kingdom 227, 228; United States 227, 228; universal jurisdiction cases 227–8; war crimes, legal applications of 208; Yugoslavia (former state of) 216–17

Conflict Termination Dataset (UCDP) 54

Congo Democratic Republic: ADF (Alliance of Democratic Forces) and 174–5; adverse regime change, risk for (2015–2017) 120; conflict-related violations (2015), criminal justice for 215–16; instability risk (2015–2017) 118; instability risk forecast for (2015–2017) 136; internal war, risk for (2015–2017) 124; multilateral peacekeeping missions in 181; non-state mass killing, risk for (2015–2017) 132; state-based mass killing, risk for (2015–2017) 128

Congo Republic: adverse regime change, risk for (2015–2017) 121; instability risk forecast for (2015–2017) 137; internal war, risk for (2015–2017) 125; non-state mass killing, risk for (2015–2017) 133; state-based mass killing, risk for (2015–2017) 128

Coppedge, Michael, John Gerring, Staffan I. Lindberg, Daniel Pemstein, et al. 70

Coppedge, Michael, John Gerring, Staffan I. Lindberg, Svend-Erik Skaaning, et al. 73

Costa Rica: adverse regime change, risk for (2015–2017) 123; instability risk forecast for (2015–2017) 139; internal war, risk for (2015–2017) 127; non-state mass killing, risk for (2015–2017) 134; state-based mass killing, risk for (2015–2017) 130

Côte d'Ivoire: adverse regime change, risk for (2015–2017) 120; conflict-related violations (2015), criminal justice for 214–15; Forces Républicaines de Côte d'Ivoire (FRCI) 192; instability risk (2015–2017) 118; instability risk forecast for (2015–2017) 136; internal war, risk for (2015–2017) 124; multilateral peacekeeping missions in 181; non-state mass killing, risk for

Index

(2015–2017) 132; state-based mass killing, risk for (2015–2017) 128

country of asylum (CoA): ethnic balance in 142–3; refugees, conflict diffusion and 147, 149–50, 151

Country Reports on Terrorism (US, 2015) 77

Cox, Arthur M. 179

CPP (Communist Party of the Philippines), Philippines and 167–8

Crisp, Jeff 146

Croatia: adverse regime change, risk for (2015–2017) 122; instability risk forecast for (2015–2017) 138; internal war, risk for (2015–2017) 126; non-state mass killing, risk for (2015–2017) 135; state-based mass killing, risk for (2015–2017) 131

Croicu, Mihai, and Joakim Kreutz 6, 26

Croicu, Mihai and Ralph Sundberg 23, 35

Cuba: adverse regime change, risk for (2015–2017) 123; instability risk forecast for (2015–2017) 138; internal war, risk for (2015–2017) 126; non-state mass killing, risk for (2015–2017) 134; state-based mass killing, risk for (2015–2017) 129

Cunningham, David 107

Cunningham, David E., Kristian S. Gleditsch, and Idean Salehyan. 46, 47

Cyprus: adverse regime change, risk for (2015–2017) 123; instability risk forecast for (2015–2017) 139; internal war, risk for (2015–2017) 127; multilateral peacekeeping missions in 181; non-state mass killing, risk for (2015–2017) 135; state-based mass killing, risk for (2015–2017) 131

Czech Republic: adverse regime change, risk for (2015–2017) 122; instability risk forecast for (2015–2017) 138; internal war, risk for (2015–2017) 126; non-state mass killing, risk for (2015–2017) 135; state-based mass killing, risk for (2015–2017) 130

Dahl, Robert 70

The Dark Side of Democracy (Mann, M.) 68

data-collection: data shortcomings, misleading exclusions and 69; integration and, coverage, quality and 8–11; integration of different types of data 11–12; need for systematic and consistent protocol for 47; process for 48; reliability and 117

Davenport, Christian 62

Davenport, Christian A., Will H. Moore, and Steven C. Poe 142

demobilization, disarmament and reintegration (DDR) programs 179

democracy, democratization and civil war 2, 68–75; association, freedom of 70, 71, 72; autocracies 68–9; case against democracy 68–9; civil war onset, democratization and 70, 71, 74; civil war onset, probability of (1946–2010) 71, 72; clean elections 70, 71, 72, 73, 74; *The Dark Side of Democracy* (Mann, M.) 68; data shortcomings, misleading exclusions and 69; democracy, attributes of 74; democratization, violent potential of 74; democratization process 68; Electoral Democracy Index 71; disaggregation of 70; electoral management body (EMB) 72, 73, 75n4; empirical analysis 71–3; expression, freedom of 70, 71, 72; inclusive and extractive political institutions, distinction between 69; Maddison Database 71; political instability 69; political participation, openness of 69; Polity indicators 70; problems with prior research 69; regime categories, disaggregating with new data 69–70; societal conflict, democracy and 68; socio-economic development 69; "sore loser" effect 69; Uppsala/PRIO Armed Conflict Dataset 71; V-Dem data, potential for 71, 72, 74; V-Dem Project 70

Denmark: adverse regime change, risk for (2015–2017) 123; instability risk forecast for (2015–2017) 139; internal war, risk for (2015–2017) 127; non-state mass killing, risk for (2015–2017) 135; state-based mass killing, risk for (2015–2017) 131

Diehl, Paul F., and Daniel Druckman 180

Djibouti: adverse regime change, risk for (2015–2017) 120; instability risk (2015–2017) 118; instability risk forecast for (2015–2017) 137; internal war, risk for (2015–2017) 126; non-state mass killing, risk for (2015–2017) 133; state-based mass killing, risk for (2015–2017) 129

Djotodia, Michel 226

DJRF (Darfur Joint Resistance Forces), Sudan and 170–71

Dominican Republic: adverse regime change, risk for (2015–2017) 121; instability risk forecast for (2015–2017) 138; internal war, risk for (2015–2017) 126; non-state mass killing, risk for (2015–2017) 133; state-based mass killing, risk for (2015–2017) 130

Donetsk People's Republic 80, 175

Donnay, Karsten xi, 1, 4–15

Donnay, Karsten, and Ravi Bhavnani 4, 23

Donnay, Karsten, and Vladimir Filimonov 6

Donnay, Karsten, Elena Gadjanova, and Ravi Bhavnani 4, 5

Donnay, Karsten, Eric Dunford, Erin C. McGrath, David Backer, and David E. Cunningham 8

Donnay, Karsten and Andrew Linke 12

Doyle, Michael W., and Nicholas Sambanis 180

Dugan, Laura xii, 2, 77–87

Dunford, Eric xii, 1, 23–33

Dyilo, Lubanga 215

Eastern Europe 82, 204; communist era in 208–9; countries in 85

Eck, Kristine and Lisa Hultman 32n4, 107, 108

Economic Community Mission in Bissau (ECOMIB) 181, 200–201

Economic Community of Central African States (ECCAS) 203

Economic Community of West African States (ECOWAS) 179, 181, 190, 191, 200, 201, 221; ECOWAS Mission in Liberia (ECOMIL) 190

Ecuador: adverse regime change, risk for (2015–2017) 121; instability risk forecast for (2015–2017) 137; internal war, risk for (2015–2017) 125; non-state mass killing, risk for (2015–2017) 133; state-based mass killing, risk for (2015–2017) 129

Egypt: adverse regime change, risk for (2015–2017) 121; instability risk (2015–2017) 118; instability risk forecast for (2015–2017) 136; internal war, risk for (2015–2017) 124; multilateral peacekeeping missions in Sinai 181; Multi-national Force and Observers (MFO) in Sinai 181, 186–7; non-state mass killing, risk for (2015–2017) 132; state-based mass killing, risk for (2015–2017) 128

Eifert, Benn, Edward Miguel, and Daniel N. Posner 69

El Salvador: adverse regime change, risk for (2015–2017) 121; instability risk forecast for (2015–2017) 138; internal war, risk for (2015–2017) 125; non-state mass killing, risk for (2015–2017) 134; state-based mass killing, risk for (2015–2017) 130; terrorist attacks (1970–2014) 80

Electoral Democracy Index 71; disaggregation of 70

electoral management body (EMB) 72, 73, 75n4

Elfversson, Emma 26

Elkins, Zachary, and Beth Simmons 143

ELN (Ejército de Liberación Nacional), Colombia and 158

Enders, Walter, Gary A. Hoover, and Todd Sandler 43

Equatorial Guinea: adverse regime change, risk for (2015–2017) 120; instability risk forecast for (2015–2017) 137; internal war, risk for (2015–2017) 126; non-state mass killing, risk for (2015–2017) 133; state-based mass killing, risk for (2015–2017) 128

Eritrea: adverse regime change, risk for (2015–2017) 120; instability risk (2015–2017) 118; instability risk forecast for (2015–2017) 136; internal war, risk for (2015–2017) 124; non-state mass killing, risk for (2015–2017) 132; state-based mass killing, risk for (2015–2017) 128

Estonia: adverse regime change, risk for (2015–2017) 122; instability risk forecast for (2015–2017) 139; internal war, risk for (2015–2017) 126; non-state mass killing, risk for (2015–2017) 135; state-based mass killing, risk for (2015–2017) 131

Estrada. Joseph 168

Ethiopia: adverse regime change, risk for (2015–2017) 122; instability risk (2015–2017) 118; instability risk forecast for (2015–2017) 136; internal war, risk for (2015–2017) 124; non-state mass killing, risk for (2015–2017) 132; OLF (Oromo Liberation Front) and 159; state-based mass killing, risk for (2015–2017) 128

ethnic balance argument: ethnic linkages of refugees to host population, role of 145–6; testing against new refugee data 146–7

Ethnic Power Relations (EPR) dataset 149

European Court of Human Rights (ECHR) 209

European Union (EU): EUFOR-Althea in Bosnia and Herzegovina 181, 194; Military Force - République Centrafricaine (EUFOR-RCA) 181, 202–3; multilateral peacekeeping operations active (2015) 179, 189; Rule of Law Mission (EULEX) 190

expression, freedom of 70, 71, 72

false negatives 112

false positives 109, 112

FARC (Fuerzas Armadas Revolucionarias de Colombia), Colombia and 158

Fariss, Christopher J. 62; global human rights conditions 89, 90, 94, 96, 99

fatalities: infliction of, rebel force size and (1975–2014) 56; organized armed violence and (PRIO-GRID, 1989–2015) 29; from terrorist attacks by region (1970–2014) 81–2; worldwide trends in 79

Fearon, James, and David Laitin 106, 108, 143

Fiji: adverse regime change, risk for (2015–2017) 122; instability risk forecast for (2015–2017) 138; internal war, risk for (2015–2017) 126; non-state mass killing, risk for (2015–2017) 134; state-based mass killing, risk for (2015–2017) 129

Findley, Michael, and Joseph Young 106

Finland: adverse regime change, risk for (2015–2017) 123; conflict-related violations (2015), criminal justice for 227; instability risk forecast for (2015–2017) 139; internal war, risk for (2015–2017) 127; non-state mass killing, risk for (2015–2017) 135; state-based mass killing, risk for (2015–2017) 131

Fjelde, Hanne xii, 1–2, 26, 34–45, 69

Fjelde, Hanne, Lisa Hultman, and Margareta Sollenberg 31, 34, 38

Fjelde, Hanne, Lisa Hultman, and Sara Lindberg Bromley 26

Fjelde, Hanne and Gudrun Østby 26

Fjelde, Hanne and Lisa Hultman 26, 34, 36, 39

Fjelde, Hanne and Nina von Uexkull 26

Fleitz, Frederick H. 180

Flores, Judge Patricia 218

forced displacement: levels of 142; political violence and 142

Forces Démocratiques de Libération du Rwanda (FDLR) 197

Forces Républicaines de Côte d'Ivoire (FRCI) 192

Forsberg, Erika 143, 144, 146

Fortna, Virginia Page 180

Fortna, Virginia Page, and Lise Morjé Howard 204n1

France: adverse regime change, risk for (2015–2017) 122; conflict-related violations (2015), criminal justice for 228; instability risk forecast for (2015–2017) 138; internal war, risk for (2015–2017) 127; non-state mass killing, risk for (2015–2017) 134; state-based mass killing, risk for (2015–2017) 130

Friedman, Jeffrey A. 47

Gabon: adverse regime change, risk for (2015–2017) 120; conflict-related violations (2015), criminal justice for 226–7; instability risk (2015–2017) 118; instability risk forecast for (2015–2017) 136; internal war, risk for (2015–2017) 126; non-state mass killing, risk for (2015–2017) 133; state-based mass killing, risk for (2015–2017) 129

Gaddafi, Muammar 220

Gaddafi, Saif Al-Islam 220

Gaibulloev, Khusrav, Justin George, Todd Sandler, and Hirofumi Shimizu 180

Gaibulloev, Khusrav, Todd Sandler, and Hirofumi Shimizu 180

The Gambia: adverse regime change, risk for (2015–2017) 121; instability risk forecast for (2015–2017) 137; internal war, risk for (2015–2017) 126; non-state mass killing, risk for (2015–2017) 133; state-based mass killing, risk for (2015–2017) 129

Gamboru Ngala, fatalities in 80

Garcia Arredondo, Pedro 218

Gassebne, Martin, Jerg Gutmann, and Stefan Voigt 106

Gbagbo, Laurent 214–15

Gbagbo, Simone 215

gender inequality, sexual violence and 58

generalizability from micro-level research 4–5

Geneva Agreements on Cessation of Hostilities in Indochina 179

Georeferenced Event Dataset (GED, UCDP) 1; see also Uppsala Conflict Data Program (UCDP) 1

Georgia: adverse regime change, risk for (2015–2017) 121; conflict-related violations (2015), criminal justice for 226; instability risk forecast for (2015–2017) 138; internal war, risk for (2015–2017) 125; non-state mass killing, risk for (2015–2017) 134; state-based mass killing, risk for (2015–2017) 129

Gerardi, Bishop Juan José 218

Germany: adverse regime change, risk for (2015–2017) 123; conflict-related violations (2015), criminal justice for 228; instability risk forecast for (2015–2017) 139; internal war, risk for (2015–2017) 127; non-state mass killing, risk for (2015–2017) 134; state-based mass killing, risk for (2015–2017) 131

Ghana: adverse regime change, risk for (2015–2017) 121; instability risk forecast for (2015–2017) 137; internal war, risk for (2015–2017) 126; non-state mass killing, risk for (2015–2017) 132; state-based mass killing, risk for (2015–2017) 129

Gibney, Mark xii, 2, 88–100

Gikoro, fatalities in 80

Gilligan, Michael, and Stephen John Stedman 180

Gilligan, Michael J., and Ernest J. Sergenti 180

Girardin, Luc, Philipp Hunziker, Lars-Erik Cederman, Nils-Christian Bormann, and Manuel Vogt 149

Gisenyi, fatalities in 80

Gleditsch, Kristian, and Håvard Hegre 68, 69

Gleditsch, Kristian Skrede 143

Gleditsch, Kristian Skrede, and Andrea Ruggeri 69

Gleditsch, Nils Petter, and Ida Rudolfsen 20, 21, 22

Gleditsch, Nils Petter, Peter Wallensteen, Mikael Eriksson, Margareta Sollenberg, and Håvard Strand 16, 19, 20, 21, 27, 32n4, 71, 142, 147

Global Database of Events, Language and Tone (GDELT) 23

global terrorism, evolution of 2, 77–87; Abadan, fatalities in 80; al-Qaeda 80, 81; armed assault 83–4; assassination 83–4; attack concentration, shift in 85–7; Badush, fatalities in 80; Bedi, fatalities in 80; Beslan, fatalities in 80; Boko Haram 80; bombings 83–4; Burundi, fatalities in 80; Caribbean, countries in 85–6; casualties of terrorist attacks, annual numbers (1970–2014) 79; Chechen Martyrs 80; chemical, biological, radiological and nuclear (CBRN) agents 84–5; Christian Extremists 80; Communist Party of Nepal-Maoist (CPN-M) 80, 81; Country Reports on Terrorism (US, 2015) 77; deadliest attacks (1970–2014) 80–85; Donetsk People's

Index

Republic 80; East and Central Asia, countries in 85; Eastern Europe, countries in 85; fatalities, worldwide trends in 79; fatalities from terrorist attacks by region (1970–2014) 81–2; Gamboru Ngala, fatalities in 80; Gikoro, fatalities in 80; Gisenyi, fatalities in 80; Global Terrorism Database (GTD) 77, 78, 79, 80, 82, 84, 85, 87n2–3; hijacking 83–4; Homoine, fatalities in 80; hostage taking 83–4; Hrabove, fatalities in 80; Hutu Extremists 80; infractrusture attack 83–4; Islamic State of Iraq and the Levant (ISIL) 80, 81; Islamic State of Iraq on the Levant (ISIL) 77; Kilinochchi, fatalities in 80; Kivyuka, fatalities in 80; Latin America, countries in 85–6; lethality of attacks across targets, variations in 83; Liberation Tigers of Tamil Eelam (LTTE) 80; Middle East, countries in 86; Mozambique National Resistance Movement (MNR) 80; Mujahedin-e Khalq (MEK) 80; New York City, fatalities in 80, 81, 87n3; North Africa, countries in 86; North America, countries in 86; Oceania, countries in 86; Palmyra, fatalities in 80; Raqqah, fatalities in 80; regional distribution of fatalities 82; regions, countries in 85–7; Sikh Extremists 80; Sinjar, fatalities in 80; South Asia, countries in 86; Southeast Asia, countries in 86; Study of Terrorism and Responses to Terrorism (START), National Consortium for 77; Sub-Saharan Africa, countries in 86–7; Suchitoto, fatalities in 80; tactics of terror 83–4; targets of terrorism 82–3; terrorism, worldwide trends in 77–9; terrorist attacks, annual numbers (1970–2014) 78; Tikrit, fatalities in 80; Toronto, fatalities in 80; Tutsi Extremists 80; Uaskeing, fatalities in 80; unarmed assault 84; US Department of Homeland Security (DHS) 87n1; weapons of terror 84–5; Western Europe, countries in 86–7

Global Terrorism Database (GTD) 13; global terrorism, evolution of 77, 78, 79, 80, 82, 84, 85, 87n2–3; organized armed violence, geography of 23; violence against civilians, spatial patterns of 44n1

global trends in organized armed violence 28–31

Goldstone, Jack, Robert Bates, David Epstein, Ted Gurr, Michael Lustik, Monty Marshall, et al. 69, 106

Goldstone, Jack A. 144, 146

Gomez, Margarita Puerto, Asger Christensen, Yonatan Yehdego Araya, and Niels Harild 144

granularity: geographic and temporal manifestations 23; granular coverage of conflict 27–8

Greece: adverse regime change, risk for (2015–2017) 123; civil war in 34; instability risk forecast for (2015–2017) 139; internal war, risk for (2015–2017) 127; non-state mass killing, risk for (2015–2017) 134; state-based mass killing, risk for (2015–2017) 130

Greig, J. Michael 26

Guatemala: adverse regime change, risk for (2015–2017) 121; conflict-related violations (2015), criminal justice for 209, 217–19; instability risk forecast for (2015–2017) 137; internal war, risk for (2015–2017) 125; non-state mass killing, risk for (2015–2017) 133; state-based mass killing, risk for (2015–2017) 130

guerrilla warfare 46

Guinea: adverse regime change, risk for (2015–2017) 120; conflict-related violations (2015), criminal justice for 227; instability risk (2015–2017) 118; instability risk forecast for (2015–2017) 136; internal war, risk for (2015–2017) 125; non-state mass killing, risk for (2015–2017) 132; state-based mass killing, risk for (2015–2017) 128

Guinea-Bissau: adverse regime change, risk for (2015–2017) 120; Economic Community Mission in Bissau (ECOMIB) 181, 200–201; instability risk forecast for (2015–2017) 137; internal war, risk for (2015–2017) 126; multilateral peacekeeping missions in 181; non-state mass killing, risk for (2015–2017) 133; state-based mass killing, risk for (2015–2017) 129

Guyana: adverse regime change, risk for (2015–2017) 120; instability risk (2015–2017) 118; instability risk forecast for (2015–2017) 137; internal war, risk for (2015–2017) 125; non-state mass killing, risk for (2015–2017) 134; state-based mass killing, risk for (2015–2017) 129

Haas, Ernst B., Robert Lyle Butterworth, and Joseph S. Nye 179

Haber, Stephen, and Victor Menaldo 71

Habré, Hissène 213–14

Hadžic, Goran 216

Hainmueller, Jens, and Chad Hazlett 100n2

Haiti: adverse regime change, risk for (2015–2017) 120; instability risk (2015–2017) 118; instability risk forecast for (2015–2017) 136; internal war, risk for (2015–2017) 124; multilateral peacekeeping missions in 181; non-state mass killing, risk for (2015–2017) 133; state-based mass killing, risk for (2015–2017) 128

Hallberg, Johan Dittrich 27

Hanmer, Michael J., and Kerem Ozan Kalkan 149

Harbom, Lotta, and Peter Wallensteen 66

Harpviken, Kristian Berg, and Sarah Kenyon Lischer 144

Harun, Ahmad 224

Haschke, Peter xii, 2, 88–100

Hegre, Håvard 68, 69, 70, 74

Hegre, Håvard, and Nicholas Sambanis 143

Hegre, Håvard, Gudrun Østby, and Clionadh Raleigh 43

Hegre, Håvard, Joakim Karlsen, Håvard Nygård, Håvard Strand, and Henrik Urdal 106

Hegre, Håvard, Tanja Ellingsen, Scott Gates, and Nils Petter Gleditsch 68

Heldt, Birger, and Peter Wallensteen 179, 204n2

Heston, Alan, Robert Summers, and Bettina Aten 149

Hewitt, J. Joseph 101

Higgins, Rosalyn 179

hijacking 83–4

Hill, Stuart, and Donald Rothchild 143

Hodis, Vasile 222

Hodler, Roland and Paul A. Raschky 26

Högbladh, Stina, Thérése Pettersson, and Lotta Themnér 108

Höglund, Kristine, Erik Melander, Margareta Sollenberg, and Ralph Sundberg 41

Holtermann, Helge 57n9

Homoine, fatalities in 80

Homosteanu, George 222

Honduras: adverse regime change, risk for (2015–2017) 121; conflict-related violations (2015), criminal justice for 227; instability risk forecast for (2015–2017) 137; internal war, risk for (2015–2017) 125; non-state mass killing, risk for (2015–2017) 134; state-based mass killing, risk for (2015–2017) 129

Horowitz, Donald 69

hostage taking 83–4

Hrabove, fatalities in 80

Hultman, Lisa xii, 1–2, 34–45, 46, 107, 108

Hultman, Lisa, Jacob D. Kathman, and Megan Shannon 26, 180

human rights conditions 2, 88–100; accountability, changing standard of 89; Amnesty International 88; analytical design 90–91; bias in measures of 99; Cingranelli and Richards Physical Integrity Rights Index (CIRI) 88, 89, 99; high-priority issue 88; Human Rights Watch (HRW) 88; information, quantity and quality of 88–9; kernel regularized least squares (KRLS) regressions 92, 95, 97, 98, 99, 100n2; Latin America, information about 90; ordinary least squares (OLS) regressions 92, 95, 97, 98, 100n2; Political Terror Scale (PTS) 88, 89, 99; full report word counts by PTS scores 96–7; global annual average scores (1976–2014) 89; relationship between PTS scores and word count estimates (1999–2014) 98; report length and 94–9; within-country effects of word counts on PTS scores (1999–2014) 99; selective data 89–90; time, report length over 91–4; US State Department 88, 90, 99; growth rates of human rights reports (1999–2015) 93, 94; time effects for word counts (1999–2015) 92; within-country effects of word counts on PTS scores (1999–2014) 99; within-country time effects of human rights reports (1999–2015) 95, 96; within-country variability of human rights reports (1999–2015) 98; word counts in human rights reports (1999–2015) 90, 91, 92

Human Rights Watch (HRW) 88, 213, 228n15
Humphreys, Macartan, and Jeremy Weinstein 108
Hungary: adverse regime change, risk for (2015–2017) 123; instability risk forecast for (2015–2017) 139; internal war, risk for (2015–2017) 127; non-state mass killing, risk for (2015–2017) 134; state-based mass killing, risk for (2015–2017) 131
Huntington, Samuel P. 69
Hussein, Abdel Raheem Muhammed 224
Hussein, Saddam 20, 22n2, 161
Huth, Paul K. xi, 1–3, 46–57, 101–41
Hutu Extremists in Rwanda 80

ICSC-Cambodia (International Commissions for Supervision and Control in Cambodia) 179
ICSC-Laos (International Commissions for Supervision and Control in Laos) 179
ICSC-Vietnam (International Commissions for Supervision and Control in Vietnam) 179
Ide, Tobias, Janpater Schilling, Jasmin S. A. Link, Jürgen Scheffran, Grace Ngaruiya, and Thomas Weinzierl 25, 26
Iliescu, Ion 222
India: adverse regime change, risk for (2015–2017) 121; instability risk (2015–2017) 118; instability risk forecast for (2015–2017) 136; internal war, risk for (2015–2017) 124; Kashmir insurgents and 160; multilateral peacekeeping missions in 181; non-state mass killing, risk for (2015–2017) 132; Pakistan and 160–61; state-based mass killing, risk for (2015–2017) 129
Indonesia: adverse regime change, risk for (2015–2017) 121; instability risk forecast for (2015–2017) 137; internal war, risk for (2015–2017) 124; non-state mass killing, risk for (2015–2017) 132; state-based mass killing, risk for (2015–2017) 129
information, quantity and quality of 88–9
infractrusture attack 83–4
instability: institutional level instability risk factors 106; international instability risk factors 106; measures of 102–3; overall instability risk factors 114; political instability 69; Political Instability Task Force (PITF) 101, 102, 103; risk factors 114–17; risk of, factors in models of 106–8; structural country-level instability risk factors 106
Integrated Conflict Early Warning System (ICEWS) 23
Inter-American Commission for Human Rights 209, 219
internal conflicts, rebel and state armed forces in 2, 46–57; coercion, engagement in 46; conflict outcomes: rebel force size and distribution of (1975–2005) 55; size of rebel groups and 46; Conflict Termination Dataset (UCDP) 54; counterinsurgency, median share of state forces committed to (1985–2014) 53; data-collection, need for systematic and consistent protocol for 47; data-collection process 48; fatalities inflicted, rebel force size and (1975–2014) 56; favourable outcomes 54; guerrilla warfare 46; impact of size of rebel and state fighting forces, assessment of 54–6; *Keesings Record of World Events* 48; lethality in internal conflicts, size of rebel forces and 54–6; median size of rebel forces: comparison by conflict duration 52; trends by region (1975–2014) 49; trends

by type of warfare (1975–2014) 51; military capabilities 46; mixed outcomes 54; Monte Carlo simulation 54, 57n10; Non-State Actor Dataset 46, 48; patterns and trends in size of rebel and state fighting forces 48–54; Peace Agreement Dataset (UCDP) 54; rebel forces, definition of 47; regional trends in size of rebel forces 49; size of rebel and state fighting forces, new dataset on 47–8; size of rebel and state forces, variation during conflict of 50–52, 56; size of rebel forces and outcomes during internal conflicts 54; state forces, definition of 47–8; state forces committed to fighting insurgencies, variation in share of 52–3; Stockholm International Peace Research Institute (SIPRI) 48; technology of conflict 48; size of rebel forces and 50; triangulation of information 48; UCDP Armed Conflict Dataset (ACD) 47; unfavourable outcomes 54; Uppsala Conflict Data Program (UCDP) Georeferenced Event Dataset (UCDP-GED) 46, 47
internal war: data sources 103, 104; dyad-year model of offset of 105; global map of risk of 115; onset model 105–9; risk factors 114
International Committee of the Red Cross (ICRC) 185
International Criminal Court (ICC) 208, 209, 212–15, 219, 220, 221, 224–5, 226, 227; conflict-related sexual violence and 59; ICC Office of the Prosecutor (OTP) 209, 220, 224, 226, 227; investigations 226–7
International Criminal Tribunal for Former Yugoslavia (ICTY) 209
International Criminal Tribunal for Rwanda (ICTR) 209
International Monitoring Team (IMT) in Philippines (Mindanao) 179, 181, 193–4
IPI (International Peace Institute) 108
Iran: adverse regime change, risk for (2015–2017) 122; instability risk (2015–2017) 118; instability risk forecast for (2015–2017) 136; internal war, risk for (2015–2017) 124; non-state mass killing, risk for (2015–2017) 133; state-based mass killing, risk for (2015–2017) 128; terrorist attacks (1970–2014) 80
Iraq: adverse regime change, risk for (2015–2017) 120; instability risk (2015–2017) 118; instability risk forecast for (2015–2017) 136; internal war, risk for (2015–2017) 124; IS (Islamic State) and 161–2; non-state mass killing, risk for (2015–2017) 132; state-based mass killing, risk for (2015–2017) 128; terrorist attacks (1970–2014) 80
Ireland: adverse regime change, risk for (2015–2017) 123; instability risk forecast for (2015–2017) 139; internal war, risk for (2015–2017) 127; non-state mass killing, risk for (2015–2017) 135; state-based mass killing, risk for (2015–2017) 131
IS (Islamic State) 174, 178n4; armed conflict over time 16, 19, 20, 21, 25; Iraq and 161–2; Nigeria and 164; Syria and 171, 172, 173
Islamic State of Iraq and the Levant (ISIL) 77, 80, 81, 85, 87n3
Islamism 16, 20, 21; militant Islam, increase in dominance of 20–22
Israel: adverse regime change, risk for (2015–2017) 121; instability risk (2015–2017) 118; instability risk forecast for (2015–2017) 136; internal war, risk for (2015–2017) 124; Israeli Defense Force (IDF) 185; multilateral peacekeeping missions in Golan 181; non-state mass killing, risk for (2015–2017) 132; Palestine-Israel 208; state-based mass killing, risk for (2015–2017) 130
Italy: adverse regime change, risk for (2015–2017) 123; instability risk forecast for (2015–2017) 138; internal war, risk for (2015–2017) 127; non-state mass killing, risk for (2015–2017) 134; state-based mass killing, risk for (2015–2017) 130

Jacobsen, Karen 145
Jamaica: adverse regime change, risk for (2015–2017) 122; instability risk forecast for (2015–2017) 138; internal war, risk

Index

for (2015–2017) 126; non-state mass killing, risk for (2015–2017) 134; state-based mass killing, risk for (2015–2017) 130

Japan: adverse regime change, risk for (2015–2017) 123; instability risk forecast for (2015–2017) 138; internal war, risk for (2015–2017) 127; non-state mass killing, risk for (2015–2017) 134; state-based mass killing, risk for (2015–2017) 131

Jett, Dennis C. 180

Johnston, Patrick 107

Joint Border Verification and Monitoring Mechanism (JBVMM) 198

Joint Control Commission (JCC) in Moldova 181, 188–9

Joint Monitoring Mission/Joint Military Commission (JMM/JMC) in Sudan 179

Jordan: adverse regime change, risk for (2015–2017) 122; instability risk forecast for (2015–2017) 138; internal war, risk for (2015–2017) 126; non-state mass killing, risk for (2015–2017) 134; state-based mass killing, risk for (2015–2017) 130

Kabila, Joseph 215

Kabila, Laurent 215

Kagwanja, Peter, and Monica Juma 146

Kalyvas, Stathis N. 4, 34, 46

Kalyvas, Stathis N., and Laia Balcells 48, 50, 57n5, 106

Kambanda, Jean 223

Karadžic, Radovan 216

Kashmir insurgents, India and 160

Katanga, Germain 215

Kathman, Jacob D. 180

Kathman, Jacob D. and Reed M. Wood 26, 180

Kazakhstan: adverse regime change, risk for (2015–2017) 122; instability risk forecast for (2015–2017) 137; internal war, risk for (2015–2017) 125; non-state mass killing, risk for (2015–2017) 134; state-based mass killing, risk for (2015–2017) 129

Keesings Record of World Events 48

Kemal, Mustafa 173

Kenya: adverse regime change, risk for (2015–2017) 121; conflict-related violations (2015), criminal justice for 209, 219–20; instability risk forecast for (2015–2017) 137; internal war, risk for (2015–2017) 125; non-state mass killing, risk for (2015–2017) 132; state-based mass killing, risk for (2015–2017) 129

kernel regularized least squares (KRLS) regressions 92, 95, 97, 98, 99, 100n2

Khan, General Yahya 210–11

Khan, Shaharyan 144

Kiir, Salva 169–70

Kilinochchi, fatalities in 80

King, Gary 14

KIO (Kachin Independence Organization), Myanmar and 162–3

Kirchner, Néstor 210

Kivyuka, fatalities in 80

Knutsen, Carl Henrik, Jørgen Møller, and Svend-Erik Skaaning 74

Konstanz, Gerald, Margit Bussmann, and Constantin Ruhe 108

Kony, Joseph 174, 225

Koos, Carlo and Matthias Basedau 26

Kosovo: Kosovo Liberation Army (KLA) 189; multilateral peacekeeping missions in 181; NATO-led Kosovo Force (KFOR) 189

Krcmaric, Daniel 146

Kreutz, Joakim 26

Krishnarajan, Suthan xii, 2, 68–76

Kulkarni, Anupma xii, 2–3, 208–33

Kuwait: adverse regime change, risk for (2015–2017) 122; instability risk forecast for (2015–2017) 138; internal war, risk for (2015–2017) 126; non-state mass killing, risk for (2015–2017) 135; state-based mass killing, risk for (2015–2017) 130

Kyrgyzstan: adverse regime change, risk for (2015–2017) 120; instability risk forecast for (2015–2017) 137; internal war, risk for (2015–2017) 125; non-state mass killing, risk for (2015–2017) 134; state-based mass killing, risk for (2015–2017) 130

LaFree, Gary xii, 2, 77–87

LaFree, Gary, Laura Dugan, and Erin Miller 84, 87n2

Lake, David, and Donald Rothchild 143, 145

Lama, Colonel Kumar 222

Laos: adverse regime change, risk for (2015–2017) 121; ICSC-Laos (International Commissions for Supervision and Control in Laos) 179; instability risk forecast for (2015–2017) 137; internal war, risk for (2015–2017) 125; non-state mass killing, risk for (2015–2017) 133; state-based mass killing, risk for (2015–2017) 128

Latin America: countries in 85–6; information about human rights conditions 90

Latvia: adverse regime change, risk for (2015–2017) 122; instability risk forecast for (2015–2017) 138; internal war, risk for (2015–2017) 126; non-state mass killing, risk for (2015–2017) 135; state-based mass killing, risk for (2015–2017) 130

Lawrence, Christopher 47

Lebanon: adverse regime change, risk for (2015–2017) 120; instability risk (2015–2017) 118; instability risk forecast for (2015–2017) 136; internal war, risk for (2015–2017) 124; multilateral peacekeeping missions in 181; non-state mass killing, risk for (2015–2017) 134; South Lebanon Army (SLA) 185; state-based mass killing, risk for (2015–2017) 130

Lebson, Mike 144

Ledwidge, Frank 52

Leiby, Michele L. 63

Leiby, Michele L., Gudrun Østby, and Ragnhild Nordås 59

Lesotho: adverse regime change, risk for (2015–2017) 121; instability risk forecast for (2015–2017) 137; internal war, risk for (2015–2017) 126; non-state mass killing, risk for (2015–2017) 133; state-based mass killing, risk for (2015–2017) 130

lethality: of armed conflict over time 16; of attacks across targets, variations in 83; in internal conflicts, size of rebel forces and 54–6

Liberation Tigers of Tamil Eelam (LTTE) 80

Liberia: adverse regime change, risk for (2015–2017) 120; ECOWAS Mission in Liberia (ECOMIL) 190; instability risk forecast for (2015–2017) 137; internal war, risk for (2015–2017) 126; Liberians United for Reconciliation and Democracy (LURD) 190; Movement for Democracy in Liberia (MODEL) 190; multilateral peacekeeping missions in 181; National Transitional Government of Liberia (NTGL) 190; non-state mass killing, risk for (2015–2017) 133; state-based mass killing, risk for (2015–2017) 130

Libya: adverse regime change, risk for (2015–2017) 120; conflict-related violations (2015), criminal justice for 220; instability risk (2015–2017) 118; instability risk forecast for (2015–2017) 136; internal war, risk for (2015–2017) 124; non-state mass killing, risk for (2015–2017) 132; state-based mass killing, risk for (2015–2017) 128

Linas-Marcoussis Agreement (2003) 191

Linke, Andrew, Frank Witmer, and John O'Loughlin 107

Linke, Andrew M. xii, 1, 4–15

Linzer, Drew, and Jeffrey Staton 106

Lischer, Sarah Kenyon 144, 145, 150

Lithuania: adverse regime change, risk for (2015–2017) 123; instability risk forecast for (2015–2017) 139; internal war, risk for (2015–2017) 127; non-state mass killing, risk for (2015–2017) 135; state-based mass killing, risk for (2015–2017) 131

locations of violence against civilians: characteristics of 41–3, 44; spatial data on 34

Loescher, Gil, and James Milner 146

lootable resources, one-sided violence (OSV) and (2005–2013) 43
Lord's Resistance Army (LRA) 174, 197, 198, 225; OSV committed by 37–8
Lucas García, Fernando Romeo 219
Lucas García, Manuel Benedicto 219
Lujala, Päivi 107
Lujala, Päivi, Nils Petter Gleditsch, and Elisabeth Gilmore 107
Lukwiya, Raska 225
Luxembourg: adverse regime change, risk for (2015–2017) 123; instability risk forecast for (2015–2017) 139; internal war, risk for (2015–2017) 127; non-state mass killing, risk for (2015–2017) 135; state-based mass killing, risk for (2015–2017) 131
Lyall, Jason, and Isaiah Wilson 108

Macedonia, FYR: adverse regime change, risk for (2015–2017) 122; instability risk forecast for (2015–2017) 138; internal war, risk for (2015–2017) 126; non-state mass killing, risk for (2015–2017) 135; state-based mass killing, risk for (2015–2017) 130
Machar, Riek 170
Mackinlay, John 179
Madagascar: adverse regime change, risk for (2015–2017) 120; instability risk (2015–2017) 118; instability risk forecast for (2015–2017) 136; internal war, risk for (2015–2017) 125; non-state mass killing, risk for (2015–2017) 133; state-based mass killing, risk for (2015–2017) 129
Maddison Database 71
Malawi: adverse regime change, risk for (2015–2017) 120; instability risk (2015–2017) 118; instability risk forecast for (2015–2017) 137; internal war, risk for (2015–2017) 125; non-state mass killing, risk for (2015–2017) 133; state-based mass killing, risk for (2015–2017) 129
Malaysia: adverse regime change, risk for (2015–2017) 120; instability risk forecast for (2015–2017) 137; internal war, risk for (2015–2017) 124; non-state mass killing, risk for (2015–2017) 134; state-based mass killing, risk for (2015–2017) 129
Mali: adverse regime change, risk for (2015–2017) 120; conflict-related violations (2015), criminal justice for 208, 221; instability risk (2015–2017) 118; instability risk forecast for (2015–2017) 136; internal war, risk for (2015–2017) 124; multilateral peacekeeping missions in 181; non-state mass killing, risk for (2015–2017) 132; state-based mass killing, risk for (2015–2017) 128
Mangenda Kabongo, Jean-Jacques 213
Mann, Michael 68
Manrique-Vallier, Daniel, Megan E. Price, and Anita Gohdes 11
Mansfield, Edward, and Jack Snyder 69, 74
Marcos, Ferdinand 168
Mariam, Mengistu Haile 159
Marshall, Monty 106
Marshall, Monty; Ted Gurr, and Keith Jaggers 69
Martin, Adrian 144
Mauritania: adverse regime change, risk for (2015–2017) 121; instability risk forecast for (2015–2017) 137; internal war, risk for (2015–2017) 125; non-state mass killing, risk for (2015–2017) 133; state-based mass killing, risk for (2015–2017) 128
Mauritius: adverse regime change, risk for (2015–2017) 123; instability risk forecast for (2015–2017) 139; internal war, risk for (2015–2017) 127; non-state mass killing, risk for (2015–2017) 135; state-based mass killing, risk for (2015–2017) 131
Mbarushimana, Callixte 215
McGrath, John J. 47, 107
Melander, Erik xiii, 1, 23–33
Melander, Erik, and Magnus Öberg 142
Melander, Erik, Therése Pettersson, and Lotta Themnér 25, 27, 31, 66; armed conflict over time 16, 19, 20, 21; Peace and Conflict Instability Ledger 106, 107

Melander, Pettersson, and Themnér 2016 154
Menem, Carlos 210
Menéndez, General Luciano Benjamín 210
Mexico: adverse regime change, risk for (2015–2017) 121; instability risk (2015–2017) 118; instability risk forecast for (2015–2017) 136; internal war, risk for (2015–2017) 124; non-state mass killing, risk for (2015–2017) 132; state-based mass killing, risk for (2015–2017) 129
Michalopoulos, Selios and Elias Papaioannou 26
micro-level research, generalization from 1, 4–14; Afghanistan, integrating conflict event data in (2008) 10; challenges 5–7; consistent empirical bases, establishment of 7–12; data integration, coverage, quality and 8–11; detailed micro-level studies 4; different empirical strategies 6–7; different spatial units of analysis, data at 13; divergent theoretical bases 5; generalizability 4–5; inconsistency in findings across studies 4; integration of different types of data 11–12; trade-offs in research, navigation of 4; variation in methodological approaches 7
Middle East 2, 16, 18, 22, 28, 31, 49, 50, 53, 82, 85, 102, 114, 115, 144, 176; countries of 86; spatial distribution of OSV in 35–7, 44; UN Truce Supervision Organization (UNTSO) in 181, 182
Miguel, Edward, Shanker Satyanath, and Ernest Sergenti 144
Mikulaschek, Christoph, and Jacob N. Shapiro. 46
MILF (Moro Islamic Liberation Front), Philippines and 166–7
Milner, James 142
Milton, Daniel, Megan Spencer, and Michael Findley 144
Misuari, Nur 167
Mladić, Ratko 216
Moldova: adverse regime change, risk for (2015–2017) 122; instability risk forecast for (2015–2017) 138; internal war, risk for (2015–2017) 125; Joint Control Commission (JCC) in 181, 188–9; multilateral peacekeeping missions in 181; non-state mass killing, risk for (2015–2017) 134; state-based mass killing, risk for (2015–2017) 130
Møller, Jørgen xiii, 2, 68–76
Møller, Jørgen, and Svend-Erik Skaaning 68
Mongolia: adverse regime change, risk for (2015–2017) 122; instability risk forecast for (2015–2017) 138; internal war, risk for (2015–2017) 127; non-state mass killing, risk for (2015–2017) 134; state-based mass killing, risk for (2015–2017) 130
Monte Carlo simulation 54, 57n10
Montenegro: adverse regime change, risk for (2015–2017) 122; instability risk forecast for (2015–2017) 138; internal war, risk for (2015–2017) 126; non-state mass killing, risk for (2015–2017) 135; state-based mass killing, risk for (2015–2017) 130
Morocco: adverse regime change, risk for (2015–2017) 122; instability risk forecast for (2015–2017) 137; internal war, risk for (2015–2017) 124; non-state mass killing, risk for (2015–2017) 133; state-based mass killing, risk for (2015–2017) 128
Most, Benjamin A., and Harvey Starr 143
Mouvement national pour la libération de l'Azawad (MNLA) 201
Mouvement pour l'unicité et le jihad en Afrique de l'Ouest (MUJAO) 201
Movement for Democracy in Liberia (MODEL) 190
Mozambique: adverse regime change, risk for (2015–2017) 120; instability risk forecast for (2015–2017) 137; internal war, risk for (2015–2017) 125; Mozambique National Resistance Movement (MNR) 80; non-state mass killing, risk for (2015–2017) 132; state-based mass killing, risk for (2015–2017) 128; terrorist attacks (1970–2014) 80
Mudacumura, Sylvestre 215–16
Mueller, John 19
Muggah, Robert, and Edward Mogire 144
Mujahedin-e Khalq (MEK) 80

Index

Mullenbach, Mark J. 180

Muller, Edward, and Erich Weede 68

multilateral peacekeeping operations active (2015) 2, 179–206; African-led International Support Mission in Mali (AFISMA) 201; African Union (AU) 179, 200; African Union Mission in Somalia (AMISOM) 181, 195–6; African Union Mission in Sudan (AMIS) 196; Angolan Military Mission to Guinea-Bissau (MISSANG) 200; Ansar Dine, al-Qaeda in the Islamic Maghreb (AQIM) 201; AU/UN Hybrid operation in Darfur (UNAMID) 181, 196–7; Cold War era peacekeeping missions 179; demobilization, disarmament and reintegration (DDR) programs 179; deployment of UN mission personnel, regional trends (1990–2015) 180; Economic Community Mission in Bissau (ECOMIB) 181, 200–201; Economic Community of Central African States (ECCAS) 203; Economic Community of West African States (ECOWAS) 179, 191, 200; ECOWAS Mission in Liberia (ECOMIL) 190; EU Rule of Law Mission (EULEX) 190; EUFOR-Althea in Bosnia and Herzegovina 181, 194; European Union (EU) 179, 189; European Union Military Force - République Centrafricaine (EUFOR-RCA) 181, 202–3; Forces Démocratiques de Libération du Rwanda (FDLR) 197; Forces Républicaines de Côte d'Ivoire (FRCI) 192; Geneva Agreements on Cessation of Hostilities in Indochina 179; ICSC-Cambodia (International Commissions for Supervision and Control in Cambodia) 179; ICSC-Laos (International Commissions for Supervision and Control in Laos) 179; ICSC-Vietnam (International Commissions for Supervision and Control in Vietnam) 179; International Committee of the Red Cross (ICRC) 185; International Monitoring Team (IMT) in Philippines (Mindanao) 179, 181, 193–4; Israeli Defense Force (IDF) 185; Joint Border Verification and Monitoring Mechanism (JBVMM) 198; Joint Control Commission (JCC) in Moldova 181, 188–9; Joint Monitoring Mission/Joint Military Commission (JMM/JMC) in Sudan 179; Kosovo Liberation Army (KLA) 189; Liberians United for Reconciliation and Democracy (LURD) 190; Linas-Marcoussis Agreement (2003) 191; Lord's Resistance Army (LRA) 197; Mouvement national pour la libération de l'Azawad (MNLA) 201; Mouvement pour l'unicité et le jihad en Afrique de l'Ouest (MUJAO) 201; Movement for Democracy in Liberia (MODEL) 190; Multinational Force and Observers (MFO) in Sinai 181, 186–7; National Transitional Government of Liberia (NTGL) 190; NATO-led Kosovo Force (KFOR) 189; NATO-led Stabilization Force (SFOR) in Bosnia 194; Observer Group Golan (OGG) 182; Organization for Security and Co-operation in Europe (OSCE) 179, 189; Organization of African Unity (OAU) 187; Organization of American States (OAS) 179; Organization of the Islamic Conference (OIC) 193; overview of 181; Palestine Liberation Organization (PLO) 185; peacekeeping operations, advances in understanding of 180–81; Philippines and the Moro Islamic Liberation Front (MILF) 193; Popular Front for the Liberation of Saguia el Hamra and Rio de Oro (POLISARIO) 187; South Lebanon Army (SLA) 185; UN Children's Fund (UNICEF) 197; UN Commission for India and Pakistan (UNCIP) 183; UN Development Program (UNDP) 193; UN Disengagement Observer Force (UNDOF) in Golan Heights 181, 182, 184–5; UN High Commissioner for Refugees (UNHCR) 189; UN Integrated Peacebuilding Office in the Central African Republic (BINUCA) 203; UN Interim Administration Mission in Kosovo (UNMIK) 181, 189–90; UN Interim Force in Lebanon (UNIFIL) 181, 185–6; UN Interim Security Force for Abyei, Sudan (UNISFA) 181, 198–9; UN Military Observer Group in India and Pakistan (UNMOGIP) 181, 183; UN Mission for Ebola Emergency Response (UNMEER) 191; UN Mission for the Referendum in Western Sahara (MINURSO) 181, 187–8; UN Mission in Liberia (UNMIL) 181, 190–91; UN Mission in the Republic of South Sudan (UNMISS) 181, 199–200; UN Multi-dimensional Integrated Stabilization Mission in Mali (MINUSMA) 181, 201–2; UN Multidimensional Integrated Stabilization Mission in the Central African Republic (MINUSCA) 181, 203–4; UN Observer Group for the Verification of the Elections in Haiti (ONUVEH) 192; UN Operation in Côte d'Ivoire (UNOCI) 181, 191–2; UN Organization Mission in the Democratic Republic of the Congo (MONUC) 197; UN Organization Stabilization Mission in the Democratic Republic of Congo (MONUSCO) 181, 197–8; UN Peacekeeping Force in Cyprus (UNFICYP) 181, 184; UN Stabilization Mission in Haiti (MINUSTAH) 181, 192–3; United Nations Truce Supervision Organization (UNTSO), Middle East 181, 182; United Nations (UN) 200; United Nations (UN) peacekeeping missions 179; World Food Program (WFP) 197

Munyakazi, Leopold 223

Murdoch, James C., and Todd Sandler 143

Musamba, Aimé Kilolo 213

Museveni, Yoweri 174, 225

Muth, Meas 212

Myanmar: adverse regime change, risk for (2015–2017) 121; instability risk (2015–2017) 118; instability risk forecast for (2015–2017) 136; internal war, risk for (2015–2017) 124; KIO (Kachin Independence Organization) and 162–3; non-state mass killing, risk for (2015–2017) 132; state-based mass killing, risk for (2015–2017) 128

Nagorno-Karabakh, Azerbaijan and 157

Najibullah, Mohammad 155

Namibia: adverse regime change, risk for (2015–2017) 121; instability risk forecast for (2015–2017) 137; internal war, risk for (2015–2017) 125; non-state mass killing, risk for (2015–2017) 133; state-based mass killing, risk for (2015–2017) 129

National Transitional Government of Liberia (NTGL) 190

NATO-led Kosovo Force (KFOR) 189

NATO-led Stabilization Force (SFOR) in Bosnia 194

natural resources, extraction of 34

Nepal: adverse regime change, risk for (2015–2017) 120; Communist Party of Nepal-Maoist (CPN-M) 80, 81; conflict-related violations (2015), criminal justice for 221–2; instability risk (2015–2017) 118; instability risk forecast for (2015–2017) 137; internal war, risk for (2015–2017) 125; non-state mass killing, risk for (2015–2017) 133; state-based mass killing, risk for (2015–2017) 129; terrorist attacks (1970–2014) 80

Netherlands: adverse regime change, risk for (2015–2017) 123; conflict-related violations (2015), criminal justice for 228; instability risk forecast for (2015–2017) 139; internal war, risk for (2015–2017) 127; non-state mass killing, risk for (2015–2017) 134; state-based mass killing, risk for (2015–2017) 131

New York City, fatalities in 80, 81, 87n3

New Zealand: adverse regime change, risk for (2015–2017) 123; instability risk forecast for (2015–2017) 139; internal war, risk for (2015–2017) 127; non-state mass killing, risk for (2015–2017) 135; state-based mass killing, risk for (2015–2017) 131

Newland, Kathrin 145, 146

Nicaragua: adverse regime change, risk for (2015–2017) 121; instability risk forecast for (2015–2017) 138; internal war, risk for (2015–2017) 125; non-state mass killing, risk for (2015–2017) 134; state-based mass killing, risk for (2015–2017) 130

Niger: adverse regime change, risk for (2015–2017) 120; instability risk forecast for (2015–2017) 137; internal war, risk for (2015–2017) 126; non-state mass killing, risk for (2015–2017) 132; state-based mass killing, risk for (2015–2017) 129

Nigeria: adverse regime change, risk for (2015–2017) 121; Boko Haram and 163–4; conflict-related violations (2015), criminal justice for 227; instability risk (2015–2017) 118; instability risk forecast for (2015–2017) 136; internal war, risk for (2015–2017) 124; IS (Islamic State) and 164; non-state mass killing, risk for (2015–2017) 132; state-based mass killing, risk for (2015–2017) 128; terrorist attacks (1970–2014) 80

Nizami, Motiur Rahman 211

Nkurunziza, Pierre 226

Non-State Actor Dataset 46, 48

non-state mass killing: data sources 103, 104; dyad-year model of 109; global map of risk of 116; risk factors 114

Nordås, Ragnhild xiii, 2, 58–67

Nordås, Ragnhild, and Dara Kay Cohen 62

Nordhaus, William D. 42

North Africa 2, 16, 22, 36, 57, 82, 85

North Korea: adverse regime change, risk for (2015–2017) 121; instability risk forecast for (2015–2017) 137; internal war, risk for (2015–2017) 125; non-state mass killing, risk for (2015–2017) 133; state-based mass killing, risk for (2015–2017) 128

Norway: adverse regime change, risk for (2015–2017) 123; conflict-related violations (2015), criminal justice for 228; instability risk forecast for (2015–2017) 139; internal war, risk for (2015–2017) 127; non-state mass killing, risk for (2015–2017) 135; state-based mass killing, risk for (2015–2017) 131

Nourain, Abdallah Banda Abakaer 224

Ntaganda, Bosco 215–16

Obote, Milton 174

Observer Group Golan (OGG) 182

Öcalan, Abdullah 173

Oceania, countries in 86

Odiambo, Okot 225

Ogata, Sadako 145

OLF (Oromo Liberation Front), Ethiopia and 159

Oli, K.P. Sharma 222

O'Loughlin, John, Andrew Martin Linke, and Frank D. Witmer 25, 26

O'Loughlin, John, Pauliina Raento, Joanne P. Sharp, James D. Sidaway, and Philip E. Steinberg 14

Oman: adverse regime change, risk for (2015–2017) 122; instability risk forecast for (2015–2017) 138; internal war, risk for (2015–2017) 126; non-state mass killing, risk for (2015–2017) 134; state-based mass killing, risk for (2015–2017) 129

Omar, Mohammed, Mullah 156

one-sided violence (OSV) 1–2, 23, 25, 31, 32n3, 34–5, 42, 66, 105, 154, 173; Africa, spatial distribution of OSV in 36; Asia, spatial distribution of OSV in 35; lootable resources and (2005–2013) 43; Lord's Resistance Army (LRA), OSV committed by 37–8; Middle East, spatial distribution of OSV in 36; rural vs. urban lovatioons for OSV (2005–2013) 41; South Asia, spatial distribution of OSV in 35; spatial overlap between OSV and type of conflict 39; spatial overlap of state-based conflict with (2005–2013) 40; Uppsala Conflict Data Program (UCDP) Georeferenced Event Dataset (UCDP-GED) 25

Ongwen, Dominic 225

Openshaw, Stan 7

Openshaw, Stan, and Peter J. Taylor 7

ordinary least squares (OLS) regressions 92, 95, 97, 98, 100n2

Organization for Economic Cooperation and Development (OECD) 113, 114

Organization for Security and Co-operation in Europe (OSCE) 179, 189

Organization of African Unity (OAU) 187

Organization of American States (OAS) 179

Organization of the Islamic Conference (OIC) 193

organized armed violence, geography of 1, 23–32; Armed Conflict Location and Event Data (ACLED) Project 23; event data, availability of 23; fatalities due to organized armed violence (PRIO-GRID, 1989–2015) 29; Global Database of Events, Language and Tone (GDELT) 23; global patterns of categories 31; Global Terrorism Database 23; global trends 28–31; granular coverage of conflict 27–8; granularity, geographic and temporal 23; Integrated Conflict Early Warning System (ICEWS) 23; mapping global impact 27–31; severity of categories of organized armed violence by administrative divisions (1989–2015) 30; Social, Political, and Economic Event Database (SPEED) 23; Social Conflict Analysis Database (SCAD) 23; Uppsala Conflict Data Program (UCDP) Georeferenced Event Dataset (UCDP-GED) 23, 24–5, 31, 32n4–5; categories, definitions of 25; contributions and innovations using 25–6; data collection, definitions and 24–5; Geographic Information Systems (GIS) software 25; motivations 24; non-state conflict 25; one-sided violence (OSV) 25; state-based conflict 24–5

Østby, Gudrun 59

Otis, John 49

Otti, Vincent 225

Ouattara, Alassane 214

Pakistan: adverse regime change, risk for (2015–2017) 120; BLA (Balochistan Liberation Army) and 165–6; BLF (Baloch Liberation Front) and 165–6; BRA (Balochistan Republican Army) and 165–6; India and 160–61; instability risk (2015–2017) 118; instability risk forecast for (2015–2017) 136; internal war, risk for (2015–2017) 124; multilateral peacekeeping missions in 181; non-state mass killing, risk for (2015–2017) 132; state-based mass killing, risk for (2015–2017) 128; Tehrik-i-Taleban Pakistan (TTP) and 164–5

Palestine: conflict-related violations (2015), criminal justice for 208, 227; Palestine Liberation Organization (PLO) 185

Palmyra, fatalities in 80

Panama: adverse regime change, risk for (2015–2017) 122; instability risk forecast for (2015–2017) 138; internal war, risk for (2015–2017) 127; non-state mass killing, risk for (2015–2017) 134; state-based mass killing, risk for (2015–2017) 130

Papua New Guinea: adverse regime change, risk for (2015–2017) 122; instability risk forecast for (2015–2017) 138; internal war, risk for (2015–2017) 125; non-state mass killing, risk for (2015–2017) 133; state-based mass killing, risk for (2015–2017) 130

Paraguay: adverse regime change, risk for (2015–2017) 121; instability risk forecast for (2015–2017) 138; internal war, risk for (2015–2017) 125; non-state mass killing, risk for (2015–2017) 134; state-based mass killing, risk for (2015–2017) 130

Parvulescu, Marian 222

Patassé, Ange-Félix 212

Peace Agreement Dataset (UCDP) 54

Peace and Conflict Instability Ledger (2017) 2, 101–40, 141n1; actor-level instability risk factors 107–8; adverse regime change, global map of risk of 115; adverse regime change data sources 103, 104; adverse regime change model 105; adverse regime change risk factors 114; Africa, risks on instability in 115; analysis, framework for 103–4; AUC score 109, 112; Center for International Development and Conflict Management (CIDCM) 101, 102, 104, 117, 140n1;

Index

conflict-level instability risk factors 106–7; consequential differences 115; country-year model of non-state mass killing 109; country-year model of offset of internal war 109; data reliability 117; diagnostics of models of instability risk 112; discussion 115–17; estimation procedure 105; false negatives 112; false positives 109, 112; high-risk categorization 115; historical associations, empirical analysis and 101; instability, measures of 102–3; instability risk, factors in models of 106–8; instability risk factors 114–17; institutional level instability risk factors 106; interdependencies 117; internal war, dyad-year model of offset of 105; internal war, global map of risk of 115; internal war data sources 103, 104; internal war onset model 105–9; internal war risk factors 114; international instability risk factors 106; model diagnostics 109–13; model specification 104–5; model specification, shortcomings in 102; models of instability risk, estimations from 110–11; non-state mass killing, dyad-year model of 109; non-state mass killing, global map of risk of 116; non-state mass killing data sources 103, 104; non-state mass killing risk factors 114; Organization for Economic Cooperation and Development (OECD) 113, 114; overall instability risk factors 114; Peace and Conflict Instability Ledger (PCIL) 101–6, 108, 109, 112, 113, 115, 117, 140n1; peer-reviewed empirical research 117; Political Instability Task Force (PITF) 101, 102, 103; previous methodology 101; rankings and classification of countries, improvement in 117; risk classifications, generation of 113–14; risk scores, calculation of 113; single model, reliance on 102; state-based mass killing, global map of risk of 116; state-based mass killing data sources 103, 104; state-based mass killing model 109; state-based mass killing risk factors 114; statistical estimation, restriction on 102; structural country-level instability risk factors 106; training models, results of estimations from 105–14; true negatives 112; true positives 109; updated methodology 102–14, 117; Uppsala Conflict Data Program (UCDP) 102, 103, 105, 107; USAID 112; World Bank 106

Pelcovits, Nathan Albert 179

Pérez Molina, Otto 219

Peru: adverse regime change, risk for (2015–2017) 122; instability risk forecast for (2015–2017) 137; internal war, risk for (2015–2017) 124; non-state mass killing, risk for (2015–2017) 133; state-based mass killing, risk for (2015–2017) 130

Petković, Milivoj 216–17

Pettersson, Thérése, and Peter Wallensteen 47

Philippines: adverse regime change, risk for (2015–2017) 121; ASG (Abu Sayyaf Group) and 166–7; BIFM (Bangsamoro Islamic Freedom Movement) and 166–7; CPP (Communist Party of the Philippines) and 167–8; instability risk (2015–2017) 118; instability risk forecast for (2015–2017) 136; internal war, risk for (2015–2017) 124; International Monitoring Team (IMT) in Mindanao 179, 181, 193–4; MILF (Moro Islamic Liberation Front) and 166–7, 193; multilateral peacekeeping missions in 181; non-state mass killing, risk for (2015–2017) 132; state-based mass killing, risk for (2015–2017) 129

Phillips, Christopher 144

Pickering, Steve 12

Pierskalla, Jan H., and Florian M. Hollenbach 5, 6, 7, 25, 26

Pinker, Steven 16, 19

Pinochet, Augusto 214

PKK (Partiya Karkeren Kurdistan: Kurdistan Workers' Party), Turkey and 173–4

Poe, Steven C., Sabine C. Carey, and Tonya C. Vazquez 90

Poland: adverse regime change, risk for (2015–2017) 123; instability risk forecast for (2015–2017) 139; internal war, risk for (2015–2017) 127; non-state mass killing, risk for (2015–2017) 134; state-based mass killing, risk for (2015–2017) 131

Political Instability Task Force (PITF) 101, 102, 103

Political Terror Scale (PTS) 88, 89, 99; full report word counts by PTS scores 96–7; global annual average scores (1976–2014) 89; relationship between PTS scores and word count estimates (1999–2014) 98; report length and 94–9; violence against civilians, spatial patterns of 44n1; within-country effects of word counts on PTS scores (1999–2014) 99

Polity indicators 70

Popular Front for the Liberation of Saguia el Hamra and Rio de Oro (POLISARIO) 187, 188

Portugal: adverse regime change, risk for (2015–2017) 123; instability risk forecast for (2015–2017) 139; internal war, risk for (2015–2017) 127; non-state mass killing, risk for (2015–2017) 135; state-based mass killing, risk for (2015–2017) 131

Postelnicu, Tudor 222

Praljak, Slobodan 216–17

previous methodology 101

Price, Megan, Anita Gohdes, and Patrick Ball 8

PRIO-GRID dataset of Oslo Peace Research Institute 12, 28, 29, 33; violence against civilians, spatial patterns of 35

Prlić, Jadranko 216–17

Prorok, Alyssa 107

Przeworski, Adam 68

Qatar: adverse regime change, risk for (2015–2017) 122; instability risk forecast for (2015–2017) 138; internal war, risk for (2015–2017) 126; non-state mass killing, risk for (2015–2017) 135; state-based mass killing, risk for (2015–2017) 129

Quintana, Carmen Gloria 214

Raleigh, Clionadh 34

Raleigh, Clionadh, and Hegre, Håvard 41

Raleigh, Clionadh, and Henrik Urdal 144

Raleigh, Clionadh, Andrew Linke, Håvard Hegre, and Joakim Karleson 6, 23

Raqqah, fatalities in 80

refugees, conflict diffusion and 2, 142–51; civil conflict, spread of 143–4; closing borders 151; conflict onset for countries with refugees, estimated risk for (1975–2009) 150; contentious inter-ethnic group relations 151; country of asylum (CoA) 147, 149–50, 151; country of asylum (CoA), ethnic balance in 142–3; ethnic balance argument, testing against new refugee data 146–7; ethnic linkages of refugees to host population, role of 145–6; Ethnic Power Relations (EPR) dataset 149; forced displacement, high levels of 142; forced displacement, political violence and 142; impact of refugees on conflict onset, estimations of 148; irregular migration, increases in 142; political challenge 150; protection for refugees, lack of 151; refugee count and prevalence of armed conflict (1960–2015) 143; refugee outflows, political violence and 142; refugee-related conflict diffusion 144; refugee-related conflict diffusion, analytical framework 147–9; refugee-related conflict diffusion, results of analysis 149–50, 150–51; refugees with co-ethnics in asylum countries relative to total numbers (1975–2009) 145; transborder ethnic kin (TEK) groups 143, 145–6, 147, 149, 150–51; transborder ethnic kin (TEK) ties to asylum countries 146; UCDP/PRIO Dataset 142; UN Convention on Status of Refugees (1951) 142

Reiter, Dan 52

Reyes Girón, Colonel Esteelmer 218

Richardson, Lewis F. 17

Ríos Montt, Efraín 217, 218

Rodríguez Sánchez, José Mauricio 217, 218

Rojas de Negri, Rodrigo 214

Romania: adverse regime change, risk for (2015–2017) 122; conflict-related violations (2015), criminal justice for 208, 222; instability risk forecast for (2015–2017) 138; internal war, risk for (2015–2017) 125; non-state mass killing, risk for (2015–2017) 134; state-based mass killing, risk for (2015–2017) 130

Rome Statute (2004) 208, 209, 224–5, 226, 227, 232n142

Ron, James 63

Rørbæk, Lasse Lykke xiii, 2, 68–76

Ross, Michael 14n1

Rüegger, Seraina xiii, 2, 142–53

Rüegger, Seraina, and Heidrun Bohnet 145, 147

Ruggeri, Andrea, Han Dorussen, and Theodora-Ismene Gizelis 180

Ruhe, Constantin 26

Russia: adverse regime change, risk for (2015–2017) 121; instability risk (2015–2017) 118; instability risk forecast for (2015–2017) 136; internal war, risk for (2015–2017) 124; non-state mass killing, risk for (2015–2017) 132; state-based mass killing, risk for (2015–2017) 128; terrorist attacks (1970–2014) 80

Ruto, William 219–20

Rwanda: adverse regime change, risk for (2015–2017) 122; conflict-related violations (2015), criminal justice for 222–3; Forces Démocratiques de Libération du Rwanda (FDLR) 197; Hutu Extremists in 80; instability risk forecast for (2015–2017) 138; internal war, risk for (2015–2017) 125; International Criminal Tribunal for Rwanda (ICTR) 209; non-state mass killing, risk for (2015–2017) 133; state-based mass killing, risk for (2015–2017) 129; terrorist attacks (1970–2014) 80; Tutsi extremists in 80

Saleh, Ali Abdullah 177

Salehyan, Idean 144

Salehyan, Idean, and Kristian Skrede Gleditsch 106, 144, 146, 147, 149

Salehyan, Idean, Cullen S. Hendrix, Jesse Hamner, Christina Case, Christopher Linebarger, Emily Stull, and Jennifer Williams 6, 23

Sambanis, Nicholas 143

Sang, Joshua Arap 219–20

Sanogo, Amadou Haya 221

Saudi Arabia: adverse regime change, risk for (2015–2017) 122; instability risk forecast for (2015–2017) 137; internal war, risk for (2015–2017) 124; non-state mass killing, risk for (2015–2017) 133; state-based mass killing, risk for (2015–2017) 128

Schmeidl, Susanne 142

Schutte, Sebastian 46

Selassie, Haile 159

Selway, Bianca 180

Senegal: adverse regime change, risk for (2015–2017) 120; conflict-related violations (2015), criminal justice for 228; instability risk forecast for (2015–2017) 137; internal war, risk for (2015–2017) 126; non-state mass killing, risk for (2015–2017) 133; state-based mass killing, risk for (2015–2017) 129

Al-Senussi, Abdullah 220

Serbia: adverse regime change, risk for (2015–2017) 121; instability risk forecast for (2015–2017) 137; internal war, risk for (2015–2017) 125; non-state mass killing, risk for (2015–2017) 134; state-based mass killing, risk for (2015–2017) 129

Sese Seko, Mobutu 215

Šešelj, Vojislav 216

sexual violence: concern about 58; conflict actors' perpetration of 62–4; occurrence in many conflicts 66; regional variation in 64–5; Sexual Violence and Armed Conflict (SVAC) dataset 58, 62, 66; by state and non-state forces, correspondence between (1989–2009) 62; by states and militias, correspondence between (1989–2009) 62

Shapiro, Jacob N., and Nils B. Weidmann 5, 6, 7

Shekau, Abubakar 163

Shimizu, Hirofumi, and Todd Sandler 180

Sierra Leone: adverse regime change, risk for (2015–2017) 120; instability risk forecast for (2015–2017) 137; internal war, risk for (2015–2017) 125; non-state mass killing, risk for (2015–2017) 132; Special Court for Sierra Leone (SCSL) 209; state-based mass killing, risk for (2015–2017) 129

Significant Activities (SIGACTS) data 6, 9, 11–13, 14n4, 26

Sikh extremists in Canada 80

Silva, Romesh, and Patrick Ball 8

Simatović, Franko 216

Singapore: adverse regime change, risk for (2015–2017) 122; instability risk forecast for (2015–2017) 138; internal war, risk for (2015–2017) 126; non-state mass killing, risk for (2015–2017) 135; state-based mass killing, risk for (2015–2017) 130

Sinjar, fatalities in 80

Sison, Jose Maria 167

Sivakumaran, Sandesh 58, 59

Skaaning, Svend-Erik xiii, 2, 68–76

Slantchev, Branislav 107

Slovak Republic: adverse regime change, risk for (2015–2017) 122; instability risk forecast for (2015–2017) 139; internal war, risk for (2015–2017) 127; non-state mass killing, risk for (2015–2017) 135; state-based mass killing, risk for (2015–2017) 130

Slovenia: adverse regime change, risk for (2015–2017) 123; instability risk forecast for (2015–2017) 139; internal war, risk for (2015–2017) 127; non-state mass killing, risk for (2015–2017) 135; state-based mass killing, risk for (2015–2017) 131

Sobek, David 74

Social, Political, and Economic Event Database (SPEED) 23

Social Conflict Analysis Database (SCAD) 23

Sollenberg, Margareta xiii, 1–2, 34–45, 154–78

Solomon Islands: adverse regime change, risk for (2015–2017) 122; instability risk forecast for (2015–2017) 138; internal war, risk for (2015–2017) 126; non-state mass killing, risk for (2015–2017) 134; state-based mass killing, risk for (2015–2017) 131

Somalia: adverse regime change, risk for (2015–2017) 120; Al-Shabaab (The Youth) and 168–9; instability risk (2015–2017) 118; instability risk forecast for (2015–2017) 136; internal war, risk for (2015–2017) 124; multilateral peacekeeping missions in 181; non-state mass killing, risk for (2015–2017) 132; state-based mass killing, risk for (2015–2017) 128

"sore loser" effect 69

South Africa: adverse regime change, risk for (2015–2017) 121; conflict-related violations (2015), criminal justice for 228; instability risk forecast for (2015–2017) 138; internal war, risk for (2015–2017) 126; non-state mass killing, risk for (2015–2017) 133; state-based mass killing, risk for (2015–2017) 130

South Asia: countries in 86; spatial distribution of OSV in 35

South Korea: adverse regime change, risk for (2015–2017) 122; instability risk forecast for (2015–2017) 138; internal war, risk for (2015–2017) 126; non-state mass killing, risk for (2015–2017) 134; state-based mass killing, risk for (2015–2017) 130

South Lebanon Army (SLA) 185

South Sudan: adverse regime change, risk for (2015–2017) 120; instability risk (2015–2017) 118; instability risk forecast for (2015–2017) 136; internal war, risk for (2015–2017) 124; multilateral peacekeeping missions in 181; non-state mass killing, risk for (2015–2017) 132; SPLM/A-In Opposition (Sudan People's Liberation Movement/Army-In Opposition) and 169–70; state-based mass killing, risk for (2015–2017) 128

Southeast Asia: countries in 86; spatial distribution of OSV in 35

Spain: adverse regime change, risk for (2015–2017) 123; conflict-related violations (2015), criminal justice for 228;

instability risk forecast for (2015–2017) 139; internal war, risk for (2015–2017) 127; non-state mass killing, risk for (2015–2017) 134; Spanish civil war 34; state-based mass killing, risk for (2015–2017) 131

Special Court for Sierra Leone (SCSL) 209

SRF (Sudanese Revolutionary Front), Sudan and 170–71

Sri Lanka: adverse regime change, risk for (2015–2017) 121; instability risk forecast for (2015–2017) 137; internal war, risk for (2015–2017) 124; Liberation Tigers of Tamil Eelam (LTTE) 80; non-state mass killing, risk for (2015–2017) 134; state-based mass killing, risk for (2015–2017) 129; terrorist attacks (1970–2014) 80

Stanišić, Jovica 216

START (National Consortium for the Study of Terrorism and Responses to Terrorism) 6, 23, 77

state and non-state actors: spatial overlap of OSV by (2005–2013) 37; spatial overlap of state-based conflict with OSV by (2005–2013) 40

state-based mass killing: data sources 103, 104; global map of risk of 116; model of 109; risk factors 114

Stedman, S. J., and F. Tanner 144, 150

Stein, Barry N. 144, 145

stigmatization, fear of 62

Stockholm International Peace Research Institute (SIPRI) 48

Stojić, Bruno 216–17

Strand, Håvard xiii, 1, 16–22

Strand, Håvard and Halvard Buhaug 24–5

Straus, Scott 5, 6, 7

Sub-Saharan Africa 5, 16, 23, 36, 82, 85, 101, 117

Suchitoto, fatalities in 80

Sudan: Abeyi, multilateral peacekeeping missions in 181; adverse regime change, risk for (2015–2017) 121; Christian Extremists in 80; conflict-related violations (2015), criminal justice for 209, 224–5; Darfur, multilateral peacekeeping missions in 181; DJRF (Darfur Joint Resistance Forces) and 170–71; instability risk (2015–2017) 118; instability risk forecast for (2015–2017) 136; internal war, risk for (2015–2017) 124; Joint Monitoring Mission/Joint Military Commission (JMM/JMC) in 179; non-state mass killing, risk for (2015–2017) 132; SRF (Sudanese Revolutionary Front) and 170–71; state-based mass killing, risk for (2015–2017) 128; terrorist attacks (1970–2014) 80

Sullivan, Patricia, and Johannes Karreth 107

Sundberg, Ralph xiii, 1–2, 34–45

Sundberg, Ralph, and Erik Melander 6, 23, 25, 34, 41, 46

Sundberg, Ralph, Kristine Eck, and Joakim Kreutz 32n4, 44n6

Suriname: adverse regime change, risk for (2015–2017) 121; instability risk forecast for (2015–2017) 138; internal war, risk for (2015–2017) 126; non-state mass killing, risk for (2015–2017) 135; state-based mass killing, risk for (2015–2017) 130

Svolik, Milan 68

Swaziland: adverse regime change, risk for (2015–2017) 121; instability risk forecast for (2015–2017) 137; internal war, risk for (2015–2017) 126; non-state mass killing, risk for (2015–2017) 133; state-based mass killing, risk for (2015–2017) 129

Sweden: adverse regime change, risk for (2015–2017) 123; conflict-related violations (2015), criminal justice for 228; instability risk forecast for (2015–2017) 139; internal war, risk for (2015–2017) 127; non-state mass killing, risk for (2015–2017) 135; state-based mass killing, risk for (2015–2017) 131

Switzerland: adverse regime change, risk for (2015–2017) 123; conflict-related violations (2015), criminal justice for 228; instability risk forecast for (2015–2017) 139; internal war, risk for (2015–2017) 127; non-state mass killing, risk for (2015–2017) 135; state-based mass killing, risk for (2015–2017) 131

Syria: adverse regime change, risk for (2015–2017) 122; instability risk (2015–2017) 118; instability risk forecast for (2015–2017) 136; internal war, risk for (2015–2017) 124; IS (Islamic State) and 171; non-state mass killing, risk for (2015–2017) 132; state-based mass killing, risk for (2015–2017) 128; Syrian insurgents and 172–3; terrorist attacks (1970–2014) 80

tactics of terror 83–4

Tajikistan: adverse regime change, risk for (2015–2017) 121; instability risk forecast for (2015–2017) 137; internal war, risk for (2015–2017) 125; non-state mass killing, risk for (2015–2017) 133; state-based mass killing, risk for (2015–2017) 128

Taliban 21, 163, 164, 165, 176, 226; Afghanistan and 155–6

Tanzania: adverse regime change, risk for (2015–2017) 120; instability risk forecast for (2015–2017) 136; internal war, risk for (2015–2017) 124; non-state mass killing, risk for (2015–2017) 132; state-based mass killing, risk for (2015–2017) 128

targets of terrorism 82–3

terrorism: targets of 82–3

Tavares, Rodrigo 143

technology of conflict 48; size of rebel forces and 50

Tehrik-i-Taleban Pakistan (TTP): Afghanistan and 164–5; Pakistan and 164–5

Teorell, Jan, Michael Coppedge, Staffan Lindberg, and Svend-Erik Skaaning 70

terrorism 55, 176, 210; Caribbean terrorism 85–6; Country Reports on Terrorism (US, 2015) 77; Global Terrorism Database (GTD) 13, 23, 44n1, 77, 78, 79, 80, 82, 84, 85, 87n2–3; START (National Consortium for the Study of Terrorism and Responses to Terrorism) 6, 23, 77; terrorist attacks, annual numbers (1970–2014) 78; worldwide trends in 77–9; see also global terrorism, evolution of

Terry, Fiona 144

Thailand: instability risk (2015–2017) 118; instability risk forecast for (2015–2017) 136; internal war, risk for (2015–2017) 124; non-state mass killing, risk for (2015–2017) 132; state-based mass killing, risk for (2015–2017) 129

Tiernay, Michael 26

Tikrit, fatalities in 80

Timor-Leste: adverse regime change, risk for (2015–2017) 121; instability risk forecast for (2015–2017) 138; internal war, risk for (2015–2017) 126; non-state mass killing, risk for (2015–2017) 133; state-based mass killing, risk for (2015–2017) 130

Toft, Monica 40

Togo: adverse regime change, risk for (2015–2017) 121; instability risk forecast for (2015–2017) 137; internal war, risk for (2015–2017) 125; non-state mass killing, risk for (2015–2017) 133; state-based mass killing, risk for (2015–2017) 128

Tollefsen, Andreas Forø, Håvard Strand and Halvard Buhaug 12, 28, 35, 108

Toronto, fatalities in 80

Touré, Amadou Toumani 221

training models, results of estimations from 105–14

transborder ethnic kin (TEK) groups 143, 145–6, 147, 149, 150–51; ties to asylum countries 146

triangulation of information 48

Trinidad and Tobago: adverse regime change, risk for (2015–2017) 122; instability risk forecast for (2015–2017) 139; internal war, risk for (2015–2017) 127; non-state mass killing, risk for (2015–2017) 134; state-based mass killing, risk for (2015–2017) 131

true negatives 112

true positives 109

Tunisia: adverse regime change, risk for (2015–2017) 121; instability risk forecast for (2015–2017) 137; internal war, risk for (2015–2017) 126; non-state mass killing, risk for (2015–2017) 134; state-based mass killing, risk for (2015–2017) 129

Turkey: adverse regime change, risk for (2015–2017) 120; instability risk (2015–2017) 118; instability risk forecast for (2015–2017) 136; internal war, risk for (2015–2017) 125; non-state mass killing, risk for (2015–2017) 132; PKK (Partiya Karkeren Kurdistan: Kurdistan Workers' Party) and 173–4; state-based mass killing, risk for (2015–2017) 130

Turkmenistan: adverse regime change, risk for (2015–2017) 121; instability risk (2015–2017) 118; instability risk forecast for (2015–2017) 137; internal war, risk for (2015–2017) 125; non-state mass killing, risk for (2015–2017) 133; state-based mass killing, risk for (2015–2017) 128

Tutsi extremists in Rwanda 80

Uaskeing, fatalities in 80

Uganda: ADF (Alliance of Democratic Forces) and 174–5; adverse regime change, risk for (2015–2017) 122; conflict-related violations (2015), criminal justice for 225; instability risk (2015–2017) 118; instability risk forecast for (2015–2017) 136; internal war, risk for (2015–2017) 124; non-state mass killing, risk for (2015–2017) 132; SPLM/A-In Opposition (Sudan People's Liberation Movement/ Army-In Opposition) and 169–70; state-based mass killing, risk for (2015–2017) 128

Uhuru Kenyatta, Mugai 219–20

Ukraine: adverse regime change, risk for (2015–2017) 120; conflict-related violations (2015), criminal justice for 227; instability risk (2015–2017) 118; instability risk forecast for (2015–2017) 136; internal war, risk for (2015–2017) 124; non-state mass killing, risk for (2015–2017) 132; state-based mass killing, risk for (2015–2017) 129; terrorist attacks (1970–2014) 80; United Armed Forces of Novorossiya and 175

ul-Haq, Zia 166

unarmed assault 84

United Arab Emirates: adverse regime change, risk for (2015–2017) 122; instability risk forecast for (2015–2017) 138; internal war, risk for (2015–2017) 126; non-state mass killing, risk for (2015–2017) 134; state-based mass killing, risk for (2015–2017) 130

United Armed Forces of Novorossiya, Ukraine and 175

United Kingdom: adverse regime change, risk for (2015–2017) 123; conflict-related violations (2015), criminal justice for 227, 228; instability risk forecast for (2015–2017) 139; internal war, risk for (2015–2017) 127; non-state mass killing, risk for (2015–2017) 134; state-based mass killing, risk for (2015–2017) 130

United Nations (UN) 19; Children's Fund (UNICEF) 197; Commission for India and Pakistan (UNCIP) 183; Convention on Status of Refugees (1951) 142; Development Program (UNDP) 193; Disengagement Observer Force (UNDOF) on Golan Heights 181, 182, 184–5; Food and Agriculture Organization (FAO) 12; High Commissioner for Refugees (UNHCR) 142, 144, 146–7, 189; Integrated Peacebuilding Office in the Central African Republic (BINUCA) 203; Interim Administration Mission in Kosovo (UNMIK) 181, 189–90; Interim Force in Lebanon (UNIFIL) 181, 185–6; Interim Security Force for Abyei, Sudan (UNISFA) 181, 198–9; Military Observer Group in India and Pakistan (UNMOGIP) 181, 183; Mission for Ebola Emergency Response (UNMEER) 191; Mission for the Referendum in Western Sahara (MINURSO) 181, 187–8; Mission in Liberia (UNMIL) 181, 190–91; Mission in the Republic of South Sudan (UNMISS) 181, 199–200; Multidimensional Integrated Stabilization Mission in Mali (MINUSMA) 181, 201–2; Multidimensional Integrated Stabilization Mission in the Central African Republic (MINUSCA) 181, 203–4; multilateral peacekeeping operations active (2015) 200;

Observer Group for the Verification of the Elections in Haiti (ONUVEH) 192; Operation in Côte d'Ivoire (UNOCI) 181, 191–2; Organization Mission in the Democratic Republic of the Congo (MONUC) 197; Organization Stabilization Mission in the Democratic Republic of Congo (MONUSCO) 181, 197–8; Peacekeeping Force in Cyprus (UNFICYP) 181, 184; peacekeeping missions 179; Security Council Resolution 1889 (2009) 59; Stabilization Mission in Haiti (MINUSTAH) 181, 192–3; Truce Supervision Organization (UNTSO), Middle East 181, 182

United States: adverse regime change, risk for (2015–2017) 123; al-Qaida and 176; Committee for Refugees and Immigrants 2009 144; conflict-related violations (2015), criminal justice for 227, 228; Country Reports on Terrorism (2015) 77; Department of Homeland Security (DHS) 87n1; instability risk forecast for (2015–2017) 138; internal war, risk for (2015–2017) 127; non-state mass killing, risk for (2015–2017) 133; Significant Activities (SIGACTS) data 6, 9, 11–13, 14n4, 26; state-based mass killing, risk for (2015–2017) 131; State Department: human rights conditions 88, 90, 99; growth rates of human rights reports (1999–2015) 93, 94; time effects for word counts (1999–2015) 92; within-country effects of word counts on PTS scores (1999–2014) 99; within-country time effects of human rights reports (1999–2015) 95, 96; within-country variability of human rights reports (1999–2015) 98; word counts in human rights reports (1999–2015) 90, 91, 92; State Department Human Rights Reports (1999–2015) 90, 91, 92, 93, 94, 96, 97; terrorist attacks (1970–2014) 80; USAID 112

universal jurisdiction cases 227–8

updated methodology 102–14, 117

Uppsala Conflict Data Program (UCDP) 1, 102, 103, 105, 107; active armed conflicts (2015) 154; Armed Conflict Dataset (ACD) 47; armed conflict over time 16; Battle-Related Deaths Dataset (2015) 18; compilation of data 154; definitions and data 154; UCDP/PRIO Armed Conflict Dataset 17, 19, 20, 21, 31n1, 71, 142

Uppsala Conflict Data Program (UCDP) Georeferenced Event Dataset (UCDP-GED) 13, 29, 30, 31n1; internal conflicts, rebel and state armed forces in 46, 47; organized armed violence, geography of 23, 24–5, 31, 32n4–5; categories, definitions of 25; contributions and innovations using 25–6; data collection, definitions and 24–5; Geographic Information Systems (GIS) software 25; motivations 24; non-state conflict 25; one-sided violence (OSV) 25; state-based conflict 24–5; violence against civilians, spatial patterns of 34–5, 35, 36, 37, 38, 39, 40, 41, 42, 43, 44n1

Ursu, Gheorghe 222

Uruguay: adverse regime change, risk for (2015–2017) 123; instability risk forecast for (2015–2017) 139; internal war, risk for (2015–2017) 127; non-state mass killing, risk for (2015–2017) 135; state-based mass killing, risk for (2015–2017) 131

Uzbekistan: adverse regime change, risk for (2015–2017) 121; instability risk (2015–2017) 118; instability risk forecast for (2015–2017) 136; internal war, risk for (2015–2017) 124; non-state mass killing, risk for (2015–2017) 132; state-based mass killing, risk for (2015–2017) 128

Uzonyi, Gary 180

Valdez Asig, Heriberto 218

Valentino, Benjamin, Paul Huth, and Dylan Balch-Lindsay 36

Vasijlković, Dragan 217

V-Dem Project 70; potential for 71, 72, 74

Venezuela: adverse regime change, risk for (2015–2017) 120; instability risk (2015–2017) 118; instability risk forecast for (2015–2017) 136; internal war, risk for (2015–2017) 124;

non-state mass killing, risk for (2015–2017) 133; state-based mass killing, risk for (2015–2017) 128

Vergez, Héctor Pedro 210

Videla, General Jorge 210

Vietnam: adverse regime change, risk for (2015–2017) 122; ICSC-Vietnam (International Commissions for Supervision and Control in Vietnam) 179; instability risk forecast for (2015–2017) 137; internal war, risk for (2015–2017) 124; non-state mass killing, risk for (2015–2017) 133; state-based mass killing, risk for (2015–2017) 129

violence against civilians, spatial patterns of 1–2, 34–44; Africa, spatial distribution of OSV in 36; armed conflict, one-sided violence (OSV) and 38–41; armed conflict, relationship between civilian victimization and 34; armed conflict, spatial overlap between OSV and type of conflict (2005–2013) 39; Asia, spatial distribution of OSV in 35; cross-national studies 34; economic development levels, spatial relationship between OSV and (2005–2013) 42; extraction of valuable natural resources 34; Global Terrorism Database (GTD) 44n1; Greek civil war 34; locations of violence, characteristics of 41–3, 44; locations of violence, spatial data on 34; lootable resources, one-sided violence (OSV) and (2005–2013) 43; Lord's Resistance Army (LRA), OSV committed by 38; Middle East, spatial distribution of OSV in 36; one-sided violence (OSV) 1–2, 34–5; Political Terror Scale (PTS) data 44n1; PRIO-GRID 35; rural vs. urban locations of OSV (2005–2013) 41; South Asia, spatial distribution of OSV in 35; Southeast Asia, spatial distribution of OSV in 35; Spanish civil war 34; spatial patterns of OSV 35–8; state and non-state actors, spatial overlap of state-based conflict with OSV by (2005–2013) 40; state and non-state armed actors, spatial overlap of OSV by (2005–2013) 37; Uppsala Conflict Data Program (UCDP) Georeferenced Event Dataset (UCDP-GED) 34–5, 44n1

Visinescu, Alexandru 222

Vogt, Manuel, Nils-Christian Bormann, Seraina Rüegger, Lars-Erik Cederman, et al. 108

Vogt, Manuel, Nils-Christian Bormann, Seraina Rüegger, Lars-Erik Cederman, Philipp Hunziker, and Luc Girardin 147, 149

von Uexkull, Nina 26

von Uexkull, Nina, Mihai Croicu, Hanne Fjelde, and Halvard Buhaug 26

Vreeland, James 69, 72, 73

Wallensteen, Peter and Margareta Sollenberg 44n6, 143

Walter, Barbara F. 107, 180

Ward, Hugh, and Han Dorussen 180

Ward, Michael D., and Kristian Skrede Gleditsch 143

Warren, T. Camber 25

weapons of terror 84–5

Weidmann, Nils B. 6, 8, 9, 11, 12, 14n4–5, 26

Weiner, Myron 142, 144, 145

Weinstein, Jeremy M. 43

Western Europe, countries in 86–7

Western Sahara: multilateral peacekeeping missions in 181; Popular Front for the Liberation of Saguia el Hamra and Rio de Oro (POLISARIO) 187, 188; UN Mission for the Referendum in Western Sahara (MINURSO) 181, 187–8

Whitaker, Reg 144

Wig, Tore and Andreas Forø Tollefsen 25

Wilkenfeld, Jonathan, and Michael Brecher 179

Wood, Elisabeth Jean 58, 59, 62

Wood, Reed M. 26, 46

Wood, Reed M. and Christopher Sullivan 26

Wood, Reed M. and Jacob D. Kathman 26

Wood, Reed M. and Mark Gibney 88, 90

Wood, William 142

World Bank 19, 106

World Food Program (WFP) 197

worring trend, entrenchment of 16–19

Wright, Thorin M. and J. Michael Greig 180

Yanagizawa-Drott, David 5, 6, 7

Yanukovych, Viktor 175

Yemen: adverse regime change, risk for (2015–2017) 120; Ansarallah (Supporters of God) and 177–8; AQAP (al-Qaeda in the Arabian Peninsula) and 177–8; instability risk (2015–2017) 118; instability risk forecast for (2015–2017) 136; internal war, risk for (2015–2017) 124; non-state mass killing, risk for (2015–2017) 132; state-based mass killing, risk for (2015–2017) 128

Yugoslavia (former state of): conflict-related violations (2015), criminal justice for 216–17; International Criminal Tribunal for Former Yugoslavia (ICTY) 209

Yussuf, Mohammed 163

Zambia: adverse regime change, risk for (2015–2017) 120; instability risk forecast for (2015–2017) 137; internal war, risk for (2015–2017) 126; non-state mass killing, risk for (2015–2017) 133; state-based mass killing, risk for (2015–2017) 129

Zelaya, José Manuel 227

Ziblatt, Daniel 74

Zimbabwe: adverse regime change, risk for (2015–2017) 120; instability risk (2015–2017) 118; instability risk forecast for (2015–2017) 136; internal war, risk for (2015–2017) 125; non-state mass killing, risk for (2015–2017) 132; state-based mass killing, risk for (2015–2017) 128

Zolberg, Aristide R., Astri Suhrke, and Sergio Aguayo 142, 144